DATE DUE

Language Arts

Language Arts: Patterns of Practice grounds readers in real classroom teaching and learning. To feel comfortable and confident in teaching, you will need more than just an understanding of the language arts concepts and familiarity with the best teaching methods. You will need to be able to see yourself successfully teaching in a language arts classroom. The text's many examples from real classrooms model best practice and teacher decision-making.

◆ *Authentic student artifacts*, the student samples from each of the four patterns of practice, found in almost every chapter, help preservice teachers learn what to expect from young readers and writers.

◆ *Seeing Common Threads* allows readers to look more closely at issues important to elementary and middle school teachers, giving them an opportunity to apply what they're learning through questions provoking reflection and analysis. To encourage a dialogue on these issues, readers are encouraged to compare their thoughts with those of other preservice teachers online in our Companion Website's Threaded Message Board, available at **www.prenhall.com/tompkins**.

◆ *Meeting the Needs of Every Student* features help prepare pre-service teachers for the diverse needs of today's students by providing ideas for adapting lessons to fit students' needs. This special feature contains explicit suggestions for scaffolding and modifying the learning experiences for students with special learning needs so they can be successful. Visit the Companion Website at **www.prenhall.com/tompkins** for even more resources for adapting instruction to better suit the needs of all students.

◆ *NEW! Free CD-ROM* will help you experience the effective instruction that takes place in classroom communities by analyzing video footage of master teachers who integrate minilessons and strategy and skill development in the use of writing workshops. Users can examine, re-examine, and manipulate genuine classroom footage to develop a deep and lasting understanding of these instructional approaches and the ways they are effectively carried out in classrooms.

  • Margin notes throughout the text integrate the CD footage and lessons with chapter content to better apply the reading.
  • *New!* A colorful insert in Chapter 10 walks you through using the CD to the fullest.
  • *New!* CD-ROM Activities on our Companion Website, found at **www.prenhall.com/tompkins** help to deepen and solidify your understanding of research-based language arts teaching.

Helping students learn to communicate effectively is an ongoing challenge, especially given the cultural and linguistic diversity of today's classrooms and the swift changes in technological environments. For those of you who are pre-service teachers, anxious to work with students from kindergarten through the eighth grade, you will find in *Language Arts: Patterns of Practice* consistent models of instruction to help you make those difficult decisions you may at first find overwhelming. For those of you who are experienced teachers, the text is infused with a rich array of strategies and ideas, adaptable to suit your personal instructional style and your students' individual needs.

Language Arts: Patterns of Practice also provides teachers with a seamless presentation of practical methods for developing and assessing specific strategies and skills

◆ *Piecing a Lesson Together* shows how to teach strategies and skills with detailed descriptions. These features list lesson topics to help teachers plan meaningful *minilessons*, illustrating fully realized minilessons, to demonstrate how classroom teachers follow certain sequences to teach skills. Additional minilessons accompany chapter modules on the text's Companion Website.

◆ *Weaving Assessment Into Practice* features take readers into the classroom to witness the regular integration of assessment in masterful language arts teaching. Here are authentic artifacts and guidelines for assessing students' language arts learning and development.

◆ *Step by Step* features in every chapter give teachers the tools they need to prepare and carry out specific instructional procedures for myriad research-based strategies. Providing detailed instructions, these features become a clear and precise map for teachers to use in their classrooms.

◆ *LA Essentials* provide *guidelines, lists, tools,* and *resources* ready to take right into the classroom. These practical, informative teaching tips are foundational tools all teachers can refer to again and again as they teach.

◆ *Classroom Library* features are another excellent tool for teachers, providing lists of books to use in teaching language arts, addressing the needs of different grades, different reading levels, and different topics.

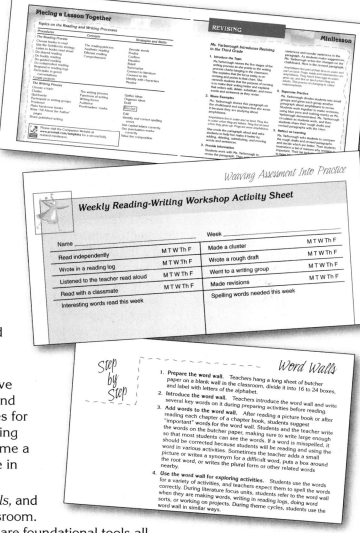

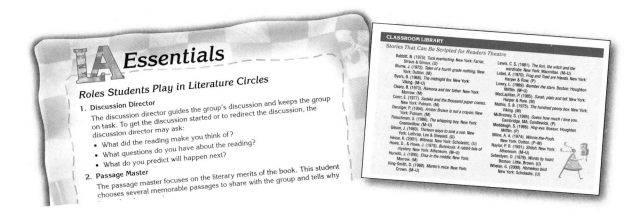

Throughout the chapters, the text illustrates how to use patterns of practice to:

1. Establish a community of learners
2. Engage students in "real" children's literature
3. Teach children the language arts strategies and skills that enable them to learn to communicate effectively
4. Integrate the six language arts skills into classroom instruction by threading them through this entire text with discussions, examples, and specific features

◆ *New! Chapter opening vignettes* begin new chapter discussions by describing how classroom teachers use one of the instructional approaches to develop students' language arts competencies associated specifically with the new chapter's content. These intimate looks at classrooms model masterful language arts teaching while offering a contextual understanding of how patterns of instructional practice actually work in real classrooms.

◆ *Colorful inserts* in Chapter 2 provide detailed classroom examples of teachers in action, identifying procedures and processes for using each instructional approach. These colorful classroom glimpses illustrate how motivating and engaging each approach can be for students learning language arts.

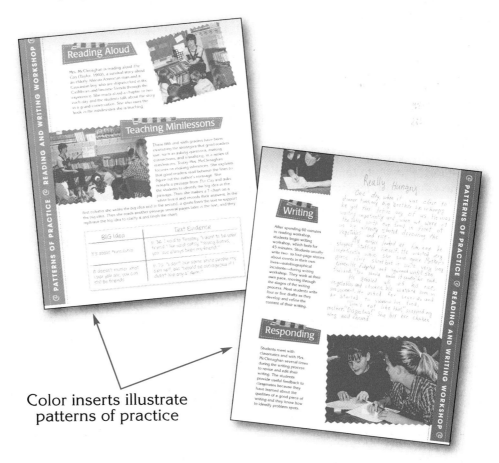

Color inserts illustrate
patterns of practice

PREFACE

Current research identifies six language arts: reading, writing, listening, talking, viewing, and visually representing. Most textbooks cover only four. *Language Arts: Patterns of Practice* not only introduces the six language arts but also *models their integration into the curriculum*. Helping children and adolescents master all six language competencies and learn to communicate effectively in our culturally diverse, technologically changing society can seem like an overwhelming task for a new or even an experienced teacher. This text will help you fully understand how best to teach these language arts in kindergarten through eighth grade.

These six language arts can be meaningfully integrated into the curriculum through four instructional approaches, or *patterns of practice*. This text intricately weaves the teaching of the six language arts through four instructional approaches and, just like creating a quilt, you learn how to put the pieces together to form a complete whole.

PATTERNS OF PRACTICE

Encouraging you as a teacher to actively engage your students in personally meaningful, functional activities, *Language Arts: Patterns of Practice* highlights the four well-respected instructional approaches best suited to integrating the six language arts. These are:

- *Literature focus units*—students read and study a high-quality children's book together as a class.
- *Literature circles*—students choose, read, and respond to a book in small groups.
- *Reading and writing workshops*—students work independently to read self-selected books and use the writing process to independently write books and other compositions.
- *Theme cycles*—students use an integrated approach to engage in a content area study, such as a unit for social studies or science topics.

For the Instructor

- **Syllabus Manager**™ provides you, the instructor, with an easy, step-by-step process to create and revise syllabi, with direct links into Companion Website and other online content without having to learn HTML.
- Students may log on to your syllabus during any study session. All they need to know is the web address for the Companion Website and the password you've assigned to your syllabus.
- After you have created a syllabus using **Syllabus Manager**™, students may enter the syllabus for their course section from any point in the Companion Website.
- Clicking on a date, the student is shown the list of activities for the assignment. The activities for each assignment are linked directly to actual content, saving time for students.
- Adding assignments consists of clicking on the desired due date, then filling in the details of the assignment—name of the assignment, instructions, and whether or not it is a one-time or repeating assignment.
- In addition, links to other activities can be created easily. If the activity is online, a URL can be entered in the space provided, and it will be linked automatically in the final syllabus.
- Your completed syllabus is hosted on our servers, allowing convenient updates from any computer on the Internet. Changes you make to your syllabus are immediately available to your students at their next log on.

Instructor's Manual

Free to instructors, this useful tool provides additional support, including a substantial bank of tests, transparency masters, and online integration. This ancillary is available both in a print version and electronically. A media guide to help professors make the most of the accompanying CD-ROM is included.

Other Merrill Books by Gail Tompkins

- *Literacy for the 21st Century*
- *Teaching Writing: Balancing Process and Product*
- *50 Literacy Strategies*
- *Literacy for the 21st Century*
- *Teaching Reading and Writing in Pre-kindergarten Through Grade 4*
- *Literacy for the 21st Century: Teaching Reading and Writing in Grades 4 Through 8*

Dr. Tompkins is also a contributing author on two Merrill texts:

- *Sharing the Pen: Interactive Writing with Young Children*
- *Teaching Vocabulary: 50 Creative Strategies, Grades K–12*
- *50 Ways to Develop Strategic Writers*

TEACHING AND LEARNING SUPPORT
CD-ROM

The free Writing Workshop CD-ROM, packaged in every text, contains classroom footage of four different language arts classrooms, each following a master teacher through the stages of a lesson. Unlike any field experience, you can watch each lesson as many times as you'd like, reflecting on the decisions made and the strengths and weaknesses in each procedure. The many learning possibilities include:

* Classroom footage, lesson plans, and quotes from the stakeholders.
* A notepad feature allowing you to take notes.
* An Internet button to do more research on the topics being covered.
* The Study Builder and Custom Studies features, allowing you to think through your observations, assess and deepen your understandings, and share your conclusions by creating your own studies.

Companion Website

Built on and enhancing this edition's content, the Companion Website offers many valuable tools for broadening and deepening the reader's feel for inquiry science teaching.

For the Student

* **Chapter Objectives**—outline key concepts from the text
* **Dear Reader**—letters from the author help users see exactly how teachers can get the most from each chapter
* **CD-ROM Activities**—help users broaden and deepen their understanding of both chapter concepts and the classroom footage on the CD.
* **Minilessons**—a second fully realized minilesson from the topics listed in each Piecing a Lesson Together feature is available on the Companion Website.
* **Seeing Common Threads**—dialog with other preservice teachers about the issues and concerns language arts teachers face.
* **Meeting the Needs of Every Student**—more adaptation ideas are provided in this module to help all students find success in their language arts instruction.
* **Extension Activities**—help readers apply information, and many invite them to observe and interact with students in elementary and middle school classrooms. Others ask them to prepare instructional materials, consult outside readings, or examine how they use language.
* **Interactive Self-quizzes**—complete with hints and automatic grading that provide immediate feedback for students
* **Web Destinations**—links to www sites that relate to chapter content
* **Message Board**—serves as a virtual bulletin board to post—or respond to—questions or comments to/from a national audience

Gail Tompkins   I have spent my life teaching. Currently I teach as a professor at California State University, Fresno, where I was awarded the Provost's Award for Excellence in Teaching. Prior to that I taught at the University of Oklahoma in Norman, where I received the Regents' Award for Superior Teaching; Miami University of Ohio; and before that, I taught elementary school in Virginia for 8 years. Today I direct the San Joaquin Valley Writing Project and work regularly with teachers, both by teaching model lessons in classrooms and by leading staff development programs.

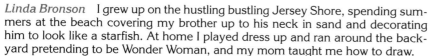

Every day, I write. *Language Arts: Patterns of Practice* is one of six texts I author for Merrill Education. I am also a contributing author for three other Merrill texts, and I've written numerous articles related to reading and language arts for *The Reading Teacher, Language Arts,* and other professional journals. For both teaching and writing I was recently honoured with an induction to California Reading Association's Reading Hall of Fame.

Teaching and writing are my life, as quilting is my hobby. I use a quilt design to carry the theme of this text. Many users recognized the underlying message embedded in this theme—effective language arts instruction weaves the teaching of the language arts into the whole curriculum, and acknowledges that instructional strategies and practices must meet the needs of the diverse language and multicultural backgrounds of students. Just like a quilt, the pieces come together to form a complete whole. To help me convey this message, I have enlisted the help of quilter Laurence Martin and designer Linda Bronson, whose beautiful craft you can see on the cover of this text as well as inside the book.

Laurence Martin   I spent my childhood in Morocco, Africa. Morocco is a land of deep saturated colours and this is reflected in the fine craftsmanship produced in ceramics, fabric, wood, clay, glass, leather, wool, and many others. When I began quilting and painting ten years ago, to my own amazement, I saw colours and shapes from my childhood surface in my work.

A self-taught artist, I practice several forms of art. Creating is as vital to my soul as breathing is to my body, and I love discovering what emerges from deep within me. I remain in awe with the process.

I love colours, fabrics, and threads of all sorts! I enjoy playing with them and at some point in the process they become quilts. Starting a new project is always exciting, as I never know what the end result will look like. You can view more of my quilts at **www.laurencemartin.ca**

Linda Bronson   I grew up on the hustling bustling Jersey Shore, spending summers at the beach covering my brother up to his neck in sand and decorating him to look like a starfish. At home I played dress up and ran around the backyard pretending to be Wonder Woman, and my mom taught me how to draw.

It wasn't until attending art college at the Rhode Island School of Design that I truly blossomed. Suddenly, I was expected to spend all of my time making art! What a treat! I was like a kid in a candy shop! I took so many interesting classes—everything from photography and graphic design to stained glass and ceramics! I learned that an artist could make a career out of doing what they love!

Nowadays, you can find my paintings in picture books, magazines, advertisements, posters and greeting cards. I think I have the world's best job! You can see more of my work at **www.lindabronson.com/**

Library of Congress Cataloging in Publication Data
Tompkins, Gail E.
    Language arts : patterns of practice / by Gail E. Tompkins.
       p. cm.
    Includes bibliographical references and index.
    ISBN 0-13-117735-4
    1. Language arts (Elementary) I. Title.

LB1576.T655 2005
376.2—dc22

                        2004044301

Vice President and Executive Publisher: Jeffery W. Johnston
Editor: Linda Ashe Montgomery
Editorial Assistant: Laura Weaver
Development Editor: Hope Madden
Production Editor: Mary M. Irvin
Design Coordinator: Diane C. Lorenzo
Photo Coordinator: Cynthia Cassidy
Text Design: Grannan Art and Design
Cover Designer: Terry Rohrbach
Cover Image: Linda Bronson
Photo Coordinator: Valerie Schultz
Production Manager: Pamela D. Bennett
Director of Marketing: Ann Castel Davis
Marketing Manager: Darcy Betts Prybella
Marketing Coordinator: Tyra Poole

This book was set in Galliard by Carlisle Communications, Ltd. It was printed and bound by Courier Kendallville, Inc. The cover was printed by Phoenix Color Corp.

Photo Credits: Michael Newman/PhotoEdit: 24; Bob Daemmrich/The Image Works: 60; Anthony Magnacca/Merrill: 117, 265, 548, 617; Anne Vega/Merrill: 164, 417; Scott Cunningham/Merrill: 232, 439; Laima Druskis/PH College: 297; Gail E. Tompkins: 347, 496; Linda Peterson/Merrill: 574; Meeting the Needs feature photos by Barbara Schwartz/Merrill, Anne Vega/Merrill, Linda Peterson/Merrill, Brad Feinknopf/Merrill, and Scott Cunningham/Merrill. All color insert photos by Gail E. Tompkins.

Pearson Education Ltd.
Pearson Education Singapore Pte. Ltd.
Pearson Education Canada, Ltd.
Pearson Education—Japan

Pearson Education Australia Pty. Limited
Pearson Education North Asia Ltd.
Pearson Educación de Mexico, S.A. de C.V.
Pearson Education Malaysia Pte. Ltd.

10 9 8 7 6 5 4 3 2 1
ISBN: 0-13-117735-4

Language Arts

Patterns of Practice

SIXTH EDITION

Gail E. Tompkins
California State University, Fresno

Middle School of Plainville LIC
Plainville, CT

PEARSON

Merrill
Prentice Hall

Upper Saddle River, New Jersey
Columbus, Ohio

ACKNOWLEDGMENTS

Many people helped and encouraged me during the development of this text and during the revisions. My heartfelt thanks go to each of them. First, I thank my students at California State University, Fresno, who have taught me while I taught them. Their insightful questions challenged and broadened my thinking, and their willingness to experiment with the teaching strategies that I was developing furthered my own writing.

I want to express my appreciation to the teachers who invited me into their classrooms and shared their expertise with me. In particular I thank the teachers featured in the Patterns in Practice features: Judith Kenney, Jackson Elementary School, Selma, California; Laurie Goodman, Pioneer Middle School, Hanford, California; Laura McCleneghan, Tarpey Elementary School, Clovis, California; and Susan McCloskey and Pam Papaleo, Greenberg Elementary School, Fresno, California, and also teachers Manuel Hernandez, Kathleen Kakutani, Arnold Keogh, Patty LaRue, Mike Martinez, Kristie McNeal, Ro Meinke, and Jennifer Miller McColm. I also want to acknowledge the teachers who are spotlighted in the Patterns in Practice vignettes in the chapters and other teachers who have influenced my teaching over the years: Eileen Boland, Kimberly Clark, Stephanie Collom, Pat Daniel, Roberta Dillon, Whitney Donnelly, Sandy Harris, Terry Kasner, Kristi McNeal, Carol Ochs, Judy Reeves, Jenny Reno, and Susan Zumwalt. Thanks, too, to the children whose writing samples and photographs appear in the book.

I also want to thank my colleagues who served as reviewers for this and previous editions: Helen Abadiano, Central Connecticut State University; Doreen Bardsley, Arizona State University; Bobbie W. Berry, Clarion University of Pennsylvania; Lonnie R. McDonald, Henderson State University; Betty Goerss, Indiana University East; Gail Gerlach, Indiana University of Pennsylvania; Scott Busley, Grand Canyon University; Marjorie S. Wynn, University of South Florida, Lakeland; Catherine Kurkjian, Central Connecticut State University; Irene Cota, California State University, Northridge; and Janet R. Young, Brigham Young University. I appreciate their thoughtful analyses and insights and I have worked to incorporate their suggestions into this edition.

Finally, I want to express my sincere appreciation to the people at Merrill in Columbus, Ohio. I want to thank Jeff Johnston, who was my first editor and started me on this odyssey; my current editor, Linda Montgomery, who helped me create a new vision for this edition; and my development editor, Hope Madden, who was my cheerleader, encouraging me every step of the way and spurring me toward impossible deadlines. Thanks, also, to the production team: Mary Irvin, my production editor, who moved this edition through the maze of production details so efficiently; Melissa Gruzs, who polished the text during copyediting; Cynthia Cassidy, who searched for the perfect photographs; and Jenifer Cooke, who dealt with the last-minute details. I value each of you.

EDUCATOR LEARNING CENTER:
AN INVALUABLE ONLINE RESOURCE

Merrill Education and the Association for Supervision and Curriculum Development (ASCD) invite you to take advantage of a new online resource, one that provides access to the top research and proven strategies associated with ASCD and Merrill—the Educator Learning Center. At www.EducatorLearningCenter.com you will find resources that will enhance your students' understanding of course topics and of current educational issues, in addition to being invaluable for further research.

How the Educator Learning Center will help your students become better teachers

With the combined resources of Merrill Education and ASCD, you and your students will find a wealth of tools and materials to better prepare them for the classroom.

Research

- More than 600 articles from the ASCD journal *Educational Leadership* discuss everyday issues faced by practicing teachers.
- A direct link on the site to Research Navigator™ gives students access to many of the leading education journals, as well as extensive content detailing the research process.
- Excerpts from Merrill Education texts give your students insights on important topics of instructional methods, diverse populations, assessment, classroom management, technology, and refining classroom practice.

Classroom Practice

- Hundreds of lesson plans and teaching strategies are categorized by content area and age range.
- Case studies and classroom video footage provide virtual field experience for student reflection.
- Computer simulations and other electronic tools keep your students abreast of today's classrooms and current technologies.

Look into the value of Educator Learning Center yourself

A four-month subscription to Educator Learning Center is $25 but is FREE when used in conjunction with this text. To obtain free passcodes for your students, simply contact your local Merrill/Prentice Hall sales representative, and your representative will give you a special ISBN to give your bookstore when ordering your textbooks. To preview the value of this website to you and your students, please go to www.EducatorLearningCenter.com and click on "Demo."

CONTENTS

Chapter 3   *The Reading and Writing Processes*   *102*

Chapter 4   *Emerging Into Literacy*   *156*

Chapter 7   *Listening to Learn*   288

SPECIAL FEATURES

Step by Step

Meeting the Needs of Every Student

Learning and the Language Arts

PATTERNS OF PRACTICE

Reading and Writing Workshop

Literature Focus Units

Literature Circles

Theme Cycles

The first graders in Mrs. McNeal's classroom reread their collaborative retelling of Maurice Sendak's *Where the Wild Things Are* (2003). Their retelling is written on three large charts, one for the beginning, one for the middle, and one for the end. Here is their retelling:

Beginning   *Max wore his wolf suit and made mischief. His mother called him, "Wild Thing!" He was sent to bed without any supper!*

Middle   *Max went to his room and a forest grew. Max got into his private boat and sailed to where the wild things are.*

End   *Max wanted to go home to where somebody loved him best of all. When he got home his supper was waiting for him and it was still hot!*

Mrs. McNeal used interactive writing to write the retelling so that all of the words would be spelled correctly, and the students could easily reread it. The chart of

the middle is shown on page 4. The boxes around some of the letters and words represent the correction tape that Mrs. McNeal and her students used to correct spelling errors and poorly formed letters.

Japmeet holds the pointer and leads the class in rereading the beginning chart. She moves the pointer from word to word as the students read aloud. Next, Henry leads the rereading of the middle chart, and Noelle does the end chart. As they finish reading, the students clap their hands. They are proud of their retelling of a favorite story.

Mrs. McNeal and her students are studying stories, and they know that stories have beginnings, middles, and ends. They can pick out the three parts of stories that Mrs. McNeal reads aloud, and they are learning to incorporate all three parts in the stories they write.

The first graders participate in a variety of language arts activities, including an hourlong writing workshop each day. They begin writing workshop with a 15-minute word work lesson that focuses on learning to read and write high-frequency words. Next, Mrs. McNeal teaches a 15-minute minilesson on a writing concept, such as adding details, writing titles, or using punctuation marks correctly. A 25-minute writing period follows. On most days, students write stories and other compositions independently, but sometimes students work together to write class collaboration compositions, such as the retelling of *Where the Wild Things Are.*

How do teachers incorporate the six language arts in their teaching?

Listening, talking, reading, writing, viewing, and visually representing are the six language arts. Two of the language arts are oral, two are written, and two are visual. Teachers incorporate opportunities for students to use all six every day in their language arts programs. They don't teach each language art separately; instead, they integrate them and provide many opportunities for students to use language actively during the school day. As you read this vignette about first graders participating in writing workshop, notice that Mrs. McNeal provides opportunities for her students to use all six language arts.

For the last 5 minutes of the workshop, students celebrate their newly published compositions by reading them aloud to their classmates.

For the word work lesson, the first graders sit on the floor in front of the word wall, a bulletin-board display with 24 sheets of construction paper on

which the letters are printed in alphabetical order and word cards with high-frequency words are posted according to beginning letter. Currently, 52 words are posted on the word wall, and several new words are added each week. The word wall is shown on page 5.

The lesson begins with a review of the words. Hanna holds the pointer and leads the students in reading the words. Next, Mrs. McNeal passes out small dry-erase boards, pens, and erasers, and the students play a word game: Mrs. McNeal gives phonological, semantic, and syntactic cues about a word on the word wall, and the first graders identify the word. Mrs. McNeal begins, "I'm thinking of a word with three letters. It begins with /y/ and it fits in this sentence: _____ are my friend. What is the word?" The students identify *you* and write it on their dry-erase boards. They hold up their boards so Mrs. McNeal can check their work. Then the students erase their boards and the game continues.

Mrs. McNeal says, "This word has two claps [syllables], it rhymes with *running,* and it fits in this sentence: I am _____ to the movies tomorrow. What is the word?" The students write *going* on their boards, and the teacher checks their progress. They continue the game, listening to cues for *went* and *how* and writing the words. Then the students move to the other side of the classroom for a minilesson.

For today's minilesson, Mrs. McNeal reviews beginning, middle, and end. She asks Sachit to read his draft aloud. He reads:

I love school. I have lots of friends. One is Yaman. He is a good friend to me. We play with Alex. We play basketball. We are good friends. I can't get a ball in the hoop.

Mrs. McNeal's Word Wall			
Aa at any and are all	Bb by	Cc can can't	Dd do don't
Ee eat	Ff fun friend	Gg got get going	Hh house had her have him how
Ii I	Jj jump	Kk	Ll like look
Mm me make	Nn new	Oo other one of or	Pp/Qq play people quiet
Rr run	Ss sister some said	Tt they there time then	Uu used us
Vv very	Ww went with want was	Xx/Yy you	Zz

The students pick out the beginning and middle sections of the story but decide that Sachit's story needs an ending. After several students suggest possible endings, Sachit decides to use Yaman's suggestion and finishes his story this way: *But I still play basketball anyway.*

Students write in their writing workshop notebooks during the writing period. Some students are ready to begin new stories. They sit knee-to-knee with a classmate and plan their stories by telling them aloud. Some students work on stories they began the previous day, and others meet with Mrs. McNeal to share their writings. They read their stories to Mrs. McNeal and talk about them, checking that they make sense and have a beginning, a middle, and an end. If the story is ready to be published, Mrs. McNeal types it on the computer, leaving space at the top for an illustration and correcting spelling and other mechanical errors so that students can read it.

IwenTToSAVrLAK.

I sWiDaNDICLaM uP.

A roK.

Mrs. McNeal prepares progressively more sophisticated writing workshop notebooks. For the first quarter, she makes their notebooks by compiling 15 sheets of unlined 12 × 18-inch paper, adding a construction paper cover, and stapling the notebook together across the 18-inch top so that students can flip through the pages. Students draw pictures in the top two-thirds of the page and write a sentence or two at the bottom. As students get ready to begin each new story, Mrs. McNeal folds the bottom third of the next page horizontally several times to create three or four lines, each approximately 1 1/4 inches apart. These fold lines help students to direct their writing left-to-right across the page. One story from Yousef's first-quarter notebook is shown above. (Transcription of his writing: I went to Shaver Lake. I swimmed and I climbed up a rock.) Yousef's writing is difficult to decipher because he doesn't leave space between words and he uses invented spellings that reflect his phonics knowledge.

For the second quarter, Mrs. McNeal makes their notebooks using legal-size paper (14 × 8 1/2 inches), legal-size file folders, and 3-inch metal paper fasteners. The pages are placed in the notebooks horizontally. The top of the paper is blank for illustrations, and six lines, each 3/4 inch apart, are drawn below. She compiles 12 sheets of paper in a legal-size folder, punches two holes in the top of the sheets and in the folded edge of the file folder, 3 inches apart, and uses the fasteners to secure the notebook. These are the notebooks that Mrs. McNeal's first graders are currently using.

For the third and fourth quarters, Mrs. McNeal will use pocket folders with three brads in the center to hold notebook paper. She will place writing workshop guidelines in the center section; these guidelines include information about writing workshop, revision suggestions, a proofreading checklist, the 100 high-frequency words arranged in alphabetical order, and a sheet for listing published compositions. The students put the composition they are currently

The Birthday Party

Once it was my grandpa's birthday. We had a party.
We played lots of games. My dad played and my sister
played and my cousin played. All of us had fun.

working on in the front section of the folder and finished writings that are waiting to be published in the back section.

During the last 5 minutes of writing workshop, the first graders gather together in the front of the classroom, and students who have just had their writing published read it aloud, show the illustration, and accept compliments from
classmates. Noelle shares her story, "The Birthday Party," which is shown
above. The students like her story because it reminds them of the times they
spend with their grandparents. Mrs. McNeal ceremoniously hangs Noelle's
story in a special section of the bulletin board for everyone to read.

View the CD-ROM that accompanies this text to see Mrs.
McNeal's writing workshop in
action

Understanding how children learn and, particularly, how they learn language
influences how we teach language arts. The instructional program should never
be construed as a smorgasbord of materials and activities; instead, teachers
design instruction based on what they know about how children learn. The
teacher's role in the elementary classroom is changing. Teachers are now decision makers, empowered with both the obligation and the responsibility to
make curricular decisions. In the language arts program, these curricular decisions have an impact on the content (information being taught) and the teaching strategies (techniques for teaching content).

My approach in this textbook incorporates both the constructivist theory
of learning proposed by Jean Piaget and the sociolinguistic theory of Lev
Vygotsky. These two theorists have postulated that students learn best using
authentic materials, through social interaction, and with the support and guidance of their teachers. As you read this chapter, think about these questions:

As you begin
reading this
chapter, you may
want to read the
"Dear Reader"
letter in Chapter 1 on the
Companion Website at
www.prenhall.com/tompkins

◆ How do children learn?

◆ What are the roles of language and culture in learning?

◆ What are the language arts?

◆ How do children learn language arts?

HOW CHILDREN LEARN

Swiss psychologist Jean Piaget (1886–1980) developed a new theory of learning that radically changed our conceptions of child development. His constructivist framework (1969) differed substantially from the behavioral theories that had influenced education for decades. Piaget described learning as the modification of students' cognitive structures as they interact with and adapt to their environment. He believed that children construct their own knowledge from their experiences. Related to Piaget's theory is information-processing theory (Flavell, 1985; Siegler, 1986), which focuses on how learners use cognitive processes and think about what and how they are learning. This view of learning requires a reexamination of the teacher's role. Instead of being primarily dispensers of knowledge, teachers provide students with reading and writing experiences and opportunities to manipulate objects such as storyboards, magnetic letters, and objects in book boxes in order for students to construct their own knowledge (Pearson, 1993).

Sociolinguists emphasize the importance of language in learning and view learning as a reflection of the culture and community in which students live (Heath, 1983; Vygotsky, 1978, 1986). According to Vygotsky, language helps to organize thought, and children use language to learn as well as to communicate and share experiences with others. Understanding that children use language for social purposes, teachers plan instructional activities that incorporate a social component, such as having students share their writing with classmates. And, because children's language and concepts of literacy reflect their cultures and home communities, teachers must respect students' language and appreciate cultural differences in their attitudes toward learning—and toward learning language arts in particular.

The Cognitive Structure

Children's knowledge is not just a collection of isolated bits of information; it is organized in the brain, and this organization becomes increasingly integrated and interrelated as their knowledge grows. The organization of knowledge is the cognitive structure, and knowledge is arranged in category systems called *schemata*. (A single category is called a *schema*.) Within the schemata are three components: categories of knowledge, the features or rules for determining what constitutes a category and what will be included in each category, and a network of interrelationships among the categories.

These schemata can be likened to a conceptual filing system in which children and adults organize and store the information derived from their past experiences. Taking this analogy further, information is filed in the brain in "file folders." As children learn, they add file folders to their filing system, and as they study a topic, its file folder becomes thicker.

As children learn, they invent new categories, and although different people have many similar categories, schemata are personalized according to individual experiences and interests. Some people, for example, may have only one general category, bugs, into which they lump their knowledge of ants, butterflies, spiders, and bees, whereas other people distinguish between insects and spiders and develop a category for each. Those who distinguish between insects and spiders also develop a set of rules based on the distinctive characteristics of these animals for classifying them into one category or the other. In addition, a network of interrelationships connects the insect and spider categories to other categories. Networks, too, are individualized, depending on each person's unique knowledge and experiences. The category of spiders might be networked as a subcategory of arachnids, and the class relationship between scorpions and spiders might be made. Other networks, such as a connection to a poisonous animals category or a webs and nests category, could be established. The networks that link categories, characteristics, and examples with other categories, characteristics, and examples are extremely complex.

As children adapt to their environment, they add new information about their experiences that requires them to enlarge existing categories or to construct new ones. According to Piaget (1969), two processes make this change possible. Assimilation is the cognitive process by which information from the environment is integrated into existing schemata. In contrast, accommodation is the cognitive process by which existing schemata are modified or new schemata are restructured to adapt to the environment. Through assimilation, children add new information to their picture of the world; through accommodation, they change that picture on the basis of new information.

The Process of Learning

Piaget recognized that children are naturally curious about their world and are active and motivated learners. New experiences are necessary for learning. Children experiment with the objects they encounter and try to make sense out of their experiences; that is to say, they construct their own knowledge from interactions and experiences rather than through passively receiving environmental stimulation. Oral and written language work the same way: Children interact with language just as they experiment with bicycles they ride.

Learning occurs through the process of equilibration (Piaget, 1975). When a child encounters something he or she does not understand or cannot assimilate, disequilibrium, or cognitive conflict, results. This disequilibrium typically produces confusion and agitation, feelings that impel children to seek equilibrium, or a comfortable balance with the environment. In other words, when confronted with new or discrepant information, children (as well as adults) are intrinsically motivated to try to make sense of it. If the child's schemata can accommodate the new information, then the disequilibrium caused by the new experience will motivate the child to learn. Equilibrium is thus regained at a higher developmental level. These are the steps of this process:

1. Equilibrium is disrupted by the introduction of new or discrepant information.
2. Disequilibrium occurs, and the dual processes of assimilation and accommodation function.
3. Equilibrium is attained at a higher developmental level.

The process of equilibration happens to us again and again during the course of a day. In fact, it is occurring right now as you are reading this chapter. If you are already familiar with the constructivist learning theory and have learned about Piaget in other education courses, your mental filing cabinet has been activated and you are assimilating the information you are reading into the file folder on "Piaget" or "learning theories" already in your filing cabinet. On the other hand, if you aren't familiar with constructivist learning theories, your mind is actively creating a new file folder in which to put the information you are reading. Learning doesn't always occur when we are presented with new information, however. If the new information is too difficult and we cannot relate it to what we already know, we do not learn. This is true for both children and adults. The important implication for teachers is that new information must be puzzling, challenging, or, in Piaget's words, "moderately novel." Information that is too familiar is quickly assimilated, and information that is too unfamiliar cannot be accommodated and will not be learned.

Learning Strategies

We all have skills that we use automatically as well as self-regulated strategies for things that we do well—driving defensively, playing volleyball, training a new pet, or maintaining classroom discipline. We unconsciously apply skills we have learned and choose among skills as we think strategically. The strategies we use in these activities are problem-solving mechanisms that involve complex thinking processes. When we are just learning how to drive a car, for example, we learn both skills and strategies. Some of the first skills we learn are how to start the engine, make left turns, and parallel park. With practice, these skills become automatic. Some of the first strategies we learn are how to pass another car and how to stay a safe distance behind the car ahead of us. At first we have only a small repertoire of strategies, and we don't always use them effectively. That's one reason why we take lessons from a driving instructor and have a learner's permit that requires a more experienced driver to ride along with us. These seasoned drivers teach us defensive driving strategies. We learn strategies for driving on interstate highways, on slippery roads, and at night. With practice and guidance, we become more successful drivers, able to anticipate driving problems and take defensive actions.

During the elementary grades, children develop a number of learning strategies or methods for learning. Rehearsal—repeating information over and over—is one learning strategy or cognitive process children can use to remember something. Other learning strategies include:

Predicting: anticipating what will happen

Organizing: grouping information into categories

Elaborating: expanding on the information presented

Monitoring: regulating or keeping track of progress

Information-processing theory suggests that as children grow older, their use of learning strategies improves (Flavell, 1985).

As they acquire more effective methods for learning and remembering information, children also become more aware of their own cognitive processes and better able to regulate them. Elementary students can reflect on their literacy processes and talk about themselves as readers and writers. For example, third grader Mario reports that "it's mostly after I read a book that I write" (Muhammad, 1993, p. 99), and fifth grader Hobbes reports that "the pictures in my head help me when I write stuff down 'cause then I can get ideas from my pictures" (Cleary, 1993, p. 142). Eighth grader Chandra talks about poetry: "Poetry is a fine activity, and it can get you in tune with yourself. . . . I think that my favorite person who does poetry is Maya Angelou" (Steinbergh, 1993, p. 212).

Students become more realistic about the limitations of their memories and more knowledgeable about which learning strategies are most effective in particular situations. They also become increasingly aware of what they know and don't know. The term *metacognition* refers to this knowledge children acquire about their own cognitive processes and to children's regulation of their cognitive processes to maximize learning.

Teachers play an important role in developing children's metacognitive abilities. During large-group activities, teachers introduce and model learning strategies. In small-group lessons, teachers provide guided practice, talk with children about learning strategies, and ask students to reflect on their own use of these cognitive processes. Teachers also guide students about when to use particular strategies and which strategies are more effective with various activities.

Social Contexts of Learning

Children's cognitive development is enhanced through social interaction. Russian psychologist Lev Vygotsky (1896–1934) asserted that children learn through socially meaningful interactions and that language is both social and an important facilitator of learning. Children's experiences are organized and shaped by society, but rather than merely absorbing these experiences, children negotiate and transform them as a dynamic part of culture. They learn to talk through social interactions and to read and write through interactions with literate children and adults (Dyson, 1993; Harste, 1990). Community is important for both readers and writers. Students talk about books they are reading with classmates, and they turn to classmates for feedback about their writing (Zebroski, 1994).

Through interactions with adults and collaboration with classmates, children learn things they could not learn on their own. Adults guide and support children as they move from their current level of knowledge toward a more advanced level. Vygotsky (1978) described these two levels as (1) the actual developmental level, the level at which children can perform a task independently, and (2) the level of potential development, the level at which children can perform a task with assistance. Children can typically do more difficult things in collaboration than they can on their own, and this is why teachers are important models for their students and why children often work with partners and in small groups.

A child's "zone of proximal development" (Vygotsky, 1978) is the range of tasks that the child can perform with guidance from others but cannot yet perform independently. Vygotsky believed that children learn best when what they are attempting to learn is within this zone. He felt that children learn little by performing tasks they can already do independently—tasks at their actual developmental level—or by attempting tasks that are too difficult or beyond their zone of proximal development.

Vygotsky and Jerome Bruner (1986) both used the term *scaffold* as a metaphor to describe adults' contributions to children's learning. Scaffolds are support mechanisms that teachers, parents, and others provide to help children successfully perform a task within their zone of proximal development. Teachers serve as scaffolds when they model or demonstrate a procedure, guide children through a task, ask questions, break complex tasks into smaller steps, and supply pieces of information. As children gain knowledge and experience about how to perform a task, teachers gradually withdraw their support so that children make the transition from social interaction to internalized, independent functioning.

The teacher's role in guiding students' learning within the zone of proximal development has three components, according to Dixon-Krauss (1996):

1. Teachers mediate or augment children's learning through social interaction.
2. Teachers are flexible and provide support based on feedback from the children as they are engaged in the learning task.
3. Teachers vary the amount of support from very explicit to vague, according to children's needs.

Language, according to Vygotsky, can be used for purposes other than social. Piaget (1975) described how young children engage in egocentric speech—talking aloud to themselves as they pursue activities, such as building with blocks. Vygotsky (1986) noticed that older children and adults sometimes talk to themselves while performing a difficult or frustrating task, and he noted that this talking aloud seemed to guide or direct their thinking. From these observations, Vygotsky concluded that language is a mechanism for thought and that children's egocentric speech (which he called "self-talk") gradually becomes inner speech, when children talk to themselves mentally rather than orally. Self-talk is the link between talk used for social purposes and talk used for intellectual purposes. According to Vygotsky, children use both self-talk and inner speech to guide their learning.

Implications for Learning Language Arts

Students interact with their environment and actively construct knowledge using the processes of assimilation and accommodation. Students learn when their existing schemata are enlarged because of assimilated information and when their schemata are restructured to account for new experiences being acted on and accommodated.

As students engage in learning activities, they are faced with learning and discovering some new element in an otherwise known or familiar system of information. Students recognize or seek out the information embedded in a situation that makes sense and is moderately novel. When students are forced to contend with the novel part of the information, their schemata are disrupted, or put in a state of disequilibrium. Accommodation of the novel information causes a reorganization of the schemata, resulting in students' having more complex schemata and being able to apply more complex information than they could previously.

Vygotsky's (1978) concept of the zone of proximal development emphasizes the importance of talk and explains how children learn through social interactions with adults. Adults use scaffolds to help children move from their current stage of development toward their potential, and teachers provide a similar type of assistance as they support students in learning language arts (Applebee & Langer, 1983).

In the lessons they prepare for their students, teachers can create optimal conditions for learning. When students do not have the schemata for predicting and interpreting the new information, teachers must help them relate what they know to what they do not know. Therefore, the new information must appear in a situation that makes sense and must be moderately novel; it must not be too difficult for students to accommodate it.

How children learn has important implications for how students learn language arts in school and how teachers teach language arts. Contributions from the constructivist and sociolinguistic learning theories include these ideas:

- Students are active participants in learning.
- Students learn by relating the new information to prior knowledge.
- Students organize their knowledge in schemata.
- Students use skills automatically and strategies consciously as they learn.
- Students learn through social interactions with classmates and the teacher.
- Teachers provide scaffolds for students.

LANGUAGE LEARNING AND CULTURE

Language is a complex system for creating meaning through socially shared conventions (Halliday, 1978). Before children enter elementary school, they learn the language of their community. They understand what community members say to them, and they share their ideas with others through that language. In an amazingly short period of 3 or 4 years, children master the exceedingly complex system of their native language, which allows them to understand sentences they have never heard before and to create sentences they have never said before. Young children are not taught how to talk; this knowledge about language develops tacitly, or unconsciously.

The Four Language Systems

Language is organized using four systems, sometimes called *cueing systems*, which together make oral and written communication possible. The four language systems are

- The phonological or sound system of language
- The syntactic or structural system of language
- The semantic or meaning system of language
- The pragmatic or social and cultural use system of language

As children learn to talk, they develop an implicit understanding of the systems, and they apply their knowledge of the four systems whenever they use words—whether for listening or talking, reading or writing, or viewing or visually representing. Students integrate information simultaneously from these four language systems in order to communicate. No one system is more important than any other one even though the phonological system plays a prominent role in early literacy.

The Phonological System.

There are approximately 44 speech sounds in English. Children learn to pronounce these sounds as they learn to talk, and they learn to associate the sounds with letters as they learn to read and write. Sounds are called phonemes, and they are represented in print with diagonal lines to differentiate them from graphemes, or letter combinations. Thus, the first letter in *mother* is written *m,* and the phoneme is represented by /m/; the phoneme in *soap* represented by the grapheme *oa* is represented by/ō/.

The phonological system is important in both oral and written language. Regional and cultural differences exist in the way people pronounce phonemes. For example, Jimmy Carter's speech is characteristic of the southeastern United States, and John F. Kennedy's is typical of New England. Similarly, the English spoken in Australia is different from American English. Children who are learning English as a second language must learn to pronounce English sounds, and sounds that are different from those in their native language are particularly difficult for children to learn. For example, Spanish does not have /th/, and children who have immigrated to the United States from Mexico and other Spanish-speaking countries have difficulty pronouncing this sound. They often substitute /d/ for /th/ because both sounds are articulated in similar ways (Nathenson-Mejia, 1989). Younger children usually learn to pronounce the difficult sounds more easily than do older children and adults.

To learn more about phonics, see Chapter 4, "Emerging Into Literacy."

Children use their knowledge of the phonological system as they learn to read and write. In a purely phonetic language, there would be a one-to-one correspondence between letters and sounds, and teaching students to sound out words would be a simple process. But English is not a purely phonetic language, because there are 26 letters and 44 sounds and many ways to combine the letters—especially the vowels—to spell some of the sounds. Consider the different ways of spelling long *e* in these words: *sea, green, Pete, me,* and *people.* And sometimes the patterns used to spell long *e* don't work, as in *head* and *great.* Phonics, which describes the phoneme-grapheme correspondences and related spelling rules, is an important part of reading instruction, because students use phonics information to decode words. However, because not all words can be easily decoded, and because good readers do much more than simply decode words when they read, phonics instruction cannot be an entire reading program, even though the advertisements for some commercial phonics programs claim that they are complete programs.

See Chapter 12, "Learning to Spell Conventionally," to learn more about invented spelling.

Students in the primary grades also use their understanding of the phonological system to create invented or temporary spellings. First graders, for example, might spell *home* as *hm* or *hom,* and second graders might spell *school* as *skule,* based on their developing knowledge of phoneme-grapheme relationships and the spelling patterns. As students learn more phonics and gain more experience reading and writing, their spellings become more sophisticated and finally become conventional. Also, the spellings of students who are learning English as a second language often reflect their pronunciations of words (Nathenson-Mejia, 1989).

The Syntactic System.   The syntactic system is the structural organization of English. This system is the grammar that regulates how words are combined into sentences. The word *grammar* here means the rules governing how words are combined in sentences, not the grammar of English textbooks or the conventional etiquette of language. Children use the syntactic system as they combine words to form sentences. Word order is important in English, and English speakers must arrange words into a sequence that makes sense. Young Spanish-speaking children who are learning English as a second language, for example, learn to say, "This is my red sweater," not, "This is my sweater red," which is the literal translation from Spanish. Children also learn to comprehend and produce statements, questions, and other types of sentences before they come to school.

Students use their knowledge of the syntactic system as they read. They anticipate that the words they are reading have been strung together into sentences. When they come to an unfamiliar word, they recognize its role in the sentence even if they don't know the terms for parts of speech. In the sentence "The horses galloped through the gate and out into the field," students may not be able to decode the word *through,* but they can easily substitute a reasonable word or phrase, such as *out of* or *past.* Many of the capitalization and punctuation rules that elementary students learn reflect the syntactic system of language. Similarly, when students learn about simple, compound, and complex sentences, they are learning about the syntactic system.

Another component of syntax is word forms. Words such as *dog* and *play* are morphemes, the smallest meaningful units in language. Word parts that change the meaning of a word are also morphemes. When the plural marker -*s* is added to *dog* to make *dogs,* for instance, or the past-tense marker -*ed* is added to *play* to make *played,* these words now contain two morphemes because the inflectional endings changed the meaning of the words. The words *dog* and *play* are free morphemes because they convey meaning while standing alone. The endings -*s* and -*ed* are bound morphemes because they must be attached to a free morpheme to convey meaning. As they learn to talk, children quickly learn to combine words and word parts, such as adding -*s* to *cookie* to create a plural and adding -*er* to *high* to indicate a comparison. They also learn to combine two or more free morphemes to form compound words. *Birthday,* for example, is a compound word created by combining two free morphemes.

During the elementary grades, students learn to add affixes to words. Affixes added at the beginning of a word are prefixes, and affixes added at the end are suffixes. Both kinds of affixes are bound morphemes. For example, the prefix *un-* in *unhappy* is a bound morpheme, whereas *happy* is a free morpheme because it can stand alone as a word.

The Semantic System.   The third language system is the semantic or meaning system. Vocabulary is the key component of this system. As children learn to talk, they acquire a vocabulary that is continually increasing through the preschool years and the elementary grades. Researchers estimate that children have a vocabulary of 5,000 words by the time they enter school, and they continue to acquire 3,000 words each year during the elementary grades (Lindfors, 1987; Nagy, 1988). Considering how many words students learn each

To read about teaching grammar in the elementary grades, see Chapter 13, "Learning About Grammar and Usage."

year, it is unreasonable to assume that they learn words only through formal instruction. Students learn many, many words informally through reading and through social studies, science, and other curricular areas. Students probably learn 7 to 10 words a day. A remarkable achievement!

At the same time children are learning new words, they are also learning that many words have more than one meaning. Meaning is usually based on the context, or the surrounding words. The common word *run,* for instance, has more than 30 meanings. Read these sentences to see how the meaning of the word *run* is tied to the context in which it is used:

> *Will the mayor run for reelection?*
>
> *The bus runs between Dallas and Houston.*
>
> *The advertisement will run for three days.*
>
> *Did you run in the 50-yard dash?*
>
> *The plane made a bombing run.*
>
> *Will you run to the store and get a loaf of bread for me?*
>
> *The dogs are out in the run.*
>
> *Oh, no! I got a run in my new pair of pantyhose!*

Children often don't have the full, adult meaning of many words; rather, they learn meanings through a process of refinement. They add features, or layers of meaning.

Children learn other sophisticated concepts about words as well. They learn about shades of meaning—for example, the differences among these *sad* words: *unhappy, crushed, desolate, miserable, disappointed, cheerless, down,* and *grief stricken.* They also learn about synonyms and antonyms, wordplay, and figurative language, including idioms.

The Pragmatic System. The fourth language system is pragmatics, which deals with the social and cultural aspects of language use. People use language for many different purposes, and how they talk or write varies according to purpose and audience.

Language variety is also part of the pragmatic system. Language use varies among social classes, cultural and ethnic groups, and geographic regions. These varieties are known as dialects. School is one cultural community, and the language of school is Standard English. This register, or style, is formal—the one used in textbooks, newspapers, and magazines and by television newscasters. Other forms, including those spoken in urban ghettos, in Appalachia, and by Mexican Americans in the Southwest, are generally classified as nonstandard English. These nonstandard forms of English are alternatives in which the phonology, syntax, and semantics differ from those of Standard English, but they are neither inferior nor substandard. They reflect the communities of the speakers, and the speakers communicate as effectively as those who use Standard English in their communities. The goal is for students to add Standard English to their repertoire of language registers, not to replace their home dialect with Standard English.

As students who speak nonstandard English read texts written in Standard English, they often translate what they read into their own dialect. Sometimes this occurs when they are reading aloud. For example, a sentence that is written "They

See Chapter 5, "Looking Closely at Words," for more information about vocabulary.

are going to school" might be read aloud this way: "They be goin' to school." Emergent or beginning readers are not usually corrected when they translate words into nonstandard dialects without changing the meaning, but older, more fluent readers should be directed to read the words as they are printed in the book.

Many trade books include dialogue written in nonstandard English. *Shiloh* (Naylor, 1991), for example, is set in West Virginia, and some of the characters speak nonstandard English. *Mirandy and Brother Wind* (McKissack, 1988) is an African American folktale, and some of the characters speak Black English. *White Dynamite and Curly Kidd* (Martin & Archambault, 1986) is a rodeo story, rich with the vocabulary, rhyme, and sentence structure of this truly American institution. As students read these books, they learn about the richness and variety of English dialects in the United States.

The four language systems and their terminology are summarized in Figure 1–1. Both children and adults use the four language systems as they communicate through oral and written language.

Culturally and Linguistically Diverse Students

The United States is a culturally pluralistic society, and our ethnic, racial, and socioeconomic diversity is increasingly being reflected in elementary classrooms. Today more than a quarter of the population in the United States classify themselves as non-European Americans (*The World Almanac and Book of Facts 2001*; 2000). The percentage of culturally diverse children is even higher: In California, 51% of school-age children belong to ethnic minority groups, and in New York State, 40% do. Given current birthrates of minority groups and immigration patterns, it has been estimated that within a few years, Hispanic American as well as Asian American populations will have grown by more than 20%, and the African American population will have grown by 12%. These changing demographic realities will have a significant impact on elementary classrooms, as more and more students come from linguistically and culturally diverse backgrounds. More than ever before, today's students will live in a global society, and they need the skills and knowledge to live harmoniously with other cultural groups.

The United States is a nation of immigrants, and dealing with cultural diversity is not a new responsibility for public schools; however, the magnitude of diversity is much greater now. In the past, the United States was viewed as a melting pot in which language and cultural differences would be assimilated or combined to form a new, truly American culture. What actually happened, though, was that the European American culture rose to the top because it was the dominant immigrant group, and the cultures of other groups sank (Banks, 1994). The concept of cultural pluralism has replaced the idea of assimilation. According to cultural pluralism, people have the right to retain their cultural identity within American society, and each culture contributes to and enriches the total society. This concept is an outgrowth of the Civil Rights movement of the 1960s. Other ethnic cultures have been inspired by the Civil Rights movement, and they have been empowered, too.

Children of diverse cultures come to school with a broad range of language and literacy experiences, even if those experiences are not the same as those of mainstream or European American children (Samway & McKeon, 1999). Minority children have already learned to communicate in at least one language,

FIGURE 1-1

Overview of the Four Language Systems

System	Description	Terms	Uses in the Elementary Grades
Phonological System	The sound system of English with approximately 44 sounds	• Phoneme (the smallest unit of sound) • Grapheme (the written representation of a phoneme using one or more letters) • Phonological awareness (knowledge about the sound structure of words, at the phoneme, onset-rime, and syllable levels) • Phonemic awareness (the ability to manipulate the sounds in words orally) • Phonics (instruction about phoneme-grapheme correspondences and spelling rules)	• Pronouncing words • Detecting regional and other dialects • Decoding words when reading • Using invented spelling • Reading and writing alliterations and onomatopoeia
Syntactic System	The structural system of English that governs how words are combined into sentences	• Syntax (the structure or grammar of a sentence) • Morpheme (the smallest meaningful unit of language) • Free morpheme (a morpheme that can stand alone as a word) • Bound morpheme (a morpheme that must be attached to a free morpheme)	• Adding inflectional endings to words • Combining words to form compound words • Adding prefixes and suffixes to root words • Using capitalization and punctuation to indicate beginnings and ends of sentences • Identifying the parts of speech • Writing simple, compound, and complex sentences • Combining sentences
Semantic System	The meaning system of English that focuses on vocabulary	• Semantics (meaning)	• Learning the meanings of words • Discovering that some words have multiple meanings • Studying synonyms, antonyms, and homonyms • Using a dictionary and a thesaurus • Reading and writing comparisons (metaphors and similes) and idioms
Pragmatic System	The system of English that varies language according to social and cultural uses	• Function (the purpose for which a person uses language) • Standard English (the form of English used in textbooks and by television newscasters) • Nonstandard English (other forms of English)	• Varying language to fit specific purposes • Reading and writing dialogue in dialects • Comparing standard and nonstandard forms of English

and, if they don't speak English, they want to learn English in order to make friends, learn, and communicate just like their classmates. Teachers of culturally and linguistically diverse students must implement a language arts program that is sensitive to and reflective of these students' backgrounds and needs. In fact, all teachers must be prepared to work with this ever-growing population, and teachers who have no minority students in their classrooms still need to incorporate a multicultural perspective in their curriculum to prepare their students to interact effectively in the increasingly multicultural American society.

Teachers should not view cultural and linguistic diversity as a problem to overcome; instead, it provides an opportunity to enhance and enrich the learning of all students. Teachers need to provide literacy experiences that reflect the multitude of backgrounds from which their students come, and multicultural literature plays an important role in filling that need (Yokota, 1993).

Bilingual Students and Students Who Are Learning English

Students who are learning English are a diverse group. Some are fluent in both English and their native language, whereas others know little or no English. Some learn to speak English quickly, and others learn more slowly. It often takes 4 to 7 years or longer to become a proficient speaker of English; the more similar the first language is to English, the easier it is to learn English (Allen, 1991).

One conflict for bilingual students is that learning and speaking Standard English are often perceived by family and community members as a rejection of family and the culture of the home. Cultural pluralism has replaced the melting-pot point of view, and people in minority ethnic groups are no longer as willing to give up their culture and language to join the mainstream culture. Often they choose to live and function in both cultures, with free access to their cultural patterns, switching from one culture to the other as the situation demands.

Valuing Students' Native Language.   Until recently, most non-English-speaking students were submerged into English-speaking classrooms and left to sink or swim (Spangenberg-Urbschat & Pritchard, 1994). Unfortunately, many students sank and dropped out before graduating from high school. To better meet the needs of linguistically diverse students, teachers now value students' native language and help their students develop a high level of proficiency in their native language as well as in English. Instruction in students' native language is effective and equitable for large groups of language-minority students (Faltis, 1993).

Whether language arts instruction is in English or in students' native language, teachers can support and value students' native language (Freeman & Freeman, 1993). Suggestions for supporting and valuing students' native language are presented in the LA Essentials feature on page 21. Even teachers who do not speak or write students' native language themselves can follow most of these guidelines using a foreign-language dictionary. For example, they can use a foreign-language dictionary to post signs in the classroom and encourage students to read and write books in their native language. The activities also help students expand their native-language proficiency, develop greater self-confidence, and value their own language.

Learning a Second Language.

Learning a second language is a constructive process, just as learning a native language is, and children develop language in a predictable way through interactions with other children and with adults. Research suggests that second-language acquisition is similar to first-language acquisition (Spangenberg-Urbschat & Pritchard, 1994). Urzua (1980) lists three principles culled from the research:

1. People use many similar language-learning strategies, whether they are small children learning their native language or older children or adults learning a second language.
2. Just as children learning to speak their native language move through a series of developmental stages, second-language learners move through several stages as they learn a new language.
3. First- or second-language learning takes place only when learners have the opportunity to use language for meaningful, functional, and genuine purposes.

When children and adults arrive in the United States, they generally go through a silent period (Krashen, 1982) of several months during which they observe others communicating prior to talking or writing in English themselves. Then they begin tentatively to use language to communicate, and through listening, talking, reading, and writing, their language use becomes more cognitively and linguistically complex. The English spoken by newcomers is syntactically less complex; in addition, newcomers enunciate words clearly, speak more slowly, and avoid using idiomatic expressions.

New English speakers use very short sentences, often with two or three key words, much like the telegraphic speech of young children. For example, newcomers might say "No pencil" for "I don't have a pencil," or "Book table" for "The book is on the table." They also may overgeneralize and call all adults in the school "teachers." As second-language learners acquire labels for more concepts and more sophisticated syntactic structures, they use progressively longer and more complex sentences. They move out of the here-and-now, present-tense verb constructions to past and future constructions; however, many students learning English as a second language have difficulty adding the *-ed* past-tense marker to verbs, as in "Yesterday I play ball."

When parents talk with preschool children learning to speak their native language, they scaffold and extend the children's language. Parents also understand their children's special words for things. These adaptations are called "motherese." There are striking parallels between the adaptations made by people who interact effectively with EL students and those described for motherese.

English learners often mix English with their native language, shifting back and forth even within sentences. This often-misunderstood phenomenon is called code switching (Lara, 1989; Troika, 1981). Sometimes students read the text in English but mentally translate it into their native language in order to understand it. This takes a little more time than native speakers need, so teachers must allow more time for EL students to translate teachers' and classmates' questions and comments from English into their native language and translate

LA Essentials

Guidelines for Supporting and Valuing Students' Native Language

1. Use Environmental Print in Students' Native Language

Teachers post signs and other environmental print written in students' native language in the classroom. In a primary-grade classroom, posters with color words, numbers, and the days of the week should be written both in English and in students' native language. Bulletin-board titles and captions on posters can also be translated into students' native language.

2. Add Native-Language Reading Materials to the Classroom Library

Teachers add books, magazines, and other reading materials written in the students' native language in the library center. Quality books for children written in a variety of languages are becoming increasingly available in the United States. Also, award-winning books of children's literature are being translated into other languages, especially Spanish and Chinese. Books such as *Where the Wild Things Are* (Sendak, 2003) have been translated for younger children, and *Tuck Everlasting* (Babbitt, 1988) for older children. Sometimes parents and other members of the community are willing to lend books written in a child's native language for the child to use in school. Or, sometimes parents can translate a book being used in class for their child.

3. Encourage Students to Write Books in Their Native Language

Students can write and publish books in their native language. They use the writing process just as English-speaking students do, and they can share their published books with classmates and place them in the classroom library.

4. Use Bilingual Tutors

Students can read and write with tutors, older students, classmates, and parents who speak their native language. Some classrooms have native-language aides who read and write with students in the native language. In other classrooms, parents or older native-speaking students come into the classroom to work with students.

5. View Native-Language Videotapes

Teachers can use videotapes of students reading and dramatizing stories in their native language. In addition, students can dramatize events in history or demonstrate how to do something in their native language. Creating and viewing these videotapes are useful for building students' proficiency in their native language.

Adapted from Freeman & Freeman, 1993.

their ideas from their native language into English. Too often, teachers assume that students have not understood or do not know the answer when they do not respond immediately. Code switching is a special linguistic and social skill; it is not a confusion between languages or a corruption of students' native language.

After approximately 2 years, many students are fluent enough in English to carry on everyday conversations, but it can take these students 5, 6, or 7 years to achieve the same level of fluency in English that their mainstream classmates have (Cummins, 1989). Interestingly, Wong-Fillmore (1985) has found that EL students learn English in class from teachers and classmates who speak fluent English rather than from their cultural peer group. Moreover, school may be the only place where students speak English!

Critical Literacy

It's easy for teachers to focus on teaching students how to read and write without considering how language works in our society. Language is more than just a means of communication; it shapes our perceptions of society, justice, and acceptance. Standard English is the language of school, but today, many students speak a different language or a nonstandard form of English at home. These language differences and the way that teachers and classmates respond to them affect how students think about themselves and their expectations for success at school. Some students are more eager to share their ideas than others, and research suggests that teachers call on boys more often than girls. Also, classmates encourage some students to participate more than others. These language behaviors silence some students and marginalize others.

Language is not neutral. The reasons why people use language are another consideration. Both children and adults use language for a variety of purposes—to entertain, inform, control, and persuade, for example. Language used for these purposes can affect our beliefs, opinions, and behavior. Martin Luther King Jr.'s "I Have a Dream" speech, for example, had a great impact on American society, calling people to action in the Civil Rights movement. Essays, novels, and other written materials also affect us in powerful ways. Think about the impact of *Anne Frank: The Diary of a Young Girl* (Frank, 1995): The madness of the Holocaust appalled us.

Critical literacy focuses on the empowering role of both oral and written language. This theory emphasizes the use of all six language arts to communicate, solve problems, and persuade others to a course of action. It emphasizes the interactions of students in the classroom and in their neighborhoods, and the relationship between language and students in the context of the classroom, the neighborhood, and society.

Critical literacy grew out of the critical pedagogy theory that suggests that teachers and students ask fundamental questions about knowledge, justice, and equity (Wink, 2000). Language becomes a means for social action. Teachers do more than just teach students to use the six language arts; both teachers and students become agents of social change. The increasing social and cultural diversity in our society adds urgency to resolving inequalities and injustices.

Language arts instruction does not take place in a vacuum; the content that teachers teach and the ways they teach it occur in a social, cultural, political and historical context (Freire & Macedo, 1987). Consider the issue of grammar instruction, for example. Some people argue that grammar shouldn't be taught in the elementary grades because it is too abstract and won't help students become better readers or writers; however, other people believe that not teaching grammar is one way the majority culture denies access to non-standard English speakers. Both proponents and detractors of grammar instruction want what is best for children, but their views are diametrically opposed. Think about these issues related to teaching and learning in the elementary grades:

> *Does school perpetuate the dominant culture and exclude others?*
>
> *Do all students have equal access to learning opportunities?*
>
> *How are students who speak nonstandard English treated?*
>
> *Is school more like family life in some cultures than others?*
>
> *Do teachers interact differently with boys and girls?*
>
> *Are some students silenced in classrooms?*
>
> *Do teachers have different expectations for minority students?*
>
> *Are English learners marginalized?*
>
> *Does the literature that students read reflect diverse voices?*

Language arts is not simply a body of knowledge, but rather is a way of organizing knowledge within a cultural and political context. Giroux (1988) challenges teachers not to accept the status quo, but to be professionals and to take control of their own teaching and consider the impact of what they do in the classroom.

Luke and Freebody's (1997) model of reading includes critical literacy as the fourth level. I have adapted their model to include both reading and writing:

1. Students become code breakers—they learn phonics, word-identification strategies, and high-frequency words to read and write fluently.
2. Students become text participants—they comprehend what they are reading, learn about text structures and genres, and develop coherent ideas in the texts they write.
3. Students become text users—they read and write multigenre texts and compare the effect of genre and purpose on texts.
4. Students become text critics—they examine the issues raised in books and other texts they read and write.

Teachers take students to the fourth level, text critics, when they read and discuss books such as *Fly Away Home* (Bunting, 1991), the story of a homeless boy and his father who live at the airport; *The Breadwinner* (Ellis, 2000), the story of a girl in Taliban-controlled Afghanistan who must pretend to be a boy to support her family; *The Watsons Go to Birmingham—1963* (Curtis, 1995), the story of an African American family caught in the Birmingham church bombing; and *Homeless Bird* (Whelan, 2000), the story of an Indian girl who has no future when she is widowed. These stories describe injustices that primary-, middle-, and upper-grade students can understand and discuss (Foss, 2002; Lewison, Flint, & Sluys, 2002). In fact, teachers report that their students are often more engaged in reading stories about social issues than other books and that students' interaction patterns change after reading them.

Implications for Learning Language Arts

Children come to school with an intuitive understanding of the four language systems based on having learned to speak their native language. Listening to parents tell and read aloud stories also contributes to this knowledge. During the elementary grades, students learn more about the phonological system as they learn phonics and spelling, more about the semantic system as their vocabularies expand, more about the syntactic system through grammar instruction, and more about the pragmatic system as they learn to vary the language they use according to purpose and audience.

Think about writing and how the four language systems work together as writers express ideas through words. Writers gather and organize ideas and choose specific words and phrases to express their ideas. They use the semantic system as they choose words to express their ideas, and the syntactic system to organize the words into sentences, paragraphs, and various writing forms, such as letters, reports, and stories. The pragmatic system comes into play as writers consider their audience and purpose for writing. They decide whether to craft longer or shorter sentences and consider the impact of informal or more formal word choices, jargon, nonstandard English, or technical vocabulary on their readers. They consider the style of their composition and decide whether to state facts objectively, use persuasive

The four language systems. *These Spanish-speaking first graders use the four language systems as they learn to speak, read, and write in English. They have already developed the language systems in their native language, and now they add information about English. Their teacher helps them understand how English is similar to their native language and how it is different. The errors that these English learners make, such as pronouncing j like h and placing modifiers after the noun instead of before it (e.g., the baby little instead of the little baby), often reflect the language systems of their native language.*

language, or create wordplays, rhymes, or poetic images to express their ideas. As they transcribe their ideas into words and sentences, writers use their knowledge of the phonological system to spell words. Without any one of the language systems, writers would be hampered in their attempt to use language to express ideas.

Culture affects the way people think and the way they use language. In her study of three culturally different U.S. communities, Shirley Brice Heath (1983) found that because of different lifestyles and child-rearing practices, children come to school with radically different literacy experiences and expectations about learning. The American families in Heath's study had dramatically different experiences with written language in their English-speaking homes; the diversity of experiences of children from homes where English is not the primary language would be even greater.

Children from each cultural group bring their unique backgrounds of experience to the process of learning, and they have difficulty understanding concepts outside their backgrounds of experience. This difficulty is greater for students who are learning English. Think, for example, of the different experiences and language knowledge that children of Vietnamese refugees, Native American children, and children of Russian Jewish immigrants bring to school. No matter what ethnic group they belong to or what language they speak, all students use the same cognitive and linguistic processes to learn.

Children of diverse ethnic groups have met with varying degrees of success in schools, depending on their previous cultural experiences, the expectations students and their parents have, and the expectations teachers have for them. Often a discrepancy exists between the way classrooms operate and the ways students from various ethnic groups behave (Law & Eckes, 1990). Four common cultural behaviors that differ from mainstream behaviors are:

1. *No eye contact.* In some Asian and Hispanic cultures, avoiding eye contact is polite and respectful behavior. Mainstream teachers sometimes mistakenly assume that when students avoid eye contact, they are not paying attention or are sullen and uncooperative.
2. *Cooperation.* Students from many Southeast Asian, Polynesian, and Native American cultures are taught to cooperate and help each other, and in school, they often assist classmates with their work. In contrast, many mainstream students are more competitive than cooperative, and sometimes mainstream teachers view cooperating on assignments as cheating.
3. *Fear of making mistakes.* Mainstream teachers encourage students to take risks and view making mistakes as a natural part of the learning process. In some cultures, especially the Japanese culture, correctness is valued above all else, and students are taught not to guess or take risks.
4. *Informal classroom environment.* In some cultures, including European and Asian cultures, the school environment is much more formal than it is in U.S. schools. Students from these cultures view U.S. schools as chaotic, and they interpret the informality as permission to misbehave.

Many Asian American students have been taught to keep a social distance between the teacher and themselves. For example, out of respect to the teacher, they look down when they are spoken to and feel more comfortable remaining in their assigned seats. Literature discussions called grand conversations, as well as other informal activities, can make these students feel uncomfortable because the lack of structure appears to indicate disrespect for the teacher. Asian American parents typically equate learning and knowledge with memorizing factual information, and they expect a great deal of homework (Cheng, 1987).

Hakuta and Garcia (1989) found that the most effective classrooms for Mexican American students have a discourse style similar to the one they know at home. Many Mexican American students are familiar with the give-and-take of cooperative learning, and they value working together and learning in a warm, responsive environment. These students work well in a child-centered, integrated program that is responsive to children's needs.

African American and Native American students have special needs, too. For too long, schools have neglected and failed these students. Teachers understand and build on these students' abilities, appreciate their varied backgrounds, and nurture their potential for learning (Brooks, 1985). Teachers must also take into account historical, economic, psychological, and linguistic barriers that have led to oppression and low expectations. One way to help raise children's self-esteem and build pride in their cultural groups is by incorporating literature about African Americans and Native Americans into their instructional programs. Teachers' acceptance of students' nonstandard English dialects is also important.

Language and culture have important implications for how children learn language arts in school and how teachers teach language arts. Some implications are:

- Children use the four language systems simultaneously as they communicate.
- Children from each cultural group bring their unique backgrounds of experience to the process of learning.
- Children's cultural and linguistic diversity provides an opportunity to enhance and enrich the learning of all students.
- Children use language arts to reflect on cultural, social, and political injustices and work to change the world.

Guidelines for teaching English learners are presented in the LA Essentials feature on page 27.

HOW CHILDREN LEARN LANGUAGE ARTS

Language arts instruction is changing to reflect greater oral, written, and visual communication needs (*Standards for the English Language Arts,* 1996). The Steering Committee of the Elementary Section of the National Council of Teachers of English (NCTE, 1996) has identified seven characteristics of competent language users that are presented in Figure 1–2. Students exemplify these characteristics of competent language users as they:

- Compare the video and book versions for the same story
- Interview community resource people who have special knowledge, interests, or talents in connection with literature focus units and social studies and science theme cycles
- Examine propaganda techniques used in print advertisements and television commercials

LA Essentials

Guidelines for Teaching English Learners

1. **Provide Comprehensible Input**
   - Use language that is neither too hard nor too easy for students.
   - Embed language in context-rich activities.
   - Speak more slowly, and rarely use idioms.
   - Highlight key words.
   - Expand the two- and three-word sentences that students produce.

2. **Create a Stress-Free Environment**
   - Show genuine interest in students, their language, and their culture.
   - Allow students to speak and write their own language.
   - Avoid forcing students to speak.
   - Encourage risk-taking.
   - Don't correct grammatical errors.
   - Understand that diverse students are caught between two cultures.

3. **Provide Opportunities to Use English**
   - Provide many opportunities for students to listen to and speak English and to read and write English in low-risk situations.
   - Have students work together with buddies and in cooperative groups.
   - Promote friendships among students.

4. **Examine Your Prejudice**
   - Avoid stereotyping any linguistic or cultural group.
   - Do not lower your expectations for certain groups of students.
   - Encourage bilingualism.
   - Consider your tolerance for nonstandard English and code switching.

5. **Alleviate Home-School Mismatches**
   - Consider the contrast between how children use language in home communities and at school.
   - Smooth the transition between home and school.
   - Expect students to be uncomfortable in unfamiliar activities.

6. **Involve Students' Parents**
   - Make home visits.
   - Encourage parents to participate in school activities.
   - Translate letters, information sheets, and memos into native languages.
   - Have translators available for school meetings and conferences.
   - Plan parent-child and home-school activities.

Adapted from Faltis, 1993; Gibbons, 1991; Law & Eckes, 1990; Scarcella, 1990.

- Use the Internet to gather information as part of social studies and science theme cycles
- Assume the role of a character while reading a story, and write simulated journal entries as that character
- Use the writing process to write stories, and share the stories with classmates
- Analyze an author's writing style during an author unit, or an artist's drawing style during an illustrator unit

These activities exhibit the three characteristics—meaningful, functional, and genuine—of all worthwhile experiences with language. First, they use language in meaningful rather than contrived situations. Second, they are functional, or real-life, activities. And third, they are genuine rather than artificial (such as worksheets) activities, because they communicate ideas.

Creating a Community of Learners

Language arts classrooms are social settings. Together, students and their teacher create the classroom community, and the type of community they create strongly

---

FIGURE 1-2

Characteristics of Competent Language Users

1. Personal Expression

Students use language to express themselves, to make connections between their own experiences and their social world, to choose books they want to read and topics they want to write about, and to create a personal voice.

2. Aesthetic Appreciation

Students use language aesthetically to read literature, talk with others, and enrich their lives.

3. Collaborative Exploration

Students use language as a learning tool as they investigate concepts and issues in collaboration with classmates.

4. Strategic Language Use

Students use strategies as they create and share meaning through language.

5. Creative Communication

Students use text forms and genres creatively as they share ideas through language.

6. Reflective Interpretation

Students use language to organize and evaluate learning experiences, question personal and social values, and think critically.

7. Thoughtful Application

Students use language to solve problems, persuade, and take action.

influences students' learning. Effective teachers establish a community of learners in which students are motivated to learn and are actively involved in language arts activities. Teachers and students work collaboratively and purposefully. Perhaps the most striking quality of classroom communities is the partnership that the teacher and students create. Students are a "family" in which all the members respect one another and support each other's learning. Students value culturally and linguistically diverse classmates and recognize that all students can make important contributions to the classroom (Wells & Chang-Wells, 1992).

Students and the teacher work together for the good of the community. Consider the differences between renting and owning a home. In a classroom community, students and the teacher are joint owners of the classroom. Students assume responsibility for their own learning and behavior, work collaboratively with classmates, complete assignments, and care for the classroom. In contrast, in traditional classrooms, the classroom is the teacher's, and students are simply renters for the school year. This doesn't mean that in a classroom community, teachers abdicate their responsibility to students. On the contrary, teachers retain their roles as organizer, facilitator, participant, instructor, model, manager, diagnostician, evaluator, coordinator, and communicator. These roles are often shared with students, but the ultimate responsibility remains with the teacher.

Researchers have identified many characteristics of classroom communities. Ten of these characteristics, which are described in Figure 1–3, show how the learning theories presented at the beginning of this chapter are translated into practice.

For more information about creating a community of learners, turn to Chapter 2, "Teaching and Assessing Language Arts."

FIGURE 1–3

Ten Characteristics of Classroom Communities

1. Responsibility

Students are responsible for their learning, their behavior, and the contributions they make in the classroom. They see themselves as valued and contributing members of the classroom community. Students become more self-reliant when they make choices about the language arts activities in which they are involved.

2. Opportunities

Students have opportunities to participate in language arts activities that are meaningful, functional, and genuine. They read real books and write books for real audiences—their classmates, their parents and grandparents, and other members of their community. They rarely use workbooks or drill-and-practice sheets.

3. Engagement

Students are motivated to learn and to be actively involved in language arts activities. In a student-centered classroom, the activities are interesting, and students sometimes choose which books to read, how they will respond to a book, topics for writing, and the writing form they will use.

4. Demonstration

Students learn procedures, concepts, skills, and strategies through demonstrations—with modeling and scaffolding—that teachers provide.

Continues

FIGURE 1-3

Continued

5. Risk Taking

Students are encouraged to explore topics, make guesses, and take risks. Rather than having students focus on correct answers, teachers promote students' experimentation with new skills and strategies.

6. Instruction

Teachers are expert language users, and they provide instruction through minilessons on procedures, skills, strategies, and other concepts related to language arts. These minilessons are planned and taught to small groups, the whole class, or individual students so that students can apply what they are learning in meaningful literacy projects.

7. Response

Students have opportunities to respond after reading and viewing and to share their interpretations of stories. Through writing in reading logs and participating in discussions called grand conversations, students share personal connections to the story, make predictions, ask questions, and deepen their comprehension. When they write, students share their rough drafts in writing groups to get feedback on how well they are communicating, and they celebrate their published books by sharing them with classmates and other "real" audiences.

8. Choice

Students often make choices about the language arts activities in which they are involved. They choose what books they will read and what projects they will create after reading. Students make choices within the parameters set by the teacher. When they are given the opportunity to make choices, students are often more highly motivated to do the activity, and they value their learning experience more. It is more meaningful to them.

9. Time

Students need large chunks of time to pursue language arts activities. It doesn't work well for teachers to break the classroom schedule into many small time blocks for phonics, reading, spelling, handwriting, grammar, and writing. Students need two or three hours of uninterrupted time each day for language arts instruction. It is important to minimize disruptions during the time set aside, and administrators should schedule computer, music, art, and other pull-out programs so that they do not interfere. This is especially important in the primary grades.

10. Assessment

Teachers and students work together to establish guidelines for assessment, and students monitor their own work and participate in the evaluation. Rather than imposing assessment on students, teachers share with their students the responsibility for monitoring and evaluating their progress.

Adapted from Cambourne & Turbill, 1987.

Motivation for Learning

Motivation is intrinsic and internal—a driving force within us. Children in the primary grades are usually eager to learn. They are enthusiastic participants in classroom activities and confident that they will be successful in school. Their teachers play a crucial role in engaging them, monitoring their progress, and providing encouragement. They plan instructional activities that are interesting, incorporate authentic materials, and often involve students in cooperative groups. Pressley, Dolezal, Raphael, Mohan, Roehrig, and Bogner (2003) studied nine second-grade teachers, examined the most engaging teachers' instructional practices, and identified these motivating teacher behaviors:

- Teachers create a community of learners.
- Teachers create a positive classroom environment with books, charts, and posters used as teaching tools, colorful bulletin board displays, and a display of student work.
- Teachers set clear expectations for behavior and learning, and students know what is expected of them.
- Teachers encourage cooperation rather than competition.
- Teachers provide positive feedback and compliment students for good behavior and learning.
- Teachers encourage students to take risks and be persistent.
- Teachers plan instruction thoroughly with little "down time" between activities.
- Teachers provide authentic, hands-on activities.
- Teachers model and scaffold learning.
- Teachers teach strategies and skills through direct instruction and modeling.
- Teachers monitor students' behavior and learning.
- Teachers stimulate students' creativity, curiosity, and critical thinking.
- Teachers emphasize depth over breadth as they teach.
- Teachers make home–school connections.
- Teachers model interest and enthusiasm for learning.
- Teachers emphasize the value of education.
- Teachers genuinely enjoy being with students and communicate that they care for them.

Often students' motivation for language arts diminishes as they reach the upper grades. Penny Oldfather (1995) conducted a 4-year study to examine the factors influencing students' motivation and found that when students had opportunities for authentic self-expression as part of language arts activities, they were more highly motivated. Students she interviewed reported that they were more highly motivated when they had ownership of the learning activities. Specific activities that they mentioned included opportunities to:

- Express their own ideas and opinions
- Choose topics for writing and books for reading
- Talk about books they are reading
- Share their writings with classmates
- Pursue "authentic" activities—not worksheets—using the language arts

Some students are not strongly motivated for language arts, and they adopt strategies for avoiding failure rather than strategies for making meaning. These strategies are defensive tactics (Dweck, 1986; Paris, Wasik, & Turner, 1991). Unmotivated students often give up or remain passive, uninvolved in reading and other language arts activities (Johnston & Winograd, 1985). Some students feign interest or pretend to be involved even though they are not. Others don't think language arts is important, and they choose to focus on other curricular areas—math or physical education, for instance. Some students complain about feeling ill or that other students are bothering them. They place the blame on anything other than themselves.

There are other students who avoid language arts entirely. They just don't do it. Another group of students read books that are too easy for them or write short pieces so that they don't have to exert much effort. Even though these strategies are self-serving, students use them because they lead to short-term success. The long-term result, however, is devastating because these students fail to learn to read and write.

The Six Language Arts

Traditionally, language arts educators have defined the language arts as the study of the four modes of language: listening, talking, reading, and writing. In 1996, however, the National Council of Teachers of English and the International Reading Association (*Standards,* 1996) proposed two additional language arts—viewing and visually representing. These new language arts reflect the growing importance of visual literacy (Ernst, 1993; Whitin, 1996). Also, thinking is sometimes referred to as an additional language art, but, more accurately, it permeates all the language arts.

Chapter 7, "Listening to Learn," explores these concepts and describes strategies for teaching listening.

Listening.   Beginning at birth, a child's contact with language is through listening. Listening instruction is often neglected in elementary classrooms because teachers feel that students have already learned how to listen and that instructional time should be devoted to reading and writing. This book presents an alternative view of listening and listening instruction and focuses on these key concepts:

- Listening is a process of which hearing is only one part.
- Students listen differently according to their purpose.
- Students listen aesthetically to stories, efferently to learn information as part of across-the-curriculum theme cycles, and critically to persuasive appeals.
- Students use listening strategies and monitor their comprehension in order to listen more effectively.

To learn more about the role of talk in the elementary grades, see Chapter 8, "Sustaining Talk in the Classroom."

Talking.   As with listening, teachers often neglect instruction in talk during the elementary grades because they feel students already know how to talk. Recent research emphasizes the importance of talk in the learning process (Dwyer, 1991; Newkirk & McLure, 1992). For example, students use talk to respond to literature, provide feedback about classmates' writing in writing groups, and present oral reports as part of social studies and science theme cycles. The key concepts about talk are:

- Talk is an essential part of the language arts curriculum.
- Students use talk for both aesthetic and efferent purposes.
- Students participate in grand conversations as they respond to literature.

Seeing Common Threads

Do you think that one of the language arts is more important than the others?

Stacy Shasky responds:

I think that speaking is the most important language art. If students are able to organize their thoughts and use appropriate vocabulary, they are already one step toward being successful readers and writers. Without the ability to speak well, students struggle with word usage and grammar. Students who do not speak well struggle to sound out words when reading that they might have known through conversation. Finally, I think that students who speak well are able to think well. If they have experience with conversation, they are able to think critically and spontaneously, and this is an essential ability that is needed in all the language arts.

What do you think?

In each chapter, you will find a question and a response written by one of Dr. Tompkins's students. Consider other comments, or respond to the question yourself, by visiting the Threaded Message Board in Chapter 1 on the Companion Website at www.prenhall.com/tompkins

Companion Website

- Students give presentations, including oral reports and debates.
- Drama, including storytelling and role-playing, provides a valuable method of learning and a powerful way of communicating.

Reading.   Reading is a process, and students use skills and strategies to decode words and comprehend what they are reading. Students vary the way they read according to their purpose. They read for pleasure differently from how they read to locate and remember information (Rosenblatt, 1991). The key concepts about reading are:

- Reading is a strategic process.
- The goal of reading instruction is comprehension, or meaning making.
- Students read differently for different purposes.
- Students participate in five types of reading: independent reading, shared reading, guided reading, buddy reading, and reading aloud to students.

> The reading process is presented in Chapter 3, and in later chapters, you will learn about teaching students to read stories (Ch. 9), informational books (Ch. 10), and poems (Ch. 11).

Writing.   Like reading, writing is a strategic process. Students use the writing process as they write stories, reports, poems, and other types of writing. Students also do informal writing, such as writing in reading logs and making clusters. As you continue reading, you will learn about these key concepts about writing:

- Writing is a process in which students cycle recursively through the stages of prewriting, drafting, revising, editing, and publishing.
- Students experiment with many written language forms.
- Informal writing is used to develop writing fluency and as a learning tool.
- Spelling and handwriting are tools for writers.

> You will learn about the writing process in Chapter 3 and in later chapters, and about teaching students to write stories (Ch. 9), reports (Ch. 10), and poems (Ch. 11).

Viewing.   Visual media include film and videos, print advertisements and commercials, photographs and book illustrations, the Internet, and CD-ROM. Because visual media, including the Internet, are commonplace in American life today, children need to learn how to comprehend them and to integrate visual knowledge with other literacy knowledge. Heide and Stilborne (1999) explain that the Internet has "a wide range of resources available for electronic field trips involving pictures, text, sound, and sometimes interactivity" (p. 19). The key concepts about viewing are:

- Viewing is an important component of literacy.
- Students view visual media for a variety of purposes.
- Viewing is much like reading, and students use comprehension strategies in both reading and viewing.
- Students use the Internet as a learning tool.
- Students learn about propaganda techniques in order to critically analyze commercials and advertisements.

Visually Representing.   Students create meaning through multiple sign systems such as video productions, Inspiration and other computer programs, dramatizations, story quilts, and illustrations on charts, posters, and books they are writing (Daniels & Bizar, 1998; Moline, 1995). According to Harste, "Seeing something familiar in a new way is often a process of gaining new insights" (1993, p. 4). Projects involving visual texts are often completed as part of literature focus units, literature circles, and theme cycles. Key concepts about visually representing presented in this book are:

- Students consider audience, purpose, and form as they create visual texts.
- Visual texts, like writing, can be created to share information learned during literature focus units and theme cycles.

Relationships Among the Language Arts.   Discussing the language arts one by one suggests a division among them, as though they could be used separately. In reality, they are used simultaneously and reciprocally, just as Mrs. McNeal's students in the vignette at the beginning of the chapter used all six language arts during writing workshop. Almost any language arts activity involves more than one of the language arts. In a seminal study, researcher Walter Loban (1976) documented the language growth and development of a group of 338 students from kindergarten through 12th grade (ages 5–18). Two purposes of his longitudinal study were, first, to examine differences between students who used language effectively and those who did not, and, second, to identify predictable stages of language development. Three of Loban's conclusions are especially noteworthy to our discussion of the language arts. First, he reported positive correlations among listening, talking, reading, and writing. Second, he found that students with less effective oral language abilities tended to have less effective written language abilities. And third, he found a strong relationship between students' oral language ability and their overall academic ability. Loban's study demonstrates clear relationships among the language arts and emphasizes the need to teach listening and talking during the elementary grades.

Literature focus units, literature circles, reading and writing workshop, and across-the-curriculum theme cycles are four ways to make language arts instruction meaningful. Students use all six language arts as they read and respond to literature in focus units. For example, as fifth graders read and respond to *Number the Stars* (Lowry, 1989), a story about friendship between a Christian girl and a Jewish girl set in Denmark during World War II, they use listening, talking, reading, writing, viewing, and visually representing in some of the ways shown in Figure 1–4. Across-the-curriculum connections are also possible given the historical setting of the story.

Similarly, students use the six language arts as they learn and share their learning in social studies and science theme cycles. As second graders learn about the desert in a theme cycle, they use the six modes to explore the concepts they are learning as well as to share what they have learned. Some of these across-the-curriculum connections for a theme on the desert are shown in Figure 1–5.

Language Arts Strategies and Skills

Students learn both strategies and skills through language arts instruction. Strategies are problem-solving methods or behaviors. Students develop and use both general learning strategies and specific strategies related to language arts. Although there is no definitive list of language arts strategies, researchers have identified a number of strategies that capable readers and writers use (Lewin, 1992; Paris & Jacobs, 1984; Schmitt, 1990). I focus on 12 of these strategies:

tapping prior knowledge	applying fix-up strategies
predicting	revising meaning
organizing ideas	monitoring
figuring out unknown words	playing with language
visualizing	summarizing
making connections	evaluating

These strategies are described in Figure 1–6. Students often use more than one of these strategies for a language arts activity, but they rarely, if ever, use all the strategies for a single activity. Students choose the appropriate strategies to accomplish the activities in which they are engaged.

These strategies are applied in all six language arts. Consider revising meaning, for example. Probably the best-known application is in writing: Students revise meaning as they add, substitute, delete, and move information in their rough drafts. Revising meaning in visual representations works the same way. But students also revise meaning as they listen to a speaker, view a videotape, or read a book. They revise their understanding as they continue listening, viewing, or reading and get more information. And, students revise meaning while they are talking on the basis of feedback from the audience.

Skills, in contrast, are information-processing techniques that students use automatically and unconsciously as they construct meaning. Many skills focus at the word level, but some require students to attend to larger chunks of text.

FIGURE 1-4

Ways Fifth Graders Use the Six Language Arts in a Literature Focus Unit on Number the Stars

1. Listening

Students listen to *Number the Stars* as it is read aloud, and they listen to classmates' comments during literature discussions. They listen and watch as classmates dramatize events from the story and as classmates share reports of information or projects.

2. Talking

Students talk as they make predictions about what will happen in upcoming chapters and as they share their responses to the story during literature discussions. They may share the results of their research into World War II or report on the geography of Denmark and trace the trip the girls took from Copenhagen to the seacoast. Students also use talk as they dramatize story events and share projects they create after reading the story.

3. Reading

Students read *Number the Stars* aloud, with a buddy, or independently. They may reread brief excerpts from the story during discussions or read-arounds and read other books by the author, Lois Lowry, or other books about World War II and the Holocaust. Students read aloud their journal entries and quickwrites to share them with classmates. During writing groups, students read aloud sequels, poems, reports, or other projects they are writing.

4. Writing

Students write their predictions about and reactions to each chapter in reading logs or keep simulated journals written from the viewpoint of one of the characters. Students write quickwrites on topics related to the story. They also make notes during presentations by the teacher about World War II and the Holocaust. Students also use the writing process as they write sequels, poems, reports, and other compositions after reading *Number the Stars*.

5. Viewing

Students observe as classmates dramatize scenes from the story. They examine large black-and-white photos of war scenes that the teacher has collected and talk about the impact of the black-and-white photos. They consider how the impact would differ if they were in color. They also watch videotapes about World War II and take notes after viewing and talking about them.

6. Visually Representing

Students make setting maps of Denmark and include sites mentioned in the story, and they make a story quilt to celebrate students' favorite quotes from the story. They also make open-mind portraits of the main characters. For these portraits, students draw a large picture of the character's face and cut it out. Then they cut a second piece of paper the same size and glue it on a piece of construction paper. They draw pictures and write words on this piece of paper to represent the character's thoughts. Then they staple the character's face paper on top so that it flips open to reveal the character's thoughts.

FIGURE 1-5

*Ways Second Graders Use the Six Language Arts in a
Theme Cycle on the Desert*

1. Listening

Students listen to the teacher read books about the desert. They listen to *Mojave* (Siebert, 1988), a book-length poem about one special desert, and picture books by Byrd Baylor that depict life in the desert, including *Desert Voices* (1981). Students also listen as the teacher presents information about the desert.

2. Talking

Students talk about the desert and what they are learning in the theme cycle. After reading or listening to the teacher read a book, they participate in grand conversations in which they share their responses to the book. They also create their own riddles after listening to the teacher read the riddles in *Desert* (Hirschi, 1992). Later, students will write their riddles and add them to a desert mural they are creating.

3. Reading

Students read *Cactus Hotel* (Guiberson, 1991) in small groups and then diagram the life cycle of the cactus in their learning logs. Students read storyboards the teacher has made by cutting apart two copies of *Desert Life* (Taylor, 1992) and backing the pages with cardboard and laminating them. Each page in the book presents a close-up look at a desert animal or plant, including tortoises, cacti, locusts, and scorpions. Students read and examine three of the pages and record facts in their learning logs. Also, using books from the classroom library, students read and reread other stories, informational books, and poems about deserts and desert life.

4. Writing

Students write in learning logs and make clusters, diagrams, and other charts in the logs, too. Then they use the writing process to research and write reports about the cacti and animals. They post their finished reports next to the large papier-mâché cactus hotel they create. Some students work together to write an alphabet book about deserts. Each student chooses a letter and writes one page, and then the pages are compiled and bound into a book. Other students write a cumulative book following the pattern in *Here Is the Southwestern Desert* (Dunphy, 1995). Each student prepares one page for the book, and then the pages are compiled and bound into a book.

5. Viewing

Students view videos and films about desert life, and they examine prints of several of Georgia O'Keeffe's desert scenes.

6. Visually Representing

As they learn about the plants and animals that live in the desert, students take notes and draw diagrams to help them remember important information. After reading *Cactus Hotel*, students make a large papier-mâché saguaro cactus and desert animals mentioned in the book. They hang their reports next to this display.

FIGURE 1-6

Language Arts Strategies

1. Tapping Prior Knowledge

Students think about what they already know about the topic as they listen, read, view, or write. This knowledge includes information and vocabulary about content-area topics, such as whales or the solar system, as well as language arts information about authors, types of literature, and literal and figurative meanings.

2. Predicting

Students make predictions about what will happen as they read or view. These guesses are based on students' knowledge about the topic and the type of literature or what they have read or viewed thus far. Students also make predictions as they talk, write, and visually represent. They make plans and set purposes.

3. Organizing Ideas

Students organize ideas and sequence story events when they read, write, view, or listen to stories read aloud. Students organize ideas for writing using clusters and demonstrate comprehension after reading or viewing using other graphic organizers. Students organize ideas differently depending on whether they are exploring stories, informational books, or poetry.

4. Figuring Out Unknown Words

Students figure out unknown words as they read, listen, and view. Depending on the particular situation, students choose whether to use word-attack skills or context clues or to skip over a word. Writers use "sound it out" and "think it out" strategies to spell unfamiliar words.

5. Visualizing

Students draw pictures in their minds of what they are listening to, reading, or writing. Often film versions of stories are disappointing because they don't match students' visualizations.

6. Making Connections

Students relate what they are listening to, reading, or viewing to their own lives and to books they have read. Similarly, students make connections between their writing or oral presentations and books they have read and experiences they have had.

7. Applying Fix-up Strategies

When students are listening, reading, viewing, writing, talking, or visually representing and something doesn't make sense, they apply fix-up strategies. They may assume that things will make sense soon and continue with the activity or they may ask a question, go back or skip ahead when reading or viewing, or talk to a classmate.

8. Revising Meaning

Students continuously revise meaning as they proceed with a language arts activity. When reading, for example, students reread for more information or because something doesn't make sense, they study the illustrations, or they get ideas from classmates during discussions. Writers meet in writing groups to get feedback on their rough drafts in order to revise their writing and make it stronger. Students also get feedback when they create visual representations.

FIGURE 1–6

Continued

9. Monitoring

Students ask themselves questions to monitor their understanding as they participate in language arts activities. They monitor their comprehension as they read,
view, and listen. They recognize when comprehension breaks down and use other
strategies to regain comprehension. When they give oral presentations or participate in discussions, students monitor what they are saying and the reactions of
classmates.

10. Playing With Language

Students notice figurative and novel uses of language as they listen, read, and view.
When they give oral presentations and write, students incorporate interesting language in their presentations and compositions.

11. Summarizing

Students summarize as they choose important ideas to remember while reading.
Similarly, as they give oral presentations and write, students often state their big
ideas at the beginning of a paragraph and then support them with facts. They want
their readers to be able to pick out the important ideas. Summarizing is important
because big ideas are easier to remember than lots of details.

12. Evaluating

Students make judgments about, reflect on, and value the language arts activities in
which they participate. They also think about themselves as language users and reflect on what they do as listeners, talkers, readers, and writers.

For example, readers use skills such as decoding unfamiliar words, noting details, and sequencing events, and writers employ skills such as forming contractions, using punctuation marks, and capitalizing people's names. Skills and
strategies are not the same thing. The important difference between skills and
strategies is how they are used: Skills are used unconsciously, and strategies
are used deliberately (Paris et al., 1991).

During the elementary grades, students learn to use five types of skills. Although many of the skills are oriented to reading and writing, some are used for
listening, talking, viewing, and visually representing. The five types of skills are:

1. *Comprehension skills.* These include separating facts and opinions,
   comparing and contrasting, and recognizing literary genres and
   structures. Students use comprehension skills as they create meaning
   using all six language arts.
2. *Print skills.* These include sounding out words, noticing word families,
   using root words and affixes to decode and spell words, and using
   abbreviations. Students use print skills as they decode words when
   reading and as they spell words when writing.
3. *Study skills.* These include skimming and scanning, taking notes,
   making clusters, and previewing a book before reading. Students use

---

FIGURE 1–7

Language Arts Skills

Category	Skills	
Print	Sound out words using phonics Notice word families Decode by analogy Use classroom resources Consult a dictionary or glossary	Apply spelling rules Recognize high-frequency words Divide words into syllables Capitalize proper nouns and adjectives Use abbreviations
Comprehension	Chunk words into phrases Sequence Categorize Classify Separate facts and opinions Note details Identify cause and effect Compare and contrast	Use context clues Notice organizational patterns of poetry, plays, business and friendly letters, stories, essays, and reports Recognize literary genres (traditional stories, fantasies, science fiction, realistic fiction, historical fiction, biography, autobiography, and poetry)
Language	Notice compound words Use contractions Use possessives Notice propaganda Use similes and metaphors Notice idioms and slang Choose synonyms Recognize antonyms Differentiate among homonyms Use root words and affixes Appreciate rhyme and other poetic devices	Use punctuation marks (period, question mark, exclamation point, quotation marks, comma, colon, semicolon, and hyphen) Use simple, compound, and complex sentences Combine sentences Recognize parts of sentences Avoid sentence fragments Recognize parts of speech (nouns, pronouns, verbs, adjectives, adverbs, conjunctions, prepositions, and interjections)
Reference	Sort in alphabetical order Use a glossary or dictionary Locate etymologies in the dictionary Use the pronunciation guide in the dictionary Locate synonyms in a thesaurus Locate information in an encyclopedia, atlas, or almanac	Use a table of contents Use an index Use a card catalog Read and make graphs, tables, and diagrams Read and make time lines Read newspapers and magazines Use bibliographic forms
Study	Skim Scan Preview Follow directions	Make outlines and clusters Take notes Paraphrase

study skills during across-the-curriculum theme cycles, while reading informational books, and while collecting information to use in writing reports.

4. *Language skills.* These include identifying and inferring meanings of words, noticing idioms, dividing words into syllables, and choosing synonyms. Students are continuously interacting with words as they use the language arts, and they use language skills to analyze words when

they are listening and reading and to choose more precise language when they are talking and writing.

5. *Reference skills.* These include alphabetizing a list of words, using a dictionary, and reading and making graphs and other diagrams. Elementary students learn to use reference skills to read newspaper articles, locate information in encyclopedias and other informational books, and use library resources.

Examples of each of the five types of skills are presented in Figure 1–7. Students use these skills for various language arts activities. For example, students use some of the skills when giving an oral report and others when making a square for a class story quilt or comparing several versions of a folktale. It is unlikely that students would use every skill listed in Figure 1–7 for any particular language arts activity, but capable students are familiar with most of these skills and can use them automatically whenever they are needed.

Teachers often wonder when they should teach the skills listed in Figure 1–7. School districts often prepare frameworks and curriculum guides that include the skills to be taught at each grade level, and skills are usually listed on scope-and-sequence charts that accompany textbook programs. On scope-and-sequence charts, textbook makers identify the grade level at which the skill should be introduced and the grade levels at which it is practiced and tested. These resources provide guidelines, but teachers decide which skills to teach based on their students' level of development and the activities in which their students are involved.

Teachers use both direct and indirect instruction to provide information that students need to know about skills and strategies. Both types of instruction are presented in context so that students see a reason to learn the skills and are able to apply what they are learning in meaningful ways (Calkins, 1980; Routman, 1996). When teachers model how to do something, scaffold students' use of a strategy or skill, or respond to a student's question, they are using indirect instruction. In contrast, direct instruction is planned. Teachers often teach minilessons, brief 10- to 30-minute lessons in which they explicitly explain a particular skill or strategy, model its use, and provide examples and opportunities for practice. Then students apply what they have learned using meaningful, functional, and genuine activities.

In upcoming chapters, you will find lists of topics, including strategies and skills, for minilessons as well as descriptions of sample minilessons.

Review

Language arts instruction should be based on theories and research about how children learn. Language and culture also have an impact on how elementary students learn language arts. The goal of language arts instruction is for students to develop communicative competence in the six language arts—listening, talking, reading, writing, viewing, and visually representing. Key concepts presented in this chapter are:

1. Language arts instruction should be based on how children learn.
2. Constructivist, information-processing, and sociolinguistic theories of learning inform our understanding of how children learn language arts.
3. Students learn through active involvement in listening, talking, reading, writing, viewing, and visually representing activities.

Visit Chapter 1 on the Companion Website at www.prenhall. com/tompkins to:

- **Check your understanding of the concepts presented in the chapter**
- **Access the Extensions (activities and a list of related readings)**
- **Link to related websites**

4. Teachers should provide instruction within children's zone of proximal development.
5. Teachers scaffold or support children's learning.
6. Students use all four language systems: phonological, syntactic, semantic, and pragmatic.
7. Students need opportunities to participate in language arts activities that are meaningful, functional, and genuine.
8. Teachers create a community of learners in their classrooms.
9. Students learn and use language arts strategies, including predicting, visualizing, revising meaning, summarizing, and monitoring.
10. Students learn and use language arts skills, including choosing synonyms, skimming, capitalizing words, and using a dictionary.

Professional References

Allen, V. A. (1991). Teaching bilingual and ESL children. In J. Flood, J. M. Jensen, D. Lapp, & J. R. Squire (Eds.), *Handbook of research on teaching the English language arts* (pp. 356–364). Upper Saddle River, NJ: Merrill/Prentice Hall.

Applebee, A. N., & Langer, J. A. (1983). Instructional scaffolding: Reading and writing and natural language activities. *Language Arts, 60,* 168–175.

Banks, J. A. (1994). *An introduction to multicultural education.* Boston: Allyn & Bacon.

Bishop, R. S. (1992). Extending multicultural understanding. In B. Cullinan (Ed.), *Invitation to read: More children's literature in the reading program* (pp. 80–91). Newark, DE: International Reading Association.

Brooks, C. K. (Ed.). (1985). *Tapping potential: English and language arts for the black learner.* Urbana, IL: National Council of Teachers of English.

Bruner, J. (1986). *Actual minds, possible worlds.* Cambridge, MA: Harvard University Press.

Calkins, L. M. (1980). When children want to punctuate: Basic skills belong in context. *Language Arts, 57,* 567–573.

Cambourne, B., & Turbill, J. (1987). *Coping with chaos.* Rozelle, New South Wales, Australia: Primary English Teaching Association.

Cheng, L. R. (1987). *Assessing Asian language performance.* Rockville, MD: Aspen.

Cleary, L. M. (1993). Hobbes: "I press rewind through the pictures in my head." In S. Hudson-Ross, L. M. Cleary, & M. Casey (Eds.), *Children's voices: Children talk about literacy* (pp. 136–143). Portsmouth, NH: Heinemann.

Cummins, J. (1989). *Empowering minority students.* Sacramento: California Association for Bilingual Education.

Daniels, H., & Bizar, M. (1998). *Methods that matter: Six structures for best practice classrooms.* York, ME: Stenhouse.

Dixon-Krauss, L. (1996). *Vygotsky in the classroom: Mediated literacy instruction and assessment.* White Plains, NY: Longman.

Dweck, C. S. (1986). Motivational processes affecting learning. *American Psychologist, 41,* 1040–1048.

Dwyer, J. (Ed.). (1991). *A sea of talk.* Portsmouth, NH: Heinemann.

Dyson, A. H. (1993). *Social worlds of children learning to write in an urban primary school.* New York: Teachers College Press.

Ernst, K. (1993). *Picturing learning.* Portsmouth, NH: Heinemann.

Faltis, C. J. (1993). *Joinfostering: Adapting teaching strategies for the multilingual classroom.* Upper Saddle River, NJ: Merrill/Prentice Hall.

Flavell, J. H. (1985). *Cognitive development* (2nd ed.). Upper Saddle River, NJ: Prentice Hall.

Foss, A. (2002). Peeling the onion: Teaching critical literacy with students of privilege. *Language Arts, 79,* 393–403.

Freeman, D. E., & Freeman, Y. S. (1993). Strategies for promoting the primary languages of all students. *The Reading Teacher, 46,* 552–558.

Freire, P., & Macedo, D. (1987). *Literacy: Reading the word and the world.* South Hadley, MA: Bergin & Garvey.

Gibbons, P. (1991). *Learning to learn in a second language.* Portsmouth, NH: Heinemann.

Giroux, H. (1988). *Teachers as intellectuals: Toward a critical pedagogy of learning.* South Hadley, MA: Bergin & Garvey.

Hakuta, K., & Garcia, E. (1989). Bilingualism and education. *American Psychologist, 44,* 374–379.

Halliday, M. A. K. (1978). *Language as social semiotic: The social interpretation of language and meaning.* Baltimore: University Park Press.

Harste, J. (1990). Jerry Harste speaks on reading and writing. *The Reading Teacher, 43,* 316–318.

Harste, J. (1993, April). Inquiry-based instruction. *Primary Voices K–6, 1,* 2–5.

Heath, S. B. (1983). *Ways with words: Language, life, and work in communities and classrooms.* Cambridge: Cambridge University Press.

Heide, A., & Stilborne, L. (1999). *The teacher's complete and easy guide to the Internet.* New York: Teachers College Press.

Johnston, P., & Winograd, P. (1985). Passive failure in reading. *Journal of Reading Behavior, 17,* 279–301.

Krashen, S. (1982). *Principles and practices of second language acquisition.* Oxford: Pergamon Press.

Lara, S. G. M. (1989). Reading placement for code-switchers. *The Reading Teacher, 42,* 278–282.

Law, B., & Eckes, M. (1990). *The more than just surviving handbook: ESL for every classroom teacher.* Winnipeg, Canada: Peguis.

Lewin, L. (1992). Integrating reading and writing strategies using an alternating teacher-led/student-selected instructional pattern. *The Reading Teacher, 45,* 586–591.

Lewison, M., Flint, A. S., & Sluys, K. V. (2002). Taking on critical literacy: The journey of newcomers and novices. *Language Arts, 79,* 382–392.

Lindfors, J. W. (1987). *Children's language and learning* (2nd ed.). Upper Saddle River, NJ: Prentice Hall.

Loban, W. (1976). *Language development: Kindergarten through grade twelve* (Research Report No. 18). Urbana, IL: National Council of Teachers of English.

Luke, A., & Freebody, P. (1997). Shaping the social practices of reading. In S. Muspratt, A. Luke, & P. Freebody (Eds.), *Constructing critical literacies* (pp. 185–225). Cresskill, NJ: Hampton.

Moline, S. (1995). *I see what you mean: Children at work with visual information.* York, ME: Stenhouse.

Muhammad, R. J. (1993). Mario: "It's mostly after I read a book that I write." In S. Hudson-Ross, L. M. Cleary, & M. Casey (Eds.), *Children's voices: Children talk about literacy* (pp. 92–99). Portsmouth, NH: Heinemann.

Nagy, W. E. (1988). *Teaching vocabulary to improve reading comprehension.* Urbana, IL: ERIC Clearinghouse on Reading and Communication Skills and the National Council of Teachers of English and the International Reading Association.

Nathenson-Mejia, S. (1989). Writing in a second language: Negotiating meaning through invented spelling. *Language Arts, 66,* 516–526.

NCTE Elementary Section Steering Committee. (1996). Exploring language arts standards within a cycle of learning. *Language Arts, 73,* 10–13.

Newkirk, T., & McLure, P. (1992). *Listening in: Children talk about books (and other things).* Portsmouth, NH: Heinemann.

Oldfather, P. (1995). Commentary: What's needed to maintain and extend motivation for literacy in the middle grades? *Journal of Reading, 38,* 420–422.

Paris, S. G., & Jacobs, J. E. (1984). The benefits of informed instruction for children's reading awareness and comprehension skills. *Child Development, 55,* 2083–2093.

Paris, S. G., Wasik, B. A., & Turner, J. C. (1991). The development of strategic readers. In R. Barr, M. L. Kamil, P. B. Mosenthal, & P. D. Pearson (Eds.), *Handbook of reading research* (Vol. 2, pp. 609–640). New York: Longman.

Pearson, P. D. (1993). Teaching and learning reading: A research perspective. *Language Arts, 70,* 502–511.

Piaget, J. (1969). *The psychology of intelligence.* Totowa, NJ: Littlefield, Adams.

Piaget, J. (1975). *The development of thought: Equilibration of cognitive structures.* New York: Viking.

Pressley, M., Dolezal, S. E., Raphael, L. M., Mohan, L., Roehrig, A. D., & Bogner, K. (2003). *Motivating primary-grade students.* New York: Guilford Press.

Rosenblatt, L. M. (1991). Literature: S.O.S.! *Language Arts, 68,* 444–448.

Routman, R. (1996). *Literacy at the crossroads: Crucial talk about reading, writing, and other teaching dilemmas.* Portsmouth, NH: Heinemann.

Samway, K. D., & McKeon, D. (1999). *Myths and realities: Best practices for language minority students.* Portsmouth, NH: Heinemann.

Scarcella, R. (1990). *Teaching language minority students in the multicultural classroom.* Upper Saddle River, NJ: Merrill/Prentice Hall.

Schmitt, M. C. (1990). A questionnaire to measure children's awareness of strategic reading processes. *The Reading Teacher, 43,* 454–461.

Siegler, R. S. (1986). *Children's thinking.* Upper Saddle River, NJ: Prentice Hall.

Spangenberg-Urbschat, K., & Pritchard, R. (Eds.). (1994). *Kids come in all languages: Reading instruction for ESL students.* Newark, DE: International Reading Association.

Standards for the English Language Arts. (1996). Urbana, IL: National Council of Teachers of English and the International Reading Association.

Steinbergh, J. W. (1993). Chandra: "To live a life of no secrecy." In S. Hudson-Ross, L. M. Cleary, & M. Casey (Eds.), *Children's voices: Children talk about literacy* (pp. 202–214). Portsmouth, NH: Heinemann.

Troika, R. C. (1981). Synthesis of research on bilingual education. *Educational Leadership, 38,* 498–504.

Urzua, C. (1980). Doing what comes naturally: Recent research in second language acquisition. In G. S. Pinnell (Ed.), *Discovering language with children* (pp. 33–38). Urbana, IL: National Council of Teachers of English.

Vygotsky, L. S. (1978). *Mind in society.* Cambridge, MA: Harvard University Press.

Vygotsky, L. S. (1986). *Thought and language.* Cambridge, MA: MIT Press.

Wells, G., & Chang-Wells, G. L. (1992). *Constructing knowledge together: Classrooms as centers of inquiry and literacy.* Portsmouth, NH: Heinemann.

Whitin, P. E. (1996). *Sketching stories, stretching minds.* Portsmouth, NH: Heinemann.

Wink, J. (2000). *Critical pedagogy: Notes from the real world* (2nd ed.). New York: Longman.

Wong-Fillmore, L. (1985). When does teacher talk work as input? In S. M. Gass & C. G. Madden (Eds.), *Input in second language acquisition* (pp. 17–50). Rowley, MA: Newbury House.

The World Almanac and book of facts 2001. (2000). Mahwah, NJ: World Almanac Books.

Yokota, J. (1993). Issues in selecting multicultural children's literature. *Language Arts, 70,* 156–167.

Zebroski, J. T. (1994). *Thinking through theory: Vygotskian perspectives on the teaching of writing.* Portsmouth, NH: Boynton/Cook.

Children's Book References

Babbitt, N. (1988). *Tuck everlasting.* New York: Farrar, Straus & Giroux.

Baylor, B. (1981). *Desert voices.* New York: Scribner.

Bunting, E. (1991). *Fly away home.* New York: Clarion.

Curtis, C. P. (1995). *The Watsons go to Birmingham—1963.* New York: Delacorte.

Dunphy, M. (1995). *Here is the southwestern desert.* New York: Hyperion.

Ellis, D. (2000). *The breadwinner.* Toronto: Groundwood Books.

Frank, A. (1995). *Anne Frank: The diary of a young girl* (new ed.). New York: Doubleday.

Guiberson, B. Z. (1991). *Cactus Hotel.* New York: Henry Holt.

Hirschi, R. (1992). *Desert.* New York: Bantam.

Lowry, L. (1989). *Number the stars.* Boston: Houghton Mifflin.

Martin, B., Jr., & Archambault, J. (1986). *White Dynamite and Curly Kidd.* New York: Henry Holt.

McKissack, P. C. (1988). *Mirandy and Brother Wind.* New York: Knopf.

Naylor, P. R. (1991). *Shiloh.* New York: Atheneum.

Sendak, M. (2003). *Where the wild things are.* New York: HarperCollins.

Siebert, D. (1988). *Mojave.* New York: HarperCollins.

Taylor, B. (1992). *Desert life.* New York: Dorling Kindersley.

Whelan, G. (2000). *Homeless bird.* New York: Scholastic.

Teaching and Assessing Language Arts

PATTERNS OF PRACTICE

Mrs. Miller-McColm sits down on her teacher's stool and picks up Natalie Babbitt's *Tuck Everlasting* (1988), the highly acclaimed story of a family who drinks from a magical spring and becomes immortal. "Yesterday, we stopped halfway through Chapter 6," she says to her sixth graders. "Who remembers what was happening?" A sea of hands go up, and Mrs. Miller-McColm calls on Junior. "Winnie wanted to run away from home, but she got kidnapped by the Tucks. I don't know why though," he says. Next Isabel says, "I think she goes with the Tucks because she wants to. I think she wants an adventure so she'll stay with them forever."

The students continue talking about the story for several minutes, and then Mrs. Miller-McColm begins reading aloud. She's a strong oral reader, and her students listen intently. After she reads the middle of page 34, she stops and asks, "Why does Mae Tuck say, 'We're not bad people, truly we're not. We had to bring you away—you'll see why in a minute—and we'll take you back just as soon as we can. Tomorrow. I promise'?" The students break into small groups

Reading and Writing Workshop

Literature Focus Units

Literature Circles

Theme Cycles

to talk for several minutes about whether the Tucks are "bad" people for kidnapping Winnie and to speculate about why they abducted her. The students' desks are arranged in five groups of five or six students each, and the classmates in each table group talk eagerly. After several minutes, Mrs. Miller-McColm brings the class back together to continue the discussion. "We don't think the Tucks are bad people," Noemi offers, "because bad people aren't nice, and Mae Tuck is. They must have a good reason for what they did." Donavon says, "They may be nice people but we don't think Winnie will get free 'tomorrow.'" Iliana agrees, "Winnie won't get free until the book ends, and there are a lot of pages still to read." After the students share their ideas, the teacher reads to the end of this chapter and continues reading the next chapter, where the Tucks explain to Winnie about their "changelessness" and why they abducted her. She finishes reading the last page of Chapter 7, puts the book down, and looks at the students. They look back at her, dazed; no one says a word.

To help the sixth graders sort out their ideas and feelings, Mrs. Miller-McColm asks them to quickwrite their reactions in their reading logs. The students take about 5 minutes to write, and then they're ready to talk. Some students read aloud their reading log entries, and others share their ideas. Mrs. Miller-McColm asks, "Do you believe the Tucks? Are they telling the truth?" About half of the students agree that the Tucks are telling the truth; other students aren't so sure. Next, she asks them to write in their reading logs again, this time about whether they believe the Tucks' story.

> ## How do teachers organize for instruction?
>
> Teachers organize for language arts instruction using the four patterns of practice—literature focus units, literature circles, reading and writing workshop, and theme cycles. Teachers vary in the patterns they choose, and some teachers add other programs, such as basal readers, to their instructional plan. No matter which patterns of practice teachers choose to use, they combine direct instruction, small-group activities, and opportunities for students to use the language arts independently in each day's plan. As you read this vignette, notice how Mrs. Miller-McColm incorporates all four patterns of practice in her language arts program.

Mrs. Miller-McColm uses the novels she reads aloud to teach students about the structure of stories. Her focus is on plot development as she reads

Tuck Everlasting. She has talked about how authors develop stories, and the students understand that in the beginning, authors introduce the problem; in the middle, the problem gets worse; and in the end, it is resolved. Yesterday, the students learned the problem in this story—Winnie Foster is abducted by the Tucks. The teacher has also taught them about conflict situations, and they know the four kinds of conflict in stories: with nature, with society, between characters, and within a character. At this point in the story, they think the conflict is between characters—between Winnie and the Tucks. Later in the story, they'll see that the conflict is within Winnie herself as she decides whether to drink from the spring and live with the Tucks forever.

The students also create projects after each book. After they finish reading *Tuck Everlasting,* Mrs. Miller-McColm will ask students to think about the advantages and disadvantages of living forever, decide if they would want to live forever, and write persuasive essays detailing their choice. After reading other books, students do other types of projects. Sometimes they perform skits, write poems, create storyboards on butcher paper, make theme collages, and write sequels.

Mrs. Miller-McColm spends the first hour of the language arts period teaching a literature focus unit using a book from her district's list of "core" literature selections. She reads the book aloud because about half of her students couldn't read it on their own. She has already read *Holes* (Sachar, 1998), *A Wrinkle in Time* (L'Engle, 1962), and *Julie of the Wolves* (George, 1972), and by the end of the school year, she will have read 11 or 12 novels.

Mrs. Miller-McColm's daily schedule is shown in the box on page 49. She involves her students in a variety of language arts activities using the four patterns of practice during the morning and connects language arts to content-area learning through social studies and science theme cycles in the afternoon.

Next, Mrs. Miller-McColm's students participate in book groups, another name for literature circles. Her students read at fourth- through eighth-grade levels, and she divides them into seven book groups according to reading level. Then students choose novels to read after their teacher gives book talks to introduce several choices for each group. Currently, students are reading these books:

Stone Fox (Gardiner, 1980) (level 4)

Sarah, Plain and Tall (MacLachlan, 1985) (level 4)

Shiloh (Naylor, 1991) (level 5)

Ralph the Mouse (Cleary, 1993) (level 5)

Maniac Magee (Spinelli, 1990) (level 6)

The BFG (Dahl, 1982) (level 6)

Harry Potter and the Goblet of Fire (Rowling, 2002) (level 8)

The box on page 50 shows other books at each reading level that students read during the year.

Students meet with their groups to set reading schedules. They read during this period and at home and meet with Mrs. Miller-McColm two or three times each week for 15 to 20 minutes to talk about the book they're reading. Students also create displays about the books on a bulletin board on one side of the classroom. The long bulletin board is divided into eight sections. In one section, Mrs. Miller-McColm posts the directions for book groups, and the book groups each take responsibility for one of the other sections. For this round of book groups, the focus is on plot development. Each group makes a sign with

MRS. MILLER-McCOLM'S DAILY SCHEDULE

8:30–8:45 *Opening*

8:45–9:45 *Literature Focus Unit*
Mrs. Miller-McColm reads aloud a featured book, involves students in response activities, and teaches story structure, vocabulary, and other strategies and skills.

9:45–10:30 *Book Groups*
Students divide into groups according to reading level and participate in literature circles. They choose books to read, read them independently, and meet with Mrs. Miller-McColm to discuss them. They also apply what they are learning about story structure during the literature focus unit to the books they are reading now and create graphic displays that they post on a special bulletin board.

10:30–10:45 *Recess*

10:45–11:15 *Word Work*
Mrs. Miller-McColm teaches minilessons on word-identification and spelling strategies and skills, including idioms, synonyms, syllabication, root words, and affixes. Students also study spelling words and take weekly spelling tests.

11:15–12:15 *Writing Workshop*
Students use the writing process to write stories and other genres. They meet in writing groups to revise their writing and editing conferences to correct spelling, capitalization, punctuation, and sentence structure errors. They share their published writing from the author's chair. Mrs. Miller-McColm also teaches minilessons on writing procedures, concepts, strategies, and skills.

12:15–1:00 *Lunch and Recess*

1:00–2:00 *Math*

2:00–3:15 *Social Studies/Science*
Mrs. Miller-McColm alternates teaching monthlong social studies and science theme cycles. Students apply what they are learning in language arts as they participate in content-area study and develop projects to share their learning.

3:15–3:25 *Clean-up and Dismissal*

| Other Book Sets for Literature Circles ||
Reading Level	Books
4	Bruchac, J. (1997). *Eagle son.* New York: Dial. Clements, A. (1996). *Frindle.* New York: Simon & Schuster. Coerr, E. (1977). *Sadako and the thousand paper cranes.* New York: Putnam. Dahl, R. (1980). *The twits.* New York: Puffin. George, J. C. (1995). *There's an owl in the shower.* New York: HarperCollins. King-Smith, D. (1995). *The school mouse.* New York: Hyperion.
5	Creech, S. (1994). *Walk two moons.* New York: HarperCollins. Fleischman, S. (1986). *The whipping boy.* New York: Morrow. George, J. C. (1980). *The cry of the crow.* New York: HarperCollins. Paterson, K. (1996). *Jip, his story.* New York: Putnam. Spinelli, J. (1996). *Crash.* New York: Knopf. Taylor, M. D. (1995). *The well.* New York: Dial.
6	Anaya, R. (1999). *My land sings: Stories from the Rio Grande.* New York: HarperCollins. Beatty, P. (1987). *Charley Skedaddle.* New York: Morrow. Cooney, C. B. (2000). *Mummy.* New York: Scholastic. Hesse, K. (1997). *Out of the dust.* New York: Scholastic. Paterson, K. (1977). *Bridge to Terabithia.* New York: HarperCollins. Raskin, E. (1978). *The westing game.* New York: Putnam.
7–8	Barrett, T. (1999). *Anna of Byzantium.* New York: Delacorte. Cormier, R. (1974). *The chocolate war.* New York: Random House. McGraw, E. J. (1961). *The golden goblet.* New York: Puffin. Norton, M. (1980). *The borrowers.* Orlando, FL: Harcourt Brace. Steig, W. (1976). *Abel's island.* New York: Farrar, Straus & Giroux. Taylor, M. D. (1976). *Roll of thunder, hear my cry.* New York: Viking.

the title and author of the book and then creates a graphic display emphasizing the conflict situations in their novel.

Mrs. Miller-McColm meets with the group reading *Sarah, Plain and Tall,* a story about a mail-order bride in the early 1900s. She begins by asking the students to summarize the story so far, and Gabrielle says, "A woman named Sarah is coming to stay at a farm. She might marry the dad and be a mom for the children, Anna and Caleb." "Has she arrived yet?" Mrs. Miller-McColm asks, and April responds, "She just arrived. She came on a train and everyone is very nervous." Then students make connections between the story and their own lives, the world around them, and other literature, and Mrs. Miller-McColm helps them analyze the plot and identify the conflict situation; it's between Sarah and the other characters. The students decide to draw open-mind portraits of the characters to post in their section of the bulletin board. For their portraits, they will draw pictures of the characters and attach three sheets of paper behind the pictures where they will draw and write about the conflict each character feels at the beginning of the story, in the middle, and at the end.

Next, she meets with the group reading *Shiloh*. These students have just finished reading the novel about a boy who sticks out his neck to save an abused dog. The students are eager to talk about the book, and they make connections to personal experiences and to other dog stories they've read. Mrs. Miller-McColm asks them to think more deeply about the story and rereads the last paragraph of the story aloud:

> I look at the dark closing in, sky getting more and more purple, and I'm thinking how nothing is as simple as you guess—not right or wrong, not Judd Travers, not even me or this dog I got here. But the good part is I saved Shiloh and opened my eyes some. Now that ain't bad for eleven. (p. 144)

She asks what Marty, the main character in the story, means when he says, "nothing is as simple as you guess . . . " Omar begins, "At first Marty thought he was all good and Judd Travers was all bad, but then Marty did something dishonest to get Shiloh. He didn't like doing bad things but he did them for a good reason so I think that's ok." The students continue talking about being responsible for your own actions, both good and bad. After the discussion ends, the teacher checks the group's section of the bulletin board, and the students make plans to finish it before the end of the week. The teacher also takes them over to the classroom library and introduces them to *Shiloh Season* (Naylor, 1996) and *Saving Shiloh* (Naylor, 1997), the second and third books in the Shiloh trilogy, and the students eagerly decide to read these two books next. Mrs. Miller-McColm passes out copies of the books to students.

Students take a recess break, and after the break, Mrs. Miller-McColm teaches a word work lesson on suffixes, beginning with the word *changelessness* from *Tuck Everlasting*. She points out the two suffixes, -*less,* meaning "without," and -*ness,* meaning "state of being." The students talk about the word's meaning and how the suffixes affect the root word. Then the teacher presents a list of other words ending in -*less,* including *weightless, effortless, heartless,* and *careless.* The students talk about the meaning of each word and identify which ones can add on the suffix -*ness,* such as *weightlessness.* Then students use the last 10 minutes of the period to practice their spelling words with partners.

Next, Mrs. Miller-McColm begins writing workshop with a 10- to 15-minute minilesson on a writing procedure, concept, strategy, or skill. Today is the first in a series of three minilessons on writing narrative leads. She displays a chart of four techniques that writers use to hook their audience and explains each one:

To see Mrs. Miller-McColm's writing workshop in action, view the CD-ROM that accompanies this text.

1. *Action.* The main character does something interesting.
2. *Dialogue.* The main character says something interesting.
3. *A thought or a question.* The main character shares something that he or she is thinking or asks a question.
4. *A sound.* The author begins with an interesting sound related to the story.

She reads aloud the first sentences from *Chocolate Fever* (Smith, 1972), *Freaky Friday* (Rodgers, 1972), *The Sign of the Beaver* (Speare, 1983), *Stone Fox* (Gardiner, 1980), *The Breadwinner* (Ellis, 2000), and *Bridge to Terabithia* (Paterson, 1977), and the students identify which hook the author used in each story. Tomorrow, the students will work together as a class to write sample leads using each technique, and on the third day, the students will write leads with partners and share them with the class.

After the minilesson, students use the writing process approach to write independently for 40 minutes. For the past month, students have been writing on self-selected topics, and many are writing stories, but some students are writing poetry and informational books. Mrs. Miller-McColm has already announced that students should finish the pieces they are working on by Friday because beginning next week, students will be using writing workshop time to write reports as part of their theme on ancient Egypt.

Some students are working independently at their desks and others are meeting with small groups of classmates to revise their writing, conferencing with the teacher, or working with partners to proofread and correct errors in their writing. The four computers are all occupied, too, as students word process their compositions and print out final copies. They place their final copies in a box on Mrs. Miller-McColm's desk and she binds their compositions—handwritten or word processed—into books for them.

During the last 5 minutes of writing workshop, students take turns sitting in the author's chair to read aloud their completed writings. The students sit on the floor around the author's chair and listen attentively as their classmate reads. Ricky, who wants to be a race car driver, reads an informational book he has researched and written about the Winston Cup Series. He's also included this year's schedule of races and a map of the United States showing where the tracks are. After he finishes reading, the students clap and they ask questions. Junior asks, "What does NASCAR stand for?" and Ricky explains that it is an acronym for the National Association for Stock Car Automobile Racing. Omar asks for more clarification about how the races are run, and Briana asks how winners of each race gain points. The students get so interested in the topic that they don't want to end the discussion even though it is lunchtime!

In the afternoon, Mrs. Miller-McColm teaches alternating theme cycles on social studies and science topics. Currently they are learning about the civilization of ancient Egypt. The students are reading from a text set of books, Internet articles, and other materials and making notes of important information about ancient Egypt in their learning logs. These logs are divided into sections on geography, culture, people and their work, government, religion, and history, and students take notes in the appropriate sections as they read. Mrs. Miller-McColm taught a series of minilessons on notetaking at the beginning of the theme, and students have been applying what they learned as they read and take notes. For the first 30 minutes of the period, students finish reading text set materials and taking notes. As they work, the teacher circulates around the classroom for a final check that students have adequate notes in each section of their logs.

Next, Mrs. Miller-McColm brings the class together to explain about the reports they will write. She begins by asking them to highlight the achievements of the ancient Egyptian civilization and they brainstorm a list, including:

the remarkable pyramids

gods and goddesses

how the Egyptians farmed near the Nile River

the mummification process

the hieroglyphic system of writing

how the Egyptians traveled on the Nile

the tools the Egyptians made and used

Egyptian women's make-up and jewelry

Then she explains that she wants students to choose one achievement that particularly interests them, continue to research it, and share what they learn in a report. They will also make an artifact to go with the report. If their topic is hieroglyphics, for example, they might make a scroll. The students are excited; they eagerly choose topics and suggest artifacts they can make. Mrs. Miller-McColm distributes the rubric that students will use to self-assess their projects and that she will use to grade them and they read it together. Then she passes around several reports and artifacts from last year. The students examine them and compare them to the rubric to better understand what their teacher wants them to do.

Over the next 3 weeks, students will create reports and artifacts, working during the writing workshop and theme cycle periods, and Mrs. Miller-McColm will provide support and guidance as they work through minilessons, demonstrations, and conferences.

Language arts instruction and assessment should be based on how children learn. Donald Graves (1991) admonishes teachers to build a literate environment that facilitates the development of lifelong readers and writers. Certainly, the classroom environment reflects teachers' goals for their students. Classrooms with publishing centers and author's chairs, libraries filled with books, and computer banks with word-processing programs and modem hookups, for example, reflect teachers' expectations for their students to effectively use all six language arts.

As you begin reading this chapter, you may want to read the "Dear Reader" letter in Chapter 2 on the Companion Website at www.prenhall.com/tompkins

Teachers use the four patterns of practice to involve students in meaningful, functional, and genuine language-learning activities. These four approaches are literature focus units, literature circles, reading and writing workshop, and theme cycles. Teachers should incorporate a combination of these approaches in their instructional programs. No longer is it enough to teach using a language arts textbook and have students complete the worksheets and other assignments that accompany the textbook.

Assessment is a crucial component of the instructional program. It should be authentic and reflect how children learn. Teachers begin by determining students' background knowledge before instruction, and they continue as they monitor students' progress during instruction. Teachers and students collaborate to document students' learning and collect artifacts in portfolios. Assigning grades is a fact of life in classrooms, and there are innovative ways to involve students in assessing their own learning and determining grades.

As you read this chapter, you will learn how to create a language arts classroom, organize for instruction, and assess students' learning. Think about these questions as you continue reading:

◆ How do teachers arrange classrooms to facilitate learning?

◆ What are literature focus units?

◆ What are literature circles?

◆ What is reading and writing workshop?

◆ What are theme cycles?

◆ How do teachers assess students' learning?

LANGUAGE ARTS CLASSROOMS AND MATERIALS

Elementary classrooms should be authentic language environments that encourage students to listen, talk, read and write, view, and visually represent; that is, they should be communities of learners. As Susan Hepler explains, "The real challenge to teachers . . . is to set up the kind of classroom community where children pick their own ways to literacy" (1991, p. 179). The physical arrangement and materials provided in the classroom play an important role in setting the stage for language arts instruction (Morrow, 1996).

In the past, textbooks were the primary instructional material, and students sat in desks arranged in rows facing the teacher. Now a wide variety of instructional materials are available in addition to textbooks, including trade books and multimedia materials. Students' desks are more often arranged in small groups, materials are set out in centers, and classrooms are visually stimulating with signs, posters, charts, and other teacher- and student-made displays related to the four patterns of practice. These are components of a language arts classroom:

- Desks arranged in groups to facilitate talk and learning
- Classroom libraries stocked with a variety of reading materials
- Posted messages about the current day
- Displays of student work and projects
- A chair designated as the author's chair
- Displayed signs, labels for items, and quotations
- Posted directions for activities or use of equipment
- An abundant supply of materials for recording language, including pencils, pens, paper, journals and logs, books, and computers
- Centers for reading and writing activities
- Reference materials for literature focus units, literature circles, and theme cycles
- Computer and listening centers stocked with multimedia equipment and software

---

FIGURE 2–1

Characteristics of a Language Arts Classroom

1. Classroom Organization

- Desks are arranged in groups to facilitate interaction and cooperative work.
- There is open space for class meetings.
- Parts of the classroom are organized into centers, such as the library center, writing center, and theme center.

2. Classroom Library Center

- There are at least four times as many books as students in the classroom.
- Stories, informational books, and poetry are included.
- Multicultural books and other reading materials are included.
- Information about authors and illustrators is displayed.
- Some of the books were written by students.
- Books related to literature focus units and theme cycles are highlighted.
- Students monitor the center.

3. Message Center

- Schedules and announcements about the current day are posted.
- Some of the announcements are student initiated.
- Mailboxes and/or a message board are available for students to use.
- Students are encouraged to write notes or send e-mail to classmates.

4. Display of Student Work and Projects

- All students have work displayed in the classroom.
- Student work reflects a variety of curricular areas.
- Students' projects and other student-made displays are exhibited in the classroom.
- There is an area where students can display their own work.
- Other student work is stored in portfolios.

5. Author's Chair

- One chair in the classroom is designated as the author's chair for students to use when sharing their writing.
- The author's chair is labeled.

6. Signs, Labels, and Quotations

- Equipment and other classroom items are labeled.
- Words, phrases, and sentences are posted in the classroom.
- Some signs, labels, and quotations are written by students.

Continues

- A puppet stage or an area for presenting plays and storytelling
- Charts for recording information (e.g., sign-in charts for attendance or writing-group charts)
- World-related print (e.g., newspapers, maps, and calendars)
- Reading and writing materials in young children's literacy play centers

Figure 2–1 elaborates on these components of a language arts classroom.

FIGURE 2-1

Characteristics of a Language Arts Classroom—Continued

7. Directions

- Directions are provided in the classroom so that students can work independently.
- Some of the directions are written by students.

8. Materials for Writing

- Pencils, pens, paper, journals, books, computers, dry-erase boards, and other materials are available for recording language.
- Students have access to these materials.

9. Places for Reading and Writing

- Special places are designated in the classroom for reading and writing activities.
- These areas are quiet and separated from other areas.

10. Reference Materials

- Word walls list important words related to literature focus units and theme cycles.
- Lists, clusters, pictures, charts, books, models, and other reference materials are available for content-area study.
- Artifacts and other items related to theme cycles are labeled and displayed.
- Dictionaries and thesauri are available for students to use.

11. Multimedia Technology

- A listening center with tapes of stories and informational books is available for students to use.
- Computers with word-processing, illustration, and PowerPoint software, a CD-ROM drive, a modem, a scanner, and other related technology are available.
- Multimedia materials—such as videotapes and DVDs—related to literature focus units and theme cycles and the related equipment are available.
- A camcorder and VCR playback system are available for student use.

12. Dramatic Center

- A puppet stage is set up in the classroom.
- Art materials are available for making puppets and other props.
- An area is accessible for presenting plays and telling stories.
- Props are available in the classroom.
- Primary-grade classrooms have literacy play centers with reading and writing materials.

The Physical Arrangement

No one physical arrangement best represents a language arts classroom, but the configuration of any classroom can be modified to include many characteristics to facilitate learning. Student desks or tables should be grouped to encourage students to talk, share, and work cooperatively. Separate areas are needed for reading and writing, a classroom library, a listening center, a computer center, centers for materials related to content-area theme cycles, and a center for dramatic activities. Kindergarten classrooms also need literacy play

Literacy play centers are discussed in Chapter 4, "Emerging Into Literacy."

FIGURE 2-2 *Classroom Arrangements*

KINDERGARTEN CLASSROOM

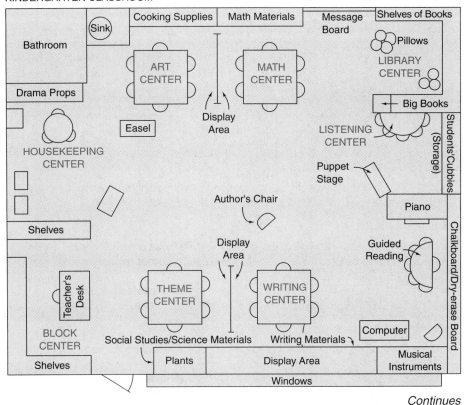

Continues

centers. Some variations obviously occur at various grade levels; older students, for example, use reference centers with materials related to the units and themes they are studying. The three diagrams in Figure 2–2 suggest ways to set up the classroom to facilitate learning.

Centers

Teachers arrange centers in their classrooms with language arts materials, and students participate in meaningful, functional, and genuine language activities independently and in small groups at these centers (Ford & Opitz, 2002). It is crucial that students engage fully with these activities so that they are learning and not wasting their time at the center (Cambourne, 2001). At the library center, students select books for independent reading; at the listening center, they listen to stories; and at the writing center, they write and construct books. At other centers, students practice language arts strategies and skills that teachers have introduced in minilessons or watch videotapes to learn about authors. Some centers, such as library and listening centers, are part of the physical arrangement of the classroom, and other centers are set up on students' desks or anywhere in the classroom where there is available space.

FIGURE 2-2   *Classroom Arrangements—Continued*

THIRD-GRADE CLASSROOM

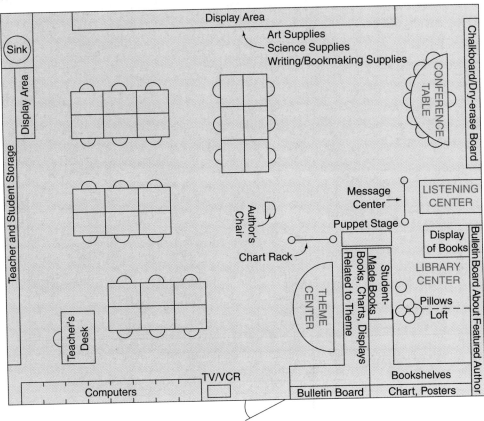

Library centers are stocked with trade books that are attractively displayed and available for students to peruse. These books might be from the teacher's own collection or borrowed from the school or public library. Many of the books should relate to units of study, and these should be changed periodically. Other books for students to read independently are also included in the library center. After studying library centers in primary classrooms, Leslie Morrow (1989) makes these recommendations:

1. Make the library center inviting.
2. Define the library center with shelves, carpets, benches, sofas, or other partitions.
3. Make the center large enough to accommodate five or six students comfortably at one time.
4. Use two kinds of bookshelves: Most of the collection should be shelved with the spines facing outward, but some books should be set so that the front covers are displayed.
5. Shelve books by category, and color-code books by type.

FIGURE 2-2   *Classroom Arrangements—Continued*

SIXTH-GRADE CLASSROOM

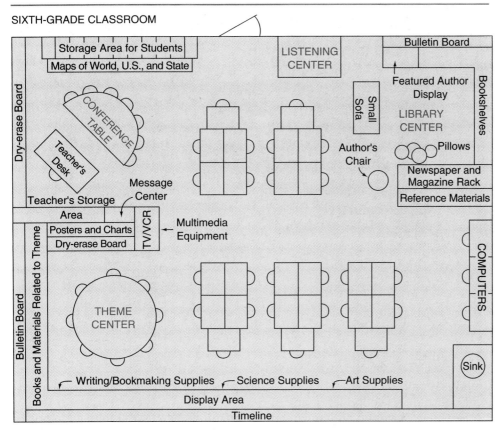

6. Display books written by one author or related to a theme being studied, and change the displays regularly.
7. Cover the floor with a rug and furnish the area with pillows, beanbag chairs, or comfortable furniture.
8. Stock the center with at least four times as many books as there are students in the classroom.
9. Provide a variety of types of reading materials, including books, newspapers, magazines, posters, and charts.
10. Display posters that encourage reading in the library center.

These recommendations are based on research done in primary-grade classrooms, but they are equally appropriate for older students.

Listening centers are equipped with tape players and headphones. Students listen to cassette tapes of stories, poems, and informational books and sometimes follow along in books, if they are available. Many commercially prepared tape recordings of children's books are available, and teachers can tape-record their own reading of books so that students can reread books and listen again and again to their favorites. Too often, teachers think of listening centers as equipment for primary-grade classrooms and do not realize their potential

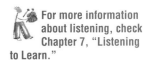

For more information about listening, check Chapter 7, "Listening to Learn."

Classroom space. *This third-grade teacher has carefully organized her classroom with a combination of large-group, small-group, and independent work spaces. Students' desks are arranged in small groups, centers provide opportunities for students to work with partners or in small groups, and there is space for small-group instruction and whole-class activities. She has also thought about how students move from one area to another. As teachers arrange their classrooms, they consider the patterns of practice they incorporate into their language arts program and the classroom spaces needed to facilitate teaching and learning.*

usefulness with older students, especially struggling readers or students learning English as a second language.

Supplies of writing and art materials for students to use as they write books and respond to books they read are stored in writing centers. These materials include:

- A variety of pens, pencils, crayons, markers, and other writing and drawing instruments
- Lined and unlined paper of varied sizes and colors
- Materials for making and binding books
- Computers with word-processing and graphic programs, modems and Internet access, and printers
- A camera and film for taking illustration photos and photos of students for their "All About the Author" pages
- Scrap art materials for illustrations and covers

In primary-grade classrooms, a table is included in the center so that students can gather to write and share their writing. In middle- and upper-grade classrooms, however, writing materials are often stored on shelves or in cabinets, and students usually write at their own desks. They gather in small groups to revise their writing wherever there is space in the classroom, and they meet with the teacher at a conference table to edit their writing.

Teachers also set up centers for students to work in small groups to practice skills and explore literacy concepts. Groups of students manipulate literacy materials, such as a box of small objects for sorting according to beginning sound, flannel-board pictures to use in retelling a story, strips of paper on which lines of a poem have been written for students to sequence, or magnetic letters to use for spelling words. Students might apply what the teacher presented in a recent minilesson. For instance, students might write group poems using the format the teacher introduced in a minilesson, or they might compile individual books or charts of compound words using the class word list created during a minilesson. Students also participate in exploring activities related to the book the class is reading at centers. They might examine brochures, watch a video, or read an autobiography about the author of the book the class is reading, read informational books about a related concept, or experiment with the artistic techniques the illustrator used in the book.

Textbooks

Textbooks are one tool for teaching language arts concepts, strategies, and skills. They are the most accessible resource and have some benefits. Textbooks provide information about language arts topics and a sequence of topics for each grade level. They present models, examples, and practice activities. Although these tools provide security for beginning teachers, they have drawbacks. The textbook's format is probably its greatest drawback, because textbooks are inappropriate for many activities. Also, the six language arts involve much more than can be contained in a single textbook. Other weaknesses are:

- Little attention to listening, talking, and viewing
- Excessive emphasis on grammar and usage skills
- Emphasis on rote memorization rather than on effective communication
- Focus on correctness rather than on experimentation with language
- Few opportunities to individualize instruction
- Difficulty in connecting textbook activities to literature focus units, across-the-curriculum theme cycles, and other instructional patterns

Teachers should consider these weaknesses when they adopt language arts textbooks and decide whether to use textbooks in their language arts programs. If teachers are going to use language arts textbooks, they should choose textbooks that:

1. Center on children's own language
2. Emphasize the social uses of language
3. Integrate the six language arts
4. Recognize the developmental aspects of students' learning
5. Assist teachers in assessing students' learning
6. Develop students' creative and critical thinking
7. Respect cultural and linguistic diversity
8. Emphasize the language arts as tools for learning across the curriculum (Shanahan & Knight, 1991)

These characteristics should permeate the textbook; they should not be addressed superficially in only one chapter or in isolated examples.

Teachers should never assume that textbooks are equivalent to the total language arts program. Teachers who start on the first page of the language arts textbook on the first day of school and continue page by page through it fail to consider the students' language-learning needs. One of the best ways to use language arts textbooks is as a resource for minilessons. As part of a minilesson on how to present an oral report, for example, students might create a rubric using the guidelines presented in the textbook; during a minilesson on how to form plurals, students might use the information presented in the textbook to make a class chart; or students might check the examples of graphs in the textbook before making a graph to chart the plot of a story they are reading. Students can also make notes, write rules, list examples, and draw diagrams in their language arts notebooks to create their own handbook or textbook.

Check Chapter 6, "Personal Writing," for more information on language arts notebooks.

Trade Books

Books written for children that are not textbooks are called trade books, and thousands of excellent trade books are currently available. Teachers collect stories, informational books, and books of poetry for their classroom libraries and to use in teaching language arts and across-the-curriculum theme cycles.

For more information about stories, see Chapter 9, "Reading and Writing Stories."

Stories.   Most stories for younger children, such as *Sylvester and the Magic Pebble* (Steig, 1969) and *Officer Buckle and Gloria* (Rathmann, 1995), are picture books, and many stories for older children, including Natalie Babbitt's *Tuck Everlasting* (1988) and Gary Paulsen's *Hatchet* (1987), are novels. A number of picture-book stories appeal to older students, however, such as *Pink and Say* (Polacco, 1994) and Chris Van Allsburg's fantasies. Many stories feature multicultural characters and themes, such as *Smoky Night* (Bunting, 1994), about the Los Angeles riot; *Abuela* (Dorros, 1991), a fanciful story about a Hispanic child and her grandmother; and *The Bracelet* (Uchida, 1993), about a Japanese American family's experiences in an internment camp during World War II.

Chapter 10, "Reading and Writing Information," tells more about informational books and how to use them in elementary classrooms.

Informational Books.   Informational books provide information on social studies, science, math, art, music, and other topics. Some are written in a story format, such as *The Magic School Bus Inside a Hurricane* (Cole, 1995) and *Castle* (Macaulay, 1977), whereas others are written in a more traditional informational style, with a table of contents, an index, and a glossary. Examples of traditional informational books are *Red-Tail Angels: The Story of the Tuskegee Airmen of World War II* (McKissack & McKissack, 1995) and *Summer Ice: Life Along the Antarctic Peninsula* (McMillan, 1995). Some informational books are written for young children, with a phrase or sentence of text presented on each page along with a photograph or illustration. *Giant Sequoia Trees* (Wadsworth, 1995) is an easy-to-read description of the life cycle of these giant trees and is illustrated with color photographs on every page. In *I See Animals Hiding* (1995), Jim Arnosky explains camouflage using watercolor illustrations of wild animals in natural settings and simple sentences about animals who blend in with their environments.

Another type of informational book presents language arts concepts, including homonyms, parts of speech, and figurative language. One example is *It Figures! Fun Figures of Speech* (Terban, 1993), which explains similes, metaphors, onomatopoeia, alliteration, hyperbole, and personification. Alphabet books are informational books, too. Although many alphabet books are designed for very young children, others are appropriate for elementary students, such as *A for Antarctica* (Chester, 1995).

Biographies are another type of informational book. Most biographies are chapter books, such as Russell Freedman's *Eleanor Roosevelt: A Life of Discovery* (1993), but several authors have written shorter biographies that resemble picture books. Perhaps the best-known biographer for younger children is David Adler, who has written *A Picture Book of Helen Keller* (1990), *A Picture Book of Patrick Henry* (1995), and other biographies of important historical figures. Jean Fritz has written a very popular series of biographies, including *You Want Women to Vote, Lizzie Stanton?* (1995) and *Will You Sign Here, John Hancock?* (1976). A few autobiographies have also been written for children, and books by children's authors, such as Eve Bunting's *Once Upon a Time* (1995), are popular.

To learn more about using biographies in the language arts program, turn to Chapter 10, "Reading and Writing Information."

Books of Poetry.   Many delightful books of poetry for children are available. Some are collections of poems on a single topic written by one poet, such as *The Dragons Are Singing Tonight* (Prelutsky, 1993) and Fleischman's *Joyful Noise: Poems for Two Voices* (1988), which is about insects. Other collections of poetry on a single topic selected by a compiler are Hopkins's *Hand in Hand: An American History Through Poetry* (1994) and Carle's *Animals, Animals* (1989). An excellent anthology (a collection of poems written by different poets on a variety of topics) is *The Random House Book of Poetry for Children* (Prelutsky, 2000).

Chapter 11, "Reading and Writing Poetry," focuses on ways to engage elementary students in poetry activities.

Teachers create text sets of stories, informational books, and poetry books to use in teaching language arts and other content areas. By using all three types of trade books, students learn more about a topic than they could if they read only stories or only informational books or poems. The Classroom Library on page 64 presents three text sets (or collections of books). One text set is for a primary-grade unit on insects, the second is for a middle-grade unit on cowboys, and the third is for an upper-grade unit on the Middle Ages. The main drawback to using trade books is that they are not sequenced and prepackaged as textbooks are, so teachers must make choices and design activities to accompany the books. Similar text sets of trade books can be collected for almost any topic.

Check Chapter 15, "Putting It All Together," to learn more about using text sets in theme cycles.

Multimedia Technology

Computers with word-processing programs and speech synthesizers, modems for Internet access, CD-ROMs, digital cameras, and other electronic media are becoming an integral part of language arts classrooms. New multimedia equipment has replaced record players and film projectors, and software programs are expanding the ways teachers and students use the new technology. Students are often more eager to use technology than their teachers are, but the power of technology to expand our communicative competence in the 21st century is undeniable.

For the past thousand years, print has been the preeminent technology, but the technology of the future is digital media (Rose & Meyer, 1994). Digital information—text, sounds, images, recorded language, movie clips, and animation—can be manipulated, transformed, customized, and copied. In contrast, print is fixed, not malleable. With digital media, students play

Three Text Sets

Text Set on Insects

Stories

Brinckloe, J. (1985). *Fireflies!* New York: Aladdin.

Carle, E. (1969). *The very hungry caterpillar.* New York: Philomel.

Carle, E. (1977). *The grouchy ladybug.* New York: Crowell.

Carle, E. (1990). *The very quiet cricket.* New York: Philomel.

Carle, E. (1995). *The very lonely firefly.* New York: Philomel.

Informational Books

Facklam, M. (1996). *Creepy, crawly caterpillars.* Boston: Little, Brown.

Fowler, A. (1990). *It's a good thing there are insects.* Chicago: Childrens Press.

Gibbons, G. (1989). *Monarch butterfly.* New York: Holiday House.

Godkin, C. (1995). *What about ladybugs?* New York: Sierra.

Heiligman, D. (1996). *From caterpillar to butterfly.* New York: HarperCollins.

Heller, R. (1985). *How to hide a butterfly and other insects.* New York: Grosset & Dunlap.

Micucci, C. (2003). *The life and times of the ant.* Boston: Houghton Mifflin.

Books of Poetry

Moses, A. (1992). *If I were an ant.* Chicago: Childrens Press.

Ryder, J. (1989). *Where butterflies grow.* New York: Lodestar.

Walton, R. (1995). *What to do when a bug climbs in your mouth: And other poems to drive you buggy.* New York: Lothrop & Lee.

Text Set on Cowboys

Stories

Antle, N. (1995). *Sam's Wild West show.* New York: Dial.

Brusca, M. C., & Wilson, T. (1995). *Three friends: A counting book/Tres amigos: Un cuento para contar.* New York: Holt.

Martin, B., Jr., & Archambault, J. (1986). *White Dynamite and Curly Kidd.* New York: Henry Holt.

Scott, A. H. (1989). *Someday rider.* New York: Clarion.

Scott, A. H. (1993). *Cowboy country.* New York: Clarion.

Van Allsburg, C. (1995). *Bad day at Riverbend.* Boston: Houghton Mifflin.

Informational Books

Christian, M. (1993). *Hats are for watering horses: Why the cowboy dressed that way.* New York: Kendrick.

Freedman, R. (1985). *Cowboys of the Wild West.* New York: Clarion.

Johnson, N. (1993). *Jack Creek cowboy.* New York: Dial.

Murdoch, D. H. (1993). *Eyewitness books: Cowboy.* New York: Knopf.

Scott, A. H. (1990). *One good horse: A cowpuncher's counting book.* New York: Greenwillow.

Winter, J. (1995). *Cowboy Charlie: The story of Charles M. Russell.* San Diego: Harcourt Brace.

Books of Poetry

Geis, J. (1992). *Where the buffalo roam.* New York: Ideals.

Grossman, B. (1993). *Cowboy Ed.* New York: HarperCollins.

Sullivan, C. (1993). *Cowboys.* New York: Rizzoli.

Text Set on the Middle Ages

Stories

Cushman, K. (1994). *Catherine, called Birdy.* New York: HarperCollins.

Cushman, K. (1995). *The midwife's apprentice.* New York: Clarion.

Mayer, M. (1987). *The pied piper of Hamelin.* New York: Macmillan.

Morpurgo, M. (1995). *Arthur, high king of Britain.* San Diego: Harcourt Brace.

Shannon, M. (1994). *Gawain and the Green Knight.* New York: Putnam.

Vaes, A. (1994). *Reynard the fox.* New York: Turner.

Informational Books

Aliki. (1983). *A medieval feast.* New York: Crowell.

Gibbons, G. (1995). *Knights in shining armor.* Boston: Little, Brown.

Howarth, S. (1993). *The Middle Ages.* New York: Viking.

Howe, J. (1995). *Knights.* New York: Orchard.

Hunt, J. (1989). *Illuminations.* New York: Bradbury Press.

Lasker, J. (1976). *Merry ever after.* New York: Viking.

Macaulay, D. (1977). *Castle.* Boston: Houghton Mifflin.

Steele, P. (1995). *Castles.* New York: Kingfisher.

Books of Poetry

Yolen, J. (1994). *Here there be unicorns.* San Diego: Harcourt Brace.

simulation games on the computer using CD-ROM, write using word-processing programs, and develop PowerPoint presentations for their oral reports. They view dramatizations of stories or other films on DVD. They create visual representations using Hypercard programs and scan their drawings to add them to books they are writing on the computer. Sound has been digitized, too: Students can add their own voice to projects they create and listen to a story or other text that uses synthetic speech on the computer. Movies and news films and videotapes have been digitized, and students can watch movie clips, listen to authors talk about the books they have written, and listen to the speeches of historical figures; for example, they can hear Martin Luther King Jr. giving his "I Have a Dream" speech. Interviews, guest speakers, dramatic productions, and oral reports can be videotaped and added to multimedia productions, too.

Computers and related technologies give students new powers and incentives (Marcus, 1990). Students use computers with word-processing programs to write and use drawing programs to add illustrations. These programs simplify revising and editing and eliminate the tedium of recopying compositions. Several word-processing programs, such as Bank Street Writer III, Writing Workshop, FirstWriter, Magic Slate, and Quill, have been developed especially for elementary students and are easy to use. Because of the limited number of computers available in classrooms, students often work collaboratively, talking about ideas, planning their writing project, deciding how to spell words and use writing formats, and rereading to check what they have written. When students compose collaboratively, they work longer at the computer and write longer compositions than they do with paper and pencil. Spellcheckers are useful proofreading tools that allow students to interact with their own texts in new ways.

Even first graders can use the computer to write stories (Butler & Cox, 1992; Eisenwine & Hunt, 2000). Butler and Cox note that an added benefit is that children learn keyboarding skills, including how to use the shift key, how to delete and move text, and how to break pages of text. Because changing text is easy on the computer, students show interest in revising earlier than they might when writing with paper and pencil.

Computers are also used to take young children's dictation. Teachers take children's dictation as they do in traditional language experience activities, but using a computer rather than paper and pencil. After entering the child's dictation, the child and the teacher read the text and make revisions. Next, the text is printed out, and the child adds an illustration. If the child has already drawn a picture, the printout can be cut and taped onto the drawing. The computer simplifies the process of taking children's dictation—teachers can record dictation more quickly than they can write, the dictation can be revised easily, and a clean copy of the revised text can be printed out.

Students can use modems to send e-mail and transmit information from their computer to another computer through the Internet. One application is to create a pen pals program so that students write back and forth to students in another classroom across town or in another state. Another possibility is for students to dialogue electronically with college students enrolled in a language arts course at a local university. Students can correspond about books they are both reading (Moore, 1991). Networks that enable students in classrooms across the United States to participate in interdisciplinary programs and share what they learn with each other are becoming increasingly available (Mulligan & Gore, 1992). Kids

For more information on word processing programs, see Chapter 3, "The Reading and Writing Processes."

To learn about keyboarding programs, turn to Chapter 14, "Developing Legible Handwriting."

Read more about the language experience approach in Chapter 4, "Emerging Into Literacy."

FIGURE 2-3 *A Frame From an Upper-Grade Student's Hypercard Report*

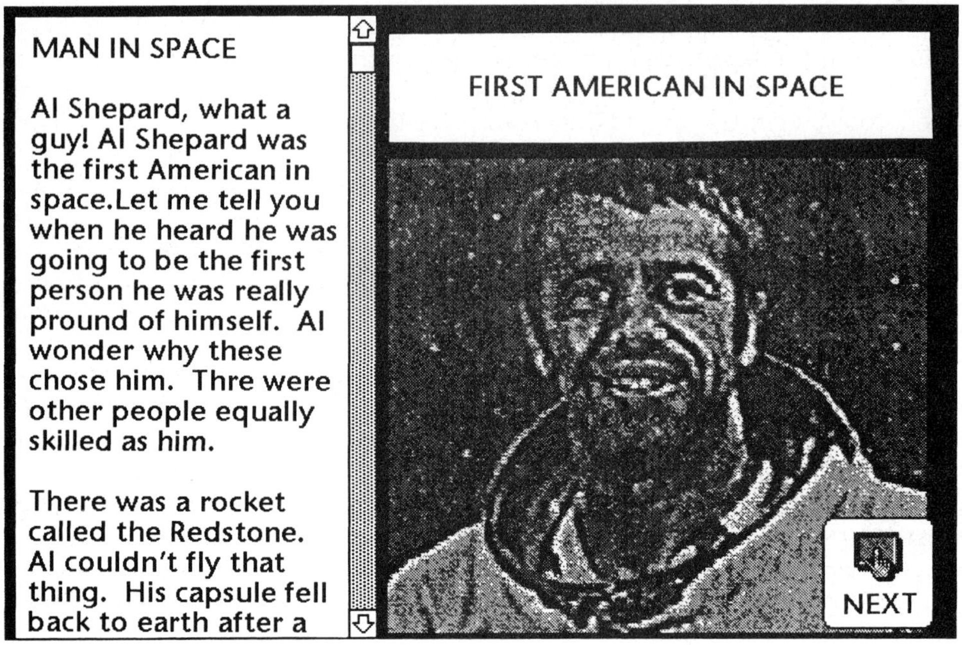

MAN IN SPACE

Al Shepard, what a guy! Al Shepard was the first American in space.Let me tell you when he heard he was going to be the first person he was really pround of himself. Al wonder why these chose him. Thre were other people equally skilled as him.

There was a rocket called the Redstone. Al couldn't fly that thing. His capsule fell back to earth after a

FIRST AMERICAN IN SPACE

NEXT

Network by the National Geographic Society is one telecommunication-based program, and other programs are available on the Internet.

Hypercard is a computer application that students can use to create databases with text and graphics. The information is stored in stacks that appear as cards on separate screens. These cards can be arranged and accessed in different ways. Information from laser discs and digitized pictures and photos can be added, and students can add sounds or their own voices to their productions. Elementary students create reports, biographies, files on favorite authors, and other types of writing projects using Hypercard (J. Smith, 1991). Figure 2–3 presents a frame from an eighth grader's Hypercard report on space.

Interactive electronic books are available on CD-ROM. These electronic books use hypertext technology to organize information and provide options for readers. Beginning readers read interactive electronic books. The text and illustrations are displayed page by page on the computer screen. The selection can be read aloud for students, with each word or phrase highlighted as it is read; students can read the book themselves and ask the computer to identify unfamiliar words; or students can read along with the computer to develop reading fluency. Music and sound effects accompany each program. Many electronic books include reading logs, word-identification activities, and other reading and writing activities. Scholastic's WiggleWorks and Broderbund's The Living Books Framework are two of the best-known programs, and they use trade books written by well-known children's authors such as Mercer Mayer and Jack Prelutsky. Electronic encyclopedias also take advantage of hypertext technology in ways that a print encyclopedia cannot. One example is Compton's Multimedia Encyclopedia (26 volumes in book format), which is contained on a single CD-ROM. Students can search an electronic encyclopedia for information on a particular topic and use hypertext capabilities to:

- Ask the computer to pronounce or define unfamiliar words
- View color photographs, diagrams, and animated illustrations
- Listen to sounds related to the topic
- View film clips
- Check related articles in the encyclopedia
- Print hard copies of the information

Because of the format and search capabilities of electronic encyclopedias, students explore topics in more depth than is possible with print encyclopedias.

Another innovative technology is captioning. Captions on videotapes and television programs that are designed for hearing-impaired adults can be used for reading practice. Students view captioned video and television programs and read along with the captions (Koskinen, Wilson, Gambrell, & Neuman, 1993). Captioned television programs provide students with opportunities for reading practice that are entertaining and self-correcting. Koskinen and her colleagues found that less fluent readers and bilingual students become more motivated readers when they use captioned television and video.

On captioned TV programs, sentences corresponding to the words spoken on the video are printed on the screen, much like the subtitles on foreign films. The captions can be seen on television sets that are equipped with special electronic TeleCaption decoders. These decoders can be purchased for less than $200 and can easily be attached to a television. All new televisions have the built-in circuitry to decode and display closed-captioned programming. Some captioned videos, such as *Reading Rainbow* programs, can be purchased from video stores and educational publishers. Captioned programs can be videotaped from television, but copyright laws restrict the length of time they can be saved and the number of times the tapes can be used.

New multimedia technology expands the range of language arts materials and the tools students have available for learning. The traditional language arts—listening, talking, reading, and writing—have not been abandoned, but technology provides new tools for learning and using these language arts as well as for redefining what the language arts are. The recent addition of viewing and visually representing as the fifth and sixth language arts illustrates the changes brought by technology.

Technology is not just a toy for playing games or completing an electronic workbook. Teachers must find ways to use technology to support their programs rather than supplanting their programs with technology (Lapp, Flood, & Lungren, 1995). Children are excited about technology and enthusiastic about using it. They adapt easily to using hardware and software and use technology for valuable language-learning activities. Teachers are learners, too, as they learn the capabilities of the technology and find ways to incorporate it into their instructional programs.

PATTERNS OF PRACTICE

Just as there are many quilt patterns, there are many ways to organize language arts instruction. This text focuses on these four patterns or instructional approaches for teaching language arts: literature focus units, literature circles,

---

FIGURE 2-4

Overview of the Four Patterns of Practice

Features	Literature Focus Units	Literature Circles
Description	Teachers and students read and respond to one text together as a class or in small groups. Teachers choose texts that are high-quality literature, either trade books or from a basal reader textbook. After reading, students explore the text and apply their learning by creating projects.	Teachers choose five or six books and collect multiple copies of each book. Students choose the book they want to read and form groups or "book clubs" to read and respond to the book. They develop a reading and discussion schedule, and the teacher often participates in the discussions.
Strengths	• Teachers develop units using the reading process. • Teachers select picture books or chapter books or use selections from basal reader textbooks for units. • Teachers scaffold reading instruction as they read with the whole class or small groups. • Teachers teach minilessons on reading skills and strategies. • Students explore vocabulary and literary language. • Students develop projects to apply their reading.	• Books are available at a variety of reading levels. • Students are more strongly motivated because they choose the books they read. • Students have opportunities to work with their classmates. • Students participate in authentic literacy experiences. • Activities are student directed, and students work at their own pace. • Teachers may participate in discussions to help students clarify misunderstandings and think more deeply about the book.
Drawbacks	• Students all read the same book whether they like it or not or whether it is at their reading level or not. • Many of the activities are teacher directed.	• Teachers often feel a loss of control since students are reading different books. • Students must learn to be task oriented and to use time wisely in order to be successful. • Sometimes students choose books that are too difficult or too easy for them.

Look for the color section that shows teachers and elementary students participating in each of the four patterns of practice.

reading and writing workshop, and theme cycles. All four patterns embody the characteristics of learning described in Chapter 1 and provide opportunities for students to be involved in meaningful, functional, and genuine activities. Teachers organize their instructional programs in different ways, but students need to have opportunities to participate in all four approaches during each school year. Figure 2–4 provides an overview of the four patterns.

Teachers can organize their daily schedule to include two or more of the instructional approaches. When teachers don't have that much time available, Lewin (1992) recommends alternating teacher-led literature focus units with student-selected literature circles or reading and writing workshop. Both teacher-led and student-selected instructional patterns provide valuable language-learning opportunities, and no one approach provides all the opportunities that students need. The logical solution is to use a combination of patterns.

FIGURE 2-4

Continued

Features	Reading and Writing Workshop	Theme Cycles
Description	Students choose books and read and respond to them independently during reading workshop and write books on self-selected topics during writing workshop. Teachers monitor students' work through conferences. Students share the books they read and the books they write with classmates during a sharing period.	Students study social studies or science topics, and they use the six language arts as learning tools as they participate in a variety of activities and to demonstrate learning. Although content-area textbooks may be used, they are only one resource for the theme cycle. Students also identify topics they want to study, so theme cycles are authentic learning opportunities.
Strengths	• Students read books appropriate for their reading levels. • Students are more strongly motivated because they choose the books they read. • Students work through the steps of the writing process during writing workshop. • Teachers teach minilessons on reading skills and strategies. • Activities are student directed, and students work at their own pace. • Teachers have opportunities to work individually with students during conferences.	• Students read text sets of stories, informational books, and poetry related to the theme. • Students write in learning logs. • Teachers and students make clusters, Venn diagrams, and other charts to organize information. • Teachers scaffold instruction as students work independently, in small groups, and as a class. • Students use talk to clarify meanings and give presentations. • Students use computers and technology tools to enhance learning. • Students create projects to apply their learning.
Drawbacks	• Teachers often feel a loss of control since students are reading different books and working at different stages of the writing process. • Students must learn to be task oriented and to use time wisely in order to be successful.	• Teachers must design theme cycles and locate needed resources and other materials. • Theme cycles are more time-consuming than textbook-driven social studies and science units.

Literature Focus Units

Teachers organize literature focus units around a featured selection or several related books. In the vignette at the beginning of the chapter, for example, Mrs. Miller-McColm was teaching a literature focus unit on *Tuck Everlasting* (Babbitt, 1988). Students read the featured selection using a five-stage reading process in which they prepare, read, respond, explore, and apply their reading. Because students are reading together in groups or as a class, they share their interpretations of the story and become a community of learners. Four components of literature focus units are:

The first pages of the color section show Mrs. Kenney and her fourth graders participating in a literature focus unit on Roald Dahl's *Charlie and the Chocolate Factory*.

1. *Reading.* Students read books together as a class or in small groups. Students may read independently or together with a partner, or they may read along as the teacher reads the book aloud or guides their reading.

2. *Responding.* Students respond to the selection to record their initial impressions of it and to develop their comprehension. Students write in reading logs and participate in discussions called grand conversations.

3. *Teaching minilessons.* Teachers teach minilessons on language arts procedures, concepts, strategies, and skills and connect the minilessons to books students are reading or compositions they are writing (Atwell, 1998). These minilessons usually last 15 to 30 minutes, and may be taught over a period of several days. The steps in teaching a minilesson are shown in the LA Essentials box on page 71.

    The purpose of a minilesson is to highlight the topic and teach it in the context of authentic literacy activities, not to isolate it or provide drill-and-practice activities. Worksheets are rarely used in minilessons; instead, students apply the minilesson to their own language arts activities. Minilessons can be conducted with the whole class, with small groups of students who have indicated that they need to learn more about a particular topic, and with individual students. Teachers also plan minilessons on a regular basis to introduce or review topics.

4. *Creating projects.* Students create projects to apply their reading. Projects may involve any of the language arts, but students usually choose the projects they create based on their interests and the opportunities the selection presents to them. For example, after reading *Jumanji* (Van Allsburg, 1981), students often choose to write sequels; after reading *Sylvester and the Magic Pebble* (Steig, 1969), students may work together as a small group to dramatize the story, or they may choose to read other books by William Steig.

To learn more about developing literature focus units, turn to Chapter 15, "Putting It All Together."

Literature Circles

Students meet in small-group literature circles to read and respond to self-selected books (Daniels, 2002; Day, Spiegel, McLellan, & Brown, 2002). What matters most is that students are reading and discussing something that interests them and is manageable in a supportive community of learners. As students participate in literature circles, they learn to view themselves as readers. Students have opportunities to read high-quality books that they might not have chosen on their own and read widely (Evans, 2001). They also learn responsibility for completing assignments and to self-assess their learning and work habits (Hill, Johnson, & Noe, 1995; Samway & Whang, 1996). The four components of literature circles are:

The second part of the color section shows Mrs. Goodman and her eighth graders participating in literature circles.

1. *Reading.* Teachers collect five or six copies of each of six books and give a book talk to introduce each book. Students sign up for the book they want to read and form literature circles to read the book. After working together as a group to create a reading and responding schedule for the book, students read the first part of the book to be ready to participate in the discussion.

2. *Responding.* Students meet to discuss the book and reflect on their reading. To facilitate their responding, students often assume roles ranging from discussion leader to artist and word wizard, and they prepare for their roles before they meet to discuss the book. A list of seven roles that students often assume is presented in the LA Essentials box on page 73.

LA Essentials

Steps in a Minilesson

A minilesson usually consists of five steps, and teachers move through the steps during the lesson. Often teachers complete the lesson in one 15- to 30-minute session, but sometimes teachers spread the lesson over 2 or 3 days when it is more involved or when students need additional practice. The five steps are:

1. **Introduce the Topic**

   Teachers introduce the language arts topic, which might be a procedure, such as how to make a double-entry journal, a concept, such as synonyms, a strategy, such as visualization, or a skill, such as using quotation marks. Teachers identify and name the topic and make a connection between the topic and activities going on in the classroom.

2. **Share Examples**

   Teachers share examples of the topic using children's writing or trade books written for children. Often teachers write word and sentence examples on chart paper for students to read and examine, or for longer examples, they make copies of a page from a trade book or textbook for students to read. Drawing authentic examples from children's own writing and books they are reading is important because it makes the lesson more relevant.

3. **Provide Information**

   Teachers provide information about the topic and make connections to trade books or to children's writing, often using the examples presented to students in the second step. They might demonstrate the steps in a procedure, explain the rules for how to use a skill, or collect more examples of the concept.

4. **Supervise Practice**

   Students practice the topic with teacher supervision. They may collect more examples of the topic or apply what they have learned in books they are reading or in their own writing. Students also make notes about the procedure, concept, strategy, or skill on a poster to be displayed in the classroom or in their language arts notebooks.

5. **Assess Learning**

   Teachers monitor students' progress and evaluate their use of newly learned procedures, concepts, skills, and strategies. Teachers also ask students to reflect or speculate on how they can use what they have learned in language arts activities and across the curriculum.

3. *Creating projects.* After finishing a book, students prepare projects to present when they share the book with classmates. Students choose the type of project they create. Projects range from murals and dramatizations to poems and choral readings of excerpts.

4. *Sharing.* Students meet as a class, and each group shares its book. Sometimes students prepare a book talk to share the book; sometimes they create projects to tell about the book. Students provide enough information to create interest in the book, but they never tell the ending because they want to encourage classmates to read the book through the sharing activity.

Mrs. Miller-McColm's students in the vignette at the beginning of the chapter participated in literature circles they called book clubs. The sixth graders participated in activities representing all four components of literature circles.

Reading and Writing Workshop

The third part of the color section shows Mrs. McClenaghan's fifth and sixth graders participating in reading and writing workshop.

Two types of workshops are reading workshop and writing workshop. Reading workshop fosters real reading of self-selected stories, poems, and informational books, and writing workshop fosters real writing for genuine purposes and authentic audiences (Atwell, 1998; Cohle & Towle, 2001). Teachers often use the two workshops concurrently, but if their schedule does not allow them to do so, they may alternate the two. Schedules for reading and writing workshop at the second-, fifth-, and eighth-grade levels are presented in Figure 2–5.

Many teachers fear that their students' standardized achievement test scores will decline if they implement a workshop approach in their classrooms, even though many teachers have reported either an increase in test scores or no change at all (Five, 1988; Swift, 1993). Kathleen Swift reported the results of a yearlong study comparing two groups of her students. One group read basal reader stories, and the other participated in reading workshop. The workshop group showed significantly greater improvement, and Swift also reported that students participating in reading workshop showed more positive attitudes toward reading.

Reading Workshop. In reading workshop, students read self-selected books independently or in small groups and respond to books by writing in reading logs and by discussing the book if a small group of students are reading the same book (Atwell, 1998; Hornsby, Sukarna, & Parry, 1986). Through reading workshop, students become more fluent readers and deepen their appreciation of books and reading. They develop lifelong reading habits, are introduced to different genres, and choose favorite authors. Most important, students come to think of themselves as readers (Daniels, 1994). The components of reading workshop are:

1. *Reading and responding.* Students spend 30 to 60 minutes independently reading books and other reading materials. They also keep reading logs for writing responses to their reading and participate in conferences with the teacher to enrich their understanding of favorite books.

2. *Sharing.* For the last 15 minutes of reading workshop, the class gathers together to share books and response projects.

Reading

Literature Focus Unit

The fifth graders in Mrs. Kenney's class are reading Roald Dahl's delicious fantasy, *Charlie and the Chocolate Factory* (1964). It's the story of Charlie Bucket, an honest and kind boy, who finds the fifth winning Golden Ticket, entitling him to a visit inside Willy Wonka's famous chocolate factory. Charlie and the four other children who also found winning tickets have a wild time visiting the factory, and, in the end, Mr. Wonka gives Charlie the best present of all—his factory!

Mrs. Kenney varies the ways students read each chapter. She reads the first chapter aloud, using whole-class shared reading, and students follow along in their copies of the book. For the other chapters, students alternate reading independently, reading with a buddy, reading in small groups, and reading together as a class.

Create your own Wonka goodie.

Responding

Mrs. Kenney's students respond to the story in two ways. They participate in small-group and whole-class discussions called grand conversations. In these lively discussions, they share their ideas about the story, ask questions to clarify misunderstandings, and make connections to their own lives. Mrs. Kenney participates in the whole-class grand conversations and often asks students to think about Charlie and compare him to the other four children who visit Willy Wonka's chocolate factory.

The fifth graders also write in double-entry reading logs. At the beginning of the literature focus unit, students staple together booklets of paper for their journals and divide each page into two columns. After reading each chapter, they choose a quote and write it in the left column and then write a response in the right column.

Quote	Response
Ch. 19 Pg. 94 "The place was like a witch's kitchen!"	I chose this quote because did you know — it's a simile!

QUOTE	MY THOUGHTS
Ch 11 Pg 50 "You've got a Golden Ticket! You found the last Golden Ticket! Hey, what do you know?"	I feel excited and happy because Charlie never had anything much in his life. Maybe now his life will take a turn for the better.

Teaching Minilessons

Mrs. Kenney and her students choose important words from each chapter as they read *Charlie and the Chocolate Factory*. The words are organized by parts of speech on the word wall because Mrs. Kenney is teaching a series of minilessons about the parts of speech. The noun list includes *hooligan*, *precipice*, and *verdict*; the verb list includes *beckoned*, *revolt*, *stammer*, and *criticize*. The adjective list includes *despicable*, *scraggy*, and *repulsive*; *ravenously*, *violently*, and *frantically* are on the adverb list.

Mrs. Kenney also uses the words from the word wall as she teaches minilessons on root words and affixes to small groups of students. Students take turns choosing a word from the word wall and breaking apart the word's prefix, root, and suffix as Mrs. Kenney writes the information on the white board. Then students record the information on small, individual white boards.

During this literature focus unit, Mrs. Kenney is focusing on character. During a series of minilessons, students investigate how Roald Dahl developed Charlie's character and compare him with Willy Wonka and the other four children with winning Golden Tickets.

After studying about the characters, students create open-mind portraits of one of the characters. One student's open-mind portrait of Willy Wonka is shown here. The portrait goes on top and the page showing his thoughts goes underneath.

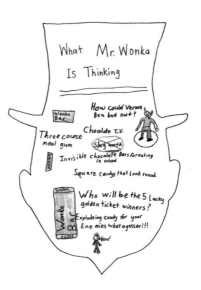

Creating Projects

Students create a variety of projects to extend the book and apply their learning. These two boys created a model of Willy Wonka's chocolate factory. Other students researched how chocolate is made and created a poster to display what they learned, wrote poems about each of the characters in *Charlie and the Chocolate Factory*, or read another of Roald Dahl's stories.

As the concluding activity, Mrs. Kenney and her students view *Willy Wonka and the Chocolate Factory*, the film version of the story starring Gene Wilder, and work in small groups to create Venn diagrams comparing the book and the film versions.
One student's Venn diagram is shown below. After discussing the differences, most students agree that they preferred the book.

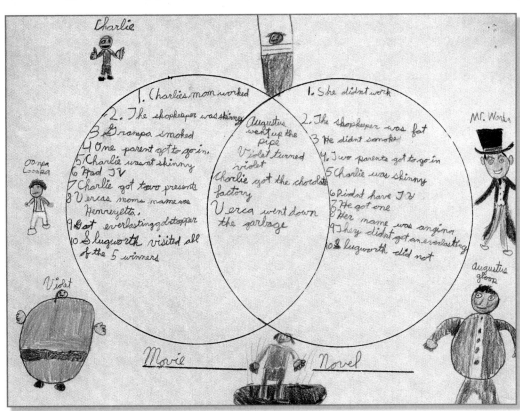

Reading

Literature Circles

Mrs. Goodman's eighth graders participate in literature circles. Mrs. Goodman introduces eight books written at varying levels of difficulty, and students sign up for the book they want to read. The students are currently reading these books:

- *The Outsiders* by S. E. Hinton (1967)
- *The Face on the Milk Carton* by Caroline Cooney (1990)
- *Holes* by Louis Sachar (1998)
- *I Am the Cheese* by Robert Cormier (1977)
- *To Kill a Mockingbird* by Harper Lee (1960)
- *What Jamie Saw* by Carolyn Coman (1995)

Students have set a schedule for reading the book, and they spend time reading during class and at home.

Students in each literature circle assume roles to deepen their understanding of the story and ensure the smooth functioning of their group. They rotate these roles each day so that everyone has the opportunity to experience all roles.

ROLES IN A LITERATURE CIRCLE	
1 Discussion Leader	This student keeps classmates focused on the big ideas in the story.
2 Harmonizer	This student helps everyone stay on task and show respect to classmates.
3 Wordsmith	This student identifies important words in the story and checks the meaning of words in a dictionary.
4 Connector	This student connects events in the story with real life experiences.
5 Illustrator	This student draws pictures to help classmates visualize events in the story.

Responding

Students frequently meet in their literature circles to discuss the story they are reading, and students fulfill their roles. They talk about what is happening in the story, ask questions to clarify confusions, make connections to their own lives, and predict what will happen next. As students talk, Mrs. Goodman circulates around the classroom, joining each group for a few minutes.

Students also write in reading logs. Sometimes they write summaries and make predictions, and at other times they write reflections and ask questions. After writing, students often divide into groups of two or three to read their entries to classmates.

Reading Log

I am liking <u>To Kill a Mockingbird</u> a lot. But it's very different from other books I've read. Instead of describing the scenery and how the people look, it tells the history of everything. The book tells you what has happened. That makes it harder to picture what is happening but easier to make up what you want. I don't think I've ever read a description of Scout anywhere in the book. I didn't quite understand the beginning of the book because it was introducing everything really fast. But now, I'm beginning to understand what is going on.

Reading Log

My questions are:

- Why don't Scout and Jim call their father Dad but use his real name (Atticus)?

- Why doesn't Scout play with other girls?

- What does everyone look like?

- Why doesn't anyone search for the truth about the Radleys?

Creating Projects

Students create projects after they finish reading and discussing a story. They write poems and sequels, research a topic on the Internet, develop PowerPoint presentations, create artifacts related to the story, and design story quilts.

After students identify a project they want to develop, they meet with Mrs. Goodman and she approves their choice and helps them get started.

"When Jamie saw Van Throw Nin"

This picture is a square from a story quilt about *What Jamie Saw*, a story about child abuse. Students in the literature circle draw pictures to represent events from the book and put them together to make the quilt, which presents a strong message about the effects of child abuse.

Sharing

Sharing is the concluding activity. Students in each literature circle share the book they have read and their project with Mrs. Goodman and the class. Sometimes students work together to give a group presentation to the class, and sometimes students develop individual presentations. The students demonstrate their understanding of the story through their presentation, and they hope to interest their classmates in choosing the book and reading the story.

Mrs. Goodman explains how students will be graded before the literature circle begins and posts the criteria in the classroom. For this literature circle, students are graded on four items; each item is worth 25 points. At the end of the literature circle, Mrs. Goodman prepares a grading sheet with the criteria, grades students' work, and assigns the grades.

GRADING SHEET

Name _Laura_

Book _To Kill A Mockingbird_

1. Reading Log — _20_

2. Roles in the Literature Circle — _25_

3. Working Together in a Group — _25_

4. Project at the End — _22_

_(92)_

Reading and Writing Workshop

You will be able to watch writing workshop in action in four different classrooms on the accompaying CD-ROM.

Reading & Responding

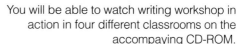

Mrs. McClenaghan's fifth and sixth graders participate in reading workshop for an hour each morning. The students read books they have selected from the classroom library, including *A Wrinkle in Time* (L'Engle, 1962), *The Sign of the Beaver* (Speare, 1983), *Harry Potter and the Sorcerer's Stone* (Rowling, 1997), *Missing May* (Rylant, 1992), and *Tuck Everlasting* (Babbitt, 1975).

Students also respond to the books they are reading, and their response activities vary according to what Mrs. McClenaghan is teaching. This week's focus is on a reading strategy—forming interpretations. The students identify a big idea in the chapter they are reading and provide evidence from the text to support the idea on T-charts they have made.

Conferencing

As her students read and respond, Mrs. McClenaghan moves around the classroom, stopping to conference with students. She asks students to read a short excerpt and tell about their reading experience and the reading strategies they are using. They talk about the story so Mrs. McClenaghan can monitor their comprehension and clarify any misunderstandings. She carries a clipboard with her and writes notes about each student, including what book the student is reading and the progress he or she is making.

Reading Aloud

Mrs. McClenaghan is reading aloud *The Cay* (Taylor, 1969), a survival story about an elderly African American man and a Caucasian boy who are shipwrecked in the Caribbean and become friends through the experience. She reads aloud a chapter or two each day and the students talk about the story in a grand conversation. She also uses the book in the minilessons she is teaching.

Teaching Minilessons

These fifth and sixth graders have been examining the strategies that good readers use, such as asking questions, making connections, and visualizing, in a series of minilessons. Today Mrs. McClenaghan focuses on making inferences. She explains that good readers read between the lines to figure out the author's message. She rereads a passage from *The Cay* and asks the students to identify the big idea in the passage. Then she makes a T-chart on a white board and records their answers. In the first column she writes the big idea and in the second, a quote from the text to support the big idea. Then she reads another passage several pages later in the text, and they rephrase the big idea to clarify it and finish the chart.

BIG Idea	Text Evidence
It's about friendship.	p. 76 I said to Timothy, "I want to be your friend." He said softly, "Young bahss, you 'ave always been my friend."
It doesn't matter what color you are, you can still be friends.	p. 79 "I don't like some white people my own self, but 'twould be outrageous if I didn't like any o' dem."

Writing

After spending 60 minutes in reading workshop, students begin writing workshop, which lasts for 45 minutes. Students usually write two- to four-page stories about events in their own lives—autobiographical incidents—during writing workshop. They work at their own pace, moving through the stages of the writing process. Most students write four or five drafts as they develop and refine the content of their writing.

Responding

Students meet with classmates and with Mrs. McClenaghan several times during the writing process to revise and edit their writing. The students provide useful feedback to classmates because they have learned about the qualities of a good piece of writing and they know how to identify problem spots.

Really Hungry

One day, when it was close to dinner time, my big brother was so hungry he got there before any of us. He was waiting impatiently and when we were at the table with our food in front of us he already started devouring the vegetables and rice.

My mother looked at him, and he stopped stuffing himself. He waited very impatiently while she said grace. Mother's grace isn't short but it isn't very long either. He fidgeted and squirmed untill she finished. "You should make it shorter," he said.

He gobbled all of his rice, vegetables and chicken. We watched him in amazement. He asked for seconds and he started to swallow his food.

"Don't eat like that," snapped my mother. "Disgusting!" She bit her chicken wing and chewed.

Teaching Minilessons

In this writing minilesson, Mrs. McClenaghan shares an essay written by a student from another class. She asks the students to rate it using their district's six-point writing rubric. They raise their hands and show with their fingers the score they would give the paper. Most students rate it a 4, and Mrs. McClenaghan agrees. They talk about the strong points in the paper and the areas where improvement is needed.

Then Mrs. McClenaghan reviews the asking-questions and magnifying-a-sentence revision strategies and the symbols students use to represent the two strategies. Next, students reread the essay and attach small sticky notes to the paper with the symbols written on them to indicate revision points. Students also underline the specific sentence to which each sticky note refers.

Sharing

During the last five minutes of writing workshop, one student sits in the author's chair and shares a newly published composition. The classmates clap and offer compliments after the student finishes reading. They are an appreciative audience because Mrs. McClenaghan and her students have developed a supportive classroom community.

Reading

Ms. McCloskey works with 40 kindergarten through third-grade students in their multi-age classroom. The students are engaged in a theme cycle on insects, integrating all areas of the curriculum. They participate in a variety of reading activities. They listen to Ms. McCloskey read books aloud and read along with Ms. McCloskey as she shares big books. During centers time, they reread familiar books with buddies and read independently. They also read other books at their own reading levels during guided reading.

Learning Logs

Each day students write entries for their learning logs at the writing center. They meet with Ms. Russell, a student teacher working in the classroom, to write about insects. Many of the students are learning English as a second language, so Ms. Russell helps them to expand their sentences and include science words in their entries. She also reviews spelling, capitalization, punctuation, and grammar skills with individual students. Then students file their papers in their learning log folders, which are kept at the writing center. At the end of the theme cycle, students compile their learning logs and decorate the covers.

This entry, titled "Wings," was written by a kindergartner who is still learning about capital letters and punctuation marks. He added the second part "because it has wings" in response to Ms. Russell's question, "How can a ladybug fly?"

Wfs

A LadeBug can fly,
BeKCSe it hS wfs.

Visual Representations

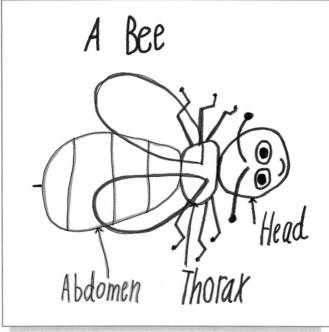

A Bee

Abdomen   Thorax   Head

SPIDERS

2 body parts
1. head
2. abdomen

8 Legs

No wings

Spin webs

INSECTS

3 body parts
1. head
2. thorax
3. Abdomen

6 legs

Wings

No webs

The students make diagrams, charts, and drawings to record information they are learning about insects. They learn to draw insects accurately with three body parts and six legs. They use diagrams to organize information they are learning as Ms. McCloskey reads a book or presents a demonstration. They also use attribute charts to record descriptive words as they observe insects in the "Look and Learn" science center.

Creating Projects

The students are creating a multigenre display on insects. Each student writes a story, poem, or report for the display, which will cover an entire wall of the classroom. The students use the writing process to develop their compositions, and all students, even the kindergartners, type their final copies on the computer with Ms. McCloskey's assistance.

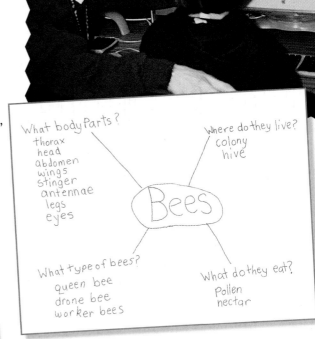

What body Parts?
thorax
head
abdomen
wings
stinger
antennae
legs
eyes

Where do they live?
colony
hive

Bees

What type of bees?
queen bee
drone bee
worker bees

What do they eat?
Pollen
nectar

The Bees

Bees have three body parts: a thorax, an abdomen, and a head. On their body they have some little and big wings, a stinger, two antennae, six legs, and two large black eyes.

The bees live in a hive. Sometimes bees live in a group of bees, and it is called a colony. A lot of bees live in a colony and a lot of bees live in a hive.

There are three kinds of bees. There a queen bee, a drone bee, and worker bees. The queen lays eggs on the hive and the worker bees take care of the baby bees. One of the worker bees gets pollen from the flowers. When the worker bees get pollen, they dance because they can't talk.

Bees eat pollen and nectar to ma honey. When bees make honey they have to go get pollen and nectar. W need bees because bees could mal honey for us. If bees is not in this state there will be no honey for us.

Dragonfly

Dragonfly fly, fly, fly.

Dragonfly fly around the pond.

Dragonfly fly by the flower.

Dragonfly fly by me.

Dragonfly fly, fly, fly.

Essentials

Roles Students Play in Literature Circles

1. **Discussion Director**

    The discussion director guides the group's discussion and keeps the group on task. To get the discussion started or to redirect the discussion, the discussion director may ask:

    -   What did the reading make you think of?
    -   What questions do you have about the reading?
    -   What do you predict will happen next?

2. **Passage Master**

    The passage master focuses on the literary merits of the book. This student chooses several memorable passages to share with the group and tells why he or she chose each one.

3. **Word Wizard**

    The word wizard is responsible for vocabulary. This student identifies four to six important, unfamiliar words from the reading and looks them up in the dictionary. The word wizard selects the most appropriate meaning and other interesting information about the word to share.

4. **Connector**

    The connector makes meaningful personal, world, or literary connections. These connections might include events at school or in the community, current events or historical events, or something from the connector's own life. Or the connector can make comparisons with other books.

5. **Summarizer**

    The summarizer prepares a brief summary of the reading to convey the main ideas to share with the group. This student often begins the discussion by reading the summary aloud to the group.

6. **Illustrator**

    The illustrator draws a picture or diagram related to the reading. It might relate to a character, an event, or a prediction. The student shares the illustration with the group, and the group talks about it before the illustrator explains it.

7. **Investigator**

    The investigator locates some information about the book, the author, or a related topic to share with the group. This student may search the Internet, check an encyclopedia, or interview a person with special expertise.

FIGURE 2-5

Schedules for Reading and Writing Workshop

Second-Grade Schedule

15 minutes	Reading aloud to students
15 minutes	Teaching a minilesson (on a reading or writing topic)
30 minutes	Reading and responding
15 minutes	Sharing
	—Later—
30 minutes	Writing
15 minutes	Sharing

This 2-hour schedule is broken into two parts. The first 75 minutes, scheduled in the morning, focuses on reading, and the second 45 minutes, scheduled after lunch, is devoted to writing.

Fifth-Grade Schedule

40 minutes	Reading and responding
20 minutes	Teaching a minilesson (on a reading or writing topic)
40 minutes	Writing
20 minutes	Sharing

This schedule is also planned for 2 hours. The minilesson separates the two independent work sessions, and during the sharing session, students share books they have read, response projects they have created, and compositions they have published.

Eighth-Grade Schedule

40 minutes	Reading and responding or writing
15 minutes	Teaching a minilesson (on Mondays–Thursdays)
	Sharing (on Fridays)

The eighth-grade schedule is for 55 minutes. Because of time limitations, students alternate reading and writing workshop, minilessons are scheduled for 4 days each week, and sharing is held on Fridays.

---

3. *Teaching minilessons.* The teacher spends approximately 15 minutes teaching minilessons on reading workshop procedures, literary concepts, and reading strategies and skills.

Writing Workshop. Writing workshop is a way of implementing the writing process (Atwell, 1998; Calkins, 1994; Fletcher & Portalupi, 2001; Graves, 1983). Students usually write on topics they choose themselves, and they assume ownership of their learning. The classroom becomes a community of writers who write and share their writing, and students come to see themselves as writers (Samway et al., 1991). They practice writing skills and strategies and learn to choose words carefully to articulate their ideas. Perhaps most important, they see firsthand the power of writing to entertain, inform, and persuade.

Students' writing grows out of their personal experiences, books they have read or listened to read aloud, and content-area study (Gillet & Beverly, 2001).

To see how four teachers use writing workshop, view the CD-ROM that accompanies this text.

They write personal narratives about experiences and events in their lives, create sequels to favorite books, and retell stories from different viewpoints. Young children often use the pattern or refrain from a familiar book, such as *Brown Bear, Brown Bear, What Do You See?* (Martin, 1992), *The Important Book* (Brown, 1990), and *Mary Wore Her Red Dress and Henry Wore His Green Sneakers* (Peek, 1993), to structure their stories. Students experiment with other genres, such as poetry and scripts, during writing workshop after reading examples of the genre and learning about them. Students also use writing workshop to write letters, book reviews, reports, and other projects as part of theme cycles. In the vignette at the beginning of the chapter, Mrs. Miller-McColm's sixth graders were writing reports on ancient Egypt during writing workshop.

In a writing workshop classroom, students have writing folders in which they keep all papers related to the writing project they are working on. They also keep writing notebooks in which they jot down images, impressions, dialogue, and experiences that they can build on for writing projects. Students also have access to different kinds of paper, some lined and some unlined, and various writing instruments, including pencils and red and blue pens.

Students sit at desks or tables arranged in small groups as they write. The teacher circulates around the classroom, conferencing briefly with students, and the classroom atmosphere is free enough that students converse quietly with classmates and move around the classroom to assist classmates or share ideas. There is space for students to get together for writing groups, and often a sign-up sheet for writing groups is posted in the classroom. A table is available for the teacher to meet with individual students or small groups for conferences, writing groups, proofreading, and minilessons.

To learn more about the writing process, see Chapter 3, "The Reading and Writing Processes."

Writing workshop is a 60- to 90-minute period scheduled each day. During this time, the teacher and the students are involved in three activities:

1. *Writing.* Students spend 30 to 45 minutes working independently on writing projects. They move through all five stages of the writing process—prewriting, drafting, revising, editing, and publishing—at their own pace. Many times, students compile their final copies to make books during writing workshop, but sometimes they attach their writing to artwork, make posters, write letters that are mailed, or perform scripts as skits or puppet shows.

2. *Sharing.* After writing, the students gather together to share their new publications with the class and to make related announcements. A student who has just finished writing a puppet-show script and making puppets may ask for volunteers to help perform the puppet show, which could be presented several days later during sharing time. Younger students often sit in a circle or gather together on a rug for sharing time. If an author's chair is available, each student sits in the special chair to read his or her composition. After the reading, classmates clap and offer compliments. They may also make other comments and suggestions, but the focus is on celebrating completed writing projects, not on revising the composition to make it better.

3. *Teaching minilessons.* During this 15- to 30-minute period, teachers provide minilessons on writing workshop procedures, literary concepts, and writing skills and strategies (Fletcher & Portalupi, 1998; Portalupi & Fletcher, 2001). They also talk about authors of children's trade books and the writing strategies and skills these authors use.

Teachers often add a fourth component to writing workshop, in which they read literature aloud to share examples of good writing with students. This activity helps students to feel a part of the community of writers. Teachers can also connect reading workshop with writing workshop.

Theme Cycles

The last part of the color section shows Ms. McCloskey's multigrade primary students participating in a theme cycle on insects.

Theme cycles are interdisciplinary units that integrate language arts with social studies, science, math, and other curricular areas (Altwerger & Flores, 1994; Cordeiro, 1995; Lindquist & Selwyn, 2000). They often extend across most or all of the school day, and students are involved in planning the direction for the theme. Topics for theme cycles are broad and encompass many possible directions for exploration. Possible topics include inventions, laws, wild animals, houses and homes, natural disasters, and civilizations.

Students use all the language arts as they investigate, solve problems, and learn during theme cycles (Rief, 1999). They also use language arts to demonstrate their new learning at the end of the theme. Four types of language arts activities occur during theme cycles:

1. *Reading.* Students read informational books and magazines, stories, and poems related to the theme as well as content-area textbooks. They also research topics on the Internet.
2. *Keeping learning logs.* Students keep learning logs in which they write entries about new concepts they are learning, record new and interesting words, make charts and diagrams, and reflect on their learning.
3. *Making visual representations.* Students create clusters, maps, time lines, Venn diagrams, data charts, and other diagrams and displays. They use these visual representations as tools to organize information and represent relationships about the topic they are studying (Moline, 1995).
4. *Creating projects.* Students create projects to apply their learning and demonstrate their new knowledge. These projects range from alphabet books and oral reports to posters and dramatizations.

Chapter 15, "Putting It All Together," presents more information about how to develop a theme cycle.

In the vignette, Mrs. Miller-McColm's students were involved in a theme cycle on ancient Egypt, and they participated in all four types of language arts activities during the theme.

The Teacher's Role

The teacher's role in a language arts classroom is complex and multidimensional. No longer are teachers simply providers of knowledge. Nor do teachers assign an endless series of worksheets and busywork. Instead, teachers understand that children's literacy develops most effectively through purposeful and meaningful social contexts. These teachers carefully create the classroom environment and a community of learners that will enhance students' learning. They plan the language arts curriculum using the four patterns of practice to meet the needs of their increasingly diverse classrooms of students. Their goal is to help students develop communicative competence and to excite students about literacy.

Language arts teachers direct the life of the classroom. They are instructors, coaches, facilitators, and managers. Figure 2–6 presents a list of some of the roles teachers assume.

FIGURE 2-6

Teachers' Roles During Language Arts Instruction

Role	Description
Organizer	Creates a language-rich environment. Sets time schedules. Uses the four patterns of practice. Uses the language arts as tools for learning across the curriculum.
Facilitator	Develops a community of learners. Stimulates students' interest in language and literacy. Allows students to choose books to read and topics for projects. Provides opportunities for students to use language for meaningful, functional, and genuine activities. Involves parents in classroom and out-of-classroom literacy activities.
Participant	Reads and writes with students. Learns along with students. Asks questions and seeks answers to questions.
Instructor	Provides information about books, authors, and illustrators. Explains language arts procedures. Teaches minilessons on concepts, skills, and strategies. Activates and builds background knowledge before reading, writing, and viewing. Groups students flexibly for instruction.
Model	Demonstrates procedures, skills, and strategies. Reads aloud to students every day.
Manager	Sets expectations and responsibilities. Monitors students' progress. Keeps records. Arranges the classroom to facilitate learning. Provides technology hardware and software to support language arts activities.
Diagnostician	Conferences with students. Observes students participating in language arts activities. Assesses students' strengths and weaknesses. Plans instruction based on students' needs.
Evaluator	Assesses students' progress in language arts. Helps students self-assess their learning. Assigns grades. Examines the effectiveness of the language arts program.
Coordinator	Works with librarians, aides, and parent volunteers. Works with other teachers on grade-level projects, pen pal programs, and cross-age reading programs.
Communicator	Expects students to do their best. Encourages students to become lifelong readers and writers. Communicates the language arts program to parents and administrators. Shares language arts goals and activities with parents and the community.

Establishing a Community of Learners. Teachers begin the process of establishing a community of learners when they make deliberate decisions about the kind of classroom culture they want to create (Whatley & Canalis, 2002). School is "real" life for students, and they learn best when they see a purpose for learning to read and write. The social contexts that teachers create are key. Teachers must think about their roles and the kind of language arts instruction they want in their classrooms. They must decide to have a democratic classroom where students' abilities in reading and writing develop through purposeful and meaningful literacy activities.

Teachers are more successful when they take the first 2 weeks of the school year to establish the classroom environment (Sumara & Walker, 1991). Teachers can't assume that students will be familiar with the procedures and routines used in language arts or that students will instinctively be cooperative, responsible, and respectful of classmates. Teachers explicitly explain classroom routines, such as how to get supplies out and put them away and how to work with classmates in a cooperative group, and set the expectation that students will adhere to the routines. Next, they demonstrate literacy procedures, including how to choose a book from the classroom library, how to provide feedback in a writing group, and how to participate in a grand conversation or discussion about a book. Third, teachers model ways of interacting with students, responding to literature, respecting classmates, and assisting classmates with reading and writing projects.

Teachers are the classroom managers or administrators. They set expectations and clearly explain to students what is expected of them and what is valued in the classroom. The classroom rules are specific and consistent, and teachers also set limits. For example, students might be allowed to talk quietly with classmates when they are working, but they are not allowed to shout across the classroom or talk when the teacher is talking or when students are making a presentation to the class. Teachers also model classroom rules themselves as they interact with students. According to Sumara and Walker, the process of socialization at the beginning of the school year is planned, deliberate, and crucial to the success of the language arts program.

Not everything can be accomplished during the first 2 weeks, however, so teachers must continue to reinforce classroom routines and language arts procedures. One way is to have student leaders model the desired routines and behaviors and encourage other students to follow the lead. Teachers also continue to teach additional literacy procedures as students are involved in new types of activities. The classroom community evolves during the school year, but the foundation is laid during the first 2 weeks.

Teachers develop a predictable classroom environment with familiar routines and procedures and a set routine. Students feel comfortable, safe, and more willing to take risks and experiment in a predictable classroom environment. This is especially true for students from varied cultures, students learning English as a second language, and less capable readers and writers.

What About Teaching? We could say that everything a teacher does during the four patterns of practice is teaching, and in a sense it is. If, however, we define teaching as providing information, literature-based reading teachers do two kinds of teaching. One kind is called direct instruction. In this kind of teaching, teachers provide systematic, planned minilessons in which they explicitly present information, provide an opportunity for supervised practice, and then have students apply what they have learned through authentic reading and writing activities (Slaughter, 1988). Teachers often use direct instruction during minilessons in which they teach students about reading and writing procedures, skills, and strategies. Direct instruction has been associated with skill-and-drill activities, but it doesn't have to be. This kind of teaching is necessary to provide information and opportunities for students to apply what they are learning with guidance from the teacher. Some examples of direct-instruction minilessons are:

- Presenting a biographical sketch of Chris Van Allsburg during a unit featuring the author and his fantasy stories
- Highlighting important vocabulary from *Bud, Not Buddy* (Curtis, 1999) on the classroom word wall
- Choosing a word from an across-the-curriculum theme and using the letters to teach Latin and Greek root words (e.g., *transportation*)
- Teaching a minilesson on pourquoi (or "why") tales before reading *Iktomi and the Boulder* (Goble, 1988)
- Demonstrating how to proofread a piece of writing to identify spelling, punctuation, and capitalization errors

The second kind of teaching is indirect teaching (Slaughter, 1988). Teachers use indirect teaching for brief, on-the-spot minilessons as they respond to students' questions or when students demonstrate the need to know something. These minilessons take place during whole-class activities, during conferences with students, and while working with small groups. Teachers also do indirect teaching as they model reading when reading aloud to the class and as they model writing when students are writing a class collaboration. Other examples include:

- Demonstrating how to use an index when a student says he or she can't find anything about scorpions in the informational book *Desert Life* (Taylor, 1992)
- Teaching a student how to use quotation marks while editing the student's piece of writing
- Explaining what a prologue and an epilogue are during a conference with a child who is reading *Tuck Everlasting* (Babbitt, 1988)
- Explaining the spelling rule that *y* at the end of a word is usually changed to *i* before adding *-es* when a child asks how to spell *cries.*
- Showing a child how to write an innovation (new text following the same pattern) for *Dogs Don't Wear Sneakers* (Numeroff, 1993)

Whereas direct instruction is planned, teachers seize the teachable moment for indirect instruction. Both kinds of teaching are valuable and should be included in language arts programs. Sometimes teachers ask how they should balance the two types of teaching. It is important to remember that most instructional time is devoted to real reading and writing—perhaps as much as 70–80% (Y. M. Goodman, Watson, & Burke, 1987). Of the remaining 20–30%, probably half is spent on unplanned, indirect instruction and the other half on planned, direct instruction. Because teachable moments may not present themselves for some important language arts strategies and skills, there is a need for both planned and unplanned instruction (Baumann, 1987).

Differentiating Instruction

Teachers know that their students vary—their interests and motivation, their background knowledge and prior experiences, and their culture and language proficiency as well as their language arts capabilities—so it's important to allow for these differences as they plan for instruction. According to Carol Ann Tomlinson (2001), differentiated instruction "means 'shaking up' what goes on in the classroom so that students have multiple options for taking information, making sense of ideas, and expressing what they learn" (p. 1). Differentiating instruction is especially important for struggling students who haven't been successful and who can't handle grade-level reading and writing assignments and for very capable students who aren't challenged by grade-level assignments.

Teachers differentiate instruction as they implement the four patterns of practice in their classrooms. Four ways to differentiate instruction are:

1. *Offer choices.* Teachers offer choices when students select books to read in literature circles and in reading workshop, and students often choose their writing topics and genres during writing workshop. Students also make choices about the projects they create during the literature focus units, literature circles, and theme cycles.
2. *Organize students into small groups.* Teachers group students flexibly for literature circles, guided reading, writing groups, and other instructional activities. Students also work in small groups to develop projects and to write reports and other compositions.
3. *Use all six language arts.* Teachers provide opportunities for students to develop expertise in all six language arts, not just reading and writing. During literature focus units, for example, students often use viewing and visually representing to support reading and writing. Many students are better able to understand and express themselves through the oral and visual language arts than through the written language arts, and using all six language arts scaffolds their learning. Other students who are capable readers and writers may have less expertise in the other language arts and need to develop those abilities, too.
4. *Incorporate projects.* Teachers involve students in creating projects as the final step in literature focus units, literature circles, and theme cycles. Through these projects, students have opportunities to explore topics that interest them, use the language arts for meaningful purposes, and demonstrate their learning in authentic ways.

When teachers consider the needs of their students and plan instruction that incorporates these four ways to differentiate instruction, students are more likely to be successful.

Meeting the Needs of Every Student

In every classroom, some students do not learn as well as their classmates or as well as the teacher believes they can. Others do not seem to be challenged by the activities they are engaged in, or they have limited proficiency in English because they are learning English as a second language. Every year, classroom teachers encounter students with a variety of strengths and needs.

The position in this text is that students with special learning needs benefit from the same language arts content and teaching strategies from which other students benefit. The material in this book capitalizes on the natural ways children learn, and it can be used effectively with almost all learners, given some adaptations.

It is important for teachers to be aware of students with special needs in their classrooms and to find ways to adapt the instructional program so that every student can be successful (Wood, 1993). Special educators continue to point out that no one way exists to teach students with special needs that is significantly different from how other students are taught. Moreover, educators recommend an integrated approach as especially valuable for learning-disabled and remedial learners (Rhodes & Dudley-Marling, 1988; Stires, 1991b) and for students learning English as a second language (Freeman & Freeman, 1992; Kucer, Silva, & Delgado-Larocco, 1995). And gifted students benefit from opportunities to create projects in order to delve more deeply into literature focus units, literature circles, and theme cycles.

The Meeting the Needs of Every Student box on page 82 presents a list of 10 general instructional recommendations for adapting the language arts program so that every student can be successful. These recommendations echo many of the main points presented in this chapter and in Chapter 1. When teachers create a community of learners in their classrooms, for example, all students benefit from being in a learning environment where they can talk with classmates, assist one another, and work individually or in small groups. Look for Meeting the Needs of Every Student boxes in the chapters that follow to learn ways to adapt language arts instruction and assessment for students with special needs.

ASSESSING STUDENTS' LEARNING

Assessing students' learning in the language arts is a difficult task. Although it may seem fairly easy to develop and administer a criterion-referenced test, tests measure language skills rather than students' ability to use language in authentic ways. Nor do tests measure listening, talking, and viewing very well. A test on punctuation marks, for example, does not indicate students' ability to use punctuation marks correctly in their own writing. Instead, such a test typically evaluates students' ability to add punctuation marks to a set of sentences created by someone else, or to proofread and spot punctuation errors in someone else's writing. An alternative and far better approach is to examine how students use punctuation marks in their own writing.

Traditional assessment reflects outdated views of how students learn to read and write and offers an incomplete assessment of students' language abilities. Tests focus on only a few aspects of what readers do as they read, what listeners do as they listen, and what writers do as they write. Traditional assessment fails to use authentic language tasks or to help teachers find ways to help students succeed.

Assessment should resemble real language use (Valencia, Hiebert, & Afflerbach, 1994). A better approach is authentic assessment, in which teachers examine both the processes that students use as they listen, talk, read, write, view, and visually represent and the artifacts or products that students create,

Meeting the Needs of Every Student

How Do Teachers Adapt Instruction and Assessment?

1. Classroom Environment

Create a community of learners so students feel comfortable taking risks and admitting when they are confused or need assistance. In addition, teachers model how students can encourage and assist their classmates.

2. Text Sets

Create text sets of books for each unit to provide students with choices. Include reading materials that vary in reading level and genre.

3. Grouping Patterns

Vary grouping patterns so students have regular opportunities to work in small groups, individually, and with the whole class. When students work in small groups, they collaborate and learn from their classmates.

4. Minilessons

Teach minilessons regularly, and reteach the minilessons to small groups of students and to individual students who need a review and additional practice.

5. Visuals

Integrate visuals, including realia, photographs, charts, maps, and diagrams, into the language arts program. These visuals are especially helpful to English learners.

6. Background Knowledge

Take time to build students' background knowledge, and introduce related vocabulary words before teaching difficult concepts. Teachers can read books, use visuals, brainstorm ideas, show videos, and talk about experiences to build background knowledge.

7. Oral Language

Focus on oral language because listening and talking are easier for most students than reading and writing. Teachers include oral language activities in all four patterns of practice.

8. Centers

Incorporate centers so students have an opportunity to work collaboratively on activities and projects and learn from their classmates.

9. Computers

Use computer and other technology tools to stimulate students' interest in language arts activities and to delve more deeply into topics.

10. Monitor Students

Monitor students' progress closely and provide assistance when needed so that students can be successful. When students don't get assistance, they often become frustrated and give up or lose their self-confidence.

Seeing Common Threads

Why aren't tests a complete assessment program?

Susan Miller responds:

Tests are not a complete method of measuring student progress because they measure only a narrow band of abilities and are not authentic assessments of what a child can do. Authentic assessments, in contrast, influence instruction by allowing teachers to learn about their students and the impact of their instruction on those students. Tests do not help teachers find ways to help students succeed. For these reasons, teachers need to use such authentic assessments as classroom observations, anecdotal notes, portfolios, conferences, and checklists in addition to tests to create a complete assessment program.

What do you think?

Each chapter presents a question and a response written by one of Dr. Tompkins's students. Consider other comments, or respond to the question yourself, by visiting the Threaded Message Board in Chapter 2 on the Companion Website at www.prenhall.com/tompkins

such as projects and reading logs. Students, too, participate in reflecting on and assessing their own learning. Authentic assessment has five purposes:

- To document milestones in students' language and literacy development
- To identify students' strengths in order to plan for instruction
- To document students' language arts activities and projects
- To determine grades
- To help teachers learn more about how students become strategic readers and writers

Assessment is more than testing; it is an integral part of teaching and learning (K. S. Goodman, Goodman, & Hood, 1989). The purpose of classroom assessment is to inform and influence instruction. Through authentic assessment, teachers learn about their students, about themselves as teachers, and about the impact of the instructional program. Similarly, when students reflect on their learning and use self-assessment, they learn about themselves as learners and also about their learning. The LA Essentials box on page 84 presents guidelines for authentic assessment and describes how teachers use authentic assessment tools in their classrooms.

Monitoring Students' Progress

Teachers monitor students' progress as they are involved in language arts and across-the-curriculum activities during literature focus units, literature circles, reading and writing workshop, and theme cycles, and they use the results of their monitoring to inform their teaching (Baskwill & Whitman, 1988;

Guidelines for Authentic Assessment

1. Choose Appropriate Assessment Tools

Teachers identify their purpose for assessment and choose an appropriate assessment tool. To judge students' spelling development, for example, teachers examine students' spelling in books they write and their use of proofreading, as well as students' performance on spelling tests.

2. Use a Variety of Assessment Tools

Teachers regularly use a variety of authentic assessment tools that reflect current theories about how children learn, including anecdotal notes.

3. Integrate Instruction and Assessment

Teachers use the results of assessment to inform their teaching. They observe and conference with students as they teach and supervise students during language arts activities.

4. Keep a Positive Focus

Teachers focus on what students can do, not what they can't do. They focus on how to facilitate students' development as readers, writers, and users of language.

5. Consider Both Processes and Products

Teachers examine both the language processes students use and the products they create. They notice the strategies students use for language activities as well as assess the quality of students' work.

6. Consider Multiple Contexts

Teachers assess students' language arts development in a variety of contexts, including literature focus units, theme cycles, and reading and writing workshop. Multiple contexts are important because students often do better in one context than in another.

7. Focus on Individual Students

In addition to whole-class assessments, teachers make time to observe, conference with, and do other assessment procedures with individual students in order to develop clear understandings of each student's development.

8. Teach Students to Self-Assess Their Learning

Self-assessment is an integral part of assessment. Students reflect on their progress in reading, writing, and the other language arts.

K. S. Goodman et al., 1989). Four ways to monitor students' progress are classroom observations, anecdotal notes, conferences, and checklists (Baskwill & Whitman, 1988).

Classroom Observations.

Language arts teachers engage in "kid watching," a term that Yetta Goodman coined and defined as "direct and informal observation of students" (1978, p. 37). To be an effective kid watcher, teachers must understand how children develop language and must understand the role of errors in language learning. Teachers use kid watching spontaneously when they interact with children and are attentive to their behavior and comments. Other observation times should be planned when the teacher focuses on particular students and makes anecdotal notes about the students' involvement in literacy events and other language arts activities. The focus is on what students do as they use oral and written language, not on whether they are behaving properly or working quietly. Of course, little learning can occur in disruptive situations, but during these observations, the focus is on language, not behavior.

Anecdotal Notes.

Teachers write brief notes as they observe students, and the most useful notes describe specific events, report rather than evaluate, and relate the events to other information about the students (Rhodes & Nathenson-Mejia, 1992). Teachers make notes about students' performance in listening, talking, reading, writing, viewing, and visually representing activities; about the questions students ask; and about the strategies and skills they use fluently or indicate confusion about. These records document students' growth and pinpoint problem areas for future minilessons and conferences. A yearlong collection of records provides a comprehensive picture of a student's learning in language arts. An excerpt from a fifth-grade teacher's anecdotal notes about one student's progress during a unit on the American Revolution appears in the Weaving Assessment Into Practice feature on page 86.

Several organizational schemes for anecdotal notes are possible, and teachers should use the format that is most comfortable for them. Some teachers make a card file with dividers for each child and write anecdotes on notecards. They feel comfortable jotting notes on these small cards or even carrying around a set of cards in a pocket. Other teachers divide a spiral-bound notebook into sections for each child and write anecdotes in the notebook, which they keep on their desk. A third technique is to write anecdotes on small sheets of paper and clip the sheets into students' assessment folders.

Conferences.

Teachers talk with students to monitor their progress in language arts activities as well as to set goals and help students solve problems (Gill, 2000). Seven types of conferences are described in the LA Essentials box on page 87. Often these conferences are brief and impromptu, held at students' desks as the teacher moves around the classroom; at other times, the conferences are planned, and students meet with the teacher at a designated conference table.

The teacher's role is to be listener and guide. Teachers can learn a great deal about students and their learning if they listen as students talk about their

Notes About Matthew

March 5	Matthew selected Ben Franklin as historical figure for American Revolution project.
March 11	Matthew fascinated with information he has found about B. F. Brought several sources from home. Is completing B. F.'s lifeline with many details.
March 18	Simulated journal. Four entries in four days! Interesting how he picked up language style of the period in his journal. Volunteers to share daily. I think he enjoys the oral sharing more than the writing.
March 25	Nine simulated journal entries, all illustrated. High level of enthusiasm.
March 29	Conferenced about cluster for B. F. biography. Well-developed with five rays, many details. Matthew will work on "contributions" ray. He recognized it as the least developed one.
April 2	Three chapters of biography drafted. Talked about "working titles" for chapters and choosing more interesting titles after writing that reflect the content of the chapters.
April 7	Drafting conference. Matthew has completed all five chapters. He and Dustin are competitive, both writing on B. F. They are reading each other's chapters and checking the accuracy of information.
April 12	Writing group. Matthew confused Declaration of Independence with the Constitution. Chapters longer and more complete since drafting conference. Compared with autobiography project, writing is more sophisticated. Longer, too. Reading is influencing writing style—e.g., "Luckily for Ben." He is still somewhat defensive about accepting suggestions except from me. He will make 3 revisions—agreed in writing group.
April 15	Revisions: (1) eliminated "he" (substitute), (2) resequenced Chapter 3 (move), and (3) added sentences in Chapter 5 (add).
April 19	Proofread with Dustin. Working hard.
April 23	Editing conference—no major problems. Discussed use of commas within sentences, capitalizing proper nouns. Matthew and Dustin more task-oriented on this project; I see more motivation and commitment.
April 29	Final copy of biography completed and shared with class..

reading, writing, or other activities. When students explain a problem they are having, the teacher is often able to decide on a way to work through it. Graves (1994) suggests that teachers balance the amount of their talk with the student's talk during the conference and, at the end, reflect on what the student has taught them, what responsibilities the student can take, and whether the student understands what to do next.

Checklists. Teachers use checklists as they observe students; as they track students' progress during literature focus units, literature circles, reading and writing workshop, and theme cycles; and as they document students' use of language arts skills, strategies, procedures, and concepts. For example, when students participate in writing conferences in which they read their compositions to small groups of classmates and ask for suggestions for im-

Essentials

Seven Types of Conferences

1. On-the-Spot Conferences

Teachers visit with students at their desks to monitor some aspect of the students' work or to check on progress. These conferences are brief; the teacher may spend less than a minute at each student's desk.

2. Prereading or Prewriting Conferences

The teacher and student make plans for reading or writing at the conference. At a prereading conference, they may talk about information related to the book, difficult concepts or vocabulary words related to the reading, or the reading log the student will keep. At a prewriting conference, they may discuss possible writing topics or how to narrow a broad topic.

3. Revising Conferences

A small group of students and the teacher meet to get specific suggestions about revising their compositions. These conferences offer student writers an audience to provide feedback on how well they have communicated.

4. Book Discussion Conferences

Students and the teacher meet to discuss the book they have read. They may share reading log entries, discuss plot or characters, compare the story to others they have read, or make plans to extend their reading.

5. Editing Conferences

The teacher reviews students' proofread compositions and helps them correct spelling, punctuation, capitalization, and other mechanical errors.

6. Minilesson Conferences

The teacher meets with students to explain a procedure, strategy, or skill (e.g., writing a table of contents, using the visualization strategy when reading, or capitalizing proper nouns).

7. Assessment Conferences

The teacher meets with students after they have completed an assignment or project to talk about their growth as readers or writers. Students reflect on their competencies and set goals.

proving their writing, teachers can note whether students participate fully in the group, share their writing with classmates, gracefully accept suggestions about improving their writing, and make substantive changes in their writing based on some of their classmates' suggestions. Students can even help develop the checklists so that they understand what types of behavior are expected of them.

A "Weekly Reading-Writing Workshop Activity Sheet" appears in the Weaving Assessment Into Practice feature on page 89. Third graders complete this checklist each week to monitor their work during reading and writing workshop. Notice that students are directed to write a letter to the teacher on the back of the sheet, reflecting on their work during that week. Another checklist is shown in the Weaving Assessment Into Practice feature on page 90. Fifth graders use the "Projects Checklist" to keep track of the types of projects they choose to create after reading.

Implementing Portfolios in the Classroom

Portfolios are systematic and meaningful collections of artifacts documenting students' language arts learning and development over a period of time (De Fina, 1992; Graves & Sunstein, 1992; Porter & Cleland, 1995). These collections are dynamic and reflect students' day-to-day learning activities in language arts and across the curriculum. Students' work samples provide windows on the strategies students employ as language users—readers, writers, listeners, viewers, and talkers.

Portfolio programs complement language arts instruction in many ways. The most important benefit is that students become more involved in the assessment of their work and more reflective about the quality of their reading, writing, and other language use. Other benefits include:

- Students feel ownership of their work.
- Students become more responsible about their work.
- Students set goals and are motivated to work toward accomplishing them.
- Students reflect on their accomplishments.
- Students make connections between learning and assessing.
- Students' self-esteem is enhanced.
- Students recognize the connection between process and product.

In addition, portfolios eliminate the need to grade all student work. Portfolios are useful for student and parent conferences and complement the information provided in report cards.

Collecting Work in Portfolios.   Portfolios are folders, large envelopes, or boxes that hold students' work. Teachers often have students label and decorate large folders and then store them in plastic crates or large cardboard boxes. Students date and label items as they place them in their portfolios, and they attach notes to the items to explain the context for the activity and why they selected a particular item for inclusion in the portfolio. Students' portfolios should be stored in the classroom in a place where they are readily accessible to students. Students review their portfolios periodically and add new pieces to them.

Weaving Assessment Into Practice

Weekly Reading-Writing Workshop Activity Sheet

Name _____   Week _____

Read independently	M T W Th F	Made a cluster	M T W Th F
Wrote in a reading log	M T W Th F	Wrote a rough draft	M T W Th F
Listened to the teacher read aloud	M T W Th F	Went to a writing group	M T W Th F
Read with a classmate	M T W Th F	Made revisions	M T W Th F
Read at the listening center	M T W Th F	Proofread my own writing	M T W Th F
Had a reading conference	M T W Th F	Had a writing conference	M T W Th F
Shared a book with classmates	M T W Th F	Shared my writing with classmates	M T W Th F
Other		Other	
Interesting words read this week		Spelling words needed this week	
Titles of books read		Titles of writings	

Write a letter on the back, thinking about the week and your reading and writing.

Students usually choose the items to place in their portfolios within the guidelines the teacher provides. Some students submit the original piece of work; others want to keep the original, so they place a copy in the portfolio instead. In addition to the writing and art samples that can go directly into portfolios, students also record oral language and drama samples on audio- and videotapes to place in their portfolios. Large-size art and writing projects can

Weaving Assessment Into Practice

Projects Checklist

Name _____   Grading Period   1   2   3   4

alphabet book	oral reading
book jacket	oral report
bookmark	plot diagram
cluster	poem
commercial or ad	point-of-view retelling
cube	portrait of character
data chart	poster
diorama	puppets
dramatization	quilt
dress as character	quotable quotes
exhibit	read other books
Internet research	report
interview	script
letter to author	sequel
literary opposites	simulated journal
map or diagram	simulated letter
mobile	storyboards
multigenre project	story box
mural	story map
newspaper article	travel brochure
open-mind portrait	Venn diagram

be photographed, and the photographs placed in the portfolio. The following types of student work might be placed in a portfolio:

"All About Me" books

alphabet books

autobiographies

biographies

books

choral readings (on audiotape)

clusters

copies of letters to pen pals, businesses, and authors, along with replies received

drawings, diagrams, and charts

learning log entries

lists of books read

multimedia programs

oral reading (on audio- or videotape)

oral reports (on audio- or videotape)

poems

projects

puppets (in photographs)

puppet shows (on videotape)

quickwrites

readers theatre performances (on audio- or videotape)

reading log entries

reports

simulated-journal entries

stories

time lines and lifelines

Venn diagrams comparing stories and their film versions

This variety of work samples takes into account all six language arts. Also, samples from workshops, literature focus units, literature circles, and across-the-curriculum theme cycles should be included.

Not all work that is placed in a student's portfolio needs to be graded for quality. Teachers will, of course, be familiar with most pieces, but it is not necessary to correct them with a red pen. Many times, students' work is simply graded as "done" or "not done." When a piece of work is to be graded, students should choose it from the items being placed in their portfolios.

Many teachers collect students' work in folders, and they assume that portfolios are basically the same as work folders; however, the two types of collections differ in several important ways. Perhaps the most important difference is that portfolios are student oriented, whereas work folders are usually teachers' collections. Students choose which samples will be placed in portfolios, and teachers often place all completed assignments in work folders (Clemmons, Lasse, Cooper, Areglado, & Dill, 1993). Next, portfolios focus on students' strengths, not their weaknesses. Because students choose items for portfolios, they choose samples that they feel best represent their language development. Another difference is that portfolios involve reflection (D'Aoust, 1992). Through reflection, students become aware of their strengths as readers, writers, and language users. They also use their work samples to identify the language arts skills, strategies, procedures, and concepts they already know and the ones they need to focus on.

Involving Students in Self-Assessment.

Portfolios are a useful vehicle for engaging students in self-reflection and goal setting (Clemmons et al., 1993). Students can learn to reflect on and assess their own reading and writing activities and their development as readers and writers (Stires, 1991a). Teachers begin by asking students to think about their language arts abilities in terms of contrast. For example, in reading, students identify the books they have read that they liked most and least and ask themselves what these choices suggest about themselves as readers. They also identify what they do well in reading and what they need to improve about their reading. By making these comparisons, students begin to reflect on their language arts development.

Teachers use minilessons and conferences to talk with students about the characteristics of good listeners, good writers, good storytellers, and good viewers. In particular, they discuss:

- What good listeners do as they listen
- How to view a film or videotape
- What fluent reading is
- How to prepare to give an oral report
- Which language arts skills and strategies students use
- How students choose books for reading workshop
- How students demonstrate comprehension
- What makes a good project to extend reading
- How students decide what to write in journals
- How students adapt their writing to their audience
- How students visually represent important concepts
- How to use writing rubrics
- How to participate in a grand conversation

As students learn about what it means to be effective language users, they acquire the tools they need to reflect on and evaluate their own language development, and they acquire vocabulary to use in their reflections, such as *goal, strategy,* and *rubric.*

Students write notes on items they choose to put into their portfolios. In these self-assessments, students explain the reasons for their selections and identify strengths and accomplishments in their work. In some classrooms, students write their reflections and other comments on index cards; in other classrooms, students design special comment sheets that they attach to the items in their portfolios. A first grader wrote this reflection to explain why she chose to make a poster about author Eric Carle and his books and include it in her portfolio: "I have a favorite author. Mr. Eric Carle. I read five of his books!" A fifth grader chose to put the reading log he wrote while reading *Shiloh* (Naylor, 1991) in his portfolio. He wrote this reflection: "I put my journal on the computer. It looks good! I used the SPELCHEK. I put in lots of details like I was him. I should of put some illustrations in the book."

Showcasing Students' Portfolios. At the end of the school year, many teachers organize "Portfolio Share Days" to celebrate students' accomplishments and to provide an opportunity for students to share their portfolios with classmates and the wider community (Porter & Cleland, 1995). Often family members, local businesspeople and politicians, school administrators, college students, and others are invited to attend. Students and community members form small groups, and students share their portfolios, pointing out their accomplishments and strengths. This activity is especially useful in involving community members in the school and showing them the types of language arts activities in which students are involved as well as how students are becoming effective readers, writers, and language users.

These sharing days also help students accept responsibility for their own learning—especially those students who have not been as motivated as their classmates. When less motivated students listen to their classmates talk about their work and how they have grown as readers, writers, and language users, these students often decide to work harder the next year.

Assigning Grades

Assigning grades is one of the most difficult responsibilities placed on teachers. "Grading is a fact of life," according to Donald Graves (1983, p. 93), but he adds that teachers should use grades to encourage students, not to hinder their achievement. The authentic assessment procedures described in this chapter encourage students because they document how students are using all the language arts in authentic ways. Reviewing and translating this documentation into grades is the difficult part.

Assignment Checklists. One way for students to keep track of assignments during literature focus units and theme cycles is to use assignment checklists. Teachers create the assignment checklist as they plan the unit. Students receive a copy of the checklist at the beginning of the unit and keep it in their unit folder. As students complete the assignments, they check them off, so it is easy for the teacher to review students' progress periodically. At the end of the unit, the teacher collects the unit folders and grades the work.

A checklist for a second-grade theme cycle on hermit crabs is presented in the Weaving Assessment Into Practice feature on page 94. Eight assignments on the checklist include both science and language arts activities. Students put a check in the boxes in the "Student's Check" column when they complete each assignment, and the teacher adds the grade in the right-hand column.

Teachers of middle- and upper-grade students often assign points to each activity in the unit checklist so that the total point value for the unit is 100 points; activities that involve more time and effort earn more points. The checklist shown in the Weaving Assessment Into Practice feature on page 95 is for a fifth-grade literature focus unit on *Number the Stars* (Lowry, 1989). The point value for each activity is listed in parentheses. Students make check

Weaving Assessment Into Practice

Checklist for Theme Cycle on Hermit Crabs

Name _____   Begin _____

End _____

	Student's Check	Teacher's Grades

1. Keep an observation log on the hermit crab on your table for 10 days.   ☐   _____

2. Make a chart of a hermit crab and label the parts.   ☐   _____
3. Make a map of the hermit crab's habitat.   ☐   _____
4. Read three books about hermit crabs and do quickwrites about them.   ☐   _____
   _____ *Hermit Crabs*
   _____ *A House for Hermit Crab*
   _____ *Is This a House for Hermit Crab?*
5. Do two science experiments and write lab reports.   ☐   _____
   _____ Wet-Dry Experiment
   _____ Light-Dark Experiment
6. Write about hermit crabs. Do one.   ☐   _____
   _____ *All About Hermit Crabs* book
   _____ A poem about hermit crabs
   _____ A story about hermit crabs
7. Do a project about hermit crabs. Share it.   ☐   _____
8. Keep everything neatly in your hermit crab folder.   ☐   _____

marks on the lines on the left side of the grading sheet, and the teacher marks the numerical grades on the right side.

Rubrics.   Teachers and students develop rubrics or scoring guides to assess students' growth as writers or to evaluate other language arts activities (Farr & Tone, 1994; Skillings & Ferrell, 2000). Rubrics make the analysis of writing simpler and the assessment process more reliable and consistent. Rubrics may have 3, 4, 5, or 6 levels, with descriptors at each level related to ideas, organization, language, and mechanics. Some rubrics are general and appropriate for almost any writing project, whereas others are designed for a specific writing assignment.

The Weaving Assessment Into Practice feature on page 96 shows a general, 5-level writing rubric that teachers and students can use to assess almost any type of formal writing assignment. In contrast, the rubric shown in the Weaving Assessment Into Practice feature on page 97 is designed to assess a particular writing assignment. A class of sixth graders designed the 4-level rubric to assess their reports on ancient Egypt. In contrast to the general

Weaving Assessment Into Practice

Number the Stars *Grading Sheet*

Name _____   Date _____

_____	1. Read *Number the Stars*.		_____
_____	2. Write 5 entries in a reading log or simulated journal.	(25)	_____
_____	3. Talk about your reading in 5 grand conversations.	(25)	_____
_____	4. Make a Venn diagram to compare characters. Summarize what you learned from the diagram in an essay.	(10)	_____
_____	5. Make a cluster about one word on the word wall.	(5)	_____
_____	6. Make a square with a favorite quote for the story quilt.	(10)	_____
_____	7. Do a response project.	(25)	_____
	Total	(100)	_____

rubric, the report rubric lists specific components that students were to include in their reports.

Both teachers and students can assess writing with rubrics. They read the composition and highlight words or check statements in the rubric that best describe the composition. It is important to note that rarely are all the highlighted words or checked statements at the same level. The score is determined by examining the highlighted words or checked statements and determining which level best represents the overall quality of the composition.

To assess students' learning systematically, teachers should use at least three evaluation approaches. Approaching an evaluation from at least three viewpoints is called triangulation. In addition to tests, teachers can use kid watching, anecdotal records, conferences, portfolios, assignment checklists, and rubrics. Using a variety of techniques enables teachers to be much more accurate in charting and assessing students' language growth.

Review

This chapter focused on how teachers teach language arts. Creating a classroom that facilitates learning is an important prerequisite. Teachers plan language arts instruction using four patterns of practice: literature focus units, literature circles, reading and writing workshop, and theme cycles. Assessment is an integral part of instruction, and instruction should be authentic. Key points presented in this chapter include:

1. Classrooms should be authentic learning environments that encourage students to use all six language arts.
2. Textbooks should never be equivalent to the total language arts program.

Writing Rubric

5   Exceptional Achievement

- Creative and original
- Clear organization
- Precise word choice and figurative language
- Sophisticated sentences
- Essentially free of mechanical errors

4   Excellent Achievement

- Some creativity, but more predictable than an exceptional paper
- Definite organization
- Good word choice but little figurative language
- Varied sentences
- Only a few mechanical errors

3   Adequate Achievement

- Predictable paper
- Some organization
- Adequate word choice
- Little variety of sentences and some run-on sentences
- Some mechanical errors

2   Limited Achievement

- Brief and superficial
- Little organization
- Imprecise language
- Incomplete and run-on sentences
- Many mechanical errors

1   Minimal Achievement

- No ideas communicated
- Lacks organization
- Inadequate word choice
- Sentence fragments
- Overwhelming mechanical errors

Rubric for Assessing Reports on Ancient Egypt

4 Excellent Report

_____ Three or more chapters with titles
_____ Main idea clearly developed in each chapter
_____ Three or more illustrations
_____ Effective use of Egypt-related words in text and illustrations
_____ Very interesting to read
_____ Very few mechanical errors
_____ Table of contents

3 Good Report

_____ Three chapters with titles
_____ Main idea somewhat developed in each chapter
_____ Three illustrations
_____ Some Egypt-related words used
_____ Interesting to read
_____ A few mechanical errors
_____ Table of contents

2 Average Report

_____ Three chapters
_____ Main idea identified in each chapter
_____ One or two illustrations
_____ A few Egypt-related words used
_____ Some mechanical errors
_____ Sort of interesting to read
_____ Table of contents

1 Poor Report

_____ One or two chapters
_____ Information in each chapter rambles
_____ No illustrations
_____ Very few Egypt-related words used
_____ Many mechanical errors
_____ Hard to read and understand
_____ No table of contents

Visit Chapter 2 on the Companion Website at www.prenhall. com/tompkins to:

- **Check your understanding of the concepts presented in the chapter**
- **Access the Extensions (activities and a list of related readings)**
- **Link to related websites**

3. Teachers collect three types of trade books—stories, informational books, and books of poetry—for text sets related to literature focus units and theme cycles.

4. Literature focus units include four components: reading books, responding, teaching minilessons, and creating projects.

5. In literature circles, students read and discuss self-selected books in small groups and then share their books with classmates.

6. Reading workshop components are reading and responding, sharing, and teaching minilessons; writing workshop components are writing, sharing, and teaching minilessons.

7. Theme cycles are interdisciplinary units that integrate language arts with social studies, science, math, and other curricular areas.

8. Teachers play many roles during language arts instruction: organizer, facilitator, participant, instructor, model, manager, diagnostician, evaluator, coordinator, and communicator.

9. Students with special learning needs benefit from the same language arts program that benefits other students, given some adaptations.

10. Teachers use authentic assessment procedures, including observations, anecdotal notes, conferences, checklists, portfolios, and rubrics.

Professional References

Altwerger, B., & Flores, B. (1994). Theme cycles: Creating communities of learners. *Primary Voices K–6, 2,* 2–6.

Atwell, N. (1998). *In the middle: New understandings about writing, reading, and learning* (2nd ed.). Portsmouth, NH: Heinemann.

Baskwill, J., & Whitman, P. (1988). *Evaluation: Whole language, whole child.* New York: Scholastic.

Baumann, J. F. (1987). Direct instruction reconsidered. *Journal of Reading, 31,* 712–718.

Butler, S., & Cox, B. (1992). Writing with a computer in grade one: A study in collaboration. *Language Arts, 69,* 633–640.

Calkins, L. M. (1991). *Living between the lines.* Portsmouth, NH: Heinemann.

Calkins, L. M. (1994). *The art of teaching writing* (2nd ed.). Portsmouth, NH: Heinemann.

Cambourne, B. (2001). What do I do with the rest of the class? The nature of teaching-learning activities. *Language Arts, 79,* 124–135.

Clemmons, J., Lasse, L., Cooper, D., Areglado, N., & Dill, M. (1993). *Portfolios in the classroom: A teacher's sourcebook.* New York: Scholastic.

Cohle, D. M., & Towle, W. (2001). *Connecting reading and writing in the intermediate grades: A workshop approach.* Newark, DE: International Reading Association.

Cordeiro, P. (Ed.). (1995). *Endless possibilities: Generating curriculum in social studies and literacy.* Portsmouth, NH: Heinemann.

Daniels, H. (2002). *Literature circles: Voice and choice in book clubs and reading groups* (2nd ed.). Portland, ME: Stenhouse.

D'Aoust, C. (1992). Portfolios: Process for students and teachers. in K. B. Yancy (Ed.), *Portfolios in the writing classroom* (pp. 39–48). Urbana, IL: National Council of Teachers of English.

Day, J., Spiegel, D. L., McLellan, J., & Brown, V. (2002). *Moving forward with literature circles.* New York: Scholastic.

De Fina, A. A. (1992). *Portfolio assessment: Getting started.* New York: Scholastic.

Eisenwine, M. J., & Hunt, D. A. (2000). Using a computer in literacy groups with emergent readers. *The Reading Teacher, 53,* 456–458.

Evans, K. S. (2001). *Literature discussion groups in the intermediate grades: Dilemmas and possibilities.* Newark, DE: International Reading Association.

Farr, R., & Tone, B. (1994). *Portfolio and performance assessment.* Orlando, FL: Harcourt & Brace.

Five, C. L. (1988). From workbook to workshop: Increasing children's involvement in the reading process. *The New Advocate, 1,* 103–113.

Fletcher, R., & Portalupi, J. (1998). *Craft lessons: Teaching writing K–8.* Portland, ME: Stenhouse.

Fletcher, R., & Portalupi, J. (2001). *Writing workshop: The essential guide.* Portsmouth, NH: Heinemann.

Ford, M. P., & Opitz, M. F. (2002). Using centers to engage children during guided reading time: Intensifying learning experiences away from the teacher. *The Reading Teacher, 55,* 710–717.

Freeman, Y. S., & Freeman, D. E. (1992). *Whole language for second language learners.* Portsmouth, NH: Heinemann.

Gill, R. S. (2000). Reading with Amy: Teaching and learning through reading conferences. *The Reading Teacher, 53,* 500–509.

Gillet, J. W., & Beverly, L. (2001). *Directing the writing workshop: An elementary teacher's handbook.* New York: Guilford Press.

Goodman, K. S., Goodman, Y. M., & Hood, W. J. (Eds.). (1989). *The whole language evaluation book.* Portsmouth, NH: Heinemann.

Goodman, Y. M. (1978). Kid watching: An alternative to testing. *National Elementary Principals Journal, 57,* 41–45.

Goodman, Y. M., Watson, D. J., & Burke, C. L. (1987). *Reading miscue inventory: Alternative procedures.* Katonah, NY: Richard C. Owen.

Graves, D. H. (1983). *Writing: Teachers and children at work.* Portsmouth, NH: Heinemann.

Graves, D. H. (1991). *Build a literate classroom.* Portsmouth, NH: Heinemann.

Graves, D. H. (1994). *A fresh look at writing.* Portsmouth, NH: Heinemann.

Graves, D. H., & Sunstein, B. S. (Eds.). (1992). *Portfolio portraits.* Portsmouth, NH: Heinemann.

Hepler, S. (1991). Talking our way to literacy in the classroom community. *The New Advocate, 4,* 179–191.

Hill, B. C., Johnson, N. J., & Noe, K. L. S. (Eds.). (1995). *Literature circles and response.* Norwood, MA: Christopher-Gordon.

Hornsby, D., Sukarna, D., & Parry, J. (1986). *Read on: A conference approach to reading.* Portsmouth, NH: Heinemann.

Koskinen, P. S., Wilson, R. M., Gambrell, L. B., & Neuman, S. B. (1993). Captioned video and vocabulary learning: An innovative practice in literacy instruction. *The Reading Teacher, 47,* 36–43.

Kucer, S. B., Silva, C., & Delgado-Larocco, E. L. (1995). *Curricular conversations: Themes in multilingual and monolingual classrooms.* York, ME: Stenhouse.

Lapp, D., Flood, J., & Lungren, L. (1995). Strategies for gaining access to the information superhighway: Off the side street and on to the main road. *The Reading Teacher, 48,* 432–436.

Lewin, L. (1992). Integrating reading and writing strategies using an alternating teacher-led/student-selected instructional pattern. *The Reading Teacher, 45,* 586–591.

Lindquist, T., & Selwyn, D. (2000). *Social studies at the center: Integrating kids, content, and literacy.* Portsmouth, NH: Heinemann.

Marcus, S. (1990). Computers in the language arts: From pioneers to settlers. *Language Arts, 67,* 519–524.

Moline, S. (1995). *I see what you mean: Children at work with visual information.* York, ME: Stenhouse.

Moore, M. A. (1991). Electronic dialoguing: An avenue to literacy. *The Reading Teacher, 45,* 280–287.

Morrow, L. M. (1989). Designing the classroom to promote literacy development. In D. S. Strickland & L. M. Morrow (Eds.), *Emerging literacy: Young children learn to read and write.* Newark, DE: International Reading Association.

Morrow, L. M. (1996). *Motivating reading and writing in diverse classrooms* (NCTE Research Report No. 28). Urbana, IL: National Council of Teachers of English.

Mulligan, P. A., & Gore, K. (1992). Telecommunications: Education's missing link? *Language Arts, 69,* 379–384.

Parry, J., & Hornsby, D. (1985). *Write on: A conference approach to writing.* Portsmouth, NH: Heinemann.

Phenix, J., & Hannan, E. (1984). Word processing in the grade one classroom. *Language Arts, 61,* 804–812.

Portalupi, J., & Fletcher, R. (2001). *Nonfiction craft lessons: Teaching information writing K–8.* Portland, ME: Stenhouse.

Porter, C., & Cleland, J. (1995). *The portfolio as a learning strategy.* Portsmouth, NH: Heinemann.

Rhodes, L. K., & Dudley-Marling, C. (1988). *Readers and writers with a difference: A holistic approach to teaching learning disabled and remedial students.* Portsmouth, NH: Heinemann.

Rhodes, L. K., & Nathenson-Mejia, S. (1992). Anecdotal records: A powerful tool for ongoing literacy assessment. *The Reading Teacher, 45,* 502–511.

Rief, L. (1999). *Vision and voice: Extending the literacy spectrum.* Portsmouth, NH: Heinemann.

Rose, D. H., & Meyer, A. (1994). The role of technology in language arts instruction. *Language Arts, 71,* 290–294.

Samway, K. D., & Whang, G. (1996). *Literacy study circles in a multicultural classroom.* York, ME: Stenhouse.

Samway, K. D., Whang, G., Cade, C., Gamil, M., Lubandina, M. A., & Phommachanh, K. (1991). Reading the skeleton, the heart, and the brain of a book: Students' perspectives on literature study circles. *The Reading Teacher, 45,* 196–205.

Shanahan, T., & Knight, L. (1991). *Guidelines for judging and selecting language arts textbooks: A modest proposal* (NCTE Concept Paper No. 1). Urbana, IL: National Council of Teachers of English.

Skillings, M. J., & Ferrell, R. (2000). Student-generated rubrics: Bringing students into the assessment process. *The Reading Teacher, 53,* 452–455.

Slaughter, H. (1988). Indirect and direct teaching in a whole language program. *The Reading Teacher, 41,* 30–34.

Smith, J. (1991). Going wild in hypercard. *Language Arts, 68,* 674–680.

Stires, S. (1991a). Thinking through the process: Self-evaluation in writing. In B. M. Power & R. Hubbard (Eds.), *The Heinemann reader: Literacy in process* (pp. 295–310). Portsmouth, NH: Heinemann.

Stires, S. (Ed.). (1991b). *With promise: Redefining reading and writing for "special" students.* Portsmouth, NH: Heinemann.

Sumara, D., & Walker, L. (1991). The teacher's role in whole language. *Language Arts, 68,* 276–285.

Swift, K. (1993). Try reading workshop in your classroom. *The Reading Teacher, 46,* 366–371.

Tomlinson, C. A. (2001). *How to differentiate instruction in mixed-ability classrooms* (2nd ed.). Alexandria, VA: Association for Supervision and Curriculum Development.

Valencia, S. W., Hiebert, E. H., & Afflerbach, P. P. (1994). *Authentic reading assessment: Practices and possibilities.* Newark, DE: International Reading Association.

Whatley, A., & Canalis, J. (2002). Creating learning communities through literacy. *Language Arts, 79,* 478–487.

Wood, J. W. (1993). *Mainstreaming: A practical approach for teachers* (2nd ed.). Upper Saddle River, NJ: Merrill/Prentice Hall.

Children's Book References

Adler, D. A. (1990). *A picture book of Helen Keller.* New York: Holiday House.

Adler, D. A. (1995). *A picture book of Patrick Henry.* New York: Holiday House.

Arnosky, J. (1995). *I see animals hiding.* New York: Scholastic.

Babbitt, N. (1988). *Tuck everlasting.* New York: Farrar, Straus & Giroux.

Brown, M. W. (1990). *The important book.* New York: HarperCollins.

Bunting, E. (1994). *Smoky night.* San Diego: Harcourt Brace.

Bunting, E. (1995). *Once upon a time*. Katonah, NY: Richard C. Owen.

Carle, E. (1989). *Animals, animals*. New York: Philomel.

Chester, J. (1995). *A for Antarctica*. New York: Tricycle.

Cole, J. (1995). *The magic school bus inside a hurricane*. New York: Scholastic.

Cleary, B. (1993). *Ralph the mouse*. New York: Morrow.

Curtis, C. P. (1999). *Bud, not Buddy*. New York: Delacorte.

Dahl, R. (1982). *The BFG*. New York: Knopf.

Dorros, A. (1991). *Abuela*. New York: Dutton.

Ellis, D. (2000). *The breadwinner*. Toronto: Groundwood Books.

Fleischman, P. (1988). *Joyful noise: Poems for two voices*. New York: Harper & Row.

Freedman, R. (1993). *Eleanor Roosevelt: A life of discovery*. New York: Clarion.

Fritz, J. (1976). *Will you sign here, John Hancock?* New York: Coward-McCann.

Fritz, J. (1995). *You want women to vote, Lizzie Stanton?* New York: Putnam.

Gardiner, J. R. (1980). *Stone Fox*. New York: HarperCollins.

George, J. C. (1972). *Julie of the wolves*. New York: HarperCollins.

Goble, P. (1988). *Iktomi and the boulder*. New York: Orchard.

Hopkins, L. B. (1994). *Hand in hand: An American history through poetry*. New York: Simon & Schuster.

L'Engle, M. (1962). *A wrinkle in time*. New York: Farrar, Straus & Giroux.

Lowry, L. (1989). *Number the stars*. Boston: Houghton Mifflin.

Macaulay, D. (1977). *Castle*. Boston: Houghton Mifflin.

MacLachlan, P. (1985). *Sarah, plain and tall*. New York: HarperCollins.

Martin, B., Jr. (1992). *Brown bear, brown bear, what do you see?* New York: Holt.

McKissack, P. C., & McKissack, F. (1995). *Red-tail angels: The story of the Tuskegee airmen of World War II*. New York: Walker.

McMillan, B. (1995). *Summer ice: Life along the Antarctic peninsula*. Boston: Houghton Mifflin.

Naylor, P. R. (1991). *Shiloh*. New York: Atheneum.

Naylor, P. R. (1996). *Shiloh season*. New York: Atheneum.

Naylor, P. R. (1997). *Saving Shiloh*. New York: Atheneum.

Numeroff, L. J. (1993). *Dogs don't wear sneakers*. New York: Simon & Schuster.

Paterson, K. (1977). *Bridge to Terabithia*. New York: HarperCollins.

Paulsen, G. (1987). *Hatchet*. New York: Viking.

Peek, M. (1993). *Mary wore her red dress and Henry wore his green sneakers*. New York: Clarion.

Polacco, P. (1994). *Pink and Say*. New York: Philomel.

Prelutsky, J. (1993). *The dragons are singing tonight*. New York: Greenwillow.

Prelutsky, J. (Sel.). (2000). *The Random House book of poetry for children*. New York: Random House.

Rathmann, P. (1995). *Officer Buckle and Gloria*. New York: Putnam.

Rodgers, M. (1972). *Freaky Friday*. New York: HarperCollins.

Rowling, J. K. (2002). *Harry Potter and the goblet of fire*. New York: Scholastic.

Sachar, L. (1998). *Holes*. New York: Farrar, Straus & Giroux.

Smith, R. K. (1972). *Chocolate fever*. New York: Dell.

Speare, E. G. (1983). *The sign of the beaver*. Boston: Houghton Mifflin

Spinelli, J. (1990). *Maniac Magee*. Boston: Little, Brown.

Steig, W. (1969). *Sylvester and the magic pebble*. New York: Simon & Schuster.

Taylor, B. (1992). *Desert life*. New York: Dorling Kindersley.

Terban, M. (1993). *It figures! Fun figures of speech*. New York: Clarion.

Uchida, Y. (1993). *The bracelet*. New York: Philomel.

Van Allsburg, C. (1981). *Jumanji*. Boston: Houghton Mifflin.

Wadsworth, G. (1995). *Giant sequoia trees*. Minneapolis: Lerner.

3 The Reading and Writing Processes

Reading and
Writing
Workshop

Literature
Focus Units

Literature
Circles

Theme
Cycles

During the first week of school, Ms. Kakutani reads aloud *Granny Torrelli Makes Soup* (Creech, 2003) to her fourth graders. It's a story about friendship, which is her theme for the first month of school. In the story, Granny Torrelli helps her granddaughter Rosie smooth out her relationship with best friend Bailey. Ms. Kakutani makes connections between what Rosie learns about being a friend and how she wants the students to behave toward their classmates. It's the teacher's first step in creating a community of learners in the classroom.

After they finish the book, Ms. Kakutani and her students prepare spaghetti and meatballs and invite parents, grandparents, and siblings to join them for a lunch. The students write invitations, and parents volunteer to supply many of the ingredients and help prepare the food in the classroom. Others bring salad, bread, fruit, and dessert to complete the meal. It's a festive occasion where children introduce their families to Ms. Kakutani and show them around their classroom.

For the next 2 weeks, Ms. Kakutani and her students read *Amber Brown Goes Fourth* (Danziger, 1995), the third in a series of chapter-book stories about a spunky girl with a two-color name. The books are written at the third-grade reading level, and they're appropriate for this class because the students read a year below grade level. The teacher has a class set of the chapter books that she distributes to students and a text set with multiple copies of the other books in the Amber Brown series that she places in the classroom library for students to read independently. An annotated list of the books in the Amber Brown series is presented in the box on page 104.

Ms. Kakutani chooses to read the story with her students using shared reading because she wants to ensure that all students can read the story, and she wants to introduce the strategies that she will emphasize as she teaches comprehension. The students follow along in their copies of the book as she reads aloud, chapter by chapter. The class spends 9 days reading the 14 chapters in the book; on some days, they read one chapter, and on other days, they read two chapters. As they read, Ms. Kakutani pauses off and on to think aloud about the comprehension strategies she is using—monitoring, visualizing, connecting, summarizing, and evaluating.

After they finish reading, the students participate in a grand conversation with Ms. Kakutani. Participating in a free-flowing discussion about the story is new to many students. The teacher explains the activity, models it for them, and teaches them how to ask questions, offer opinions, and make connections to their own lives and to *Granny Torrelli Makes Soup.* They talk about the events in the story, the

How do teachers use the reading process to organize literature focus units?

Good teaching is not accidental. Teachers organize and plan literature focus units so that students can comprehend what they are reading. Some activities introduce the book and activate background knowledge, some activities guide students as they interpret the story, and others provide opportunities to teach students about literature and for students to apply what they are learning. These activities represent the five stages of the reading process. As you read this vignette, notice how Ms. Kakutani incorporates the prereading, reading, responding, exploring, and applying stages of the reading process in her literature focus unit.

Ms. Kakutani's Annotated Text Set of Amber Brown Stories

Danziger, P. (1994). *Amber Brown is not a crayon.* New York: Putnam.
Amber's life changes when her parents divorce and her best friend Justin moves away.

Danziger, P. (1995). *Amber Brown goes fourth.* New York: Putnam.
Amber begins fourth grade without a best friend.

Danziger, P. (1995). *You can't eat your chicken pox, Amber Brown.* New York: Putnam.
Amber goes to Europe with her Aunt Pam but doesn't get to visit her divorced father because she gets chicken pox.

Danziger, P. (1996). *Amber Brown wants extra credit.* New York: Putnam.
Amber has trouble getting her work done at school because she's upset that her mother is dating Max.

Danziger, P. (1997). *Amber Brown sees red.* New York: Putnam.
Amber is torn between her future stepdad who is there for her and her absentee dad who is not.

Danziger, P. (1997). *Forever Amber Brown.* New York: Putnam.
More changes are in store for Amber when her divorced mother and her boyfriend get engaged.

Danziger, P. (1998). *Amber Brown is feeling blue.* New York: Putnam.
Amber is having trouble adjusting to a new classmate—Kelly Green—who also has a two-color name.

Danziger, P. (1999). *I, Amber Brown.* New York: Putnam.
Amber's parents have joint custody of her, and she feels like she's losing control of her life and identity.

Danziger, P. (2003). *Amber Brown is green with envy.* New York: Putnam.
Amber is facing more changes as her divorced parents create new lives for themselves.

---

importance of having friends, and their own nervousness about beginning fourth grade.

When the grand conversation slows down, Ms. Kakutani often returns to the book and rereads a sentence or paragraph to redirect the conversation. After reading Chapters 6 and 7, for example, she rereads the bottom part of page 47 and asks, "What does Brandi mean when she says, 'I am NOT Justin'"? At first the students are unsure, but as they talk about how Brandi might feel, they recognize that one child cannot replace another one. Then the teacher asks, "Do you think Brandi and Amber will become best friends?"

The students make predictions that guide their reading for the second half of the story.

After reading and discussing Chapter 14, Ms. Kakutani rereads Amber's comment, "I guess there will always be changes in my life" (p. 100) and asks students what they think it means. The students reflect on the changes in Amber's life—her friend Justin moving away, her parents getting divorced, her father moving to Paris, her mother dating Max, and Amber starting fourth grade. Then Ms. Kakutani asks students if they expect to have changes in their lives, and the conversation continues for more than 30 minutes as students talk about the changes in their lives—parents who are soldiers leaving for Iraq, new babies born into their families, mothers going to work, families moving to a new community, grandparents dying, older siblings being sent to prison, and, of course, starting fourth grade.

After they talk about the story, the students write entries in their reading logs. Ms. Kakutani provides questions to guide students' responses. She makes her questions open-ended to encourage students to continue to think more deeply about the story and make connections to their own lives. Here are Ms. Kakutani's questions:

Chapters 1 and 2	*What have you learned about Amber?*
	How do you think her life is going to change?
Chapter 3	*What's hard about starting fourth grade?*
Chapters 4 and 5	*How is Amber's fourth grade different from third grade?*
	How is it different for you?
Chapters 6 and 7	*Do you think Amber and Brandi will become best friends?*
	Do you agree with Amber that everyone should have a best friend?
Chapter 8	*What have you wanted to do over?*
	What funny things have you done with your mom or dad?
	What has your mom or dad taught you how to do?
Chapter 9	*Do you think it was fair for the girls to get detention for laughing?*
Chapters 10 and 11	*Why do you think Brandi and Amber are getting to be better friends?*
	Would you want to be the Burp Queen or Burp King of fourth grade?
Chapters 12 and 13	*What should Amber do to be a good friend?*
	Do you think Amber is ever going to like Max?
Chapter 14	*Do you think Max was trying to bribe Amber with the mermaid?*
	What changes have you had in your life?

When there are two or more questions, the teacher encourages students to choose one question to respond to.

The students make small journals by stapling together sheets of lined paper and adding construction paper covers. They illustrate the covers to reflect the book they are reading. They begin each entry on a new page and add the chapter number, a title, and the date at the top of the page. Bella writes this entry after reading Chapters 6 and 7, in response to the question, "Do you think Amber and Brandi will become best friends?":

> *I feel sorry for Amber Brown. She has too many changes in her life. She needs a new best friend. Her old best friend moved away and she is lonely. I am thinking Brandi will be her best friend because she needs one, too. I hope there are no more changes for her!*

Jordan writes this entry after reading Chapter 14 and adds this title—"The Change in My Life":

> *I'm having a change right now and it scares me. My Dad is in Iraq. He is a sergeant. I pray to God to watch over him. He says he's safe but I think he could get killed. I'm proud of him because he is brave. I pray he comes back safe.*

Students write reading log entries after participating in grand conversations, and the ideas developed during the conversations are often reflected in their entries. Through these reading log entries, the students clarify their thoughts and share their ideas about the story. Ms. Kakutani reads them to gauge her students' understanding of the story, see what connections they are making to their own lives, and respond to the students' ideas and questions.

Ms. Kakutani also emphasizes the important vocabulary in the story. She posts a word wall—a large chart divided into 16 alphabetized sections—and after reading each chapter or two, students choose the words that are most important to add to the word wall. They take turns writing the words on the chart, and they refer to the word wall whenever they need help thinking of a word or spelling it. The class word wall is shown in the box on page 107.

The teacher also points out the word play in the story. The students get interested in reading jokes after reading the ones in Chapter 1 and Chapter 6, and Ms. Kakutani locates several joke books in the classroom library to share with them.

Ms. Kakutani also shares information with students about author Paula Danziger that she has downloaded from the Internet and does a book talk to introduce the other Amber Brown books. Then students spend the last week in the unit reading other Amber Brown stories individually, with partners, and in small groups. Ms. Kakutani circulates around the classroom as students read, stopping to talk with them about the books they're reading and to answer questions.

On the last day of the unit, the class has a read-around to share their favorite sentences and paragraphs from the books they are reading. Students prepare by choosing a favorite part to read, marking the excerpt with a bookmark, and rehearsing so that they can read it fluently. The class comes together and sits in a circle. One student begins by reading an excerpt aloud, and then other students take turns reading their excerpts until everyone has had an opportunity to share. Even after the unit ends, many students will trade books and continue reading about Amber Brown's adventures during independent reading time.

The Word Wall for *Amber Brown Goes Fourth*			
AB Amber Brown best friend Brandi Colwin Burp Queen braids bossy	**CD** colorful change divorce do-over detention	**EF** empty feeling feet-feat fourth-forth fiend	**GH** Hannah Burton Her Dweebness humongous
IJ Justin Daniels immature	**KL** London knapsack laughing	**M** Max musical mermaid Mrs. Holt	**NO** nervous name dropper
PQ Paris	**R**	**S** sole-soul scared snap fingers spaghetti-slurping contest	**T** trophy
UV vacancies	**W**	**XY**	**Z**

Both reading and writing are meaning-making processes. According to constructivist and sociolinguistic learning theories, readers create meaning through negotiation with the texts they are reading, and, similarly, writers create meaning through negotiation with the texts they are writing. Readers use their life and literature experiences and knowledge of written language as they read, and writers bring similar knowledge and experiences to writing. It is quite common for two people to read the same story and come away with different interpretations and for two writers to write different accounts of the same event. Meaning does not exist on the pages of the book that a reader is reading or in the words of the composition that a writer is writing; instead, meaning is created through the transaction between readers and what they are reading or between writers and what they are writing.

The reading process involves a series of stages during which readers construct interpretations—known as comprehension—as they read and then respond

 As you begin reading this chapter, you may want to read the "Dear Reader" letter in Chapter 3 on the Companion Website at www.prenhall.com/tompkins

to the text they have read. "Text" includes all reading materials—stories, maps, newspapers, cereal boxes, textbooks, and so on—and is not limited to basal reader textbooks. The writing process is a similar recursive process involving a variety of activities as students gather and organize their ideas, draft their compositions, revise and edit the drafts, and, finally, publish their writings.

Reading and writing have long been thought of as the flip sides of a coin, as opposites: Readers decoded or deciphered written language, and writers encoded or produced written language. Then researchers noted similarities between reading and writing and began to talk of both of them as processes. Now reading and writing are viewed as parallel processes of meaning construction and readers and writers as using similar strategies for making meaning with text.

In this chapter, you will read about the reading and writing processes and see how teachers use these processes in designing language arts instruction. As you continue reading, think about these questions:

◆ What are the stages in the reading process?

◆ What are the stages in the writing process?

◆ How are the two processes alike?

◆ How do teachers use these two processes in teaching language arts?

THE READING PROCESS

Reading is a transactive process in which a reader negotiates meaning in order to comprehend, or create an interpretation. During reading, the meaning does not go from the page to the reader. Instead, reading involves a complex negotiation between the text and the reader that is shaped by many factors: the reader's knowledge about the topic; the reader's purpose for reading; the language community the reader belongs to and how closely that language matches the language used in the text; the reader's culturally based expectations about reading; and the reader's expectations about reading based on his or her previous experiences (Weaver, 1994).

Aesthetic and Efferent Reading

To compare aesthetic and efferent reading with similar stances for listening, see Chapter 7, "Listening to Learn."

Readers read for different purposes, and the way they approach the reading process varies according to their purpose. Often they read for enjoyment, but at other times, they read to carry away information. When reading for enjoyment or to be entertained, readers assume an aesthetic stance and focus on the lived-through experience of reading. They concentrate on the thoughts, images, feelings, and associations evoked during reading. Readers also respond to these thoughts, images, feelings, and associations. For example, as children read Cynthia Rylant's story *The Relatives Came* (1985), they may relate the events in the book to a time when their relatives visited; as they read Diane Siebert's *Sierra* (1991), they may respond to the language of the text; or as they read *Catherine, Called Birdy* (Cushman, 1994), they may imagine themselves in Birdy's medieval world.

Seeing Common Threads

Why is the idea that reading and writing are processes so critical to our current understanding of how children learn?

Kristi Garcia responds:

When I was a beginning teacher, I often gave my students topics to write about. These topics were not related to anything specific to their lives or what we were studying. Often they complained that they didn't know what to write about, so I would write a topic on the chalkboard and expect masterpieces in return. Most days I was completely disappointed. It was only after learning more about literacy that I learned the importance of reading and writing as transactive processes. The processes of reading and writing together help students make meaning. And they make meaning only with experiences they can relate to. As my students began writing about books we were reading and themes we were studying, I saw a marked increase in the quality of my students' work.

What do you think?

Each chapter presents a question and a response written by one of Dr. Tompkins's students. Consider other comments, or respond to the question yourself, by visiting the Threaded Message Board in Chapter 3 on the Companion Website at www.prenhall.com/tompkins

When reading to carry away information, readers assume an efferent stance: They concentrate on the public, common referents of the words and symbols in the text. For example, as children read Patricia Lauber's *Seeing Earth From Space* (1990), with its breathtaking photographs of the earth taken by satellites, their focus is on the information in the text and illustrations, not on the experience of reading.

Almost every reading experience calls for a balance between aesthetic and efferent reading (Rosenblatt, 1978, 1991). Readers do not simply read stories and poems aesthetically and informational books efferently. As they read, readers move back and forth between the aesthetic and efferent stances. Literature, however, should be read primarily from the aesthetic stance.

During both aesthetic and efferent reading, readers move through the five stages of the reading process: prereading, reading, responding, exploring, and applying. The key features of each stage are summarized in the LA Essentials box on page 110. Many of the features are characteristic of both aesthetic and efferent reading, but a few features exemplify one stance or the other.

Stage 1: Prereading

The reading process begins before readers open a book to read. The first stage is prereading. As readers prepare to read, they:

- Choose books
- Activate background knowledge
- Set purposes
- Plan for reading

Essentials

Key Features of the Reading Process

Stage 1: Prereading

- Choose a book.
- Activate or build background knowledge.
- Connect to prior personal and literary experiences.
- Connect to theme cycles or special interests.
- Set purposes for reading.
- Make predictions.
- Preview the text.
- Consult the index to locate information.

Stage 2: Reading

- Make predictions.
- Apply skills and strategies.
- Read independently, with a buddy, using shared reading, or through guided reading, or listen to the text read aloud.
- Read the illustrations, charts, and diagrams.
- Read the entire text from beginning to end.
- Read one or more sections of the text to learn specific information.
- Take notes.

Stage 3: Responding

- Write in a reading log.
- Participate in a grand conversation or an instructional conversation.

Stage 4: Exploring

- Reread and think more deeply about the text.
- Make connections with personal experiences.
- Make connections with other literary experiences.
- Examine the author's craft.
- Identify memorable quotes.
- Learn new vocabulary words.
- Participate in minilessons.

Stage 5: Applying

- Use information in theme cycles.
- Connect with related books.
- Create a project.
- Value the reading experience.

Choosing Books. Readers often begin the reading process by choosing the book they will read. Choosing an appropriate book is not easy. First of all, students need to know about themselves as readers. What types of books do they like? Who are their favorite authors? As they become readers, students learn the answers to these questions. They can also point to books they have read and can tell about them and explain why they enjoyed reading them.

Students need to learn to choose books they can read. Ohlhausen and Jepsen (1992) developed a strategy for choosing books called the "Goldilocks strategy." These teachers developed three categories of books—"too easy," "too hard," and "just right"—using "The Three Bears" folktale as their model. The books in the "too easy" category were books students had read before or could read fluently. "Too hard" books were unfamiliar and confusing, and books in the "just right" category were interesting and had just a few unfamiliar words. The books in each category vary according to the students' reading levels. This approach was developed with a second-grade class, but the categorization scheme can work at any grade level. Figure 3–1 presents a chart about choosing books using the Goldilocks strategy developed by a third-grade class. Sometimes teachers choose books for students, but it is important that readers have many opportunities to choose books they are interested in reading.

Activating Background Knowledge. Readers activate their background knowledge or schemata about the book (or other selection) before beginning to read. The topic of the book, the title, the author, the genre, the cover illustration, a comment someone makes about the book, or something else may trigger this activation. When students are reading independently—during reading workshop, for example—they choose the books they will read and activate their background knowledge themselves. For instance, readers who love horses often choose horse books such as *Misty of Chincoteague* (Henry, 1963) to read.

At other times, such as during literature focus units, teachers teach mini-lessons to help students activate and build their background knowledge. They share information on a topic related to the book or introduce a book box with a collection of objects related to the book. Or, they show a video or film, tell about the author, read the first paragraph aloud, or ask students to make a prediction about the book. For instance, before reading Paula Danziger's *Amber Brown Is Not a Crayon* (1994), teachers talk about missing friends when they move away; before reading Jan Brett's *The Mitten* (1989), teachers show students a white mitten and several stuffed animals representing characters in the story—a bear, a fox, a rabbit, and an owl—and ask students whether they think these animals could fit into the mitten.

For readers to make meaning from the selection they are reading, their schemata must be activated. When students are preparing to read a book on an unfamiliar topic, they need to build background knowledge. By building a new schema before reading and being introduced to key vocabulary, students are more likely to be successful when they read. For example, teachers show a video on hermit crabs before reading *A House for Hermit Crab* (Carle, 1987); or, before reading *The Giver* (Lowry, 1993), they build a concept of what a "perfect" society might be like by having students brainstorm a list of problems in today's society and think of possible remedies.

FIGURE 3-1

A Third-Grade Chart Applying the Goldilocks Strategy

How to Choose the Best Books for YOU

"Too Easy" Books

1. The book is short.
2. The print is big.
3. You have read the book before.
4. You know all the words in the book.
5. The book has a lot of pictures.
6. You are an expert on this topic.

"Just Right" Books

1. The book looks interesting.
2. You can decode most of the words in the book.
3. Mrs. Donnelly has read this book aloud to you.
4. You have read other books by this author.
5. There's someone to give you help if you need it.
6. You know something about this topic.

"Too Hard" Books

1. The book is long.
2. The print is small.
3. There aren't many pictures in the book.
4. There are a lot of words that you can't decode.
5. There's no one to help you read this book.
6. You don't know much about this topic.

Another part of activating knowledge before reading is to make connections to personal experiences and to literary experiences. The more connections students make between the book they are about to read and personal experiences, the better. Students who have a hermit crab as a pet, for instance, will be better prepared to read *A House for Hermit Crab* than students who have never seen a hermit crab. Similarly, students who have read other books by Eric Carle and know about his fabulous collage illustrations will be better prepared to read *A House for Hermit Crab.*

Setting Purposes. The two overarching purposes for reading are pleasure and information. When students read for pleasure or enjoyment, they read aesthetically, to be carried into the world of the text; when they read a selection to locate and remember information or for directions about how to do something, they read efferently (Rosenblatt, 1978). Often readers use elements of both purposes as they read, but usually one purpose is more primary to the reading experience than the other. For example, when students pick up *The Sweetest Fig* (1993) or *The Garden of Abdul Gasazi* (1979), two of Chris Van Allsburg's picture book fantasies, their primary purpose is enjoyment. They want to experience the story, but at the same time, they search for the white dog, a trademark that Van Allsburg includes in all of his books, and they compare these books with others of his that they have read. As they search for the white dog or make comparisons, they add efferent purposes to their primarily aesthetic reading experience.

Readers are more successful when they have a single purpose for reading the entire selection. During literature focus units, purpose setting is usually directed by the teacher, but in reading workshop, students set their own purposes because everyone is reading different self-selected books. For teacher-directed purpose setting, teachers explain how students are expected to read and what they will do after reading. The goal of teacher-directed purpose setting is to help students learn how to set personally relevant purposes when they are reading independently (Blanton, Wood, & Moorman, 1990). Students should always have a purpose for reading, whether they are reading aesthetically or efferently, whether reading a selection for the first time or the tenth.

When readers have a purpose for reading, comprehension of the selection they are reading is enhanced in three ways (Blanton et al., 1990). First, the purpose guides the reading process that students use. Having a purpose provides motivation and direction for reading as well as a mechanism students use for monitoring their reading. As they monitor their reading, students ask themselves whether they are fulfilling their purpose. Second, purpose setting activates a plan for teachers to use in teaching reading. They help students draw on background knowledge as they set purposes, consider strategies they might use as they read, and think about the structure of the text they are reading. Third, students are better able to sort out important from unimportant information as they read when they have a purpose for reading. Teachers direct students' attention to relevant concepts as they set purposes for reading and show them how to connect the concepts they are reading about to their background knowledge.

Planning for Reading.   Students often preview the reading selection as they prepare to read. They look through the selection and check its length, the reading difficulty of the selection, and the illustrations in order to judge the general suitability of the selection for themselves as readers. Previewing serves an important function as students connect their background knowledge, identify their purpose for reading, and take their first look at the selection.

Teachers set the guidelines for the reading experience. They explain how the book will be read—independently, in small groups, or as a class—and set the schedule for reading. Setting the schedule is especially important when students are reading a chapter book. Often teachers and students work together to create a 2- or 3-week schedule for reading and responding and then write the schedule on a calendar to which students can refer.

When students are preparing to read informational books, they preview the selection by flipping through the pages and noting section headings, illustrations, diagrams, and other charts. Sometimes they examine the table of contents to see how the book is organized or consult the index to locate specific information they want to read. They may also notice unfamiliar terminology and other words they can check in the glossary, ask a classmate or the teacher about, or look up in a dictionary.

Stage 2: Reading

Students read the book or other selection in the second stage. They use their knowledge of word identification, sight words, reading strategies and skills, and vocabulary while they read. Fluent readers are better able to understand what they are reading because they identify most words automatically and use decoding skills when necessary (LaBerge & Samuels, 1976). They also apply their knowledge of the structure of text as they create meaning. They continue reading as long as what they are reading fits the meaning they are constructing. When something doesn't make sense, fluent readers slow down, back up, and reread until they are making meaning again.

Students may read the entire selection or read only sections. When students are reading aesthetically, they usually read the entire selection, but when they are reading efferently, they may be searching for specific information and read only until they locate that information. Also, students may decide to put a book down if it does not capture their interest, if it is too difficult to read, or if it does not contain the information they are searching for. It is unrealistic to assume that students will always read entire selections or finish reading every book they begin.

Outside of school, readers usually read silently and independently. Sometimes, however, people listen as someone else reads. Young children often sit in a parent's lap and look at the illustrations as the parent reads a picture book aloud. Adults also listen to books read aloud on cassette tapes or CDs. In the classroom, teachers and students use five types of reading:

- Shared reading
- Guided reading
- Independent reading
- Buddy reading
- Reading aloud to students

See Chapter 4, "Emerging into Literacy," to read more about big books and how to use shared reading with young children.

Shared Reading.   Teachers use shared reading during literature focus units to introduce a book or other reading selection before the students read the selection with partners or individually (Fisher & Medvic, 2000). In this type of reading, students follow along as the teacher reads the selection aloud. Kindergarten teachers and other primary-grade teachers often use big books—enlarged versions of the selection—for shared reading (Holdaway, 1979). Students sit so that they can see the book, and they either listen to the teacher read aloud or join in and read along with the teacher. The teacher or a student points to each line of text as it is read to draw students' attention to the words, to show the direction of print on a page, and to highlight important concepts about letters, words, and sentences.

Teachers also use shared reading when students have individual copies of the reading selection. Students follow along in their copies as the teacher or another fluent reader reads aloud. This "first" reading is preparation for students so that they become familiar enough with the story line and the vocabulary that they can read the selection independently later during the literature focus unit.

When students are reading chapter books, shared reading is used as the main reading approach during the unit if students can't read the selection independently. The teacher and other fluent readers take turns reading aloud as students follow along in their copies of the selection. To ensure that all the students are following along in their copies of the book, teachers sometimes ask all students or a group of students to read aloud very softly or "mumble" along as they read aloud. Sometimes teachers read the first chapter or two of a chapter book together with the class, using shared reading, and then students use other types of reading as they read the rest of the book. Only students for whom the book is too difficult continue to use shared reading and read along with the teacher.

There are several variations of shared reading (Slaughter, 1993). One is choral reading, when students divide into groups to read poems aloud. Another is readers theatre, in which students read play scripts aloud. A third type of shared reading is the listening center, where students can listen to a book read aloud as they follow along in the book. Listening centers are a good way to provide additional reading practice to help students become fluent readers.

Guided Reading.   Teachers scaffold students' reading to enable them to develop and use reading skills and strategies in guided reading (Clay, 1991; Fountas & Pinnell, 1996, 2001). This type of reading is teacher directed and usually done in small groups with students who read at the same level or who use similar reading skills and strategies.

Selections used for guided reading should be written at students' instructional reading levels, that is, slightly beyond their ability to read the text independently or at their level of proximal development. Students usually read the selection silently, and if the selection is too difficult, shared reading might be a better approach. If the selection is too easy, then independent reading might be a better choice. Teachers often group and regroup students for guided reading so that the book selected is appropriate for all students in a group. The steps in guided reading, according to Fountas and Pinnell (1996), are shown in the Step by Step feature on page 116.

Guided reading is used in literature focus units. Teachers read the featured selection with students in small groups, which provides teachers with opportunities to demonstrate reading strategies, clarify misconceptions as students read, point out key vocabulary words, and take advantage of many teachable moments. The small-group arrangement also allows teachers to observe individual students as they read, monitor their comprehension, and informally assess their reading progress.

Independent Reading.   When students read independently, they read silently by themselves and at their own pace (Hornsby, Sukarna, & Parry, 1986; Taylor, 1993). For students to read independently, the reading selections must be at their reading level. Students read the featured selection independently during

Guided Reading

1. **Choose an appropriate book for the small group of students.**   The students should be able to read the book with 90–94% accuracy. Teachers collect copies of the book for each student in the group.

2. **Introduce the book to the group.**   Teachers show the cover, reading the title and author, and activating students' prior knowledge on a topic related to the book. They often use key vocabulary as they talk about the book, but they don't use vocabulary flash cards to drill students on new words before reading. Students also "picture walk" through the book, looking at the illustrations and talking about them.

3. **Have students read the book independently.**   Teachers provide support to students with decoding and reading strategies as needed. Students either read silently or "mumble" read softly. Teachers observe students as they read and assess their use of word-identification and comprehension strategies. They help individual students decode unfamiliar words, deal with unfamiliar sentence structures, and comprehend ideas presented in the text whenever they require assistance.

4. **Provide opportunities for students to respond to the book.**   Students talk about the book, ask questions, and relate it to others they have read, as in a grand conversation.

5. **Involve students in one or two teacher-directed exploring activities.**   Teachers involve students in strategy instruction, literary analysis, and word work activities. They review and reinforce the reading strategy students used in reading the selection, they explain genres, present information about text structures, and review vocabulary from the selection.

6. **Provide opportunities for independent reading.**   Teachers place the book in a book basket or in the classroom library so that students can reread it independently during reading workshop.

literature focus units, but this is often after they have already read the selection once or twice with assistance from the teacher. They also read related books from the text set independently as part of these units.

During reading workshop, students almost always read independently. They choose the books they want to read, and they need to learn how to choose books that are written at an appropriate level of difficulty. Even young children in kindergarten can do a variation of independent reading when they look at books, creating their own text to accompany the illustrations.

Independent reading is an important part of language arts instruction because it is the most authentic type of reading. This type of reading is what most

Buddy reading. *These two good friends like to read chapter books together during DEAR time (Drop Everything And Read, a 20-minute daily independent reading time). They choose the books together from the classroom library and take turns doing the reading. Their teacher has taught them several strategies for cooperative reading, so they help each other with unfamiliar words, stop reading when necessary to ask clarifying questions, and often make personal and literary connections to the story. Buddy reading is a good alternative to independent reading for students who are very social or students who don't like to read.*

people do when they read, and this is the way students develop a love of reading and come to think of themselves as readers. The reading selection, however, must be either at an appropriate level of difficulty or very familiar so that students can read it independently. Otherwise, teachers use one of the other four types of reading to support students and make it possible for them to participate in the reading experience.

Buddy Reading.   In buddy reading, students read or reread a selection with a classmate. Sometimes students read with buddies because it is an enjoyable social activity, and sometimes they read together to help each other. Often students can read selections together that neither one could read individually. By working together, they are often able to figure out unfamiliar words and talk out comprehension problems.

During literature focus units, students often reread the featured selection with buddies after the teacher has presented it using shared reading. Students read and reread books from the text set this way, too. Buddy reading is used less often during reading workshop, but students might decide to read a book together, especially if it is a book they both want to read and neither could read independently.

As teachers introduce buddy reading, they show students how to read with buddies and how to support each other as they read. Unless the teacher has explained and modeled the approach and taught students how to work collaboratively, buddy reading often deteriorates into the better reader reading aloud to the other student, and that is not the intention of this type of reading. Students need to take turns reading aloud to each other or read in unison. They often stop and help each other identify an unfamiliar word or take a minute or two at the end of each page to talk about what they have read. Buddy reading is a valuable way of providing the practice that beginning readers need to become fluent readers, and it is also an effective way to work with students with special learning needs and students who are learning English.

Reading Aloud to Students.   In kindergarten through eighth grade, teachers read aloud to students for a variety of purposes each day. During literature focus units, teachers read aloud featured selections that are appropriate for students' interest level but too difficult for students to read by themselves. Teachers also read aloud the featured selection if only one copy of the book is available. Sometimes it is appropriate to read the featured selection aloud before distributing copies for students to read with buddies or independently. When they read aloud, teachers model what good readers do and how good readers use reading strategies (Cochran-Smith, 1984).

During reading workshop, teachers also read aloud stories and other books to introduce students to literature they might not choose to read on their own. The reading-aloud component of reading workshop provides students with a shared social experience and an opportunity to talk about literature and reading. In addition, teachers read aloud books related to science, social studies, and other across-the-curriculum themes.

Reading aloud to students is not the same as round-robin reading, in which students take turns reading paragraphs aloud as the rest of the class listens. Round-robin reading has been used for reading chapter books aloud, but it is more commonly used for reading chapters in content-area textbooks, even though there are more effective ways to teach content-area information and read textbooks.

Round-robin reading is no longer recommended, for several reasons (Opitz & Rasinski, 1998). First, students should read fluently if they are going to read aloud to the class. When less capable readers read, their reading is often difficult to listen to and embarrassing to them personally. Less capable readers need reading practice, but performing in front of the entire class is not the most productive way for them to practice. They can read with buddies and in small groups during guided reading. Second, if the selection is easy enough for students to read aloud, they should read independently instead. During round-robin reading, many students follow along only just before it is their turn to read, so they don't do much reading. Third, round-robin reading is often tedious and boring, and students lose interest in reading.

The advantages and disadvantages of each type of reading are outlined in Figure 3–2.

Stage 3: Responding

Readers respond to their reading and continue to negotiate meaning in order to deepen their comprehension. Two ways for students to make tentative and exploratory comments immediately after reading are:

- Writing in reading logs
- Participating in grand conversations

FIGURE 3-2

Advantages and Disadvantages of the Five Types of Reading

Type	Advantages	Disadvantages
Shared Reading Teacher reads aloud while students follow along using individual copies of a book, a class chart, or a big book.	• Students have access to books they could not read independently. • Teachers model fluent reading. • Teachers model reading strategies. • A community of readers is developed.	• Multiple copies, a class chart, or a big book version of the text is needed. • Text may not be appropriate for all students. • Some students may not be interested in the text.
Guided Reading Teacher supports students as they read texts at their reading levels. Students are grouped homogeneously.	• Teachers provide direction and scaffolding. • Students practice reading strategies. • Students read independently. • Students practice the prediction cycle.	• Multiple copies of the text are needed. • Teachers control the reading experience. • Some students may not be interested in the text.
Independent Reading Students read a text independently and often choose the text themselves.	• Students develop responsibility and ownership. • Students self-select texts. • Readers have a more authentic experience.	• Students may need assistance to read the text. • Teachers have little involvement or control.
Buddy Reading Two students read or reread a text together.	• Students are encouraged to collaborate. • Students reread familiar texts. • Students develop reading fluency. • Students talk about texts to deepen comprehension.	• Teachers' involvement and control are limited. • One student may depend on the other to do the reading.
Reading Aloud to Students Teacher or other fluent reader reads aloud to students.	• Students have access to books they could not read independently. • Teachers model fluent reading. • Teachers model reading strategies. • A community of readers is developed. • Only one copy of the text is required.	• Students have no opportunity to read. • Text may not be appropriate for some students. • Some students may not be interested in the text.

Writing in Reading Logs.   Students write and draw thoughts and feelings about what they have read in reading logs. Rosenblatt (1978) explains that as students write about what they have read, they unravel their thinking and at the same time elaborate on and clarify their responses. When students read informational books, they sometimes write in reading logs just as they do after reading stories and poems, but at other times, they make notes of important information or draw charts and diagrams to use in theme cycles.

To learn more about reading logs, see Chapter 6, "Personal Writing."

Students usually make reading logs by stapling together 10 to 12 sheets of paper at the beginning of a literature focus unit or reading workshop. At the beginning of a theme cycle, students make learning logs to write in during the unit. They decorate the covers in keeping with the theme of the unit, write entries related to their reading, and make notes related to what they are learning in minilessons.

Students usually choose their own topics for reading log entries, but at times, teachers offer a list of prompts from which students may choose. Students are never expected to respond to all prompts. Many teachers make a list of prompts to hang in the classroom or for students to place in their language arts notebooks. Possible prompts include:

I really don't understand . . .

I like/dislike (character) because . . .

This book reminds me of . . .

(Character) reminds me of myself because . . .

I think (character) is feeling . . .

I wonder why . . .

(Event) makes me think about the time I . . .

I like this quote because . . .

If I were (character), I'd . . .

I noticed that (the author) is . . .

I predict that . . .

These prompts are open-ended and allow students to make connections to their own lives. Sometimes, teachers ask a specific question to direct students' attention to some aspect of a book. For example, as upper-grade students are reading Lois Lowry's Newbery Medal book *The Giver* (1993), teachers often ask questions like these:

After Chapter 2	*Does Jonas's community seem more perfect than ours?*
After Chapter 6	*What assignment do you think Jonas will get?*
After Chapter 11	*Would you like to have Jonas's assignment?*
After Chapter 19	*What does "release" mean?*
After Chapter 23	*What happened to Jonas and Gabe?*

These questions, like the prompts listed earlier, are open-ended and ask for students' interpretations—even the questions for Chapters 19 and 23, which may at first seem like literal questions.

Teachers monitor students' entries, often reading and responding to those entries. Because these journals are learning tools, teachers rarely correct students' spellings. They focus their responses on the students' ideas, but they expect students to spell the title of the book, the names of characters, and high-frequency words accurately. At the end of the unit, teachers review students' work and often grade the journals based on whether students completed all the entries and on the quality of the ideas in their entries.

Participating in Grand Conversations.   Students also talk about the text with classmates in discussions called grand conversations. Peterson and Eeds (1990) explain that in this type of discussion, students share their personal responses and tell what they liked about the selection. After sharing personal reactions, they shift the focus to "puzzle over what the author has written and . . . share what it is they find revealed" (p. 61). Often students make connections between the selection and their own lives, the world around them, or other literature they have read. If they are reading a chapter book, they also make predictions about what will happen in the next chapter.

For more information about grand conversations, turn to Chapter 8, "Sustaining Talk in the Classroom."

Martinez and Roser (1995) have researched students' grand conversations and found that students often talk about story events or characters and explore the themes of the story but less often delve into the author's craft to explore the way the author structured the book, the arrangement of text and illustrations on the page, or the author's use of figurative or repetitive language. The researchers call these three conversation directions experience, message, and object. They suggest that stories help to shape students' talk about books and that some books lend themselves to talk about message and others to talk about experience or object. Stories with dramatic plots or stories that present a problem to which students can relate, such as *Chrysanthemum* (Henkes, 1991), *Jeremy Thatcher, Dragon Hatcher* (Coville, 1991), and *Hatchet* (Paulsen, 1987), focus the conversation on the book as experience. Multilayered stories or books in which main characters deal with dilemmas, such as *Smoky Night* (Bunting, 1994), *Sarah, Plain and Tall* (MacLachlan, 1985), and *The Giver* (Lowry, 1993), focus the conversation on the message. Books with distinctive structures or language features, such as *Black and White* (Macaulay, 1990), *Tuesday* (Wiesner, 1991), and *Maniac Magee* (Spinelli, 1990), focus the conversation on the object.

Teachers often participate in grand conversations, but they act as interested participants, not as leaders. Although the talk is primarily among the students, teachers ask open-ended questions regarding things they are genuinely interested in learning more about and share information in response to questions students ask. Possible questions include (Daniels, 1994):

Which character is most like you?

What would you have done if . . . ?

What did that make you think of?

In the past, many discussions were "gentle inquisitions" during which students recited answers to factual questions teachers asked about books students were reading (Eeds & Wells, 1989). Teachers dominated the talk and asked these questions to determine whether students had read the assignment. In contrast, the focus in grand conversations is on clarifying and deepening students' understanding or comprehension of the selection they have read.

Grand conversations can be held with the whole class or with small groups. Young children usually meet as a class, whereas older students often prefer to talk with classmates in small groups. When students get together as a class, there is a feeling of community, and the teacher can be part of the group. When students meet in small groups, students have more opportunities to participate in the discussion and share their responses, but fewer viewpoints are expressed in each group and teachers must move around, spending only a few minutes with each group. Some teachers compromise and have students begin their discussions in small groups and then come together as a class and have the groups share what they discussed.

Stage 4: Exploring

Students go back into the text to explore it more analytically. They participate in some of these activities:

- Rereading the selection
- Examining the author's craft
- Focusing on new vocabulary words
- Participating in minilessons

Rereading the Selection.   Through repeated readings, students reread the selection and think again about what they have read. Each time they reread, students benefit in specific ways (Yaden, 1988). They enrich their comprehension and make further connections between the selection and their own lives or between the selection and other literature they have read. Students often reread a selection several times. If the teacher used shared reading to read the selection with students in the reading stage, students might reread it with a buddy once or twice, read it with their parents, and after these experiences, read it independently.

To learn more about the elements of story structure, turn to Chapter 9, "Reading and Writing Stories."

Examining the Author's Craft.   Teachers plan exploring activities to focus students' attention on the structure of the text and the literary language that authors use (Eeds & Peterson, 1995). Students notice opposites in the story, use storyboards (pages of the book cut apart and glued on tagboard cards) to sequence the events in the story, and make story maps to visually represent the plot, characters, and other story elements (Bromley, 1996). Another way students learn about the structure of stories is by writing books based on the selection they have read. Students write sequels, telling what happened to the characters after the story ends. Some stories, such as *Jumanji* (Van Allsburg, 1981), end in a way that seems to invite students to create a sequel. Students also write innovations, or new versions, for the selection by following the sentence pattern. First graders often write innovations for Bill Martin Jr.'s *Brown Bear, Brown Bear, What Do You See?* (1983) and *Polar Bear, Polar Bear, What Do You Hear?* (1992), and older students write innovations for *Alexander and the Terrible, Horrible, No Good, Very Bad Day* (Viorst, 1977).

Teachers share information about the author of the featured selection and introduce other books by that author. Sometimes teachers have students compare several books written by a particular author. To focus on literary language, students often reread favorite excerpts in a read-around and write memorable quotes on story quilts that they create.

When students are reading picture books, they also learn about illustration and the illustrator's craft. Students can learn about the media and techniques the artist used and experiment with the media themselves. They can examine the illustrations using storyboards to find out about the illustrator's stylistic choices and think more deeply about the story (Kiefer, 1994, 1995).

Focusing on Words.   Teachers and students add "important" words to word walls after reading and post these word walls in the classroom. Students refer to the word walls when they write, using these words for a variety of activities during the exploring stage. Researchers emphasize the importance of immersing students in words, teaching strategies for learning words, and personalizing word learning (Blachowicz & Fisher, 1996). Students make word clusters and posters to highlight particular words. They also make word chains, sort words, create a semantic feature analysis to analyze related words, and play word games.

Teachers choose words from word walls to use in minilessons, too. Words are used to teach phonics skills, such as beginning sounds, rhyming words, vowel patterns, *r*-controlled vowels, and syllabication (Bear, Invernizzi, Templeton, & Johnston, 2004). Other concepts, such as root words and affixes, compound words, and metaphors, can also be taught using examples from word walls. Teachers often teach a minilesson on a particular concept, such as the -*ly* suffix, because five or six words representing the concept are listed on the word wall.

Teaching Minilessons.   Teachers present minilessons on reading procedures, concepts, strategies, and skills during the exploring stage. A list of topics for minilessons about the reading process is presented on page 124. In a minilesson, teachers introduce the topic and make connections between the topic and examples in the featured selection. In this way, students are better able to connect the information teachers are presenting with their own reading process. Students need to learn about the process approach to reading—both aesthetic and efferent—and about ways to develop interpretations.

Stage 5: Applying

Readers move beyond comprehension to deepen their interpretations, reflect on their understanding, and value the reading experience in this last stage of the reading process. Students build on their reading, the responses they made immediately after reading, and the exploring activities as they create projects. These projects can involve reading, writing, talk and drama, viewing, visually representing, or research, and may take many forms, including murals, readers theatre scripts, oral presentations, and individual books and reports, as well as reading other books by the same author. A list of projects is presented in Figure 3–3. The wide variety of project options offers students choices and takes into account Howard Gardner's (1993) theory of multiple intelligences, that students have preferred ways of learning and showing knowledge. Usually students choose which projects they will do rather than working as a class on the same project. Sometimes, however, the class decides to work together on a project.

Teaching the Reading Process

Teachers apply the five-stage reading process in the reading lessons they teach, whether they organize instruction into literature focus units, literature circles, reading workshop, or theme cycles. Successful language arts instruction doesn't just happen (Hickman, 1995); teachers bring students together as

Check Chapter 5, "Looking Closely at Words," to read more about word walls and teaching vocabulary.

Piecing a Lesson Together

Topics on the Reading and Writing Processes

Procedures	Concepts	Strategies and Skills
The Reading Process		
Choose books to read	The reading process	Decode words
Use the Goldilocks strategy	Aesthetic reading	Predict
Listen to books read aloud	Efferent reading	Confirm
Do shared reading	Comprehension	Visualize
Do buddy reading		Retell
Do guided reading		Summarize
Do independent reading		Connect to literature
Respond in reading logs		Connect to life
Participate in grand		Identify with characters
conversations		Monitor
Create projects		
The Writing Process		
Choose a topic	The writing process	Gather ideas
Cluster	Functions of writing	Organize ideas
Quickwrite	Writing forms	Draft
Participate in writing groups	Audience	*Revise*
Proofread	Proofreaders' marks	
Make hardcover books		Edit
Write "All About the Author"		Identify and correct spelling
pages		errors
Share published writing		Use capital letters correctly
		Use punctuation marks
		correctly
		Value the composition

Please visit the Companion Website at **www.prenhall.com/tompkins** for a second fully realized minilesson.

---

a community of learners and teach them the procedures for various language arts activities. Each pattern of practice—literature focus unit, literature circle, reading workshop, or theme cycle—requires that teachers carefully structure activities, provide appropriate books and other materials, and create time and space for students to work. Teachers, too, assume a variety of roles as they scaffold students' learning.

In Literature Focus Units.   Students move through the five stages of the reading process as they read a book in a literature focus unit. A sixth-grade

Turn back to Chapter 2, "Teaching and Assessing Language Arts," to learn more about literature focus units and the other three patterns of practice.

REVISING

Minilesson

Ms. Yarborough Introduces Revising to the Third Grade

1. **Introduce the Topic**

   Ms. Yarborough names the five stages of the writing process as she points to the writing process charts hanging in the classroom. She explains that the focus today is on revising and points to that chart. She reminds students that the purpose of revising is to make their writing better and explains that writers add, delete, substitute, and move words and sentences as they revise.

2. **Share Examples**

   Ms. Yarborough shares this paragraph on the chalkboard and explains that she wrote it because they are studying about amphibians:

   Amphibians live in water and on land. They live in water when they are babies. They live on land when they grow up. Frogs are some amphibians.

   She reads the paragraph aloud and asks students to help her make it better by adding, deleting, substituting, and moving words and sentences.

3. **Provide Information**

   Students work with Ms. Yarborough to revise the paragraph. They add words and sentences and reorder sentences in the paragraph. As students make suggestions, Ms. Yarborough writes the changes on the chalkboard. Here is the revised paragraph:

   Amphibians live part of their lives in water and part on land. Frogs, toads and salamanders are amphibians. They hatch from eggs in water, grow up, and live on land when they are adults. This process of changing is called metamorphosis.

4. **Supervise Practice**

   Ms. Yarborough divides students into small groups and gives each group another paragraph about amphibians to revise. Students work together to make revisions, using blue pens and making marks as Ms. Yarborough demonstrated. Ms. Yarborough circulates as students work, and then students share their rough drafts and revised paragraphs with the class.

5. **Reflect on Learning**

   Ms. Yarborough asks students to compare the rough drafts and revised paragraphs and decide which are better. Then students brainstorm a list of reasons why revision is important. Their list includes: "The writing is more interesting," "It's more fun to read," and "The words are more scientific."

class read *Bunnicula: A Rabbit-Tale of Mystery* (Howe & Howe, 1979), a story of a family and its unusual pets—a dog, a cat, and a bunny that is believed to be a vampire. The teacher used a book box with a stuffed rabbit dressed like a vampire, plastic vegetables that had been painted white, and a children's version of the Dracula story. Students used shared and independent reading to read the chapter book; then they responded to their reading and participated in exploration activities. The teacher presented minilessons on homophones (e.g., *steak–stake*) and portmanteau words (*bunny + dracula = Bunnicula; smoke + fog = smog*), and shared information about the author, James Howe.

FIGURE 3–3

Projects for the Applying Stage of the Reading Process

Visually Representing Projects

1. Experiment with the illustration techniques (e.g., collage, watercolor, line drawing) used in a favorite book.
2. Make a diagram or model using information from a book.
3. Create a collage to represent the theme of a book.
4. Design a book jacket for a book, laminate it, and place it on the book.
5. Make a story can or box. Decorate a coffee can or cardboard box using scenes from a book. Fill the can with objects and quotes related to the book.
6. Construct a shoe box or other miniature scene of an episode for a favorite book (or use a larger box to construct a diorama).
7. Make a set of storyboards with one card for each episode or chapter. Include an illustration and a paragraph describing the section of the book.
8. Make a map or relief map of a book's setting or something related to the book.
9. Construct a mobile illustrating a book.
10. Make a comic strip to illustrate the sequence of events in a book.
11. Prepare bookmarks for a book and distribute them to classmates.
12. Use or prepare illustrations of the events in the story for clothesline props to use in retelling the story.
13. Make a mural of the book.
14. Make an open-mind portrait of a character in the story.
15. Create a Venn diagram to compare the book and film versions of a story.
16. Make a data chart to analyze several versions of a story or a text set of books by one author.
17. Create a quilt about a book.
18. Draw a graphic organizer of the main ideas in an informational book.
19. Make a plot profile of the book.
20. Make a sketch-to-stretch poster.

Writing Projects

21. Write a review of a favorite book for a class review file.
22. Write a postcard or letter about a book to a classmate, friend, or pen pal.
23. Write another episode or a sequel for a book.
24. Create a newspaper with news stories and advertisements based on characters and episodes from a book.
25. Write and mail a letter to a favorite author.
26. Write a simulated letter from one book character to another.
27. Copy five quotable quotes from a book and list them on a poster.
28. Make a scrapbook about the book. Label all items in the scrapbook, and write a short description of the most interesting ones.
29. Create a found poem, or write a poem related to the book.
30. Write a time line or lifeline related to the book, the era, a character, or the author.
31. Write a business letter to a company or organization requesting information on a topic related to the book.
32. Keep a simulated journal from the perspective of one character in the book.
33. Write a dictionary defining specialized vocabulary in a book.
34. Rewrite the story from another point of view.
35. Make a class collaboration book. Each child dictates or writes one page.
36. Prepare a multigenre project.
37. Create an alphabet book on a topic related to the book.
38. Make a cube with information about the book or a related topic.

FIGURE 3–3

Continued

Reading Projects

39. Read another book by the same author.
40. Read another book by the same illustrator.
41. Read another book on the same theme.
42. Read another book in the same genre.
43. Read and compare two versions of a story.
44. Read a biography about the author or illustrator of the book.

Viewing Projects

45. View a video version of the book.
46. Compare the illustrations in several versions of a book. (Multiple versions of folktales are available.)
47. Analyze the illustrator's craft.
48. Choose a piece of art (e.g., painting or sculpture) that represents the book and share the art with the class.

Talk and Drama Projects

49. Present a book talk about the book to the class.
50. Read a poem that complements the book aloud to the class. Place a copy of the poem in the book.
51. Give a readers theatre presentation of a book.
52. Create a song about a book, or choose a tune for a poem and sing the song for the class.
53. Write a script and present a play about a book.
54. Make puppets and use them in retelling a book.
55. Dress as a character from the book and answer questions from classmates about the character.
56. Write and present a rap about the book.
57. Videotape a commercial for a book.

Research Projects

58. Interview someone in the community who is knowledgeable about a topic related to the book.
59. Research the author or illustrator of the book on the Internet and compile information in a chart or summary. Post the chart or summary in the library center.
60. Research a topic related to the book. Present the information in an oral or written report.

Students also constructed projects to apply their learning. Figure 3–4 shows how this literature focus unit fits into the five stages of the reading process.

In Literature Circles.   Students use the five stages of the reading process as they read self-selected books in literature circles. In a seventh-grade classroom, for example, one group of students chose to read Christopher Paul Curtis's Newbery Award–winning book, *Bud, Not Buddy* (1999), a Depression-era story of a spunky, motherless boy who escapes from a bad foster home to search for his father. After students chose the book they wanted to read, they got together to set the schedule and make plans for reading and discussing the book. Then students read the book independently or with buddies and met periodically as a small group with the teacher to discuss the book. During these meetings, students also examined vocabulary words and explored Bud's character traits. After they finished reading *Bud, Not Buddy,* students prepared a

---

FIGURE 3–4

How the Reading Process Fits into the Four Patterns of Practice

	Sixth-Grade Literature Focus Unit on *Bunnicula: A Rabbit-Tale of Mystery*	Seventh-Grade Literature Circles for *Bud, Not Buddy*
Prereading	The teacher shares a box of objects related to the book, and students make predictions about the story.	Students form a small group to read the book and set a schedule for reading and discussing the book. They also choose roles and clarify assignments.
Reading	The teacher uses shared reading and independent reading alternately to read the chapter book.	Students read independently or with a buddy and prepare their assignment for the group meeting.
Responding	Students write in reading logs and participate in grand conversations to talk about the story and make connections between the story and their own lives.	Students meet to talk about their reading, and the teacher often participates. They talk about the book, ask questions, and deepen their understanding of the story.
Exploring	Students write important words on the word wall and use the words in word sorts and other activities. The teacher shares information about author James Howe and teaches minilessons on characterization, homophones, and portmanteau words.	At the group meeting, students share the assignments they have prepared with classmates, including important vocabulary words, quotes, and character sketches.
Applying	Students create projects from the list of choices posted in the classroom. Some students read another book by James Howe, and others write letters to the author, write and perform a play about a favorite episode, make book boxes, and research Dracula and vampires.	Students prepare a project—a character cluster—to share with classmates at the class meeting when each group presents its book.

---

project—a character cluster—to share with classmates during a class meeting. Figure 3–4 shows how these activities also fit into the five stages of the reading process.

In Reading Workshop.   Although the focus in reading workshop is on reading and responding to books, students are also involved in the other stages of the reading process, but to a lesser degree. In a fourth-grade classroom, for example, students used the Goldilocks strategy to choose books from the classroom library. After getting the teacher's approval, students read the book they had chosen independently. They stopped periodically to write in reading logs and talk about the books they were reading in conferences with the teacher. If students especially liked the book, they created a project to apply and extend

FIGURE 3-4

Continued

	Reading Workshop in a Fourth-Grade Classroom	***It's a Good Thing There Are Insects* During a Second-Grade Theme Cycle on Insects**
Prereading	Students use the Goldilocks strategy to choose books from the classroom library to read, and have the teacher approve their choice.	Students build background about insects through a variety of theme-cycle activities, and the teacher and students "text walk" through the book before reading.
Reading	Students read independently the books they have chosen.	The teacher and students read the book three times. First, they use shared reading; next, students reread the book with buddies; and then they read the book independently.
Responding	Students write in reading logs and note unfamiliar words and favorite quotes. They also conference with the teacher, individually or in small groups, to discuss the book they are reading.	Students discuss the book in an instructional conversation and then brainstorm a list of reasons why insects are beneficial.
Exploring	Teachers teach minilessons to individuals, small groups, or the whole class on reading concepts, procedures, strategies, and skills. Then students apply what they have learned to books they are reading.	The teacher teaches a series of minilessons on informational books, including the difference between stories and informational books, features of an informational book, and how to read efferently.
Applying	Students share the books they have read at a whole-class sharing session, and sometimes they create and share projects related to the book.	Students write their own informational books about insects, incorporating many of the features of informational books.

their learning. Students also talked about the books they read during sharing time and shared their completed projects with classmates. The teacher also taught minilessons during which students learned reading concepts, procedures, strategies, and skills. These activities are also summarized according to the five stages of the reading process in Figure 3–4.

In Theme Cycles.   Teachers often coordinate the books students are reading with topics they are studying during theme cycles. For example, during a theme cycle on insects in a second-grade classroom, students read *It's a Good Thing There Are Insects* (Fowler, 1990), and they moved through all five stages of the reading process. What students were learning during the theme cycle built background knowledge that they used as they read the book. Before beginning to read, the teacher and students did a text walk, during which they looked through the book and noted key features; then they read the easy-to-read informational book using shared reading and read it a second time with reading buddies. The third time they read it independently. After students read the book the first time, they participated in a grand conversation and brainstormed a list of reasons why it's a good thing there are insects. The teacher also used this book to teach mini-lessons about the differences between stories and informational books. *It's a Good Thing There Are Insects* is a good example of an informational book because it is illustrated with photographs and it contains a glossary and an index. Later, students wrote their own informational books about insects and used many of the features of informational books in their own writing. Figure 3–4 shows how these activities fit into the five stages of the reading process.

Meeting the Needs of Every Student.   Reading process activities are flexible and can be adapted to help every student become a more successful reader. For students with limited experiences or for those who are learning English as a second language, more time should be spent in the prereading stage. During reading, teachers often read books aloud or use shared reading when working with students who are not yet fluent readers. Many easy-to-read stories and informational books that are well written and enticing to students are currently available, so it is possible to have several books at different reading levels on almost any topic. During the responding stage, students can draw rather than write their responses in reading logs, and grand conversations take on an even greater importance for students who need to clarify misconceptions about their reading. Students can reread the text with a buddy during the exploring stage. The fifth stage is important for all students, and many students who find reading difficult are very successful in creating art projects and dramatic productions. Suggestions for adapting the reading process to meet the needs of every student are presented on page 131.

THE WRITING PROCESS

The focus in the writing process is on what students think and do as they write; it is writer-centered (Gillet & Beverly, 2001). The five stages are prewriting, drafting, revising, editing, and publishing, and the key features of each stage are shown in the LA Essentials box on page 132. The labeling and numbering of the stages does not mean, however, that the writing process is a linear series of neatly packaged categories. Research has shown that the process involves recurring cycles, and labeling is only an aid to identifying and discussing writing activities (Barnes, Morgan, & Weinhold, 1997; Graves, 1994; Perl, 1994). In the classroom, the stages merge and recur as students write.

Stage 1: Prewriting

Prewriting is the getting-ready-to-write stage. The traditional notion that writers have a topic completely thought out and ready to flow onto the page is ridiculous. If writers wait for ideas to fully develop, they may wait forever. Instead, writers begin tentatively—talking, reading, writing—to discover what they know and decide what direction they want to take (Flower & Hayes, 1994). Prewriting has probably been the most neglected stage in the writing process; how-

Meeting the Needs of Every Student

How Do Teachers Adapt the Reading Process?

Teachers add more support during the reading process so that every student can be successful. Try these suggestions:

Stage 1: Prereading

- Spend more time activating background knowledge.
- Use concrete experiences, multimedia presentations, and photos.
- Introduce important vocabulary related to the topic, but not necessarily the vocabulary in the text.
- Do a text walk to preview the book.

Stage 2: Reading

- Read books aloud.
- Use shared reading or buddy reading.
- Use guided reading.
- Have students listen to the book at the listening center.
- Use easy-to-read books on the same topic.
- Break the reading time into smaller chunks.
- Provide more challenging alternative texts.

Stage 3: Responding

- Have students draw responses instead of writing in reading logs.
- Take time in grand conversations to clarify misconceptions.

Stage 4: Exploring

- Role-play important events in the book.
- Have students reread the text with a buddy.
- Teach minilessons to individual students and small groups of students.

Stage 5: Applying

- Encourage students to create art projects.
- Encourage students to present dramatic productions.
- Set out clear expectations about the projects students develop.
- Encourage students to pursue projects that interest and challenge them.

ever, it is as crucial to writers as a warm-up is to athletes. Murray (1982) believes that at least 70% of writing time should be spent in prewriting. During the prewriting stage, students:

- Choose a topic
- Consider purpose, form, and audience
- Generate and organize ideas for writing

Essentials

Key Features of the Writing Process

Stage 1: Prewriting

- Students write on topics based on their own experiences.
- Students engage in rehearsal activities before writing.
- Students identify the audience for whom they will write.
- Students identify the purpose of the writing activity.
- Students choose an appropriate genre or form for their compositions based on audience and purpose.

Stage 2: Drafting

- Students write a rough draft.
- Students mark their writing as a rough draft.
- Students emphasize content rather than mechanics.

Stage 3: Revising

- Students reread their own writing.
- Students share their writing in writing groups.
- Students participate constructively in discussions about classmates' writing.
- Students make changes in their compositions to reflect the reactions and comments of both teacher and classmates.
- Between the first and final drafts, students make substantive rather than only minor changes.

Stage 4: Editing

- Students proofread their own compositions.
- Students help proofread classmates' compositions.
- Students increasingly identify and correct their own mechanical errors.
- Students meet with the teacher for a final editing.

Stage 5: Publishing

- Students make the final copy of their writing, often using word processing.
- Students publish their writing in an appropriate form.
- Students share their finished writing with an appropriate audience.
- Students sit in the author's chair to share their writing.

Choosing a Topic.   Choosing a topic for writing can be a stumbling block for students who have become dependent on teachers to supply topics. For years, teachers have supplied topics by suggesting gimmicky story starters and relieving students of the "burden" of topic selection. Often, these "creative" topics stymied students, who were forced to write on topics they knew little about or had no interest in. Graves (1976) calls this "writing welfare." Instead, students need to choose their own writing topics.

Some students complain that they do not know what to write about, but teachers can help them brainstorm a list of three, four, or five topics and then identify the one topic they are most interested in and know the most about. Students who feel they cannot generate any writing topics are often surprised that they have so many options. Then, through prewriting activities, students talk, draw, read, and even write to develop information about their topics.

Asking students to choose their own topics for writing doesn't mean that teachers never give writing assignments; teachers do provide general guidelines. Sometimes they may specify the writing form, and at other times, they may establish the function, but students should choose their own specific content.

Considering Purpose.   As students prepare to write, they need to think about their purpose for writing. Are they writing to entertain? to inform? to persuade? Understanding the purpose of a piece of writing is important because it influences other decisions students make about audience and form. When students have no purpose in mind other than to complete the assignment, their writing is usually lackluster—without a strong voice or controlling idea.

Considering Audience.   Students may write primarily for themselves—to express and clarify their ideas and feelings—or they may write for others. Possible audiences include classmates, younger children, parents, foster grandparents, children's authors, and pen pals. Other audiences are more distant and less well known. For example, students write letters to businesses to request information, write articles for the local newspaper, and compose stories and poems for publication in literary magazines.

Children's writing is influenced by their sense of audience. Britton, Burgess, Martin, McLeod, and Rosen define sense of audience as "the manner in which the writer expresses a relationship with the reader in respect to the writer's understanding" (1975, pp. 65–66). Students adapt their writing to fit their audience, just as they vary their speech to meet the needs of the people who are listening to them.

Considering Form.   One of the most important considerations is the form the writing will take: a story? a letter? a poem? a journal entry? Writing activities can be handled in any one of these ways. As part of a theme cycle on hermit crabs, for instance, students write a story or a poem about a hermit crab, write a report on hermit crabs with information about how they obtain shells to live in, or write a description of the pet hermit crabs in the classroom. During the elementary grades, students learn to use six genres as they write descriptions, directions, comparisons, poems, learning logs, e-mail messages, stories, and letters. Figure 3–5 explains the six genres and lists some writing activities exemplifying each one.

Through reading and writing, students develop a strong sense of these genres and how they are structured. Langer (1985) found that by third grade, students responded in distinctly different ways to story- and report-writing

FIGURE 3-5

Writing Genres

Genre	Purpose	Activities
Descriptive Writing	Children become careful observers and choose precise language when they use description. They take notice of sensory details and learn to make comparisons (metaphors and similes) in order to make their writing more powerful.	Character sketches Comparisons Descriptive paragraphs Descriptive sentences Five-senses poems Found poems Observations
Informational Writing	Children collect and synthesize information for informative writing. This writing is objective, and reports are the most common type of informative writing. Children use informational writing to give directions, sequence steps, compare one thing to another, explain causes and effects, or describe problems and solutions.	Alphabet books Autobiographies Biographies Data charts Dictionaries Directions Interviews Posters Reports Summaries
Journals and Letters	Children write to themselves and to specific, known audiences in journals and letters. Their writing is personal and often less formal than other genres. They share news, explore new ideas, and record notes. Letters and envelopes require special formatting, and children learn these formats during the primary grades.	Business letters Courtesy letters E-mail messages Friendly letters Learning logs Personal journals Postcards Reading logs
Persuasive Writing	Persuasion is winning someone to your viewpoint or cause. The three ways people are persuaded are by appeals to logic, moral character, and emotion. Children present their position clearly and then support it with examples and evidence.	Advertisements Book and movie reviews Persuasive letters Persuasive posters
Poetry Writing	Children create word pictures and play with rhyme and other stylistic devices as they create poems. As children experiment with poetry, they learn that poetic language is vivid and powerful but concise, and they learn that poems can be arranged in different ways on a page.	Acrostic poems Cinquain poems Color poems Diamante poems Five-senses poems Found poems Free verse Haiku "I am" poems "If I were . . ." poems "I wish . . ." poems Riddles
Story Writing	Children retell familiar stories, develop sequels for stories they have read, write stories called personal narratives about events in their own lives, and create original stories. They include a beginning, middle, and end in the narratives they write. In the beginning, they introduce the characters, identify a problem, and interest readers in the story. In the middle, the problem becomes worse or additional roadblocks are set up to thwart the main character as he/she attempts to solve the problem. In the end, the problem is resolved.	Original short stories Personal narratives Retellings of stories Sequels to stories Scripts of stories

assignments; they organized the writing differently and included varied kinds of information and elaboration. Similarly, Hidi and Hildyard (1983) found that elementary students could differentiate between stories and persuasive essays. Because children are clarifying the distinctions between various writing forms during the elementary grades, it is important that teachers use the correct terminology and not label all children's writing "stories."

Decisions about purpose, audience, and form influence one another. For example, if the function is to entertain, an appropriate form might be a story, poem, or script, and these three forms look very different on a piece of paper. Whereas a story is written in the traditional block format, scripts and poems have unique page arrangements. Scripts are written with the character's name and a colon, and the dialogue is set off. Action and dialogue, rather than description, carry the story line in a script. In contrast, poems have unique formatting considerations, and each word and phrase is chosen to convey a maximum amount of information.

Gathering and Organizing Ideas.   Students engage in activities to gather and organize ideas for writing. Graves (1994) calls what writers do to prepare for writing "rehearsal" activities. When students read books, take field trips, view videos and CDs, and dramatize stories, for example, they are participating in rehearsal activities because they are building and activating background knowledge. Just before beginning to write, students participate in other types of rehearsal activities.

Young children use drawing to gather and organize ideas for writing. Primary-grade teachers notice that students often draw before they write, and, thinking that the children are eating dessert before the meat and vegetables, the teachers may insist that they write first. But many young children cannot because they don't know what to write until they see what they draw (Dyson, 1986).

The most important way middle- and upper-grade students prepare for writing is by making clusters—weblike diagrams—in which they write the topic in a center circle and draw out rays for each main idea (Rico, 1983). Then they add details and other information on rays drawn out from each main idea. Through clustering, students organize their ideas for writing. Clustering is a better prewriting strategy than outlining because it is nonlinear.

Stage 2: Drafting

Students write and refine their compositions through a series of drafts. During the drafting stage, students focus on getting their ideas down on paper (Gillet & Beverly, 2001). Just as writers do not begin writing with their compositions already composed in their minds, students begin with tentative ideas developed through prewriting activities. The drafting stage is the time to pour out ideas, with little concern about spelling, punctuation, and other mechanical aspects of writing.

When students write their rough drafts, they write on every other line to leave space for revisions (Lane, 1993). They use arrows to move sections of text, cross-outs to delete sections, and scissors and tape to cut apart and rearrange text, just as adult writers do. They write on only one side of a sheet of paper so that it can be cut apart or rearranged. Because word processors are available in many elementary classrooms, revising, with all its shifting and deleting text, is much easier. However, for students who handwrite their compositions, the wide spacing is crucial. Teachers might make small *x*s on every other line of students' papers as a reminder to skip lines as students draft their compositions.

Students label their drafts by writing "Rough Draft" in ink at the top of the paper or by stamping them with a ROUGH DRAFT stamp. This label indicates to the writer, other students, parents, and administrators that the composition is a draft in which the emphasis is on content, not mechanics. It also explains why the teacher has not graded the paper or marked mechanical errors.

During drafting, students may need to modify their earlier decisions about purpose, audience, and, especially, the form their writing will take. For example, a composition that began as a story may be transformed into a report, a letter, or a poem if the new format allows the student to communicate more effectively. The process of modifying earlier decisions continues into the revising stage.

As students write rough drafts, it is important not to emphasize correct spelling and neatness. In fact, pointing out mechanical errors during the drafting stage sends students a message that mechanical correctness is more important than content (Sommers, 1994). Later, during editing, students can clean up mechanical errors and put their composition into a neat, final form.

Stage 3: Revising

During the revising stage, writers clarify and refine ideas in their compositions. Students often break the writing process cycle as soon as they complete a rough draft, believing that once they have jotted down their ideas, the writing task is complete. Experienced writers, however, know that they must turn to others for reactions and revise on the basis of these comments (Sommers, 1994). Revision is not just polishing; it is meeting the needs of readers by adding, substituting, deleting, and rearranging material. The word *revision* means "seeing again," and in this stage, writers see their compositions again with the help of their classmates and teacher. Activities in the revising stage are:

- Rereading the rough draft
- Sharing the rough draft in a writing group
- Revising on the basis of feedback
- Conferencing with the teacher

Rereading the Rough Draft.   After finishing the rough draft, writers need to distance themselves from it for a day or two, then reread it from a fresh perspective, as a reader might. As they reread, students make changes—adding, substituting, deleting, and moving—and place question marks by sections that need work. It is these trouble spots that students ask for help with in their writing groups.

Sharing in Writing Groups.   Students meet in writing groups to share their compositions with classmates. Because writing must meet the needs of readers, feedback is crucial. Mohr (1984) identifies four general functions of writing groups: to offer the writer choices; to provide the writer with group members' responses, feelings, and thoughts; to show different possibilities in revising; and to speed up revising. Writing groups provide a scaffold in which teachers and classmates talk about plans and strategies for writing and revising (Calkins, 1994). The Step by Step feature on page 137 describes the procedures for writing groups.

Writing Groups

Step
by
Step

1. **The writer reads.** Students take turns reading their compositions aloud to the group. All students listen politely, thinking about compliments and suggestions they will make after the writer finishes reading. Only the writer looks at the composition, because when classmates and the teacher look at it, they quickly notice and comment on mechanical errors, even though the emphasis during revising is on content. Listening to the writing read aloud keeps the focus on content.

2. **Listeners offer compliments.** Writing-group members say what they liked about the writing. These positive comments should be specific, focusing on strengths, rather than the often heard "I liked it" or "It was good." Comments may focus on organization, leads, word choice, voice, sequence, dialogue, theme, and so on.

3. **The writer asks questions.** After a round of positive comments, writers ask for assistance with trouble spots they identified earlier when rereading their writing, or they may ask questions that reflect more general concerns about how well they are communicating.

4. **Listeners offer suggestions.** Members of the writing group ask questions about things that were unclear to them, and they make suggestions about how to revise the composition. Almost any writer resists constructive criticism, and it is especially difficult for elementary students to appreciate suggestions. It is important to teach students what kinds of comments and suggestions are acceptable so that they will word what they say in helpful rather than hurtful ways.

5. **The process is repeated.** The first four steps are repeated for each student's composition. This is the appropriate time for teachers to provide input as well. They should react to the piece of writing as any other listener would—not error hunting with red pen in hand (Sommers, 1994). Most teachers prefer to listen to students read their compositions aloud, because teachers may become frustrated by the numerous misspelled words and nearly illegible handwriting common in rough drafts if they read them themselves.

6. **Writers plan for revision.** At the end of the writing-group session, all students make a commitment to revise their writing based on the comments and suggestions of the group members. The final decisions on what to revise always rest with the writers themselves, but with the understanding that their rough drafts are not perfect comes the realization that some revision will be necessary. When students verbalize their planned revisions, they are more likely to complete the revision stage. Some students also make notes for themselves about their revision plans. After the group disbands, students make the revisions.

FIGURE 3-6   *Sixth Graders' List of Writing-Group Comments*

Compliments	Questions	Suggestions
I liked the part where _____ .	Did my introduction grab your attention?	Could you add more about _____ ?
Your lead grabbed my attention because _____ .	What do you want to know more about?	The part about _____ isn't clear to me.
My favorite sentence is _____ .	Did you understand my organization?	I think the part about _____ is long, and you could delete some of that.
I like the way you described _____ .	What do you think the best part of my paper is?	
I noticed this metaphor: _____ .	Are there some words that I need to change?	Which part is your conclusion?
I could hear your "voice" when you wrote _____ .	Did you like my title?	I think you should substitute a better word for _____ , such as _____ .
I like your conclusion because _____ .	Does my dialogue sound "real" to you?	
I liked your organization because _____ .	Is there something that isn't clear to you?	Your organization isn't clear to me because _____ .
Your sequence is _____ .	Is there something that I need to delete?	I think you might try moving the part about _____ to _____ .
Your writing is powerful because it made me feel _____ .	Is there something I should move from one part of my writing to another part?	I suggest that you add transition words like _____ in the part where _____ .
		I suggest that you use a metaphor or simile to explain about _____ .
		I think you used _____ too many times. Can you combine some sentences?

Teaching students how to work in writing groups takes patience and practice. Teachers begin by explaining the purpose of writing groups and the steps in the procedure. Next, they model the steps using a rough draft they have written and ask for comments from students in the class. Then small groups of students model the steps while their classmates watch, and teachers point out how to provide useful feedback to writers. Teachers often have students develop a list of meaningful comments and post it in the classroom for students to refer to during this stage of the writing process. Figure 3–6 shows a sixth-grade class list of compliments, questions, and suggestions that students can offer to provide useful feedback to classmates. Teachers also need to coach students on how to accept their classmates' compliments and suggestions for revision.

Writing groups can form spontaneously when several students have completed drafts and are ready to share their compositions, or they can be formal groupings with identified leaders. In some classrooms, writing groups form when four or five students finish writing their rough drafts. Students gather around a conference table or in a corner of the classroom. They take turns reading their rough drafts aloud, and classmates in the group listen and respond, offering compliments and suggestions for revision (Gere & Abbott, 1985). Sometimes the teacher joins the writing group, but if the teacher is involved in something else, students work independently.

In other classrooms, the writing groups are established. Students get together when all students in the group have completed their rough drafts and are ready to share their writing. Sometimes the teacher participates in these groups, providing feedback along with the students. At other times, the writing groups can function independently. Four or five students are assigned to each group, and a list of groups and their members is posted in the classroom. The teacher puts a star by one student's name, and that student serves as group leader. The leader changes every quarter.

Making Revisions.   Students make four types of changes: additions, substitutions, deletions, and moves (Faigley & Witte, 1981). As they revise, students might add words, substitute sentences, delete paragraphs, and move phrases. Students often use a blue or red pen to cross out, draw arrows, and write in the space left between the double-spaced lines of their rough drafts so that revisions will show clearly. That way teachers can examine the types of revisions students make by examining their revised rough drafts. Revisions are another gauge of students' growth as writers.

Conferencing With the Teacher.   Sometimes the teacher participates in the writing groups and provides revision suggestions along with the students. Sometimes the teacher conferences individually with students about their rough drafts. The teacher's role during conferences is to help students make choices and define directions for revision. Barry Lane (1993) offers these suggestions for talking with students about their papers:

- Have students come to a conference prepared to begin talking about their concerns. Students should talk first in a conference.
- Ask questions rather than give answers. Ask students what is working well for them, what problems they are having, and what questions they have.
- React to students' writing as a reader, not as a teacher. Offer compliments first; give suggestions later.
- Keep the conference short, and recognize that not all problem areas or concerns can be discussed.
- Limit the number of revision suggestions, and make all suggestions specific.
- Have students meet in writing groups before conferencing. Then students can share the feedback they received from classmates.
- To conclude the conference, ask students to identify the revisions they plan to make.

- Take notes during conferences and summarize students' revision plans. These notes are a record of the conference, and the revision plans can be used in assessing students' revisions.

It is time-consuming to meet with every student, but many teachers believe it is worth the time (Calkins, 1994; Graves, 1994). In a 5-minute conference, teachers listen to students talk about their writing processes, guide students as they make revision plans, and offer feedback during the writing process, when it is most usable.

Stage 4: Editing

Editing is putting the piece of writing into its final form. Until this stage, the focus has been primarily on the content of students' writing. Once the focus changes to mechanics, students polish their writing by correcting misspellings and other mechanical errors. The goal here is to make the writing "optimally readable" (Smith, 1982). Writers who write for readers understand that if their compositions are not readable, they have written in vain because their ideas will never be read.

Mechanics are the commonly accepted conventions of written Standard English; they include capitalization, punctuation, spelling, sentence structure, usage, and formatting considerations specific to poems, scripts, letters, and other writing forms. The use of these commonly accepted conventions is a courtesy to those who will read the composition.

Mechanical skills are best taught during the editing stage, not through workbook exercises. When editing a composition that will be shared with a genuine audience, students are more interested in using mechanical skills correctly so that they can communicate effectively. In a study of two third-grade classes, Calkins (1980) found that the students in the class who learned punctuation marks as a part of editing could define or explain more marks than the students in the other class, who were taught punctuation skills in a traditional manner, with instruction and practice exercises on each punctuation mark. In other words, the results of this research, as well as of other studies (Graves, 1994; Routman, 1996; Weaver, 1996), suggest that students learn mechanical skills better as part of the writing process than through practice exercises.

Students move through three activities in the editing stage:

- Getting distance from the composition
- Proofreading to locate errors
- Correcting errors

Getting Distance.   Students are more efficient editors if they set the composition aside for a few days before beginning to edit. After working so closely with a piece of writing during drafting and revising, they are too familiar with it to be able to locate many mechanical errors. With the distance gained by waiting a few days, children are better able to approach editing with a fresh perspective and gather the enthusiasm necessary to finish the writing process by making the paper optimally readable.

Proofreading.   Students proofread their compositions to locate and mark possible errors. Proofreading is a unique type of reading in which students read slowly, word by word, hunting for errors rather than reading quickly for meaning (M. King, 1985). Concentrating on mechanics is difficult because our nat-

FIGURE 3-7 *Proofreaders' Marks*

Delete	↙	There were cots to sleep on and food to eat ~~on~~ at the shelter.
Insert	⋀	Mrs. Kim's cat is the color of carrots.
Indent paragraph	⁋	⁋Riots are bad. People can get hurt and buildings can get burned down but good things can happen too. People can learn to be friends.
Capitalize	≡	Daniel and his mom didn't like mrs. Kim or her cat.
Change to lowercase	/	People were Rioting because they were angry.
Add period	⊙	I think Daniel's mom and Mrs. Kim will become friends ⊙
Add comma	⋀	People hurt other people they steal things and they burn down buildings in a riot.
Add apostrophe	⋎	Daniels cat was named Jasmine.

ural inclination is to read for meaning. Even experienced proofreaders often find themselves reading for meaning and thus overlooking errors that do not inhibit meaning. It is important, therefore, to take time to explain proofreading and demonstrate how it differs from regular reading.

To demonstrate proofreading, a teacher copies a piece of student writing on the chalkboard or displays it on an overhead projector. The teacher reads it several times, each time hunting for a particular type of error. During each reading, the teacher reads the composition slowly, softly pronouncing each word and touching the word with a pencil or pen to focus attention on it. The teacher marks possible errors as they are located.

Errors are marked or corrected with special proofreaders' marks. Students enjoy using these marks, the same ones that adult authors and editors use. Proofreaders' marks that elementary students can learn to use in editing their writing are presented in Figure 3–7. Editing checklists help students focus on particular types of errors. Teachers can develop checklists with two to six items appropriate for the grade level. A first-grade checklist, for example, might contain only two items—perhaps one about capital letters at the beginning of sentences and another about periods at the end of sentences. In contrast, a middle-grade checklist might have items such as using commas in a series, indenting paragraphs, capitalizing proper nouns, and spelling homonyms correctly. Teachers can revise the checklist during the school year to focus attention on skills that have recently been taught.

A third-grade editing checklist is presented in Figure 3–8. First, students proofread their own compositions, searching for errors in each category on the checklist; after proofreading, they check off each item. Then, after completing

FIGURE 3-8   *A Third-Grade Editing Checklist*

Editing Checklist

Author   Editor

☐   ☐   1. I have circled the words that might be misspelled.

☐   ☐   2. I have checked that all sentences begin with a
                          capital letter.

☐   ☐   3. I have checked that all sentences end with a
                          punctuation mark.

☐   ☐   4. I have checked that all proper nouns begin with a
                          capital letter.

Signatures

Author: _____   Editor: _____

the checklist, students sign their names and trade checklists and compositions. Now they become editors and complete each other's checklists. Having both writer and editor sign the checklist helps them take the activity seriously.

Correcting Errors.   After students proofread their compositions and locate the errors, they correct the errors individually or with an editor's assistance. Some errors are easy to correct, some require use of a dictionary, and others involve instruction from the teacher. It is unrealistic to expect students to locate and correct every mechanical error in their compositions. Not even published books are error free! Once in a while, students may change a correct spelling or punctuation mark and make it incorrect, but they correct far more errors than they create.

Editing can end after students and their editors correct as many mechanical errors as possible, or after students meet with the teacher in a conference for a final editing. When mechanical correctness is crucial, this conference is important. Teachers proofread the composition with the student, and they identify and make the remaining corrections together, or the teacher makes check marks in the margin to note errors for the student to correct independently.

Stage 5: Publishing

In this stage, students bring their compositions to life by publishing them or sharing them orally with an appropriate audience. When they share their writing with real audiences of classmates, other students, parents, and community members, students come to think of themselves as authors. In this stage, students:

- Make books
- Read from the author's chair
- Share their writing

Making Books.   One of the most popular ways for children to publish their writing is by making books (L. King & Stovall, 1992). Simple booklets can be made by folding a sheet of paper into quarters, like a greeting card. Students write the title on the front and use the three remaining sides for their compositions. They can also construct booklets by stapling sheets of writing paper together and adding construction paper covers. Sheets of wallpaper cut from old sample books also make sturdy covers. These stapled booklets can be cut into various shapes, too. Students can make more sophisticated books by covering cardboard covers with contact paper, wallpaper samples, or cloth. Pages are sewn or stapled together, and the first and last pages (endpapers) are glued to the cardboard covers to hold the book together. Directions for making one type of hardcover book are shown in Figure 3–9.

The Author's Chair.   Teachers designate a special chair in their classroom as "the author's chair" (Graves & Hansen, 1983). This chair might be a rocking chair, a lawn chair with a padded seat, a wooden stool, or a director's chair, and it should be labeled "Author's Chair." Students sit in the chair to read aloud books they have written, and this is the only time anyone sits there.

View the CD-ROM on writing workshop that accompanies this text to see how four teachers use the author's chair in their classrooms.

When students share their writing, one student sits in the author's chair and a group of classmates sit on the floor or in chairs in front of the author's chair (Karelitz, 1993). The student sitting in the author's chair reads the book or other piece of writing aloud and shows the accompanying illustrations. After the reading, classmates who want to make a comment raise their hands, and the author chooses several classmates to ask questions, give compliments, and make comments. Then the author chooses another student to share and takes a seat in the audience.

Most students really enjoy reading their writing aloud to their classmates, and they learn about the importance of audience as they watch for their classmates' reactions. And classmates benefit from the experience as well. They get ideas for their own writing as they listen and hear other students use sentence patterns and vocabulary that they might not be familiar with. The process of sharing their writing brings closure to the writing process and energizes students for their next writing project.

Sharing Writing.   In addition to reading their writing to classmates, students share their writing in other ways, too. They may share it with larger audiences through hardcover books placed in the class or school library, plays performed for classmates, or letters sent to authors, businesses, and other correspondents. Other ways to share writing are:

- Submit the piece to writing contests
- Display the writing as a mobile
- Contribute to a class anthology

FIGURE 3-9 *Directions for Making Hardcover Books*

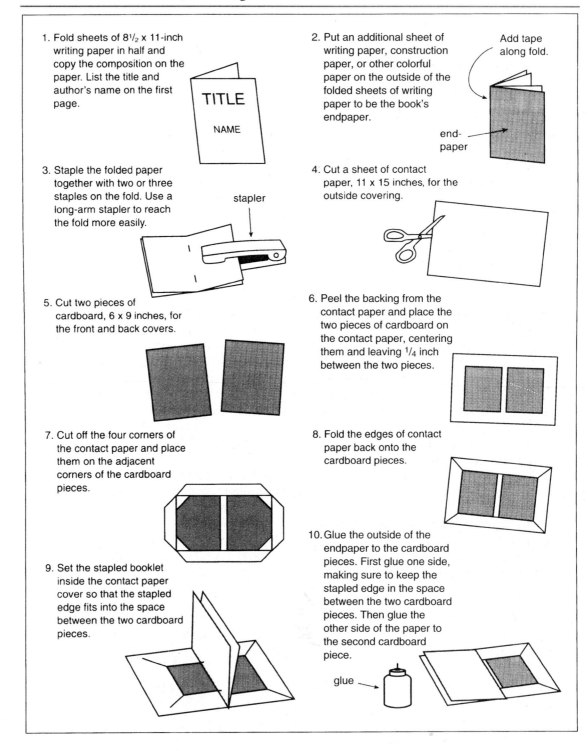

1. Fold sheets of 8½ x 11-inch writing paper in half and copy the composition on the paper. List the title and author's name on the first page.

   TITLE

   NAME

2. Put an additional sheet of writing paper, construction paper, or other colorful paper on the outside of the folded sheets of writing paper to be the book's endpaper.

   Add tape along fold.

   end-paper

3. Staple the folded paper together with two or three staples on the fold. Use a long-arm stapler to reach the fold more easily.

   stapler

4. Cut a sheet of contact paper, 11 x 15 inches, for the outside covering.

5. Cut two pieces of cardboard, 6 x 9 inches, for the front and back covers.

6. Peel the backing from the contact paper and place the two pieces of cardboard on the contact paper, centering them and leaving ¼ inch between the two pieces.

7. Cut off the four corners of the contact paper and place them on the adjacent corners of the cardboard pieces.

8. Fold the edges of contact paper back onto the cardboard pieces.

9. Set the stapled booklet inside the contact paper cover so that the stapled edge fits into the space between the two cardboard pieces.

10. Glue the outside of the endpaper to the cardboard pieces. First glue one side, making sure to keep the stapled edge in the space between the two cardboard pieces. Then glue the other side of the paper to the second cardboard piece.

    glue

144

- Contribute to the local newspaper
- Make a shape book
- Record the writing on a cassette tape
- Submit it to a literary magazine
- Read it at a school assembly
- Share at a read-aloud party
- Share with parents and siblings
- Produce a videotape of it
- Display poetry on a "poet-tree"
- Send it to a pen pal
- Make a hardbound book
- Produce it as a roller movie
- Display it on a bulletin board
- Post it on the Internet
- Make a big book
- Design a poster about the writing
- Read it to foster grandparents
- Share it as a puppet show
- Display it at a public event
- Read it to children in other classes

Through this sharing, students communicate with genuine audiences who respond to their writing in meaningful ways.

Sharing writing is a social activity that helps children develop sensitivity to audiences and confidence in themselves as authors. Dyson (1985) advises that teachers consider the social interpretations of sharing—students' behavior, teacher's behavior, and interaction between students and teacher—within the classroom context. Individual students interpret sharing differently. More than just providing the opportunity for students to share writing, teachers need to teach students how to respond to their classmates. Teachers themselves serve as a model for responding to students' writing without dominating the sharing.

Students can share their writing with wide audiences when they post their writing on the Internet. Figure 3–10 presents a list of websites that publish elementary students' writing free of charge. These websites vary in their submission requirements, so it is important to read the guidelines for submissions listed on-line. Many of these websites offer special programs, including information about writing genres, guidelines about revising and editing, and chat rooms so that students can talk about their writing.

Teaching the Writing Process

Students learn to use the writing process as they write compositions in literature focus units and theme cycles and as they participate in writing workshop. Learning to use the writing process is more important than any particular writing projects students might be involved in, because the writing process is a tool. Students need many opportunities to learn to use the writing process. Teachers model the writing process by writing class collaborations, and they teach minilessons on the procedures, concepts, and strategies and skills that writers use.

One way to introduce the writing process is to write a collaborative or group composition. The teacher models the writing process and provides an opportunity for students to practice the process approach to writing in a supportive

---

FIGURE 3–10

On-line Publishing Opportunities for Children

Children's Express. http://www.childrens-express.org
Students serve as guest reporters and submit news articles, profiles, and opinion pieces for this journalistic website.

Co-nect to Kids. http://www.co-nect.net/legacy/schools/webzine
Students submit their writings to The Link, a webzine created by students for students.

Cyberkids. http://www.cyberkids.com/index.html
Students ages 7–12 are invited to submit stories, poems, and articles. Jokes, games, and multimedia presentations are also accepted.

Frodo's Notebook. http://www.frodosnotebook.com/
This website publishes essays and poetry written by students ages 13–19.

Kid News. http://kidnews.com/
Students submit stories, poems, news, and opinions. This site also sponsors an international pen pal program.

Kids Online Magazine. http://www.kidsonlinemagazine.com/
Students are invited to submit writing, music, and art to this online 'zine created by a child and her mother.

KidsViews. http://www.eduplace.com/kids/rdg/chall.html
Children are invited to write and submit "KidView" book reviews about favorite books that are published on-line at Houghton Mifflin's Eduplace website.

MidLink Magazine. http://longwood.cs.ucf.edu/~MidLink/
This website is an interdisciplinary magazine for children and teenagers. Student writing is published according to themes being highlighted.

Teen Lit. http://www.teenlit.com/
Poems, essays, short stories, and book reviews by teenage writers are published at this website.

White Barn Press. http://www.whitebarnpress.com
This on-line 'zine is for students who want to publish their writing for a wide audience. This site also offers ideas for teachers who want to encourage their students to write.

Writing With Writers. http://teacher.scholastic.com/writewit/index.htm
On-line seminars are presented by well-known authors of children's books about writing different genres, and some student work is published.

Young Writer's Club. http://www.cs.bilkent.edu.tr/~david/derya/ywc.html
This website publishes a wide range of stories, poems, movie and book reviews, and reports.

---

environment. As students and teacher write a composition together, they move through the five stages of the writing process, just as writers do when they work independently. The teacher demonstrates the strategies writers use and clarifies misconceptions during the group composition, and students offer ideas for writing as well as suggestions for tackling common writing problems.

The teacher begins by introducing the idea of writing a group composition and reviewing the project. Students dictate a rough draft, which the teacher records on the chalkboard or on chart paper. The teacher notes any misunderstandings students have about the writing assignment or process and, when necessary, reviews concepts and offers suggestions. Then the teacher and students read the composition and identify ways to revise it. Some parts of the composition will need reworking, and other parts may be deleted or moved. More specific words will be substituted for less specific ones, and redundant words and sentences will be deleted. Students may also want to add new parts to the composition. After making the necessary content changes, students proofread the composition, checking for mechanical errors, for paragraph breaks, and for sentences to combine. They correct errors and make changes. Then the teacher or a student copies the completed composition on chart paper or on a sheet of notebook paper. Copies can be made and given to each student.

Collaborative compositions are an essential part of many writing experiences, especially when students are learning to use the writing process or a new writing form. Group compositions serve as a dry run during which students' questions and misconceptions can be clarified.

Teachers also use minilessons to teach students how to gather and organize ideas for writing, how to participate in writing groups, how to proofread, and how to share their writing. Teachers teach these procedures, concepts, and strategies and skills during minilessons. Minilessons can be taught as part of class collaborations, during literature focus units and theme cycles, and in writing workshop. Topics for minilessons on the writing process are listed in the Piecing a Lesson Together feature on pages 124 and 125, and a minilesson on teaching revising to third graders is also presented. Many teachers use the editing stage as a time to informally assess students' spelling, capitalization, punctuation, and other mechanical skills and to give minilessons on a skill that students are having trouble with.

In Literature Focus Units.   Students use the writing process as they create projects during the applying stage of the reading process. Sometimes the class works together to write a class collaboration; sometimes students work in small groups on the same writing project; and at other times, students work on a variety of writing projects. Here are three examples:

- After reading Freeman's teddy bear story, *Corduroy* (1968), first graders work together to write a retelling of the story, which they publish as a big book.
- During an author unit on Chris Van Allsburg, fifth graders each choose an illustration from *The Mysteries of Harris Burdick* (1984) and write a story about it.
- As part of a unit on point of view, seventh-grade students rewrite familiar folktales from the viewpoint of one character after reading *The True Story of the 3 Little Pigs!* (Scieszka, 1989), which is told from the wolf's viewpoint.

In each of these projects, students used the writing process and moved through all five stages as they collected ideas, drafted, revised, edited, and published their compositions.

In Writing Workshop.   Students regularly move through the stages of the writing process during the writing time. It would be convenient if the writing process equated to prewriting on Monday, drafting on Tuesday, revising on Wednesday, editing on Thursday, and publishing on Friday, but it does not. Writers move back and forth through the stages as they develop, refine, and polish

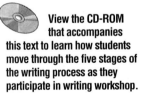
View the CD-ROM that accompanies this text to learn how students move through the five stages of the writing process as they participate in writing workshop.

their compositions, and they participate in some activities, such as revising, throughout the writing process (Flower & Hayes, 1994). A special sharing time is set aside for students to share their published writing projects with classmates. Sharing is a social experience, and when students share their writing with real audiences, they feel the satisfaction of a job well done.

In Theme Cycles.   Teachers often plan writing projects in connection with theme cycles. Sometimes all students in the classroom work together on a single project, such as making an alphabet book about the ocean as part of a theme on oceans, or writing a collection of animal poems to put with the animal sculptures they made.

At other times, however, students choose projects and work independently. For example, during a theme cycle on pioneers, students might create a variety of projects, such as:

- Keep a simulated journal from the viewpoint of a pioneer.
- Write a story about a pioneer family.
- Prepare an informational book about covered wagons.
- Write poems about life on the Oregon Trail.
- Write an explanation to accompany a relief map of the pioneer trails across the United States.
- Make a time line for the westward expansion, with notes about important dates and events.
- Write an essay comparing pioneers in the 1800s with immigrants coming to the United States today.
- Make posters about pioneer legends or tall-tale heroes (e.g., Johnny Appleseed, Pecos Bill, and Paul Bunyan).

For each of these projects, students use the writing process to develop their compositions. They meet in writing groups to share their rough drafts and revise their pieces using feedback from classmates. They also edit their compositions to identify and correct as many mechanical errors as possible. Then they make final copies of their compositions and share them with classmates or other audiences.

Meeting the Needs of Every Student.   Teachers adapt the activities involved in each stage of the writing process to make writing a successful experience for all students. Teachers often shorten the writing process to three stages—prewriting, drafting, and publishing—for young children and for students with few successful writing experiences. Then, as students become more confident and more fluent writers and develop audience awareness, teachers add the revising and editing stages.

Teachers can develop checklists with activities for each stage of the writing process so that students with short attention spans or students who have trouble completing an assignment can stay on task. Other suggestions for adapting each stage are listed in the Meeting the Needs of Every Student box on page 149.

Responding to Student Writing.   The teacher's role should not be restricted to that of evaluator. Again and again, researchers report that although teachers are the most common audience for student writing, they are also one of the worst audiences, because they read with a red pen in hand. Teachers

Meeting the Needs of Every Student

How Do Teachers Adapt the Writing Process?

Learning to use the writing process effectively is a struggle for some students. You can provide additional support in these ways:

Stage 1: Prewriting

- Use drawing as a rehearsal activity.
- Have students "talk out" their compositions before beginning to write.
- Draw a cluster for students, using the ideas and words they suggest.

Stage 2: Drafting

- Have students dictate their rough drafts.
- Mark students' papers so that they write on every other line.
- Reassure students that spelling and other mechanical skills are not important in this stage.

Stage 3: Revising

- Participate in writing groups with students.
- Focus on compliments rather than on suggestions for revisions when students begin writing groups.
- Expect students to make only one or two revisions at first.

Stage 4: Editing

- Teach students how to proofread.
- Have students mark possible errors; then correct errors with them.
- Have students identify and correct errors on the first page of their compositions; then correct remaining errors for students.

Stage 5: Publishing

- Use a word processor for final copies.
- Handwrite the final copy for students.
- Provide opportunities for students to share their writing with a trusted group of classmates.
- Do not correct any remaining errors on the final copy.

should instead read their students' writing for information, for enjoyment, and for all the other purposes readers have for reading. Much of students' writing does not need to be assessed; it should simply be shared with the teacher as a "trusted adult" (Martin, D'Arcy, Newton, & Parker, 1976).

When children use a process approach to writing, they are less likely to plagiarize because they have developed their compositions step-by-step—from prewriting and drafting to revising and editing. Nonetheless, at some time or other, most teachers fear that a composition they are reading is not the student's own work. Jackson, Tway, and Frager (1987) cite several reasons why children

See Chapter 10, "Reading and Writing Information," to read about how to teach students to write reports so that they won't plagiarize.

might plagiarize. First, some students simply internalize a piece of writing through repeated readings so that months or years later, they do not realize that it is not their own work. Second, some students plagiarize because of competition to succeed. Third, some students plagiarize by accident, not realizing the consequences of their actions. A final reason some students plagiarize is that they have not been taught to use a process approach, so they don't know how to synthesize information for a report from published sources. The two best ways to avoid having students copy work from another source and pass it off as their own are to teach the writing process and to have students write at school rather than at home. Students who work at school and move through the various writing process activities know how to complete the writing project.

CONNECTIONS BETWEEN READING AND WRITING

Reading and writing are both meaning-making processes, and readers and writers are involved in remarkably similar activities. It is important that teachers plan literacy activities so that students can connect reading and writing because they enhance students' learning when used together.

Comparing the Two Processes

The reading and writing processes have comparable activities at each stage (Butler & Turbill, 1984). In both reading and writing, the goal is to construct meaning, and, as shown in Figure 3–11, the activities at each stage are similar. For example, notice the similarities between the activities listed for the third stage of reading and writing—responding and revising, respectively. Fitzgerald (1989) analyzed these activities and concluded that they draw on similar processes of author-reader-text interactions. Similar analyses can be made for activities in the other stages as well.

Tierney (1983) explains that reading and writing are multidimensional and involve concurrent, complex transactions between readers and writers. Writers participate in several types of reading activities: They read other authors' works to obtain ideas and to learn about the structure of stories, informational books, and poetry, but they also read and reread their own work to discover, monitor, and clarify. The quality of these reading experiences seems closely tied to success in writing. Readers are writers, too. They participate in many of the same activities that writers use—generating ideas, organizing, monitoring, problem solving, and revising.

Classroom Connections

Teachers can help students appreciate the similarities between reading and writing. Tierney explains: "What we need are reading teachers who act as if their students were developing writers and writing teachers who act as if their students were readers" (1983, p. 151). Here are some ways to point out the relationships between reading and writing:

- Help writers assume alternative points of view as potential readers.
- Help readers consider the writer's purpose and viewpoint.
- Point out that reading is much like composing, so that students will view reading as a process, much like the writing process.

FIGURE 3–11

A Comparison of the Reading and Writing Processes

	What Readers Do	**What Writers Do**
Stage 1	*Prereading*	*Prewriting*
	Readers use knowledge about	Writers use knowledge about
	• the topic • reading • literature • language systems	• the topic • writing • literature • language systems
	Readers' expectations are cued by	Writers' expectations are cued by
	• previous reading/writing experiences • format of the text • purpose for reading • audience for reading	• previous reading/writing experiences • format of the text • purpose for writing • audience for writing
	Readers preview the text and make predictions.	Writers gather and organize ideas.
Stage 2	*Reading*	*Drafting*
	Readers	Writers
	• use word-identification strategies • use comprehension strategies • monitor reading • create meaning	• use spelling strategies • use comprehension strategies • monitor writing • create meaning
Stage 3	*Responding*	*Revising*
	Readers	Writers
	• respond to the text • clarify misunderstandings • develop interpretations	• respond to the text • clarify misunderstandings • develop interpretations
Stage 4	*Exploring*	*Editing*
	Readers examine the text by	Writers examine the text by
	• considering the impact of words and literary language • exploring structural elements • comparing the text to others	• correcting mechanical errors • reviewing paragraph and sentence structure
Stage 5	*Applying*	*Publishing*
	Readers	Writers
	• develop projects to extend knowledge • share projects with classmates • reflect on the reading process • make connections to life and literature • value the piece of literature • feel success • want to read again	• produce the finished copy of their compositions • share their compositions with genuine audiences • reflect on the writing process • value the composition • feel success • want to write again

Source: Adapted from Butler & Turbill, 1984.

- Talk with students about the similarities between the reading and writing processes.
- Talk with students about reading and writing strategies.

To review the 12 reading and writing strategies, see Chapter 1, "Learning and the Language Arts."

Readers and writers use similar strategies for constructing meaning as they interact with print. As readers, we use a variety of problem-solving strategies to make decisions about an author's meaning and to construct meaning for ourselves. As writers, we also use problem-solving strategies to decide what our readers need as we construct meaning for them and for ourselves. Tierney and Pearson (1983) compare reading to writing by describing reading as a composing process because readers compose and refine meaning through reading, much as writers do.

There are practical benefits of connecting reading and writing. Reading contributes to students' writing development, and writing contributes to students' reading development. Shanahan (1988) outlined seven instructional principles for relating reading and writing so that students develop a clear concept of literacy:

1. Involve students in daily reading and writing experiences.
2. Introduce reading and writing processes in kindergarten.
3. Plan instruction that reflects the developmental nature of the reading-writing relationship.
4. Make the reading-writing connection explicit to students.
5. Emphasize both the processes and the products of reading and writing.
6. Emphasize the purposes for which students use reading and writing.
7. Teach reading and writing through meaningful, functional, and genuine literacy experiences.

Review

Reading and writing are similar processes of constructing meaning. Teachers organize reading and writing instruction using the five stages of the reading and writing processes. Students learn to use the reading and writing processes through literature focus units, literature circles, reading and writing workshop, and theme cycles. The key concepts presented in this chapter are:

1. Students use aesthetic reading when they read for enjoyment and efferent reading when they read for information.
2. The five stages of the reading process are prereading, reading, responding, exploring, and applying.
3. Students use the Goldilocks strategy to choose books at their reading level.
4. Five ways to read a selection are shared reading, guided reading, independent reading, buddy reading, and listening as it is read aloud.
5. Students use the reading process during literature focus units, literature circles, reading workshop, and theme cycles.
6. The five stages of the writing process are prewriting, drafting, revising, editing, and publishing.
7. Purpose, form, and audience influence students' compositions.
8. Students use the writing process as they write during literature focus units, writing workshop, and theme cycles.

Visit Chapter 3 on the Companion Website at www.prenhall. com/tompkins to:

- **Check your understanding of the concepts presented in the chapter**
- **Access the Extensions (activities and a list of related readings)**
- **Link to related websites**

9. Teachers present minilessons on procedures, concepts, skills, and strategies in the reading and writing processes.
10. The goal of both reading and writing is to construct meaning, and the two processes have comparable activities at each stage.

Professional References

Barnes, D., Morgan, K., & Weinhold, K. (Eds.). (1997). *Writing process revisited: Sharing our stories.* Urbana, IL: National Council of Teachers of English.

Bear, D. R., Invernizzi, M., Templeton, S., & Johnston, F. (2004). *Words their way: Word study for phonics, vocabulary, and spelling instruction.* (3rd ed.). Upper Saddle River, NJ: Merrill/Prentice Hall.

Blachowicz, C., & Fisher, P. (1996). *Teaching vocabulary in all classrooms.* Upper Saddle River, NJ: Merrill/Prentice Hall.

Blanton, W. E., Wood, K. D., & Moorman, G. B. (1990). The role of purpose in reading instruction. *The Reading Teacher, 43,* 486–493.

Britton, J., Burgess, T., Martin, N., McLeod, A., & Rosen, H. (1975). *The development of writing abilities, 11–18.* London: Schools Council Publications.

Bromley, K. D. (1996). *Webbing with literature: Creating story maps with children's books* (2nd ed.). Boston: Allyn & Bacon.

Butler, A., & Turbill, J. (1984). *Towards a reading-writing classroom.* Portsmouth, NH: Heinemann.

Calkins, L. M. (1980). When children want to punctuate: Basic skills belong in context. *Language Arts, 57,* 567–573.

Calkins, L. M. (1994). *The art of teaching writing* (2nd ed.). Portsmouth, NH: Heinemann.

Clay, M. M. (1991). *Becoming literate: The construction of inner control.* Portsmouth, NH: Heinemann.

Cochran-Smith, M. (1984). *The making of a reader.* Norwood, NJ: Ablex.

Daniels, H. (1994). *Literature circles: Voice and choice in the student-centered classroom.* York, ME: Stenhouse.

Dyson, A. H. (1985). Second graders sharing writing: The multiple social realities of a literacy event. *Written Communication, 2,* 189–215.

Dyson, A. H. (1986). The imaginary worlds of childhood: A multimedia presentation. *Language Arts, 63,* 799–808.

Eeds, M., & Peterson, R. L. (1995). What teachers need to know about the literary craft. In N. L. Roser & M. G. Martinez (Eds.), *Book talk and beyond: Children and teachers respond to literature* (pp. 10–23). Newark, DE: International Reading Association.

Eeds, M., & Wells, D. (1989). Grand conversations: An exploration of meaning construction in literature study groups. *Research in the Teaching of English, 23,* 4–29.

Faigley, L., & Witte, S. (1981). Analyzing revision. *College Composition and Communication, 32,* 400–410.

Fisher, B. & Medvic, E. F. (2000). *Perspectives on shared reading: Planning and practice.* Portsmouth, NH: Heinemann.

Fitzgerald, J. (1989). Enhancing two related thought processes: Revision in writing and critical thinking. *The Reading Teacher, 43,* 42–48.

Flower, L., & Hayes, J. R. (1994). The cognition of discovery: Defining a rhetorical problem. In S. Perl (Ed.), *Landmark essays on writing process* (pp. 63–74). Davis, CA: Heragoras Press.

Fountas, I. C., & Pinnell, G. S. (1996). *Guided reading: Good first teaching for all children.* Portsmouth, NH: Heinemann.

Fountas, I. C., & Pinnell, G. S. (2001). *Guiding readers and writers, grades 3–6.* Portsmouth, NH: Heinemann.

Gardner, H. (1993). *Frames of mind: The theory of multiple intelligences.* New York: Basic Books/HarperCollins.

Gere, A. R., & Abbott, R. D. (1985). Talking about writing: The language of writing groups. *Research in the Teaching of English, 19,* 362–381.

Gillet, J. W., & Beverly, L. (2001). *Directing the writing workshop: An elementary teacher's handbook.* New York: Guilford Press.

Graves, D. H. (1976). Let's get rid of the welfare mess in the teaching of writing. *Language Arts, 53,* 645–651.

Graves, D. H. (1994). *A fresh look at writing.* Portsmouth, NH: Heinemann.

Graves, D. H., & Hansen, J. (1983). The author's chair. *Language Arts, 60,* 176–183.

Hickman, J. (1995). Not by chance. In N. L. Roser & M. G. Martinez (Eds.), *Book talk and beyond: Children and teachers respond to literature* (pp. 3–9). Newark, DE: International Reading Association.

Hidi, S., & Hildyard, A. (1983). The comparison of oral and written productions in two discourse modes. *Discourse Processes, 6,* 91–105.

Holdaway, D. (1979). *The foundations of literacy.* Portsmouth, NH: Heinemann.

Hornsby, D., Sukarna, D., & Parry, J. (1986). *Read on: A conference approach to reading.* Portsmouth, NH: Heinemann.

Jackson, L. A., Tway, E., & Frager, A. (1987). Dear teacher, Johnny copied. *The Reading Teacher, 41,* 22–25.

Karelitz, E. B. (1993). *The author's chair and beyond: Language and literacy in a primary classroom.* Portsmouth, NH: Heinemann.

Kiefer, B. Z. (1994). *The potential of picture books: From visual literacy to aesthetic understanding.* Upper Saddle River, NJ: Merrill/Prentice Hall.

Kiefer, B. Z. (1995). Responding to literature as art in picture books. In N. L. Roser & M. G. Martinez (Eds.), *Book talk and beyond: Children and teachers respond to literature* (pp. 191–200). Newark, DE: International Reading Association.

King, L., & Stovall, D. (1992). *Classroom publishing.* Hillsboro, OR: Blue Heron.

King, M. (1985). Proofreading is not reading. *Teaching English in the Two-Year College, 12,* 108–112.

LaBerge, D., & Samuels, S. J. (1976). Toward a theory of automatic information processing in reading. In H. Singer & R. Ruddell (Eds.), *Theoretical models and processes of reading* (pp. 548–579). Newark, DE: International Reading Association.

Lane, B. (1993). *After the end: Teaching and learning creative revision.* Portsmouth, NH: Heinemann.

Langer, J. A. (1985). Children's sense of genre. *Written Communication, 2,* 157–187.

Lee, G. (2000). Getting into line to publish online. *Voices from the Middle, 8*(1), 23–34.

Martin, N., D'Arcy, P., Newton, B., & Parker, R. (1976). *Writing and learning across the curriculum.* London: Schools Council Publications.

Martinez, M. G., & Roser, N. L. (1995). The books make a difference in story talk. In N. L. Roser & M. G. Martinez (Eds.), *Book talk and beyond: Children and teachers respond to literature* (pp. 32–41). Newark, DE: International Reading Association.

Mohr, M. M. (1984). *Revision: The rhythm of meaning.* Upper Montclair, NJ: Boynton/Cook.

Murray, D. H. (1982). *Learning by teaching.* Montclair, NJ: Boynton/Cook.

Ohlhausen, M. M., & Jepsen, M. (1992). Lessons from Goldilocks: "Somebody's been choosing my books but I can make my own choices now!" *The New Advocate, 5,* 31–46.

Opitz, M. F., & Rasinski, T. V. (1998). *Good-bye round robin: Twenty-five effective oral reading strategies.* Portsmouth, NH: Heinemann.

Perl, S. (1994). Understanding composing. In S. Perl (Ed.), *Landmark essays on writing process* (pp. 99–106). Davis, CA: Heragoras Press.

Peterson, R., & Eeds, M. (1990). *Grand conversations: Literature groups in action.* New York: Scholastic.

Rico, G. L. (1983). *Writing the natural way.* Los Angeles: Tarcher.

Rosenblatt, L. M. (1978). *The reader, the text, the poem: The transactional theory of the literary work.* Carbondale: Southern Illinois University Press.

Rosenblatt, L. M. (1991). Literature: S.O.S.! *Language Arts, 68,* 444–448.

Routman, R. (1996). *Literacy at the crossroads: Crucial talk about reading, writing, and other teaching dilemmas.* Portsmouth, NH: Heinemann.

Shanahan, T. (1988). The reading-writing relationship: Seven instructional principles. *The Reading Teacher, 41,* 636–647.

Slaughter, J. P. (1993). *Beyond storybooks: Young children and the shared book experience.* Newark, DE: International Reading Association.

Smith, F. (1982). *Writing and the writer.* New York: Holt, Rinehart and Winston.

Sommers, N. (1994). Revision strategies of student writers and experienced adult writers. In S. Perl (Ed.), *Landmark essays on writing process* (pp. 75–84). Davis, CA: Heragoras Press.

Taylor, D. (1993). *From the child's point of view.* Portsmouth, NH: Heinemann.

Tierney, R. J. (1983). Writer-reader transactions: Defining the dimensions of negotiation. In P. L. Stock (Ed.), *Forum: Essays on theory and practice in the teaching of writing* (pp. 147–151). Upper Montclair, NJ: Boynton/Cook.

Tierney, R. J., & Pearson, P. D. (1983). Toward a composing model of reading. *Language Arts, 60,* 568–580.

Weaver, C. (1994). *Reading process and practice: From sociopsycholinguistics to whole language* (2nd ed.). Portsmouth, NH: Heinemann.

Weaver, C. (1996). *Teaching grammar in context.* Portsmouth, NH: Heinemann.

Yaden, D. B., Jr. (1988). Understanding stories through repeated read-alouds: How many does it take? *The Reading Teacher, 41,* 556–560.

Children's Book References

Brett, J. (1989). *The mitten.* New York: Putnam.

Bunting, E. (1994). *Smoky night.* San Diego: Harcourt Brace.

Carle, E. (1987). *A house for hermit crab.* Saxonville, MA: Picture Book Studio.

Coville, B. (1991). *Jeremy Thatcher, dragon hatcher.* San Diego: Harcourt Brace.

Creech, S. (2003). *Granny Torrelli makes soup.* New York: HarperCollins.

Curtis, C. P. (1999). *Bud, not Buddy.* New York: Delacorte.

Cushman, K. (1994). *Catherine, called Birdy.* New York: HarperCollins.

Danziger, P. (1994). *Amber Brown is not a crayon.* New York: Putnam.

Danziger, P. (1995). *Amber Brown goes fourth.* New York: Putnam.

Fowler, A. (1990). *It's a good thing there are insects.* Chicago: Childrens Press.

Freeman, D. (1968). *Corduroy.* New York: Viking.

Henkes, K. (1991). *Chrysanthemum.* New York: Greenwillow.

Henry, M. (1963). *Misty of Chincoteague.* Chicago: Rand McNally.

Howe, D., & Howe, J. (1979). *Bunnicula: A rabbit-tale of mystery.* New York: Atheneum.

Lauber, P. (1990). *Seeing Earth from space.* New York: Orchard.

Lowry, L. (1993). *The giver.* Boston: Houghton Mifflin.

Macaulay, D. (1990). *Black and white.* Boston: Houghton Mifflin.

MacLachlan, P. (1985). *Sarah, plain and tall.* New York: Harper & Row.

Martin, B., Jr. (1983). *Brown bear, brown bear, what do you see?* New York: Holt, Rinehart and Winston.

Martin, B., Jr. (1992). *Polar bear, polar bear, what do you hear?* New York: Holt, Rinehart and Winston.

Paulsen, G. (1987). *Hatchet.* New York: Viking.

Rylant, C. (1985). *The relatives came.* New York: Bradbury Press.

Scieszka, J. (1989). *The true story of the 3 little pigs!* New York: Viking.

Siebert, D. (1991). *Sierra.* New York: HarperCollins.

Spinelli, J. (1990). *Maniac Magee.* Boston: Little, Brown.

Van Allsburg, C. (1979). *The garden of Abdul Gasazi.* Boston: Houghton Mifflin.

Van Allsburg, C. (1981). *Jumanji.* Boston: Houghton Mifflin.

Van Allsburg, C. (1984). *The mysteries of Harris Burdick.* Boston: Houghton Mifflin.

Van Allsburg, C. (1993). *The sweetest fig.* Boston: Houghton Mifflin.

Viorst, J. (1977). *Alexander and the terrible, horrible, no good, very bad day.* New York: Atheneum.

Wiesner, D. (1991). *Tuesday.* New York: Clarion.

4 Emerging Into Literacy

PATTERNS OF PRACTICE

In Mrs. Kirkpatrick's kindergarten–first grade multiage classroom, the students participate in weeklong literature focus units. She uses the featured book for shared reading and center activities that students work on while she teaches guided reading groups using leveled books at students' reading levels. This week's featured book is *If You Give a Mouse a Cookie* (Numeroff, 1985), a circular story about a mouse who, after receiving a cookie, wants a glass of milk, a straw, a napkin, other items, and finally another cookie. Mrs. Kirkpatrick has copies of both the regular-size and the big book versions of the story as well as copies of four other books by the same author, *If You Give a Moose a Muffin* (Numeroff, 1991), *If You Give a Pig a Pancake* (Numeroff, 1998), *If You Take a Mouse to the Movies* (Numeroff, 2000), and *If You Take a Mouse to School* (2002), that incorporate the same circular pattern.

Mrs. Kirkpatrick teaches language arts for 2 1/2 hours each morning. She begins with a shared reading activity. Students sample cookies and talk about their favorite cookies on Monday before Mrs. Kirkpatrick begins to read the fea-

Diagram labels: Reading and Writing Workshop / Literature Circles / Literature Focus Units / Theme Cycles

tured book using shared reading. Children read and reread the big book version of the story several times, and each time they are able to read more of the words themselves. The predictable pattern of the text and picture clues make it easier for the children to be successful. Later in the week, the children read the regular-size versions of the book individually or with buddies. Mrs. Kirkpatrick moves through the reading process as children respond to the story in a grand conversation, compare it to other circular stories that Laura Numeroff has written, and draw pictures and write in reading logs.

The children also participate in exploring-stage activities. Mrs. Kirkpatrick draws children's attention to specific words in the story, and together they write vocabulary words on a word wall. She also teaches high-frequency words, which are posted on another word wall in the classroom. One of the high-frequency words this week is *you*. The children locate the word again and again in the story and reread all the high-frequency words that have been posted on the word wall in the classroom. Mrs. Kirkpatrick teaches minilessons on phonics concepts, using sample words from the featured book to make the connection that phonics knowledge is useful for reading and writing. She also teaches minilessons about irregular plurals after children ask whether *mouses* or *mice* is the correct plural form. They also practice reading skills at centers.

Children work on two culminating projects. They write pages for a class book following Laura Numeroff's pattern and using their own names. For example: *If you give Graciela a bag of popcorn, she will want a glass of juice.* They also make a cookie quilt to hang on the wall of the classroom. Each child

How do teachers support students' emergence into reading and writing?

In kindergarten and first grade, children acquire phonemic awareness and phonics knowledge, learn to recognize and print the letters of the alphabet, and develop concepts about print as they learn to read and write. Literature focus units are an excellent way to support students' emergence into literacy because a book provides the foundation for the unit and because teachers use a combination of direct instruction and authentic reading and writing activities to teach reading and writing. As you read this vignette, notice how Mrs. Kirkpatrick provides instruction and opportunities to support her students' emergence into reading and writing.

157

Outline for a Literature Focus Unit on *If You Give a Mouse a Cookie*

1. Prereading

- The teacher brings in several types of cookies for children to sample. Students talk about their favorite cookies, and they create a graph and chart their favorite cookies.
- The teacher introduces the book using a big book version of the story.
- The teacher shares a book box of objects or pictures of objects mentioned in the story (cookie, glass of milk, straw, napkin, mirror, scissors, broom, etc.), and children talk about how some of the items might be used in the story.
- Students and the teacher begin the word wall with *cookie* and *mouse*.

2. Reading

- The teacher reads the big book version of *If You Give a Mouse a Cookie* using shared reading.
- The teacher rereads the book, and students join in reading and use echo reading to repeat each sentence after the teacher reads it.

3. Responding

- The students and teacher participate in a grand conversation about the book.
- Students dramatize the story using objects in the book box.
- Students draw pictures in reading logs and add words (using invented spelling) to record their reactions to the book.

4. Exploring

- Students and teacher add interesting and important words to the word wall.
- Students read regular-size versions of the book with partners and reread the book independently.
- The teacher teaches minilessons on the /m/ sound or other phonemic awareness or phonics concepts.
- The teacher explains the concept of a circular story, and students sequence picture cards of the events in the story to make a circle diagram.
- The teacher presents a minilesson about the author, Laura Numeroff, and reads other books by the author.
- Students make word posters of words on the word wall.
- The teacher teaches a minilesson on irregular plurals (e.g., *mouse–mice, child–children*).
- The teacher sets up centers for students to sort objects related to the phonics lesson, listen to *If You Give a Moose a Muffin* (Numeroff, 1991) and other books by the author, write books about cookies, and use cards to sequence story events.

5. Applying

- Students write their own versions of the story or original circle stories.
- Students create a cookie quilt.

The Centers in Mrs. Kirkpatrick's Classroom

1. Comprehension Center
Children wear a mouse hand puppet as they sequence objects and retell *If You Give a Mouse a Cookie.* Copies of the book are available at the center to use to check the order of events in the story.

2. Phonics Center*
Children sort a collection of objects into baskets labeled with letters. *Mm* is this week's featured letter and sound, and Mrs. Kirkpatrick has set out these *Mm* objects: toy mouse, milk carton, marble, toy monkey, macaroni, play money, mitten, and toy man. In addition, she sets out books with other phonics activities that are appropriate for students in each of the reading groups.

3. Listening Center
Children listen to books written by Laura Numeroff and write and draw pictures in their reading logs.

4. Writing Center*
Children make books about cookies, write a retelling of the story, or write a new version of the story. A poster with cookie labels and names of cookies and a word wall with words related to the story are posted nearby.

5. Quilt Center
Children make cookie blocks for the class paper quilt. A variety of art materials are available at the center for children to use.

6. High-Frequency Word Center
Children mark *you,* the high-frequency word of the week, and other familiar high-frequency words on charts posted at the center using Wikki-Stix (pipe cleaners covered in wax) shaped into circles. They also use magnetic letters, plastic linking letters, or foam letters to practice spelling the words.

7. Reading Center*
Children select and read leveled books independently. Leveled books arranged in plastic tubs are available at the center for children to choose from.

*Required centers

---

makes a square for the paper quilt by designing a cookie in the center of the square and writing or dictating a sentence that is written underneath. The figure on page 158 presents a stage-by-stage outline showing how Mrs. Kirkpatrick teaches the book *If You Give a Mouse a Cookie.*

Later in the morning, Mrs. Kirkpatrick meets with students in small groups for guided reading while other students work in centers. Two sixth graders come to the classroom to help supervise centers so Mrs. Kirkpatrick can concentrate on the reading groups. The activities at most of the centers are related to the featured book. For example, at one center, students retell the story by sequencing objects or cards with pictures of objects related to the story. A list of the centers in Mrs. Kirkpatrick's classroom is shown on this page. Three of the centers are required, and they are marked with an asterisk in the figure. All students must complete these centers. The others are free choice, and students must complete at least two of them during the week. Students work at their own pace and move freely from center to center. They put their work in a folder that they carry from center to center. Stapled inside the folder is a weekly list of centers, and the sixth-grade aides put a stamp beside the name of the center when children complete work there.

As you begin reading this chapter, you may want to read the "Dear Reader" letter in Chapter 4 on the Companion Website at www.prenhall.com/tompkins

Is there a magic age when children become readers and writers? Researchers used to think that at the age of 6, most children were ready to learn to read and write. We now know that children begin the process of becoming literate gradually during the preschool years. Very young children notice signs, logos, and other environmental print. Who hasn't observed children making scribbles on paper as they try to "write"? As children are read to, they learn how to hold a book and turn pages, and they observe how the text is read. Most children come to kindergarten and first grade with sophisticated knowledge about written language and experiences with reading and writing.

The process of becoming literate begins well before the elementary grades and continues into adulthood, if not throughout life. It used to be that 5-year-old children came to kindergarten to be "readied" for reading and writing instruction, which would formally begin in first grade. The implication was that there was a point in children's development when it was time to begin teaching them to read and write. Those not ready participated in a variety of "readiness" activities to prepare them for reading and writing. Since the 1970s, this view has been discredited by teachers' and researchers' observations (Clay, 1991). Even children considered not ready have demonstrated that they could recognize signs and other environmental print, retell stories, scribble letters, invent printlike writing, and listen to stories read aloud to them.

This current approach to language arts instruction in kindergarten through second grade reflects the process known as emergent literacy. New Zealand educator Marie Clay is credited with coining the term. Studies from 1966 on have shaped the current outlook (Clay, 1967; Durkin, 1966; Holdaway, 1979; Taylor, 1983; Teale, 1982; Teale & Sulzby, 1989). Now, researchers are looking at literacy learning from the child's point of view. The age range has been extended to include children as young as 12 or 14 months of age who listen to stories being read aloud, notice labels and signs in their environment, and experiment with pencils. The concept of literacy has been broadened to incorporate the cultural and social aspects of language learning, and children's experiences with and understanding of written language—both reading and writing—are included as part of emergent literacy.

Teale and Sulzby (1989) paint a portrait of young children as literacy learners with these characteristics:

- Learning the functions of literacy through observing and participating in real-life settings in which reading and writing are used

- Developing reading and writing abilities concurrently and interrelatedly through experiences in reading and writing

- Constructing their understanding of reading and writing through active involvement with literacy materials

Teale and Sulzby describe young children as active learners who construct their own knowledge about reading and writing with the assistance of parents and other literate people. These caregivers help by demonstrating literacy as they read and write, by supplying materials, and by structuring opportunities for children to be involved in reading and writing. The environment is positive, with children experiencing reading and writing in many facets of their everyday lives and observing others who are engaged in literacy activities.

President George W. Bush's No Child Left Behind Act of 2001 has brought unprecedented attention to how young children learn to read and write. Teachers and administrators, parents, researchers, and policy makers are all focused on ensuring that every child reads at grade level by the end of third grade. Although all of the interested groups have the same goal, they are divided on the most effective ways to teach language arts in the primary grades. Many state and national policy makers contend that "scientific" evidence specifies that a skills-based, direct instruction approach is the most effective way, but many teachers and researchers believe in a balanced approach of blending direct instruction with reading and writing (Barone & Morrow, 2003; Burns, Griffin, & Snow, 1999; International Reading Association/ National Association for the Education of Young Children, 1998; Moats, 1999; National Reading Panel, 2000; Stanovich, 2000). The approach taken in this book is that children are more successful when teachers use research-based practices to provide direct instruction within the context of meaningful and authentic literacy activities.

As you read this chapter about young children's literacy development, think about these questions:

◆ How do teachers foster young children's interest in literacy?

◆ How do young children develop as readers and writers?

◆ What teaching strategies do teachers use in teaching reading and writing?

FOSTERING YOUNG CHILDREN'S INTEREST IN LITERACY

Children's introduction to written language begins before they come to school. Parents and other caregivers read to young children, and the children observe adults reading. They learn to read signs and other environmental print in their community. Children experiment with writing and have parents write for them. They also observe adults writing. When young children come to kindergarten, their knowledge about written language expands quickly as they participate in meaningful, functional, and genuine experiences with reading and writing.

Students also grow in their ability to stand back and reflect on language. The ability to talk about concepts of language is called metalinguistics (Yaden & Templeton, 1986), and children's ability to think metalinguistically is developed by their experiences with reading and writing (Templeton & Spivey, 1980).

Seeing Common Threads

Are kindergartners too young to learn to read and write?

Jennie Alameida responds:

Johnny, one of my kindergarten students, rushed in to see me one day during our third month of school. He was brimming with excitement and eager to share this discovery with me: Did I know *for* is everywhere? I told him I was teaching important words that he would see everywhere; the word *for* was one of our high-frequency words. He was so pleased that he made this reading discovery on a trip to the grocery store. He found meaning in the grown-up world, and this profound discovery drove his reading and writing. Giving kindergartners motivation and connections to the previously unclear world of adult literacy is a gift that I am pleased to share—because I believe that kindergartners are not too young to read and write.

What do you think?

Each chapter presents a question and a response written by one of Dr. Tompkins's students. Consider other comments, or respond to the question yourself, by visiting the Threaded Message Board in Chapter 4 on the Companion Website at www.prenhall.com/tompkins

Concepts About Written Language

Through experiences in their homes and communities, young children learn that print carries meaning and that reading and writing are used for a variety of purposes. They read menus in restaurants to know what foods are being served, write and receive letters to communicate with friends and relatives, and read (and listen to) stories for enjoyment. Children also learn as they observe parents and teachers using written language for all of these purposes.

Children's understanding about the purposes of reading and writing reflects how written language is used in their community. Although reading and writing are part of daily life for almost every family, families use written language for different purposes in different communities (Heath, 1983). It is important to realize that children have a wide range of literacy experiences in both middle- and working-class families, even though those experiences might be different (Taylor, 1983; Taylor & Dorsey-Gaines, 1987). In some communities, written language is used mainly as a tool for practical purposes, such as paying bills, and in some communities, reading and writing are also used for leisure-time activities. In other communities, written language serves even wider functions, such as debating social and political issues.

Teachers demonstrate the purposes of written language and provide opportunities for students to experiment with reading and writing by:

- Posting signs in the classroom
- Making a list of classroom rules
- Using literacy materials in dramatic play centers
- Writing notes to students in the class

- Exchanging messages with classmates
- Reading and writing stories
- Making posters about favorite books
- Labeling classroom items
- Drawing and writing in journals
- Writing morning messages
- Recording questions and information on charts
- Writing notes to parents
- Reading and writing letters to pen pals
- Reading and writing charts and maps

Concept of a Word.   Children's understanding of the concept of a "word" is an important part of becoming literate. Young children have only vague notions of language terms, such as *word, letter, sound,* and *sentence,* that teachers use in talking about reading and writing (Downing, 1971–1972; Invernizzi, 2003). Researchers have found that young children move through several levels of awareness and understanding about this terminology during the primary grades (Downing & Oliver, 1973–1974).

Preschoolers equate words with the objects the words represent. As they are introduced to reading and writing experiences, children begin to differentiate between objects and words, and finally they come to appreciate that words have meanings of their own. Templeton (1980) explains children's development with these two examples:

When asked if "dog" were a word, a four-year-old acquaintance of mine jumped up from the floor, began barking ferociously, and charged through the house, alternately panting and woofing. Confronted with the same question, an eight-year-old friend responded "of course 'dog' is a word," and went on to explain how the spelling represented spoken sounds and how the word *dog* stood for a particular type of animal. (p. 454)

Several researchers have investigated children's understanding of a word as a unit of language. Papandropoulou and Sinclair (1974) identified four stages of word consciousness. At the first level, young children do not differentiate between words and things. At the next level, children describe words as labels for things. They consider words that stand for objects as words, but do not classify articles and prepositions as words because words such as *the* and *with* cannot be represented with objects. At the third level, children understand that words carry meaning and that stories are built from words. At the fourth level, more fluent readers and writers describe words as autonomous elements having meanings of their own with definite semantic and syntactic relationships. Children might say, "You make words with letters." Also, at this level, children understand that words have different appearances—they can be spoken, listened to, read, and written.

Environmental Print.   Young children's "reading" experiences often begin with environmental print. Many children begin reading by recognizing logos on fast-food restaurants, department stores, grocery stores, and commonly used household items within familiar contexts (Harste, Woodward, & Burke, 1984). They recognize the golden arches of McDonald's and say "McDonald's," but when they are shown the word *McDonald's* written on a sheet of paper without the familiar sign and restaurant setting, they cannot yet read the word.

Researchers have found that young emergent readers depend on context to read familiar words and memorized texts (Dyson, 1984; Sulzby, 1985). Slowly, children develop relationships linking form and meaning as they learn concepts about written language and gain more experience reading and writing.

When children begin writing, they use scribbles or single letters to represent complex ideas (Clay, 1991; Schickedanz, 1990). As they learn about letter names and phoneme-grapheme correspondences, they use one, two, or three letters to stand for a word. At first they run their writing together, but they slowly learn to segment words and leave spaces between words. They sometimes add dots or lines as markers between words, or they draw circles around words. They also move from capitalizing words randomly to using a capital letter at the beginning of a sentence and to mark proper nouns. Similarly, children move from using periods at the end of each line of writing to marking the ends of sentences with periods. Then they learn about other end-of-sentence markers and, finally, about punctuation marks that are embedded in sentences.

Literacy Play Centers.   Young children learn about the functions of reading and writing as they use written language in their play. As they construct block buildings, children write signs and tape them on the buildings; as they play doctor, they write prescriptions on slips of paper; and as they play teacher, they read stories aloud to friends who are pretending to be students or to doll and stuffed-animal "students." Young children use these activities to reenact familiar, everyday activities and to pretend to be someone or something else.

To learn more about the power of drama as a learning tool, see Chapter 8, "Sustaining Talk in the Classroom."

Literacy-enriched centers.
These kindergartners use reading and writing as they play in the housekeeping center. They read recipes and food-package labels as they cook, for example, and write telephone messages when they answer the telephone. They also leave messages for classmates who will visit this center. After "baking" clay cookies, these children wrote this message using invented spelling: GD KE R U (good cookies for you). Through these activities, young children practice the literacy skills they are learning and learn to value reading and writing because of the important role literacy can play in their lives.

Through these literacy-enriched play activities, children use reading and writing for a variety of functions.

Kindergarten teachers adapt play centers and add literacy materials to enhance their value for literacy learning. Housekeeping centers are probably the most common play centers in kindergarten classrooms, but teachers can transform them into grocery stores, post offices, or medical centers by changing the props. Materials for reading and writing can be included in each of these centers. Food packages, price stickers, and money are props in grocery store centers; letters, stamps, and mailboxes in post office centers; and appointment books, prescription pads, and folders for patient records in medical centers. A variety of literacy play centers can be set up in classrooms to coordinate with units and theme cycles. Ideas for literacy play centers are offered in Figure 4–1.

FIGURE 4-1

Literacy Play Centers With Reading and Writing Materials

Post Office Center

mailboxes	wrapping paper	package seals
envelopes	tape	address labels
stamps (stickers)	packages	cash register
pens	scale	money

Hairdresser Center

hair rollers	towel	curling iron (cordless)
brush and comb	posters of hairstyles	ribbons, barrettes, clips
mirror	wig and wig stand	appointment book
empty shampoo bottle	hair dryer (cordless)	open/closed sign

Restaurant Center

tablecloth	napkins	aprons/vests for waitstaff
dishes	menus	hat and apron for chef
glasses	tray	
silverware	order pad and pencil	

Medical Center

appointment books	stethoscope	folders (for patient
white shirt/jacket	thermometer	records)
medical bag	tweezers	prescription bottles
hypodermic syringe	bandages	and labels
(play)	prescription pad	walkie-talkie

Grocery Store Center

grocery cart	price stickers	marking pen
food packages	cash register	cents-off coupons
plastic fruit and	money	advertisements
artificial foods	grocery bags	

Each center includes authentic literacy materials that children can experiment with and use to learn more about the functions of written language.

Concepts About the Alphabet

Turn back to Chapter 1, "Learning and the Language Arts," to review the four language systems.

Young children also develop concepts about the alphabet and how letters are used to represent phonemes. Children use this phonics knowledge to decode unfamiliar words as they read and to create spellings for words as they write. Too often it is assumed that phonics instruction is the most important component of the reading program for young children, but phonics is only one of the four language systems. Emergent readers and writers use all four language systems—phonological, semantic, syntactic, and pragmatic—as well as their knowledge about written language concepts as they read and write.

The Alphabetic Principle.   The one-to-one correspondence between the phonemes (or sounds) and graphemes (or letters), such that each letter consistently represents one sound, is known as the alphabetic principle. In phonetic languages, there is a one-to-one correspondence; however, English is not a purely phonetic language. The 26 letters represent approximately 44 phonemes, and three letters—*c, q,* and *x*—are superfluous because they do not represent unique phonemes. The letter *c,* for example, can represent either /k/ as in *cat* or /s/ as in *city,* and it can be joined with *h* for the digraph /ch/. To further complicate matters, there are more than 500 spellings to represent the 44 phonemes. Consonants are more consistent and predictable than vowels. Long *e,* for instance, is spelled 14 ways in common words (Horn, 1957).

Researchers estimate that words are spelled phonetically approximately half the time (Hanna, Hanna, Hodges, & Rudorf, 1966). The nonphonetic spellings of many words reflect morphological information. The word *sign,* for instance, is a shortened form of *signature,* and the spelling shows this relationship. Spelling the word phonetically (i.e., *sine*) might seem simpler, but the phonetic spelling lacks semantic information (Venezky, 1999).

Check Chapter 14, "Developing Legible Handwriting," to learn more about teaching hand-writing to young children.

Letter Names.   The most basic information children learn about the alphabet is how to identify and form the letters in handwriting. They notice letters in environmental print, and they often learn to sing the ABC song. By the time children enter kindergarten, they can usually recognize some letters, especially those in their own names, in names of family members and pets, and in common words in their homes and communities. Children can also write some of these familiar letters.

Young children associate letters with meaningful contexts—names, signs, T-shirts, and cereal boxes. Baghban (1984) notes that the letter *M* was the first letter her daughter noticed. She pointed to *M* in the word *K Mart* and called it "McDonald's." Even though the child confused a store and a restaurant, this account demonstrates how young children make associations with letters. Research suggests that children do not learn alphabet letter names in any particular order or by isolating letters from meaningful written language. McGee and Richgels (2001, 2003) conclude that learning letters of the alphabet requires many, many experiences with meaningful written language.

They recommend that teachers take three steps to encourage children's alphabet learning:

1. *Capitalize on children's interests.* Teachers provide letter activities that children enjoy and talk about letters when children are interested in talking about them. Teachers know what features to comment on because they observe children during reading and writing activities to find out which letters or features of letters children are exploring. Children's questions also provide insights into what they are curious about.
2. *Talk about the role of letters in reading and writing.* Teachers talk about how letters represent sounds and how letters combine to spell words, and they point out capital and lowercase letters. Teachers often talk about the role of letters as they write with children.
3. *Teach routines and provide a variety of opportunities for alphabet learning.* Teachers use children's names and environmental print in literacy activities, do interactive writing, encourage children to use invented spellings, share alphabet books, and play letter games.

Teachers begin teaching letters of the alphabet using two sources of words—children's own names and environmental print. They also teach children to sing the alphabet song so that children will have a strategy to use to identify a particular letter. Children learn to sing the alphabet song and point to each letter on an alphabet chart until they reach the unfamiliar letter. This is an important strategy because it gives them a real sense of independence in identifying letters. Teachers also provide routines, activities, and games for talking about and manipulating letters. During these familiar, predictable activities, teachers and children say letter names, manipulate magnetic letters, and write letters on white boards. At first the teacher structures and guides the activities, but with experience, the children internalize the routine and do it independently, often at a literacy center. Figure 4–2 presents 10 routines or activities to teach the letters of the alphabet.

What is important about teaching students to identify and print the letters of the alphabet is that instruction is embedded in meaningful and authentic reading and writing experiences (McGee & Richgels, 2003). Instruction is meaningful when children can tie what they are learning to their own world and authentic when children can apply what they are learning to reading and writing stories and other books. Children recognize and write the letters found in environmental print and in their classmates' names, find familiar letters and words on classroom signs and in books, write letters and words as they respond to literature, and make books.

Being able to name the letters of the alphabet is a good predictor of beginning reading achievement, even though knowing the names of the letters does not directly affect a child's ability to read (Adams, 1990). A more likely explanation for this relationship between letter knowledge and reading is that children who have been actively involved in reading and writing activities before entering first grade know the names of the letters, and they are more likely to begin reading quickly. Simply teaching children to name the letters without the accompanying reading and writing experiences does not have this effect.

Phonemic Awareness.   Phonemic awareness is children's basic understanding that speech is composed of a series of individual sounds, and it provides the

FIGURE 4–2

Routines to Teach the Letters of the Alphabet

1. Environmental Print
Teachers collect food labels, toy traffic signs, and other environmental print for children to use in identifying letters. Children sort labels and other materials to find examples of a letter being studied.

2. Alphabet Books
Teachers read aloud alphabet books to build vocabulary and teach students the names of words that represent each letter. Then children reread the books and consult them to think of words when making books about a letter.

3. Magnetic Letters
Children pick all examples of one letter from a collection of magnetic letters or match upper- and lowercase letter forms of magnetic letters. They also arrange the letters in alphabetical order and use the letters to spell their names and other familiar words.

4. Letter Stamps
Students use letter stamps and ink pads to stamp letters on paper or in booklets. They also use letter-shaped sponges to paint letters and letter-shaped cookie cutters to make cookies and to cut out clay letters.

5. Key Words
Teachers use alphabet charts with a picture of a familiar object for each letter. It is crucial that children be familiar with the objects or they won't remember the key words. Teachers recite the alphabet with children, pointing to each letter and saying, "A—apple, B—bear, C—cat," and so on.

6. Letter Containers
Teachers collect coffee cans or shoe boxes, one for each letter of the alphabet. They write upper- and lowercase letters on the outsides of the containers and place several familiar objects or pictures of objects that represent the letter in each one. Teachers use these containers to introduce the letters, and children use them at a center for sorting and matching activities.

7. Letter Frames
Teachers make circle-shaped letter frames from tagboard, collect large plastic bracelets, or shape pipe cleaners or Wikki-Stix (pipe cleaners covered in wax) into circles for students to use to highlight particular letters on charts or in big books.

8. Letter Books and Posters
Children make letter books with pictures of objects beginning with a particular letter on each page. They add letter stamps, stickers, or pictures cut from magazines. For posters, the teacher draws a large letter form on a chart and children add pictures, stickers, and letter stamps.

9. Letter Sorts
Teachers collect objects and pictures representing two or more letters. Then children sort the objects and place them in containers marked with the specific letters.

10. White Boards
Children practice writing upper- and lowercase forms of a letter and familiar words on white boards.

foundation for phonics (Yopp, 1992). When children can choose a duck as the animal that begins with /d/ from a collection of toy animals, identify *duck* and *luck* as two words that rhyme, or blend the sounds /d/, /ŭ/, and /k/ to pronounce *duck,* they are phonemically aware. (Note that the emphasis is on the sounds of spoken words, not reading letters or pronouncing letter names.) Developing phonemic awareness enables children to use sound-symbol correspondences to read and spell words. Phonemic awareness is not sounding out words for reading, nor is it using spelling patterns to write words; rather, it is the ability to manipulate sounds orally.

Understanding that words are composed of smaller units—phonemes—is a significant achievement for young children because phonemes are abstract language units. Phonemes carry no meaning, and children think of words according to their meanings, not their linguistic characteristics (Griffith & Olson, 1992). When children think about ducks, for example, they think of animals covered with feathers that swim in ponds, fly through the air, and make noises we describe as "quacks." They don't think of *duck* as a word with three phonemes or four graphemes or as a word beginning with /d/ and rhyming with *luck.* Phonemic awareness requires that children treat speech as an object and that they shift their attention away from the meaning of words to the linguistic features of speech. This focus on phonemes is even more complicated because phonemes are not discrete units in speech. Often they are blended or slurred together; think about the blended initial sound in *tree* and the ending sound in *eating.*

Children develop phonemic awareness in two ways. They learn playfully as they sing songs, chant rhymes, and listen to parents and teachers read word-play books to them (Griffith & Olson, 1992). Yopp (1995) recommends that teachers read books with wordplay aloud and encourage students to talk about the books' language. Teachers ask questions and make comments, such as "Did you notice how _____ and _____ rhyme?" and "This book is fun because of all the words beginning with the /m/ sound." Once students are very familiar with the book, they can create new verses or make other variations. Books such as *Cock-a-doodle-moo!* (Most, 1996), *Jamberry* (Degen, 1983), and *The Baby Uggs Are Hatching* (Prelutsky, 1982) stimulate children to experiment with sounds, create nonsense words, and become enthusiastic about reading. When teachers read books with alliterative or assonant patterns, such as *Faint Frogs Feeling Feverish and Other Terrifically Tantalizing Tongue Twisters* (Obligado, 1983), children attend to the smaller units of language.

Teachers also teach lessons to help students understand that their speech is composed of sounds (Ball & Blachman, 1991; Lundberg, Frost, & Petersen, 1988). The goal of phonemic awareness activities is to break down and manipulate spoken words. Students who have developed phonemic awareness can manipulate spoken language in these five ways:

- Match words by sounds
- Isolate a sound in a word
- Blend individual sounds to form a word
- Substitute sounds in a word
- Segment a word into its constituent sounds (Yopp, 1992)

Teachers teach minilessons focusing on each of these tasks using familiar songs with improvised lyrics, riddles and guessing games, and wordplay books.

These activities should be playful and gamelike, and they should be connected to literature focus units and theme cycles whenever possible. Five types of activities are described in Figure 4–3.

Teachers often use Elkonin boxes to teach phonemic awareness. This activity comes from the work of Russian psychologist D. B. Elkonin (Clay, 1985). As illustrated in Figure 4–4, the teacher displays an object or picture of an object and draws a series of boxes, with one box for each sound in the name of the object. Then the teacher or a child moves a marker onto each box as the sound is pronounced. Children can move small markers onto cards on their desks, or the teacher can draw the boxes on the chalkboard and use tape or small magnets to hold the larger markers in place. Elkonin boxes can also be used for spelling activities. When a child is trying to spell a word, such as *duck,* the teacher can draw three boxes and then have the child write the letters representing each sound in the boxes.

Children experiment with oral language in phonemic awareness activities. Teachers have typically avoided having children read and write letters and words during these activities because the focus is on speech. More recently, however, teachers are finding that once students develop a rudimentary level of phonemic awareness, the activities are most effective when teachers begin with an oral language activity and then students apply what they are learning to decoding and spelling words.

The relationship between phonemic awareness and learning to read is extremely important, and researchers have concluded that at least some level of phonemic awareness is a prerequisite for learning to read (Gillon, 2004). In fact, phonemic awareness seems to be both a prerequisite for and a consequence of learning to read (Perfitti, Beck, Bell, & Hughes, 1987; Stanovich, 1980). As they become phonemically aware, children recognize that speech can be segmented into smaller units, and this knowledge is very useful when children learn about sound-symbol correspondences and spelling patterns.

Moreover, phonemic awareness has been shown to be the most powerful predictor of later reading achievement (Juel, Griffith, & Gough, 1986; Lomax & McGee, 1987; Tunmer & Nesdale, 1985). In a study comparing children's progress in learning to read in whole-language and traditional reading instruction, Klesius, Griffith, and Zielonka (1991) found that children who began first grade with strong phonemic awareness did well regardless of the kind of reading instruction they received. And neither type of instruction was better for children who were low in phonemic awareness at the beginning of first grade.

Phonics. Phonics is the set of relationships between phonology (the sounds in speech) and orthography (the spelling patterns of written language). Sounds are spelled in different ways, for several reasons. One reason is that sounds, especially vowels, vary according to their location in a word (e.g., *go–got*). Adjacent letters often influence how letters are pronounced (e.g., *bed–bead*), as do vowel markers such as the final *e* (e.g., *bit–bite*) (Shefelbine, 1995).

Phonics is a very controversial topic. Ken Goodman calls it "the most widely misunderstood aspect" of reading instruction (1993, p. 1). Some parents and politicians, as well as even a few teachers, believe that most of the educational ills in the United States could be solved if children were taught to read using phonics. A few people still argue that phonics is a complete reading program, but that view ignores what we know about the interrelatedness of the four

FIGURE 4–3

Five Types of Phonemic Awareness Activities

1. Sound-Matching Activities

Teachers create matching games using familiar objects and toys as well as pictures of familiar objects. From a collection of objects and pictures, including a football, a car, a fish, and a toothbrush, children choose the two that begin with the same sound. Or, children choose one of several items beginning with a particular sound. Children also identify rhyming words. They name a word that rhymes with a given word and identify rhyming words from familiar songs and stories.

2. Sound-Isolation Activities

Children identify the sounds at the beginning, middle, or end of the word, or teachers can set out a tray of objects and ask children to choose the one object that doesn't belong because it doesn't begin with the sound. From a tray with a toy pig, a puppet, a teddy bear, and a pen, for example, the teddy bear doesn't belong. Yopp (1992) created new verses to the tune of "Old MacDonald Had a Farm":

> What's the sound that starts these words:
> Chicken, chin and cheek?
> (wait for response)
> /ch/ is the sound that starts these words:
> Chicken, chin, and cheek.
> With a /ch/, /ch/ here, and a /ch/, /ch/ there,
> Here a /ch/, there a /ch/, everywhere a /ch/, /ch/.
> /ch/ is the sound that starts these words:
> Chicken, chin, and cheek. (p. 700)

Teachers change the question at the beginning of the verse to focus on medial and final sounds.

3. Sound-Blending Activities

Children play the "What am I thinking of?" guessing game. The teacher identifies several characteristics of an object and then pronounces its name, articulating each of the sounds separately (Yopp, 1992). Then children blend the sounds together and identify the word using both the phonological and semantic information that the teacher provided. For example:

> I am thinking of an animal that lives in a pond when it is young, but that lives on land when it is an adult. It is a /f/, /r/, /o/, /g/. What is it?

The children blend the sounds together to pronounce the word *frog*.

4. Sound Addition or Substitution Activities

Students create nonsense words as they add or substitute sounds in words in songs they sing or in books that are read aloud to them. Teachers read wordplay books, such as Hutchins's *Don't Forget the Bacon!* (1976), in which a boy leaves for the store with a mental list of four items to buy. As he walks, he repeats his list, substituting sounds and creating new words each time. "A cake for tea" changes to "a cape for me" and then to "a rake for leaves." Children suggest other substitutions, such as "a pail for maple sugar trees." They also substitute sounds in refrains of songs (Yopp, 1992). For example, students can change the "Ee-igh, ee-igh, oh!" refrain in "Old MacDonald Had a Farm" to "Bee-bigh, bee-bigh, boh!" to focus on the initial /b/ sound. Teachers choose one sound, such as /sh/, and have children substitute this sound for the beginning sound in their names and in familiar words. For example, *José* becomes *Shosé* and *clock* becomes *shock*.

5. Segmentation Activities

Children slowly pronounce a word, identifying all its sounds. Yopp (1992) suggests singing a song to the tune of "Twinkle, Twinkle, Little Star" in which children segment entire words. Here is one example:

> Listen, listen, to my word.
> Then tell me all the sounds you heard: *coat*
> /k/ is one sound, /o/ is two
> /t/ is last in coat; it's true. (p. 702)

After several repetitions of the verse segmenting other words, the song ends this way:

> Thanks for listening to my words
> And telling all the sounds you heard! (p. 702)

FIGURE 4-4

How to Use Elkonin Boxes

1. The teacher shows students an object or the picture of an object, such as a duck, a bed, a game, a bee, a cup, or a cat.

2. The teacher prepares a diagram with a series of boxes, corresponding to the number of sounds heard in the name of the object. For example, the teacher draws three boxes side by side to represent the three sounds heard in the word *duck*. The teacher can draw the boxes on the chalkboard or on small cards for each child to use. The teacher also prepares markers to place on the boxes.

3. The teacher or students say the word slowly and move markers onto the boxes as each sound is pronounced.

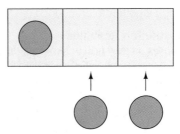

4. Elkonin boxes can also be used when spelling words. The teacher draws a series of boxes corresponding to the number of sounds heard in the word, and then the child and teacher pronounce the word, pointing to each box or sliding markers onto each box. Then the child writes the letters representing each sound or spelling pattern in the boxes.

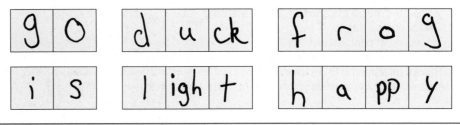

cueing systems. Reading is a complex process, and the phonological system works in conjunction with the semantic, syntactic, and pragmatic systems, not in isolation.

The controversy now centers on how to teach phonics. Marilyn Adams (1990), in her landmark review of the research on phonics instruction, recommends that phonics be taught within a balanced approach that integrates instruction in reading skills and strategies with meaningful opportunities for reading and writing. She emphasizes that phonics instruction should focus on the most useful information for identifying words and that it be systematic, intensive, and completed by the third grade.

Teachers teach sound-symbol correspondences, how to blend sounds together to decode words and segment sounds for spelling, and the most useful phonics generalizations, or "rules." Phonics concepts build on phonemic awareness. The most important concepts that primary-grade students learn are:

1. Consonants. Letters are classified as either consonants or vowels. The consonants are *b, c, d, f, g, h, j, k, l, m, n, p, q, r, s, t, v, w, x, y,* and *z.* Most consonants represent a single sound consistently, but there are some exceptions. *C,* for example, does not represent a sound of its own. When it is followed by *a, o,* or *u,* it is pronounced /k/ (e.g., *castle, coffee, cut*) and when it is followed by *e, i,* or *y,* it is pronounced /s/ (e.g., *cell, city, cycle*). *G* represents two sounds, as the word *garbage* illustrates. It is usually pronounced /g/ (e.g., *glass, go, green, guppy*), but when *g* is followed by *e* or *i,* it is pronounced /j/, as in *giant. Gy* is not a common English spelling, but when *g* is followed by *y* (e.g., *energy, gypsy, gymnasium*), it is usually pronounced /j/. *X* is also pronounced differently according to its location in a word. When *x* is at the beginning of a word, it is often pronounced /z/, as in *xylophone,* but sometimes the letter name is used, as in *X ray.* At the end of a word, *x* is pronounced /ks/, as in *box.*

The letters *w* and *y* are particularly interesting. At the beginning of a word or syllable, they are consonants (e.g., *wind, yard*), but when they are in the middle or at the end of a word or syllable, they are vowels (e.g., *saw, flown, day, by*).

Two kinds of combination consonants are blends and digraphs. Consonant blends are two or three consonants that appear next to each other in words and whose individual sounds are blended together, as in *grass, belt,* and *spring.* Consonant digraphs are letter combinations that represent single sounds. The four most common are *ch* as in *chair* and *each, sh* as in *shell* and *wish, th* as in *father* and *both,* and *wh* as in *whale.* Another consonant digraph is *ph,* as in *graph* and *photo.*

2. Vowels. The remaining five letters—*a, e, i, o,* and *u*—represent vowels, and *w* and *y* are vowels when used in the middle and at the end of syllables and words. Vowels represent several sounds. The most common are short and long vowels. The short-vowel sounds are /ă/ as in *cat,* /ĕ/ as in *bed,* /ĭ/ as in *win,* /ŏ/ as in *hot,* and /ŭ/ as in *cup.* The long-vowel sounds are the same as the letter names, and they are illustrated in the words *make, feet, bike, coal,* and *suit.* Long vowels are usually spelled with two vowels, except when *e* or *y* is used at the end of a word or syllable (e.g., *before, try*).

When *y* is a vowel at the end of a word, it is pronounced as long *e* or long *i,* depending on the length of the word. In one-syllable words, such as *by* and

For more information about how young children learn to spell, see Chapter 12, "Learning to Spell Conventionally."

try, the *y* is pronounced as long *i,* but in most longer words, such as *baby* and *happy,* the *y* is pronounced as long *e.*

Vowel sounds are more complicated than consonant sounds, and many vowel combinations represent long vowels and other vowel sounds. Consider these combinations:

> *ai* as in *nail*
>
> *au* as in *laugh* and *caught*
>
> *aw* as in *saw*
>
> *ea* as in *peach* and *bread*
>
> *ew* as in *sew* and *few*
>
> *ia* as in *dial*
>
> *ie* as in *cookie*
>
> *oa* as in *soap*
>
> *oi* as in *oil*
>
> *oo* as in *cook* and *moon*
>
> *ou* as in *house* and *through*
>
> *ow* as in *now* and *snow*
>
> *oy* as in *toy*

Most vowel combinations are vowel digraphs or diphthongs. When two vowels represent a single sound, the combination is a vowel digraph (e.g., *nail, snow*), and when two vowels represent a glide from one sound to another, the combination is a diphthong. Two vowel combinations that are consistently diphthongs are *oi* and *oy,* but other combinations, such as *ou* in *house* (but not in *through*) and *ow* as in *now* (but not in *snow*) are diphthongs when they represent a glided sound. In *through,* the *ou* represents the $\overline{oo}$ sound as in *moon,* and in *snow* the *ow* represents the $\overline{o}$ sound.

When *r* follows one or more vowels in a word, it influences the pronunciation of the vowel sound, as in *car, air, are, ear, bear, first, for, more, murder,* and *pure.* These sounds are called *r*-controlled vowels. Because they are difficult to sound out, students learn many of these words as sight words.

The vowels in the unaccented syllables of multisyllabic words are often softened and pronounced "uh," as in the first syllable of *about* and *machine* and the final syllable of *pencil, tunnel, zebra,* and *selection.* This vowel sound is called a *schwa* and is represented in dictionaries with a ə, which looks like an inverted *e.*

3. Rimes and Rhymes.   One-syllable words and syllables in longer words can be divided into two parts, the onset and the rime. The onset is the consonant sound, if any, that precedes the vowel and the rime is the vowel and any consonant sounds that follow it. For example, in *show, sh* is the onset and *ow* is the rime, and in *ball, b* is the onset and *all* is the rime. For *at* and *up,* there is no onset; the entire word is the rime. Research has shown that children make more errors decoding and spelling final consonants than initial consonants and that they make more errors on vowels than on consonants (Treiman, 1985). These problem areas correspond to rimes, and educators now speculate that onsets and rimes could provide a key to unlocking phonemic awareness.

Children can focus their attention on a rime, such as *ay*, and create rhyming words, including *bay, day, lay, may, play, say,* and *way*. These words can be read and spelled by analogy because the vowel sounds are consistent in rimes. Wylie and Durrell (1970) identified 37 rimes that can be used to produce nearly 500 words that primary-grade students read and write. These rimes and some common words using them are presented in the LA Essentials box on page 176.

4. Phonics Generalizations. Because English does not have a one-to-one correspondence between sounds and letters, both linguists and educators have tried to create rules or generalizations to clarify English spelling patterns. One rule is that *q* is followed by *u* and pronounced /kw/ (e.g., *queen* and *earthquake*). There are very few exceptions to this rule. Another generalization that has few exceptions relates to *r*-controlled vowels: *r* influences the preceding vowel so that its sound is neither long nor short (e.g., *car, market, birth,* and *four*). There are exceptions, however, for instance, *fire*.

Many generalizations aren't very useful because there are more exceptions to the rule than words that conform (Clymer, 1996). A good example is this long-vowel rule: When there are two vowels side by side, the long-vowel sound of the first one is pronounced and the second is silent. Teachers sometimes call this the "when two vowels go walking, the first one does the talking" rule. Examples of words conforming to this rule are *meat, soap,* and *each*. There are many more exceptions, however, including *food, said, head, chief, bread, look, soup, does, too, again,* and *believe*.

Only a few phonics generalizations have a high degree of utility for readers. The generalizations that work most of the time are the ones that students should learn because they are the most useful (Adams, 1990). Eight high-utility generalizations are listed in the LA Essentials box on page 177. Even though these rules are fairly reliable, very few of them approach 100% utility. The *r*-controlled vowel rule is useful in 78% of words in which the letter *r* follows the vowel (Adams, 1990). Other commonly taught, useful rules have even lower percentages of utility. The CVC pattern rule—which says that when a one-syllable word has only one vowel and the vowel comes between two consonants, it is usually short, as in *bat, land,* and *cup*—is estimated to work 62% of the time. Exceptions include *told, fall, fork,* and *birth*. The CVCe pattern rule—which says that when there are two vowels in a one-syllable word and one vowel is an *e* at the end of the word, the first vowel is long and the final *e* is silent—is estimated to work in 63% of CVCe words. Examples of conforming words are *came, hole,* and *pipe,* and two very common exceptions are *have* and *love*.

Students learn phonics as a natural part of reading and writing activities, and teachers also teach phonics directly and systematically. Teachers explain many phonics concepts as they engage children in authentic literacy activities using children's names, titles of books, and environmental print in the classroom. During these teachable moments, teachers answer students' questions about words, model how to use phonics knowledge to decode and spell words, and have students share the strategies they use for reading and writing (Mills, O'Keefe, & Stephens, 1992). For example, as part of a literature focus unit on *The Very Hungry Caterpillar* (Carle, 1969), teachers might point out that *Very* begins with *v* but that not many words start with *v*. Children might mention other *v* words, such as *valentine*. Teachers also demonstrate

LA Essentials

Thirty-Seven Common Rimes

-ack
black, pack, quack, stack

-ail
mail, nail, sail, tail

-ain
brain, chain, plain, rain

-ake
cake, shake, take, wake

-ale
male, sale, tale, whale

-ame
came, flame, game, name

-an
can, man, pan, than

-ank
bank, drank, sank, thank

-ap
cap, clap, map, slap

-ash
cash, dash, flash, trash

-at
bat, cat, rat, that

-ate
gate, hate, late, plate

-aw
claw, draw, jaw, saw

-ay
day, play, say, way

-eat
beat, heat, meat, wheat

-ell
bell, sell, shell, well

-est
best, chest, nest, west

-ice
ice, mice, nice, rice

-ick
brick, pick, sick, thick

-ide
bride, hide, ride, side

-ight
bright, fight, light, might

-ill
fill, hill, kill, will

-in
chin, grin, pin, win

-ine
fine, line, mine, nine

-ing
king, sing, thing, wing

-ink
pink, sink, think, wink

-ip
drip, hip, lip, ship

-ir
fir, sir, stir

-ock
block, clock, knock, sock

-oke
choke, joke, poke, woke

-op
chop, drop, hop, shop

-or
for, or

-ore
chore, more, shore, store

-uck
duck, luck, suck, truck

-ug
bug, drug, hug, rug

-ump
bump, dump, hump, lump

-unk
bunk, dunk, junk, sunk

Essentials

The Most Useful Phonics Generalizations

Pattern	Description	Examples	
1. Two sounds of *c*	The letter *c* can be pronounced as /k/ or /s/. When *c* is followed by *a*, *o*, or *u*, it is pronounced /k/—the hard *c* sound. When *c* is followed by *e*, *i*, or *y*, it is pronounced /s/—the soft *c* sound.	cat cough cut	cent city cycle
2. Two sounds of *g*	The sound associated with the letter *g* depends on the letter following it. When *g* is followed by *a*, *o*, or *u*, it is pronounced as /g/—the hard *g* sound. When *g* is followed by *e*, *i*, or *y*, it is usually pronounced /j/—the soft *g* sound. Exceptions include *get* and *give*.	gate go guess	gentle giant gypsy
3. CVC pattern	When a one-syllable word has only one vowel and the vowel comes between two consonants, it is usually short. One exception is *told*.	bat cup land	
4. Final *e* or CVCe pattern	When there are two vowels in a one-syllable word and one of them is an *e* at the end of the word, the first vowel is long and the final *e* is silent. Two exceptions are *have* and *love*.	home safe cute	
5. CV pattern	When a vowel follows a consonant in a one-syllable word, the vowel is long. Exceptions include *the, to,* and *do*.	go be	
6. *R*-controlled vowels	Vowels that are followed by the letter *r* are overpowered and are neither short nor long. One exception is *fire*.	car for birthday	
7. *-igh*	When *gh* follows *i*, the *i* is long and the *gh* is silent. Two exceptions are *neighbor* and *eight*.	high night	
8. *Kn-* and *wr-*	In words beginning with *kn-* and *wr-*, the first letter is not pronounced.	knee write	

Adapted from Clymer, 1996.

how to apply phonics information as they read big books with the class and do interactive writing. As they read and spell words, teachers break words apart into sounds and apply phonics rules and generalizations.

Teachers also present minilessons on specific high-utility phonics concepts, skills, and generalizations as part of a systematic program. According to Shefelbine, the program should be "systematic and thorough enough to enable most students to become independent and fluent readers; yet still efficient and streamlined" (1995, p. 2). Phonics instruction is always tied to reading and writing because without meaningful reading and writing activities, children see little reason to learn phonics (Cunningham, 2000; Freppon & Dahl, 1991).

YOUNG CHILDREN EMERGE INTO READING

Children move through three stages as they learn to read: emergent reading, beginning reading, and fluent reading (Juel, 1991). In emergent reading, children gain an understanding of the communicative purpose of print. They notice environmental print, dictate stories for the teacher to record, and reread predictable books after they have memorized the pattern. From this foundation, children move into the beginning reading stage. In this stage, children learn phoneme-grapheme correspondences and begin to decode words. In the third stage, fluent reading, children have learned how to read. They recognize most words automatically and can decode unfamiliar words quickly. Children should reach this fluent stage by third grade. Once they are fluent readers, children are able to concentrate more of their cognitive energy on comprehension. This accomplishment is significant because beginning in fourth grade, children read more informational books and content-area textbooks as reading becomes a learning tool.

Primary-grade teachers organize language arts instruction into the same four patterns of practice that teachers of middle- and upper-grade students use, but they make special adaptations to accommodate young children's developing literacy abilities. Two instructional adaptations that primary-grade teachers use are shared reading and the language experience approach. Through these approaches, kindergartners, first graders, and second graders read big books aloud with classmates, read independently books appropriate for their reading levels, and create texts by dictating their own words for the teachers to record. Teachers use these two approaches to support or scaffold young children's learning. Teachers model how fluent readers read and guide children as they practice reading skills and strategies. Through a multifaceted language arts program of literature, daily reading and writing experiences, and instruction in phonics, skills, and strategies, young children develop into fluent readers and writers.

Shared Reading

Teachers and children read books together in shared reading. Usually the teacher reads aloud as children follow along in regular-size or enlarged, big book picture books. Teachers use this approach to share the enjoyment of high-quality literature when students cannot read the books independently (Fisher & Medvic, 2000; Holdaway, 1979). As they read, teachers also demonstrate how print works, provide opportunities for children to use the prediction

Shared Reading

1. **Introduce the book.** Teachers introduce the book by activating children's prior knowledge about the topic or by presenting new information on a topic related to the book, and then by showing the cover of the book and reading the title and author's name. Then children make predictions about what will happen in the book. The purpose of these introductory activities is to involve children in the reading activity and to build their background knowledge.

2. **Read the book.** The teacher reads the book aloud while children follow along in individual copies or on a big book positioned on a chart rack beside the teacher. The teacher models fluent reading and uses a dramatic style to keep the children's attention. Teachers encourage children to chime in on words they can predict and for phrases, sentences, and refrains that are repeated. Periodically, teachers stop to ask children to make predictions about the story or to redirect their attention to the text.

3. **Respond to the book.** Children respond to the book by drawing and writing in reading logs and by sharing their responses in grand conversations. During shared reading, enjoyment is the primary goal. Afterward, children use the book to learn more about written language.

4. **Reread the book.** Children take turns turning pages and using the pointer to track the reading. Teachers invite children to join in reading familiar and predictable words. Also, they take opportunities to teach and use graphophonic cues and reading strategies while reading.

5. **Continue the process.** Teachers continue to reread the book with children several more times over a period of several days, again having them turn pages and take turns using the pointer to track the text while reading. They encourage children who can read the text to read along with them.

6. **Have students read independently.** After children become familiar with the text, teachers distribute individual copies of the book or other text for them to read independently and use for a variety of activities.

strategy, and increase children's confidence in their ability to read. Shared reading is often used with emergent readers; however, teachers also use shared reading with older students who cannot read independently. The steps in shared reading are listed in the Step by Step feature above.

Predictable Books. The stories and other books teachers use for shared reading with young children often have repeated words and sentences, rhyme, or other patterns. Books that use these patterns are known as predictable books. They are a valuable tool for emergent readers because the repeated words and sentences, patterns, and sequence enable children to predict the next sentence or episode in the story or other book (Heald-Taylor, 1987; Tompkins & Webeler, 1983). Four characteristics of predictable books are:

Repetition.   Phrases and sentences are repeated over and over to create a predictable pattern in many books for young children. Examples include *I Went Walking* (Williams, 1989), *Barnyard Banter* (Fleming, 1994), and *Polar Bear, Polar Bear, What Do You Hear?* (Martin, 1992). Sometimes each episode or section of the text ends with the same words or a refrain, and in other books, the same statement or question is repeated. For example, in *The Little Red Hen* (Galdone, 1973), the animals repeat "Not I" when the Little Red Hen asks them to help her plant the seeds, harvest the wheat, and bake the bread. After their refusals to help, the hen each time says, "Then I will."

Cumulative Sequence.   In other books, phrases or sentences are repeated and expanded in each episode. In *The Gingerbread Boy* (Galdone, 1975), for instance, Gingerbread Boy repeats and expands his boast as he meets each character on his run away from Little Old Man and Little Old Woman. Other examples include *Jack's Garden* (Cole, 1995) and *Jump, Frog, Jump!* (Kalan, 1995).

Rhyme and Rhythm.   Rhyme and rhythm are important devices in some books. Many of the popular Dr. Seuss books, such as *Hop on Pop* (1963), are good examples. The sentences have a strong beat, and rhyme is used at the end of each line or in another poetic scheme. Also, some books have an internal rhyme—within lines rather than at the ends of lines. Other books in this category include familiar songs, such as *Skip to My Lou* (Westcott, 1989), and booklong verses, such as *Sailaway Home* (Degen, 1996).

Sequential Patterns.   Some books use a familiar sequence—such as months of the year, days of the week, numbers 1 to 10, or letters of the alphabet—to structure the text. For example, *The Very Hungry Caterpillar* (Carle, 1969) combines number and day-of-the-week sequences as the caterpillar eats through an amazing array of foods. Laura Numeroff's *If You Give a Mouse a Cookie* (1985) is another example of a predictable sequence.

A list of predictable books illustrating each of these patterns is presented in the Classroom Library box on page 181.

Big Books.   Teachers use enlarged picture books called big books in shared reading, most commonly with primary-grade students. In this technique, developed in New Zealand, teachers place the enlarged picture book on an easel or chart rack where all children can see it; the teacher reads the big book with small groups of children or with the whole class (Holdaway, 1979). Trachtenburg and Ferruggia (1989) used big books with their class of transitional first graders and found that making and reading big books dramatically improved children's reading scores on standardized achievement tests. The teachers reported that children's self-concepts as readers were decidedly improved as well.

Many popular picture books, including *Tar Beach* (Ringgold, 1991), *How Much Is a Million?* (Schwartz, 1994), *Wilfred Gordon McDonald Partridge* (Fox, 1988), *The Mitten* (Brett, 1989), *Rosie's Walk* (Hutchins, 1987), and *Eating the Alphabet: Fruits and Vegetables From A to Z* (Ehlert, 1994), are available in big book editions. Teachers and children can also make big books themselves by printing the text of a book on large sheets of posterboard and adding illustrations. These books can be retellings of published books, innovations or new versions of familiar stories, or original stories or informational books that children have created. The steps in making a big book are shown in Figure 4–5.

Young Children's Books With Predictable Patterns

Repetitive Sentences

Bennett, J. (1985). *Teeny tiny.* New York: Putnam.

Carle, E. (1973). *Have you seen my cat?* New York: Philomel.

Carle, E. (1990). *The very quiet cricket.* New York: Philomel.

Carle, E. (1995). *The very lonely firefly.* New York: Philomel.

Cohen, C. L. (1996). *Where's the fly?* New York: Greenwillow.

Fleming, D. (1994). *Barnyard banter.* New York: Henry Holt.

Florian, D. (2000). *A pig is big.* New York: Greenwillow.

Fox, M. (1998). *Boo to a goose.* New York: Dial.

Galdone, P. (1973). *The little red hen.* New York: Seabury.

Guarino, D. (1989). *Is your mama a llama?* New York: Scholastic.

Hill, E. (1980). *Where's Spot?* New York: Putnam.

Hoberman, M. A. (2001). *"It's simple," said Simon.* New York: Knopf.

Hutchins, P. (1972). *Good-night, owl!* New York: Macmillan.

Hutchins, P. (1986). *The doorbell rang.* New York: Morrow.

Kalan, R. (1993). *Stop, thief!* New York: Greenwillow.

Lyon, G. E. (1989). *Together.* New York: Orchard.

Martin, B., Jr. (1983). *Brown bear, brown bear, what do you see?* New York: Holt, Rinehart and Winston.

Martin, B., Jr. (1992). *Polar bear, polar bear, what do you hear?* New York: Holt, Rinehart and Winston.

Peek, M. (1981). *Roll over!* Boston: Houghton Mifflin.

Peek, M. (1985). *Mary wore her red dress.* New York: Clarion.

Root, P. (2001). *Rattletrap car.* Cambridge, MA: Candlewick Press.

Rosen, M. (1989). *We're going on a bear hunt.* New York: Macmillan.

Souhami, J. (1996). *Old MacDonald.* New York: Orchard.

Weiss, N. (1987). *If you're happy and you know it.* New York: Greenwillow.

Weiss, N. (1989). *Where does the brown bear go?* New York: Viking.

Westcott, N. B. (1988). *The lady with the alligator purse.* Boston: Little, Brown.

Williams, S. (1989). *I went walking.* San Diego, CA: Harcourt Brace Jovanovich.

Cumulative Sequence

Brett, J. (1989). *The mitten.* New York: Putnam.

Fox, H. (1986). *Hattie and the fox.* New York: Bradbury.

Galdone, P. (1975). *The gingerbread boy.* New York: Seabury.

Kalan, R. (1995). *Jump, frog, jump!* New York: Greenwillow.

Neitzel, S. (2001). *I'm not feeling well today.* New York: Greenwillow.

Robart, R. (1992). *The cake that Mack ate.* Boston: Houghton Mifflin.

Thomas, S. M. (1995). *Putting the world to sleep.* Boston: Houghton Mifflin.

West, C. (1996). *"I don't care!" said the bear.* Cambridge, MA: Candlewick.

Westcott, N. B. (1980). *I know an old lady who swallowed a fly.* Boston: Little, Brown.

Westcott, N. B. (1990). *There's a hole in the bucket.* New York: HarperCollins.

Zemach, M. (1983). *The little red hen.* New York: Farrar, Straus & Giroux.

Rhyme and Rhythm

Archambault, J. (1996). *A beautiful feast for a big king cat.* New York: HarperCollins.

Martin, B., Jr., & Archambault, J. (1989). *Chicka chicka boom boom.* New York: Aladdin.

Raffi. (1999). *Down by the bay.* New York: Crown.

Seuss, Dr. (1963). *Hop on Pop.* New York: Random House.

Seuss, Dr. (1988). *Green eggs and ham.* New York: Random House.

Westcott, N. B. (1989). *Skip to my Lou.* Boston: Little, Brown.

Sequential Patterns

Carle, E. (1969). *The very hungry caterpillar.* Cleveland: Collins-World.

Carle, E. (1984). *The very busy spider.* New York: Philomel.

Carle, E. (1987). *A house for Hermit Crab.* New York: Simon & Schuster.

Galdone, P. (1986). *Over in the meadow.* New York: Simon & Schuster.

Kraus, R. (1995). *Come out and play, little mouse.* New York: HarperCollins.

Mack, S. (1974). *10 bears in my bed.* New York: Pantheon.

Martin, B., Jr. (1970). *Monday, Monday, I like Monday.* New York: Holt, Rinehart and Winston.

Numeroff, L. J. (1985). *If you give a mouse a cookie.* New York: HarperCollins.

Numeroff, L. J. (2002). *If you take a mouse to school.* New York: HarperCollins.

Wood, A. (1984). *The napping house.* San Diego, CA: Harcourt Brace Jovanovich.

FIGURE 4–5

The Steps in Making a Big Book

1. Collect materials, including sheets of posterboard or chart paper, pens, crayons, paints, and other art materials.

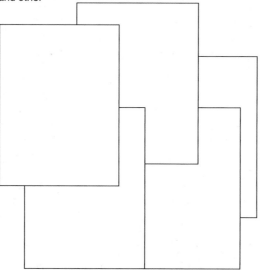

2. Print the text of the story, nursery rhyme, song, or poem on the large sheets of paper, dividing the text evenly across the pages of the book and leaving at least half of each page for illustration.

Birds lived in nests in the big old tree.

Squirrels played in the big old tree.

3. Add illustrations, which can be drawn by children or teachers. Teachers can also use opaque projectors to reproduce illustrations from picture books.

Birds lived in nests in the big old tree.

Squirrels played in the big old tree.

FIGURE 4-5

Continued

4. Add a title page with names of authors and illustrators and copyright. When students adapt books, that should also be stated on the title page.

5. Design a cover.

6. Put the pages into sequence.

Front Cover
Title Page

Back Cover

7. Bind the book together with metal rings, yarn, or clips.

Cross-Age Reading Buddies.   One way to use shared reading in a kinder-garten or first-grade classroom is with cross-age reading buddies. A class of upper-grade students is paired with a class of emergent readers, and the students become reading buddies. Older students read books with younger children, using shared reading techniques so that the younger children do more and more of the reading as they become familiar with the book. Research supports the effectiveness of cross-age tutoring, and teachers report that students' reading fluency increases and their attitudes toward school and learning become more positive (Caserta-Henry, 1996; Labbo & Teale, 1990; Morrice & Simmons, 1991).

Teachers arranging a buddy reading program decide when the students will get together, how long each session will last, and what the reading schedule will be. Primary-grade teachers explain the program to their students and talk about activities the buddies will be doing together. Upper-grade teachers teach a series of minilessons about how to work with young children, how to read aloud and encourage children to make predictions, how to use shared reading, how to select books to appeal to younger children, and how to help them respond to books. Then older students choose books to read aloud and practice reading them until they can read the books fluently.

At the first meeting, the students pair off, get acquainted, and read together. They also talk about the books they have read and perhaps write in special reading logs. Buddies also may want to go to the library and choose the books they will read at the next session.

There are significant social benefits to cross-age tutoring programs. Children get acquainted with other children that they might otherwise not meet, and they learn how to work with older or younger children. As they talk about books they have read, they share personal experiences. They also talk about reading strategies, how to choose books, and their favorite authors or illustration styles. Sometimes reading buddies write notes back and forth, or the two classrooms plan holiday celebrations together, and these activities strengthen the social connections between the children.

Traveling Bags of Books.   Another way to encourage shared reading is to involve parents by using traveling bags of books. Teachers collect text sets of three, four, or five books on various topics for children to take home and read with their parents (Reutzel & Fawson, 1990). For example, teachers might collect copies of *The Gingerbread Boy* (Galdone, 1975), *Flossie and the Fox* (McKissack, 1986), *Red Fox Dances* (Baron, 1996), and *Rosie's Walk* (Hutchins, 1968) for a traveling bag of fox stories. Then children and their parents read one or more of the books and draw or write a response to the books they have read in the reading log that accompanies the books in the traveling bag. One family's response after reading *The Gingerbread Boy* is shown in Figure 4–6. In this entry, the kindergartner drew a picture of Gingerbread Boy, an older sibling wrote the sentence the kindergartner dictated to accompany the picture, and the children's mother also wrote a comment. Children keep the bag at home for several days and then return it to school so that another child can borrow it. Text sets for 10 traveling bags are listed in the Classroom Library box on page 186. Many of these text sets include combinations of stories, informa-

FIGURE 4–6 *A Family's Reading Log Entry Written After Reading* The Gingerbread Boy

tional books, and poems. Teachers can also add small toys, stuffed animals, au-diotapes of one of the books, or other related objects to the bags.

Teachers often introduce traveling bags at a special parents' meeting or an open house get-together and explain how parents use shared reading to read with their children. It is important for parents to understand that their children may not be familiar with the books and that the children are not expected to be able to read them independently. Teachers also talk about the responses that children and parents write in the reading log and show sample entries from the previous year.

Language Experience Approach

The language experience approach (LEA) is based on children's language and experiences (Ashton-Warner, 1965; Stauffer, 1970). Children dictate words and sentences about their experiences, and the teacher takes down the dicta-tion for the children. The text they develop becomes the reading material. Be-cause the language comes from the children themselves, and because the content is based on their experiences, they are usually able to read the text eas-ily. Reading and writing are connected as students are actively involved in read-ing what they have written. The steps are shown in the Step by Step feature on page 187.

The language experience approach is an effective way to help children emerge into reading. Even students who have not been successful with other types of reading activities can read what they have dictated. There is a drawback, however: Teachers provide a "perfect" model when they take

Text Sets for Traveling Bags of Books

Books About Airplanes

Barton, R. (1982). *Airport.* New York: Harper & Row.

Maynard, C. (1995). *Airplane.* New York: Dorling Kindersley.

McPhail, D. (1987). *First flight.* Boston: Little, Brown.

Ziegler, S. (1988). *A visit to the airport.* Chicago: Childrens Press.

Books About Dogs

Barracca, D., & Barracca, S. (1990). *The adventures of taxi dog.* New York: Dial.

Bridwell, N. (1963). *Clifford the big red dog.* New York: Greenwillow.

Cole, J. (1991). *My puppy is born.* New York: Morrow.

Reiser, L. (1992). *Any kind of dog.* New York: Greenwillow.

Books by Ezra Jack Keats

Keats, E. J. (1962). *The snowy day.* New York: Viking.

Keats, E. J. (1964). *Whistle for Willie.* New York: Viking.

Keats, E. J. (1967). *Peter's chair.* New York: Harper & Row.

Keats, E. J. (1969). *Goggles.* New York: Macmillan.

Keats, E. J. (1970). *Hi cat!* New York: Macmillan.

Books About Frogs and Toads

Lobel, A. (1970). *Frog and Toad are friends.* New York: Harper & Row.

Mayer, M. (1974). *Frog goes to dinner.* New York: Dial.

Pallotta, J. (1990). *The frog alphabet book: And other awesome amphibians.* Watertown, MA: Charlesbridge.

Watts, B. (1991). *Frog.* New York: Lodestar.

Yolen, J. (1980). *Commander Toad in space.* New York: Coward-McCann.

Books About Mice

Cauley, L. B. (1984). *The city mouse and the country mouse.* New York: Putnam.

Henkes, K. (1991). *Chrysanthemum.* New York: Greenwillow.

Lionni, L. (1969). *Alexander and the wind-up mouse.* New York: Pantheon.

Lobel, A. (1977). *Mouse soup.* New York: Harper & Row.

Numeroff, L. J. (1985). *If you give a mouse a cookie.* New York: Harper & Row.

Books About Numbers

Aker, S. (1990). *What comes in 2's, 3's, & 4's?* New York: Simon & Schuster.

Bang, M. (1983). *Ten, nine, eight.* New York: Greenwillow.

Giganti, P., Jr. (1992). *Each orange had 8 slices: A counting book.* New York: Greenwillow.

Tafuri, N. (1986). *Who's counting?* New York: Greenwillow.

Books About Plants

Bunting, E. (1994). *Flower garden.* San Diego: Harcourt Brace.

Ehlert, L. (1987). *Growing vegetable soup.* San Diego: Harcourt Brace Jovanovich.

Ford, M. (1995). *Sunflower.* New York: Greenwillow.

Lobel, A. (1990). *Alison's zinnia.* New York: Greenwillow.

Books About Rain

Branley, F. M. (1985). *Flash, crash, rumble, and roll.* New York: Harper & Row.

Polacco, P. (1990). *Thunder cake.* New York: Philomel.

Shulevitz, U. (1969). *Rain rain rivers.* New York: Farrar, Straus & Giroux.

Spier, P. (1982). *Rain.* New York: Doubleday.

Books About the Three Bears

Cauley, L. B. (1981). *Goldilocks and the three bears.* New York: Putnam.

Galdone, P. (1972). *The three bears.* New York: Clarion Books.

Tolhurst, M. (1990). *Somebody and the three Blairs.* New York: Orchard Books.

Turkle, B. (1976). *Deep in the forest.* New York: Dutton.

Books About Trucks

Crews, D. (1980). *Truck.* New York: Greenwillow.

Llewellyn, C. (1995). *Truck.* New York: Dorling Kindersley.

Rockwell, A. (1984). *Trucks.* New York: Dutton.

Rotner, S. (1995). *Wheels around.* Boston: Houghton Mifflin.

Siebert, D. (1984). *Truck song.* New York: Harper & Row.

Language Experience Approach

1. **Provide an experience.** A meaningful experience is identified to serve as the stimulus for the writing. For group writing, it can be a school experience, a book read aloud, a field trip, or some other experience—such as having a pet or playing in the snow—that all children are familiar with. For individual writing, the stimulus can be any experience that is important for the particular child.

2. **Talk about the experience.** Students and teacher discuss the experience prior to writing. The purpose of the talk is to generate words and review the experience so that the children's dictation will be more interesting and complete. Teachers often begin with an open-ended question, such as, "What are you going to write about?" As children talk about their experiences, they clarify and organize ideas, use more specific vocabulary, and extend their understanding.

3. **Record the dictation.** Teachers write down the child's dictation. Texts for individual children are written on sheets of writing paper or in small booklets, and group texts are written on chart paper. Teachers print neatly and spell words correctly, but they preserve students' language as much as possible. For individual texts, teachers continue to take the child's dictation and write until the child finishes or hesitates. If the child hesitates, the teacher rereads what has been written and encourages the child to continue. For group texts, children take turns dictating sentences, and after writing each sentence, the teacher rereads it.

4. **Read the text.** After the text has been dictated, the teacher reads it aloud, pointing to each word. This reading reminds children of the content of the text and demonstrates how to read it aloud with appropriate intonation. Then children join in the reading. After reading group texts together, individual children can take turns rereading. Group texts can also be copied so that each child has a copy to read independently.

children's dictation—they write neatly and spell all words correctly. After language experience activities, some young children are not eager to do their own writing, because they prefer their teacher's "perfect" writing to their own childlike writing. To avoid this problem, teachers have young children do their own writing in personal journals and take part in other writing activities concurrently with the language experience activities. In this way, children learn that sometimes they do their own writing, and at other times the teacher takes their dictation.

YOUNG CHILDREN EMERGE INTO WRITING

Many young children become writers before entering kindergarten; others are introduced to writing during their first year of school (Harste et al., 1984; Temple, Nathan, Burris, & Temple, 1988). Young children's writing development follows a pattern similar to their reading development: emergent writing, beginning writing, and fluent writing. In the first stage, emergent writing, children make scribbles to represent writing. At first, the scribbles may appear randomly on a page, but with experience, children line up the letters or scribbles from left to right and from top to bottom. Children also begin to "read," or tell what their writing says. The next stage is beginning writing, and it signals children's growing awareness of the alphabetic principle. Children use invented spelling to represent words, and as they learn more about phoneme-grapheme correspondences, their writing approximates conventional spelling. They move from writing single words to writing sentences and experiment with capital letters and punctuation marks. The third stage is fluent writing, when children write in paragraphs and vary their writing according to genre. They use mainly correct spelling and other conventions of written language, including capital letters and punctuation marks.

Opportunities for writing begin on the first day of kindergarten and continue daily throughout the primary grades, regardless of whether children have already learned to read or write letters and words. Children often begin using a combination of art and scribbles or letterlike forms to express themselves. Their writing moves toward conventional forms as they apply concepts that they are learning about written language.

Four samples of young children's writing are shown in Figure 4–7. The first sample is a kindergartner's letter to the Great Pumpkin. The writing is at the emergent stage. The child wrote using scribbles, much like cursive, and followed the left-to-right, top-to-bottom orientation. The Great Pumpkin's comment, "I love you all," can be deciphered. The second sample is characteristic of the beginning stage. A kindergartner wrote this list of favorite foods as part of a literature focus unit on *The Very Hungry Caterpillar* (Carle, 1969). The list reads, "orange, strawberry, apple, pizza, birthday cake." The third sample is another example of beginning-stage writing. It was taken from a first grader's reading log. The child used invented spelling to list the animal characters that appear in *The Mitten* (Brett, 1989). The fifth animal from the top is a badger. The fourth sample is a page from a first grader's dinosaur book. The text reads, "No one ever saw a real dinosaur," and this child used a capital letter to begin the sentence and a period to mark the end. This sample shows the transition from beginning to fluent writing.

Introducing Young Children to Writing

Young children's writing grows out of talking and drawing. As they begin to write, their writing is literally their talk written down, and children can usually express in writing the ideas they talk about. At the same time, children's letterlike marks develop from their drawing. With experience, children learn to differentiate between their drawing and their writing. Kindergarten teachers often explain to children that they should use crayons when they draw and pencils when they write. Teachers

FIGURE 4-7 *Four Samples of Young Children's Writing*

To: The Great Pumpkin
From: melissa

I ♥ U ALL

orange
sdribare
apple
pizza
Brfeday ka

Mole
Ra bot
Hajhaog
oawl
Blre
Focs
Brae
mous

No one
evur sae
a rel dinsur.

also differentiate where on a page children will write and draw: The drawing might go at the top of a page and the writing at the bottom, or children can use paper with space for drawing at the top and lines for writing at the bottom.

Teachers help children emerge into writing beginning on the first day of kindergarten when they give children pencils and encourage them to write. We can call the writing of young children "kid writing" and contrast it with teachers' writing, or adult writing. When young children understand that their writing is allowed to look different from adults' writing, they are more willing to experiment with writing. Teachers show children how to hold a pencil and do kid writing with scribbles; random, letterlike marks; or letters. During kindergarten and first grade, children's writing gradually comes more closely to approximate adult writing because teachers are modeling adult writing for children, teaching minilessons about written language, and involving them in writing activities.

Kid writing takes many different forms. It may be scribbles or a collection of random marks on paper. Sometimes children imitate adults' cursive writing as they scribble. Children string together letters that have no phoneme-grapheme correspondences, or they use one or two letters to represent entire words. Children with more experience with written language invent spellings that represent more sound features of words and apply some spelling rules. A child's progressive writings of "Abbie is my dog. I love her very much" over a period of eighteen months are presented in Figure 4–8. The child moves from using scribbles, to using single letters to represent words (top two entries), to spelling phonetically and misapplying a few spelling rules (third and fourth entries). Note that in the fourth example, the child is experimenting with using periods to mark spaces between words. In the fifth example, the child's writing is more conventional, and more than half of the words are spelled correctly. The message is written as two sentences, which are marked at the beginning with capital letters and at the end with periods.

Kid writing is important for young children to understand because it gives them permission to experiment with written language when they draw and write. Too often, children assume that they should write and spell like adults do, and they cannot. Without this ability, children do not want to write, or they ask teachers to spell every word or copy text out of books or from charts. Kid writing offers students several strategies for writing and gives them permission to invent spellings that reflect their knowledge of written language.

Interactive Writing

Teachers use interactive writing to model adult or conventional writing (Button, Johnson, & Furgerson, 1996; Tompkins & Collom, 2004). In this teaching strategy, children and the teacher collaborate on constructing the text to be written. Teachers reinforce concepts about written language, provide opportunities to create texts, and focus children's attention on individual words and sounds within words. This teaching strategy grew out of the language experience approach, and conventional writing is used so that everyone can read the completed text.

Topics for interactive writing can come from stories students have read, classroom news, and information learned during theme cycles. Children take

Turn to Chapter 12, "Learning to Spell Conventionally," to read more about the stages of invented spelling.

To view an interactive writing lesson in action, check the CD-ROM that accompanies this text.

FIGURE 4-8   *The Development of One Child's Kid Writing*

Scribble Writing

One-Letter Labeling

Invented Spelling Without Spacing

More Sophisticated Invented Spelling With Spacing

More Conventional Writing in Sentences

turns holding the marking pen and doing the writing themselves. They usually sit in a circle on the carpet and take turns writing the text they construct on chart paper that is displayed on an easel. While one student is writing at the easel, the others are writing on small chalkboards or white boards in their laps.

Teachers begin by collecting the necessary materials. For whole-class or small-group activities, they collect chart paper, colored marking pens, white correction tape, an alphabet chart, magnetic letters, and a pointer. They also collect small white boards, dry-erase pens, and erasers for children to use. The steps in interactive writing are shown in the Step by Step feature on page 192.

When students begin interactive writing in kindergarten, they write letters to represent the beginning sounds in words and write familiar words such as *the, a,*

Step by Step

1. **Collect materials.**   Teachers collect chart paper, colored marking pens, white correction tape, an alphabet chart, magnetic letters or letter cards, and a pointer. They also collect small white boards, dry-erase pens, and erasers for individual students' writing.

2. **Set a purpose.**   Teachers present a stimulus activity or set a purpose for the interactive writing activity. Often they read or reread a trade book, but students also write daily news, compose a letter, or brainstorm information they are learning in a theme cycle.

3. **Choose a sentence to write.**   Teachers negotiate the text—often a sentence or two—with students. Students repeat the sentence several times and segment it into words. The teacher also helps the students remember the sentence as it is being written.

4. **Pass out writing supplies.**   Teachers distribute individual white boards, dry-erase pens, and erasers for students to use to write the text individually as it is written on chart paper. They periodically ask students to hold their white boards up so they can see what the students are writing.

5. **Write the first sentence word by word.**   Before writing the first word, teachers slowly pronounce the word, "pulling" it from their mouths or "stretching" it out. Then students take turns writing the letters in the first word. The teacher chooses students to write a sound or the entire word, depending on students' knowledge of phonics and spelling. Teachers often have students use one color of pen for the letters they write, and they use another color and write the parts of words that students can't spell. In that way, teachers can keep track of how much writing students are able to do. Teachers keep a poster with the upper- and lowercase letters of the alphabet to refer to when students are unsure about a letter form, and they use white correction tape (sometimes called "boo-boo" tape) when students write a letter incorrectly or write the wrong letter. After writing each word, one student serves as the "spacer"; this student uses his or her hand to mark the space between words and sentences. Teachers have students reread the sentence from the beginning each time a new word is completed. When appropriate, teachers call children's attention to capital letters, punctuation marks, and other conventions of print. They repeat this procedure to write additional sentences to complete the text.

6. **Display the interactive writing.**   After the writing is completed, teachers post the chart in the classroom and have students reread the text using shared or independent reading. Students often reread interactive charts when they "read the room." They may also add artwork to "finish" the chart.

FIGURE 4-9   *A Kindergarten Class Interactive Writing Chart*

Brushing Teeth
Brush your teeth after
You eat food.
Brush your teeth in the morning
and at night.
If You don't you will get
cavities.

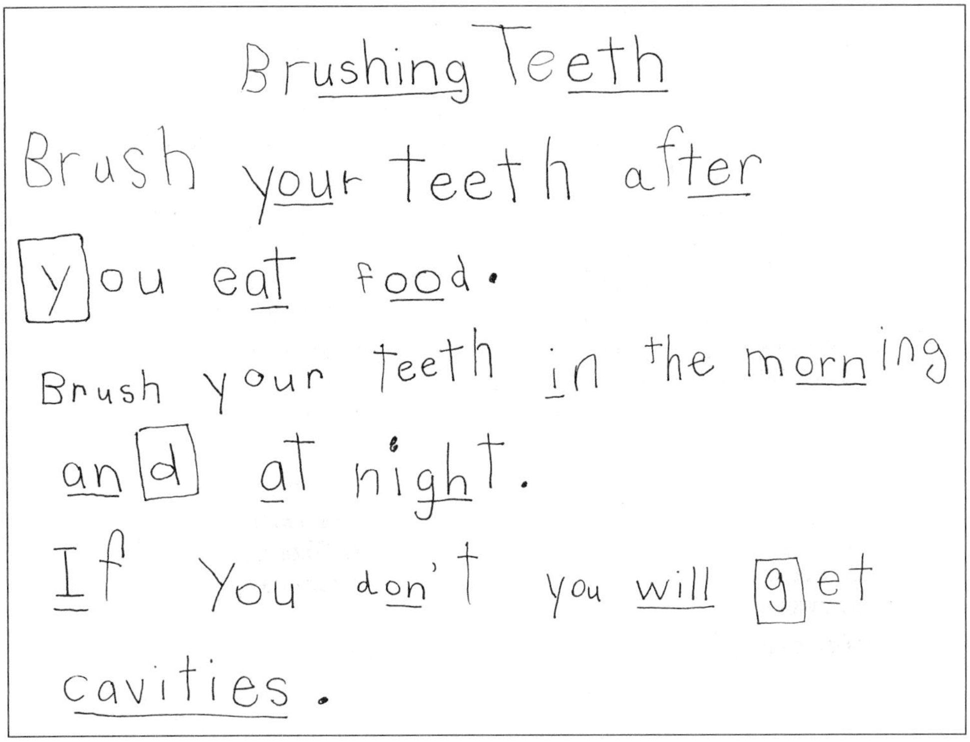

and *is*. The first letters that students write are often the letters in their own names. As students learn more about sound-symbol correspondences and spelling patterns, they do more of the writing. Once students are writing words fluently, they can continue to do interactive writing as they work in small groups. Each student in the group uses a particular color pen, and students take turns writing letters, letter clusters, and words. They also get used to using the white correction tape to correct poorly formed letters and misspelled words.

Figure 4–9 presents an interactive writing chart about brushing teeth. It was written over several days by a kindergarten class after a visit to a dentist. Notice that the children knew most beginning and ending sounds and the sight words *you* and *the*. Underlining has been added to show the letters the teacher wrote, and the boxes around letters indicate the use of correction tape.

Minilessons About Reading and Writing

Teachers teach minilessons about written language concepts and other reading and writing topics to young children in kindergarten and the primary grades. Children learn about how reading and writing are used to convey messages and how children behave as readers and writers. A list of minilesson topics is presented on pages 194 and 195 along with the steps for teaching a minilesson about making predictions. These minilessons can be taught during literature focus units, in reading and writing workshop, and through other activities.

Piecing a Lesson Together

Emergent Literacy Topics

Procedures	Concepts	Strategies and Skills
Hold a book correctly	Direction of print	Sing ABC song to identify a letter
Turn pages correctly	A word	Identify letter names
Separate words into onsets and rimes	A sentence	Match upper- and lowercase letter forms
Point at words as they are read	Uppercase letters	Identify phoneme-grapheme correspondences
Match printed words with words read aloud	Lowercase letters	"Stretch" words
Do buddy reading	Alphabetic principle	Read environmental print
Do shared reading	Rhyming words	*Make predictions*
Dictate language experience stories	The author's chair	Notice repetition patterns
Do interactive writing	Kid writing	Copy familiar words and environmental print
Use writing in play activities	Adult spelling	Use capital letters to begin sentences
		Use punctuation marks to end sentences
		Use invented spelling

 Please visit the Companion Website at **www.prenhall.com/tompkins** for a second fully realized minilesson.

Review

Emergent literacy is based on research about how children learn to read and write. Young children learn concepts about written language as they experiment with reading and writing, and teachers demonstrate reading and writing through shared reading, interactive writing, and other teaching strategies. Children emerge into writing as they learn to use graphic symbols to represent their thoughts, and they refine their kid writing as they learn about phoneme-grapheme correspondences. The key concepts presented in this chapter are:

1. Emergent literacy has replaced the traditional readiness approach.
2. As children learn about words, they move from recognizing environmental print to reading decontextualized words in books.
3. Children use phonics as well as information from the other three language systems as they learn to read.

MAKING PREDICTIONS

Mr. Voss's Kindergartners Learn to Predict

1. **Introduce the Topic**

   Mr. Voss explains to his kindergarten class that before he begins to read a book, he thinks about it. He looks at the illustration on the book cover, reads the title, and makes a prediction or guess about the story.

2. **Share Examples**

   Mr. Voss shows the cover of *The Wolf's Chicken Stew* (Kasza, 1987) and thinks aloud about it. He says, "This book is about a wolf who is going to cook some delicious chicken stew. Yes, that makes sense because I know that wolves like to eat chickens. I think the wolf on the cover is looking for chickens to cook in the stew." Then Mr. Voss asks the kindergartners to agree or disagree. Most agree, but one child suggests that the wolf is looking for a supermarket to buy the chickens.

3. **Provide Information**

   Mr. Voss reads the book aloud, stopping several times to confirm or revise predictions. Children confirm the prediction once the hen and her chicks are introduced, but by the end, no one is surprised when the wolf befriends the chickens. After reading, they talk about how their predictions changed as they read the story.

4. **Supervise Practice**

   During story time for 5 days, the kindergartners make predictions before reading aloud. If the prediction seems far-fetched, Mr. Voss asks the child to relate it to the book or make a new prediction. Children confirm or revise predictions as they listen and discuss their predictions after reading.

5. **Reflect on Learning**

   Mr. Voss's students make a chart about predicting. The kindergartners dictate these sentences for the chart: *You have to turn on your brain to think before you read. You can make a prediction. Then you want to find out if you are right.*

---

4. Both reading and writing development have three stages: emergent, beginning, and fluent.
5. Two ways to read books with young children are shared reading and guided reading.
6. Beginning readers often read leveled books, books written at an appropriate level of difficulty, so that they can be successful.
7. Teachers use children's own language to create reading materials in the language experience approach.
8. Children are introduced to writing as they watch their parents and teachers write and as they experiment with writing.
9. Children use kid writing to experiment with written language concepts and invented spelling.
10. Teachers use interactive writing to teach concepts about print, phonics, spelling, high-frequency words, and written language conventions.

Visit Chapter 4 on the Companion Website at www.prenhall. com/tompkins to:

- **Check your understanding of the concepts presented in the chapter**
- **Access the Extensions (activities and a list of related readings)**
- **Link to related websites**

Professional References

Adams, M. J. (1990). *Beginning to read: Thinking and learning about print.* Cambridge, MA: MIT Press.

Ashton-Warner, S. (1965). *Teacher.* New York: Simon & Schuster.

Baghban, M. J. M. (1984). *Our daughter learns to read and write: A case study from birth to three.* Newark, DE: International Reading Association.

Ball, E., & Blachman, B. (1991). Does phoneme segmentation training in kindergarten make a difference in early word recognition and developmental spelling? *Reading Research Quarterly, 26,* 49–86.

Barone, D. M., & Morrow, L. M. (2003). *Literacy and young children: Research-based practices.* New York: Guilford Press.

Burns, S., Griffin, P., & Snow, C. E. (1999). *Starting out right: A guide to promoting children's reading success.* Washington, DC: National Academy Press.

Button, K., Johnson, M. J., & Furgerson, P. (1996). Interactive writing in a primary classroom. *The Reading Teacher, 49,* 446–454.

Caserta-Henry, C. (1996). Reading buddies: A first-grade intervention program. *The Reading Teacher, 49,* 500–503.

Clay, M. M. (1967). The reading behavior of five-year-old children: A research report. *New Zealand Journal of Education Studies,* 11–31.

Clay, M. M. (1985). *The early detection of reading difficulties* (3rd ed.). Portsmouth, NH: Heinemann.

Clay, M. M. (1991). *Becoming literate: The construction of inner control.* Portsmouth, NH: Heinemann.

Clymer, T. (1996). The utility of phonic generalizations in the primary grades. *The Reading Teacher, 50,* 182–187.

Cunningham, P. A. (2000). *Phonics they use: Words for reading and writing* (3rd ed.). New York: Longman.

Depree, H., & Iversen, S. (1996). *Early literacy in the classroom: A new standard for young readers.* Bothell, WA: The Wright Group.

Downing, J. (1971–1972). Children's developing concepts of spoken and written language. *Journal of Reading Behavior, 4,* 1–19.

Downing, J., & Oliver, P. (1973–1974). The child's conception of "a word." *Reading Research Quarterly, 9,* 568–582.

Durkin, D. (1966). *Children who read early.* New York: Teachers College Press.

Dyson, A. H. (1984). "N spells my grandmama": Fostering early thinking about print. *The Reading Teacher, 38,* 262–271.

Fisher, B., & Medvic, E. F. (2000). *Perspectives on shared reading: Planning and practice.* Portsmouth, NH: Heinemann.

Fountas, I. C., & Pinnell, G. S. (1996). *Guided reading: Good first teaching for all children.* Portsmouth, NH: Heinemann.

Fountas, I. C., & Pinnell, G. S. (1999). *Matching books to readers: Using leveled books in guided reading, K–3.* Portsmouth, NH: Heinemann.

Fountas, I. C., & Pinnell, G. S. (2001). *Guiding readers and writers: Grades 3–6.* Portsmouth, NH: Heinemann.

Freppon, P. A., & Dahl, K. L. (1991). Learning about phonics in a whole language classroom. *Language Arts, 68,* 190–197.

Gillon, G. T. (2004). *Phonological awareness: From research to practice.* New York: Guilford Press.

Goodman, K. S. (1993). *Phonics phacts.* Portsmouth, NH: Heinemann.

Griffith, F., & Olson, M. (1992). Phonemic awareness helps beginning readers break the code. *The Reading Teacher, 45,* 516–523.

Hanna, P. R., Hanna, J. S., Hodges, R. E., & Rudorf, E. H. (1966). *Phoneme-grapheme correspondences as cues to spelling improvement.* Washington, DC: US Government Printing Office.

Harste, J. C., Woodward, V. A., & Burke, C. L. (1984). *Language stories and literacy lessons.* Portsmouth, NH: Heinemann.

Heald-Taylor, G. (1987). How to use predictable books for K–2 language arts instruction. *The Reading Teacher, 40,* 656–661.

Heath, S. B. (1983). *Ways with words: Language, life, and work in communities and classrooms.* Cambridge: Cambridge University Press.

Holdaway, D. (1979). *The foundations of literacy.* Portsmouth, NH: Heinemann.

Horn, E. (1957). Phonetics and spelling. *Elementary School Journal, 57,* 425–432.

International Reading Association and the National Association for the Education of Young Children. (1998). Learning to read and write: Developmentally appropriate practices for young children. A joint position statement of the International Reading Association and the National Association for the Education of Young Children. *Young Children, 53,* 524–546.

Invernizzi, M. (2003). Concepts, sounds, and the ABCs: A diet for a very young reader. In D. M. Barone & L. M. Morrow (Eds.), *Literacy and young children: Research-based practices* (pp. 140–156). New York: Guilford Press.

Juel, C. (1991). Beginning reading. In R. Barr, M. L. Kamil, P. Mosenthal, & P. D. Pearson (Eds.), *Handbook of reading research* (Vol. 2, pp. 759–788). New York: Longman.

Juel, C., Griffith, P. L., & Gough, P. B. (1986). Acquisition of literacy: A longitudinal study of children in first and second grade. *Journal of Educational Psychology, 78,* 243–255.

Klesius, J. P., Griffith, P. L., & Zielonka, P. (1991). A whole language and traditional instruction comparison: Overall effectiveness and development of the alphabetic principle. *Reading Research and Instruction, 30,* 47–61.

Labbo, L. D., & Teale, W. H. (1990). Cross-age reading: A strategy for helping poor readers. *The Reading Teacher, 43,* 362–369.

Lomax, R. G., & McGee, L. M. (1987). Young children's concepts about print and meaning: Toward a model of word reading acquisition. *Reading Research Quarterly, 22,* 237–256.

Lundberg, I., Frost, J., & Petersen, O. (1988). Effects of an extensive program for stimulating phonological awareness in preschool children. *Reading Research Quarterly, 23,* 263–284.

McGee, L. M., & Richgels, D. J. (2001). *Literacy's beginnings: Supporting young readers and writers* (3rd ed.). Boston: Allyn & Bacon.

McGee, L. M., & Richgels, D. J. (2003). *Designing early literacy programs.* New York: Guilford Press.

Mills, H., O'Keefe, T., & Stephens, D. (1992). *Looking closely: Exploring the role of phonics in one whole language classroom.* Urbana, IL: National Council of Teachers of English.

Moats, L. (1999). *Teaching reading* is *rocket science.* Washington, DC: American Federation of Teachers.

Morrice, C., & Simmons, M. (1991). Beyond reading buddies: A whole language cross-age program. *The Reading Teacher, 44,* 572–578.

National Reading Panel. (2000). *Report of the National Reading Panel.* Washington, DC: National Institute of Child Health and Human Development Clearinghouse.

Opitz, M. F., & Rasinski, T. V. (1998). *Good-bye round robin: Twenty-five effective oral reading strategies.* Portsmouth, NH: Heinemann.

Papandropoulou, I., & Sinclair, H. (1974). What is a word? Experimental study of children's ideas on grammar. *Human Development, 17,* 241–258.

Perfitti, C., Beck, I., Bell, L., & Hughes, C. (1987). Phonemic knowledge and learning to read are reciprocal: A longitudinal study of first grade children. *Merrill-Palmer Quarterly, 33,* 283–319.

Peterson, B. (1991). Selecting books for beginning readers. In D. DeFord, C. Lyons, & G. S. Pinnell (Eds.), *Bridges to literacy: Learning from Reading Recovery* (pp. 119–147). Portsmouth, NH: Heinemann.

Reutzel, D. R., & Fawson, P. C. (1990). Traveling tales: Connecting parents and children in writing. *The Reading Teacher, 44,* 222–227.

Schickedanz, J. A. (1990). *Adam's righting revolutions: One child's literacy development from infancy through grade one.* Portsmouth, NH: Heinemann.

Shefelbine, J. (1995). *Learning and using phonics in beginning reading* (Literacy research paper, vol. 10). New York: Scholastic.

Stanovich, K. (1980). Toward an interactive-compensatory model of individual differences in the development of reading fluency. *Reading Research Quarterly, 16,* 37–71.

Stanovich, K. E. (2000). *Progress in understanding reading: Scientific foundations and new frontiers.* New York: Guilford Press.

Stauffer, R. G. (1970). *The language experience approach to the teaching of reading.* New York: Harper & Row.

Sulzby, E. (1985). Kindergartners as readers and writers. In M. Farr (Ed.), *Advances in writing research, vol. 1: Children's early writing development* (pp. 127–199). Norwood, NJ: Ablex.

Taylor, D. (1983). *Family literacy: Young children learning to read and write*. Exeter, NH: Heinemann.

Taylor, D., & Dorsey-Gaines, C. (1987). *Growing up literate: Learning from inner-city families*. Portsmouth, NH: Heinemann.

Teale, W. H. (1982). Toward a theory of how children learn to read and write. *Language Arts, 59,* 555–570.

Teale, W. H., & Sulzby, E. (1989). Emerging literacy: New perspectives. In D. S. Strickland & L. M. Morrow (Eds.), *Emerging literacy: Young children learn to read and write* (pp. 1–15). Newark, DE: International Reading Association.

Temple, C., Nathan, R., Burris, N., & Temple, F. (1988). *The beginnings of writing*. Boston: Allyn & Bacon.

Templeton, S. (1980). Young children invent words: Developing concepts of "word-ness." *The Reading Teacher, 33,* 454–459.

Templeton, S., & Spivey, E. (1980). The concept of word in young children as a function of level of cognitive development. *Research in the Teaching of English, 14,* 265–278.

Tompkins, G. E., & Collom, S. (Eds.). (2004). *Sharing the pen: Interactive writing with young children*. Upper Saddle River, NJ: Merrill/Prentice Hall.

Tompkins, G. E., & Webeler, M. B. (1983). What will happen next? Using predictable books with young children. *The Reading Teacher, 36,* 498–502.

Trachtenburg, R., & Ferruggia, A. (1989). Big books from little voices: Reaching high risk beginning readers. *The Reading Teacher, 42,* 284–289.

Treiman, R. (1985). Phonemic analysis, spelling, and reading. In T. H. Carr (Ed.), *The development of reading skills* (pp. 5–18). San Francisco: Jossey-Bass.

Tunmer, W., & Nesdale, A. (1985). Phonemic segmentation skill and beginning reading. *Journal of Educational Psychology, 77,* 417–427.

Venezky, R. L. (1999). *The American way of spelling: The structure and origins of American English orthography*. New York: Guilford Press.

Wylie, R. E., & Durrell, D. D. (1970). Teaching vowels through phonograms. *Elementary English, 47,* 787–791.

Yaden, D. B., Jr., & Templeton, S. (Eds.). (1986). *Metalinguistic awareness and beginning literacy: Conceptualizing what it means to read and write*. Portsmouth, NH: Heinemann.

Yopp, H. K. (1992). Developing phonemic awareness in young children. *The Reading Teacher, 45,* 696–703.

Yopp, H. K. (1995). Read-aloud books for developing phonemic awareness: An annotated bibliography. *The Reading Teacher, 48,* 538–542.

Children's Book References

Baron, A. (1996). *Red fox dances*. Cambridge, MA: Candlewick.

Brett, J. (1989). *The mitten*. New York: Putnam.

Carle, E. (1969). *The very hungry caterpillar*. Cleveland: Collins-World.

Cole, H. (1995). *Jack's garden*. New York: Greenwillow.

Degen, B. (1983). *Jamberry*. New York: Harper & Row.

Degen, B. (1996). *Sailaway home*. New York: Scholastic.

Ehlert, L. (1994). *Eating the alphabet: Fruits and vegetables from A to Z*. San Diego: Harcourt Brace.

Fleming, D. (1994). *Barnyard banter*. New York: Henry Holt.

Fox, M. (1988). *Wilfred Gordon McDonald Partridge*. New York: Kane-Miller.

Galdone, P. (1973). *The little red hen*. New York: Seabury.

Galdone, P. (1975). *The gingerbread boy*. New York: Seabury.

Hutchins, P. (1968). *Rosie's walk*. New York: Macmillan.

Hutchins, P. (1976). *Don't forget the bacon!* New York: Mulberry.

Hutchins, P. (1987). *Rosie's walk* (big book edition). New York: Scholastic.

Kalan, R. (1995). *Jump, frog, jump!* New York: Greenwillow.

Kasza, K. (1987). *The wolf's chicken stew*. New York: Putnam.

Martin, B., Jr. (1992). *Polar bear, polar bear, what do you hear?* New York: Holt, Rinehart and Winston.

McKissack, P. C. (1986). *Flossie and the fox*. New York: Dial.

Most, B. (1996). *Cock-a-doodle-moo!* San Diego: Harcourt Brace.

Numeroff, L. J. (1985). *If you give a mouse a cookie*. New York: Harper & Row.

Numeroff, L. J. (1991). *If you give a moose a muffin*. New York: HarperCollins.

Numeroff, L. J. (1998). *If you give a pig a pancake*. New York: HarperCollins.

Numeroff, L. J. (2000). *If you take a mouse to the movies*. New York: HarperCollins.

Numeroff, L. (2002). *If you take a mouse to school*. New York: HarperCollins.

Obligado, L. (1983). *Faint frogs feeling feverish and other terrifically tantalizing tongue twisters*. New York: Puffin.

Prelutsky, J. (1982). *The baby uggs are hatching*. New York: Mulberry.

Ringgold, F. (1991). *Tar beach*. New York: Crown.

Schwartz, D. M. (1994). *How much is a million?* New York: Morrow.

Seuss, Dr. (1963). *Hop on Pop*. New York: Random House.

Westcott, N. B. (1989). *Skip to my Lou*. Boston: Little, Brown.

Williams, S. (1989). *I went walking*. San Diego: Harcourt Brace Jovanovich.

5 Looking Closely at Words

During a theme cycle on the Middle Ages, Ms. Boland's eighth graders develop a word wall. The students identify words to put on the word wall as they read books about the Middle Ages, including *Catherine, Called Birdy* (Cushman, 1994), *Castle Diary: The Journal of Tobias Burgess, Page* (Platt, 1999), *Ms. Frizzle's Adventures: Medieval Castle* (Cole, 2002), and *Castle* (Macaulay, 1977). Students choose 10 important words and draw word clusters on index cards, and they also write the words in their learning logs so that they can refer more easily to them during the theme cycle. The word wall is shown on page 202.

Ms. Boland uses the words on the word wall for a series of five vocabulary minilessons. To review the meaning of the words, she uses a semantic feature analysis chart with the categories "castle," "knights," "peasants," "Crusades," and "cathedral" and 20 words for students to categorize. For *villein,* the "peasants" category would be checked, and for *fortress,* the "castle" category would be checked, for example. For other words, such as *Black Death,* more than one

Reading and
Writing
Workshop

Literature
Focus
Units

Literature
Circles

Theme Cycles

category would be checked. She demonstrates how to fill in the chart using the first two words as examples, and then students work in small groups to complete the chart.

In the second minilesson, Ms. Boland focuses on etymology, or word history, and students learn that words about the Middle Ages come from English, French, Latin, and Greek. Ms. Boland shares some guidelines for determining the language source, such as that compound words are usually English, words in which *ch* is pronounced /sh/ are French, words that end in *-tion* are Latin, and words in which *ch* is pronounced /k/ are Greek. Then students sort these words according to language:

English: *freeman, drawbridge, landlord, knight, forenoon, heathen, sword, scabbard,* and *king*

French: *chivalry, heraldry, garderobe, lute, troubadour,* and *tournament*

Latin: *manuscript, apprentice, illumination, humor, joust, entertainment, cathedral, solar, Renaissance,* and *medieval*

Greek: *alchemy, monk,* and *monastery*

In the third minilesson, students examine root words and affixes to determine the meaning of *Renaissance* (rebirth), *monk* and *monastery* (alone), *manuscript* (handwritten), *medieval* (Middle Ages), *Crusades* (cross), *solar* (sun), *unicorn* (one horn). They also compare related English and Latin words, for example, *church* and *cathedral, Middle Ages* and *medieval, kingly* and *royal, sun* and *solar,* and *Black Death* and *plague,* to discover that the more common words in each pair are English and the more sophistical words are Latin.

What is the best way to teach vocabulary?

Students are expected to learn many technical terms in social studies and other content-area units, but in too many classrooms, having students look up the definition of words and write sentences using the words substitutes for teaching vocabulary. Researchers tell us that students learn many words incidentally through multiple exposures and others through word-study activities that go beyond looking up definitions and through meaningful use in talk and writing activities. As you read this vignette, notice how Ms. Boland involves students in selecting words for study and provides a variety of meaningful word-study activities.

A archery acre apprentice alchemy archer armorer	B breaking fast bailey barter baron battering ram Black Death battlements bloodletting	C cathedral castle constable Crusades chain mail Charlemagne coat of arms clergy chivalry	D dizzard dub drawbridge E estate entertainment earl
F fairs feudal system forenoon flying buttresses fortress fanfare fowl fresco freeman	G gatehouse garderobe guilds great hall	H heraldry heathen heraldic arms huntsman harvest humors herbs	I illumination J Jerusalem jousts K keep kings knight knighthood
L lance lord leprosy landlord lute	M manor manuscript mercenary medieval merchants Middle Ages missionaries minstrel moat Magna Carta monastery monk	N Notre Dame nave nobles O	P pagan peasant parchment pennant pike pillory plague pilgrims poacher portcullis
Q quartering quill pens R reeve royal Renaissance	S scabbard sally port serf sword suit of armor shield siege steward squire solar	T tournament trencher transepts turrets troubadours twelvemonth	U unicorn V vernacular villein W watchtower X Y yeoman Z

In the fourth minilesson, Ms. Boland compares the English word *hand* with the Latin word *manus* ("hand") and words made from these two root words. To begin, students brainstorm a list of words with the root word *hand: handwriting, handle, handy, handmade, handshake, handsome, handicraft, right-* (or *left-) handed,* and *handbag.* Then Ms. Boland introduces the Latin root word *manus,* which is used in *manuscript* and a "handful" of other words, including

CRUSADES

- A Crusade is a holy war that is started by a religious leader.
- Crusade comes from the Latin word "crux" or cross.
- So a Crusade was the War of the Cross.

manufacture, manual, and *manicure.* Students make root-word clusters for the two words in their learning logs.

In the fifth minilesson, Ms. Boland reviews synonyms and how to use a thesaurus. Together she and her students examine synonyms for *knight* and choose these five synonyms as the most appropriate ones: *warrior, defender, protector, gallant,* and *cavalier.* Next, Ms. Boland divides students into small groups, and each group investigates the synonyms for another word-wall word and chooses the five most appropriate synonyms.

After reading about the Middle Ages, students divide into research teams to learn more about a particular aspect of life at that time. One group researches the building of a castle, and other groups investigate medical practices; the Crusades; monks and life in a monastery; knighthood; the feudal social system; food, drink, and celebrations; the life of a serf, and the life of the nobles. The students in each group research their topic and develop a display with artifacts and a PowerPoint presentation to document what they have learned. A page from a PowerPoint presentation on the Crusades is shown above. This excerpt shows how students incorporated the word-history information they learned about the word C*rusades.*

At the end of the theme cycle, students transform their classroom into a museum. They dress in costumes and set up their displays at stations in the classroom. Parents and other students at the school visit the displays, and students share what they have learned about the Middle Ages.

For more information on planning theme cycles, see Chapter 15, "Putting It All Together."

Mark Twain said, "The difference between the right word and the almost right word is the difference between lightning and the lightning bug." Learning about words and how to choose the right one to express the meaning you intend is

As you begin reading this chapter, you may want to read the "Dear Reader" letter in Chapter 5 on the Companion Website at www.prenhall.com/tompkins

what vocabulary is all about. Vocabulary is not decoding or word identification; rather, the focus is on meaning. Choosing the best word to express meaning is important to all language users. When we listen and read, we must understand the meaning someone else intends, and when we talk and write, we must choose exactly the right word so that our audience will understand our message.

Words are the meaning-bearing units of language. Of the three-quarters of a million words in English, most people use only about 20,000, and most of the words we commonly use come from a body of approximately 5,000 to 7,000 words (Klein, 1988). Our personal ownership of words is quite limited. We have overlapping but separate listening, speaking, reading, and writing vocabularies. For example, most of us might recognize a word such as *obfuscate* when listening or reading, but fewer of us would use the word in talking or writing. Our reading and listening vocabularies are more extensive than our talking and writing vocabularies, for many reasons. We may fear mispronouncing or misspelling a word, or we may fear what our friends will think if we use the word in conversation. The words we use mark us in a number of ways: by our word choice, by our pronunciation, and by the way we string the words together into sentences.

As you read this chapter, think about how students use their knowledge of words in reading and writing. Ask yourself these questions:

◆ How has the development of the English language affected vocabulary?

◆ What vocabulary concepts do elementary students learn?

◆ How do teachers focus on words during the four patterns of practice?

HISTORY OF THE ENGLISH LANGUAGE

Understanding the history of English and how words entered the language contributes greatly to understanding words and their meanings. English is a historic language, which accounts for word meanings and some spelling inconsistencies (Tompkins & Yaden, 1986). English has a variety of words for a single concept, and the history of English in general and the etymology of the words in particular explain many apparent duplications. Consider these words related to water: *aquatic, hydrant, aquamarine, waterfall, hydroelectric, watercress, watery, aquarium, waterproof, hydraulic, aqualung,* and *hydrogen.* These words have one of three root words, each meaning water: *water* is English, of course, whereas *aqua* is Latin and *hydro* is Greek. The root word used depends on the people who created the word, the purpose of the word, and when the word entered English.

The development of the English language is divided into three periods: Old English, Middle English, and Modern English. The beginning and end of each period are marked by a significant event, such as an invasion or an invention. The contributions of each period to our language today are outlined in Figure 5–1.

Old English (A.D. 450–1100)

The recorded history of the English language begins in A.D. 449, when Germanic tribes, including the Angles and Saxons, invaded Britain. The invaders pushed the original inhabitants, the Celts, to the northern and western corners

FIGURE 5-1

The Development of the English Language

Period	Dates	Contributions
Old English (OE)	450–1100	Angles and Saxons bring a Germanic language to England Roman missionaries write English phonetically Vikings contribute many words and the sounds /g/, /k/, and /sk/ OE has irregular verb and plural forms Compounding is used to create new words Suffixes *-ly, -dom,* and *-hood* are used Only 15% of OE words remain in English today
Middle English (ME)	1100–1500	French contribute many loan words Many English-French synonyms French monks replace English ones and change some spellings, such as *light* *-s* is accepted as the plural marker Regular past tense and past participle forms develop for many verbs Latin and Dutch loan words enter English
Modern English (ModE)	1500–present	Wide borrowing of words from more than 50 languages Latin and Greek loan words enter English, especially scientific words With publication of dictionaries, spelling no longer changes to reflect changes in pronunciation The Great Vowel Shift in the 1500s changes the pronunciation of long vowel sounds English becomes a world language with more than 750,000 words

of the island. This annexation is romanticized in the King Arthur legends. Arthur is believed to have been a Celtic military leader who fought bravely against the German invaders.

The English language began as an intermingling of the dialects spoken by the Angles, the Saxons, and other Germanic tribes in Britain. Many people assume that English is based on Latin, but it has Germanic roots and was brought to Britain by these invaders. Although 85% of Old English words are no longer used, many everyday words remain (e.g., *child, foot, hand, house, man, mother, old,* and *sun*). In contrast to Modern English, Old English had few loan words (words borrowed from other languages and incorporated into English) and had a highly developed inflectional system for indicating number, gender, and verb tense. The Anglo-Saxons added affixes to existing words, including *be-, for-, -ly, -dom,* and *-hood.* They also invented vividly descriptive compound words. The Old English word for "music," for example, was *ear-sport;* the word for "world" was *age of man;* and the word for "folly" was *wanwit.* The folk epic *Beowulf,* the great literary work of the period, illustrates the poetic use of words; for instance, the sea is described as a "whale-path" and a "swan's road."

Foreign words also made their way into the predominantly Germanic word stock. The borrowed words came from two main sources: Romans and Vikings. A number of words were borrowed from Latin and incorporated into English.

Contact between the Roman soldiers and traders and the Germanic tribes on the continent, before they had invaded England, contributed some words, including *cheese, copper, mile, street,* and *wine.* The missionaries who reintroduced Christianity to Britain in 597 also brought with them a number of religious words (e.g., *angel, candle, hymn*).

In 787, the Vikings from Denmark and other parts of Scandinavia began a series of raids against English villages, and for the next 3 centuries, they attacked, conquered, and occupied much of England. Their influence was so great that the Danish king Canute ruled England during the first part of the 11th century. The Vikings' contributions to the English language were significant. They provided the pronouns *they, their, them;* introduced the /g/ and /k/ sounds (e.g., *get, kid*); contributed most of our *sk-* words (e.g., *skin, sky*) and some of our *sc-* words (e.g., *scalp, score*); and enriched our vocabulary with more than 500 everyday words, including *husband* and *window.*

In Old English, some consonant combinations were pronounced that are not heard today, including the /k/ in words such as *knee.* The letter *f* represented both /f/ and /v/, resulting in the Modern English spelling pattern of *wolf* and *wolves.* The pronunciation of the vowel sounds was very different, too; for example, the Old English *stan* (*a = a* in *father*) became our word *stone.*

The structure, spelling, and pronunciation of Old English were significantly different from those of Modern English, so much so that we would not be able to read an Old English text or understand someone speaking Old English. It was a highly inflected language, with many different word endings, and the arrangement of words in sentences was different, too, with verbs often placed at the end of sentences. In many ways, Old English was more like Modern German than Modern English.

Middle English (1100–1500)

An event occurred in 1066 that changed the course of the English language and ushered in the Middle English period: the Norman Conquest. In that year, William the Conqueror crossed the English Channel from the French province of Normandy and defeated the English king, Harold, at the Battle of Hastings. William claimed the English throne and established a French court in London. This event had far-reaching consequences. For nearly 300 years, French was the official language in England, spoken by the nobility and upper classes, although the lower classes continued to speak English. By 1300, the use of French had declined, and before the end of the 14th century, English was restored as the official language. Chaucer's *Canterbury Tales,* written in the late 1300s, provides evidence that English was also replacing French as the preferred written language. Political, social, and economic changes contributed to this reversal.

The Middle English period was one of tremendous change. A large portion of the Old English vocabulary was lost as 10,000 French words were added to the language, reflecting the Norman impact on English life and society (Baugh & Cable, 1978). They included military words (e.g., *soldier, victory*), political words (e.g., *government, princess*), medical words (e.g., *physician, surgeon*), and words related to the arts (e.g., *comedy, music, poet*). Many of the new loan words duplicated Old English words. Typically, one word was eventually lost; often, it was the Old English word that disappeared. If both words remained in the language, they developed slightly different meanings. For example, the words *hearty* (Old English) and *cordial* (French) were originally synonyms, both meaning "from the heart." In time they differentiated, and they now have different meanings.

Most of the French loan words were derived from Latin. In addition, a few Latin words (e.g., *individual, polite*) passed directly into English during this period. In contrast to the French loan words, Latin borrowings were more sophisticated words, used more often in writing than in speech. Also, several words (e.g., *dock, freight*) were borrowed from the Dutch as a result of trade with the Low Countries.

During this period, there was a significant reduction in the use of inflections, or word endings. Many irregular verbs were lost, and others developed regular past and past-participle forms (e.g., *climb, talk*), although Modern English still retains some irregular verbs (e.g., *sing, fly, be, have*) that contribute to our usage problems. By 1000, *-s* had become the accepted plural marker, although the Old English plural form *-en* was used in some words. This artifact remains in a few plurals, such as *children*.

Modern English (1500–Present)

The Modern English period is characterized by the development of the printing press and the tremendous upswing in exploration, colonization, and trade with countries around the world. The introduction of the printing press in England by William Caxton marked the beginning of the Modern English period. The printing press was a powerful force in standardizing English spelling, as well as a practical means for providing increasing numbers of people with books. Until the invention of the printing press, English spelling kept pace with pronunciation, but the printing press standardized and fixed spelling, and the lag between pronunciation and spelling began to widen. The tremendous increase in travel to many parts of the world resulted in a wide borrowing of words from more than 50 languages. Borrowings include *alcohol* (Arabic), *chocolate* (Spanish), *cookie* (Dutch), *czar* (Russian), *hallelujah* (Hebrew), *hurricane* (Spanish), *kindergarten* (German), *smorgasbord* (Swedish), *tycoon* (Chinese), and *violin* (Italian).

Many Latin and Greek words were added to English during the Renaissance to increase the language's prestige; for example, *congratulate, democracy,* and *education* came from Latin, and *catastrophe, encyclopedia,* and *thermometer* from Greek. Many modern Latin and Greek borrowings are scientific words (e.g., *aspirin, vaccinate*), and some of the very recently borrowed forms (e.g., *criterion, focus*) have retained their native plural forms, adding confusion about how to spell these forms in English. Also, some recent loan words from French have retained their native spellings and pronunciations, such as *hors d'oeuvre* and *cul-de-sac*.

In addition to the considerable vocabulary expansion during the Modern English period, there have also been extensive sound changes. The short vowels have remained relatively stable, but there was a striking change in the pronunciation of long vowels. This change, known as the Great Vowel Shift, has been characterized as "the most revolutionary and far-reaching sound change during the history of the language" (Alexander, 1962, p. 114). The change was gradual, occurring during the 1500s. Because spelling had become fixed before the shift, the vowel letter symbols no longer corresponded to the sounds.

For example, the word *name* had two syllables and rhymed with *comma* during the Middle English period, but during the Great Vowel Shift, the pronunciation of *name* shifted to rhyme with *game* (Hook, 1975).

The Modern English period brought changes in syntax, particularly the disappearance of double negatives and double comparatives and superlatives. Eliminations came about slowly; for instance, Shakespeare still wrote, "the most unkindest cut of all." Also, the practice of using *-er* or *-est* to form comparatives and superlatives in shorter words and *more* or *most* with longer words was not standardized until after Shakespeare's time.

Learning About Word Histories

The best source of information about word histories is an unabridged dictionary, which provides basic etymological information about words: the language the word was borrowed from, the spelling of the word in that language or the transliteration of the word into the Latin alphabet, and the original meaning of the word. Etymologies are enclosed in square brackets and appear at the beginning or the end of an entry. They are written in an abbreviated form to save space, using abbreviations for language names such as Ar for Arabic and L for Latin. Let's look at etymologies for three words derived from very different sources: *king, kimono,* and *thermometer.* Each etymology is translated and elaborated, beginning with *king:*

> *king* [bef. 900; ME, OE *cyng*]

> Elaboration: The word *king* is an Old English word originally spelled *cyng.* It was used in English before the year 900. In the Middle English period, the spelling changed to its current form.

Next, let's consider *kimono:*

> *kimono* [1885–1890; <Japn clothing, garb, equiv. to *ki* wear + *mono* thing]

> Elaboration: Our word *kimono* comes from Japanese, and it entered English between 1885 and 1890. *Kimono* means "clothing" or "garb," and it is equivalent to the Japanese words *ki,* meaning "wear," and *mono,* meaning "thing."

Finally, we examine *thermometer:*

> *thermometer* [1615–1625; thermo < Gr *thermos,* hot + meter < *metron,* measure]

> Elaboration: The first recorded use of the word *thermometer* in English was between 1615 and 1625. Our word was created from two Greek words meaning "hot" and "measure."

A list of books about the history of English that are appropriate for elementary students is shown in the Classroom Library box on page 209. The books include fascinating stories about how words grew and changed because of historical events and linguistic accidents.

Books About the History of English

Adelson, L. (1972). *Dandelions don't bite: The story of words.* New York: Pantheon. (M–U)

Arnold, O. (1979). *What's in a name: Famous brand names.* New York: Messner. (U)

Ashton, C. (1988). *Words can tell: A book about our language.* Englewood Cliffs, NJ: Julian Messner. (M–U)

Asimov, I. (1961). *Words from myths.* Boston: Houghton Mifflin. (U)

Asimov, I. (1968). *Words from history.* Boston: Houghton Mifflin. (U)

Brook, D. (1998). *The journey of English.* New York: Clarion. (M)

Clements, A. (1996). *Frindle.* New York: Simon & Schuster. (M)

Collis, H. (1987). *101 American English idioms.* Lincolnwood, IL: Passport. (M–U)

Conrad, P. (1995). *Animal lingo.* New York: HarperCollins. (P–M)

Dewey, A. (1995). *Naming colors.* New York: HarperCollins. (P–M)

Fakih, K. O. (1995). *Off the clock: A lexicon of time words and expressions.* New York: Ticknor. (M–U)

Fletcher, C. (1973). *One hundred keys: Names across the land.* Nashville, TN: Abingdon Press. (M–U)

Graham-Barber, L. (1991). *Gobble! The complete book of Thanksgiving words.* New York: Bradbury. (P–M)

Graham-Barber, L. (1991). *Mushy! The complete book of valentine words.* New York: Bradbury. (M)

Graham-Barber, L. (1995). *A chartreuse leotard in a magenta limousine: And other words named after people and places.* New York: Hyperion. (M–U)

Greenfeld, H. (1978). *Sumer is icumen in: Our ever-changing language.* New York: Crown Books. (U)

Hazen, B. S. (1979). *Last, first, middle and nick: All about names.* Englewood Cliffs, NJ: Prentice Hall. (M–U)

Juster, N. (1961). *The phantom tollbooth.* New York: Bullseye Books. (M–U)

Kaye, C. B. (1985). *Word works: Why the alphabet is a kid's best friend.* Boston: Little, Brown. (M–U)

Klausner, J. (1990). *Talk about English: How words travel and change.* New York: Crowell. (U)

Kraske, R. (1975). *The story of the dictionary.* New York: Harcourt Brace Jovanovich. (P–M)

McCrum, R., Cran, I., & MacNeil, R. (1986). *The story of English.* New York: Viking Press. (U)

Meltzer, M. (1984). *A book about names.* New York: Crowell. (M–U)

Metcalf, A., & Barnhart, D. K. (1997). *America in so many words: Words that have shaped America.* Boston: Houghton Mifflin. (U)

Pizer, V. (1976). *Ink, Ark., and all that: How American places got their names.* New York: Putnam. (M–U)

Pizer, V. (1981). *Take my word for it.* New York: Dodd, Mead. (M–U)

Sanders, E. (1995). *What's your name? From Ariel to Zoe.* New York: Holiday. (P–M)

Sarnoff, J., & Ruffins, R. (1981). *Words: A book about the origins of everyday words and phrases.* New York: Scribner. (M–U)

Sorel, N. (1970). *Word people.* New York: American Heritage. (M–U)

Sperling, S. (1979). *Poplollies and bellibones: A celebration of lost words.* New York: Penguin. (U)

Steckler, A. (1979). *101 words and how they began.* Garden City, NY: Doubleday. (P–M–U)

Steckler, A. (1981). *101 more words and how they began.* Garden City, NY: Doubleday. (P–M–U)

Terban, M. (1983). *In a pickle and other funny idioms.* Boston: Houghton Mifflin. (M–U)

Terban, M. (1988). *Guppies in tuxedos: Funny eponyms.* New York: Clarion. (M)

Terban, M. (1996). *Scholastic dictionary of idioms.* New York: Scholastic. (M–U)

Towle, W. (1993). *The real McCoy: The life of an African-American inventor.* New York: Scholastic. (M–U)

Weiss, A. E. (1980). *What's that you said: How words change.* New York: Harcourt Brace Jovanovich. (U)

Wolk, A. (1980). *Everyday words from names of people and places.* New York: Elsevier/Nelson. (M–U)

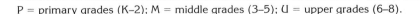

P = primary grades (K–2); M = middle grades (3–5); U = upper grades (6–8).

WORDS AND THEIR MEANINGS

Students begin kindergarten with approximately 5,000 words in their vocabularies, and their vocabularies grow at a rate of about 3,000 words a year (Nagy & Herman, 1985). Through literature focus units, literature circles, reading and writing workshop, and theme cycles, students experiment with words and concepts, and students' knowledge of words and meanings grows. Young children assume that every word has only one meaning, and words that sound alike, such as *son* and *sun*, are confusing to them. Through continuing experiences with language, students become more sophisticated about words and their literal and figurative meanings. During the elementary grades, students learn about words and word parts, words that mean the same thing as and the opposite of other words, words that sound alike, words with multiple meanings, the figurative language of idioms, and how words have been borrowed from languages around the world. They also learn about how words are created and have fun playing with words (Tompkins, 2004).

Root Words and Affixes

A root word is a morpheme, the basic part of a word to which affixes are added. Many words are developed from a single root word; for example, the Latin word *portare* ("to carry") is the source of at least nine Modern English words: *deport, export, import, port, portable, porter, report, support,* and *transportation.* Latin is one source of English root words, and Greek and Old English are two other sources.

Some root words are whole words, and others are parts of words. Some root words have become free morphemes and can be used as separate words, but others cannot. For instance, the word *act* comes from the Latin word *actus,* meaning "doing." English uses part of the word and treats it as a root word that can be used independently or in combination with affixes, as in *actor, activate, react,* and *enact.* In the words *alias, alien, inalienable,* and *alienate,* the root word *ali* comes from the Latin word *alius,* meaning "other"; it is not used as an independent root word in English. A list of English, Latin, and Greek root words appears in the LA Essentials box on page 211. Students can compile lists of words developed from these root words, and they can draw root word clusters to illustrate the relationship of the root word to the words developed from it. Figure 5–2 shows a root word cluster for the Greek root *graph,* meaning "write," made by a seventh-grade class. Recognizing basic elements from word to word helps students cut down on the amount of memorizing necessary to learn meanings and spellings.

Affixes are bound morphemes that are added to words and root words. Affixes can be prefixes or suffixes. Prefixes are added to the beginnings of words, such as *re-* in *reread,* and suffixes are added to the ends of words, such as *-ing* in *singing* and *-er* in *player.* Like root words, affixes come from English, Latin, and Greek. They often change a word's meaning, such as adding *un-* to *happy* to form *unhappy.* Sometimes they change the part of speech: For example, when *-tion* is added to *attract* to form *attraction,* the verb *attract* becomes a noun.

When an affix is "peeled off," or removed from a word, the remaining word is usually a real word. For example, when the prefix *pre-* is removed from *preview,* the word *view* can stand alone; and when the suffix *-able* is removed from *lovable,* the word *love* can stand alone (when the final *e* is added, anyway). Some words include letter sequences that might be affixes, but because

Essentials

Root Words

Root	Language	Meaning	Sample Words
ann/enn	Latin	year	anniversary, annual, centennial, millennium, perennial
arch	Greek	ruler	anarchy, archbishop, architecture, hierarchy, monarchy, patriarch
astro	Greek	star	aster, asterisk, astrology, astronaut, astronomy, disaster
auto	Greek	self	autobiography, automatic, automobile, autopsy
bio	Greek	life	biography, biohazard, biology, biodegradable, bionic, biosphere
capit/capt	Latin	head	capital, capitalize, capitol, captain, caption, decapitate, per capita
cent	Latin	hundred	bicentennial, cent, centennial, centigrade, centipede, century, percent
circ	Latin	around	circle, circular, circus, circumspect, circuit, circumference, circumstance
corp	Latin	body	corporal, corporation, corps, corpuscle
cosmo	Greek	universe	cosmic, cosmopolitan, microcosm
cred	Latin	believe	credit, creditable, creed, discredit, incredulity
cycl	Greek	wheel	bicycle, cycle, cyclist, cyclone, recycle, tricycle
dict	Latin	speak	contradict, dictate, dictator, prediction, verdict
graph	Greek	write	autobiography, biographer, cryptograph, epigraph, graphic, paragraph
gram	Greek	letter	cardiogram, diagram, grammar, monogram, telegram
jus/jud/jur	Latin	law	injury, injustice, judge, juror, jury, justice, justify, prejudice
lum/lus/luc	Latin	light	illuminate, lucid, luminous, luster
man	Latin	hand	manacle, maneuver, manicure, manipulate, manual, manufacture
mar/mer	Latin	sea	aquamarine, Margaret, marine, maritime, marshy, mermaid, submarine
meter	Greek	measure	centimeter, diameter, seismometer, speedometer, thermometer
mini	Latin	small	miniature, minibus, minimize, minor, minimum, minuscule, minute
mort	Latin	death	immortal, mortality, mortuary, postmortem
nym	Greek	name	anonymous, antonym, homonym, pseudonym, synonym
ped	Latin	foot	biped, pedal, pedestrian, pedicure
phono	Greek	sound	earphone, microphone, phonics, phonograph, saxophone, symphony
photo	Greek	light	photograph, photographer, photosensitive, photosynthesis
pod/pus	Greek	foot	octopus, podiatry, podium, tripod
port	Latin	carry	exporter, import, port, portable, porter, reporter, support, transportation
quer/ques/quis	Latin	seek	inquisitive, query, quest, question
scope	Latin	see	horoscope, kaleidoscope, microscope, periscope, telescope
scrib/scrip	Latin	write	describe, inscription, postscript, prescribe, scribble, scribe, script
sphere	Greek	ball	atmosphere, atmospheric, hemisphere, sphere, stratosphere
struct	Latin	build	construct, construction, destruction, indestructible, instruct, reconstruct
tele	Greek	far	telecast, telegram, telegraph, telephone, telescope, telethon, television
terr	Latin	land	subterranean, terrace, terrain, terrarium, terrier, territory
vers/vert	Latin	turn	advertise, anniversary, controversial, divert, reversible, versus
vict/vinc	Latin	conquer	convict, convince, evict, invincible, victim, victor, victory
vis/vid	Latin	see	improvise, invisible, revise, supervisor, television, video, vision, visitor
viv/vit	Latin	live	revive, survive, vital, vitamin, vivacious, vivid, viviparous
volv	Latin	roll	convolutions, evolve, evolution, involve, revolutionary, revolver, volume

FIGURE 5-2   *A Cluster for the Root Word* Graph

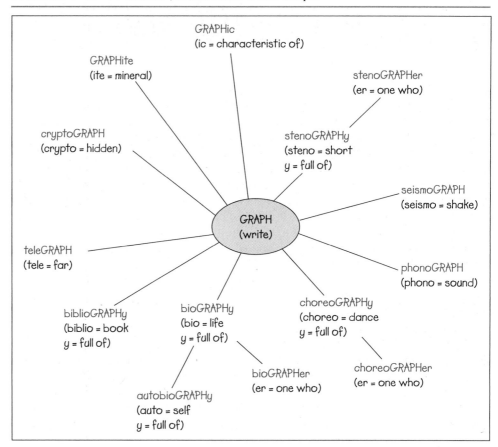

the remaining word cannot stand alone, they are not affixes. For example, the *in-* at the beginning of *include* is not a prefix because *clude* is not a word, and the *-ic* at the end of *magic* is not a suffix because *mag* cannot stand alone as a word, but the *-ic* at the end of *atomic* is a suffix because *atom* is a word. Sometimes, however, the root word cannot stand alone. One example is *legible:* The *-ible* is a suffix and *leg-* is the root word even though it cannot stand alone.

Some affixes have more than one form. For example, the prefixes *il-, im-,* and *ir-* are forms of the prefix *in-,* with the meanings of "in," "into," and "on"; these prefixes are used with verbs and nouns. The prefixes *il-, im-, ir-,* and *ig-* are also forms of the prefix *in-,* with the meaning "not"; these prefixes are used with adjectives. Both *in-* prefixes are borrowed from Latin. The prefix *a-* and its alternate form *an-* are borrowed from Greek and also mean "not." The alternate form is used when the word it is being added to begins with a vowel. Similarly, some suffixes have alternate forms; for example, the suffix *-ible* is an alternate form of *-able.* The alternate form is used in words, such as *legible,* whose root words cannot stand alone. There are exceptions, however, such as *collectible.*

A list of prefixes and suffixes is presented in the LA Essentials box on page 214. White, Sowell, and Yanagihara (1989) identified the affixes most commonly used in English words; these are marked with an asterisk in the LA Essentials feature. White and his colleagues recommend that the commonly used affixes be taught to middle- and upper-grade students because of their usefulness. Some of the most commonly used prefixes can be confusing because they have more than one meaning. The prefix *in-*, for instance, can mean either "not" or "again," and *un-* can mean "not" or it can reverse the meaning of the word (e.g., *tie–untie*).

Synonyms and Antonyms

Synonyms are words that have the same or nearly the same meaning. English has many synonyms because so many words have been borrowed from other languages. Synonyms provide options, allowing us to express ourselves precisely. Think of all the synonyms for the word *cold: cool, chilly, frigid, icy, frosty,* and *freezing,* for example. Each word has a different shade of meaning: *Cool* means moderately cold; *chilly* is uncomfortably cold; *frigid* is intensely cold; *icy* means very cold; *frosty* means covered with frost; and *freezing* is so cold that water changes into ice. Our language would be limited if we could say only that we were cold.

The largest number of synonyms entered English during the Norman occupation of Britain. Compare these pairs of synonyms: *end–finish, clothing–garments, forgive–pardon, buy–purchase, deadly–mortal.* The first word in each pair comes from Old English; the second was borrowed from the Normans. The Old English words are more basic words, and the French loan words are more sophisticated. Perhaps that is why both words in each pair have survived—they express slightly different ideas. Other pairs of synonyms come from different languages. For example, in the pair *comfortable* and *cozy, comfortable* is a Latin loan word, whereas *cozy* is English, probably of Scandinavian origin.

Students can check a dictionary or thesaurus to locate synonyms for words. A fifth-grade class examined the word *wretched* after reading Chris Van Allsburg's picture book fantasy, *The Wretched Stone* (1991), the story of a strange, glowing stone picked up on a sea voyage that captivates a ship's crew and has a terrible transforming effect on them. They guessed from context clues that the word meant something "bad" or "evil," but they didn't know the exact meaning. One student checked a dictionary and found three meanings for the word—"unfortunate," "causing misery," and "of poor quality." He reported back to his classmates, and they immediately recognized that the second meaning—"causing misery"—was the most appropriate. Then they checked the word in a thesaurus and found seven synonyms. The students divided into seven groups and each group studied one of the synonyms, checking its meaning in a dictionary and thinking about how the word was used in the story. Then the groups reported back that *terrible, miserable,* and *dreadful* were the three most appropriate synonyms. Finally, the students collaborated to make a class chart for *wretched,* which is shown in Figure 5–3. The word being studied is written at the top of the chart, the word is used in a sentence in the middle section, and the synonyms are listed in a T chart in the bottom section to indicate their appropriateness in this context.

Antonyms are words that express opposite meanings. Antonyms for *loud* include *soft, subdued, quiet, silent, inaudible, sedate, somber, dull,* and *colorless.* These words express shades of meaning just as synonyms do, and some opposites are more appropriate for one meaning of *loud* than for another. When *loud* means *gaudy,* for instance, appropriate opposites might be *somber, dull,* and *colorless.*

LA Essentials

Affixes

Language	Prefixes	Suffixes
English	*over- (too much): overflow self- (by oneself): self-employed *un- (not): unhappy *un- (reversal): untie under- (beneath): underground	-ed (past tense): played -ful (full of): hopeful -ing (participle): eating, building -ish (like): reddish -less (without): hopeless -ling (young): duckling *-ly (in the manner of): slowly *-ness (state or quality): kindness -s/-es (plural): cats, boxes *-y (full of): sleepy
Greek	a-/an- (not): atheist, anaerobic amphi- (both): amphibian anti- (against): antiseptic di- (two): dioxide hemi- (half): hemisphere hyper- (over): hyperactive hypo- (under): hypodermic micro- (small): microfilm mono- (one): monarch omni- (all): omnivorous poly- (many): polygon sym-/syn-/sys- (together): synonym	-ism (doctrine of): communism -ist (one who): artist -logy (the study of): zoology
Latin	bi- (two, twice): bifocal, biannual de- (away): detract *dis- (not): disapprove *dis- (reversal): disinfect ex- (out): export *il-/im-/in-/ir- (not): illegible, impolite, inexpensive, irrational *in- (in, into): indoor inter- (between): intermission milli- (thousand): millennium *mis- (wrong): mistake multi- (many): multimillionaire post- (after): postwar pre- (before): precede quad-/quart- (four): quadruple, quarter re- (again): repay *re-/retro- (back): replace, retroactive *sub- (under): submarine trans- (across): transport tri- (three): triangle	-able/-ible (worthy of, can be): lovable, audible *-al/-ial (action, process): arrival, denial -ance/-ence (state or quality): annoyance, absence -ant (one who): servant -ary/-ory (person, place): secretary, laboratory -cule (very small): molecule -ee (one who is): trustee *-er/-or/-ar (one who): teacher, actor, liar -ic (characterized by): angelic -ify (to make): simplify -ment (state or quality): enjoyment -ous (full of): nervous *-sion/-tion (state or quality): tension, attraction -ure (state or quality): failure

* = most common affixes.

214

FIGURE 5-3   *A Student's T-Chart of Synonyms for* Wretched

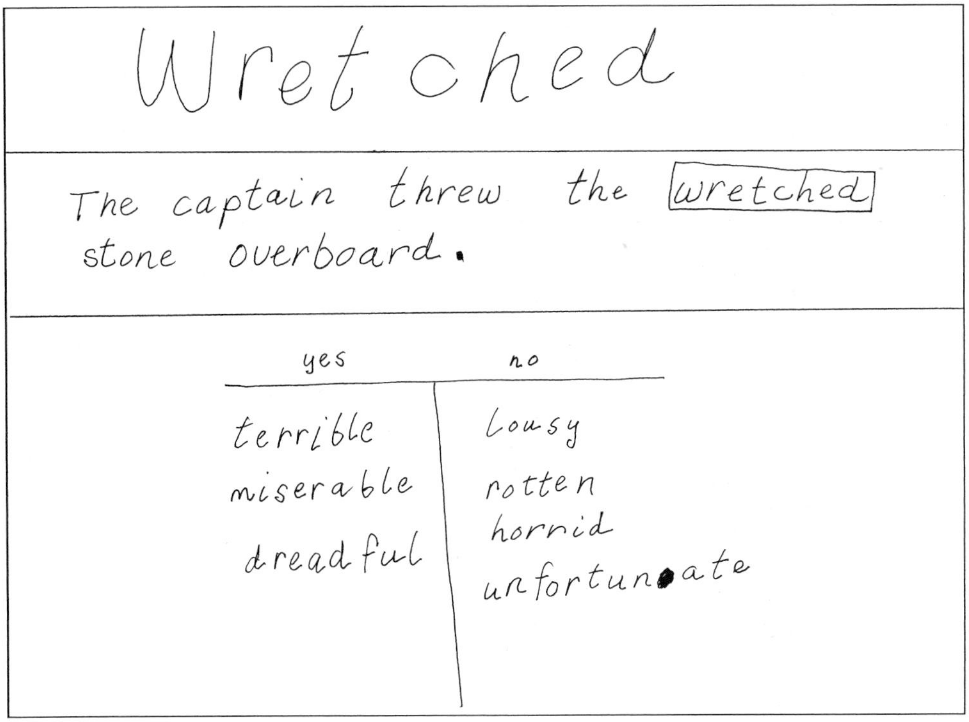

Wretched

The captain threw the [wretched] stone overboard.

yes	no
terrible	Lousy
miserable	rotten
dreadful	horrid
	unfortunoate

Two important reference books for examining the meanings of words are dictionaries and thesauri. Both list synonyms and antonyms, but dictionaries also explain the shades of meaning of related words. Series of dictionaries published by American Heritage, Macmillan, Merriam-Webster, Scholastic, and other publishing companies are available for elementary students. Most series include a first dictionary for primary-grade (K–2) students, a children's dictionary for middle-grade (3–5) students, and a student's dictionary for upper-grade (6–8) students. The *Dorling Kindersley Merriam-Webster Children's Dictionary* (2000), with over 32,000 entries and 3,000 illustrations, is an excellent reference. This dictionary takes into account children's interests and was designed with visually exciting illustrations and diagrams that expand word definitions. In addition, synonym boxes suggest word choices and word-history boxes present interesting information about how words entered English and have changed in meaning over the centuries. The same text is available as *Merriam-Webster's Elementary Dictionary* (2000), but this dictionary is not visually appealing.

An easy-to-use thesaurus for elementary students is *A First Thesaurus* (Wittels & Greisman, 2001), which contains more than 2,000 entry words. Synonyms are printed in black type for each entry word, and the antonyms follow in red type. Another good thesaurus is the *Scholastic Children's Thesaurus* (Bollard, 1998). More than 2,500 synonyms are grouped under 500 entries in the thesaurus. Under the entry *common,* for example, the synonyms *ordinary, typical, familiar, everyday,* and *widespread* are listed along with a brief definition and sample sentence for each. These and other reference books are annotated in the Classroom Library box on page 216.

Reference Books for Elementary Students

Dictionaries

The American Heritage children's dictionary. (1998). Boston: Houghton Mifflin. (M) This appealing hardcover dictionary contains 14,000 entries and more than 600 color photos and illustrations. Word history, language detective, synonym, and vocabulary-builder boxes provide additional interesting information. A 10-page phonics guide and 6-page thesaurus are also included in this reference book. This dictionary is also available on CD-ROM.

The American Heritage first dictionary. (1998). Boston: Houghton Mifflin. (P) More than 1,800 entries and 650 color photographs and graphics are presented in this attractive reference book. A clearly stated definition and an easy-to-read sentence are provided for each entry.

The American Heritage student dictionary. (1998). Boston: Houghton Mifflin. (U) This comprehensive dictionary for middle school students has 65,000 detailed entries with sentence examples and etymologies and more than 2,000 photographs. New computer and Internet terms have been included, and synonym lists, word-history boxes, and word-building features are highlighted in the text. Charts on the periodic table, geological eras, and weights and measures add to the book's usefulness.

DK Merriam-Webster children's dictionary. (2000). London: Dorling Kindersley. (M–U) This stunning volume pairs the 32,000 entries from *Merriam-Webster's Elementary Dictionary* with the striking design and color illustrations that DK is famous for.

This visually appealing book includes more than 3,000 photos and charts.

Levey, J. S. (1998). *Scholastic first dictionary.* New York: Scholastic. (P) More than 1,500 entries are in this visually appealing dictionary for beginning readers. Each entry word is highlighted, defined, and used in a sentence.

Macmillan dictionary for children. (2003). New York: Simon & Schuster. (M–U) This newly revised dictionary contains 35,000 entries presented in an uncluttered, two-column layout. Spelling hints, brief etymologies, and a reference section with a thesaurus are also included.

Merriam-Webster's elementary dictionary. (2000). Springfield, MA: Merriam-Webster. (M–U) This paperback dictionary contains 32,000 entries and 600 black-and-white illustrations. Entries are easy to read. Synonym boxes and word-history boxes provide additional useful information. In comparison to other dictionaries, this book lacks visual appeal.

Scholastic children's dictionary. (2002). New York: Scholastic. (M) More than 30,000 entries are presented with color illustrations and bright page decorations. Attractively designed boxes with information about synonyms, affixes, and word histories are featured throughout the book.

Swanson, M. (2003). *The American Heritage picture dictionary.* Boston: Houghton Mifflin. (P) The 900 common words in this book designed for kindergartners and first graders are listed alphabetically and illustrated with lively color drawings.

Thesauri

Bollard, J. K. (1998). *Scholastic children's thesaurus.* New York: Scholastic. (M) This attractive reference book for middle-grade students contains 500 entries and 2,500 synonyms grouped under the entries. All synonyms are defined and used in sample sentences. Antonyms are not listed.

Hellweg, P. (2003). *The American Heritage children's thesaurus.* Boston: Houghton Mifflin. (M–U) This well-designed and attractive reference book contains more than 4,000 entries and 36,000 synonyms. For each entry, synonyms are listed with the best matches first and each is used in a sentence to clarify its meaning. Antonym and word-group boxes provide additional information and extend the book's usefulness.

Hellweg, P. (2003). *The American Heritage student thesaurus.* Boston: Houghton Mifflin. (U) This comprehensive, dictionary-style thesaurus with

6,000 entries and more than 70,000 synonyms is designed for middle school and high school students. Clear sample sentences are provided for each synonym. In addition, word-group features list related vocabulary for words with no true synonyms.

Wittels, H., & Greisman, J. (2001). *A first thesaurus.* Racine, WI: Golden Books. (P–M) More than 2,000 entries are listed, with the main words printed in bold type in this easy-to-read reference. Synonyms are printed in regular type and antonyms in red.

Wittels, H., & Greisman, J. (1999). *The clear and simple thesaurus dictionary.* New York: Grosset & Dunlap. (M) This easy-to-use thesaurus lists 2,500 words in alphabetical order in a dictionary format. Each entry is followed by its synonyms printed in black and antonyms printed in red.

Homonyms

Homonyms, words that have sound and spelling similarities, are divided into three categories: homophones, homographs, and homographic homophones. Homophones are words that sound alike but are spelled differently. Most homophones developed from entirely different root words, and it is only by accident that they have come to sound alike; for example, the homophones *right* and *write* entered English before the year 900 and were pronounced differently. *Right* was spelled *reht* or *riht* in Old English; during the Middle English period, the spelling was changed by French scribes to the current spelling. The verb *write* was spelled *writan* in Old English and *writen* in Middle English. *Write* is an irregular verb, suggesting its Old English heritage, and the silent *w* was pronounced hundreds of years ago. In contrast, a few words were derived from the same root words, such as *flea–flee, flower–flour, stationary–stationery,* and *metal–medal–mettle,* and the similar spellings have been retained to demonstrate the semantic relationships.

Homographs are words that are spelled the same but pronounced differently. Examples of homographs are *bow, close, lead, minute, record, read,* and *wind. Bow* is a homograph that has three unrelated meanings. The verb form, meaning "to bend in respect," was spelled *bugan* in Old English; the noun form, meaning "a gathering of ribbon" or "a weapon for propelling an arrow," is of Old English origin and was spelled *boga.* The other noun form of *bow,* meaning "forward end of a ship," did not enter English until the 1600s from German.

Homographic homophones are words that are both spelled and pronounced alike, such as *bark, bat, bill, box, fair, fly, hide, jet, mine, pen, ring, row, spell, toast,* and *yard.* Some are related words; others are linguistic accidents. The different meanings of *toast,* for example, came from the same Latin source word, *torrere,* meaning "to parch or bake." The derivation of the noun *toast* as heated and browned slices of bread is obvious. However, the relationship between the source word and *toast* as a verb, "drinking to someone's honor or health," is not immediately apparent; the connection is that toasted, spiced bread flavored the drinks used in making toasts. In contrast, *bat* is a linguistic accident: *Bat* as a cudgel comes from the Old English word *batt;* the verb *to bat* is derived from the Old French word *batre;* and the nocturnal *bat* derives its name from an unknown Viking word and was spelled *bakke* in Middle English. Not only do the three forms of *bat* have unrelated etymologies, but they were borrowed from three languages!

There are many books of homonyms for children, including Gwynne's *The King Who Rained* (1970), *A Chocolate Moose for Dinner* (1976), *The Sixteen Hand Horse* (1980), and *A Little Pigeon Toad* (1988); Maestro's *What's a Frank Frank?* (1984); and Terban's *Hey, Hay! A Wagonful of Funny Homonym Riddles* (1991). Elementary students enjoy reading these books and making their own word books. Figure 5–4 shows a page from a second grader's homophone book.

Multiple Meanings

Many words have more than one meaning. The word *bank,* for example, may refer to a piled-up mass of snow or clouds, the slope of land beside a lake or river, the slope of a road on a turn, the lateral tilting of an airplane in a turn, to

FIGURE 5-4 *A Page From a Second Grader's Homophone Book*

cover a fire with ashes for slow burning, a business establishment that receives and lends money, a container in which money is saved, a supply for use in emergencies (e.g., blood bank), a place for storage (e.g., computer's memory bank), to count on, similar things arranged in a row (e.g., a bank of elevators), or to arrange things in a row. You may be surprised that there are at least 12 meanings for the common word *bank*. Why does this happen? The meanings of *bank* just listed come from three sources. The first five meanings come from a Viking word, and they are related because they all deal with something slanted or making a slanted motion. The next five meanings come from the Italian word *banca,* a money changer's table. All these meanings deal with financial banking except for the 10th meaning, to count on, which requires a bit more thought. We use the saying "to bank on" figuratively to mean "to depend on," but it began more literally from the actual counting of money on a table. The last two meanings come from the Old French word *banc,* meaning "bench." Words acquired multiple meanings as society became more complex and finer shades of meaning were necessary; for example, the meanings of *bank* as an emergency supply and a storage place are fairly new. As with many words with multiple meanings, it is a linguistic accident that three original words from three languages, with unrelated meanings, came to be spelled the same way.

Students can create posters with word clusters to show multiple meanings of words (Bromley, 1996). Figure 5–5 shows a cluster with 10 meanings of the word *hot* sketched from a poster made by three seventh graders. The students drew rays and wrote the meanings, listed examples, and drew illustrations.

Words assume additional meanings when an affix is added or when they are combined with another word, or compounded. Consider the word *fire* and the variety of words and phrases that incorporate *fire: fire hydrant, firebomb, fireproof, fireplace, firearm, fire drill, under fire, set the world on fire, fire away,* and *open fire.* Students can compile a list of words or make a booklet illustrating the words. Figure 5–6 lists more than 80 *down* words that a sixth-grade class compiled. Other common words with many variations include *short, key, water, book, rain, shoe, head, make, walk, cat,* and *side.*

FIGURE 5-5   *Seventh Graders' Poster of 10 Meanings for* Hot

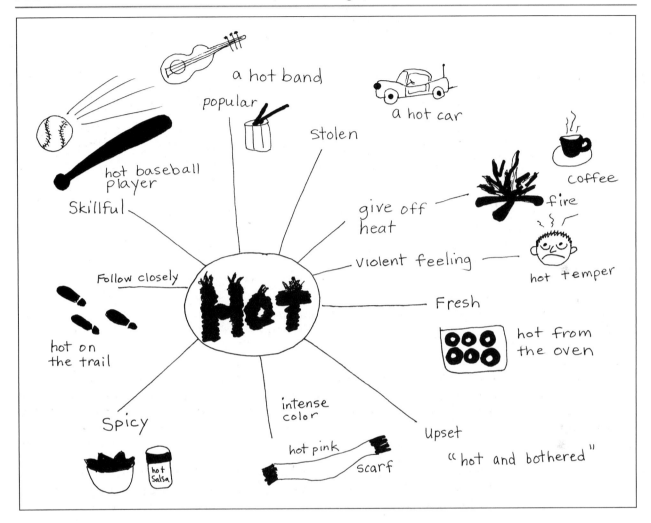

Figurative Language

Many words have both literal and figurative meanings. Literal meanings are the explicit, dictionary meanings, and figurative meanings are metaphorical or use figures of speech. For example, to describe winter as the coldest season of the year is literal, but to say that winter has icy breath is figurative. Two types of figurative language are idioms and metaphors.

Idioms are groups of words, such as "spill the beans," that have a special meaning. Idioms can be confusing to students because they must be interpreted figuratively rather than literally. "Spill the beans" dates back to ancient Greece. Cox (1980) explains that at that time, many Greek men belonged to secret clubs, and when someone wanted to join the club, the members took a vote to decide whether to admit him. They wanted the vote to remain secret, so they voted by each placing a white or brown bean in a special jar; a white bean indicated a yes vote, and a brown bean was a no vote. The club leader would then

FIGURE 5-6   *A Sixth-Grade Class's Collaboration List*

		Down Words	
downtown	climb down	reach down	downward
touchdown	down payment	write down	hunt down
get down	sit down	settle down	knock down
chow down	throw down	down it	breakdown
shake down	cut down	goose down	sundown
squat down	downhill	hop down	fall down
showdown	low-down	hands down	tear down
lie down	slow down	downfall	turn down
quiet down	downright	close down	push down
shut down	beam down	run down	downstairs
shot down	downy	pin down	look down
cool down	downer	come down	inside down
crackdown	downslope	slam down	zip down
countdown	kickdown	slap down	pour down
pass down	stare down	hoedown	downpour
pass me down	boogy down	lockdown	tape down
burn down	put down	water down	downgrade
downbeat	wrestle down	downturn	downstream
down to earth	flop down	stuff down	mow down
shimmy down	hung down	downcast	downhearted
downtrodden	chase down	hurl down	beat down

count the beans, and if all the beans were white, the person was admitted to the club. The vote was kept secret to avoid hurting the person's feelings in case the members voted not to admit him to the club. Sometimes during the voting, one member would accidentally (or not so accidentally) knock the jar over, spilling the beans, and the vote would no longer be a secret. The Greeks turned this real happening into a saying that we still use today. Another idiom with a different history but a similar meaning is "let the cat out of the bag."

There are hundreds of idioms in English, and we use them every day to create word pictures that make language more colorful. Some examples are "out in left field," "a skeleton in the closet," "stick your neck out," "a chip off the old block," and "don't cry over spilt milk." Some of these idioms are new, and others are hundreds or thousands of years old; some are American in origin, and others come from around the world.

Four excellent books of idioms for students are the *Scholastic Dictionary of Idioms, Phrases, Sayings, and Expressions* (Terban, 1996), *Put Your Foot in Your Mouth and Other Silly Sayings* (Cox, 1980), *Punching the Clock: Funny Action Idioms* (Terban, 1990), and *In a Pickle and Other Funny Idioms* (Terban, 1983). Because idioms are figurative sayings, many children—especially those who are learning English as a second language—have difficulty learning them. It is crucial that children move beyond the literal meanings, thus learning flexibility in using language. One way for students to learn flexibility is to create idiom posters showing the literal and figurative meanings of the sayings. A fourth grader's drawing of the literal meaning of "hold your horses" is shown in Figure 5–7.

Metaphors and similes compare something to something else. A simile is a comparison signaled by the use of *like* or *as:* "The crowd was as rowdy as a bunch of marauding monkeys" and "In the moonlight the dead tree looked like a skeleton" are two examples. In contrast, a metaphor compares two things by

FIGURE 5-7 *A Fourth Grader's Idiom Poster*

implying that one is something else, without using *like* or *as*. "The children were frisky puppies playing in the yard" is an example. Metaphors are a stronger comparison, as these examples show:

Simile: *The two old men crossed the street as slowly as snails.*

Metaphor: *The two old men were snails crossing the street.*

Simile: *In the moonlight, the dead tree looked like a skeleton.*

Metaphor: *In the moonlight, the dead tree was a skeleton.*

Differentiating between the terms *simile* and *metaphor* is less important than understanding the meaning of comparisons in books students are reading and having students use comparisons to make their writing more vivid.

Students begin by learning traditional comparisons, such as "happy as a clam" and "high as a kite," and then they learn to notice and invent fresh, unexpected comparisons. To introduce traditional comparisons to primary-grade students, teachers use Audrey Wood's *Quick as a Cricket* (1982). Middle- and upper-grade students locate comparisons in books they are reading and invent their own as they write poems, stories, and other types of writing.

Borrowed Words

The most common way of expanding vocabulary is to borrow words from other languages. This practice, which dates from Old English times, continues to the present day. Perhaps as many as 75% of our words have been borrowed from other languages and incorporated into English. Word borrowing has occurred during every period of language development, beginning when the Angles and Saxons borrowed over 400 words from the Romans. During the eighth and ninth centuries, the Vikings contributed approximately 900 words. The Norman conquerors introduced thousands of French words into English, reflecting every aspect of life; for example, *adventure, fork, juggler,* and *quilt.* Later, during the Renaissance, when scholars translated Greek and Latin classics into English, they borrowed many words from Latin and Greek to enrich the language, including *chaos, encyclopedia, pneumonia,* and *skeleton.* More recently, words from at least 50 languages have been added to English through exploration, colonization, and trade. These are some of the loan words from other languages (Tompkins & Yaden, 1986, p. 31):

African (many languages): *banjo, cola, gumbo, safari, zombie*

Arabic: *alcohol, apricot, assassin, magazine*

Aboriginal/Maori: *kangaroo, kiwi*

Celtic: *walnut*

Chinese: *chop suey, kowtow, tea, wok*

Czech: *pistol, robot*

Dutch: *caboose, easel, pickle, waffle*

Eskimo: *igloo, parka*

Finnish: *sauna*

French: *ballet, beige, chauffeur*

German: *kindergarten, poodle, pretzel, waltz*

Greek: *atom, cyclone, hydrogen*

Hawaiian: *aloha, hula, lei, luau*

Hebrew: *cherub, kosher, rabbi*

Hindi: *dungaree, juggernaut, jungle, shampoo*

Hungarian: *goulash, paprika*

Icelandic: *geyser*

Irish: *bog, leprechaun, shamrock*

Italian: *broccoli, carnival, macaroni, opera, pizza*

Japanese: *honcho, judo, kimono, origami*

Persian: *bazaar, divan, khaki, shawl*

Polish: *mazurka, polka*

Portuguese: *cobra, coconut, molasses*

Russian: *czar, sputnik, steppe, troika, vodka*

Scandinavian: *egg, fjord, husband, ski, sky*

Scottish: *clan, golf, slogan*

Spanish: *alligator, guitar, mosquito, potato*

Turkish: *caviar, horde, khan, kiosk, yogurt*

Yiddish: *bagel, chutzpah, pastrami*

Native Americans have also contributed a number of words to English. The early American colonists encountered many unfamiliar animals, plants, foods, and aspects of Native American life in North America. They borrowed the Native American terms for these objects or events and tried to spell them phonetically. Native American loan words include *chipmunk, hickory, moccasin, moose, muskrat, opossum, papoose, powwow, raccoon, skunk, toboggan, tomahawk,* and *tepee.*

Other Sources of New Words

New words continually appear in English, many of them created to describe new inventions and scientific projects. Some of the newest words come from the Internet, including *modem* and *e-mail*. They are created in a variety of ways, including compounding, coining, and clipping. *E-mail,* for example, is clipped, or shortened, from *electronic mail.*

Compounding means combining two existing words to create a new word. *Friendship* and *childhood* are two words that the Anglo-Saxons compounded more than a thousand years ago. Recent compoundings include *latchkey children* and *software*. Compound words usually progress through three stages: they begin as separate words (e.g., *ice cream*), then are hyphenated (e.g., *baby-sit*), and finally are written as one word (e.g., *splashdown*). There are many exceptions to this rule, such as the compound words *post office* and *high school,* which have remained separate words. Other compound words use Greek and Latin elements, for example, *stethoscope* and *television.*

Creative people have always coined new words. Lewis Carroll, author of *Alice in Wonderland* and *Through the Looking Glass,* is perhaps the best-known inventor of words. He called his new words portmanteau words (borrowing from the British word for a suitcase that opens into two halves) because they were created by blending two words into one. His most famous example, *chortle,* a blend of *snort* and *chuckle,* is from the poem "Jabberwocky." Other examples of blended words include *brunch (breakfast + lunch), electrocute (electric + execute), guesstimate (guess + estimate),* and *smog (smoke + fog).*

Two other types of coined words are trademarks and acronyms. Examples of well-known trademarks and brand names include *Kleenex, Coca-Cola, Xerox,* and *nylon.* Nylon was invented by scientists working in New York and London; they named their product by combining *ny,* the abbreviation for New York, with *lon,* the first three letters of London. Acronyms, words formed by combining the initial letters of several words, include *radar, laser,* and *scuba. Scuba,* for example, was formed by combining the initial letters of self-contained underwater breathing apparatus.

Clipping is a process of shortening existing words. For example, *bomb* is the shortened form of *bombard,* and *zoo* comes from *zoological park.* Most clipped words are only one syllable and are used in informal conversation. Although it is unlikely that your students will create new words that will eventually appear in the dictionary, they do create words to add pizzazz to their writing, and some words become part of the everyday jargon in a classroom.

Authors also create new words in their stories, and students should be alert to the possibility of finding a created word when they read or listen to stories. The Howes (1979) created *Bunnicula* to name their spooky young rabbit *(bunny + dracula),* and Chris Van Allsburg (1981) invented the word *Jumanji* to name his adventure game.

TEACHING STUDENTS ABOUT WORDS

Students' vocabularies grow at an astonishing rate—about 3,000 words a year, or roughly 7 to 10 new words every day (Nagy & Herman, 1985). By the time students finish high school, their vocabularies reach 25,000 to 40,000 words. It seems obvious that to learn words at such an astonishing rate, students learn words both in school and outside of school. Television has a significant impact on children's vocabularies, too. Teachers often assume that students learn words primarily through the lessons they teach, but students actually learn the meanings of many more words through independent reading and writing projects than through instruction. Encouraging students to read is probably the most important way teachers promote vocabulary growth (Nagy, 1988). Repeated exposure to words is crucial because students need to see and use a new word many times before it becomes a part of their ownership dictionaries—words they understand and use competently.

Not all the words students learn are equally hard or easy to learn; the degree of difficulty depends on what the student already knows about the word. Graves (1985) identifies four possible situations for unfamiliar words:

1. *Sight word.* Students know what the word means when they hear someone say it and can use it orally, but they don't recognize its written form.
2. *New word.* Students have a concept related to the word, but they are not familiar with the word, either orally or in written form.
3. *New concept.* Students have little or no background knowledge about the concept underlying the word, and they don't recognize the word itself.
4. *New meaning.* Students know the word, but they are unfamiliar with the way the word is used and its meaning in this situation.

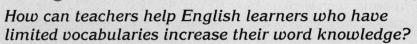

Seeing Common Threads

How can teachers help English learners who have limited vocabularies increase their word knowledge?

Jennie Alameida responds:

I think the most authentic and efficient way to learn a large number of words is through a theme cycle. Reading and listening to thematic stories and nonfiction books helps my students develop concepts and learn the meaning of new vocabulary words. My students put new words up on the word wall and use the words for many different activities. Because the amount of time within a classroom is limited, and many repetitions are required to learn a new word, I connect vocabulary with social studies and science through theme cycles.

What do you think?

Each chapter presents a question and a response written by one of Dr. Tompkins's students. Consider other comments, or respond to the question yourself, by visiting the Threaded Message Board in Chapter 5 on the Companion Website at www.prenhall.com/tompkins

New sight words are probably the easiest words for students to learn because they already use the word orally; the most difficult category of words is the one involving new concepts because students must both learn the concept and attach the word label.

Even though students learn hundreds or thousands of words incidentally through reading and content-area study each year, teaching vocabulary directly is an essential part of language arts instruction for all students and especially for struggling students and English learners (Beck, McKeown, & Kucan, 2002). Blachowicz and Fisher (2002) have reviewed the research on effective vocabulary instruction and identified these guidelines for teaching vocabulary:

1. Teachers immerse students in vocabulary by creating a word-rich environment in the classroom. When teachers post words on word walls, students are more likely to learn them incidentally and through direct instruction.
2. Teachers prepare students to become independent word learners. When teachers involve students in choosing some of the words they will study and teach word-learning tools, such as how to use root words to analyze words and how to use a dictionary, students are more likely to take control of their own learning.
3. Teachers model word-learning strategies while teaching vocabulary. When teachers demonstrate ways, such as making clusters and sorting words, to become actively involved in learning word meanings and students participate in these activities, they are more likely to personalize the words and remember their meanings.
4. Teachers assess both the depth and the breadth of vocabulary knowledge. When teachers choose assessment techniques based on their instructional goals, they can evaluate both how well students understand the words they've studied and the range of words they learned.

Vocabulary instruction has a place in all four patterns of practice. Students learn the meaning of words through a combination of reading and direct instruction. Students are involved in reading in all four patterns of practice, and in three of the patterns, they are also involved in vocabulary activities. Teachers apply Blachowicz and Fisher's guidelines as they teach vocabulary. During literature focus units and theme cycles, for example, teachers, like Ms. Boland in the vignette at the beginning of the chapter, highlight important words on word walls and teach minilessons using these words, and in literature circles, students assume a leadership role to highlight unfamiliar words, check their definitions, and use the words in their discussions.

Word Walls

The most important way to focus students' attention on words is to write important words on word-wall charts and post them in the classroom. Before beginning instruction, teachers hang up blank word walls made from large sheets of butcher paper that have been divided into alphabetized sections. Students and the teacher write on the word wall interesting, confusing, and important words from books they are reading and concepts they learn during theme cycles. Usually students choose the words to write on the word wall during the exploring stage of the reading process, and they may even do the writing themselves.

Word Walls

Step by Step

1. **Prepare the word wall.**   Teachers hang a long sheet of butcher paper on a blank wall in the classroom, divide it into 16 to 24 boxes, and label with letters of the alphabet.

2. **Introduce the word wall.**   Teachers introduce the word wall and write several key words on it during preparing activities before reading.

3. **Add words to the word wall.**   After reading a picture book or after reading each chapter of a chapter book, students suggest "important" words for the word wall. Students and the teacher write the words on the butcher paper, making sure to write large enough so that most students can see the words. If a word is misspelled, it should be corrected because students will be reading and using the word in various activities. Sometimes the teacher adds a small picture or writes a synonym for a difficult word, puts a box around the root word, or writes the plural form or other related words nearby.

4. **Use the word wall for exploring activities.**   Students use the words for a variety of activities, and teachers expect them to spell the words correctly. During literature focus units, students refer to the word wall when they are making words, writing in reading logs, doing word sorts, or working on projects. During theme cycles, students use the word wall in similar ways.

5. **Write the words on word cards.**   Teachers transfer the words from the word wall to word cards at the end of the unit. They can write the words on index cards, sentence strips, or small sheets of decorated paper that correspond to the topic of the unit. They punch holes in one corner of the cards and use metal rings or yarn to make a booklet. They place the word booklets in the writing center for students to refer to as needed.

Teachers add any key words students have not chosen. Words are added to the word wall as they come up—in books students are reading during literature focus units or during theme cycles—not in advance; also, separate charts are used for each unit. The procedure for creating a word wall is described in the Step by Step feature above.

Teachers choose the most important words from books to teach. Important words include words that are essential to understanding the text, words that may confuse students, and words students will use as they read other books. As teachers choose words for word walls and other vocabulary activities, they consider the book being read as well as the instructional context. For example, during a literature focus unit on Amy Axelrod's *Pigs Will Be Pigs* (1994), a story about a family of pigs who hunt for money around their house in order to go to a restaurant for dinner, a second-grade class created the word wall shown in Figure 5–8.

FIGURE 5-8   *A Word Wall for Pigs Will Be Pigs*

AB	C	D	EF
bank B.J. bedroom basement burritos bellyaches	closets chimichangas chef's special cozy	Dave dollar bill dime drawers downstairs	empty enchanted enchilada frijoles refritos explode
GH grocery shopping hungry	**IJ** jewelry box jalapeños	**KL** kitchen lucky laundry room	**M** Mr. Pig Mrs. Pig Mike money menu
NO nickels nacho chips	**PQ** quarter penny pennies pocketbooks pantry piglets	**R** refrigerator restaurant	**S** searched salad bar sopaipillas stuffed
T two hundred tool box taco salad	**UV** upstairs	**W** wallet waitress	**XYZ**

These words include the names of characters, rooms in the pigs' home where they search for money, amounts of money, and foods on the menu at the Mexican restaurant. They were chosen because they are important to the story, and the teacher chose to focus on the money-related words and tie in a math unit on counting money.

Even though all these words and perhaps more will be added to the word wall, not all will be directly taught to students. As they plan, teachers create lists of words that they anticipate will be written on word walls during the unit. They try to identify which words will be sight words for their students and which words represent new concepts, new words, and new meanings for their students. From this list, teachers choose the key words—the ones that are critical to understanding the book or the theme—and these are the words they plan to highlight or include in minilessons. They also choose any words that must be introduced before reading. According to Vygotsky's notion of a "zone of proximal development," teachers need to be alert to individual students and what words they are learning so that they can provide instruction when students are most interested in learning more about a word.

Identifying some words on the word wall as key words doesn't mean that the other words are unimportant. Students have many opportunities to use all the word wall words as they write and talk about what they are reading and studying. For example, students often use the word wall to locate a specific word they want to use to make a point during a discussion or to check the spelling of a word they are writing in a reading log or in a report. Teachers also use the words listed on the word wall for word-study activities.

Word-Study Activities

Word-study activities provide students with opportunities to explore the meanings of words listed on word walls, other words related to books they are reading, and words they are learning during social studies or science theme cycles. Through these activities, students explore the word meanings and make associations among words. None of these activities require students simply to write words and their definitions or to use the words in sentences or a contrived story. Here are eight types of activities:

1. *Word posters.* Students choose a word from the word wall and write it on a small poster. Then they draw and color a picture to illustrate the word. They may also want to use the word in a sentence.
2. *Word clusters.* Students choose a word to write in the center circle of a cluster. Then they draw rays, write information about the word, and make connections between the word and the literature focus unit or theme cycle. Figure 5–9 shows three types of word clusters. First graders made the first cluster after reading *The Adventures of Taxi Dog* (Barracca & Barracca, 1990). The second is a cluster that third graders made after reading *Sugaring Time,* by Kathryn Lasky (1983). For the third cluster, seventh graders considered the definition of *reminiscent,* its history or etymology, its part of speech, other related forms, its word parts, and its synonyms.
3. *Dramatizing words.* Students choose a word from the word wall and dramatize it for classmates to guess. Teachers might also want to choose a word from the word wall for a "word of the day."
4. *Word sorts.* Students sort a collection of words taken from the word wall into two or more categories (Bear, Invernizzi, Templeton, & Johnston, 2004). Usually students choose which categories they will use for the sort, but sometimes the teacher chooses. For example, words from a story might be sorted by character, or words from a theme on machines might be sorted according to whether they are machines or according to type of machine. The words can be written on cards, and then students sort a pack of word cards into piles. Or, students can cut apart a list of words, sort the words into categories, and then paste each group on a sheet of paper. Figure 5–10 shows a word sort done by a small group of fifth graders during a theme on the colonies. Students chose the three categories—New England colonies, middle colonies, and Southern

FIGURE 5-9 *Three Word Clusters*

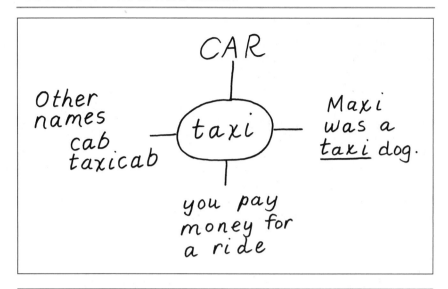

CAR

taxi

Other names
cab
taxicab

Maxi was a <u>taxi</u> dog.

you pay money for a ride

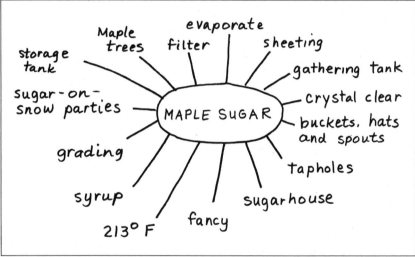

MAPLE SUGAR

Maple trees
storage tank
sugar-on-snow parties
grading
syrup
213° F
fancy
evaporate
filter
sheeting
gathering tank
crystal clear
buckets, hats and spouts
tapholes
sugarhouse

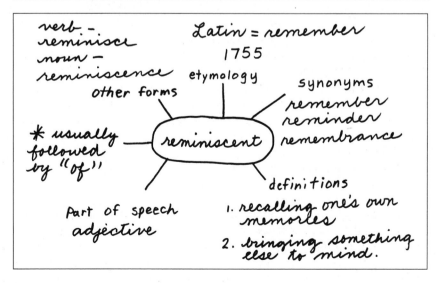

reminiscent

verb – reminisce
noun – reminiscence
other forms

Latin = remember
1755
etymology

synonyms
remember
reminder
remembrance

* usually followed by "of"

Part of speech
adjective

definitions
1. recalling one's own memories
2. bringing something else to mind.

FIGURE 5-10   *A Word Sort on the American Colonies*

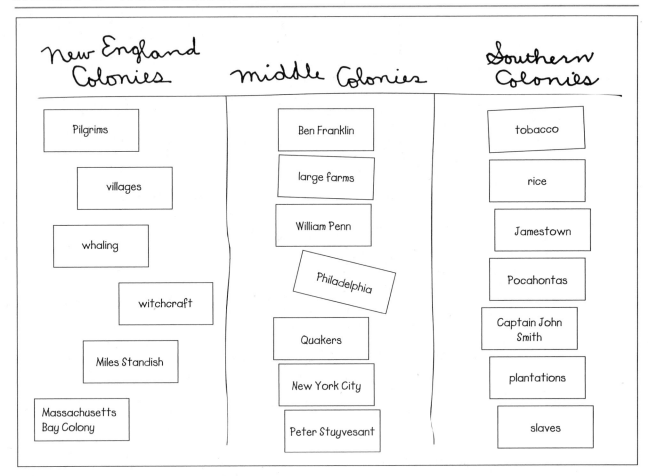

colonies—and sorted word cards for each category. Then they glued the word cards onto a large sheet of paper.

5. *Books about words.* A variety of books for children are collections of words or explain words related to particular concepts. *Zin! Zin! Zin! A Violin* (Moss, 1995), for instance, explains words for groups of musicians (e.g., *solo, duo, trio, quartet*), and Ruth Heller introduces *batch, school, fleet, bevy,* and *flock* in *A Cache of Jewels and Other Collective Nouns* (1987). Marvin Terban, the author of more than a dozen books about words, explains *hocus-pocus, razzmatazz, hodgepodge, knickknack,* and 103 other words in *Superdupers! Really Funny Real Words* (1989). These and other books about words are listed in the Classroom Library box on page 231.

Teachers often connect books about words with literature focus units and theme cycles. For example, as part of a theme cycle on birds, teachers might use Lois Ehlert's *Feathers for Lunch* (1990), which provides detailed information about and drawings of 12 backyard birds, or during a literature focus unit on *Chrysanthemum* (Henkes, 1991), a story about a girl who didn't like being named for a flower, teachers might

CLASSROOM LIBRARY

Books About Words and Wordplay

Agee, J. (2000). Elvis lives! and other anagrams. New York: Farrar, Straus & Giroux. (M–U)

Agee, J. (2002). *Palindromania!* New York: Farrar, Straus & Giroux. (M–U)

Browne, P. (1996). *A gaggle of geese: The collective names of the animal kingdom.* New York: Atheneum. (M)

Clements, A. (1996). *Frindle.* New York: Simon & Schuster. (M–U)

Dewan, T. (1992). *Inside the whale and other animals.* London: Dorling Kindersley. (M–U)

Dewey, A. (1995). *Naming colors.* New York: HarperCollins. (M)

Edwards, P. D. (2001). *Slop goes the soup: A noisy warthog word book.* New York: Hyperion. (P–M)

Ehlert, L. (1989). *Eating the alphabet: Fruits and vegetables from A to Z.* Orlando, FL: Harcourt Brace. (P–M)

Ehlert, L. (1990). *Feathers for lunch.* Orlando, FL: Harcourt Brace. (P–M)

Feder, J. (1995). *Table, chair, bear: A book in many languages.* New York: Ticknor. (P–M)

Frasier, D. (2000). *Miss Alaineus: A vocabulary disaster.* San Diego: Harcourt Brace. (M)

Gibbons, G. (1990). *Weather words and what they mean.* New York: Holiday House. (P–M)

Graham-Barber, L. (1995). *A chartreuse leotard in a magenta limousine: And other words named after people and places.* New York: Hyperion. (M–U)

Heller, R. (1983). *The reason for a flower.* New York: Sandcastle. (See other books in the series by this author.) (M)

Heller, R. (1987). *A cache of jewels and other collective nouns.* New York: Grosset & Dunlap. (M–U)

Hepworth, C. (1992). *Antics! An alphabetical anthology.* New York: Putnam. (M–U)

Hubbard, W. (1990). *C is for curious: An ABC of feelings.* San Francisco: Chronicle Books. (P–M)

Hunt, J. (1989). *Illuminations.* New York: Bradbury. (M–U)

Lobel, A. (1990). *Alison's zinnia.* New York: Greenwillow. (M)

Maestro, B., & Maestro, G. (1989). *Taxi: A book of city words.* New York: Clarion. (P–M)

Magee, D., & Newman, R. (1990). *All aboard ABC.* New York: Puffin. (P)

McMillan, B. (1989). *Super, super, superwords.* New York: Lothrop, Lee & Shepard. (P)

Moss, L. (1995). *Zin! Zin! Zin! A violin.* New York: Simon & Schuster. (P–M)

Most, B. (1980). *There's an ant in Anthony.* New York: Morrow. (P–M)

Most, B. (1991). *A dinosaur named after me.* Orlando, FL: Harcourt Brace. (P–M)

Onyefulu, I. (1993). *A is for Africa.* New York: Cobblehill Books. (M)

Pallotta, J. (1994). *The desert alphabet book.* Watertown, MA: Charlesbridge. (See other alphabet books by the same author.) (M–U)

Parker, N. W., & Wright, J. R. (1987). *Bugs.* New York: Greenwillow. (M)

Parker, N. W., & Wright, J. R. (1990). *Frogs, toads, lizards, and salamanders.* New York: Greenwillow. (M)

Rockwell, A. (1986). *Things that go.* New York: Dutton. (P)

Rotner, S. (1996). *Action alphabet.* New York: Atheneum. (P–M)

Terban, M. (1988). *Guppies in tuxedos: Funny eponyms.* New York: Clarion. (M–U)

Terban, M. (1989). *Superdupers! Really funny real words.* New York: Clarion. (M–U)

Terban, M. (1993). *It figures! Fun figures of speech.* New York: Clarion. (M)

Terban, M. (1996). *Scholastic dictionary of idioms.* New York: Scholastic. (M–U)

Trucks. (1991). London: Dorling Kindersley. (P)

Wildsmith, B. (1967). *Birds.* Oxford, England: Oxford University Press. (M–U)

use *Alison's Zinnia* (Lobel, 1990) or *The Flower Alphabet Book* (Pallotta, 1988) for a minilesson on the names of various flowers. Also, during minilessons on language concepts, teachers might use other books about words. For a minilesson on comparative and superlative forms, teachers might share *Super, Super, Superwords* (McMillan, 1989), or they might use *Action Alphabet* (Rotner, 1996) for a minilesson on verbs. After students read these books, they can make their class collaboration or individual books about words.

Minilessons. *This teacher is reviewing how to take notes using key vocabulary words with a small group of students. She taught the minilesson to the whole class, and then students were to continue to take notes as they read the next chapter. These four students were unsure how to proceed, so the teacher reviewed the steps in taking notes and next will work with students as they read, make a cluster, and take notes on the next chapter together. Teachers provide direct instruction through minilessons and are then available to give additional assistance to students who need more support.*

6. *Tea party.* Teachers prepare a set of cards with text (sentences or paragraphs) from a story or informational book students are reading. At least one "important" word from the word wall is included in each excerpt, and the word is highlighted. Students have a "tea party" and read the cards to classmates. They also talk about the highlighted word and its meaning. Sometimes teachers write the definition of the word or a synonym on the back of the card.

7. *Word chains.* Students choose a word from the word wall and then identify three or four words to sequence before or after the word to make a chain. For example, the word *tadpole* can be chained this way: *egg, tadpole, frog;* and the word *aggravate* can be chained like this: *irritate, bother, aggravate, annoy.* Students can draw and write their chains on a sheet of paper, or they can make a construction paper chain and write the words on each link.

8. *Semantic feature analysis.* Students select a group of related words, such as names of different kinds of birds, and then make a grid or chart to classify them according to distinguishing characteristics. A semantic feature analysis that Ms. Boland's class created during their theme on medieval life is presented in Figure 5–11. This activity reinforces students' organization of knowledge and related words into schemata (Pittelman, Heimlich, Berglund, & French, 1991).

Teaching Minilessons

Traditionally, vocabulary instruction involved assigning students to look up the definitions of a list of words in a dictionary and use the words in sentences, but this approach often failed to produce in-depth understanding (Nagy, 1988). In

FIGURE 5-11 *A Semantic Feature Analysis on Medieval Life*

	castle	knights	peasants	Crusades	cathedral
apprentice	O	✓	O	O	O
bailey	✓	O	O	O	O
Black Death	O	✓	✓	O	O
chivalry	O	✓	O	O	O
clergy	O	O	O	?	✓
dub	O	✓	O	O	O
flying buttress	O	O	O	O	✓
fortress	✓	O	O	O	O
garderobe	✓	O	O	O	O
Jerusalem	O	O	O	✓	O
jousts	O	✓	O	O	O
keep	✓	O	O	O	O
mercenary	O	?	O	✓	O
moat	✓	O	O	O	O
pilgrims	O	?	O	✓	O
portcullis	✓	O	O	O	O
serf	O	O	✓	O	O
siege	✓	O	O	O	O
tournament	O	✓	O	O	O
villein	O	O	✓	O	O

Code: ✓ = yes

O = no

? = don't know

Piecing a Lesson Together

Topics on Vocabulary

Procedures	Concepts	Strategies and Skills
Choose words for word walls	History of English	Use phonics to pronounce a word
Extrapolate the etymology	Root words	Use structural analysis to identify a word
"Peel off" affixes	Affixes	
Make a word poster	Prefixes	Use context clues to identify a word
Make a word cluster	Suffixes	
Do a word sort	Synonyms	Consider shades of meaning in selecting a word
Make a word chain	Antonyms	
Do a semantic feature analysis	Homophones	Use a thesaurus to choose a better word
Locate a word in a dictionary	Homographs	
Locate a word in a thesaurus	Homographic homophones	Use a dictionary to identify a word
	Multiple meanings of words	Avoid trite language
	Idioms	Consider multiple meanings of words
	Literal meanings	
	Figurative meanings	
	Borrowed words	
	Compound words	

Please visit the Companion Website at
www.prenhall.com/tompkins for a second
fully realized minilesson.

contrast to the traditional approach, teachers teach minilessons to teach specific words as well as word-learning strategies (Baumann & Kame'enui, 2004). To teach specific words, they provide in-depth information about words, provide multiple opportunities to learn a word, and get students to actively investigate words in order to deepen their level of knowledge. To teach word-learning strategies, teachers explain and demonstrate strategies for unlocking word meanings, such as peeling off affixes or using the root word to determine the word's meaning. A list of topics for minilessons and a sample minilesson showing how a sixth-grade teacher explains to her students how related words develop from English, Latin, and Greek root words is presented in the box above.

ROOT WORDS

Mrs. Monroe Teaches Her Sixth Graders About Root Words

1. **Introduce the Topic**

   Mrs. Monroe asks her sixth-grade students to brainstorm a list of words about teeth, and students suggest words, including: *teeth, toothbrush, floss, dentist, cavities, cleaning, tooth fairy, dental, orthodontist, braces,* and *dentures.* She points out that it seems unusual that words such as *toothbrush, dentist,* and *orthodontist* all relate to teeth, but look so different.

2. **Share Examples**

   Mrs. Monroe explains that many words dealing with teeth come from three root words—*tooth* (English), *dent* (Latin), and *dont* (Greek). They sort the words from the brainstormed list into four columns:

tooth	dent	dont	other
teeth	dentist	orthodontist	floss
toothbrush	dental		cavities
tooth fairy	dentures		braces

   She points out that Latin and Greek words are likely to be medical or scientific.

3. **Provide Information**

   Mrs. Monroe explains that there are other trios of related words:

   star (E), *stell* (L), and *astr* (Gr)
   sound (E), *sono* (L), and *phon* (Gr)
   people (E), *pop* (L), and *demo* (Gr)
   foot (E), *ped* (L), and *pod* (Gr)
   water (E), *aqua* (L), and *hydro* (Gr)

   The students brainstorm some examples of the trios and ask why words come from different root words. The teacher explains that many words in English come from different languages because people wanted to be able to express different ideas, and that at different historical times, the English liked to invent new words from different languages, especially Latin and Greek.

4. **Supervise Practice**

   Mrs. Monroe divides the class into five groups and gives each group a set of word cards representing a different trio of words. The students read the word cards, check the meanings of any unfamiliar words, sort the words, glue the sorted words on a poster, and add other related words.

5. **Reflect on Learning**

   Students share their posters with the class and marvel at the complexity of English.

Meeting the Needs of Every Student

Because learning about words is an important part of language arts, it is crucial that teachers find ways to help every student use the words they are learning. Having a word wall in every literature focus unit and across-the-curriculum theme cycle is probably the most important way to focus students' attention on words. Teachers also need to provide a variety of word-study activities to meet the needs of every student. Suggestions for adapting vocabulary instruction are presented on page 236. These suggestions focus on using vocabulary in meaningful, functional, and genuine ways.

Meeting the Needs of Every Student

How Can I Develop My Students' Vocabularies?

Many students today have limited vocabularies because of too much time spent watching television or too little time spent reading, impoverished home environments, or lack of opportunities to explore the world and talk with adults about their experiences. Some of these students are English learners, but it's wrong to assume that all students who are learning English have limited vocabularies. When students have rich vocabularies in their first language, they learn the English words fairly easily because translating words from one language to another is much easier than learning new words.

No matter why your students' vocabularies are limited, it is crucial that you build their word knowledge. How do you do it? The single most important way is by reading. You should read aloud both stories and informational books to students every day no matter what grade you teach, and students should read self-selected books every day, too. You should emphasize vocabulary in the lessons you teach by introducing key vocabulary at the beginning of language arts and content-area lessons and by focusing on vocabulary through word walls and word-study activities. Sometimes you will need to work with a small group of struggling students to preteach concepts and vocabulary words before introducing a lesson to the class and reteach the words after teaching the lesson. It's also important that you use new vocabulary in your conversation, and then expect your students to use the words, too, both orally and in writing.

To investigate other ways to meet the needs of every student, visit the links for this chapter on the Companion Website at www.prenhall.com/tompkins

Companion Website

Assessing Students' Use of Words

Teachers assess students' use of words related to literature focus units and across-the-curriculum themes in a variety of ways. They listen while students talk during the theme, examine students' writing and projects, and ask students to talk or write about the theme and what they have learned. Here are some specific strategies to determine whether students have learned and are applying new words:

- Check reading logs, learning logs, or simulated journals for words related to the unit or theme.
- Use these words in a conference and note the student's response.
- Listen for vocabulary when students give an oral report.
- Ask students to make a cluster or do a quickwrite about the theme or unit or about specific words.
- Ask students to brainstorm a list of words and phrases about the theme or unit.

- Check students' reports, biographies, poems, stories, or other writings for unit- or theme-related words.
- Check students' projects for these words.
- Ask students to write a letter to you, telling what they have learned in the unit or theme.

Teachers can also give tests on the vocabulary words, but this is probably the least effective approach because a correct answer on a test does not indicate whether students have ownership of a word or whether they are applying it in meaningful and genuine ways.

Review

Learning about words is an important part of language arts. Few words have only one meaning, and students in the elementary grades learn about multiple meanings as well as about root words and affixes; homonyms, synonyms, and antonyms; and figurative meanings of words, such as idioms and metaphors. The best measure of students' learning of words is their ability to use the words in meaningful, functional, and genuine activities. The key points in this chapter are:

1. English is a historic language, and its diverse origins account for word meanings and some spelling inconsistencies.
2. The fact that students' vocabularies grow at a rate of about 3,000 words a year suggests that students learn many words incidentally.
3. Students use their knowledge of root words and affixes to unlock the meaning of unfamiliar words.
4. Many words have more than one meaning, and students learn additional word meanings through the four patterns of practice.
5. Idioms and metaphors can be confusing to students because they must be interpreted figuratively rather than literally.
6. Reading and writing are the most important ways students learn vocabulary, but direct instruction is also important.
7. Students need to use a word many times in order to learn it well.
8. Words are not all equally difficult or easy to learn; the degree of difficulty depends on what the student already knows about the word.
9. Students use reference books, including dictionaries and thesauri, to learn about words.
10. Word-study activities include word walls, word posters, word clusters, word sorts, word chains, and semantic feature analysis.

Visit Chapter 5 on the Companion Website at www.prenhall.com/tompkins to:

- **Check your understanding of the concepts presented in the chapter**
- **Access the Extensions (activities and a list of related readings)**
- **Link to related websites**

Professional References

Alexander, H. (1962). *The story of our language.* Garden City, NY: Doubleday.

Baugh, A. C., & Cable, T. (1978). *The history of the English language* (3rd ed.). Upper Saddle River, NJ: Prentice Hall.

Baumann, J. F., & Kame'enui, E. J. (Eds.). (2004). *Vocabulary instruction: Research to practice.* New York: Guilford Press.

Bear, D. R., Invernizzi, M., Templeton, S., & Johnston, F. (2004). *Words their way: Word study for phonics, vocabulary, and spelling instruction* (3rd ed.). Upper Saddle River, NJ: Merrill/Prentice Hall.

Beck, I. L., McKeown, M. G., & Kucan, L. (2002). *Bringing words to life: Robust vocabulary instruction.* New York: Guilford Press.

Blachowicz, C., & Fisher, P. (2002). *Teaching vocabulary in all classrooms* (2nd ed.). Upper Saddle River, NJ: Merrill/Prentice Hall.

Bromley, K. D. (1996). *Webbing with literature: Creating story maps with children's books* (2nd ed.). Boston: Allyn & Bacon.

Carr, E., & Wixon, K. K. (1986). Guidelines for evaluating vocabulary instruction. *Journal of Reading, 29,* 588–595.

Graves, M. (1985). *A word is a word . . . or is it?* Portsmouth, NH: Heinemann.

Hook, J. N. (1975). *History of the English language.* New York: Ronald Press.

Klein, M. L. (1988). *Teaching reading comprehension and vocabulary: A guide for teachers.* Upper Saddle River, NJ: Merrill/Prentice Hall.

Nagy, W. E. (1988). *Teaching vocabulary to improve reading comprehension.* Urbana, IL: ERIC Clearinghouse on Reading and Communication Skills and the National Council of Teachers of English and the International Reading Association.

Nagy, W. E., & Herman, P. (1985). Incidental vs. instructional approaches to increasing reading vocabulary. *Educational Perspectives, 23,* 16–21.

Pittelman, S. D., Heimlich, J. E., Berglund, R. L., & French, M. P. (1991). *Semantic feature analysis: Classroom applications.* Newark, DE: International Reading Association.

Tompkins, G. E. (2004). *Teaching writing: Balancing process and product* (4th ed.). Upper Saddle River, NJ: Merrill/Prentice Hall.

Tompkins, G. E., & Yaden, D. B., Jr. (1986). *Answering students' questions about words.* Urbana, IL: National Council of Teachers of English.

White, T. G., Sowell, J., & Yanagihara, A. (1989). Teaching elementary students to use word-part clues. *The Reading Teacher, 42,* 302–308.

Children's Book References

Axelrod, A. (1994). *Pigs will be pigs.* New York: Four Winds Press.

Barracca, D., & Barracca, S. (1990). *The adventures of taxi dog.* New York: Dial.

Bollard, J. K. (1998). *Scholastic children's thesaurus.* New York: Scholastic.

Cole, J. (2002). *Ms. Frizzle's adventures: Medieval castle.* New York: Scholastic.

Cox, J. A. (1980). *Put your foot in your mouth and other silly sayings.* New York: Random House.

Cushman, K. (1994). *Catherine, called Birdy.* New York: HarperCollins.

Dorling Kindersley Merriam-Webster children's dictionary. (2000). London: Dorling Kindersley.

Ehlert, L. (1990). *Feathers for lunch.* Orlando: Harcourt Brace.

Gwynne, F. (1970). *The king who rained.* New York: Windmill Books.

Gwynne, F. (1976). *A chocolate moose for dinner.* New York: Windmill Books.

Gwynne, F. (1980). *The sixteen hand horse.* New York: Prentice Hall.

Gwynne, F. (1988). *A little pigeon toad.* New York: Simon & Schuster.

Heller, R. (1987). *A cache of jewels and other collective nouns.* New York: Grosset & Dunlap.

Henkes, K. (1991). *Chrysanthemum.* New York: Greenwillow.

Howe, D., & Howe, J. (1979). *Bunnicula: A rabbit-tale of mystery.* New York: Atheneum.

Lasky, K. (1983). *Sugaring time.* New York: Macmillan.

Lester, H. (1988). *Tacky the penguin.* Boston: Houghton Mifflin.

Lobel, A. (1990). *Alison's zinnia.* New York: Greenwillow.

Lowry, L. (1993). *The giver.* Boston: Houghton Mifflin.

Macaulay, D. (1977). *Castle.* Boston: Houghton Mifflin.

Maestro, G. (1984). *What's a frank Frank? Tasty homograph riddles.* New York: Clarion Books.

McMillan, B. (1989). *Super, super, superwords.* New York: Lothrop, Lee & Shepard.

Merriam-Webster's elementary dictionary. (2000). Springfield, MA: Merriam-Webster.

Moss, L. (1995). *Zin! Zin! Zin! A violin.* New York: Simon & Schuster.

Pallotta, J. (1988). *The flower alphabet book.* Watertown, MA: Charlesbridge.

Platt, R. (1999). *Castle diary: The journal of Tobias Burgess, page.* Cambridge, MA: Candlewick Press.

Rotner, S. (1996). *Action alphabet.* New York: Atheneum.

Terban, M. (1983). *In a pickle and other funny idioms.* New York: Clarion Books.

Terban, M. (1989). *Superdupers! Really funny real words.* New York: Clarion.

Terban, M. (1990). *Punching the clock: Funny action idioms.* New York: Clarion Books.

Terban, M. (1991). *Hey, hay! A wagonful of funny homonym riddles.* New York: Clarion.

Terban, M. (1996). *Scholastic dictionary of idioms, phrases, sayings, and expressions.* New York: Scholastic.

Van Allsburg, C. (1981). *Jumanji.* Boston: Houghton Mifflin.

Van Allsburg, C. (1991). *The wretched stone.* Boston: Houghton Mifflin.

Wittels, H., & Greisman, J. (2001). *A first thesaurus.* Racine, WI: Golden Books.

Wood, A. (1982). *Quick as a cricket.* London: Child's Play.

6 Personal Writing

PATTERNS OF PRACTICE

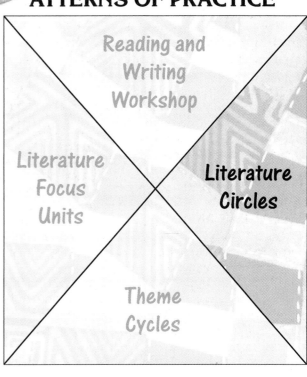

Reading and Writing Workshop

Literature Focus Units

Literature Circles

Theme Cycles

Ms. Meinke teaches seventh-grade language arts, and her students often participate in literature circles. One group of six students is reading *The Great Gilly Hopkins* (Paterson, 1978), the story of Gilly, an angry, mistrustful, disrespectful foster child who eventually finds love and acceptance. To begin their 3-week period of literature circles, the students sign up to read one of the six books that Ms. Meinke has introduced. The students divide into groups. Each group selects a group leader and sets its schedule for reading and discussing the book. Students also construct reading logs by stapling paper into booklets and adding construction paper covers.

Ms. Meinke meets with *The Great Gilly Hopkins* group to talk about the book. She explains that the story is about a girl named Gilly Hopkins who is a foster child. They talk about foster care and how children become foster children. Several children mention that they know someone who is a foster child. She also passes out a list of topics for reading log entries, and students place

the sheet in their reading logs. A copy of the topics sheet is shown on page 242.

Ms. Meinke varies the types of entries that she asks students to write in reading logs. She does this for two reasons. First of all, she believes that each chapter is different and that the content of the chapter should determine the type of activity. Also, she has found that students tire of writing straight reading logs because of their repetitiveness and predictability.

The students read in class and at home, and every 2 days, they meet to discuss their read-

> ### Should teachers provide topics for reading log entries?
>
> Sometimes teachers invite students to choose their own topics for reading log entries, and sometimes they provide the topics for students. There are benefits to each approach. When students choose their own topics, they assume more responsibility, make many connections, and probe the ideas that interest them, but when teachers provide the topics, students are often prompted to explore ideas that they might otherwise miss. As you read this vignette, think about why Ms. Meinke provides questions to direct her students' thinking about the chapter they've read and what they write in reading log entries.

ing. Often Ms. Meinke sits in on at least part of their discussions. During the discussions, students ask questions and clarify misunderstandings, share their favorite excerpts, and make predictions about what will happen next. Sometimes, too, they share their reading log entries or talk about how they will write their entries.

Timothy wrote this simulated-journal entry after reading chapter 2:

Dear Diary,

I can't live here, it's a dump. I have to live with Miss Trotter and that colored (or black) man Mr. Randolph. I will have to get out of this dump and fast. Today was the first day Mr. Randolph came and I can't escort him every day to dinner. I don't belong here, even Mrs. Nevin's house was better than here.

I cannot believe Miss Ellis took me to this awful place. I got to find a way to call Courtney Hopkins. She'll take me outta this place. Everyone's trying to be nice to me but I'll show them who's the boss, and I bet there is something wrong with W. E.

Reading Log Assignments for The Great Gilly Hopkins

Chapter 1 "Welcome to Thompson Park"
What is a foster child? How do foster children feel and behave? Why?

Chapter 2 "The Man Who Comes to Supper"
Write a diary entry from Gilly's viewpoint.

Chapter 3 "More Unpleasant Surprises"
Write a double entry with a quote from the chapter and your response.

Chapter 4 "Sarsaparilla to Sorcery"
Write a diary entry from Gilly's viewpoint.

Chapter 5 "William Ernest and Other Mean Flowers"
Do a character study on Maime Trotter. Identify and list three characteristics. Then locate and copy two quotes as evidence for each characteristic.

Chapter 6 "Harassing Miss Harris"
Write a letter to Gilly telling her what you think of what she did to Miss Harris.

Chapter 7 "Dust and Desperation"
Gilly does two things that are considered immoral: she lies and she steals. She has had a rough life, so maybe doing these things is excusable. Perhaps, however, lying and stealing are wrong under any circumstances. Take a position and support it with evidence from the book.

Chapter 8 "The One Way Ticket"
Draw a scene from the chapter and write a brief description of the scene.

Chapter 9 "Pow"
There is a definite change in Gilly's behavior and feelings in this chapter. Describe how she changes and then describe the causes of these changes using examples from the book.

Chapter 10 "The Visitor"
Draw a picture of Gilly and her family at Thanksgiving dinner. Then, in a paragraph, describe Gilly's foster family and how they make each other feel needed. Or, draw Nonnie, Gilly's grandmother. Then, in a paragraph, tell what she looks like, what kind of person she seems to be, how she behaves, and how she gets along with her daughter, Courtney.

Chapter 11 "Never and Other Canceled Promises"
So where should Gilly go? List three reasons why she should stay with Trotter and list three reasons why she should go with her grandmother Nonnie. Then write a short paragraph telling where you would like her to go and why.

Chapters 12 and 13 "The Going" and "Jackson, Virginia"
Select eight to ten images, details, interesting phrases, or parts of sentences from the book and arrange the "found" parts into a poem.

Chapters 14 and 15 "She'll Be Riding Six White Horses" and "Homecoming"
In this final response, write about your feelings. What did you like? dislike? Why?

After reading chapter 6, about how mean Gilly is to her teacher, Miss Harris, Steven wrote this simulated letter to Gilly:

Hey Gilly,

That was the best note you have ever written. That was cool because you actually made Miss Harris curse. I bet you none of the kids at this school could ever make a teacher do that. I wish I could write cards like that and make teachers curse. You are also very brave because you wrote that to a teacher. No kid is crazy enough to do something like that. That is how crazy I think you are.

Your classmate,

Steven

Johanna wrote this response about whether it is ever right to lie and steal after reading chapter 7:

I think she shouldn't be forgiven. I know she has had a horrible life, but it's never right. It is one thing to steal and it's another to steal from a blind man. That is just mean. I kind of feel bad for her because of everything she's been through. She lies, cheats, and steals. I am not sure which side to take because in one way she should be forgiven but on another side she shouldn't be because she's done too many bad things. Especially stealing from Mr. Randolph.

Sarah wrote about how Gilly has changed after reading chapter 9:

Gilly changes because she sees that Trotter really cares for her. Trotter got in an argument about what Gilly did. Miss Ellis wanted to take Gilly back but Trotter wouldn't let her. Gilly becomes more liking toward Trotter. Gilly even starts liking W. E. Gilly doesn't think he is dumb any more. Another example is "Look, W. E.," she bent over close to his ear and whispered hoarsely into it, "I'm going to teach you how to fight. No charge or anything. Then when some big punk comes up to you and tries to start something, you can just let them have it," said Gilly.

After reading chapters 12 and 13, Timothy wrote this found poem:

He tore a piece of him and gave it to you.

Don't make it harder for us, baby.

This was supposed to be a party, not a funeral.

Sometimes it's best not to go visiting.

You make me proud.

Why would anybody leave peace for war?

Stop hovering over me.

Inside her head, she was screaming.

Steven reflects on the book in his last entry:

I thought that at the end Gilly was going to go with her mom. I also thought Gilly's mom was going to be nice and sweet. I thought this was very good because it had an unexpected ending. I didn't think that Gilly's mom would be so rude and mean. Now I wish that Gilly would go back with Trotter because Courtney is mean. Those are my reasons why she should be with Trotter.

Ms. Meinke is especially interested in the students' responses in this last entry. She finds that many students, like Steven, want Gilly to stay with Trotter, but she is pleased when they realize that Nonnie, who never even knew of Gilly's existence, is family and is delighted to provide a home for her only granddaughter.

Ms. Meinke collects the students' reading logs twice—once halfway through the literature circle and again at the end—to grade them. She has found that students appreciate the opportunity to pace themselves as they read and write the entries. She awards points for each journal entry, and these points are part of students' grades for the literature circle.

As you begin reading this chapter, you may want to read the "Dear Reader" letter in Chapter 6 on the Companion Website at www.prenhall.com/tompkins

All kinds of people—artists, scientists, dancers, politicians, writers, assassins, and children—do personal writing (Mallon, 1984). They write letters and keep journals or diaries. People usually record the everyday events of their lives and the issues that concern them in both journals and letters. The difference between the two is that people usually don't expect anyone else to read their journals, and they do expect people to read their letters when they correspond with family members and friends in personal letters.

The journals and letters of some public figures have survived for hundreds of years and provide a fascinating glimpse of their authors and the times in which they lived. For example, the Renaissance genius Leonardo da Vinci recorded his daily activities, dreams, and plans for his painting and engineering projects in more than 40 notebooks. American explorers Meriwether Lewis and George Rogers Clark kept a journal of their travels across the North American continent, more for geographical than personal use. Dutch artist Vincent Van Gogh wrote more than 1,000 letters during his lifetime, many to his brother Theo; these letters, which often contained striking drawings, document the artist's tragic life. Anne Frank, who wrote while in hiding from the Nazis during World War II, is probably the best-known child diarist.

Elementary students write journals and letters, too. They write for many of the same reasons that public figures write—to record events in their lives and to share information with others. And, there are other reasons for using personal writing in elementary classrooms. Young children use personal writing to develop writing fluency. As they write in journals and write letters to the teacher and classmates, they practice writing conventions, handwriting skills, and spelling high-frequency words. Students use personal writing as a tool to enhance their learning in language arts and across the curriculum. Students write in learning logs, for instance, as part of theme cycles, and as they write, they learn to take notes, summarize, and reflect on learning.

As you continue reading about journals and letters and how to incorporate personal writing in your language arts program, think about these questions:

◆ What types of journals do elementary students use?

◆ How do students use journals as tools for learning in language arts and across the curriculum?

◆ What types of letters do elementary students write?

◆ How do teachers incorporate letter writing in their instructional programs?

WRITING IN JOURNALS

Elementary students use journals for a variety of purposes, just as adults do. Seven types of journals are described in the LA Essentials box on page 246. In each type of journal, the focus is on the writer; the writing is personal and private. Students' writing is spontaneous and loosely organized, and it often contains mechanical errors because students are focusing on thinking, not on spelling, capitalization, and punctuation. James Britton and his colleagues (1975) compare this type of writing to a written conversation, which may be with oneself or with trusted readers who are interested in the writer. Some of the purposes for journal writing are to:

- Record experiences
- Stimulate interest in a topic
- Explore thinking
- Personalize learning
- Develop interpretations
- Wonder, predict, and hypothesize
- Engage the imagination
- Ask questions
- Activate prior knowledge
- Assume the role of another person
- Share experiences with trusted readers

Toby Fulwiler (1985) shared excerpts from his daughter Megan's third-grade journal in language arts, demonstrating how she used writing for many of these functions. Later, when she was a teenager, Megan Fulwiler (1986) reflected on her journal-writing experiences and her reasons for writing. Most important, Megan described her journal as an extension of her mind that she used to work out her feelings, ask questions and find answers, and write down and organize her thoughts. She noted that as time passed, her entries grew more personal and became a record of her growing up.

As with Megan, journal writing gives students valuable writing practice. They gain fluency and confidence that they can write. They can also experiment with writing conventions that must be considered in more public writing. If they decide to make an entry "public," students can later revise and edit their writing.

Personal Journals

Students often keep personal journals in which they recount events in their lives and write about topics of their choosing. Students choose to write about a variety of topics and explore their feelings in these entries. It is normal for students to misspell a few words in their entries; when students write in personal journals, the emphasis is on what they say, not how correctly they write.

 **Essentials**

Types of Journals

Students learn to use these seven types of journals during the elementary grades.

Personal Journals

Students write about events in their own lives and about other topics of special interest in personal journals. These journals are the most private type. Teachers respond as interested readers, often asking questions and offering comments about their own lives.

Dialogue Journals

Dialogue journals are similar to personal journals except they are written to be shared with the teacher or a classmate. Whoever receives the journal reads the entry and responds to it. These journals are like a written conversation.

Reading Logs

Students respond to stories, poems, and informational books they are reading in reading logs. They write and draw entries after reading, record key vocabulary words, make charts and other diagrams, and write memorable quotes.

Double-Entry Journals

Students divide each page of their journals into two columns and write different types of information in each column. Sometimes they write quotes from a story in one column and add reactions to the quotes in the other, or they write predictions in one column and what actually happened in the story in the other.

Language Arts Notebooks

Students take notes, write rules and examples, draw diagrams, and write lists of other useful information about language arts in these notebooks. Students use these notebooks during minilessons and refer to the information during literature focus units and reading and writing workshop.

Learning Logs

Students write in learning logs as part of social studies and science theme cycles and math units. They write quickwrites, draw diagrams, take notes, and write vocabulary words.

Simulated Journals

Students assume the role of a book character or a historical personality and write journal entries from that person's viewpoint. Students include details from the story or historical period in their entries.

FIGURE 6-1 *Fourth and Fifth Graders' List of Writing Topics*

Things to Write About in Personal Journals

my favorite place in town	if I had three wishes
boyfriends/girlfriends	my teacher
things that make me happy or sad	TV shows I watch
music	my favorite holiday
an imaginary planet	if I were stranded on an island
cars	what I want to be when I grow up
magazines I like to read	private thoughts
what if snow were hot	how to be a superhero
dreams I have	dinosaurs
cartoons	my mom/my dad
places I've been	my friends
favorite movies	my next vacation
rock stars	love
if I were a movie/rock star	if I were an animal or something else
poems	books I've read
pets	favorite things to do
football	my hobbies
astronauts	if I were a skydiver
the president	when I get a car
jokes	if I had a lot of money
motorcycles	dolls
things that happen in my school	if I were rich
current events	wrestling and other sports
things I do on weekends	favorite colors
a soap opera with daily episodes	questions answered with "never"

or ANYTHING else I want to write about

It is often helpful to develop a list of possible journal-writing topics on a chart in the classroom or on sheets of paper for students to clip inside their journal notebooks. Students choose their own topics for personal journals. Although they can write about almost anything, some students will complain that they don't know what to write about, so a list of topics gives them a crutch. Figure 6–1 shows a list of possible journal-writing topics developed by a class of fourth and fifth graders. Students can add topics to their lists throughout the year, which may include more than 100 topics by the end of the school year. Referring students to the list or asking them to brainstorm a list of topics encourages them to become more independent writers and discourages them from relying too heavily on teachers for writing topics.

Privacy becomes an important issue as students grow older. Most young children are willing to share what they have written, but by third or fourth grade, students grow less willing to read their journal entries aloud to the class, although they are usually willing to share the entries with a trusted teacher. Teachers must be scrupulous about respecting students' privacy and not insist that they share their writing when they are unwilling to do so. It is also important to talk with students about respecting each other's privacy and not reading each other's journals. To protect students' privacy, many teachers keep personal journals on an out-of-the-way shelf when they are not in use.

When students share personal information with teachers through their journals, a second issue arises: Sometimes teachers learn details about students' problems and family life that they do not know how to deal with. Entries about child abuse, suicide, or drug use may be the child's way of asking for help. Although teachers are not counselors, they do have a legal obligation to protect their students and to report possible problems to appropriate school personnel. Occasionally a student invents a personal problem in a journal entry as an attention-getting tactic; however, asking the student about the entry or having a school counselor do so will help to ensure that the student's safety is fully considered.

Dialogue Journals

Students converse in writing with the teacher or with a classmate through dialogue journals (Bode, 1989; Gambrell, 1985; Staton, 1980, 1987). These journals are interactive and conversational in tone. Most important, dialogue journals are an authentic writing activity and provide the opportunity for real communication between students or between a student and the teacher. Students write informally about something of interest, a concern, a book they are reading, or what they are learning in a theme cycle. Students choose their own topics and usually control the direction the writing takes.

When teachers or classmates respond to students' entries, they answer as they would in an oral conversation. They react to students' comments, ask questions, and offer suggestions. Staton (1987) offers these suggestions for teachers who are responding to students' writing and continuing the dialogue:

1. Acknowledge students' ideas and encourage them to continue to write about their interests.
2. Support students by complimenting them about behavior and schoolwork.
3. Provide new information about topics, so that students will want to read your responses.
4. Write less than the students do.
5. Avoid unspecific comments such as "good idea" or "very interesting."
6. Ask few questions; instead, encourage students to ask you questions.

Teachers' responses do not need to be lengthy; a sentence or two is often enough. Even so, it is time-consuming to respond to 25, 30, or more journal entries every day. As an alternative, many teachers read and respond to students' journal entries on a rotating basis; they might respond to one group of students one week and another group the next week.

In this fifth grader's dialogue journal, Daniel shares the events and problems in his life with his teacher, and she responds sympathetically. Daniel writes:

Over spring break I went down to my grandma's house and played basketball in their backyard and while we were there we went to see some of my uncles who are all Indians. Out of my whole family down there they are all Indians except Grandpa Russell.

And Daniel's teacher responds:

What a fun spring break! That is so interesting to have Indians in your family. I think I might have some Indian ancestors too. Do you still plan to go to Padre Island for the summer?

The next day Daniel writes:

My family and I plan to go to Padre Island in June and I imagine we will stay there for quite a while. I think the funnest part will probably be swimming or camping or something like that. When we get there my mom says we will probably stay in a nice motel.

Daniel's teacher responds:

That really sounds like a fun vacation. I think swimming is the most fun, too. Who will go with you?

Daniel continues to talk about his family, now focusing on the problems he and his family are facing:

Well, my mom and dad are divorced so that is why I am going to court to testify on Tuesday but my mom, me, and my sister and brother are all going and that kind of makes me sad because a couple of years ago when my mom and dad were together we used to go a lot of places like camping and hiking but now after what happened we hardly go anywhere.

His teacher responds:

I am so sorry your family is having problems. It sounds as if your mom and dad are having problems with each other, but they both love you and want to be with you. Be sure to keep talking to them about how you feel.

Daniel replies:

I wish my mom and dad did not have problems because I would have a lot more fun and get to go and do a lot more things together, but since my mom and dad are divorced I have to take turns spending time with both of them.

This journal is not a series of teacher questions and student answers; instead, the student and teacher are having a dialogue, or conversation, and the interchange is built on mutual trust and respect.

Dialogue journals can be effective in dealing with students who have behavior problems or other types of difficulties in school (Staton, 1980). The teacher and student write back and forth about the problem and identify ways to solve it. In later entries, the student reflects on his or her progress toward solving the problem. The teacher responds to the student's message, asks clarifying questions, or offers sympathy and praise.

Kreeft (1984) believes that the greatest value of dialogue journals is that they bridge the gap between talking and writing; they are written conversations. As the journal excerpts between Daniel and his teacher show, a second value is the strong bond that develops between student and teacher through their writing back and forth.

Dialogue journals are especially effective in promoting the writing development of children who are learning English as a second language. Researchers have found that these students are more successful writers when they choose their own topics for writing and when their teachers contribute to the dialogue with requests for a reply, statements, and other comments (Peyton & Seyoum, 1989; Reyes, 1991). Not surprisingly, researchers found that students wrote more when teachers requested a reply than when teachers made comments that did not require a response. Also, when a student was particularly interested in a topic, it was less important what the teacher did, and when the teacher and the student were both interested in a topic, the topic seemed to take over as they shared and built on each other's writing. Reyes also found that bilingual students were much more successful in writing dialogue journal entries than in writing in response to books they had read.

Students use dialogue journals to write to classmates or the teacher about books they are reading (Barone, 1990; Dekker, 1991; Nash, 1995). In these journal entries, students write about the books they are reading, compare the books to others by the same author or books by other authors they have read, and offer opinions about the book and whether a classmate or the teacher might enjoy reading it. They also write about their book-selection strategies and their reading behavior.

This approach is especially effective in reading workshop classrooms when students are reading different books. Students are often paired and write back and forth to their reading buddies. This activity provides the socialization that independent reading does not. Depending on whether students are reading relatively short picture books or longer chapter books, they can write dialogue journal entries every other day or once a week, and then classmates write back.

Fourth graders wrote these entries to classmates and their teacher about informational books they were reading during reading workshop:

Dear Adam,

I'm reading the coolest book. It's about snakes and it's called *A Snake's Body* [Cole, 1981]. Look at the pictures on pages 34, 35, 36, 37, 38, 39, 40, 41, and 42 to see how a python strangles and eats a chick. It's awesome.

Your Friend, Todd

Dear Mrs. Parker,

I just finished reading *The Magic School Bus Inside the Human Body* [Cole, 1989]. I think you would like it, too, because it's about a teacher named Ms. Frizzle and she's sort of magic. She takes her kids on a field trip and Ms. Frizzle drives the school bus inside a human body. The book takes a long time to read because it has lots of cartoons and extra things to read and look at. I'd say it was one of the best books I've ever read. I think everyone in our class should read it. What do you think?

Love, Ali

Trevor,

The book I'm reading is *A Wall of Names* [Donnelly, 1991]. It's ok, if you want to know about the Vietnam wall memorial. I picked this book because my Gramps was in that war and last summer we went to Washington, D.C. on vacation and I got to see the wall. It's shiny and black and all the names of the soldiers that died fighting in it are written on the wall. Have you ever heard of it?

From your friend, David

Before the students began writing dialogue journal entries, the teacher taught a minilesson about how to format their entries, about how to capitalize and underline book titles, and about the importance of asking questions in their

To learn more about reading workshop, see Chapter 2, "Teaching and Assessing Language Arts."

entries so that respondents could answer them in their replies. In their entries, most students incorporated what they had learned in the minilesson.

Reading Logs

Students write in reading logs about the stories and other books they are reading or listening to the teacher read aloud during literature focus units, literature circles, and reading workshop. Rather than simply summarize their reading, students relate their reading to their own lives or to other literature they have read. Students may also list interesting or unfamiliar words, jot down memorable quotes, and take notes about characters, plot, or other story elements; but the primary purpose of these journals is for students to think about the book, connect literature to their lives, and develop their own interpretations, as Ms. Meinke's students did in the vignette at the beginning of the chapter. These journals go by a variety of names, including literature response journals (Hancock, 1992), literature journals (Five, 1986), and reading journals (Wollman-Bonilla, 1989); but no matter what they are called, their purpose remains the same.

Teachers and researchers (Barone, 1990; Dekker, 1991; Hancock, 1992) have examined students' reading log entries and have identified these categories of responses:

- Questions related to understanding the text
- Interaction with characters
- Empathy with characters
- Prediction and validation
- Personal experiences
- Personal feelings and opinions
- Simple and elaborate evaluations
- Philosophical reflections
- Retellings and summaries

When students begin writing entries in reading logs, their first entries are often retellings and plot summaries, but as students gain experience reading and responding to literature, their entries become more interpretive and personal. Teachers can model writing "I think" reactions, share student entries that are interpretive, and respond to students' entries by asking questions.

Teachers and researchers have examined students' responses and noticed patterns in their reading log entries. Hancock (1992, 1993) identified eight categories that are listed in the LA Essentials box on page 252. The first four categories are personal meaning-making options in which students make inferences about characters, offer predictions, ask questions, or discuss confusions. The next three categories focus on character and plot development. Students are more involved with the story, and they offer reactions to the characters and events of the story. The last category is literary evaluation, in which students evaluate books and reflect on their own literary tastes.

These categories can extend the possibilities of response by introducing teachers and students to a wide variety of response options. Hancock (1992, 1993) recommends that teachers begin by assessing the kinds of responses students are currently making. They can read students' reading logs, categorize the entries, tally the categories, and make an assessment. Often students use only a few types of responses, not the wide range that is available. Teachers can

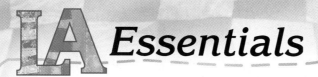

Essentials

Response Patterns in Students' Reading Log Entries

Personal Meaning-Making

Monitoring Understanding	Students get to know the characters and explain how the story is making sense to them. These responses usually occur at the beginning of a book.
Making Inferences	Students share their insights into the feelings and motives of a character. They often begin their comments with "I think."
Making, Validating, or Invalidating Predictions	Students speculate about what will happen later in the story and also confirm or deny predictions they made previously.
Expressing Wonder or Confusion	Students reflect on the way the story is developing. They ask "I wonder why" questions and write about confusions.

Character and Plot Development

Character Interaction	Students show that they are personally involved with a character, sometimes writing "If I were _____, I would . . . " They express empathy and share related experiences from their own lives. Also, they may give advice to the character.
Character Assessment	Students judge a character's actions and often use evaluative terms such as *nice* or *dumb.*
Story Involvement	Students reveal their involvement in the story as they express satisfaction with how the story is developing. They may comment on their desire to continue reading or use terms such as *disgusting, weird,* or *awesome* to react to sensory aspects of the story.

Literary Evaluation

Literary Criticism	Students offer "I liked/I didn't like" opinions and praise or condemn an author's style. Sometimes students compare the book with others they have read or compare the author with other authors with whom they are familiar.

Adapted from Hancock, 1992, 1993.

teach minilessons and model types of responses that students aren't using, and they can ask questions when they read journals to prompt students to think in new ways about the story they are reading.

Seventh graders' reading log entries about *The Giver* (Lowry, 1993) are shown in Figure 6–2. In these entries, students react to the book, make predictions, deepen their understanding of the story, ask questions, assume the role of the main character, and value the story. Each entry is categorized according to Hancock's patterns of response. As you read the students' excerpts, you might notice other patterns, too.

Double-Entry Journals

Students divide each entry into two parts when they write double-entry journals (Barone, 1990; Berthoff, 1981). Usually students divide their journal pages into two columns; in the left column, they write quotes from the story or other book they are reading, and in the right column, they relate each quote to their own life and to literature they have read. Through this type of journal, students become more engaged in what they are reading, note sentences that have personal connections, and become more sensitive to the author's language.

Students in a fifth-grade class wrote double-entry journals as they read C. S. Lewis's classic *The Lion, the Witch and the Wardrobe* (1950). After they read each chapter, students reviewed the chapter and selected one or two brief quotes. They wrote these excerpts in the left column of their journals, and they wrote reactions beside each quote in the right column. Excerpts from a fifth grader's journal are presented in Figure 6–3. This student's responses indicate that she is engaged in the story and is connecting the story to her own life.

Double-entry journals can be used in several other ways. Instead of recording quotes from the book, students can write "Reading Notes" in the left column and then add "Reactions" in the right column. In the left column, students write about the events they read about in the chapter. Then in the right column, they make personal connections to the events.

As an alternative, students can use the heading "Reading Notes" for one column and "Discussion Notes" for the other column. Students write reading notes as they read or immediately after reading. Later, after discussing the story, or chapter of a longer book, students add discussion notes. As with other types of double-entry journals, it is in the second column that students make more interpretive comments.

Younger students can use the double-entry format for a prediction journal (Macon, Bewell, & Vogt, 1991). They label the left column "Predictions" and the right column "What Happened." In the left column, they write or draw a picture of what they predict will happen in the story or chapter before reading it. Then, after reading, they draw or write what actually happened in the right column.

Language Arts Notebooks

Language arts notebooks are a specialized type of journal in which students record a variety of information about language arts. Often students use these notebooks to take notes about procedures, concepts, strategies, and skills during minilessons. Procedure entries include the steps in giving a book talk, participating in a grand conversation, and proofreading a paper. Concept entries include

FIGURE 6-2 Entries From Seventh Graders' Reading Logs About *The Giver*

Student	Excerpt	Response Pattern
Tiffany	I think the book The Giver is very scary because when you do something wrong you get released from the community. I think it would be terrible to be pushed out of your community and leave your family. Your family would be ashamed and embarrassed. It is like you are dead.	Story involvement
Scott	I don't think I could handle being a friend of Jonas's. In other words NO I would not like to be a friend of his. There would be too much pain involved and most of the time I wouldn't see Jonas.	Character interaction
Rob	The part that hooked me was when the book said Jonas took his pills and did not have feelings about Fiona.	Monitoring understanding
Jared	As I'm reading I'm wondering if they get married at twelve because they get jobs at twelve.	Expressing wonder or confusion
Elizabeth	Something that surprised me so far in the story was when Lily said she wanted to be a birthmother. Lily's mom became mad and said three years, three births, and then you're a laborer. Being a birthmother is not a good job at least after the three years. I hope that doesn't happen to Lily but I don't know what other job she should have.	Character assessment
Graciela	So far I think that the story is really sad. The story is sad because everyone has sameness except Jonas and the Giver. Jonas and the Giver are the only ones who can see color because of the memories. The story is also sad because no one has feelings.	Story involvement
Rob	Why didn't Jonas use the fire in his favorite memory to stay warmer on his long journey through the rain and snow, and the terrible coldness? Also, why didn't the author explain more about the things that are between the lines so the reader could really grasp them?	Literary criticism
Marcos	Well, I can't really make a prediction of what is going to happen because I already read the book. If I hadn't read ahead my prediction would be that Jonas would get drowned in the river because he couldn't handle the pain.	Monitoring understanding
Rob	I think Jonas will confront his father. He won't ever forget what he saw his father do and it is wrong. Just wrong, wrong, wrong. If my father ever did that to an innocent little baby I would never forgive him. It's like abortion. I would confront him and tell him that I know. I will always know and so will God.	Making, validating, or invalidating predictions
Elizabeth	I don't exactly understand what happens at the end. It sounds like they froze to death. I think they died but I wish they found freedom and happiness. It is very sad.	Expressing wonder or confusion
Mark	The ending is cool. Jonas and Gabe come back to the community but now it is changed. There are colors and the people have feelings. They believe in God and it is Christmas.	Story involvement
Graciela	At first I thought it would be good to have a perfect community. There would be no gangs and no crime and no sickness. But there is a lesson in this story. Now I think you can't have a perfect community. Even though we have bad things in our community we have love and other emotions and we can make choices.	Making inferences

FIGURE 6-3 *Excerpts From a Fifth Grader's Double-Entry Journal About The Lion, the Witch and the Wardrobe*

In the Text	My Response
Chapter 1	
I tell you this is the sort of house where no one is going to mind what we do.	I remember the time that I went to Beaumont, Texas to stay with my aunt. My aunt's house was very large. She had a piano and she let us play it. She told us that we could do whatever we wanted to.
Chapter 5	
"How do you know?" he asked, "that your sister's story is not true?"	It reminds me of when I was little and I had an imaginary place. I would go there in my mind. I made up all kinds of make-believe stories about myself in this imaginary place. One time I told my big brother about my imaginary place. He laughed at me and told me I was silly. But it didn't bother me because nobody can stop me from thinking what I want.
Chapter 15	
Still they could see the shape of the great lion lying dead in his bonds.	When Aslan died I thought about when my Uncle Carl died.
They're nibbling at the cords.	This reminds me of the story where the lion lets the mouse go and the mouse helps the lion.

information on authors and genres, contractions, homophones, parts of speech, plot diagrams, affixes, poetic formulas, and types of sentences. Strategy entries include explanations of visualization or connecting to personal experience, and student reflections about how they use the strategy during language arts activities. Skill entries include charts about forming plurals, using quotations in writing dialogue, alphabetizing a list of words, and skimming a content-area textbook.

By recording this information in a notebook, students create a permanent reference book to use during language arts activities. Teachers of upper-grade students often have students divide their language arts notebooks into several sections, and students add information to sections on authors, words, spelling, parts of speech, sentences, strategies, poetry, stories, and study skills.

Four entries from sixth graders' language arts notebooks are shown in Figure 6–4. The first page lists the steps in writing a summary; the second page lists the two parts of a sentence, with sample sentences from Naylor's award-winning *Shiloh* (1991); the third page compares *dessert* and *desert,* two easily confused spellings; and the fourth page lists prepositions that describe locations.

Learning Logs

Students write entries in learning logs to record or react to what they are learning in math, science, social studies, or other content areas. Fulwiler explains: "When people write about something they learn it better" (1987, p. 9). As students write in these journals, they reflect on their learning, discover gaps

FIGURE 6-4 *Four Excerpts From Sixth Graders' Language Arts Notebooks*

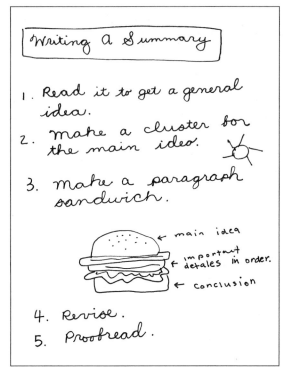

Writing a Summary

1. Read it to get a general idea.
2. make a cluster for the main idea.
3. make a paragraph sandwich.

← main idea
← important detales in order.
← conclusion

4. Revise.
5. Proofread.

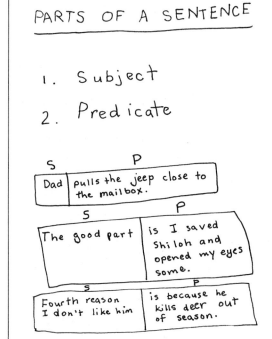

PARTS OF A SENTENCE

1. Subject
2. Predicate

S	P
Dad	pulls the jeep close to the mailbox.

S	P
The good part	is I saved Shiloh and opened my eyes some.

S	P
Fourth reason I don't like him	is because he kills deer out of season.

1 S OR **2 SS** ?

de[ss]ert

de[s]ert

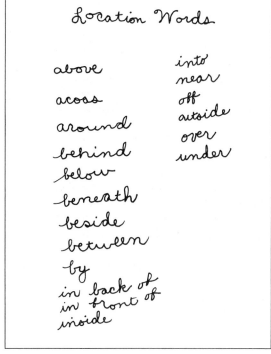

Location Words

above
acoss
around
behind
below
beneath
beside
between
by
in back of
in front of
inside

into
near
off
outside
over
under

FIGURE 6–5   *A Sixth Grader's Math Learning Log Entry*

Changing to Improper Fractions

To Change a mixed number such as $5\frac{2}{3}$, you must must multiply the denominator, which is the bottom number, times the whole number which is 5. So now we have : 3×5=15, Next you add the numerator to the problem like this! 15+2=17. Put the same denominator, the bottom number, and it should look like this! $\frac{17}{3}$. To check your answer, find out how many times 3, the bottom number, goes into the top number, 17. It goes in 5 times. There are two left over, so the answer is $5\frac{2}{3}$. It is correct.

6 Steps!

1. $5\frac{2}{3}$
2. 3×5=15
3. 15+2=17
4. $\frac{17}{3}$
5. $3\overline{)17}\,^{5}\,^{2} = 5\frac{2}{3}$
6. $5\frac{2}{3}$ – correct

in their knowledge, and explore relationships between what they are learning and their past experiences. Students use learning logs to write about what they are learning in math (Salem, 1982). They record explanations and examples of concepts presented in class and react to the mathematical concepts they are learning and any problems they may be having. Figure 6–5 presents an entry from a sixth grader's learning log in which she describes how to change improper fractions. Notice that after she describes the steps in sequence, she includes a review of the six steps. In addition, some upper-grade teachers allow students the last five minutes of math class to summarize the day's lesson and react to it in their learning logs (Schubert, 1987). Through these activities, students practice taking notes, writing descriptions and directions, and using other writing skills. They also learn how to reflect on and evaluate their own learning (Stanford, 1988).

FIGURE 6-6 *Two Entries From a Second Grader's Science Log on Caterpillars*

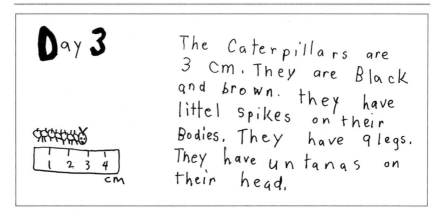

Day 3

The Caterpillars are 3 cm. They are Black and brown. they have littel spikes on their Bodies. They have 9 legs. They have untanas on their head.

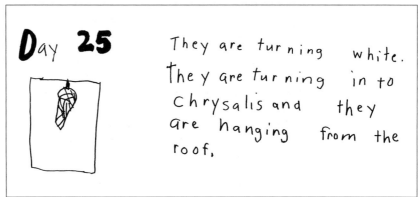

Day 25

They are turning white. They are turning into Chrysalis and they are hanging from the roof.

Science-related learning logs can take several different forms. One type is an observation log in which students make daily entries to track the growth of plants or animals. For instance, a second-grade class observed caterpillars as they changed from caterpillars to chrysalides to butterflies over a period of 4 to 6 weeks. Students each kept a log with daily entries, in which they were to describe the changes they observed using words describing shape, color, size, and other properties. Two pages from a second grader's log documenting the caterpillars' growth and change are presented in Figure 6–6. A second type of science-related learning log is one in which students make entries during a theme cycle. Students may take notes during presentations by the teacher or after reading, after viewing films, or at the end of each class period. Sometimes students make entries in list form, sometimes in clusters, charts, or maps, and at other times in paragraphs.

Students often keep learning logs as part of theme cycles in social studies. In their logs, students write in response to stories and informational books, note interesting words related to the theme, create time lines, and draw diagrams, charts, and maps. For example, as part of a theme cycle on the Civil War for eighth graders, students might include the following in their learning logs:

- Write about the causes of the war and other topics related to the war
- List words related to the theme
- Chart the major battles in the war
- Make a Venn diagram to compare the Northern and Southern viewpoints
- Draw a time line showing events related to the war
- Show the battle location on a map of the United States
- Write notes after viewing several films about the Civil War era
- Write favorite quotes from Lincoln's "Gettysburg Address"
- Write responses to chapter books such as *Charley Skedaddle* (Beatty, 1987), *Brady* (Fritz, 1987), or *Across Five Aprils* (Hunt, 1987) that are set during the Civil War

Through these learning log activities, students explore concepts they are learning and record information they want to remember about the Civil War.

Simulated Journals

Some children's books, such as *Catherine, Called Birdy* (Cushman, 1994) and *Stranded at Plimoth Plantation, 1626* (Bowen, 1994), are written as journals; the authors assumed the role of a character and wrote from the character's point of view. These books can be called simulated journals. They are rich with historical details and feature examples of both words and phrasing of the period. At the end of these books, authors often include information about how they researched the period and explanations about the liberties they took with the character, setting, or events that are recorded. Scholastic Books recently began publishing a series of historical journals appropriate for fourth- through eighth-grade students. The books include *A Journey to the New World: The Diary of Remember Patience Whipple* (Lasky, 1996), *The Journal of William Thomas Emerson: A Revolutionary War Patriot* (Denenberg, 1998), *A Picture of Freedom: The Diary of Clotee, a Slave Girl* (McKissack, 1997), and *The Journal of Ben Uchida: Citizen 13559, Mirror Lake Internment Camp* (Denenberg, 1999). Each book provides a glimpse into American history from a young girl's or a young boy's perspective and is handsomely bound to look like an old journal. The paper is heavy and rough cut around the edges, and a ribbon page marker is bound into the book.

Elementary students, too, can write simulated journals. They can assume the role of another person and write from that person's viewpoint. They can assume the role of a historical figure when they read biographies or as part of social studies theme cycles (Tompkins, 1995). As they read stories, students can assume the role of a character in the story. In this way, students gain insight into other people's lives and into historical events. A look at a series of diary entries written by a fifth grader who has assumed the role of Betsy Ross shows how she carefully chose the dates for each entry and wove in factual information:

May 15, 1773

Dear Diary,

This morning at 5:00 I had to wake up my husband John to get up for work but he wouldn't wake up. I immediately called the doc. He came over as fast as he could. He asked me to leave the room so I did. An hour later he came out and told me he had passed away. I am so sad. I don't know what to do.

June 16, 1776

Dear Diary,

Today General Washington visited me about making a flag. I was so surprised. Me making a flag! I have made flags for the navy, but this is too much. But I said yes. He showed me a pattern of the flag he wanted. He also wanted six-pointed stars but I talked him into having five-pointed stars.

July 8, 1776

Dear Diary,

Today in front of Carpenter Hall the Declaration of Independence was read by Tom Jefferson. Well, I will tell you the whole story. I heard some yelling and shouting about liberty and everyone was gathering around Carpenter Hall. So I went to my next door neighbors to ask what was happening but Mistress Peters didn't know either so we both went down to Carpenter Hall. We saw firecrackers and heard a bell and the Declaration of Independence was being read aloud. When I heard this I knew a new country was born.

June 14, 1777

Dear Diary,

Today was a happy but scary day. Today the flag I made was adopted by Congress. I thought for sure that if England found out that a new flag was taking the old one's place something bad would happen. But I'm happy because I am the maker of the first American flag and I'm only 25 years old!

Students can use simulated journals in two ways: as a tool for learning or as a project. When students use simulated journals as a tool for learning, they write the entries as they are reading a book in order to get to know the character better or during the theme cycle as they are learning about the historical period. In these entries, students are exploring concepts and making connections between what they are learning and what they already know. These journal entries are less polished than when students write a simulated journal as a project. Students might choose to write a simulated journal as a culminating project for a literature focus unit or a theme cycle. As a project, students plan out their journals carefully, choose important dates, and use the writing process to draft, revise, edit, and publish their journals.

Students can also write simulated letters (Roop, 1995). Students assume the role of a book character or historical figure, as they do for simulated journals, but they write a letter—not a journal entry—to another character in the book or to another historical figure. Students can exchange letters with classmates or the teacher and write replies.

Seeing Common Threads

Some teachers use only personal journals because they want their students to write about things they know well. Why isn't using just one kind of journal enough?

Alison Kaiser responds:

Personal journals are great for building fluency. They can also generate topics for writing workshop, but the other types of journals are great academic learning tools. Next year, I will have my students write their own language arts notebook. It will include a table of contents and an index. I think I will do the same thing with their learning logs and let them use their learning logs for quizzes. I think that way they will really understand how a table of contents and index are used. Double-entry journals help students interact with what they are reading and simulated journals help bring a real or fictional character to life. All of these kinds of journals are worthwhile, I believe.

What do you think?

Each chapter presents a question and a response written by one of Dr. Tompkins's students. Consider other comments, or respond to the question yourself, by visiting the Threaded Message Board in Chapter 6 on the Companion Website at www.prenhall.com/tompkins

Young Children's Journals

Young children can write in journals by drawing, or they can use a combination of drawing and writing (Hipple, 1985; McGee & Richgels, 2001; Nathan, 1987). Children may write scribbles, random letters and numbers, simple captions, or extended texts using invented spelling. Their invented spellings often seem bizarre by adult standards, but they are reasonable in terms of children's knowledge of phoneme-grapheme correspondences and spelling patterns. Other children want parents and teachers to take their dictation and write the text. After the text has been written, children can usually read it immediately, and they retain recognition of the words for several days.

 To read about invented spelling, turn to Chapter 12, "Learning to Spell Conventionally," and to learn more about how young children learn to write, see Chapter 4, "Emerging Into Literacy."

Kindergartners begin writing in journals early in the school year, and their writing becomes more conventional as they learn concepts about print, letters of the alphabet, and phonics skills. Hannon (1999) recommends beginning with personal or dialogue journals. Four kindergartners' journal entries are presented in Figure 6–7. The top two entries are from personal journals, and the bottom two are from reading logs. In the top left entry, the 5-year-old student focuses on the illustration, drawing a detailed picture of a football game (note that the player in the middle-right position has the ball); he adds five letters for the text so that his entry will have some writing. In the top right entry, the kindergartner writes, "I spent the night at my dad's house." The child wrote the entry on the bottom left after he listened to the teacher read *The Three Billy Goats Gruff* (Stevens, 1987) and then acted out the story. As he shared his

FIGURE 6-7 *Entries From Young Children's Journals*

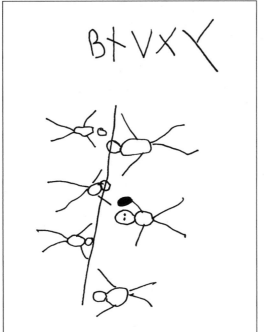

entry with classmates, he read the text this way: "You are a mean, bad troll." The kindergartner wrote the entry on the bottom right after listening to the teacher read *The Jolly Postman, or Other People's Letters* (Ahlberg & Ahlberg, 1986). This child drew a picture of the three bears receiving a letter from Goldilocks. She labeled the mom, dad, and baby bear in the picture and wrote, "I [am] sorry I ate your porridge."

Through a variety of forms and purposes, journal writing helps children discover the power of writing to record information and explore ideas. They usually cherish their journals and are amazed by the amount of writing they contain.

Teaching Students to Write in Journals

Journals are typically written in notebooks or booklets. Spiral-bound notebooks are useful for long-term personal and dialogue journals and for language arts notebooks, whereas small booklets of paper stapled together are more often used for reading logs, learning logs, and simulated journals that are used for one literature focus unit, literature circle, or theme cycle. Most teachers prefer to keep the journals in the classroom so that they will be available for students to write in each day, but students might write in journals at home as well.

Students usually write at a particular time each day. Many teachers have students make personal or dialogue journal entries while they take attendance or immediately after recess. Language arts notebooks are often used during minilessons to record information about topics such as poetic forms or quotation marks. Entries are made in reading logs during literature focus units and reading workshop. Learning logs and simulated journals can be written in as part of math class or social studies or science theme cycles.

Teachers introduce students to journal writing using minilessons in which they explain the purpose of the journal-writing activity and the procedures for gathering ideas, writing the entry, and sharing it with classmates. Teachers often model the procedure by writing a sample entry on the chalkboard or on chart paper as students observe. This sample demonstrates that the writing is to be informal, with ideas emphasized over correctness. Then students make their own first entries, and several read their entries aloud. Through this sharing, students who are still unclear about the activity have additional models on which to base their own writing.

Similar procedural minilessons are used to introduce each type of journal. Even though most types of journals are similar, the purpose of the journal, the information included in the entries, and the viewpoint of the writer vary according to type.

Journal writing can also be introduced with examples from literature. Characters in children's literature, such as Harriet in *Harriet the Spy* (Fitzhugh, 1964), Leigh in *Dear Mr. Henshaw* (Cleary, 1983), and Birdy in *Catherine, Called Birdy* (Cushman, 1994), keep journals in which they record events in their lives, their ideas, and their dreams. A list of books in which characters and

Books in Which Characters and Historical Personalities Keep Journals

Altman, S. (1995). *My worst days diary*. New York: Bantam. (P)

Anderson, J. (1987). *Joshua's westward journey*. New York: Morrow. (M)

Blos, J. (1979). *A gathering of days: A New England girl's journal, 1830–1832*. New York: Scribner. (U)

Bowen, G. (1994). *Stranded at Plimoth plantation, 1626*. New York: HarperCollins. (M–U)

Cartlidge, M. (1994). *A mouse's diary*. New York: Dutton. (P)

Cleary, B. (1983). *Dear Mr. Henshaw*. New York: Morrow. (M)

Cleary, B. (1991). *Strider*. New York: Morrow. (M)

Creech, S. (1995). *Absolutely normal chaos*. New York: HarperCollins. (U)

Cronin, D. (2000). *Click, clack, moo: Cows that type*. New York: Simon & Schuster.

Cruise, R. (1998). *The top-secret journal of Fiona Claire Jardin*. San Diego, CA: Harcourt Brace. (M)

Cummings, P. (1992). *Petey Moroni's Camp Runamok diary*. New York: Bradbury. (P)

Cushman, K. (1994). *Catherine, called Birdy*. New York: Clarion. (U)

Denenberg, B. (1996). *When will this cruel war be over? The Civil War diary of Emma Simpson*. New York: Scholastic. (M–U)

Denenberg, B. (1999). *The journal of Ben Uchida: Citizen 13559, Mirror Lake Internment Camp*. New York: Scholastic. (M–U)

Fitzhugh, L. (1964). *Harriet the spy*. New York: Harper & Row. (M)

Frank, A. (1987). *Anne Frank: The diary of a young girl*. Philadelphia: Washington Square. (U)

Garland, S. (1998). *A line in the sand: The Alamo diary of Lucinda Lawrence*. New York: Scholastic. (M–U)

George, J. C. (1959). *My side of the mountain*. New York: Dutton. (M–U)

Gregory, K. (1996). *The winter of red snow: The Revolutionary War diary of Abigail Jane Stewart*. New York: Scholastic. (M–U)

Gregory, K. (1999). *The great railroad race: The diary of Libby West*. New York: Scholastic. (M–U)

Hesse, K. (2000). *Stowaway*. New York: McElderry. (M–U)

Hest, A. (1995). *The private notebook of Katie Roberts, age 11*. Cambridge, MA: Candlewick Press. (M–U)

Hest, A. (1998). *The great green notebook of Katie Roberts: Who just turned 12 on Monday*. New York: Candlewick. (M–U)

Johnson, D. (1994). *Seminole diary: Remembrances of a slave*. New York: Macmillan. (M)

Lasky, K. (1996). *A journey to the new world: The diary of Remember Patience Whipple*. New York: Scholastic. (M–U)

Lasky, K. (1998). *Dreams in the golden country: The diary of Zipporah Feldman, a Jewish immigrant girl*. New York: Scholastic. (M–U)

Leslie, C. W. (1991). *Nature all year long*. New York: Greenwillow. (M)

Lewis, C. C. (1998). *Dilly's big sister diary*. New York: Millbrook. (P)

Lyon, G. E. (1994). *Here and then*. New York: Orchard. (M–U)

McKissack, P. C. (1997). *A picture of freedom: The diary of Clotee, a slave girl*. New York: Scholastic. (M–U)

McKissack, P. C. (2000). *Nzingha: Warrior queen of Matamba*. New York: Scholastic. (M–U)

Moss, M. (1995). *Amelia's notebook*. New York: Tricycle. (P–M)

Moss, M. (1998). *Rachel's journal: The story of a pioneer girl*. San Diego, CA: Silver Whistle/Harcourt Brace. (M)

Moss, M. (2002). *Galen: My life in imperial Rome*. San Diego: Harcourt Brace. (M–U)

Murphy, J. (1998). *The journal of James Edmond Pease: A Civil War Union soldier*. New York: Scholastic. (M–U)

Murphy, J. (1998). *West to a land of plenty: The diary of Teresa Angelino Viscardi*. New York: Scholastic. (M–U)

Myers, W. D. (1999). *The journal of Scott Pendleton Collins: A World War II soldier*. New York: Scholastic. (M–U)

Parker, S. (1999). *It's a frog's life*. Pleasantville, NY: Reader's Digest. (P)

Perez, A. I. (2002). *My diary from here to there/Mi diario de aqui hasta alla*. San Francisco: Childrens Book Press. (P)

Philbrick, R. (2001). *The journal of Douglas Allen Deeds: The Donner party expedition*. New York: Scholastic. (M–U)

Platt, R. (1999). *Castle diary: The journal of Tobias Burgess, page*. Cambridge, MA: Candlewick Press. (U)

Roop, C., & Roop, P. (2001). *The diary of David R. Leeper: Rushing for gold*. St. Paul, MN: Benchmark. (M–U)

Roop, P., & Roop, C. (1993). *Off the map: The journals of Lewis and Clark*. New York: Walker. (M–U)

Roth, S. L. (1990). *Marco Polo: His notebook*. New York: Doubleday. (U)

Ruby, L. (1994). *Steal away home*. New York: Macmillan. (U)

Thaxter, C. (1992). *Celia's island journal*. Boston: Little, Brown. (P–M)

Vasil, R. (1994). *Ever after*. New York: Orchard. (U)

Van Allsburg, C. (1991). *The wretched stone*. Boston: Houghton Mifflin. (M–U)

Veciana-Suarez, A. (2002). *Flight to freedom*. New York: Scholastic. (U)

Watts, L. (2002). *Stonecutter*. San Diego: Harcourt Brace. (U)

Whelan, G. (2002). *Fruitlands: Louisa May Alcott made perfect*. New York: HarperCollins. (U)

White, E. E. (1998). *Voyage on the great* Titanic: *The diary of Margaret Ann Brady*. New York: Scholastic. (M–U)

Whiteley, P. (1994). *Only Opal: The diary of a young girl*. New York: Philomel. (P–M)

Williams, V. B. (1981). *Three days on a river in a red canoe*. New York: Greenwillow. (P–M)

Wilson, J. (2001). *The story of Tracy Beaker*. New York: Delacorte. (M–U)

Yep, L. (2001). *Lady of Ch'iao Kuo: Warrior of the south*. New York: Scholastic. (U)

Using learning logs. A third grader takes notes in her learning log as her classmates perform a science experiment. Her focus is on capturing ideas and using the scientific vocabulary words her teacher has introduced. Students often brainstorm a list of words, draw and label diagrams, record the steps in completing a task, and answer questions in their learning logs. Because the writing is informal, it is messier than other types of writing, but it must be legible. Writing is an important tool for learning because as they write informally, students clarify ideas, learn concepts, and practice vocabulary they are learning.

historical personalities keep journals is presented in the Classroom Library box on page 264. In these books, the characters demonstrate the process of journal writing and illustrate both the pleasures and the difficulties of keeping a journal.

Students write in journals on a regular schedule, usually daily. After they know how to write the appropriate type of entry, they can write independently. Although some children prefer to write private journals, others volunteer to read their journal entries aloud each day no matter what type of journal they are writing. Young children share their picture-journal entries and talk about them. If the sharing becomes too time-consuming, students can share in small groups or with partners. Then, after everyone has had a chance to share, several students can be selected to share with the entire class. Teachers and classmates may offer compliments about the topic, word choice, humor, and so on.

Students may write in personal journals throughout the school year, or they may alternate with other types of journals, starting and stopping with particular literature focus units and social studies and science theme cycles. Sometimes students seem to lose interest in personal journals. When this happens, many teachers find it useful to put the personal journals away and try another type of journal.

Quickwriting. Much of the writing that students do in journals or other impromptu writing is quickwriting: Students reflect on what they know about a topic, ramble on paper, generate words and ideas, and make connections among the ideas. Students write about a topic for 5 to 15 minutes, letting their thoughts flow from their minds to their pens without focusing on mechanics or revisions. This strategy, originally called "freewriting" and popularized by Peter Elbow (1973), is a way to help students focus on content rather than mechanics. Even by second or third grade, students have learned that many teachers emphasize correct spelling and careful handwriting more than the content of a composition. Elbow explains that focusing on mechanics makes writing "dead" because it doesn't allow students' natural voices to come through.

During a theme cycle on the solar system, fourth graders each chose a word from the word wall (a list of vocabulary words hanging in the classroom) to quickwrite about in their learning logs. This is one student's quickwrite on Mars:

Mars is known as the red planet. Mars is Earth's neighbor. Mars is a lot like Earth. On Mars one day lasts 24 hours. It is the fourth planet in the solar system. Mars may have life forms. Two Viking ships landed on Mars. Mars has a dusty and rocky surface. The Viking ships found no life forms. Mars' surface shows signs of water long ago. Mars has no water now. Mars has no rings.

Another student wrote about the sun:

The sun is an important star. It gives the planets light. The sun is a hot ball of gas. Even though it appears large, it really isn't. It's pretty small. The sun's light takes time to travel to the planets so when you see light it's really from a different time. The closer the planet is to the sun the quicker the light reaches it. The sun has spots where gas has cooled. These are called sun spots. Sun spots look like black dots. The sun is the center of the universe.

These quickwrites, which took 10 minutes for students to draft, provide both a good way of checking on what students are learning and an opportunity to clarify misconceptions. After students write, they usually share their quickwrites in small groups, and then one student in each group shares with the class. Sharing also takes about 10 minutes, and the entire activity can be completed in approximately 20 minutes.

Before starting a new unit of study, teachers might ask students to quickwrite on the new topic to check their knowledge about the topic, to relate personal experiences about it, and to stimulate interest. For example, students can produce the following quickwrites in connection with current events, literature, social studies, and science themes:

- Before discussing a current events topic, quickwrite on freedom or on a geographic location.
- Before studying the Oregon Trail, quickwrite on a trip students have taken.
- Before studying reptiles, quickwrite on snakes.
- Before studying nutrition, quickwrite on junk food.

After completing the theme, students quickwrite again on the topic, applying what they have learned. Then they compare the two quickwrites as one measure of what they have learned.

Teaching Minilessons.   Teachers teach minilessons on procedures, concepts, and strategies and skills about writing in journals. A list of minilesson topics and a minilesson about quickwriting are presented in the box on pages 268 and 269.

It is especially important to teach a minilesson when students are learning a new type of journal or when they are having difficulty with a particular procedure or strategy, such as changing point of view for simulated journals or writing in two columns in double-entry journals.

Meeting the Needs of Every Student

Journals can easily be adapted to meet the needs of every student. Students who have not had a lot of experience with journals may be more successful in writing personal or dialogue journals in which they focus on their own lives rather than on literature they are reading or on across-the-curriculum theme cycles. Research suggests that English learners are more successful using dialogue journals than using other types of journals.

For students who have difficulty writing, spelling, or expressing themselves in English, two alternatives are drawing illustrations and dictating entries to the teacher or a cross-age tutor. Some students may benefit from talking about their reactions to stories before writing in reading logs or from talking about topics for quickwrites before writing in learning logs. No matter what type of journal students are writing, it is important to help them focus on their ideas and the interpretations they are expressing, not on mechanical correctness. Suggestions for helping struggling students write better journal entries are presented on page 270.

Assessing Students' Journal Entries

Students can write in journals independently with little or no sharing with the teacher, or they can make daily entries that the teacher monitors or reads regularly. Typically, students are accustomed to having teachers read all or most of their writing, but the quantity of writing students produce in journals is often too great for teachers to keep up with. Some teachers rarely check students' journals; others read selected entries and monitor the remaining entries; still others try to read all entries. These three management approaches can be termed private journals, monitored journals, and shared journals. When students write private journals, they write primarily for themselves, and sharing with classmates or the teacher is voluntary; the teacher does not read the journals unless invited to. When students write monitored journals, they write primarily for themselves, but the teacher monitors the writing to ensure that entries are being made regularly. The teacher simply checks that entries have been made and does not read the entries unless they are marked "Read me." Students write shared journals primarily for the teacher; the teacher regularly reads all entries, except those marked "private," and offers encouragement and suggestions.

Many teachers have concerns about how to grade journal entries. Because the writing is usually not revised and edited, teachers should not grade the quality of the entries. One option is to give points for each entry made, especially in personal journals. However, some teachers grade the content in learning logs and simulated journals because they can check to see whether the entries include particular pieces of information. For example, if students are writing simulated journals about the Crusades, they may be asked to include five pieces of historically accurate information in their entries. (It is helpful to ask students

Piecing a Lesson Together

Topics on Journal Writing

Procedures	Concepts	Strategies and Skills
Write a journal entry	Personal journals	Choose a topic
Share entries	Dialogue journals	Generate ideas
Respond in dialogue journals	Language arts notebooks	Organize ideas
Write in language arts notebooks	Reading logs	Focus on ideas
Write reading log entries	Double-entry journals	Compare
Write double-entry journals	Learning logs	Predict
Use logs in math	Simulated journals	Describe
Write science observation logs	Qualities of a good entry	Reflect on
Write simulated journals		Incorporate key vocabulary
		Assume another viewpoint

Quickwrite

 Please visit the Companion Website at **www.prenhall.com/tompkins** for a second fully realized minilesson.

to identify the five pieces of information by underlining and numbering them.) Rough-draft journal entries should not be graded for mechanical correctness. Students need to complete the writing process and revise and edit their entries if they are to be graded for mechanical correctness.

Figure 6–8 presents two first graders' reading log entries written after they listened to *Sam, Bangs, and Moonshine* (Ness, 1966) read aloud. This Caldecott Medal story is about a girl named Sam (for Samantha) who has a cat named Bangs. Sam tells "moonshine" about a make-believe baby kangaroo to

QUICKWRITE

Minilesson

Mrs. Ohashi Introduces Quickwriting to Her Third Graders

1. Introduce the Topic

Mrs. Ohashi tells her third graders that they are going to learn about a new kind of writing called quickwriting. She explains that it is the kind of writing you do after reading a book or learning something. In quickwriting, she says, you think and write fast.

2. Share Examples

Mrs. Ohashi demonstrates how to do a quickwrite. She holds up a book the students are very familiar with—*The True Story of the 3 Little Pigs!* (Scieszka, 1989), an outlandish version of "The Three Little Pigs," told from the wolf's viewpoint—and she says, "I don't believe that wolf! He's making up excuses for his horrible behavior." Then she begins to write the same words on the chalkboard. She pauses to think about the book. Then she rereads what she has written and continues writing. Here is her completed quickwrite:

I don't believe that wolf! He's not telling the truth. He's making up excuses for his horrible behavior. He knows that it is wrong to huff and puff and blow down other people's houses. I think he deserved what happened to him, but I like this story because it is so funny.

She reads her completed quickwrite aloud to the third graders.

3. Provide Information

Mrs. Ohashi explains that a quickwrite is a short piece of writing that is written quickly. You think and write, think and write, and then think and write some more. She explains that she begins by thinking about the topic and writing down the words she would say. She asks students to think about what they saw her do as she wrote the quickwrite, and they remember that she did a lot of thinking and writing.

4. Supervise Practice

Mrs. Ohashi asks the students what they would say if they were writing a quickwrite about the book. Students take turns offering suggestions. Then she asks them to write their own quickwrites about the familiar story. Mrs. Ohashi circulates, inviting students to think aloud when they have trouble thinking of something to say. The students write for 10 minutes, and then they share their writing with a partner.

5. Reflect on Learning

Mrs. Ohashi asks her third graders to reflect on what they have learned about writing a quickwrite. They talk about the cycle of thinking and writing.

---

her friend Thomas. The results are almost disastrous. The two reading logs illustrate the problems in grading students' journal entries. In her entry, Andi drew a picture of Bangs and the baby kangaroo and wrote, "If you lie you will get in big trouble and you will hurt your friends." She thoughtfully and accurately described the theme of the story. In his entry, Julio wrote from the point of view of Thomas. His picture is of the make-believe kangaroo, and the text originally read, "He is lying to me. He don't have a kangaroo." After he shared his entry with classmates and they mentioned that Sam was a girl, not a boy,

Meeting the Needs of Every Student

How Can I Help My Struggling Students Write Better Journal Entries?

Writing is very difficult for struggling students. These students often write brief entries, if any at all. Their handwriting is messy, as if they're trying to disguise their ideas, and the entries are full of misspelled words, including many high-frequency words. Too often, teachers give up on their struggling students and conclude that they just can't write, but teachers can help struggling writers write better journal entries.

First of all, teach the students how to write an entry. Demonstrate by thinking aloud about your ideas, pointing out how to use the word wall to locate the spelling of high-frequency words, and modeling how to reread what you've written. Afterward, point out the qualities that make the entry you've written a good one. In addition, before they begin writing their own journals, you and your students can practice revising poorly written journal entries that you've written.

You increase your students' chances of success when you help them talk out their ideas before beginning to write and create a word bank to use when writing. If your students aren't fluent writers, you might work with them to write the first sentence themselves and then take their dictation and write the rest of the entry for them. You may think you're providing too much help, but it's essential that you break their cycle of failure. Once your students are successful writing the first sentence themselves, gradually give them responsibility to do more of the writing themselves.

To investigate other ways to meet the needs of every student, visit the links for this chapter at the Companion Website at www.prenhall.com/tompkins

Julio changed the *he* to *she* and added the picture of Sam. Julio wrote two sentences and spelled all words correctly; Andi used invented spelling and punctuated her text as one sentence.

Which reading log entry is better? Which deserves a higher grade? It is very difficult to make these types of judgments, and such decisions are probably unnecessary. In both entries, students explored the story through illustrations and text, and both entries are remarkable in one way or another—note Andi's articulation of the theme and Julio's viewpoint and his ability to make revisions that reflect the feedback he received from classmates. Andi and Julio's teacher marked the two entries the same way. They each received a check in the gradebook for a reading log entry that was completed and that met these two requirements: first, the entry contains both an illustration and some writing; and second, the entry contains information about the story.

FIGURE 6-8 *Two First Graders' Reading Log Entries About* Sam, Bangs, and Moonshine

LETTER WRITING

Letters are a way of talking to people who live too far away to visit. Audience and purpose are important considerations, but form is also important in letter writing. Although letters may be personal, they involve a genuine audience of one or more persons. Through letter writing, students have the opportunity not only to sharpen their writing skills, but also to increase their awareness of audience. Because letters are written to communicate with a specific and important audience, students take more care to think through what they want to say, to write legibly, and to use spelling, capitalization, and punctuation conventions correctly.

Elementary students' letters are typically classified as friendly or business letters. Formats for friendly and business letters are shown in the LA Essentials box on page 272. The choice of format depends on the purpose of the letter. Friendly letters might be informal, chatty letters to pen pals or thank-you notes to a television newscaster who has visited the classroom. When students write to the National Park Service requesting information about the Grand Canyon or another park or send letters to the president expressing an opinion about current events, they use the more formal, business-letter style. Before students write both types of letters, they need to learn how to format them.

Friendly and business-letter formats are accepted writing conventions, and most teachers simply explain the formats to students and prepare a set of charts to illustrate them. Attention to format should not suggest, however, that form is more important than content; rather, it should highlight the formatting considerations of letter writing, which elementary students are typically unfamiliar with.

Essentials

Forms for Friendly and Business Letters

Friendly letter

Street
City, State ZIP
Date ← Return address

Greeting→ Dear _____ ,

_____
_____
_____
_____
Body { _____
_____
_____
_____

Your friend,

← Complimentary closing

Signature

Business letter

Street
City, State ZIP
Date ← Return address

Inside→ Person's Name
address Company Name
Street
City, State ZIP

Greeting→ Dear _____ ,

_____
_____
_____
Body { _____
_____
_____
_____
_____

Sincerely,

← Complimentary closing

Signature

Friendly Letters

After teachers have introduced the format for friendly letters, students need to choose a "real" someone to write to. Writing authentic letters that will be delivered is much more valuable than writing practice letters to be graded by the teacher. Children write friendly letters to classmates, friends who live out of town, relatives, and pen pals. Students may want to keep a list of addresses of people to write friendly letters to on a special page in their journals or in address booklets. In these casual letters, they share news about events in their lives and ask questions to learn more about the person they are writing to and to encourage that person to write back. Receiving mail is the real reward of letter writing!

Robinson, Crawford, and Hall (1991) examined the effects of personal letter writing on young children's writing development. In the study, a group of 20 kindergartners wrote back and forth to the researchers over a 2-year period. In their early letters, the children told about themselves, promised to be friends with their correspondent, and asked the correspondent questions. Over the 2-year period, they developed as letter writers and continued to be eager correspondents. Their letters became more sophisticated, and they developed letter-writing strategies that took their readers into account. The researchers concluded that authentic, purposeful, and sustained letter-writing experiences were extremely valuable for elementary students.

Sometimes students write informal, single-draft letters, but often students use the writing process in letter writing. In the prewriting stage, they decide what to include in their letters. Brainstorming and clustering are effective strategies to help students choose information to include and questions to ask. Figure 6–9 shows a cluster with four rays developed by a third-grade class for pen pal letters. As a class, the students brainstormed a list of possible topics and finally decided on the four main-idea rays (me and my family, my school, my hobbies, and questions for my pen pal). Then students completed the clusters by adding details to each main idea.

Students' rough drafts incorporated the information from one ray into the first paragraph, information from a second ray into the second paragraph, and so on, for the body of the letters. After writing their rough drafts, students met in writing groups to revise content and edit to correct mechanical errors, first with a classmate and later with the teacher. Next, they recopied their final drafts, addressed envelopes, and mailed them. A sample letter is also presented in Figure 6–9. Comparing each paragraph of the letter with the cluster reveals that using the cluster helped the student write a well-organized and interesting letter that was packed with information.

Pen Pal Letters.
Teachers can arrange for their students to exchange letters with students in another class by contacting a teacher in a nearby school or local educational associations, or by answering advertisements in educational magazines. Another possible arrangement is to have an elementary class become pen pals with college students in a language arts methods class. Over a semester, the elementary students and the preservice teachers can write back and forth four, five, or six times, and perhaps can even meet at the end of the semester. The children have the opportunity to be pen pals with college students, and

FIGURE 6-9 *A Third Grader's Cluster and Pen Pal Letter*

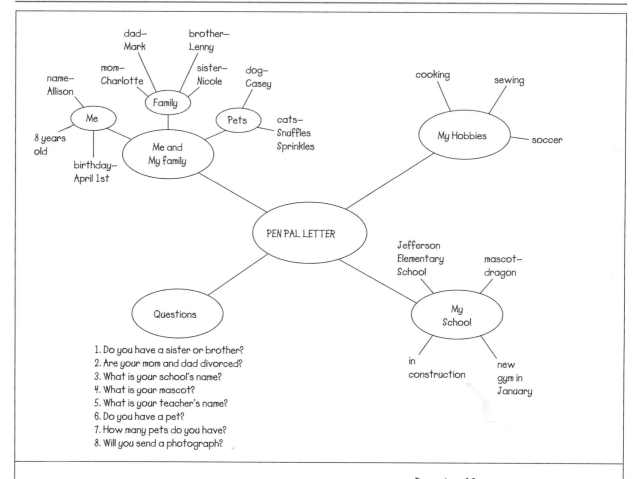

December 10

Dear Annie,

I'm your pen pal now. My name is Allison and I'm 8 years old. My birthday is on April 1st.

I go to Jefferson Elementary School. Our mascot is a dragon. We are in construction because we're going to have a new gym in January.

My hobbies are soccer, sewing, and cooking. I play soccer, sewing I do in free time, and I cook dinner sometimes.

My pets are two cats and a dog. The dog's name is Casey and he's a boy. He is two years old. The cat is a girl and her name is Snuffles. She is four years old. The kitten is a girl and her name is Sprinkles. She is two months old.

My dad's name is Mark and my mom's name is Charlotte. Her birthday is the day after Mother's Day. My brother's name is Lenny. He is 13 years old. My sister's name is Nicole. She is 3 years old.

I have some questions for you. Do you have a sister or a brother? Are your mom and dad divorced? Mine aren't. What is your school's name? What is your mascot? What is your teacher's name? Do you have a pet? How many pets do you have? Will you send me a photograph of yourself?

Your friend,
Allison

the college students have the opportunity to get to know an elementary student and examine the student's writing as they are learning to be teachers (Berrill & Gall, 1999).

In a study by Greenlee, Hiebert, Bridge, and Winograd (1986), a class of second graders became pen pals with a class of college students who were majoring in elementary education. The researchers investigated whether having a genuine audience would influence the quality of the letters the students wrote. They compared the second graders' letters to letters written by a control group who wrote to imaginary audiences and received traditional teacher comments on their letters. The researchers found that the students who wrote to pen pals wrote longer and more complex letters once they received responses to their letters. The results of this study emphasize the importance of providing real audiences for student writing.

Courtesy Letters. Invitations and thank-you notes are two other types of friendly letters that elementary students write. They may write to parents to invite them to an after-school program, to the class across the hall to invite them to visit a classroom exhibit, or to a person in the community to invite him or her to be interviewed as part of a content-area unit. Children write letters to thank people who have been helpful.

E-mail Messages. The Internet has created a completely new way for elementary students to send messages electronically to correspondents anywhere in the world. It's a fast and simple way to send and reply to mail, and messages can be saved and stored on the computer, too. Students use e-mail message forms. They type the correspondent's e-mail address in the top window, specify a subject in the subject window, and then write their message in the large window. They begin by greeting their correspondent, and then they write their message. Students keep their messages short—no longer than one or two screens—so that they can easily be read on the computer screen. They end their messages with a closing, much as in other types of letters.

Not only are e-mail messages fun to send and receive, but they can support students' learning. A fifth-grade class became e-mail pen pals with another fifth-grade class in a distant state. The students were encouraged to focus on the books they were reading in their correspondence. Here is a series of brief e-mail messages between Mikey and his pen pal, William:

Hey dude!
What book are you reading now?
    Mikey

Mikey,
I'm reading Hatchet. What are you reading?
    Your friend,
    William

Dude!
I read Hatchet, too. I liked it:) Read The River next. It's good. I want to read the new Harry Potter book. I keep begging my Mom to buy it.
    Mikey

Dude,

Our teacher Miss Horsman read us Harry Potter and the Sorcerer's Stone but I haven't read it.

> Your friend,
> William

Hey William!

My mom got me Harry Potter and the Chamber of Secrets. I'm on page 24. I'll tell you more after I read more.

> Mikey

McKeon (1999) studied the e-mail messages that a class of third graders wrote about the books they were reading and concluded that e-mail is a constructive way to enhance students' learning as well as an effective strategy for teachers to personalize their interaction with students.

Letters to Authors and Illustrators.

Students write letters to favorite authors and illustrators to share their ideas and feelings about the books they have read. They ask questions about how a particular character was developed or why the illustrator used a certain art medium. Students also describe the books they have written. Here are letters from fourth graders to Eve Bunting. These letters were written at the end of an author study, after the class had read and responded to eight of her books.

Dear Eve Bunting,

I have read some of your books. All of them had friendship in them. My favorite book is *Smoky Night.* I think the theme is get along and respect each other. My family needs to learn to respect each other and to get along because I fight with my brother and he fights with my sister.

How many picture books have you written? I have read eight of them. Have you ever met Chris Van Allsburg because we did an author study on him also. Why do you write your books?

> Sincerely,
> Jeffrey

Dear Eve Bunting,

I've read some of your books and I like them all. That's why I wanted to write to you. *The Man Who Could Call Down Owls* appealed to me because it's not like the other books. Most of your books are realistic. My favorite sentence from the book is "They came swooping on noiseless wings."

I have a few questions to ask you. Are you going to write any more books that have mysteries? I like mysteries. Is the illustrator of *The Man Who Could Call Down Owls* an Indian? I think he is because of the way he draws nature. Have you met Jerry Pallotta? I did when he came to our school. Have you written any chapter books? I would like to read some.

> Your fan,
> Brad

Most authors and illustrators reply to children's letters when possible, and Eve Bunting answered these fourth graders' letters. However, they receive thousands of letters from children every year and cannot be pen pals with students.

Beverly Cleary's award-winning book *Dear Mr. Henshaw* (1983) offers a worthwhile lesson about what students (and their teachers) can realistically expect from authors and illustrators. Here are some guidelines for writing to authors and illustrators:

- Follow the correct letter format with return address, greeting, body, closing, and signature.
- Use the process approach to write, revise, and edit the letter. Be sure to proofread and correct errors.
- Recopy the letter so that it will be neat and easy to read.
- Write the return address on both envelope and letter.
- Include a stamped, self-addressed envelope for a reply.
- Be polite in the letter; use the words *please* and *thank you.*

Students should write genuine letters to share their thoughts and feelings about the author's writing or the illustrator's artwork, and they should write only to authors and illustrators whose work they are familiar with. In their letters, students should avoid asking personal questions, such as how much money the author or illustrator earns. They should not ask for free books, because authors and illustrators usually don't have copies of their books to give away. Students send their letters to the author or illustrator in care of the publisher (the publisher's name appears on the book's title page, and the address usually appears on the copyright page, the page following the title page). If students cannot find the complete mailing address, they can check *Books in Print* or *Literary Market Place,* reference books that are available in most public libraries.

Young Children's Letters.   Young children can write individual letters, as the first grader's letter to Goldilocks in Figure 6–10 illustrates. Carrie wrote the letter after reading *The Jolly Postman, or Other People's Letters* (Ahlberg & Ahlberg, 1986), a collection of letters to nursery rhyme and storybook characters. Young children prewrite by drawing pictures before writing. A quick review of how to begin and end letters is also helpful. In contrast with older children's letters, kindergartners and first graders' letters may involve only a single draft, because invented spellings and the artwork may carry much of the message.

Primary-grade students can also compose class collaboration letters. The children brainstorm ideas, which the teacher records on a large chart. After the letter is finished, children add their signatures. They might write collaborative letters to thank community members who have visited the class, to invite another class to attend a puppet show, or to compliment a favorite author. Class collaboration letters can also serve as pen pal letters to another class.

Business Letters

Students write business letters to seek information, to complain and compliment, and to transact business. They use this more formal letter style and format (as shown in the LA Essentials box on page 272) to communicate with businesses, local newspapers, and government agencies. Students may write

FIGURE 6-10 *A First Grader's Letter to Goldilocks*

to businesses to order products, to ask questions, and to complain about or compliment specific products; they write letters to the editors of local newspapers and magazines to comment on articles and to express their opinions. It is important that students support their comments and opinions with facts if they hope to have their letters published. Students can also write to local, state, and national government officials to express concerns, make suggestions, or seek information.

Addresses of local elected officials are listed in the telephone directory, and addresses of state officials are available in the reference section of the public library. Here are the addresses of the president and U.S. senators and representatives:

President's name
The White House
Washington, DC 20500

Senator's name
Senate Office Building
Washington, DC 20510

Representative's name
House of Representatives Office Building
Washington, DC 20515

Students may also write business letters to request information and free materials. Two sources of free materials are *Freebies for Kids* (Abbett, 1996) and *Free Stuff for Kids* (Lansky, 1996). These books are updated regularly and list hundreds of free or inexpensive materials that elementary students can write for. Children can also write to NASA, the National Wildlife Federation, publishers, state tourism bureaus, and other businesses to request materials.

Simulated Letters

Students can write simulated letters, in which they assume the identity of a historical or literary figure. Simulated letters are similar to simulated journals except that they are written as letters using the friendly letter form. Students can write letters as though they were Davy Crockett or another of the men defending the Alamo, or Thomas Edison, inventor of the lightbulb. Students can write from one book character to another; for example, after reading *Sarah, Plain and Tall* (MacLachlan, 1985), students can assume the persona of Sarah and write a letter to her brother William, as a third grader did in this letter:

Dear William,

    I'm having fun here. There was a very big storm here. It was so big it looked like the sea. Sometimes I am very lonesome for home but sometimes it is very fun here in Ohio. We swam in the cow pond and I taught Caleb how to swim. They were afraid I would leave. Maggie and Matthew brought some chickens.

Love,

Sarah

Even though these letters are never mailed, they are written to a specific audience. Classmates can assume the role of the person to whom the letter is addressed and respond to the letter from that point of view. Also, these letters show clearly how well students comprehend the story, and teachers can use them to monitor students' learning.

Teaching Students to Write Letters

Teachers teach a variety of minilessons so that students will know how to write letters and how the format and style of letters differ from the format and style of stories, informational books, and journals. Topics for minilessons include using the letter-writing forms, focusing on your audience, organizing information in the letter, and asking questions. Teachers also teach minilessons on capitalizing proper nouns, addressing an envelope, using paragraphs, and being courteous. See the list of minilesson topics on page 280 for other ideas.

    Students use the process approach to write letters so that they can make their letters interesting, complete, and readable. The steps are shown in the Step by Step feature on page 282.

    A variety of books that include letters have been published for children. Some of these are stories with letters that children can take out of envelopes and read. *With Love, Little Red Hen* (Ada, 2001) is a collection of letters that tells a story, and Ann Turner's *Nettie's Trip South* (1987) is a book-length letter about the inhumanity of the antebellum South. Other books are epistolary novels in which the story is told through a collection of letters, such as *Dear Whiskers*

Piecing a Lesson Together

Topics on Letter Writing

Procedures	Concepts	Strategies
Write pen pal letters	Friendly letter format	Use letter format correctly
Write courtesy letters	Business-letter format	Ask questions to elicit
Write e-mail messages		information
Write letters to authors		Respond to correspondent's
and illustrators		questions
Write business letters		
Write simulated letters		

Please visit the Companion Website at
www.prenhall.com/tompkins for a second fully
realized minilesson.

(Nagda, 2000), the story of a fourth grader who befriends her second-grade pen pal, a Saudi Arabian girl who has recently come to the United States. The Classroom Library box on page 283 lists many of these books, which teachers can share with students as part of letter-writing activities.

Teaching Minilessons.   Teachers present minilessons about letters, including how they are formatted and how to craft letters to encourage correspondents to

SIMULATED LETTERS

Mr. Rinaldi's Eighth Graders Write Simulated Letters

1. Introduce the Topic

Mr. Rinaldi's eighth graders are studying the American Civil War, and each student has assumed the persona of someone who lived in that period. Many students have become Union or Confederate soldiers and given themselves names and identities. Today, Mr. Rinaldi asks his students to think about the war as their persona would. He explains that they will write simulated letters to Abraham Lincoln or Jefferson Davis, arguing an issue as their persona might. He explains that a simulated letter is a letter that is written as if the writer were someone else.

2. Share Examples

Mr. Rinaldi assumed the persona of a Confederate bugle boy when his students assumed personas, and he reads a letter he has written to Abraham Lincoln as that bugle boy, begging Lincoln to end the war. He gives three reasons why the war should end: the South has the right to choose its own destiny; the South is being destroyed by the war; and too many boys are dying. He ends his emotional letter this way: *I 'spect I'ma gonna die, too, Mr. President. What ya' gonna do when there be no more of us to shoot? No more Johnny Rebs to die. When the South has all died away,*

will you be a-smilin' then? The students are stunned by the power of their teacher's simulated letter.

3. Provide Information

Mr. Rinaldi explains that he did three things in his simulated letter to make it powerful: He wrote in persona—the way a scared, uneducated boy might write—he included vocabulary words about the war, and he argued his point of view persuasively. Together they brainstorm a list of arguments or persuasive appeals—for better food and clothing for soldiers and to end the war or to continue the war. He passes out a prewriting form that students use to plan their simulated letters.

4. Supervise Practice

The students write their letters using the writing process. The planning sheet serves as prewriting, and students draft, revise, and edit their letters as Mr. Rinaldi conferences with students, encouraging them to develop the voice of their personas. Afterward, students share their letters with the class.

5. Reflect on Learning

After the lesson, Mr. Rinaldi talks with his students about their simulated letters. He asks them to reflect on what they have learned, and the students emphasize that what they learned was about the inhumanity of war, even though they thought they were learning about letters.

respond. A list of minilesson topics and a sample minilesson on writing letters to favorite authors are presented in the box on these pages. These lessons are sometimes presented as part of language arts lessons. Sometimes teachers teach minilessons on letter writing as part of social studies or science lessons because students often write letters as part of theme cycles. For example, students write business letters to request information during a science unit on ecology or write simulated letters as part of a history theme cycle.

Step by Step

Writing Letters

1. **Gather and organize information for the letter.**   Students participate in prewriting activities, such as brainstorming or clustering, to decide what information to include in their letters. If they are writing friendly letters, particularly to pen pals, they also identify several questions to ask.

2. **Review the friendly or business-letter form.**   Before writing the rough drafts of their letters, students review the friendly or business-letter form.

3. **Draft the letter.**   Students write a rough draft, incorporating the information developed during prewriting and following either the friendly or the business-letter style.

4. **Revise the letter.**   Next, students meet in a writing group to share their rough drafts, receive compliments, and get feedback. They make changes based on the feedback in order to communicate more effectively.

5. **Edit the letter.**   Students edit their letters with a partner, proofreading to identify errors and correcting as many as possible. They also make sure they have used the appropriate letter format.

6. **Make the final copy of the letter.**   After making all the mechanical corrections, students recopy their letters and address envelopes. Teachers often review how to address an envelope during this step, too.

7. **Mail the letter.**   The crucial last step is to mail the letters and wait for a reply.

Assessing Students' Letters

Traditionally, students wrote letters and turned them in for the teacher to grade. The letters were returned to the students after they were graded, but they were never mailed. Educators now recognize the importance of having an audience for student writing, and research suggests that students write better when they know that their writing will be read by someone other than the teacher. Although it is often necessary to assess student writing, it would be inappropriate for the teacher to put a grade on the letter if it is going to be mailed to someone. Teachers can instead develop a checklist or rubric for evaluating students' letters without marking on them.

A third-grade teacher developed the checklist in the Weaving Assessment Into Practice feature on page 284. The checklist identifies specific behaviors and measurable products. The teacher shares the checklist with students before they begin to write so that they know what is expected of them and how they will be graded. At an evaluation conference before the letters are mailed, the teacher reviews the checklist with each student. The letters are mailed

Books That Include Letters

Ada, A. F. (1997). *Dear Peter Rabbit.* New York: Atheneum. (P)

Ada, A. F. (1998). *Yours truly, Goldilocks.* New York: Atheneum. (P)

Ada, A. F. (2001). *With love, Little Red Hen.* New York: Atheneum. (P)

Ahlberg, J., & Ahlberg, A. (1986). *The jolly postman, or other people's letters.* Boston: Little, Brown. (P)

Avi. (1991). *Nothing but the truth.* New York: Orchard. (U)

Ayres, K. (1998). *North by night: A story of the Underground Railroad.* New York: Delacorte. (M–U)

Bonners, S. (2000). *Edwina victorious.* New York: Farrar, Straus & Giroux. (M)

Boudalika, L. (1998). *If you could be my friend: Letters of Mervet Akaram Sha'ban and Galit Fink.* New York: Orchard. (M–U)

Cartlidge, M. (1993). *Mouse's letters.* New York: Dutton. (P)

Cartlidge, M. (1995). *Mouse's scrapbook.* New York: Dutton. (P)

Caswell, M. (2001). *Pioneer girl.* Toronto, Canada: Tundra Books. (M–U)

Cherry, L. (1994). *The armadillo from Amarillo.* New York: Gulliver Green. (M)

Danziger, P., & Martin, A. M. (1998). *P. S. Longer letter later.* New York: Scholastic. (M)

Danziger, P., & Martin, A. M. (2000). *Snail mail no more.* New York: Scholastic. (M)

Demas, C. (2000). *If ever I return again.* New York: HarperCollins. (M–U)

George, J. C. (1993). *Dear Rebecca, winter is here.* New York: HarperCollins. (M)

Grimes, N. (2002). *Danitra Brown leaves town.* New York: HarperCollins. (P)

Hample, S. (Comp.) (1993). *Dear Mr. President.* New York: Workman. (M)

Harrison, J. (1994). *Dear bear.* Minneapolis: Carolrhoda. (P)

Heisel, S. E. (1993). *Wrapped in a riddle.* Boston: Houghton Mifflin. (M–U)

Hesse, K. (1992). *Letters from Rifka.* New York: Holt. (U)

Hobbie, H. (1997). *Toot and Puddle.* Boston: Little, Brown. (P)

Holub, J. (1997). *Pen pals.* New York: Grosset & Dunlap. (P)

Jakobsen, K. (1993). *My New York.* Boston: Little, Brown. (P–M)

James, E., & Barkin, C. (1993). *Sincerely yours: How to write great letters.* New York: Clarion. (M–U)

Johnston, T. (1994). *Amber on the mountain.* New York: Dial. (P–M)

Klise, K. (1998). *Regarding the fountain: A tale in letters, of liars and leaks.* New York: Avon. (U)

Klise, K. (1999). *Letters from camp.* New York: Avon. (U)

Langen, A., & Droop, C. (1994). *Letters from Felix: A little rabbit on a world tour.* New York: Abbeville Press. (M)

Lorbiecki, M. (1997). *My palace of leaves in Sarajevo.* New York: Dial. (M–U)

Lyons, M. E. (1992). *Letters from a slave girl: The story of Harriet Jacobs.* New York: Scribner. (U)

Nagda, A. W. (2000). *Dear Whiskers.* New York: Holiday. (M)

Nichol, B. (1994). *Beethoven lives upstairs.* New York: Orchard. (M–U)

Nolen, J. (2002). *Plantzilla.* San Diego: Harcourt Brace. (P–M)

Olson, M. W. (2000). *Nice try, tooth fairy.* New York: Simon & Schuster. (P)

Pak, S. (1999). *Dear Juno.* New York: Viking. (P)

Pinkney, A. D. (1994). *Dear Benjamin Banneker.* San Diego, CA: Gulliver/Harcourt Brace. (M)

Potter, B. (1995). *Dear Peter Rabbit.* New York: Warne. (P–M)

Rabbi, N. S. (1994). *Casey over there.* San Diego, CA: Harcourt Brace. (P–M)

Schomp, V. (2001). *World War II.* St. Paul, MN: Benchmark. (M–U) (See other books in the Letters from the Homefront series.)

Stewart, S. (1997). *The gardener.* New York: Farrar, Straus & Giroux. (P)

Teague, M. (2002). *Dear Mrs. LaRue: Letters from obedience school.* New York: Scholastic. (P)

Tryon, L. (1994). *Albert's Thanksgiving.* New York: Atheneum. (P)

Turner, A. (1987). *Nettie's trip south.* New York: Macmillan. (M–U)

Wheeler, S. (1999). *Greetings from Antarctica.* Chicago: Peter Bedrick Books. (M–U)

Whybrow, I. (1999). *Little Wolf's book of badness.* Minneapolis: Carolrhoda. (M)

Woodruff, E. (1994). *Dear Levi: Letters from the Overland Trail.* New York: Knopf. (M–U)

Ylvisker, A. (2002). *Dear Papa.* Cambridge, MA: Candlewick Press. (M)

283

Weaving Assessment Into Practice

A Checklist for Assessing Students' Pen Pal Letters

Pen Pal Letter Checklist

Name _____

	Yes	No
1. Did you complete the cluster?	☐	☐
2. Did you include questions in your letter?	☐	☐
3. Did you put your letter in the friendly letter form?	☐	☐

_____ return address
_____ greeting
_____ 3 or more paragraphs
_____ closing
_____ salutation and name

	Yes	No
4. Did you write a rough draft of your letter?	☐	☐
5. Did you revise your letter with suggestions from people in your writing group?	☐	☐
6. Did you proofread your letter and correct as many errors as possible?	☐	☐

without evaluative comments or grades written on them, but the completed checklist goes into students' writing folders. A grading scale can be developed from the checklist; for example, points can be awarded for each check mark in the Yes column, or five check marks can equal a grade of A, four check marks a B, and so on.

Review

Two types of personal writing are journals and letters. Journals are an important learning tool that students at all grade levels can use effectively. Students use journal writing to share events in their lives and to record what they are learning in literature focus units, literature circles, and theme cycles. Students write three kinds of letters: friendly letters, business letters, and simulated letters. The key concepts presented in this chapter are:

1. Students write in seven kinds of journals: personal journals, dialogue journals, reading logs, double-entry journals, language arts notebooks, learning logs, and simulated journals.
2. Dialogue journals are especially useful for English learners.
3. Reading logs, double-entry journals, and simulated journals are often used during literature focus units and literature circles.
4. Learning logs and simulated journals are used for across-the-curriculum theme cycles.
5. Even young children can draw and write in personal journals and reading logs.

6. Teachers teach minilessons about how to write in journals.
7. Students often share entries with classmates, although personal journal entries are usually private.
8. The friendly and business letters that students write should be mailed to authentic audiences.
9. Students write simulated letters in connection with literature focus units, literature circles, and social studies and science theme cycles.
10. The focus in personal writing is on developing writing fluency and using writing for authentic purposes.

Visit Chapter 6 on the Companion Website at www.prenhall.com/tompkins to:

- **Check your understanding of the concepts presented in the chapter**
- **Access the Extensions (activities and a list of related readings)**
- **Link to related websites**

Professional References

Barone, D. (1990). The written responses of young children: Beyond comprehension to story understanding. *The New Advocate, 3,* 49–56.

Berrill, D. P., & Gall, M. (1999). On the carpet: Emergent writer/reader's letter sharing in a penpal program. *Language Arts, 76,* 470–486.

Berthoff, A. E. (1981). *The making of meaning.* Montclair, NJ: Boynton/Cook.

Bode, B. A. (1989). Dialogue journal writing. *The Reading Teacher, 42,* 568–571.

Britton, J., Burgess, T., Martin, N., McLeod, A., & Rosen, H. (1975). *The development of writing abilities, 11–18.* London: Schools Council Publications.

Dekker, M. M. (1991). Books, reading, and response: A teacher-researcher tells a story. *The New Advocate, 4,* 37–46.

Elbow, P. (1973). *Writing without teachers.* London: Oxford University Press.

Five, C. L. (1986). Fifth graders respond to a changed reading program. *Harvard Educational Review, 56,* 395–405.

Fulwiler, M. (1986). Still writing and learning, grade 10. *Language Arts, 63,* 809–812.

Fulwiler, T. (1985). Writing and learning, grade 3. *Language Arts, 62,* 55–59.

Fulwiler, T. (1987). *The journal book.* Portsmouth, NH: Boynton/Cook.

Gambrell, L. B. (1985). Dialogue journals: Reading-writing interaction. *The Reading Teacher, 38,* 512–515.

Greenlee, M. E., Hiebert, E. H., Bridge, C. A., & Winograd, P. N. (1986). The effects of different audiences on young writers' letter writing. In J. A. Niles & R. V. Lalik (Eds.), *Solving problems in literacy: Learners,* *teachers, and researchers* (pp. 281–289). Rochester, NY: National Reading Conference.

Hancock, M. R. (1992). Literature response journals: Insights beyond the printed page. *Language Arts, 61,* 141–150.

Hancock, M. R. (1993). Exploring and extending personal response through literature journals. *The Reading Teacher, 46,* 466–474.

Hannon, J. (1999). Talking back: Kindergarten dialogue journals. *The Reading Teacher, 53,* 200–203.

Hipple, M. L. (1985). Journal writing in kindergarten. *Language Arts, 62,* 255–261.

Kreeft, J. (1984). Dialogue writing: Bridge from talk to essay writing. *Language Arts, 61,* 141–150.

Macon, J. M., Bewell, D., & Vogt, M. E. (1991). *Responses to literature, Grades K–8.* Newark, DE: International Reading Association.

Mallon, T. (1984). *A book of one's own: People and their diaries.* New York: Ticknor & Fields.

McGee, L. M., & Richgels, D. J. (2001). *Literacy's beginnings: Supporting young readers and writers* (3rd ed.). Boston: Allyn & Bacon.

McKeon, C. A. (1999). The nature of children's e-mail in one classroom. *The Reading Teacher, 52,* 698–706.

Nash, M. F. (1995). "Leading from behind": Dialogue response journals. In N. L. Roser & M. G. Martinez (Eds.), *Book talk and beyond: Children and teachers respond to literature* (pp. 217–225). Newark, DE: International Reading Association.

Nathan, R. (1987). I have a loose tooth and other unphotographic events: Tales from a first grade journal. In T. Fulwiler (Ed.), *The journal book* (pp. 187–192). Portsmouth, NH: Boynton/Cook.

Peyton, J. K., & Seyoum, M. (1989). The effect of teacher strategies on students' interactive writing: The case of dialogue journals. *Research in the Teaching of English, 23,* 310–334.

Reyes, M. de la Luz. (1991). A process approach to literacy using dialogue journals and literature logs with second language learners. *Research in the Teaching of English, 25,* 291–313.

Robinson, A., Crawford, L., & Hall, N. (1991). *Someday you will no (sic) all about me: Young children's explorations in the world of letters.* Portsmouth, NH: Heinemann.

Roop, P. (1995). Keep the reading lights burning. In M. Sorensen & B. Lehman (Eds.), *Teaching with children's books: Paths to literature-based instruction* (pp. 197–202). Urbana, IL: National Council of Teachers of English.

Salem, J. (1982). Using writing in teaching mathematics. In M. Barr, P. D'Arcy, & M. K. Healy (Eds.), *What's going on? Language/learning episodes in British and American classrooms, grades 4–13* (pp. 123–134). Montclair, NJ: Boynton/Cook.

Schubert, B. (1987). Mathematics journals: Fourth grade. In T. Fulwiler (Ed.), *The journal book* (pp. 348–358). Portsmouth, NH: Boynton/Cook.

Stanford, B. (1988). Writing reflectively. *Language Arts, 65,* 652–658.

Staton, J. (1980). Writing and counseling: Using a dialogue journal. *Language Arts, 57,* 514–518.

Staton, J. (1987). The power of responding in dialogue journals. In T. Fulwiler (Ed.), *The journal book* (pp. 47–63). Portsmouth, NH: Boynton/Cook.

Tompkins, G. E. (1995). Hear ye, hear ye, and learn the lesson well: Fifth graders read and write about the American Revolution. In M. Sorensen & B. Lehman (Eds.), *Teaching with children's books: Paths to literature-based instruction* (pp. 171–187). Urbana, IL: National Council of Teachers of English.

Wollman-Bonilla, J. E. (1989). Reading journals: Invitations to participate in literature. *The Reading Teacher, 43,* 112–120.

Children's Book References

Abbett, L. (1996). *Freebies for kids.* Chicago: Contemporary Books.

Ada, A. F. (2001). *With love, Little Red Hen.* New York: Atheneum.

Ahlberg, J., & Ahlberg, A. (1986). *The jolly postman, or other people's letters.* Boston: Little, Brown.

Beatty, P. (1987). *Charley Skedaddle.* New York: Morrow.

Bowen, G. (1994). *Stranded at Plimoth plantation, 1626.* New York: HarperCollins.

Bunting, E. (1984). *The man who could call down owls.* New York: Macmillan.

Bunting, E. (1994). *Smoky night.* San Diego: Harcourt Brace.

Cleary, B. (1983). *Dear Mr. Henshaw.* New York: Morrow.

Cole, J. (1981). *A snake's body.* New York: Morrow.

Cole, J. (1989). *The magic school bus inside the human body.* New York: Scholastic.

Cushman, K. (1994). *Catherine, called Birdy.* New York: HarperCollins.

Denenberg, B. (1998). *The journal of William Thomas Emerson: A Revolutionary War patriot.* New York: Scholastic.

Denenberg, B. (1999). *The journal of Ben Uchida: Citizen 13559, Mirror Lake Internment Camp.* New York: Scholastic.

Donnelly, J. (1991). *A wall of names: The story of the Vietnam Veterans Memorial.* New York: Random House.

Fitzhugh, L. (1964). *Harriet the spy.* New York: Harper & Row.

Fritz, J. (1987). *Brady.* New York: Penguin.

Hunt, I. (1987). *Across five Aprils.* New York: Berkley.

Lansky, B. (1996). *Free stuff for kids.* New York: Simon & Schuster.

Lasky, K. (1996). *A journey to the new world: The diary of Remember Patience Whipple.* New York: Scholastic.

Lewis, C. S. (1950). *The lion, the witch and the wardrobe*. New York: Macmillan.

Lowry, L. (1993). *The giver*. Boston: Houghton Mifflin.

MacLachlan, P. (1985). *Sarah, plain and tall*. New York: Harper & Row.

McKissack, P. C. (1997). *A picture of freedom: The diary of Clotee, a slave girl*. New York: Scholastic.

Nagda, A. W. (2000). *Dear Whiskers*. New York: Holiday.

Naylor, P. R. (1991). *Shiloh*. New York: Atheneum.

Ness, E. (1966). *Sam, Bangs, and moonshine*. New York: Holt, Rinehart and Winston.

Paterson, K. (1978). *The great Gilly Hopkins*. New York: Crowell.

Scieszka, J. (1989). *The true story of the 3 little pigs!* New York: Penguin.

Stevens, J. (1987). *The three billy goats Gruff*. San Diego: Harcourt Brace Jovanovich.

Turner, A. (1987). *Nettie's trip south*. New York: Macmillan.

7 Listening to Learn

PATTERNS OF PRACTICE

Reading and Writing Workshop

Literature Focus Units

Literature Circles

Theme Cycles

The second graders in Mr. Hernandez's classroom are involved in a monthlong study of folktales, and this week they are comparing several versions of "The Little Red Hen" and reading related books. On Monday, Mr. Hernandez read aloud Paul Galdone's *Little Red Hen* (1985), and the students reread it with buddies the next day. Next, he read aloud Margot Zemach's *The Little Red Hen: An Old Story* (1983), and the second graders compared it to Galdone's version. On Wednesday and Thursday, the students read *The Little Red Hen* in their reading textbooks, in guided reading groups and compared this version with the Galdone and Zemach versions.

Parent volunteers came into the classroom on Wednesday to make bread with the students. The second graders learned how to read a recipe and use measuring cups and other cooking tools as they made the bread. They baked the bread in the school kitchen, and what the students especially enjoyed was eating their freshly baked bread—still warm from the oven—dripping with butter and jam.

The next day, Mr. Hernandez read aloud *Bread, Bread, Bread* (Morris, 1989), an informational book about the kinds of bread that people eat around the world, and parents brought in different kinds of bread for the students to sample, including tortillas, rye bread, corn bread, croissants, bagels, Jewish matzah, blueberry muffins, Indian chapatty, Italian breadsticks, and biscuits. As they sampled the breads, the students took turns talking about the kinds of bread their families eat.

Today, the students are sitting on a carpet as Mr. Hernandez prepares to read aloud *Cook-a-Doodle-Doo!* (Stevens & Crummel, 1999), the story of the Little Red Hen's great-grandson, Big Brown Rooster, who manages to bake a strawberry shortcake with the help of three friends—Turtle, Iguana, and Pig. The teacher sets out a story box of objects related to the story: a chef's hat, a flour sifter, an egg beater, a plastic strawberry, an oven mitt, a shortcake pan, a timer, a pastry blender, and measuring cups and spoons. The students identify the objects, and Mr. Hernandez prepares a word card for each one so that students can later practice matching objects and word cards at a center. Almost immediately, Mikey guesses, "I know what the story is about! Little Red Hen is going to cook something, but it isn't bread. Um . . . Maybe it is strawberry jam to put on the bread."

"That's a good prediction, Mikey, but let me get one more clue for this story box," Mr. Hernandez says, as he reaches over to a nearby rack of puppets. He selects a rooster puppet and adds it to the box. He looks at the students expectantly, and Mallory asks, "Is that a hen?" "No, it isn't," Mr. Hernandez replies. Again he waits until Cristina

> **S**hould teachers encourage discussion as they read a story aloud or postpone it until afterward?
>
> Many teachers ask students to listen quietly while they read a story aloud and then encourage them to talk about it afterward, sharing ideas, clarifying confusions, and making connections to deepen their understanding. Other teachers, however, invite students to become actively involved in the story as they are reading it aloud. These teachers stop reading periodically to pose questions to stimulate discussion, ask students to make predictions, and encourage students to offer spontaneous comments while they are listening. As you read this vignette, notice which approach Mr. Hernandez uses and think about how he uses discussion to support his second graders' comprehension.

offers, "I think it's a rooster." "You're right! A rooster is a male chicken, and a hen is a female chicken," the teacher explains. Then Mikey revises his prediction, "I know! Now I know! It's a story about a rooster who cooks something with strawberries."

Mr. Hernandez shows the cover of *Cook-a-Doodle-Doo!* and reads aloud the title. At first the students laugh at the title, and then several of them repeat it aloud. "What does the title make you think of?" Mr. Hernandez asks. Jesus jumps up and imitates a rooster as he calls, "Cock-a-doodle-doo! Cock-a-doodle-doo!" The students compare the sound a rooster makes to the book's title and conclude that the rooster in this book is going to do some cooking.

The teacher draws the students' attention back to the cover of the book and asks, "What do you think the rooster is going to cook?" Lacey and Connor both answer "strawberry pancakes" and the class agrees. Mr. Hernandez asks if anyone has ever tasted strawberry shortcake, but no one has. He explains what it is and tells the class it's his favorite dessert. Then he looks back at the cover illustration, and says, "I keep looking at this picture, and I think it looks just like strawberry shortcake."

"Let's start reading," Mr. Hernandez says, and he reads the first two pages of the story that introduce the Little Red Hen's great-grandson, Big Brown Rooster, who is the main character in the story. The students point out the similarity between Little Red Hen and Big Brown Rooster's names: They are each three words long, they each have a size word, a color word, and an animal name, and words are in the same order in each name.

Mr. Hernandez continues reading, and the students learn that the Rooster does plan to make strawberry shortcake—their teacher's favorite dessert. "What's shortcake?" Larry asks. "Is it the opposite of long cake?" Everyone laughs, including Mr. Hernandez. He explains that shortcake is flatter than cake, more like a biscuit. Mikey asks, "Is it like a brownie? Brownies are flatter than chocolate cake." "That's a good comparison," Mr. Hernandez says. Sammy offers: "A tortilla is flatter than a piece of bread." "Good! That's another good comparison," the teacher responds. "All this talk about food is making me hungry."

"Look at this," Mr. Hernandez says, and he points to the cookbook that Big Brown Rooster is holding in the illustration. "That's Little Red Hen's cookbook—*The Joy of Cooking Alone,*" he laughs. "My wife's favorite cookbook is called *The Joy of Cooking,*" he explains. "I wonder why the illustrator added the word *alone* to the title of her cookbook?" "That's because no one would help her make bread," Mallory explains.

The teacher continues reading the story aloud. He turns the page and shows students the illustration, a picture of Big Brown Rooster talking to a dog, a cat, and a goose, and the students, remembering the events from "Little Red Hen," spontaneously call out to Rooster, "No, don't ask them. They won't help you!" Big Brown Rooster does ask the three animals to help him, and as the students predicted, they refuse. As Mr. Hernandez reads the "Not I" refrain, the students join in. Sondra comments on the similarities to the "Little Red Hen" story: "There's a dog, a cat, and a goose like in the other story, and they won't listen to the Big Brown Rooster either." Then the students predict that Big Brown Rooster, like Little Red Hen, will have to cook alone.

On the next several pages, the students learn that three other animals— Turtle, who can read recipes, Iguana, who can get "stuff," and Pig, who is a tasting expert—offer to help. The students get excited. "I think this story is going to be different. It's better," Cristina comments. Mr. Hernandez wonders aloud if these three animals will be good helpers, and the students agree that they will be.

The rooster calls the four of them a "team" on the next page, and Mr. Hernandez asks, "What is a team?" The students mention basketball teams and name their favorite teams, so the teacher rephrases his question: "What makes a group of basketball players a team? What do they do when they are a team?" Students respond that players work together to make a score and win a game. "So, what kind of team are the rooster, the turtle, the iguana, and the pig?" Connor explains, "They are a cooking team. I predict they will work together to cook strawberry shortcake." Then Raymond adds, "And Mr. Hernandez is the captain of the team!"

Mr. Hernandez continues reading, as Turtle reads the recipe and Iguana collects the needed ingredients for strawberry shortcake. In the story, Iguana doesn't know the difference between a *flower* and *flour* and because the students seem confused, too, the teacher explains the homophones. Iguana doesn't know about cooking tools and procedures either. He wants to use a ruler instead of a measuring cup to measure flour and he looks for teaspoons in a teapot, for example. Because the students recently used measuring cups and spoons when they baked bread, they are more knowledgeable than Iguana, and Sammy says, "That iguana is silly. He's not very smart either." On the next page, Iguana misunderstands "stick of butter." He breaks a stick from a tree branch, and Lacey calls out, "No, Iguana, that's the wrong kind of stick."

As each ingredient is added, Pig offers to taste the batter, but Big Brown Rooster replies "not yet." Mr. Hernandez pauses after he reads this and reflects, "Pig seems very eager to taste the shortcake batter. I wonder how long he'll wait patiently for his turn to taste?" "Maybe Big Brown Rooster should give him something else to do," Sondra offers. "I'd tell him to go in the living room and watch a video because that's what my mama tells my brother," says Connor. Mr. Hernandez continues reading, and in the story, Pig is getting more desperate to taste the batter. Jesus calls out, "Oh no! Now Pig really, really wants to taste it. Something bad is going to happen." The students agree.

The teacher continues reading. The characters finish mixing the ingredients and put the batter in the oven to bake. "Wow! I'm surprised that Pig is being so good," Mallory offers. "I thought he would gobble up all the shortcake from the mixing bowl." The other students agree. "So, now you think the shortcake is going to turn out right?" Mr. Hernandez asks. Most of the students think that it will, but Jesus and Mikey predict trouble ahead.

Mr. Hernandez continues reading. In the story, the characters cut the strawberries in half and make whipped cream while the shortcake is in the oven. As he reads, some of the students spontaneously pretend to cut strawberries or pretend to use the egg beater to whip the cream. They dramatize cooking activities again and again as the teacher reads.

The next several pages tell how Rooster takes the shortcake out of the oven, lets it cool, and slices it in half, and assembles the layers of shortcake with cake, whipped cream, and strawberries. Mikey notices that Pig smells the shortcake when it comes out of the oven and really wants to taste it. "I still think that Pig is bad news," he says.

Finally the strawberry shortcake is ready to eat, and Rooster says, "If Great-Granny could see me now!" Mr. Hernandez asks what the sentence means. Connor answers, "Rooster wants her to know he is a good cook, too!" Lacey suggests, "Rooster is really proud of himself." Raymond says, "I think Rooster wants Little Red Hen to know that he has a team to help him cook."

Mr. Hernandez turns the page and the students gasp. The illustration shows the strawberry shortcake falling off the plate as Iguana carries it to the table. "Oh no, it's ruined!" Mallory says. "They can't eat it because it's on the floor." "Pig can! Yes, Pig can. Now it really is his turn," Mikey says gleefully. Jesus cheers. "Well, I guess pigs can eat food on the floor," Mallory allows.

"What about the other animals?" Mr. Hernandez asks. "Won't they get to eat strawberry shortcake?" At first the students guess that they won't, and then Jacob offers, "Well, they could go to the store and buy more food and make another strawberry shortcake." Most of the students agree that Jacob has a good idea, but Larry disagrees, "No way. 'Snip, snap, snout. This story's told out,' said Pig." Both the teacher and the students laugh as Larry suggests an alternative ending using the final words from the "The Gingerbread Man" story they read several weeks before.

Mr. Hernandez reads the last few pages in the book, and the students learn that the animals do make another delicious strawberry shortcake for everyone to eat. The students are satisfied with how the story turned out. "I'm really glad everyone got to eat some strawberry shortcake," Cristina says. "It's a really good story," Sammy reflects, "because it's funny and serious, too." "What's funny in the story?" the teacher asks. The students say that Iguana is the funniest character, and the funniest part is when the shortcake falls on the floor and Pig gobbles it up. Then Mr. Hernandez asks, "What's serious in the story?" The students recognize the authors' message and identify it as the serious part of the book. They say that the book's message is that a job is easier to do when you work together as a team. "I'm glad Rooster had a team," said Sondra. "What about us?" Mr. Hernandez asks, "Do we have a team?" Mikey says, "I never really thought of it before, but I guess our class is a team." Mr. Hernandez responds, "What do you think makes us a team?" "We help each other learn and do our work," Larry answers. The other students agree.

Finally, Mr. Hernandez shows the students the last page of the book with Little Red Hen's recipe for strawberry shortcake, and the teacher surprises the students by announcing that he brought the ingredients and that they will make strawberry shortcake after lunch.

The students regularly make charts using a combination of drawing and writing in their reading logs to help them remember an important idea about each story they read or listen to read aloud. After reading *Cook-a-Doodle-Doo!*, the students make charts about how the characters in the story were a team. One student's chart about the team is shown in the box on page 293. Mr. Hernandez helps them brainstorm a list of words they might want to use on their charts and writes the words on the chalkboard so that the students can spell them correctly. The words they brainstorm include: *team, Big Brown Rooster, Turtle, Iguana, Pig, Little Red Hen, strawberry shortcake, helper, recipe,* and *taster.*

Listening has been called the neglected language art for more than 50 years because it is rarely taught in elementary classrooms. Students are admonished

We are a Team!

Rooster	Iguana	Turtle	Pig
I need a Team.	I can get stuf!	I can read the recipe!	I am the taster! I like to eat.

to listen, but few teachers teach students how to improve their listening strategies and skills. Teachers usually assume that children come to school already
knowing how to listen. Also, some teachers feel that it is more important to
spend the limited instructional time available on reading and writing instruction. Despite these concerns about teaching listening in the elementary grades,
most teachers agree that students need to know how to listen because it is the
most used language art.

Listening is the first language mode children acquire, and it provides the
basis for the other language arts (Lundsteen, 1979). Infants use listening to
begin the process of learning to comprehend and produce language. From the
beginning of their lives, children listen to sounds in their immediate environment, attend to speech sounds, and construct their knowledge of oral language. Listening is also important in learning to read. Children are introduced
to written language by listening to stories that parents and other caregivers
read to them. When children are read to, they begin to see the connection between what they hear and what they see on the printed page and to gain an
understanding of stories. The processes of reading and listening and the strategies and skills used during reading and listening are similar in many ways
(Sticht & James, 1984).

Listening is "the most used and perhaps the most important of the language (and learning) arts" (Devine, 1982, p. 1). Researchers have found that
children and adults spend as much time listening as they do reading, writing,
and talking combined (Rankin, 1926; Werner, 1975; Wilt, 1950). Figure 7–1

As you begin reading this chapter, you may want to read the "Dear Reader" letter in Chapter 7 on the Companion Website at www.prenhall.com/tompkins

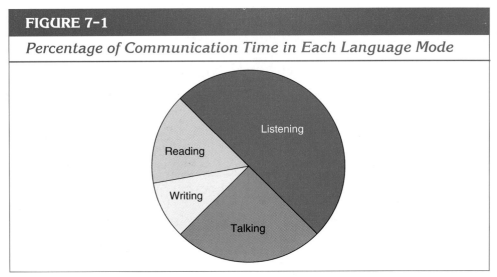

FIGURE 7-1

Percentage of Communication Time in Each Language Mode

Data from Rankin, 1926; Werner, 1975; Wilt, 1950

illustrates the amount of time we communicate in these language modes. Both children and adults spend approximately 50% of their communication time listening. Language researcher Walter Loban has described the importance of listening this way: "We listen a book a day, we speak a book a week, we read a book a month, and we write a book a year" (cited in Erickson, 1985, p. 13).

Despite its importance in our lives, listening has remained the "orphan" language art for more than half a century (Anderson, 1949). Little time has been devoted to listening instruction in most classrooms, and teachers often complain that they do not know how to teach listening (Devine, 1978; Landry, 1969; Strother, 1987).

As you continue reading, you will learn about different kinds of listening, how to teach listening, and ways to incorporate listening instruction into the language arts curriculum. Keep these points in mind as you read:

◆ What is the listening process?

◆ How do students listen aesthetically?

◆ How do students listen efferently?

◆ How do students listen critically?

◆ How is each type of listening taught and assessed?

THE LISTENING PROCESS

Listening is elusive because it occurs internally. Lundsteen (1979) describes listening as the "most mysterious" language process. Teachers often do not know whether listening has occurred until they ask students to apply what they have listened to through discussions, projects, and other assignments. Even then, there is no guarantee that the students' responses indicate that they have

Seeing Common Threads

Listening has been the neglected language art for decades. Do you think listening should receive more emphasis?

Laura Presno responds:

Yes! Listening is the most used language art for communication, yet it is taught in the classroom only as a "pay attention" tool. Students are pros at selective hearing, so teachers must teach students effective listening techniques to improve their listening strategies and skills. Good listeners can discriminate both verbal and nonverbal messages more easily and are better at recalling story events or remembering information than poor listeners are.

What do you think?

Each chapter presents a question and a response written by one of Dr. Tompkins's students. Consider other comments, or respond to the question yourself, by visiting the Threaded Message Board in Chapter 7 on the Companion Website at www.prenhall.com/tompkins

listened, because they may have known the material before listening or may have learned it from someone else at about the same time.

Listening is a complex, multistep process "by which spoken language is converted to meaning in the mind" (Lundsteen, 1979, p. 1). As this definition suggests, listening is more than just hearing, even though children and adults often use the terms *hearing* and *listening* synonymously. Rather, hearing is an integral component, but only one component, of the listening process. The crucial part is thinking, or converting to meaning what one has heard.

The listening process involves three steps: receiving, attending, and assigning meaning (Wolvin & Coakley, 1985). In the first step, listeners receive the aural stimuli or the combined aural and visual stimuli presented by the speaker. Next, listeners focus on selected stimuli while ignoring other, distracting stimuli. Because so many stimuli surround students in the classroom, they must attend to the speaker's message, focusing on the most important information in that message. In the third step, listeners assign meaning to, or understand, the speaker's message. Listeners assign meaning using assimilation and accommodation to fit the message into their existing cognitive structures or to create new structures if necessary. Responding or reacting to the message is not considered part of the listening process; the response occurs afterward, and it sets another communication process into action in which the listener becomes the message sender.

For more information about Piaget's equilibration process, refer to Chapter 1, "Learning and the Language Arts."

The second step of Wolvin and Coakley's listening-process model may be called the "paying attention" component. Elementary teachers spend a great deal of instructional time reminding students to pay attention; unfortunately, however, children often do not understand the admonition. When asked to explain what "paying attention" means, some children equate it with physical behaviors such as not kicking their feet, or cleaning off their desks. Learning to attend to the speaker's message is especially important because researchers have learned that students can listen to 250 words per minute—two to three times the normal rate of talking (Foulke, 1968). This differential allows listeners time to tune in and out as well as to become distracted during listening.

Furthermore, the intensity of students' need to attend to the speaker's message varies with the purpose for listening. Some types of listening require more attentiveness than others. Effective listeners, for example, listen differently to directions on how to reach a friend's home than they do to a poem or story being read aloud.

Purposes for Listening

Why do we listen? Students often answer that question by explaining that they listen to learn or to avoid punishment. It is unfortunate that some students have such a vague and limited view of the purposes for listening. Wolvin and Coakley (1979, 1985) delineate four broad types of listening:

- Discriminative listening
- Aesthetic listening
- Efferent listening
- Critical listening

I have applied Louise Rosenblatt's (1985, 1991) terms *aesthetic reading,* meaning "reading for pleasure," and *efferent reading,* meaning "reading to carry away information," for two of the listening categories. These terms are appropriate because reading and listening are similar language modes, except that one is written and the other is oral.

Discriminative Listening.   People use discriminative listening to distinguish sounds and to develop a sensitivity to nonverbal communication. Teaching discriminative listening involves one sort of activity in the primary grades and a different activity for older students. Having kindergartners listen to tape-recorded animal sounds and common household noises is one discriminative listening activity. Most children are able to discriminate among sounds by the time they reach age 5 or 6. Primary-grade students also use discriminative listening as they develop phonemic awareness, the ability to blend and segment the sounds in spoken words. Older students use discriminative listening to sound out spellings of words and divide words into syllables.

Students also learn to "listen" to the nonverbal messages that people communicate. Young children quickly recognize the unspoken message when a parent's expression changes from a smile to a frown or when a teacher expresses puzzlement. Older students learn the meanings of more sophisticated forms of body language, such as folding one's arms over one's chest, and they recognize how teachers emphasize that something they are teaching is important, such as by writing it on the chalkboard, raising their eyebrows, speaking more loudly, or repeating it.

When teachers read aloud books such as Dr. Seuss's *Fox in Socks* (1965) and Nancy Shaw's *Sheep Out to Eat* (1992) (and other books in the series about the cavorting sheep), they provide opportunities for young children to develop their discriminative listening abilities. Middle- and upper-grade students develop more sophisticated knowledge about the sounds of language when they read *Zin! Zin! Zin! A Violin* (Moss, 1995) and *Lots of Limericks* (Livingston, 1991).

See Chapter 9, "Reading and Writing Stories," for more information about Louise Rosenblatt's reader-response theories.

For more information on phonemic awareness, check Chapter 4, "Emerging Into Literacy."

Using listening centers. These two first graders enjoy rereading a familiar story at the listening center. After their teacher reads aloud stories and informational books, she places two or more copies of the book at the listening center along with the tape she made as she read the book aloud. As students listen to the tape and follow along in the book, they notice high-frequency words, learn vocabulary, and gain valuable reading experience. Listening centers promote students' learning when teachers teach them how to work effectively in the center and they understand what's expected of them.

Aesthetic Listening.   People listen aesthetically to a speaker or reader when they listen for enjoyment, as Mr. Hernandez's students did in the vignette at the beginning of the chapter. Listening to someone read stories aloud or recite poems is a pleasurable activity. Teachers encourage children's aesthetic listening by reading aloud and teaching students how to visualize characters and episodes and notice figurative language. Viewing videotape versions of stories and listening to classmates converse or talk about literature they have read or listened to are other examples of aesthetic listening.

As students listen to the teacher read aloud well-crafted stories such as *Charlotte's Web* (White, 1980), *Thunder Cake* (Polacco, 1990), and *The Giver* (Lowry, 1993), they engage with the text and step into the secondary world of the story. In *Charlotte's Web,* they feel the unlikely friendship between Charlotte and Wilbur. In *Thunder Cake,* they understand the granddaughter's fear of thunderstorms and the urgency with which she and her grandmother collect the ingredients and prepare the thunder cake. And in *The Giver,* students share Jonas's outrage at his community and escape with him.

Students also listen aesthetically as teachers read poems aloud, such as *Welcome to the Green House* (Yolen, 1993), a book-length poem about the rain forest, or *Sierra* (Siebert, 1991), a book-length poem about the California mountains. Another way to share poems and stories is through readers theatre presentations. In readers theatre, students read aloud play scripts dramatically. One script for second and third graders is *I Am the Dog/I Am the Cat* (Hall, 1994), in which one child assumes the perspective of the dog and a second child becomes the cat.

See Chapter 8, "Sustaining Talk in the Classroom," to read more about readers theatre.

Efferent Listening.   People listen efferently to understand a message, and this is the type of listening required in many instructional activities, particularly in theme cycles. Students determine the speaker's purpose, identify the main ideas, and then organize the information in order to remember it. Elementary students usually receive little instruction in efferent listening; rather, teachers assume that students know how to listen. Note taking is typically the one efferent listening strategy taught in the elementary grades.

Students often use efferent listening as they listen to teachers read aloud books or as they view videos as part of social studies and science theme cycles. Students learn how plants and animals coexist in the desert as they listen to the teacher read *Cactus Hotel* (Guiberson, 1991), learn about the mummification process in *Mummies Made in Egypt* (Aliki, 1979), and find out how a volcanic island is formed in *Surtsey: The Newest Place on Earth* (Lasky, 1996). Even though these three books are informational books, students don't necessarily listen to them efferently. As students are reading about the mummification process in *Mummies Made in Egypt,* for example, they often travel back in time and imagine themselves in ancient Egypt—living in the secondary world of the book. Louise Rosenblatt (1991) explains that aesthetic and efferent reading represent two ends of a continuum and that students rarely use one type of reading or the other exclusively. The same is true of listening.

Critical Listening.   People listen critically to evaluate a message. Critical listening is an extension of efferent listening. As in efferent listening, listeners seek to understand a message, but they also filter the message to detect propaganda devices, persuasive language, and emotional appeals. Critical listening is used when people listen to debates, commercials, political speeches, and other arguments.

Teachers can help students learn to think more critically as they read aloud and discuss books. When students listen to teachers read aloud stories such as *The True Story of the 3 Little Pigs!* (Scieszka, 1989) and *Nothing But the Truth* (Avi, 1991), they can critically analyze the characters' claims, and when they read informational books, such as *Antarctica* (Cowcher, 1990), and biographies, such as *My Hiroshima* (Morimoto, 1987), they can evaluate the authors' warnings about destroying the environment and about nuclear war. Students don't automatically think critically about these books, but teachers can guide them to consider the effects of viewpoint, persuasion, and emotional appeal.

Students rarely use these types of listening in isolation. For instance, as students listen to stories such as *Catherine, Called Birdy* (Cushman, 1994), set in the Middle Ages, or *The Bracelet* (Uchida, 1993), set in World War II, they often use several types of listening simultaneously. As they listen aesthetically, they step back into history and imagine they are Birdy or Emi and feel what the characters feel. They use efferent listening as they think about geographic locations, historical events, kings and other historical figures, and additional information that authors have carefully researched and included in the story. They use discriminative listening as they notice rhyme, alliteration, and other types of wordplay. Critical listening plays a role, too, as students consider the author's viewpoint, assess emotional appeals, and think about the theme. The four types of listening are reviewed in Figure 7–2.

Listening Strategies

Listening goes on every day in every classroom. Students listen to the teacher give directions and instruction, to tape-recorded stories at listening centers, to classmates during discussions, and to someone reading stories and poetry

FIGURE 7-2

Overview of the Four Types of Listening

Types	Characteristics	Examples
Discriminative	Distinguish among sounds	Participate in phonemic awareness activities Notice rhyming words in poems and songs Recognize alliteration and onomatopoeia Experiment with tongue twisters
Aesthetic	Listen for pleasure or enjoyment	Listen to stories and poems read aloud Use the Directed Listening-Thinking Approach View video versions of stories Listen to stories at a listening center Watch students perform a play or readers theatre reading Participate in grand conversations Participate in tea party activities
Efferent	Listen to understand a message	Listen to informational books read aloud or at a listening center Use anticipation guides Listen to oral reports Use clusters and graphic organizers View informational videos Listen to book talks Participate in instructional conversations Participate in writing groups Do note taking/note making Listen during minilessons Listen to students share projects
Critical	Evaluate messages	Listen to debates and political speeches View commercials and other advertisements Evaluate themes and arguments in books read aloud

aloud. Because listening plays a significant role in these and other classroom activities, listening itself is not neglected. Most of what has traditionally been called listening instruction has been merely practice. When students listen to a story at a listening center and then answer questions about it, for example, teachers assume that the students know how to listen and that they will be able to answer the questions. These activities provide opportunities for students to practice listening strategies they already possess. What has been neglected is teaching students how to become more effective listeners.

Language arts educators have repeatedly cited the need to teach listening strategies (Brent & Anderson, 1993; Devine, 1978; Lundsteen, 1979; Pearson & Fielding, 1982; Wolvin & Coakley, 1985). Listening strategies are comprehension strategies—the same strategies students use as they read. Students need to learn to vary how they listen to fit their purpose for listening and to develop specific strategies to use for different kinds of listening (Brent & Anderson, 1993; Jalongo, 1991). More capable listeners often use predicting and visualizing when listening aesthetically to stories, but many less capable listeners have only one approach to listening, no matter what the purpose. They listen as hard as they can and try to remember everything.

> For more information on strategies, turn to Chapter 1, "Learning and the Language Arts."

This strategy is destined to fail for at least two reasons: First, trying to remember everything places an impossible demand on short-term memory; and second, many items in a message are not important enough to remember. Often students equate listening with intelligence, and less capable listeners assume that they are poor listeners because they "just aren't smart enough." Kucer (1991) urges teachers to talk with students about their understanding of strategies because he found that students' interpretations often don't match those of the teacher.

AESTHETIC LISTENING

Louise Rosenblatt (1978, 1983, 1991) coined the term *aesthetic reading* to describe the stance readers take when they are concerned with the experience they are living through and with their relationship to the literature they are reading. The focus is on their experience during reading, not on the information they will carry away from the experience. The term *aesthetic listening* can be used to describe the type of listening children and adults do as they listen to storytellers tell stories, poets recite poems, actors perform a play, singers sing songs, and readers read stories aloud and as they view films and videotape versions of stories. The focus of this type of listening is on the lived-through experience and the connections the listeners are making to the literature they are listening to. More traditional names for aesthetic listening are appreciative listening and listening for pleasure.

Teachers often take aesthetic listening for granted and assume that students are experienced listeners and know how to listen to literature. Teachers should not make this assumption. It is important to explain to students that they listen differently for various purposes. For aesthetic listening, students focus on the experience of the literature—forming mental images, predicting what will happen next, appreciating the beauty of the language, and making connections to other experiences or other literature. Students do not concentrate on remembering specific information; instead, they listen for the emotional impact.

Strategies for Aesthetic Listening

Students use many of the same strategies for aesthetic listening that they use for reading and writing (Pinnell & Jaggar, 1991). Six strategies that are especially important for aesthetic listening are:

1. Predicting.   As students listen to a story read aloud or view a puppet show, they are predicting or making guesses about what will happen next in the story. Then they revise their predictions as they continue listening to or viewing the story. When they read aloud, teachers help students develop the predicting strategy by asking them what they think will happen in the story before reading and by stopping several times while reading to have students predict again.

2. Visualizing.   Students create an image or picture in their minds while listening to a story that has strong visual images, details, or descriptive words. Students practice this strategy by closing their eyes and trying to draw mental pictures while they listen to a story, and then reproducing these pictures on paper after reading.

3. Making connections.   Students make personal connections between the story they are listening to and experiences in their own lives. Students might share these connections in reading log entries and in grand conversations after reading. They also make connections between the story they are listening to and other stories they have listened to read aloud, stories they have read themselves, or videos they have viewed. Students make connections between the story they are listening to and another story with the same theme, or a character or episode in this story and a character or episode in another story. Teachers help students use this strategy by asking them to talk about any connections they are making as the story is discussed or by having them make entries in their reading logs. These literary connections are known as intertextuality.

To read more about intertextuality, turn to Chapter 9, "Reading and Writing Stories."

4. Revising meaning. Students begin to formulate meaning as soon as they see the cover of the book and hear the title of the story. As students listen to the story read aloud, their comprehension of the story expands and deepens. Comprehension doesn't happen all at once, but in layers as students listen to the story. Sometimes students misunderstand a word or phrase, don't understand a character's motivations, or miss some important information when they are distracted, and their understanding of the story goes awry. As they continue to listen, students realize that what they are listening to doesn't make sense, and they make corrections.

5. Playing with language. As they are listening, students should be sensitive to the author's choice of language, to the way sentences are phrased, and to the author's use of comparisons, alliteration, or other word-play. Children take over the language they hear and make it part of their own (Cullinan, 1987). Teachers comment on examples of powerful and beautiful language as they are reading or after reading, and students can collect examples in their reading logs, on charts, or in story quilts.

6. Summarizing. As they listen to a story read aloud or view a video version of a story, students apply their knowledge of plot, characters, setting, theme, and point of view to summarize or remember the important events in the story. Students use the basic organization of a story into beginning, middle, and end to structure their summary.

The second graders in the vignette at the beginning of this chapter used these six strategies as they listened to their teacher read aloud *Cook-a-Doodle-Doo!* (Stevens & Crummel, 1999). Mikey offered predictions spontaneously, and at key points in the story, Mr. Hernandez asked the students to make additional predictions. They revised their understanding of the story as they made predictions and listened to see if they were correct. Students refined their understanding of the story as they offered comments and listened to the comments their classmates made, such as when students reflected on the pig's role in the story. The students made personal connections to their families' cooking experiences and literary connections to the "Little Red Hen" stories they had read. The title of the book provided an opportunity for language play when Mr. Hernandez and his students compared "cock-a-doodle-doo" to "cook-a-doodle-doo." The students also noticed the similarity between the names Big Brown Rooster and Little Red Hen and the "not I" refrain from "The Little Red Hen" story. The students used the visualizing and summarizing strategies when they made character charts after listening to Mr. Hernandez read the story. Students do not always use all six strategies as they listen to a story, but this story provided opportunities for the students to use all six, and Mr. Hernandez knew how to take advantage of them.

Students also use these strategies as they listen aesthetically to poems or informational books read aloud. They create mental images and make connections between what they are listening to and their own lives and other literature they know. Instead of using story structure to help them summarize what they are listening to, they use their knowledge about how poetry or informational books are organized. Similarly, as they think about the powerful figurative language of poems, students consider the impact of alliteration and metaphors. When listening to informational books, they think about how the author's use of factual information, examples, diagrams, and photographs helps them create mental images.

Because reading and listening involve many of the same strategies, teachers can teach strategies through listening and then have students apply the strategies during reading (Pearson & Fielding, 1982). As they read aloud, teachers model how to use these strategies, and after listening, students can reflect on how they used them. It is easier for students to focus on strategy use during listening than during reading because they don't have to decode written words when listening.

Reading Aloud to Students

Sharing stories, poems, and informational books orally with students is a wonderful way to develop an appreciation of literature, model fluent reading, encourage interest in reading, and create a community of learners in the classroom. Reading stories aloud to children has always been an important component in most kindergarten and first-grade classrooms. Unfortunately, too many teachers think they need to read to children only until they learn to read for themselves; reading aloud and sharing the excitement of books, language, and reading should remain an important part of the language arts program at all grade levels.

A common complaint is that there is not enough time in the school day to read to children, but reading a story or a chapter of a longer story aloud can take as little as 15 minutes a day. Jim Trelease (2001) points out the necessity of finding time to read aloud so as to take advantage of the many benefits:

- Stimulating children's interest in books and in reading
- Broadening children's reading interests and developing their taste for quality literature
- Introducing children to the sounds of written language and expanding their vocabulary and sentence patterns
- Sharing with children books that are "too good to miss"
- Allowing children to listen to books that would be too difficult for them to read on their own or that are "hard to get into"
- Expanding children's background of experiences
- Introducing children to concepts about written language, different genres of literature, poetry, and elements of story structure
- Providing a pleasurable, shared experience
- Modeling to children that adults read and enjoy reading, to increase the likelihood that children will become lifelong readers

Guidelines for choosing literature to read aloud are simple: choose books that you like and that you think will appeal to your students. Trelease (2001) suggests four additional criteria of good read-aloud books: They should be fast-paced, to hook children's interest as quickly as possible; contain well-developed characters; include easy-to-read dialogue; and keep long descriptive passages to a minimum. A number of annotated guidebooks are available to help teachers select books for reading aloud as well as for independent reading. The Classroom Library box on page 303 lists these guides as well as journals and other resources to help teachers select books to read aloud.

Guides for Choosing Literature to Read Aloud to Students

Books

Brown, J. E., & Stephens, E. C. (Eds.). (2003). *Your reading: An annotated booklist for middle school and junior high school* (11th ed.). Urbana, IL: National Council of Teachers of English.

Cullinan, B. E. (2000). *Read to me: Raising kids who love to read.* New York: Scholastic.

Hansen-Krening, N., Aoki, E. M., & Mizokawa, D. T. (Eds.). (2003). *Kaleidoscope: A multicultural booklist for grades K–8* (4th ed.). Urbana, IL: National Council of Teachers of English.

Hearne, B. G., & Stevenson, D. (1999). *Choosing books for children: A commonsense guide.* Urbana, IL: University of Illinois Press.

Horning, K. T. (1997). *From cover to cover: Evaluating and reviewing children's books.* New York: HarperCollins.

Lipson, E. R. (2000). *The New York Times parent's guide to the best books for children.* New York: Crown/3Rivers Press.

McClure, A. M., & Kristo, J. V. (Eds.). (2002). *Adventuring with books: A booklist for pre-K–grade 6* (13th ed.). Urbana, IL: National Council of Teachers of English.

Recommended readings in literature: Kindergarten through grade eight (Rev. ed.). (1996). Sacramento: California State Department of Education.

Samuels, B. G., & Beers, G. K. (Eds.). (1995). *Your reading: An annotated booklist for middle school and junior high* (10th ed.). Urbana, IL: National Council of Teachers of English.

Sutton, W. K. (Ed.). (1997). *Adventuring with books: A booklist for pre-K–grade 6* (12th ed.). Urbana, IL: National Council of Teachers of English.

Trelease, J. (2001). *The read-aloud handbook* (5th ed.). New York: Penguin.

Journals and Newsletters

Book Links. American Library Association, 50 E. Huron Street, Chicago, IL 60611-2795.

CBC Features. The Children's Book Council, 67 Irving Place, New York, NY 10003.

The Horn Book. Park Square Building, 31 St. James Avenue, Boston, MA 02116.

Language Arts. National Council of Teachers of English, 1111 Kenyon Road, Urbana, IL 61801.

The Reading Teacher. International Reading Association, P.O. Box 8139, Newark, DE 19711.

Websites

Association for Library Service to Children (ALSC): www.ala.org/alsc/

The California Reading List: www.californiareadinglist.com/

Carol Hurst's Children's Literature Site: www.carolhurst.com

The Children's Book Council: www.cbcbooks.org

Children's Literature: Beyond Basals: www.beyondbasals.com

Children's Literature Directory: dir.yahoo.com/Arts/Humanities/Literature/Genres/Children_s/

Children's Literature Web Guide: www.ucalgary.ca/~dkbrown

Kay Vandergrift's Special Interest Page: www.scils.rutgers.edu/~kvander/childrenlit/

The New York Public Library's ON-LION for Kids: www2.nypl.org/home/branch/kids/reading/

Young Adult Library Services Association (YALSA): www.ala.org/yalsa/

Listservs

Children's Literature Criticism and Theory: listserv@rutvml.rutgers.edu

To subscribe, send this e-mail message: Subscribe CHILDLIT

Children and Youth Literature: listserv@bingvmb.cc.binghamton.edu

To subscribe, send this e-mail message: Subscribe KIDLIT-L

Books that have received awards or other acclaim from teachers, librarians, and children make good choices. Two of the most prestigious awards are the Caldecott Medal and the Newbery Medal. Lists of outstanding books are prepared annually by professional groups such as the National Council of Teachers of English and the National Council of Teachers of Social Studies. In many states, children read and vote for books to receive recognition, such as the Buckeye Book Award in Ohio and the Sequoia Book Award in Oklahoma. The International Reading Association sponsors a Children's Choices competition, in which children read and select their favorite books, and a similar Teachers' Choices competition; lists of these books are published annually in *The Reading Teacher.*

Teachers in many primary-grade classrooms read one story aloud as part of a literature focus unit and later during the day read informational books aloud as part of social studies or science theme cycles. Poems, too, are read aloud in connection with content-area themes. It is not unusual for primary-grade students to listen to their teacher read aloud three or more stories and other books during the school day. If children are read to only once a day, they will listen to fewer than 200 books during the school year, and this is not enough! More than 50,000 books are available for children, and reading stories and other books aloud is an important way to share more of this literature with children. Students in middle and upper grades should also read and listen to chapter books and poems read aloud as part of literature or author units, along with reading and listening to informational books, magazines, and newspaper articles in content-area units.

Students—especially kindergartners and primary-grade students—often beg to have a familiar book reread. Although it is important to share a wide variety of books with children, researchers have found that children benefit in specific ways from repeated readings (Yaden, 1988). Through repetition, students gain control over the parts of a story and are better able to synthesize those parts into a whole. The quality of children's responses to a repeated story changes (Beaver, 1982), and children become more independent users of the classroom library center (Martinez & Teale, 1988).

Martinez and Roser (1985) examined young children's responses to stories and found that as stories became increasingly familiar, students' responses indicated a greater depth of understanding. They found that children talked almost twice as much about familiar books that had been reread many times as they did about unfamiliar books that had been read only once or twice. The form and focus of children's talk changed, too. Whereas children tended to ask questions about unfamiliar stories, they made comments about familiar stories. Children's talk about unfamiliar stories focused on characters; the focus changed to details and word meanings when they talked about familiar stories. The researchers also found that children's comments after repeated readings were more probing and more specific, suggesting that they had greater insight into the story. Researchers investigating the value of repeated readings have focused mainly on preschool and primary-grade students, but rereading favorite stories may have similar benefits for older students as well.

Multimedia Presentation Formats

Stories, poems, and informational books can be shared with students through story telling, puppet shows, readers theatre, and plays; these oral presentation modes are discussed in Chapter 8. Students also listen to (and sometimes view) multimedia presentations of books on audiotapes, videotapes, CD-ROM, DVD, and film.

Students often view high-quality videos of children's literature as part of literature focus units and theme cycles, and it is important that teachers take advantage of the unique capabilities of this technology (Green, 1989). Teachers use videos in connection with books children are reading or books they are listening to the teacher read aloud. Teachers decide whether students view the video before or after reading, or how much of the video they watch, depending on the students' needs and interests. Students with limited background knowledge often benefit from viewing before reading or listening to the book read aloud, but for other students, watching a video before reading would curtail their interest in reading the book.

Students often make comparisons between the book and video versions of a story and choose the one they like better. Interestingly, less capable students who don't visualize the story in their minds often prefer the video version, whereas more capable readers often prefer the book version because the video doesn't meet their expectations. They can also examine some of the conventions used in video productions, such as narration, music and sound effects, the visual representation of characters and the setting, the camera's perspective, and any changes from the book version. Guidelines for using videos in the classroom are listed in the LA Essentials box on page 306.

Teaching Aesthetic Listening

Too many teachers take reading aloud for granted, assuming that it is something they do for fun in between instructional activities, but reading aloud to students is an important instructional activity. Students learn comprehension strategies as they listen that they can apply when reading independently. For aesthetic listening and for aesthetic reading, students use the same comprehension strategies. Equally important, as teachers read aloud, they provide opportunities for students to listen aesthetically and know the lived-through experience of aesthetic listening; and students who find pleasure in listening to stories read aloud are more likely to become lifelong readers.

When reading stories aloud to children, teachers have three responsibilities. First, they help students activate their background knowledge before reading. Students need to become actively involved in books they listen to read aloud, and the first step in active involvement is to connect the book to their background knowledge. Second, teachers model and teach aesthetic listening strategies as they read aloud and provide opportunities for students to practice using the strategies as they listen. And third, teachers provide opportunities for students to respond to the book after reading (Pinnell & Jaggar, 1991). Students need opportunities to share their ideas, ask questions, and bring closure to the listening experience.

In the vignette, Mr. Hernandez actively involved his second graders in listening by encouraging them to talk about the story as he read it aloud. Barrentine (1996) recommends that teachers invite brief conversations so that students can talk about their use of listening strategies, notice literary elements and other aspects of the story, and make predictions and connections. Sipe (2002) found that students make five types of responses as they interact with stories; Mr. Hernandez's second graders made these responses in the vignette:

1. *Dramatizing.* Students spontaneously act out the story in both nonverbal and verbal ways. Mr. Hernandez's second graders, for example, dramatized cutting strawberries and beating cream as their teacher read aloud.

LA Essentials

Guidelines for Using Videos in the Classroom

1. **Preview the Video**

   Before showing the video to students, teachers make sure it is suitable for them to view. It may be necessary to skip some portions because of excessive length or unsuitable content.

2. **Plan How to Use the Video**

   Students who have little background knowledge on the topic or students for whom the sentence structure or vocabulary is difficult may benefit from viewing the video before reading or listening to the book read aloud.

3. **Set the Purpose**

   Teachers explain the purpose for viewing the video and explain whether students should use primarily aesthetic, efferent, or critical listening.

4. **Use the Pause Function**

   Teachers stop the video periodically for students to make predictions, reflect on their use of a listening strategy, talk about the video, or compare the book and video versions. When students are listening to an informational video, teachers stop the video periodically to allow students to take notes.

5. **Re-view the Video**

   Teachers consider showing the video more than once because re-viewing is as beneficial as rereading. Teachers can use the rewind function to show particular scenes twice while students are viewing, or they can show the video without interruption the first time and later play it a second time.

6. **Vary the Procedure Used to Show Videos**

   Teachers sometimes show the beginning of the story on the videotape and then read aloud the entire book. Afterward, students view the entire video. Or teachers can alternate reading and viewing chapters of a longer book.

7. **Compare the Author's and Camera's Views**

   Students can examine the impact of the narration, music and sound effects, the visual representation of the characters and setting, and camera angles.

8. **Respond to the Video**

   Provide opportunities for students to respond to videos after viewing. Students can respond by participating in grand conversations or instructional conversations and writing in reading logs.

2. *Talking back.* Students talk back to the characters, giving them advice or criticizing and complimenting them. At the beginning of the story, for example, Mr. Hernandez's students tell the Rooster not to ask the cat, the dog, and the goose for help, and later in the story, they tell Iguana that he has the wrong kind of stick.

3. *Critiquing/controlling.* Students suggest alternative plots, characters, or settings to personalize the story. For example, several of Mr. Hernandez's students suggest ways that Rooster could handle Pig more effectively.

4. *Inserting.* Students insert themselves or their friends into the story. One of Mr. Hernandez's students, for example, inserts Mr. Hernandez into the story and says that he is the team captain.

5. *Taking over.* Students take over the text and manipulate it to express their own creativity. These responses are usually humorous and provide an opportunity for students to show off. For example, after Mr. Hernandez's students suggest several possible endings for the story after the pig eats the first strawberry shortcake, Larry gets a big laugh when he suggests a different ending using words from "The Gingerbread Man."

Students make these types of responses when teachers encourage their active participation in the story, and it is the teacher's responsibility to balance the time spent reading and talking.

The Directed Listening-Thinking Activity.   One of the best ways to involve students actively in listening to a story read aloud is the Directed Listening-Thinking Activity (DL-TA), which is based on the Directed Reading-Thinking Activity, a procedure developed by Russell Stauffer (1975). In DL-TA, the teacher reads the story aloud to students who are actively listening by making predictions and listening to confirm their predictions. After listening to the book read aloud, students discuss their predictions and give reasons to support them. The steps are shown in the Step by Step feature on page 308.

DL-TA is useful only when students are listening to an unfamiliar story so that predicting actively involves them in the story. This strategy can be used both when students are listening to the teacher read a story aloud and when students are doing the reading themselves; however, DL-TA is intended for aesthetic listening and reading, not for efferent or critical listening and reading. When students are listening or reading for other purposes, they use other comprehension strategies.

Responding After Reading.   Immediately after reading, students respond to a story (or a chapter of a longer book) by talking about the story or writing in a reading log (Pinnell & Jaggar, 1991). In these initial responses, students focus on voicing their personal feelings, making connections to their own lives, articulating questions and confusions, and identifying favorite characters, events, and quotations. Students need this opportunity to talk about a story after reading. They may talk about the book with a partner, in small groups, or with the entire class. The focus is on interpreting the story, not on answering the teacher's questions about the story.

Students also capture initial responses to a story by writing entries in a reading log. Primary-grade students keep a reading log by writing the title and author of the story and drawing a picture related to the story. They can also add

Step by Step

Directed Listening-Thinking Activity

1. **Activate background knowledge.** The teacher stimulates students' interest in the book by discussing the topic, showing pictures, or sharing objects related to the story to draw on students' prior knowledge. Sometimes the teacher needs to build students' background knowledge through new experiences before beginning to read.

2. **Make predictions.** The teacher shows the cover of the book, reads the title, and asks students to make predictions about the story using questions like these:

   What do you think a story with a title like this might be about?

   What do you think might happen in this story?

   Does this picture give you any ideas about what might happen in this story?

   If the title and cover illustration don't provide enough information, the teacher reads the first paragraph or two to provide more information for students to use in making their predictions. If a student makes an unreasonable prediction, the teacher follows up by asking the student to relate the prediction to the story's title or cover illustration. If the student can't make a reasonable prediction, the teacher encourages the student to consider another prediction based on the information presented.

3. **Read aloud to students.** After students make their predictions, the teacher reads part of the story aloud and then asks them to confirm or reconsider their predictions by answering questions such as:

   What do you think now?

   What do you think will happen next?

   What would happen if . . . ?

4. **Continue reading and predicting.** The teacher continues reading the story aloud, stopping at several pivotal points to repeat the third step. It is important to choose pivotal points to repeat the predicting step so that predicting really enhances students' comprehension of the story.

5. **Have students reflect on their predictions.** After listening to the story read aloud, students talk about the story, expressing their feelings and making connections to their own lives and experiences with literature. Then students reflect on the predictions they made as they listened to the story being read aloud and how those predictions influenced their understanding of the story.

a few words or a sentence. During an author unit on Eve Bunting, for instance, third graders, after listening to each story, record the title on a page in their reading logs and write a response telling what they liked about the story or what it made them think of. Figure 7–3 presents three entries from a third grader's reading log written during an author study on Eve Bunting. Older students write an entry after each chapter. After drawing and writing, students

FIGURE 7-3 *Three Entries From a Third Grader's Reading Log*

<u>Fly Away Home</u> by Eve Bunting

This book was so sad I stareted crying. Its sad to be homeless but Andrew has a lot of hope and hes going to get out just like the bird. Hes going to get a home again. I think everone shold have a home to live in.

<u>A Day's Work</u> by Eve Bunting

I liked this book alot. Francesco said his Abuelo was a fine gardner but he didn't know what to do. But they got to keep the jobs because they were honest. Weeds and flowers can look the same if your not a gardner.

weed | flower | weed

<u>The Blue And The Gray</u> by Eve Bunting

War is very sad. And the Civil War was brother agenst brother. People hate each other and solders fight and die. I think they shold always put a marker to show where they died. "I think the Angels wept." That means war is so very very very sad. I hope I am never in a war.

Piecing a Lesson Together

Topics on Aesthetic Listening

Procedures	Concepts	Strategies and Skills
Listen to a story read aloud	Aesthetic listening	Activate background knowledge
Respond to classmates' comments in a grand conversation	Difference between aesthetic and efferent listening	Predict
		Confirm
Listen to a poem read aloud	Concept of story	*Visualize*
Write a response in a reading log		Connect to personal experiences
Choose favorite quotations from a story		Connect to other stories
Work on projects		Notice the power and beauty of language
		Apply knowledge of text structure

Please visit the Companion Website at **www.prenhall.com/tompkins** for a second fully realized minilesson.

often share their reading logs with classmates, and this sharing provides another opportunity for classmates to listen aesthetically.

Minilessons.   Teachers teach minilessons to introduce, practice, and review procedures, concepts, and skills related to aesthetic listening. See these pages for a list of topics for minilessons related to aesthetic listening and the description of how Mrs. Armstrong taught a minilesson on visualization to her fourth graders. These minilessons about aesthetic listening are very important because students use the same strategies when they are reading stories independently. Often it is easier for teachers to teach strategies as students listen to

VISUALIZING

Minilesson

Mrs. Armstrong Teaches Visualizing to Her Fourth Graders

1. Introduce the Topic

Mrs. Armstrong introduces visualizing to her fourth-grade class. She explains that when she listens to a story read aloud, she makes pictures in her mind that go along with the story. She asks if they, too, make pictures in their minds, and many children agree that they do.

2. Share Examples

Mrs. Armstrong begins reading Judy Blume's *Tales of a Fourth Grade Nothing* (1972) and demonstrates how to create mind pictures of the characters and story events while reading aloud the first two chapters.

3. Provide Information

Mrs. Armstrong explains the steps she uses in creating mind pictures:

1. Close your eyes.
2. Draw a picture of a scene or character in your mind.
3. Listen for details and add them to your picture.
4. Add colors to your mind picture.

She creates a chart about visualizing, draws a person's head with a picture in it, and writes these four steps on the chart.

4. Supervise Practice

As Mrs. Armstrong continues reading the book aloud, students practice making mind pictures. She stops reading periodically to ask students to describe how they are using the strategy. The fourth graders especially enjoy creating mind pictures near the end of the book when Peter finds out that his little brother Fudge ate his turtle.

5. Reflect on Learning

After finishing the book, Mrs. Armstrong asks students to reflect on how they used the visualization strategy. One fourth grader explains:

I made a picture in my mind of how upset Peter was that Fudge ate his turtle. He was crazy for wanting to find his turtle and mad at his brother and because no one cared about his turtle, only about his brother. His face was red because he was crazy mad and he was yelling at Fudge and at his mom. He was crying and wiping at his eyes because his turtle's been eaten. Then I had a new picture in my mind when Peter got the big box with a puppy in it at the end. He was calm but not really happy. He was still sad about his turtle being dead. He had a smart look on his face because he knew it had to be a puppy and he thought to name him Turtle so he wouldn't forget. I see him holding the black and white dog and that dog is licking him all over his face.

a book read aloud than when students are reading on their own. What is important, however, is that teachers emphasize that students should apply what they are learning when they read.

Assessing Students' Aesthetic Listening

Students need to learn how to listen aesthetically so that they can engage more fully in the lived-through experience of literature. Teachers assess whether students are listening aesthetically in several ways. First, they judge the predictions students make as part of the Directed Listening-Thinking Activity to see that they are actively involved in listening to and thinking about the story being read aloud. Teachers also listen to the comments students make during grand conversations and read entries in students' reading logs to see whether they are using aesthetic listening strategies. Specifically, teachers can check that students are:

- Making predictions
- Visualizing
- Connecting to personal experience and to literature
- Revising meaning
- Playing with language from the story
- Summarizing main events of the story

Teachers can also check that students are transferring their use of these listening strategies to reading.

EFFERENT LISTENING

Efferent listening is practical listening to understand a message. The term *efferent,* first applied to language arts by Louise Rosenblatt (1978, 1983), means "carrying away." It is the most common type of listening students do in school. For example, a fifth-grade teacher who discusses the causes of the American Revolution, a first-grade teacher who explains how to dial 911 in an emergency, and an eighth-grade teacher who discusses the greenhouse effect are all providing information for students to relate to what they already know and remember. Students use efferent listening to identify and remember important pieces of information.

Whether students comprehend and remember the message is determined by many factors. Some of these factors are operative before listening, others during or after. First, students need a background of knowledge about the content they are listening to. They must be able to relate what they are about to hear to what they already know, and speakers can help provide some of these links. Second, as they listen, students use a strategy to help them remember. They organize and "chunk" the information they receive, and they may want to take notes to help them remember. Then, after listening, students should somehow apply what they have heard so that there is a reason to remember the information.

Strategies for Efferent Listening

Students use a variety of strategies as they listen efferently; some of the strategies are the same as for reading and writing, and others are unique to efferent listening. The purpose of each strategy is to help students organize and remember the information they are listening to. Six strategies elementary students use for efferent listening are:

1. Organizing. Informational presentations are usually organized in special ways called expository text structures. The five most common patterns are description, sequence, comparison, cause and effect, and problem and solution. Students learn to recognize these patterns and use them to understand and remember a speaker's message more easily. Speakers often use certain words to signal the organizational structures they are following. Signal words include *first, second, third, next, in contrast,* and *in summary.* Students can learn to attend to these signals to identify the organizational pattern the speaker is using.

• To learn more about the expository text structures, see Chapter 10, "Reading and Writing Information."

FIGURE 7-4 *A Sixth Grader's T-Chart Comparing Amphibians and Reptiles*

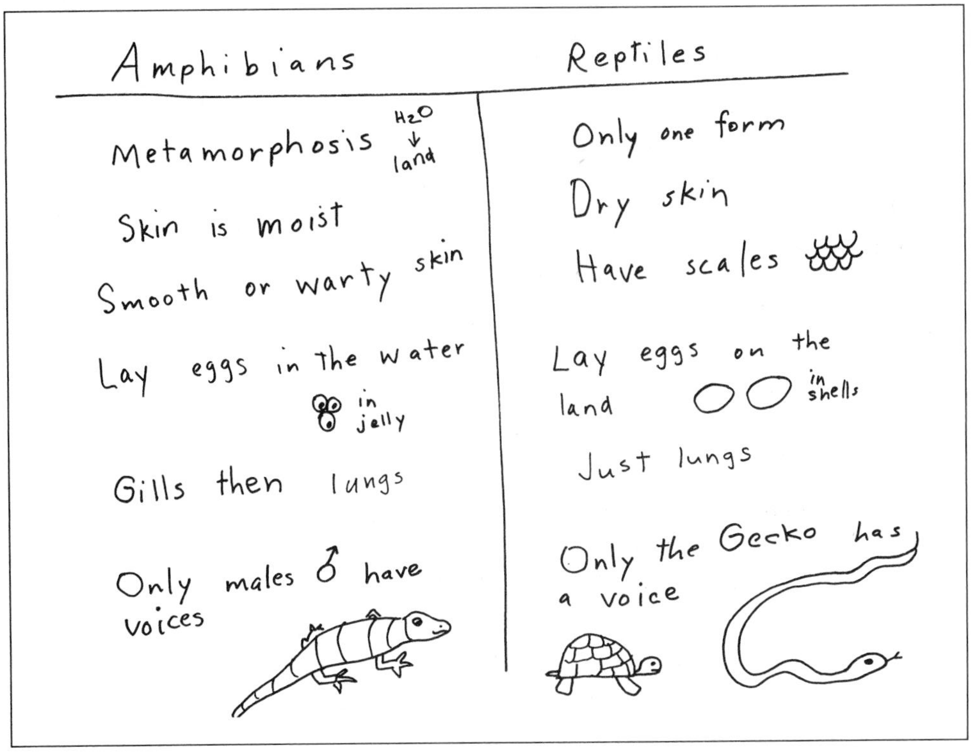

Students often use graphic organizers to visualize the organization of oral presentations, informational videos, or informational books (Yopp & Yopp, 2001). When students listen to a presentation comparing amphibians and reptiles, for example, students make T-charts or Venn diagrams to organize the information. Students can draw a two-column T-chart, labeling one column "Amphibians" and the other "Reptiles." Then students write notes in the columns while they listen to the presentation or immediately after listening. A sixth grader's T-chart comparing amphibians and reptiles is shown in Figure 7–4.

When students are listening to a presentation or an informational book that contains information on more than two or three categories, they can make a cluster diagram, write each category on a ray, and then add descriptive information. For example, when students are listening to a presentation on simple machines, they make a cluster with five rays, one for each type of simple machine. Then students add words and drawings to take notes about each type of simple machine. A fifth grader's cluster is shown in Figure 7–5.

2. Summarizing.   Speakers present several main ideas and many details during oral presentations, and students need to learn to focus on the main ideas in order to summarize. Otherwise, they try to remember everything and quickly feel overwhelmed. Once students can identify the main ideas, they can chunk the details to the main idea.

When teachers introduce the summarizing strategy, they ask students to listen for two or three main ideas. They write these ideas on the chalkboard and draw boxes around them. Then they give an oral presentation, having students raise their hands when they hear the first main idea stated. Students then raise

FIGURE 7-5   *Cluster Diagram on Simple Machines*

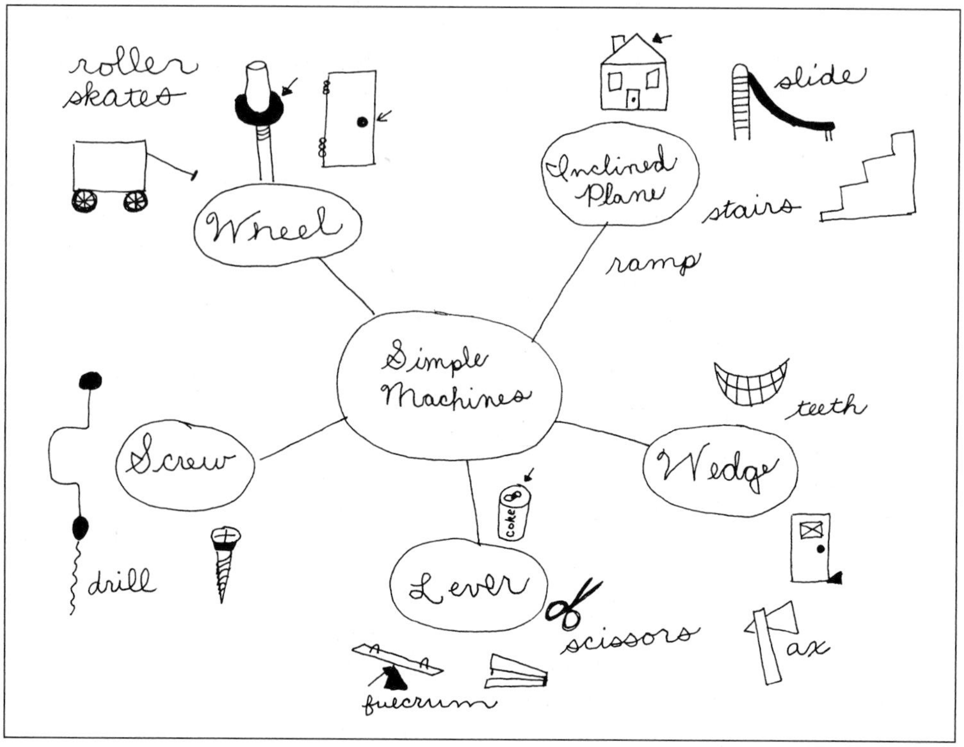

their hands when they hear the second main idea, and again for the third main idea. Once students gain practice in detecting already-stated main ideas, teachers give a very brief presentation with one main idea and ask students to identify the main idea. Once students can identify the main idea, teachers give longer oral presentations and ask students to identify two or three main ideas. A teacher might make these points when giving an oral presentation on simple machines:

1. There are five kinds of simple machines.
2. Simple machines are combined in specialized machines.
3. Machines make work easier.
4. Almost everything we do involves machines.

Once students can identify the main ideas during an oral presentation, they can chunk details to the main ideas. This hierarchical organization is the most economical way to remember information, and students need to understand that they can remember more information when they use the summarizing strategy.

   3. Note taking.   Students are more active listeners when they take notes. Devine describes note taking as "responding-with-pen-in-hand" (1981, p. 156). Students' interest in note taking begins with the realization that they cannot store unlimited amounts of information in their minds; they need some kind of external storage system. Many listening strategies require listeners to make written notes about what they are hearing. Note taking is often thought of as a listing or an outline, but notes can also be written in clusters and other diagrams.

   Teachers introduce note taking by taking notes with the class on the chalkboard. During an oral presentation, the teacher stops periodically, asks students to identify what important information was presented, and lists their responses on the chalkboard. Teachers often begin by writing notes in a list format, but the notes can also be written in outline or cluster formats. Similarly, the teacher can use key words, phrases, or sentences in recording notes. After an introduction to various note-taking strategies, students develop personal note-taking systems in which they write notes in their own words and use a consistent format.

Children's awareness of note taking as a strategy "to help you remember what you are listening to" begins in the primary grades. Teachers begin demonstrating the usefulness of note taking on the chalkboard or on charts with kindergartners and first graders. Second and third graders begin taking notes in their learning logs as a part of social studies and science classes.

Outlining is a useful note-taking strategy, but it has gained a bad reputation from misuse in secondary and college English and content-area classes (Devine, 1981). It may be preferable to introduce outlining with print materials, because oral presentations are often less structured than print materials and because students must discover the speaker's plan in order to outline. Teachers who want to teach outlining through oral presentations, however, should begin with a simple organization of perhaps three main ideas with two subordinate ideas for each main idea. Teachers can also give students a partial outline to complete during an oral presentation.

The information students include in the notes they take depends on their purpose for listening. Thus, it is essential that students understand the purpose for listening before they begin to take notes. Some listening tasks require noting main ideas or details; others require noting sequence, cause and effect, or comparisons.

Students can take notes from informational books they are reading and from reference materials; however, taking notes from a speaker is an equally important strategy. When they are taking notes from a speaker, students cannot control the speed at which information is presented. They usually cannot listen more than once to a speaker in order to complete their notes, and the structure of oral presentations is often not as formal as that of printed materials. Students need to become aware of these differences so that they can adapt their note-taking system to the mode of presentation.

4. Monitoring.   Students monitor whether they are understanding as they are listening. Monitoring is important because students need to know when they are not listening successfully or when a listening strategy is not working so that they can ask a question or apply fix-up strategies to correct the situation (Tompkins, Friend, & Smith, 1987). Students can use these self-questions to monitor their understanding as they begin to listen:

- Why am I listening to this message?
- Will I need to take notes?
- Does this information make sense to me?

These are possible questions to use during listening:

- Is my strategy still working?
- Am I organizing the information effectively?
- Is the speaker giving me cues about the organization of the message?
- Is the speaker giving me nonverbal cues, such as gestures and facial expressions?

These questions are appropriate after listening:

- Do I have questions for the speaker?
- Is any part of the message unclear?
- Are my notes complete?
- Did I make a good choice of strategies? Why or why not?

Students need to learn to select appropriate strategies for specific listening purposes. The choice depends on both the listener's and the speaker's purpose. Although students must decide which strategy to use before they begin to listen, they need to continue to monitor their selection during and after listening. Students can generate a list of questions to guide their selection of strategies and monitor their effectiveness.

5. Applying fix-up strategies.   When students are listening and something doesn't make sense, they must take action to resolve the problem. Otherwise, they are likely to become confused and frustrated. Often students ask a question to clarify information or eliminate confusion. Although asking questions can disturb other students and may interrupt the speaker's train of thought, students should usually be allowed to ask questions because confusion inhibits their listening and learning.

Asking questions is only one fix-up strategy. Other ways to fix comprehension problems include:

- Continue listening because the speaker may clarify, summarize, or review the point.
- Check any visual displays the speaker has presented.
- Make connections to what the listener already knows about the topic.
- Write down questions to ask later.

Students need to learn how to manage comprehension problems during listening to avoid becoming confused and frustrated. When readers don't understand something, they often turn back a page or two and reread, but listeners can't turn back unless they are listening to an audiotape or a video presentation.

6. Getting clues from the speaker.   Speakers use both visual and verbal cues to convey their messages and direct their listeners' attention. Visual cues include gesturing, writing or underlining important information on the chalkboard, and changing facial expressions. Verbal cues include pausing, raising or lowering the voice, slowing down speech to stress key points, and repeating important information. Surprisingly, many students are not aware of these attention-directing behaviors, so teachers must point them out. Once students are aware of these cues, they can use them to increase their understanding of a message.

Teaching Efferent Listening

Learning to listen efferently is an important school task, and students use efferent listening as they listen to presentations as part of theme cycles. Using the efferent listening strategies helps students remember information more efficiently and better understand the message they are listening to. Teachers need to explain the differences between aesthetic and efferent listening and teach students to use the efferent listening strategies.

Teachers teach students to listen more effectively by activating background knowledge before listening and using graphic organizers and note taking to remember information while listening. These approaches can also be used when students read informational books. Teachers also teach minilessons about procedures, concepts, and strategies and skills related to efferent listening. Then students use what they have learned about efferent listening as part of theme cycles and other across-the-curriculum learning.

Brainstorming Ideas.   Teachers encourage students to activate background knowledge and build on that knowledge before listening when they ask students to brainstorm ideas about a topic. Students talk about the topic and the teacher takes notes on chart paper, in list or cluster format. As students share ideas, the teacher asks them to elaborate, and the teacher clarifies any misconceptions. Or, the teacher can have students do a quickwrite on the topic, read their quickwrites in small groups, and then share them with the class. As students share with the class, the teacher takes notes on chart paper. After the oral presentation, students can add more information to the chart. Teachers often use one color of marking pen for the "before listening" information and another color for the "after listening" information to demonstrate the usefulness of the activity.

Anticipation Guides.   Teachers use anticipation guides to stimulate students' interest in a topic and activate their background knowledge before listening. Teachers present a set of statements related to the oral presentation; some of the statements are true and will be confirmed by the presentation, and other statements are false and will be corrected by the presentation. Students read and discuss each statement and mark whether they think it is true or false. Then students listen to the presentation and mark each statement again after listening (Head & Readence, 1986). An eighth-grade anticipation guide on the Crusades is presented in Figure 7–6. Notice that students mark whether they agree or disagree before listening on the left side of the paper and after listening on the right side of the paper. The steps in preparing anticipation guides are shown in the Step by Step feature on the next page.

FIGURE 7-6   *An Eighth-Grade Anticipation Guide*

Anticipation Guide on the Crusades					
Before				After	
T	F			T	F
		1. The Crusaders wanted to go to the Holy Land to meet Jesus.			
		2. The Crusades took place between 1096 and 1270.			
		3. The Crusaders fought the Muslims to recapture the Holy Land.			
		4. Only noblemen and rich people were allowed to go on the Crusades.			
		5. The Crusaders traveled to the Holy Land for religious reasons.			
		6. Because of the Crusades, Europeans were introduced to many luxuries, including sugar, silk, and glass mirrors.			

*Step
by
Step*

Anticipation Guides

1. **Identify several major concepts.**   Teachers consider their students' knowledge about the topic and any misconceptions students might have as they identify concepts related to their presentation.

2. **Develop a list of three to six statements.**   Teachers write a statement about each major concept they identified. These statements should be general enough to stimulate discussion, present major concepts, and help clarify misconceptions. The list can be written on a chart, or individual copies can be duplicated for each student.

3. **Discuss the statements on the anticipation guide.**   Teachers introduce the anticipation guide and have students respond to the statements. Students think about the statements and mark whether they are true or false.

4. **Listen to the presentation.**   Students listen to the oral presentation and note information that relates to the statements on the anticipation guide.

5. **Discuss the statements again.**   After listening, students reconsider their earlier responses to each statement and again mark whether the statements are true or false. Then students share their responses with the class. Sometimes the students also revise the false statements to make them true.

Students also use anticipation guides before reading informational books and content-area textbooks. Their purpose remains the same whether students are listening or reading.

Note Taking/Note Making.   Students often take notes as they listen efferently to oral presentations. Upper-grade students often use a special kind of note taking in which they divide their papers into two columns, labeling the left column "Take Notes" and the right column "Make Notes." They take notes in the left column, but, more important, they think about the notes, make connections, and personalize the notes in the right column (Berthoff, 1981). Students need to stop periodically and reflect on the notes they have taken. The right column should be more extensive than the left one. A sample note-taking and note-making sheet is presented in Figure 7–7. A fifth grader took these notes as she listened to a presentation about illegal drugs. Her comments in the "Make Notes" column are especially interesting because they show the connections she was making.

Reading Aloud Informational Books.   Teachers read aloud informational books during theme cycles. Informational books have the power to intrigue and excite students, and students use a combination of efferent and aesthetic listening because informational books provide both a literary and a learning experience (Vardell & Copeland, 1992). High-quality informational books, such as *Welcome to the Green House* (Yolen, 1993), *Wolves* (Simon, 1992), *Buffalo Hunt* (Freedman, 1988), *A River Ran Wild* (Cherry, 1992), and *Cleopatra* (Stanley & Vennema, 1994), cover a wide range of topics. Teachers often think about the

FIGURE 7–7 *A Fifth Grader's Note-Taking and Note-Making Sheet*

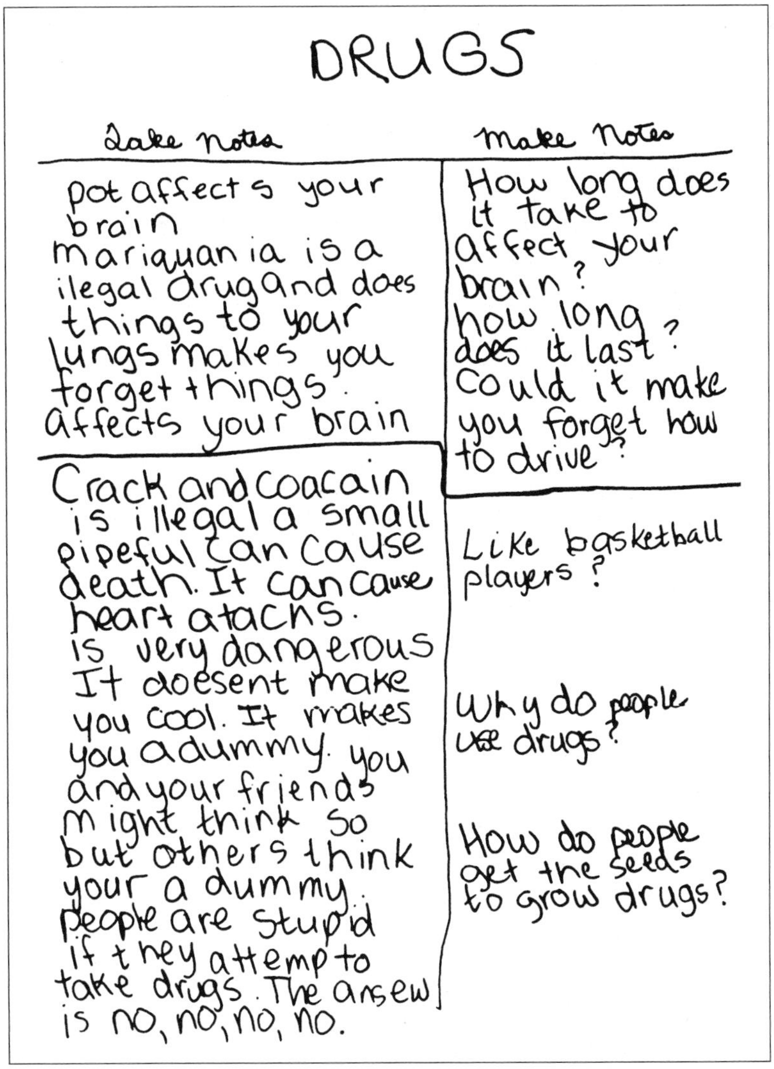

DRUGS

Take notes	Make Notes
pot affects your brain mariquania is a ilegal drug and does things to your lungs makes you forget things. affects your brain	How long does it take to affect your brain? how long does it last? Could it make you forget how to drive?
Crack and coacain is illegal a small pipeful can cause death. It can cause heart atacks. is very dangerous It doesent make you cool. It makes you a dummy. you and your friends might think so but others think your a dummy. People are stupid if they attemp to take drugs. The ansew is no, no, no, no.	Like basketball players? Why do people use drugs? How do people get the seeds to grow drugs?

instructional value of informational books when they read them aloud, but the books also captivate students' imaginations while they are learning.

Many different types of informational books can be shared with students. Some informational books incorporate a story frame, such as *The Magic School Bus in the Time of the Dinosaurs* (Cole, 1994) and others in the Magic School Bus series. Other informational books are written in rhyme. Ruth Heller's science books, including *The Reason for a Flower* (1983), and her books about words, such as *Up, Up and Away: A Book About Adverbs* (1991), are stunning. Biographies are another type of informational book, and they can be integrated into history theme cycles. Teachers also read aloud autobiographies of children's book authors, such as *Firetalking*, by Patricia Polacco (1994), and *A Letter From Phoenix Farm*, by Jane Yolen (1992b), in connection with author units.

There are many reasons to read aloud informational books (Vardell, 1996). Students learn content-area knowledge and specialized vocabulary. Teachers

Essentials

Guidelines for Reading Aloud Informational Books

1. **Choose High-Quality Books**

   Teachers choose high-quality informational books for theme-cycle text sets. Books should have visual appeal and relevance to the theme cycle or other unit.

2. **Share a Variety of Informational Books**

   Teachers read aloud storylike nonfiction, books with rhyming texts, alphabet and counting books, and biographies.

3. **Point Out Features of Informational Books**

   As teachers read aloud, they point out the unique features of informational books, including the table of contents, glossary, illustrations and diagrams, and index, and they demonstrate how to use them.

4. **Use the Reading Process**

   Although some stages may be abbreviated, teachers activate background knowledge, set purposes for listening, and provide opportunities for students to apply what they have learned.

5. **Read Books Aloud More Than Once**

   During the first reading, students may use primarily aesthetic listening; then, during the second reading, students focus on remembering information.

6. **Teach Efferent Listening Strategies**

   Teachers model and teach note taking and other efferent listening strategies when reading aloud informational books.

7. **Use Graphic Organizers**

   Teachers give students copies of a chart to complete while they listen or draw a diagram on the chalkboard to organize students' thinking before reading.

8. **Set Up a Listening Center**

   Teachers use listening centers so that students can listen to the informational book a second or third time. Listening centers can also be used instead of reading aloud to students.

9. **Plan Oral Performances**

   Teachers and students adapt informational books for readers theatre performances, choral reading, puppet shows, and other presentations.

introduce students to books they might not tackle on their own, and students often read books independently that have been read aloud to them. Students also learn about the genre of informational books and use the format when writing their own books.

Teachers use the reading process introduced in Chapter 3 to share informational books with students. Even though teachers often abbreviate some of the stages, it is important that they activate students' background knowledge and set a purpose before reading. When teachers set a purpose, students know how to focus their attention as they listen. Often teachers read an informational book twice. During the first reading, students often listen aesthetically and are immersed in the experience. Then, during the second reading, they focus their attention on the main ideas or important information. Teachers also use informational books to teach the efferent listening strategies. Guidelines for using informational books are listed in the LA Essentials box on page 320.

After reading, students need to talk about the book: They share interesting information, ask questions, clarify confusions, and respond to the listening experience. Teachers often have students complete graphic organizers, write in learning logs, and apply what they have learned. Students apply what they have learned as they create projects, including posters, oral reports, and found poems. Students can also write their own informational books and create information quilts—like story quilts, but with facts students have learned written and illustrated on each square. A class of first graders made an information quilt about penguins during a theme cycle on penguins; one square is shown in Figure 7–8.

FIGURE 7-8 *A Square for a First-Grade Information Quilt on Penguins*

Penguens like to eat lots of fish.

Piecing a Lesson Together

Topics on Efferent Listening

Procedures	Concepts	Strategies and Skills
Take notes	The listening process	Activate background knowledge
Do note taking/note making	Efferent listening	Categorize ideas
Use graphic organizers	Organizational patterns	Generalize
Participate in instructional	of informational texts	Monitor
conversations	Features of informational	Ask questions of the speaker
	books	Ask self-questions
		Note cue words

Get clues from the speaker

Make connections to the world
and other literature

 Please visit the Companion Website at
www.prenhall.com/tompkins for a second fully realized
minilesson.

Before making the quilt, students listened to the teacher read aloud several informational books on penguins and then wrote facts they learned on a class chart. Students referred to the chart when they made their quilt.

Minilessons. Because efferent listening is so important in learning across the curriculum, teachers should not assume that students already know how to listen to oral presentations of information. In addition to helping students with brainstorming ideas, using anticipation guides and graphic organizers, and note taking, teachers also teach minilessons about efferent listening. A list of minilesson topics for efferent listening is presented in the box on these pages, followed by a sample minilesson about getting clues from the speaker.

GETTING CLUES

Minilesson

Mrs. Rodriquez's Students Watch for Clues

1. **Introduce the Topic**

   Mrs. Rodriquez explains to her second graders that she often does some special things to get their attention and to tell them what information is most important when she teaches a lesson.

2. **Share Examples**

   Mrs. Rodriquez asks her students to watch her carefully as she begins a lesson about the body of an insect as part of a theme cycle on insects. Mrs. Rodriquez begins to speak, and she holds up three fingers as she explains that insects have three body parts. Next, she points to the three body parts on a nearby chart and names them, tapping each part with a pointer. Then she writes the names of the body parts on the chalkboard. Afterward, Mrs. Rodriquez asks students to remember what she did during the presentation, and the students correctly point out the three clues she used.

3. **Provide Information**

   Mrs. Rodriquez explains to students that teachers or other presenters often use clues to help listeners understand what is most important in a lesson. She explains that teachers use a variety of clues and asks her students to look for more clues as she continues the lesson. She demonstrates several more clues, including repeating an important fact and raising her voice for emphasis. Afterward, Mrs. Rodriquez asks students to identify the clues.

4. **Supervise Practice**

   The next day, Mrs. Rodriquez presents a lesson comparing insects and spiders, and she asks students to watch for her clues and to raise their hands to indicate that they noticed them. Afterward, she reviews the clues she used. She repeats this step for several additional lessons about insects.

5. **Reflect on Learning**

   Mrs. Rodriquez and her second graders make a list of clues she uses during a lesson, and students draw pictures to illustrate each clue they add to the list. Then they post the list in the classroom.

Assessing Students' Efferent Listening

Teachers often use objective tests to measure students' efferent listening. For example, if teachers have provided information about the causes of the American Revolution, how to dial 911 for an emergency, or the greenhouse effect, they can check the students' understanding of the information and infer whether students listened. However, teachers should assess students' listening more directly. Specifically, they should check how well students understand efferent listening procedures, concepts, strategies, and skills and how they apply them in listening activities. Asking students to reflect on and talk about the strategies they use and what they do before, during, and after listening provides insights into children's thinking in a way that objective tests cannot.

CRITICAL LISTENING

Students—even those in the primary grades—need to develop critical listening skills because they are exposed to many types of persuasion and propaganda. Interpreting books and films requires critical thinking and listening. And social studies and science lessons on topics such as pollution, political candidates, and drugs demand that students listen and think critically.

Television commercials are another form of persuasion and source of propaganda, and because many commercials are directed at children, it is essential that they listen critically and learn to judge the advertising claims. For example, do the jogging shoes actually help you run faster? Will the breakfast cereal make you a better football player? Will a particular toy make you a more popular child?

Persuasion and Propaganda

There are three basic ways to persuade people. The first is by reason. People seek logical conclusions, whether from absolute facts or from strong possibilities; for example, people can be persuaded to practice more healthful living as the result of medical research. It is necessary, of course, to distinguish between reasonable arguments and unreasonable appeals. To suggest that diet pills will bring about extraordinary weight loss is an unreasonable appeal.

A second means of persuasion is an appeal to character. We can be persuaded by what another person recommends if we trust that person. Trust comes from personal knowledge or the reputation of the person who is trying to persuade. We must always question whether we can believe the persuader. We can believe what scientists say about the dangers of nuclear waste, but can we believe what a sports personality says about the effectiveness of a particular sports shoe?

The third way to persuade people is by appealing to their emotions. Emotional appeals can be as strong as intellectual appeals. We have strong feelings and concern for ourselves and other people and animals. Fear, a need for peer acceptance, and a desire for freedom of expression are all potent feelings that influence our opinions and beliefs.

Any of the three types of appeals can be used to try to persuade someone. For example, when a child tries to convince her parents that her bedtime should be delayed by 30 minutes, she might argue that neighbors allow their children to stay up later—an appeal to character. It is an appeal to reason when the argument focuses on the amount of sleep a 10-year-old needs. And when the child announces that she has the earliest bedtime of anyone in her class and it makes her feel like a baby, the appeal is to emotion. The same three appeals apply to in-school persuasion. To persuade classmates to read a particular book in a book report "commercial," a student might argue that they should read the book because it is short and interesting (reason); because it is hilarious and they'll laugh (emotion); or because it is the most popular book in the second grade and everyone else is reading it (character).

Children need to learn to become critical consumers of advertisements (Lutz, 1989; Rudasill, 1986; Tutolo, 1981). Advertisers use appeals to reason, character, and emotion just as other persuaders do to promote products, ideas, and services; however, advertisers may also use propaganda to influence our beliefs and actions. Propaganda suggests something shady or underhanded. Like persuasion, propaganda is designed to influence people's beliefs and actions, but propagandists may use certain techniques to distort, conceal, and exaggerate. Two of these techniques are deceptive language and propaganda devices.

People seeking to influence us often use words that evoke a variety of responses. They claim that something is "improved," "more natural," or "50% better"—loaded words and phrases that are deceptive because they are suggestive. When a product is advertised as 50% better, for example, consumers need to ask, "50% better than what?" Advertisements rarely answer that question.

Doublespeak is another type of deceptive language characterized as evasive, euphemistic, confusing, and self-contradictory. It is language that "pretends to communicate but really does not" (Lutz, 1991, p. 17). Lutz cites a number of kinds of doublespeak, and elementary students can easily understand two kinds: euphemisms and inflated language. Euphemisms are words or phrases (e.g., "passed away") that are used to avoid a harsh or distasteful reality, often out of concern for someone's feelings rather than to deceive. Inflated language includes words intended to make the ordinary seem extraordinary. Thus, car mechanics become "automotive internists," and used cars become "pre-owned" or "experienced" cars. Examples of deceptive language are listed in Figure 7–9. Children need to learn that people sometimes use words that only pretend to communicate; sometimes they use words to intentionally misrepresent, as when someone advertises a vinyl wallet as "genuine imitation leather" or a ring with a glass stone as a "faux diamond." Children need to be able to interpret deceptive language and to avoid using it themselves.

To sell products, advertisers use propaganda devices, such as testimonials, the bandwagon effect, and rewards. Eight devices that elementary students can learn to identify are listed in Figure 7–10. Students can listen to commercials to find examples of each propaganda device and discuss the effect the device has

FIGURE 7–9

Examples of Deceptive Language

Loaded Words	Doublespeak
best buy	bathroom tissue (toilet paper)
better than	civil disorder (riot)
carefree	correctional facility (jail, prison)
discount	dentures (false teeth)
easier	disadvantaged (poor)
extra strong	encore telecast (rerun)
fortified	funeral director (undertaker)
fresh	genuine imitation leather (vinyl)
guaranteed	inner city (slum, ghetto)
improved	memorial park (cemetery)
longer lasting	mobile home (house trailer)
lowest	nervous wetness (sweat)
maximum	occasional irregularity (constipation)
more natural	passed away (died)
more powerful	people expressways (sidewalks)
new/newer	personal flotation device (life preserver)
plus	pre-owned or experienced (used)
stronger	pupil station (student's desk)
ultra	senior citizen (old person)
virtually	terminal living (dying)

Lutz, 1989.

FIGURE 7-10

Propaganda Devices

1. Glittering Generality

Generalities such as "motherhood," "justice," and "The American Way" are used to enhance the quality of a product or the character of a political figure. Propagandists select a generality (such as motherhood or patriotism) so attractive that listeners do not challenge the speaker's real point.

2. Testimonial

To persuade people to purchase a product, an advertiser associates it with a popular personality, such as an athlete or a film star. For example, "Bozo Cereal must be good because Joe Footballstar eats it every morning." Listeners consider whether the person offering the testimonial has the expertise to judge the quality of the product.

3. Transfer

Persuaders try to transfer the prestige of a person or object to another person or object that will then be accepted. A film star, for example, is shown using Super Soap, and viewers are to believe that they can have youthful skin if they use this soap. Likewise, politicians appear with famous athletes or entertainers so that the luster of the stars will rub off on them.

4. Name Calling

Advertisers try to pin a bad label on something they want listeners to dislike. In a discussion of health insurance, for example, an opponent may call the sponsor of a bill a socialist. Whether or not the sponsor is a socialist does not matter to the name caller; the purpose is to cause unpleasant associations to rub off on the victim. Listeners consider the effect the label has on the product.

5. Card Stacking

Persuaders often choose only items that favor one side of an issue. Unfavorable facts are ignored. To be objective, listeners seek information about other viewpoints.

6. Bandwagon

This technique appeals to people's need to be a part of a group. Advertisers claim that everyone is using this product and you should, too. For example, "More physicians recommend this pill than any other." Listeners ask: Does everyone really use this product? What is it better than?

7. Snob Appeal

Persuaders use snob appeal to attract the attention of people who want to be part of an exclusive group. Advertisements for expensive clothes, cosmetics, and gourmet foods often use this technique. Listeners consider whether the product is of high quality or merely has an expensive name tag.

8. Rewards

Advertisers often offer rewards for buying their products. For example, cereal products offer toys. Adults are lured by this device, too; gifts, rebates from manufacturers, and low-cost financing are offered with expensive items. Listeners consider the value of rewards and how they increase the product's cost.

Techniques 1–5 adapted from Devine, 1982.

on them. They can also investigate to see how the same devices vary in commercials directed toward youngsters, teenagers, and adults. For instance, a commercial for a snack food with a sticker or toy in the package will appeal to a youngster, and a videotape recorder advertisement offering a factory rebate will appeal to an adult. The propaganda device for both ads is the same: a reward! Propaganda devices can be used to sell ideas as well as products. Public service announcements about smoking or wearing seat belts, as well as political advertisements, endorsements, and speeches, use these devices.

When students locate advertisements and commercials they believe are misleading or deceptive, they can write letters of complaint to the following watchdog agencies:

Action for Children's Television
46 Austin St.
Newton, MA 02160

Children's Advertising Review Unit
Council of Better Business Bureaus
845 Third Ave.
New York, NY 10022

Federal Trade Commission
Pennsylvania Ave. at Sixth St. NW
Washington, DC 20580

Zillions Ad Complaints
256 Washington St.
Mt. Vernon, NY 10553

In their letters, students should carefully describe the advertisement and explain what bothers them about it. They should also tell where and when they saw or heard the advertisement or commercial.

Strategies for Critical Listening

Listening critically means evaluating the message, and the most important strategy for critical listening is evaluating (Lundsteen, 1979). Students use the evaluating strategy to determine and judge the author's message. Students consider a variety of points simultaneously:

- What is the speaker's or author's purpose?
- Is there an intellectual appeal?
- Is there a character appeal?
- Is there an emotional appeal?
- Are illustrations persuasive?
- Are propaganda devices being used?
- Are deceptive words or inflated language used?

As students listen to books read aloud, view commercials and advertisements, and listen to speakers, they need to ask themselves these questions in order to critically evaluate the message.

Students also use efferent listening strategies during critical listening because critical listening is an extension of efferent listening. They organize ideas, generalize main ideas, and monitor their understanding of the presentation. With this foundation, students evaluate the message.

Teaching Critical Listening

The steps in teaching students to be critical listeners are similar to the steps in teaching aesthetic and efferent listening strategies. In this teaching strategy, students view commercials to examine propaganda devices and persuasive language. Later, they can create their own commercials and advertisements. The steps are shown in the Step by Step feature on page 328.

Step by Step

Creating Commercials and Advertisements

1. **Introduce commercials.** Talk about commercials and ask students about familiar commercials. Videotape some commercials and view them with students. Discuss the purpose of each commercial. Use these questions about commercials to probe students' thinking about persuasion and propaganda:

   - What is the speaker's purpose?
   - What are the speaker's credentials?
   - Is there evidence of bias?
   - Does the speaker use deceptive language?
   - Does the speaker make sweeping generalizations or unsupported inferences?
   - Do opinions predominate the talk?
   - Does the speaker use any propaganda devices?
   - Do you accept the message? (Devine, 1982, pp. 41–42)

2. **Explain deceptive language.** Present the terms *persuasion* and *propaganda*. Introduce the propaganda devices and view the commercials again to look for examples of each device. Introduce loaded words and doublespeak, and view the commercials a third time to look for examples of deceptive language.

3. **Analyze deceptive language.** Have students work in small groups to critique a commercial as to type of persuasion, propaganda devices, and deceptive language. Students might also want to test the claims made in the commercial.

4. **Review concepts.** Review the concepts about persuasion, propaganda devices, and deceptive language introduced in the first three steps. It may be helpful for students to make charts about these concepts.

5. **Provide practice.** Present a new set of videotaped commercials for students to critique. Ask them to identify persuasion, propaganda devices, and deceptive language in the commercials.

6. **Create commercials.** Have students apply what they have learned about persuasion, propaganda devices, and deceptive language by creating their own products and writing and producing their own commercials to advertise them. Possible products include breakfast cereals, toys, beauty and diet products, and sports equipment. Students might also create homework and house-sitting services to advertise, or they can choose community or environmental issues to campaign for or against. As the students present the commercials, classmates act as critical listeners to detect persuasion, propaganda devices, loaded words, and doublespeak.

Using Advertisements.   Students can use the same procedures and activities with advertisements they collect from magazines and product packages. Have children collect advertisements and display them on a bulletin board. Written advertisements also use deceptive language and propaganda devices. Students examine advertisements and then decide how the writer is trying to persuade them to purchase the product. They can also compare the amount of text to the amount of pictures. Students often notice that toy advertisements feature large, colorful pictures and that cosmetic advertisements feature pictures of beautiful women, whereas advertisements for medicines devote more space to text. They also point out sports stars and entertainment personalities in many advertisements. Even primary-grade students recognize intellectual, character, and emotional appeals in these advertisements.

Students often apply what they have learned about persuasion in advertisements they create. Students can create advertisements as part of literature focus units, reading workshop, and theme cycles. Figure 7–11 shows the "Wanted" poster a second grader made after reading *Sylvester and the Magic Pebble* (Steig, 1969), the story of a donkey who is lost after he is magically turned into a stone. Before students made these posters, the teacher taught a minilesson about persuasion and shared examples of advertisements with the

FIGURE 7-11   *A Second Grader's "Wanted" Poster*

CLASSROOM LIBRARY

Books That Encourage Critical Listening

Avi. (1991). *Nothing but the truth.* New York: Orchard. (U)

Babbit, N. (1975). *Tuck everlasting.* New York: Farrar, Straus & Giroux. (U)

Bunting, E. (1994). *Smoky night.* San Diego: Harcourt Brace. (M)

Cohen, B. (1983). *Molly's pilgrim.* New York: Lothrop, Lee & Shepard. (M)

Cowcher, H. (1990). *Antarctica.* New York: Farrar, Straus & Giroux. (P–M)

Ellis, D. (2000). *The breadwinner.* Toronto: Groundwood. (M–U)

Gantos, J. (2000). *Joey Pigza loses control.* New York: Farrar, Straus & Giroux. (M–U)

Haddix, M. P. (1998). *Among the hidden.* New York: Aladdin. (U)

Hesse, K. (2001). *Witness.* New York: Scholastic. (U)

Jeffers, S. (1991). *Brother eagle, sister sky.* New York: Dial. (M)

Knight, M. B. (1993). *Who belongs here? An American story.* Gardiner, ME: Tilbury House. (M)

Lowry, L. (1993). *The giver.* Boston: Houghton Mifflin. (U)

Lowry, L. (2003). *The silent boy.* Boston: Houghton Mifflin. (U)

Meunier, B. (2003). *Pipolo and the roof dogs.* New York: Dutton. (M)

Morimoto, J. (1987). *My Hiroshima.* New York: Puffin. (M)

Naylor, P. R. (1991). *Shiloh.* New York: Macmillan. (M–U)

Ringgold, F. (1996). *My dream of Martin Luther King.* New York: Crown. (M)

Scieszka, J. (1989). *The true story of the 3 little pigs!* New York: Viking. (P–M)

Siebert, D. (1991). *Sierra.* New York: HarperCollins. (M–U)

Spinelli, J. (1997). *Wringer.* New York: HarperCollins. (M–U)

Turner, A. (1987). *Nettie's trip south.* New York: Macmillan. (M)

Van Allsburg, C. (1986). *The stranger.* Boston: Houghton Mifflin. (M)

Whelan, G. (2000). *Homeless bird.* New York: HarperCollins. (U)

Williams, S. A. (1992). *Working cotton.* Orlando, FL: Harcourt Brace. (P–M)

Yolen, J. (1992). *Encounter.* Orlando, FL: Harcourt Brace. (M)

Zolotow, C. (1972). *William's doll.* New York: Harper & Row. (P)

P = primary grades (K–2); M = middle grades (3–5); U = upper grades (6–8).

students. With this introduction, students decided to feature large pictures of the donkey, emotional appeals, reward offers, and their telephone numbers. Students can also make advertisements about their favorite books as part of reading workshop, and make recycling, antidrug, and safe-driving advertisements during theme cycles.

Teaching With Trade Books. A variety of stories, informational books, and poetry encourage critical thinking. When teachers read aloud stories such as *The Giver* (Lowry, 1993) and *The True Story of the 3 Little Pigs!* (Scieszka, 1989), students use both aesthetic and critical listening. They use critical listening to evaluate the theme of *The Giver* and to determine whether the wolf's story is believable. When students listen to informational books such as *Antarctica* (Cowcher, 1990) and *Encounter* (Yolen, 1992a), they confront important ecological and social issues. The books provide information about the issues, and classmates share their ideas during discussions. Through these activities, students think more deeply about controversial issues and challenge and expand their own beliefs. Even some books of poetry

Meeting the Needs of Every Student

How Can I Help My Students Who Aren't Good Listeners?

Teachers often read aloud grade-appropriate books that are too difficult for some students to read independently. The idea is that even if students can't read the words, they can understand the ideas presented in the book. This read-aloud strategy works for many students, but for others, it does not. Students may lack sufficient background knowledge on the topic or be overwhelmed by unfamiliar vocabulary words in the book. Students may not listen strategically or may not be interested in the book. You can solve these problems. You can build background knowledge before reading by showing a video, reading a picture book, or sharing a story box of objects. At the same time you're building background knowledge, introduce key vocabulary words, and while reading, briefly explain unfamiliar vocabulary words; sometimes providing a synonym is enough. In addition, struggling students may not know how to listen. It's important to teach the listening process and ask students to use strategies, such as visualizing, while they listen. Finally, struggling students often complain that a book is "boring," but what they mean is that they don't understand it. Making sure that students understand often takes care of their seeming disinterest; however, if the book really doesn't interest students, you can create interest by making connections with students' own lives, showing the video version of the story, or asking students to assume a role as a character and dramatize events from the story. If none of these strategies work, then choose a different book to read.

To investigate other ways to meet the needs of every student, visit the links for this chapter on the Companion Website at www.prenhall.com/tompkins

Companion Website

stimulate critical listening. *Sierra* (Siebert, 1991), for example, a book-length poem about this western mountain range, ends with a warning about the threat people pose to the environment. A list of these and other books that encourage critical listening (and thinking) is presented in the Classroom Library box on page 330.

Minilessons. Teachers also teach minilessons to introduce, practice, and review procedures, concepts, and strategies and skills related to critical listening. See pages 332–333 for a list of topics for minilessons on critical listening and a sample minilesson. These topics can be taught when students are studying commercials or writing advertisements as part of a social studies or science theme cycle, or they can be taught as minilessons during reading and writing workshop.

Piecing a Lesson Together

Topics on Critical Listening

Procedures	Concepts	Strategies and Skills
Write advertisements Make storyboards Film commercials	Critical listening **Three types of persuasion** Propaganda Persuasion compared to propaganda Deceptive language Propaganda devices	Evaluate the message Determine the speaker's purpose Recognize appeals Recognize deceptive language Identify propaganda devices

Please visit the Companion Website at **www.prenhall.com/tompkins** for a second fully realized minilesson.

Meeting the Needs of Every Student

Because listening is the language mode used most often, it is especially important that all students be effective listeners. Too often, teachers simply admonish students to listen or assume that students are listening because they are sitting quietly. To become effective listeners, students need to learn how to vary the way they listen for different purposes and how to use the listening strategies presented in this chapter. See the Meeting the Needs of Every Student feature on page 331 for suggestions about adapting listening instruction to meet the needs of all students.

PERSUASION

Ms. Scott's Students Learn the Types of Persuasion

1. **Introduce the Topic**

   Mr. Scott's seventh graders are beginning a unit on persuasion, and he explains that persuasion means that someone tries to get someone else to do something. The students offer examples of persuasion from their own lives, which Mr. Scott lists on the chalkboard.

2. **Share Examples**

   Mr. Scott shows three television commercials that he has videotaped and asks students what each is trying to persuade them to do.

3. **Provide Information**

   Mr. Scott explains that there are three ways to persuade people: information, character, and emotion. Then he plays each commercial again and asks students to name the type of persuasion and how the commercial emphasizes its appeal.

4. **Supervise Practice**

   Mr. Scott shows several additional commercials, and students work in small groups to name the type of persuasion and how the commercial emphasizes its appeal. Then Mr. Scott distributes copies of advertisements for students to examine in small groups. Again, the students work to name the type of persuasion and how the advertisement emphasizes its appeal. The students also prepare and present impromptu commercials using one of the three types of persuasion for products they created. One group, for example, advertises a candy bar that promises great intelligence, using data from report cards they created in their "information" appeal.

5. **Reflect on Learning**

   The seventh graders attend an assembly to listen to candidates running for Student Council give speeches, and as they listen to the speeches, they try to identify the type of persuasion the candidates use. After the assembly, the students return to class and analyze the candidates' use of persuasion in their speeches. Finally, they discuss how their knowledge about the types of persuasion influenced the way they listened to the speeches.

Assessing Students' Critical Listening

After teaching about persuasion and propaganda, teachers can assess students' knowledge of critical listening by having them view and critique commercials, advertisements, and other oral presentations. They can note the critical listening procedures, strategies, and skills their students use. A second way to assess students' understanding of critical listening is to have them develop their own commercials and advertisements. Critical listening goes beyond one unit, however, and is something that teachers should return to again and again during the school year.

Review

Listening is the most basic and most used of the language modes. Despite its importance, listening instruction has been neglected in elementary classrooms. Students vary the way they listen for different purposes, and they use different procedures, strategies, and skills for each type of listening. The key concepts presented in this chapter are:

1. Listening is the neglected language art because it is rarely taught; instead, teachers admonish students to listen or merely provide practice activities.
2. Listening is a three-step process: receiving, attending, and assigning meaning.
3. There are four types of listening: discriminative, aesthetic, efferent, and critical.
4. Students listen aesthetically as teachers read stories aloud and while viewing puppet shows, plays, and video versions of stories.
5. The Directed Listening-Thinking Activity (DL-TA) is one way to actively involve students in aesthetic listening.
6. During theme cycles, students use efferent listening to remember information and critical listening to evaluate a message.
7. Students need to learn to use listening strategies to enhance their listening abilities.
8. Teachers introduce listening strategies during minilessons and then provide opportunities for students to use the strategies during literature focus units and theme cycles.
9. Students need to learn to listen critically because they are exposed to many types of persuasion and propaganda.
10. Students apply what they learn about persuasion and propaganda as they create commercials and advertisements.

Visit Chapter 7 on the Companion Website at www.prenhall.com/ tompkins to:

- **Check your understanding of the concepts presented in the chapter**
- **Access the Extensions (activities and a list of related readings)**
- **Link to related websites**

Professional References

Anderson, H. (1949). Teaching the art of listening. *School Review, 57,* 63–67.

Barrentine, S. J. (1996). Engaging with reading through interactive read-alouds. *The Reading Teacher, 50,* 36–43.

Beaver, J. M. (1982). Say it! over and over. *Language Arts, 59,* 143–148.

Berthoff, A. E. (1981). *The making of meaning.* Montclair, NJ: Boynton/Cook.

Brent, R., & Anderson, P. (1993). Developing children's classroom listening strategies. *The Reading Teacher, 47,* 122–126.

Cullinan, B. E. (1987). Inviting readers to literature. In B. E. Cullinan (Ed.), *Children's*

literature in the reading program (pp. 2–14). Newark, DE: International Reading Association.

Devine, T. G. (1978). Listening: What do we know after fifty years of theorizing? *Journal of Reading, 21,* 296–304.

Devine, T. G. (1981). *Teaching study skills: A guide for teachers.* Boston: Allyn & Bacon.

Devine, T. G. (1982). *Listening skills schoolwide: Activities and programs.* Urbana, IL: ERIC Clearinghouse on Reading and Communication Skills and the National Council of Teachers of English.

Erickson, A. (1985). Listening leads to reading. *Reading Today, 2,* 13.

Foulke, E. (1968). Listening comprehension as a function of word rate. *Journal of Communication, 18,* 198–206.

Green, D. H. (1989). Beyond books: Literature on the small screen. In M. K. Rudman (Ed.), *Children's literature: Resources for the classroom* (pp. 207–217). Norwood, MA: Christopher-Gordon.

Head, M. H., & Readence, J. E. (1986). Anticipation guides: Meaning through prediction. In E. K. Dishner, T. W. Bean, J. E. Readence, & D. W. Moore (Eds.), *Reading in the content areas* (2nd ed.) (pp. 229–234). Dubuque, IA: Kendall/Hunt.

Jalongo, M. R. (1991). *Strategies for developing children's listening skills* (Phi Delta Kappan Fastback Series #314). Bloomington, IN: Phi Delta Kappa Educational Foundation.

Kucer, S. B. (1991). Authenticity as the basis for instruction. *Language Arts, 68,* 532–540.

Landry, D. (1969). The neglect of listening. *Elementary English, 46,* 599–605.

Lundsteen, S. W. (1979). *Listening: Its impact on reading and the other language arts* (Rev. ed.). Urbana, IL: National Council of Teachers of English.

Lutz, W. (1989). *Doublespeak.* New York: HarperCollins.

Lutz, W. (1991). Notes toward a description of doublespeak (Revised). In W. Gibson & W. Lutz (Eds.), *Doublespeak: A brief history, definition, and bibliography, with a list of award winners, 1974–1990* (Concept Paper No. 2). Urbana, IL: National Council of Teachers of English.

Martinez, M. G., & Roser, N. L. (1985). Read it again: The value of repeated readings during storytime. *The Reading Teacher, 38,* 782–786.

Martinez, M., & Teale, W. H. (1988). Reading in a kindergarten classroom library. *The Reading Teacher, 41,* 568–572.

Pearson, P. D., & Fielding, L. (1982). Research update: Listening comprehension. *Language Arts, 59,* 617–629.

Pinnell, G. S., & Jaggar, A. M. (1991). Oral language: Speaking and listening in the classroom. In. J. Flood, J. M. Jensen, D. Lapp, & J. R. Squire (Eds.), *Handbook of research on the teaching of the English language arts* (pp. 691–742). New York: Macmillan.

Rankin, P. R. (1926). The importance of listening ability. *English Journal, 17,* 623–640.

Rosenblatt, L. M. (1978). *The reader, the text, the poem: The transactional theory of the literary work.* Carbondale: Southern Illinois University Press.

Rosenblatt, L. M. (1983). *Literature as exploration* (4th ed.). New York: Modern Language Association.

Rosenblatt, L. M. (1985). Viewpoints: Transaction versus interaction: A terminological rescue operation. *Research in the Teaching of English, 19,* 98–107.

Rosenblatt, L. M. (1991). Literature: S.O.S.! *Language Arts, 68,* 444–448.

Rudasill, L. (1986). Advertising gimmicks: Teaching critical thinking. In J. Golub (Ed.), *Activities to promote critical thinking (Classroom practices in teaching English)* (pp. 127–129). Urbana, IL: National Council of Teachers of English.

Sipe, L. R. (2002). Talking back and taking over: Young children's expressive engagement during storybook read-alouds. *The Reading Teacher, 55,* 476–483.

Stauffer, R. G. (1975). *Directing the reading-thinking process.* New York: Harper & Row.

Sticht, T. G., & James, J. H. (1984). Listening and reading. In P. D. Pearson (Ed.), *Handbook of reading research* (pp. 293–318). New York: Longman.

Strother, D. B. (1987). Practical applications of research: On listening. *Phi Delta Kappan, 68,* 625–628.

Tompkins, G. E., Friend, M., & Smith, P. L. (1987). Strategies for more effective listening. In C. R. Personke & D. D. Johnson (Eds.), *Language arts and the beginning teacher* (Chapter 3). Upper Saddle River, NJ: Prentice Hall.

Trelease, J. (2001). *The read-aloud handbook* (5th ed.). New York: Penguin.

Tutolo, D. (1981). Critical listening/reading of advertisements. *Language Arts, 58,* 679–683.

Vardell, S. M. (1996). The language of facts: Using nonfiction books to support language growth. In A. A. McClure & J. V. Kristo (Eds.), *Books that invite talk, wonder, and play* (pp. 59–77). Urbana, IL: National Council of Teachers of English.

Vardell, S. M., & Copeland, K. A. (1992). Reading aloud and responding to nonfiction: Let's talk about it. In E. B. Freeman & D. G. Person (Eds.), *Using nonfiction trade books in the elementary classroom: From ants to zeppelins* (pp. 76–85). Urbana, IL: National Council of Teachers of English.

Werner, E. K. (1975). *A study of communication time.* Unpublished master's thesis, University of Maryland, College Park.

Wilt, M. E. (1950). A study of teacher awareness of listening as a factor in elementary

education. *Journal of Educational Research, 43,* 626–636.

Wolvin, A. D., & Coakley, C. G. (1979). *Listening Instruction* (TRIP Booklet). Urbana, IL: ERIC Clearinghouse on Reading and Communication Skills and the Speech Communication Association.

Wolvin, A. D., & Coakley, C. G. (1985). *Listening* (2nd ed.). Dubuque, IA: William C. Brown.

Yaden, D. B., Jr. (1988). Understanding stories through repeated read-alouds: How many does it take? *The Reading Teacher, 41,* 556–560.

Yopp, H. K., & Yopp, R. H. (2001). *Literature-based reading activities* (3rd ed.). Boston: Allyn & Bacon.

Children's Book References

Aliki. (1979). *Mummies made in Egypt.* New York: HarperCollins.

Avi. (1991). *Nothing but the truth.* New York: Orchard.

Blume, J. (1972). *Tales of a fourth grade nothing.* New York: Dutton.

Cherry, L. (1992). *A river ran wild.* Orlando: Harcourt Brace.

Cole, J. (1994). *The magic school bus in the time of the dinosaurs.* New York: Scholastic.

Cowcher, H. (1990). *Antarctica.* New York: Farrar, Straus & Giroux.

Cushman, K. (1994). *Catherine, called Birdy.* New York: HarperCollins.

Freedman, R. (1988). *Buffalo hunt.* New York: Holiday House.

Galdone, P. (1985). *Little Red Hen.* New York: Clarion.

Guiberson, B. Z. (1991). *Cactus hotel.* New York: Henry Holt.

Hall, D. (1994). *I am the dog/I am the cat.* New York: Dial.

Heller, R. (1983). *The reason for a flower.* New York: Putnam.

Heller, R. (1991). *Up, up and away: A book about adverbs.* New York: Grosset & Dunlap.

Lasky, K. (1996). *Surtsey: The newest place on earth.* New York: Hyperion.

Livingston, M. C. (Sel.). (1991). *Lots of limericks.* New York: McElderry Books.

Lowry, L. (1993). *The giver.* Boston: Houghton Mifflin.

Morris, A. (1989). *Bread, bread, bread.* New York: HarperCollins.

Moss, L. (1995). *Zin! Zin! Zin! A violin.* New York: Simon & Schuster.

Polacco, P. (1990). *Thunder cake.* New York: Philomel.

Polacco, P. (1994). *Firetalking.* Katonah, NY: Richard C. Owen.

Scieszka, J. (1989). *The true story of the 3 little pigs!* New York: Viking.

Seuss, Dr. (1965). *Fox in socks.* New York: Random House.

Shaw, N. (1992). *Sheep out to eat.* Boston: Houghton Mifflin.

Siebert, D. (1991). *Sierra.* New York: HarperCollins.

Simon, S. (1992). *Wolves.* New York: HarperCollins.

Speare, E. G. (1983). *The sign of the beaver.* Boston: Houghton Mifflin.

Stanley, D., & Vennema, P. (1994). *Cleopatra.* New York: Morrow Junior Books.

Steig, W. (1969). *Sylvester and the magic pebble.* New York: Simon & Schuster.

Stevens, J., & Crummel, S. S. (1999). *Cook-a-doodle-doo!* San Diego: Harcourt Brace.

Uchida, Y. (1993). *The bracelet.* New York: Philomel.

White, E. B. (1980). *Charlotte's web.* New York: HarperCollins.

Yolen, J. (1992a). *Encounter.* Orlando: Harcourt Brace.

Yolen, J. (1992b). *A letter from Phoenix Farm.* Katonah, NY: Richard C. Owen.

Yolen, J. (1993). *Welcome to the green house.* New York: Putnam.

Zemach, M. (1983). *The Little Red Hen: An old story.* New York: Farrar, Straus & Giroux.

Sustaining Talk in the Classroom

PATTERNS OF PRACTICE

Reading and
Writing
Workshop

Literature
Focus
Units

**Literature
Circles**

Theme
Cycles

In addition to guided reading lessons, the students in Mrs. Zumwalt's third-grade class participate in literature circles each day because she knows that these students need lots of reading practice and opportunities to talk about books. For 30 minutes each day, they read or talk about the easy chapter books they are reading in small groups. Most of her students are English learners (ELs) who read a year below grade level, so Mrs. Zumwalt works hard to find easy-to-read chapter books that will interest them. The box on page 340 lists 20 of the books that Mrs. Zumwalt has in her classroom.

One small group of students is reading *The Cat's Meow* (Soto, 1987), the story of a white cat named Pip who speaks Spanish to Graciela, the little girl who owns him. Spanish words are included in the text. All but one of the students in this group speak Spanish at home, so they feel very comfortable with the inclusion of the Spanish words.

Yesterday, the five students in the group read the first chapter, and now they're talking about the story. Mrs. Zumwalt joins the group for a few min-

utes. The discussion focuses on whether the cat can really speak Spanish or whether it is just Graciela's imagination at work.

Armando: That girl knows Spanish, so it could be that she is just pretending. She really could be just thinking those Spanish words. And it says that her mom and dad are weird. Maybe she comes from a weird family. That's what I think.

Maricela: I think Pip can speak Spanish, but she will just speak to that girl and no one else.

Marcos: Yeah, I think Pip can talk in Spanish. That would be cool.

Rubin: No, Armando. It's for real, man. The cat—what's his name?

Linda: Pip, and she's a girl, not a boy.

Rubin: Yeah, Pip. I think he, I mean she, can talk. And Linda, how do you know it's a girl cat?

Linda: Look, I'll show you. (She turns to the first page of the first chapter, scanning for a word.) Look, on page 1, here it is. It says "looked at *her* empty bowl." Her. That's how I know.

> ## What can you learn by listening to students talk about a book?
>
> Teachers know that they can learn a great deal through observing students as they work, listening to students participate in discussions, and talking with students during conferences. As you read this vignette about a small group of third graders discussing a book they are reading, notice Armando's role in the discussion and how the students use talk to clarify their understanding. In addition, think about how the students talk about their use of reading strategies and the connections they are making between the book and their lives, the world around them, and other literature.

Mrs. Zumwalt redirects the conversation and asks: "Do you think you'll find out for sure whether Pip can talk by the time you finish reading the book?" The

---

Books That Mrs. Zumwalt's Students Read in Literature Circles

Bang-Campbell, M. (2002). *Little rats sets sail.* San Diego: Harcourt Brace.

Benchley, P. (1994). *Small wolf.* New York: HarperCollins.

Brenner, B. (1978). *Wagon wheels.* New York: HarperCollins.

Coerr, E. (1986). *The Josefina story quilt.* New York: HarperCollins.

Coerr, E. (1988). *Chang's paper pony.* New York: HarperCollins.

Coerr, E. (1999). *Buffalo Bill and the Pony Express.* New York: HarperCollins.

Cushman, D. (2000). *Inspector Hopper.* New York: HarperCollins.

Dahl, R. (1990). *Esio trot.* New York: Puffin.

Danziger, P. (1994). *Amber Brown is not a crayon.* New York: Putnam.

Haas, J. (2001). *Runaway radish.* New York: Greenwillow.

Horowitz, R. (2001). *Breakout at the bug lab.* New York: Dial.

Laurence, D. (2001). *Captain and Matey set sail.* New York: HarperCollins.

Lewis, T. P. (1983). *Hill of fire.* New York: HarperCollins.

Livingstone, S. (2001). *Harley.* New York: North-South Books.

Lottridge, C. B. (2003). *Berta: A remarkable dog.* Toronto: Groundwood.

Lowry, L. (2002). *Gooney bird Greene.* Boston: Houghton Mifflin.

McDonald, M. (2002). *Judy Moody.* Cambridge, MA: Candlewick.

Roop, P., & Roop, C. (1985). *Keep the lights burning, Abbie.* Minneapolis, MN: Carolrhoda.

Seuling, B. (2001). *Robert and the great pepperoni.* Chicago: Cricket.

Turner, A. (1995). *Dust for dinner.* New York: HarperCollins.

---

students are sure they will find out. Then she asks them to consider possible story lines: "So, what do you think might happen in the story?"

Linda:	I think the story might be like the one about Martha the talking dog that we read last year. Martha got in trouble for talking too much so she stopped talking but then at the end when some robbers came, she called the police and was a hero.
Mrs. Zumwalt:	I know that story! It's called *Martha Speaks,* right? (The students agree.)
Armando:	I don't think Pip will talk in front of anyone except for Graciela. Not that Juanita. Pip doesn't want to be sent to be in a circus because she's a freak. She wants to be a normal white cat. I think maybe it will stay her secret.
Rubin:	I think people will find out about Pip and she will be famous. Then she'll win a million dollars on *Who Wants to Be a Millionaire?*

After everyone laughs at Rubin's comment, Mrs. Zumwalt asks about Juanita and the students respond.

Armando:	Juanita is the girl that Graciela talks to and tells that Pip can talk Spanish. She doesn't believe her, but she could still gossip about it at school.
Mrs. Zumwalt:	Is Juanita a friend of Graciela's?
Linda:	I think so.
Maricela:	They play together.
Armando:	No, I don't think they are friends. They just know each other and maybe they play together, but they are not friends. They don't act like friends.
Maricela:	I think Graciela *wants* to be friends. That's what I think.

Mrs. Zumwalt moves the conversation around to Juanita because the students seemed unaware of her when Armando mentioned her and because she will figure prominently in the book. As several of the students suggested, people will find out about Pip the talking cat, and a big problem develops.

The students continue reading and talking about the book as they learn that Graciela's neighbor, Sr. Medina, is the one who taught Pip to speak Spanish. In chapter 6, they read that Sr. Medina's nosy neighbor has called the television stations and told them about Pip and her special ability. During their discussion, the students talk about the television news crews coming to interview Sr. Medina and Pip. The students are angry that the neighbor called the television stations.

Linda:	It's not fair that that lady across the street was so nosy and she ruined everything. It got so bad that Sr. Medina had to move away.
Maricela:	I like that Graciela sprayed that lady with the hose and she got all wet. And Graciela called her a "sour old snoop." That's funny.
Mrs. Zumwalt:	In the book, it says that Graciela hoped the lady would "shrink into a puddle of nothing like the evil witch in *The Wizard of Oz*." What does that mean?
Armando:	That's what happened in *The Wizard of Oz*. I saw the movie so I know.
Rubin:	This chapter reminds me of when my neighbor's son got killed. His name was Manuel. He was 16, I think. He got killed by some gang bangers. They were in a car and they came by his house and they shot him. He was in the house and the bullet came in through the window. Then the ambulance came but he was dead. So the police came and they put up this yellow ribbon all around the house. My mom and dad made me stay in the house but I wanted to go outside and watch. Then the television reporters came and it was crowded with people. Just like in this chapter.

Marcos:	Sr. Medina had to move away and he took Pip with him.
Linda:	No, he didn't take Pip. She's Graciela's cat.
Marcos:	Look on page 69. It says, "He moved out last night and took his cat with him."
Linda:	Well, it's not *his* cat.

Mrs. Zumwalt asks the students to predict whether Graciela will get her cat back, and then they read the last chapter of the book and learn that Pip does come back, and now she's black, not white, and she speaks French, not Spanish! They talk about the ending.

Linda:	I'm happy. I knew Pip would come back. I would be so, so, so sad if anyone stole my cat.
Marcos:	I liked this book. It was funny.
Rubin:	I wish it would happen to me.
Maricela:	I would like to be Graciela.
Mrs. Zumwalt:	Why?
Maricela:	Well, her parents are weird; that's for sure. But, she does some interesting things. And I wish I had a cat who could talk to me in Spanish or in English.
Armando:	I liked the Spanish words. I'm going to write a story and put Spanish words in it. Those Spanish words made it fun to read this book.

Mrs. Zumwalt moves from group to group as they discuss the books they are reading. Her focus in these conversations is that students should use talk to deepen their comprehension. She watches to make sure that all students are participating and that the conversation explores important elements of plot, character, and theme. She asks questions to probe their thinking or redirect their attention. She also watches students' growing involvement with the story. Mrs. Zumwalt is pleased that Rubin became more involved with *The Cat's Meow.* After reading the first chapter, he didn't seem interested in the story, but by the end, he was hooked. Mrs. Zumwalt believes that it is the conversation that brings about the change.

When they come to school, most children are fluent oral language users, no matter what language they speak. They have had 4 or 5 years of extensive practice talking and listening in social settings. Because students have acquired basic oral language competencies, teachers often assume that they don't need to emphasize talk in the elementary school curriculum. Research shows, however, that students benefit from participating in talk activities for both social and academic purposes throughout the school day and that talk is a necessary ingredient for learning (Cazden, 1988; Heath, 1983; Smith, 2001; Wells & Chang-Wells, 1992).

Heath (1983) explored the value of talk in elementary classrooms and concluded that children's talk is an essential part of language arts and is necessary for academic success in all content areas. Quiet classrooms were once considered the most conducive to learning, but research now suggests that talk is a necessary ingredient for learning. Shuy (1987) says talk is often thwarted in elementary classrooms because of large class size and the mistaken assumption that silence facilitates learning. Teachers must make an extra effort to provide opportunities for children to use talk for both socialization and learning.

There are two ways of considering students' talk. First, we can classify it by purpose: Is it aesthetic or efferent? If the purpose of the talk is to tell stories or deepen students' understanding of stories, it is aesthetic, and if the purpose is to present information or understand information better, it is efferent talk. A second way to classify talk is by the level of formality: Is the talk formal or informal? Formal talk involves oral presentations, such as storytelling, readers theatre, oral reports, and debates. Informal talk usually consists of conversations, where students work in small groups and use talk to understand literature or information better or to accomplish an assignment or project.

As you continue reading, you will learn ways to encourage aesthetic and efferent talk in your classroom, with activities ranging from informal to formal. Think about these questions as you read:

As you begin reading this chapter, you may want to read the "Dear Reader" letter in Chapter 8 on the Companion Website at www.prenhall.com/tompkins

- ◆ Why is talk important in the learning process?
- ◆ How do students use aesthetic talk activities to respond to literature?
- ◆ How do students use efferent talk as a learning tool in theme cycles?
- ◆ What types of dramatic activities are appropriate for elementary students?

AESTHETIC TALK

Aesthetic talk, like aesthetic listening, deals with the lived-through experience of literature. Students use aesthetic talk to respond to literature and to deepen their comprehension of books they are reading. In literature focus units and literature circles, students use aesthetic talk as they participate in grand conversations. In these conversations, students share ideas, ask questions, and respond to classmates' comments. Elementary students also participate in more formal aesthetic talk activities as they tell stories and participate in readers theatre.

Conversations About Literature

Conversations are common occurrences in elementary classrooms. As students converse with classmates, they use talk for different purposes (Wilkinson, 1984): They try to control classmates' behavior, maintain social relationships, convey information, and share personal experiences and opinions. Students meet in small groups to respond to literature they have read, to respond to each other's writing, to work on projects, and to explore concepts they are learning. The most important feature of small-group conversations is that they promote thinking. Teachers take students' ideas seriously, and students are validated as thinkers (Nystrand, Gamoran, & Heck, 1993). The characteristics of small-group conversations are listed in Figure 8–1.

Students learn and refine their strategies and skills for socializing and conversing with classmates as they participate in small-group conversations (Cintorino, 1993; Kaufman, 2000). Students learn how to begin conversations, take turns, keep the conversation moving forward, support comments and questions that group members make, deal with conflicts, and bring the conversation to a close. And, they learn how powerful talk is in making meaning and creating knowledge.

To begin the conversation, students gather in groups at tables or other areas in the classroom, bringing with them any necessary materials. One student

---

FIGURE 8-1

Characteristics of Small-Group Conversations

1. Each group has three to six members. These groups may be permanent, or they may be established for specific activities. It is important that group members be a cohesive group and be courteous to and supportive of each other. Students in established groups often choose names for their groups.
2. The purpose of the small-group conversation or work session is to develop interpretations and create knowledge.
3. Students' talk is meaningful, functional, and genuine. Students use talk to solve problems and discover answers to authentic questions—questions that require interpretation and critical thinking.
4. The teacher clearly defines the goal of the group work and outlines the activities to be completed. Activities require cooperation and collaboration and could not be done as effectively through independent work.
5. Group members have assigned jobs. Sometimes students keep the same jobs over a period of time, and at other times, specific jobs are identified for a particular purpose.
6. Students use strategies to begin the conversation, keep it moving forward and on task, and end it.
7. Students feel ownership of and responsibility for the activities they are involved in and the projects they create.

Adapted from Cintorino, 1993; Nystrand, Gamoran, & Heck, 1993; Shafer, 1993.

in each group begins the conversation with a question or comment; students then take turns making comments and asking questions, and they support the other group members as they elaborate on and expand their comments. The tone is exploratory, and throughout the conversation, the group is progressing toward a common goal (Cintorino, 1993). The goal may be deepening students' understanding of a book they have read, responding to a question the teacher has asked, or creating a project. From time to time, the conversation slows down and there may be a few minutes of silence (Sorenson, 1993). Then a group member asks a question or makes a comment that sends the conversation in a new direction.

Students try to support one another in groups, and perhaps the most important way they do this is by calling each other by name. They also cultivate a climate of trust in the group by expressing agreement, sharing feelings, voicing approval, and referring to comments that group members made earlier. Conflict is inevitable, but students need to learn how to deal with it so that it doesn't get out of control. They learn to accept that there will be differing viewpoints and to make compromises. Cintorino (1993) reported that her eighth graders used humor to defuse disagreements in small-group conversations.

At the end of a conversation, students reach consensus and conclude that they have finished sharing ideas, explored all dimensions of a question, or completed a project. Sometimes students produce a product during the conversation. The product may be a brainstormed list, a chart, or something more elaborate, such as a set of puppets. Group members are responsible for collecting and storing materials they have used and for reporting on the group's work.

From their observational study of fifth and sixth graders conducting conversations about literature, Eeds and Wells (1989) found that through talk, students extend their individual interpretations of their reading and even create a better understanding of it. Students talk about their understanding of the story and can change their opinions after listening to classmates' alternative views. They share personal stories related to their reading in poignant ways that trigger other students to identify with them. Students also gain insights about how authors use the elements of story structure to develop their message.

An additional benefit of conversations is that when students talk in depth about literature, their writing shows the same level of inferential comprehension (Sorenson, 1993). Students seem to be more successful in conversations about literature if they have written in journals first, and they are more successful in writing journal entries if they have participated in conversations first.

Teaching Students to Talk in Small Groups.   Teachers play an important role in making the conversations successful, beginning with creating a community of learners in the classroom so that students understand that they are responsible group members (Kaufman, 2000). Teachers create a climate of trust by demonstrating to students that they trust them and their ability to learn. Similarly, students learn to socialize with classmates and to respect one another as they work together in small groups. For primary- and middle-grade students, reading Diane Stanley's *The Conversation Club* (1983) is a good way to introduce the climate of trust and to explain the roles of speakers and listeners during conversations.

Sorenson (1993) begins the school year by telling her eighth-grade students that they will participate in a different type of discussion in her classroom. She hangs a sign in the classroom that says "Teach Each Other," and she tells them that it is a quote from one of her students about why this different kind of discussion works. The students learn that what they say is just as important as what the teacher says and that through conversations, students are teaching each other.

Grand Conversations.   To dig deeper into a story and deepen their comprehension, students talk about literature they are reading in literature focus units and literature circles. These conversations are often called grand conversations (Eeds & Wells, 1989; Peterson & Eeds, 1990). Students take responsibility for their own learning as they voice their opinions and support their views with examples from the literature. They talk about what puzzles them, what they find interesting, their personal connections to the story, and connections they see between this story and others they have read. Students also encourage their classmates to contribute to the conversation. Even though teachers often sit in on conversations as a participant, not as a judge, the talk is primarily among the students.

Grand conversations can be held with the whole class or in small groups. When students meet as a class, there is a feeling of community. Young children

Grand conversation. These sixth graders are participating in a literature circle, and they meet with their teacher twice a week to talk about the novel they are reading. Their discussion is a grand conversation because it is authentic; the students share ideas, make connections, ask questions, offer predictions, and talk about the author's use of story elements and literary devices. Their teacher also participates in the grand conversation, modeling how to talk about literature, scaffolding students' comments, and asking questions to help them think more critically about the novel.

usually meet as a class, and older students get together when they are learning literature conversation procedures, participating in a literature focus unit, or listening to the teacher read a book aloud to the class. But during literature circles, they meet in small groups because they are reading different books and they want to have more opportunities to talk. When the entire class meets, students have only a few opportunities to talk, but when they meet in small groups, they have many, many more opportunities to share their responses.

Grand conversations have two parts. The first part is open-ended: Students talk about their reactions to the book, and their comments determine the direction of the conversation. Teachers do participate, however, and share their responses, ask questions, and provide information. In the second part, the teacher focuses students' attention on one or two aspects of the book that they did not talk about in the first part of the conversation. The steps are shown in the Step by Step feature on page 348.

After the grand conversation, students often write in their reading logs, or write again if they wrote before the grand conversation. Then they continue reading the book if they have read only part of it. Both participating in grand conversations and writing entries in reading logs help students think about and respond to what they have read.

Asking Questions.   Both students and the teacher ask questions to stimulate conversation and deepen understanding. The most useful questions cannot be answered with "yes" or "no"; they require students to analyze, interpret, evaluate, and offer opinions. After reading *Amber Brown Is Not a Crayon* (Danziger, 1994), the story of two best friends and what happens as one of them moves to another state, a group of third graders in Mrs. Zumwalt's class wrote their own questions. The group spent the first few minutes of the grand

Step by Step

Grand Conversations

1. **Meet in a group.** Students meet in small groups or as a class to talk about a book or a section of a book. When students meet as a class, they sit in a circle in order to see each other; when they meet in a small group, they sit close together so that they can talk without disturbing their classmates.

2. **Share responses.** To begin the conversation, a student or the teacher asks, "Who would like to begin? What did you think of the story? Who would like to share?" As students share their responses, they comment on the events in the story, on the literary elements, or on the author's language, and they might make connections to their own lives and to other literature they have read. Every student participates in the grand conversation. To ensure that everyone has an opportunity to participate, teachers often ask students to make no more than three comments until everyone has spoken at least once. Usually students don't raise their hands and are not called on by the teacher or a group leader. Instead, students take turns and speak when no one else is speaking, much as adults do when they talk with friends. Pauses and brief silences may occur, and when students indicate that they have run out of things to say, the conversation may end or continue to the next part.

3. **Ask questions.** Teachers ask open-ended questions to focus students' attention on one or two aspects of the book that have been missed. The questions teachers ask depend on the particular book and the comments students have already made about it, but teachers often ask students to make comparisons to other books they have read or to their own lives, to comment on the author's or illustrator's style, to explore the book's theme, or to respond to a quote from the book.

conversation considering the questions and deciding which ones to actually use. Their questions included:

- Why do you think Amber and Justin are best friends?
- Do you think Mr. Cohn is sort of like Ms. Frizzle [in the Magic School Bus series]?
- Do you think Mr. Cohn is a good teacher?
- Did you know from the beginning that Justin was going to move away?
- How can best friends fight and still be best friends?
- Is Justin happy or sad about moving to Alabama?
- Why is Amber so mean to Justin?
- What do you think will happen to Amber and Justin after he moves away?
- Can they still be best friends after Justin moves away?

These questions delve into the "best friends" theme of the book and require students to use higher-level thinking skills. The students who created the questions are perceptive, and their questions go far beyond the factual level. They require students to think deeply about the story and even to go back and reread portions to support their answers. If students are not going this deeply into a story, teachers should pose questions like these.

Questions can be divided into three levels: literal, inferential, and critical. Literal or "on the page" questions have a single factual answer and can usually be answered with a few words or "yes" or "no." When the questions refer to a story or other book that students are reading, the answers are directly stated in the text. The second level of questions is inferential or "between the lines." To answer these questions, students synthesize information and form interpretations using both their background knowledge and clues in the text. The answers are implicitly stated in the text. The third, most complex level of questioning is critical or "beyond the page." These questions are open-ended. They require students to go beyond the text and think creatively and abstractly about global ideas, issues, and concerns. At this level, students apply information, make connections, evaluate and value the text, and express opinions. The LA Essentials feature on page 350 reviews the three levels of questioning and lists questions about Chris Van Allsburg's *The Wretched Stone* (1991), the story of a strange glowing stone picked up on a sea voyage that captivates a ship's crew and has a terrible transforming effect on them.

Teachers use these three levels of questions for different purposes. They use literal questions during a conversation to check that students have basic information and understand the meaning of words. Literal questions are easy to ask and to answer, but, because they are the most frequently asked questions, teachers need to be careful not to use too many of them. To help students think more deeply and to challenge their thinking, teachers use inferential and critical questions. They ask inferential questions to probe students' understanding of a story and make interpretations. They ask critical questions to challenge students' thinking to go beyond the story to make connections, evaluate the story, reflect on the overall theme, and delve into the author's craft.

Minilessons.   Even though most children come to school speaking fluently, they need to learn new ways to use talk. Small-group conversations are one of these new ways. Teachers are wrong to assume that because students know how to talk, they know how to work in small groups, tell stories, participate in debates, and use talk in other ways. Teachers present minilessons on how to conduct conversations, and they also explain and demonstrate the various types of talk. A list of minilesson topics related to talk is presented on pages 352–353, along with a sample minilesson on how to sustain a conversation.

Meeting the Needs of Every Student

Talk is a useful learning tool, and it is important that activities be adapted so that every student can use talk successfully. Small-group conversations and the other activities discussed in this chapter can be adapted in many ways to meet students' needs. Perhaps the most basic way to meet the needs of students who

Essentials

Levels of Questioning

Level	Category	Description	Questions about The Wretched Stone
3	Critical or "Beyond the Page" Questions	Critical questions go beyond the text and focus on global issues, ideas, and problems. Often there are no correct answers to these questions. Students think creatively; make personal connections, world connections, and literary connections; evaluate the text; and express opinions to answer critical questions.	Why does the captain look so much like the author? Why did Chris Van Allsburg point out that the crew was clever—they could read, tell stories, and play music? How would this story be different if it were told from the crew's viewpoint instead of the captain's? Why do you think Chris Van Allsburg wrote this book? How has watching television affected reading?
2	Inferential or "Between the Lines" Questions	Inferential questions require analysis and interpretation. The answers to these questions are implicitly stated in the text. Students use a combination of background knowledge and clues in the text to answer inferential questions.	Why was the captain named Randall Ethan Hope? Why does the captain say, "We are doomed"? Why did the captain sink the ship? What does the wretched stone symbolize? Is this a true story? Why?
1	Literal or "On the Page" Questions	Literal questions are factual. The answers to these questions are stated explicitly in the text. Students answer these questions with "yes" or "no" or with a few words taken directly from the text.	What was different about this crew? What did the rock look like? What was strange about the island where they found it? What made the crew turn into apes? What made the crew turn back into men?

Meeting the Needs of Every Student

How Can I Get My Quiet Students to Talk?

Students are quiet for a number of reasons. Some reasons deal with language: Students may be self-conscious because they are English learners or speak a regional or nonstandard dialect of English. Other reasons relate to students' self-confidence or knowledge level: They may feel they have nothing to contribute or think they don't know the "right" answer. Other reasons are cultural: Students may have been taught to respect the teacher by listening, not talking. These students are not used to dialoguing with children and adults. There are other reasons, too: Some students are shy or intimidated by more popular classmates.

No matter why students are quiet, you can do several things to encourage all students to participate in talk activities. First of all, create a supportive, all-inclusive classroom community where students know that they are safe, respected, and valued. It is essential that students are confident that they will not be laughed at for their ideas or the way their comments are phrased. They need time to observe classmates participating in conversations so that they know what's expected of them. It's helpful to brainstorm a list of guidelines about how to participate in talk activities and post it in the classroom. You also need to model how to participate in talk activities because jumping into a conversation and making a useful comment can be difficult. Whole-class conversations can be intimidating to some quiet students, so small-group conversations are usually more effective until students gain confidence.

To investigate other ways to meet the needs of every student, visit the links for this chapter on the Companion Website at www.prenhall.com/tompkins

Companion Website

are uncomfortable speaking in a large group or who are hesitant to speak because they are learning English as a second language or have other language problems is to have them work in a small, comfortable group and to keep the language use informal. It is much easier to work in a small group to accomplish a project than to give an oral report in front of the class or participate in a debate. Other ways to meet students' needs are presented in the Meeting the Needs of Every Student box above.

Storytelling

The ancient art of storytelling is a valuable instructional tool. Teachers share literature with their students using storytelling techniques, and students tell stories, too. Storytelling is entertaining and stimulates children's imaginations. It expands their language abilities, and it helps them internalize the characteristics of stories and develop interpretations of stories (Morrow, 1985).

Piecing a Lesson Together

Topics on Talk and Drama

Procedures	Concepts	Strategies and Skills
Begin a conversation	Roles of speakers and listeners	Share ideas and feelings
Take turns	Working collaboratively	Refer to previous comments
Stay on task	Grand conversations	Extend a comment
Sustain a conversation	Instructional conversations	Call group members by name
End a conversation	Scripts	Look at classmates while speaking
Tell a story	Rehearsal	Vary tone of voice and pace of speech
Make K-W-L charts		Listen attentively
Make clusters		Ask questions
Make data charts		Seek clarification
Present an oral report		Express a viewpoint
Conduct an interview		Maintain the audience's interest
Role-play		Offer predictions
Create a puppet		Present main ideas coherently
Perform a puppet show		Give directions
Write a script		Use appropriate vocabulary

Please visit the Companion Website at **www.prenhall.com/tompkins** for a second fully realized minilesson.

Students learn how to tell stories as they listen to their teachers tell stories. They notice that teachers change their voices for dialogue and emphasize repetitive phrases. They also watch teachers use puppets and other props. Modeling is very important, but teachers also teach minilessons to explain the storytelling procedure. Storytelling involves four steps, shown in the Step by Step feature on page 354.

CONVERSATIONS

Ms. Shapiro Teaches Her Second Graders About Sustaining Conversations

1. Introduce the Topic

Ms. Shapiro explains to her second graders that she wants them to think about how they behave during grand conversations. She asks them to observe a grand conversation that she has planned with four students in the class. "We will be doing some good things to help the conversation and some bad things that hurt the conversation," she says. "Watch carefully so you will notice them."

2. Share Examples

Ms. Shapiro and four students have a grand conversation about a familiar story, *Hey, Al* (Yorinks, 1986). She chose a familiar story so that students could focus on the conversation itself and not get caught up in the story. The students participating in the conversation take turns making comments, but they don't expand on each other's comments nor do they call each other by name or look at classmates as they are talking. Also, some students are looking away from the group as though they are not listening.

3. Provide Information

Ms. Shapiro's students are eager to identify the strengths and weaknesses of the grand conversation they have observed. The "good things" were that "everyone talked about the story and nothing else" and "everybody was nice." The "bad things" included that "some people didn't pay attention and look at the person talking," "some people didn't say other people's names," and "some people just said things but they didn't go next to what other people said." Ms. Shapiro agrees that the students have identified the problems and she explains that she's seen some of these same problems in their conversations. Together they make a chart of "Good Things to Do in a Grand Conversation."

4. Supervise Practice

Ms. Shapiro's students participate in grand conversations as part of literature circles and after she reads a book aloud to the class. She explains that she will observe their grand conversations to make sure they are doing all the good things they listed on their chart. For the next 2 weeks, Ms. Shapiro briefly reviews the chart with them before each grand conversation and takes a few minutes afterward to talk about the changes in behavior she has observed.

5. Reflect on Learning

After 2 weeks of practice, Ms. Shapiro brings the students together to talk about their grand conversations, and she asks the second graders which of the good things from the chart they are doing better now. The students mention various points and conclude that their grand conversations have improved.

Many stories can be used for storytelling activities. Morrow (1979) suggests that the best stories embody these qualities:

- A simple, well-rounded plot
- A clear beginning, middle, and end
- An underlying theme

Storytelling

Step by Step

1. **Choose a story.**   Traditional stories, such as folktales, are often chosen for storytelling activities; however, teachers and students can choose any type of story for a storytelling activity. The most important considerations in choosing a story are that whoever will tell the story likes it, knows it well, and wants to tell it.

2. **Prepare to tell the story.**   Students plan and rehearse a familiar story before telling it. It is not necessary to memorize a story to tell it effectively. Kingore (1982) recommends that students choose a familiar story that they really like, and that they reread the story once or twice to review details about characters and to place major events in proper sequence. Then students choose interesting or repeated phrases from the story to enliven the language of their retelling and consider how to vary their speaking voice to make the story more interesting for listeners. Students also plan simple props or gestures to accompany the story. Then they prepare a brief introduction that relates the story to the audience's experiences. Students rehearse the story several times, incorporating phrases to enliven the story, varying their speaking voices, and using props or gestures. This process can be abbreviated when very young children tell stories. They choose a story they already know well and make props to guide the telling.

3. **Add props.**   Students use props to add variety and interest to stories. Props include flannel-board pictures, puppets, and small stuffed animals or other objects. For instance, to retell *The Mitten* (Brett, 1989), students can use a white mitten and pictures of the animals that squeeze into the mitten in telling the story, or they can use a Ukrainian painted egg when telling *Rechenka's Eggs* (Polacco, 1988).

4. **Tell the story.**   Students tell the stories they have prepared to small groups of classmates or to younger children. Teachers may want to divide the audience into small groups so that more students can tell stories at one time.

- A small number of well-defined characters
- Dialogue
- Repetition
- Colorful language or catchphrases

The Classroom Library box on page 355 lists recommended stories for storytelling activities, and these stories contain many of Morrow's qualities. Children can also tell stories to accompany wordless picture books. For example, Tomie dePaola's *Pancakes for Breakfast* (1978) is the charming story of a little old woman who wants to cook pancakes for breakfast but runs into a series of problems as she tries to assemble the ingredients. In the end, her neighbors invite her to their home for pancakes. The repetition of events in this story makes it easy for primary-grade children to tell.

CLASSROOM LIBRARY

Stories for Storytelling Activities

Aardema, V. (1975). *Why mosquitoes buzz in people's ears.* New York: Dial. (M–U)

Ada, A. F. (1995). *Mediopollito/Half-chicken.* New York: Doubleday. (P–M)

Brett, J. (1989). *The mitten.* New York: Putnam. (P–M)

Brett, J. (1999). *The gingerbread baby.* New York: Putnam. (P)

Carle, E. (1994). *The very hungry caterpillar.* New York: Scholastic. (P)

Demi. (1990). *The empty pot.* New York: Holt. (P–M)

Downey, L. (2000). *The flea's sneeze.* New York: Henry Holt. (P)

Ernst, L. C. (2000). *Goldilocks returns.* New York: Simon & Schuster. (P–M)

Fox, M. (1986). *Hattie and the fox.* New York: Bradbury Press. (P–M)

Gág, W. (1996). *Millions of cats.* New York: Puffin. (P)

Galdone, P. (1981). *The three billy goats Gruff.* New York: Clarion. (P)

Hamilton, V. (1995). *Her stories: African American folktales, fairy tales, and true tales.* New York: Blue Sky Press. (M–U)

Hamilton, V. (2000). *The girl who spun gold.* New York: Blue Sky Press. (M–U)

Hastings, S. (1985). *Sir Gawain and the loathly lady.* New York: Mulberry. (U)

Kasza, K. (1987). *The wolf's chicken stew.* New York: Putnam. (P–M)

Kimmel, E. A. (2000). *The runaway tortilla.* Delray Beach, FL: Winslow. (P–M)

Lionni, L. (1987). *Alexander and the wind-up mouse.* New York: Knopf. (M)

Mahy, M. (1990). *The seven Chinese brothers.* New York: Scholastic. (M)

Martin, B., Jr., & Archambault, J. (1985). *The ghost-eye tree.* New York: Holt, Rinehart and Winston. (M–U)

Mayer, M. (1978). *Beauty and the beast.* New York: Macmillan. (U)

Mayer, M. (1987). *There's an alligator under my bed.* New York: Dial. (P–M)

McDermott, G. (1997). *Musicians of the sun.* New York: Aladdin. (M)

Meddaugh, S. (1995). *Hog-eye.* Boston: Houghton Mifflin. (M)

Numeroff, L. J. (1985). *If you give a mouse a cookie.* New York: Harper & Row. (P–M–U)

Polacco, P. (1988). *Rechenka's eggs.* New York: Philomel. (M)

Slobodkina, E. (1987). *Caps for sale.* New York: HarperCollins. (P)

Wood, A. (1984). *The napping house.* San Diego, CA: Harcourt Brace Jovanovich. (P)

Xiong, B. (1989). *Nine-in-one Grr! Grr!* San Francisco: Children's Book Press. (M)

Zemach, M. (1990). *It could always be worse.* New York: Farrar, Straus & Giroux. (P–M–U)

Ziefert, H. (1995). *The teeny-tiny woman.* New York: Viking. (P–M).

P = primary grades (K–2); M = middle grades (3–5); U = upper grades (6–8).

Teachers can assess both the process students use to tell stories and the quality of the storytelling production, but the process of developing interpretations is far more important than the quality of the storytelling. Teachers check that students move through the steps of planning and rehearsing the story before telling it and that they:

- Introduce the story to the audience
- Include the beginning, middle, and end of the story
- Incorporate interesting or repeated phrases in their story
- Add dialogue
- Vary their voices for more interest
- Use props or gestures

Teachers often develop checklists of these qualities to use in assessing students' storytelling performances. The Weaving Assessment Into Practice feature on page 356 shows a grading sheet that a fourth-grade teacher used. As

Weaving Assessment Into Practice

A Fourth-Grade Storytelling Grading Sheet

Name _____

Title of Story _____

	Student	Teacher
1. Did you introduce the story?	_____	_____
2. Did you tell the TITLE?	_____	_____
3. Did you tell the BEGINNING of the story?	_____	_____
4. Did you tell the MIDDLE of the story?	_____	_____
5. Did you tell the END of the story?	_____	_____
6. Did you REPEAT some words?	_____	_____
7. Did you add DIALOGUE?	_____	_____
8. Did you change your VOICE?	_____	_____
9. Did you use PROPS?	_____	_____
10. Did you act as though you were having FUN?	_____	_____

students gain experience telling stories, they become more comfortable in front of an audience and learn ways to play to the audience.

Readers Theatre

Readers theatre is "a formalized dramatic presentation of a script by a group of readers" (Busching, 1981, p. 330). Each student assumes a role and reads the character's lines in the script. Students develop reading fluency and increased motivation for reading through this dramatic activity (Worthy & Prater, 2002). The reader's responsibility is to interpret a story without using much action. Students may stand or sit, but they must carry the whole communication of the plot, characterization, mood, and theme by using their voices, gestures, and facial expressions.

Readers theatre avoids many of the restrictions inherent in theatrical productions. Students do not memorize their parts, and elaborate props, costumes, and backdrops are not needed. Neither do students spend long, tedious hours rehearsing the performance. Students create a presentation that can be performed for their own enjoyment or as a more formal production for classmates and other audiences.

Quality play scripts exhibit the same characteristics as other types of fine literature. The essential characteristics include an interesting story, a well-paced plot, recognizable and believable characters, plausible language, and a distinct style (Manna, 1984). The arrangement of the text on the page is also an important consideration when selecting or preparing a script. There should be a clear distinction between stage directions and dialogue through adequate

CLASSROOM LIBRARY

Stories That Can Be Scripted for Readers Theatre

Babbitt, N. (1975). *Tuck everlasting.* New York: Farrar, Straus & Giroux. (U)

Blume, J. (1972). *Tales of a fourth grade nothing.* New York: Dutton. (M)

Byars, B. (1968). *The midnight fox.* New York: Viking. (M–U)

Cleary, B. (1973). *Ramona and her father.* New York: Morrow. (M)

Coerr, E. (1977). *Sadako and the thousand paper cranes.* New York: Putnam. (M)

Danziger, P. (1994). *Amber Brown is not a crayon.* New York: Putnam. (M)

Fleischman, S. (1986). *The whipping boy.* New York: Greenwillow. (M–U)

Gilson, J. (1983). *Thirteen ways to sink a sub.* New York: Lothrop, Lee & Shepard. (U)

Hesse, K. (2001). *Witness.* New York: Scholastic. (U)

Howe, D., & Howe, J. (1979). *Bunnicula: A rabbit-tale of mystery.* New York: Atheneum. (M–U)

Hurwitz, J. (1995). *Elisa in the middle.* New York: Morrow. (M)

King-Smith, D. (1988). *Martin's mice.* New York: Crown. (M–U)

Lewis, C. S. (1981). *The lion, the witch and the wardrobe.* New York: Macmillan. (M–U)

Lobel, A. (1970). *Frog and Toad are friends.* New York: Harper & Row. (P)

Lowry, L. (1989). *Number the stars.* Boston: Houghton Mifflin. (M–U)

MacLachlan, P. (1985). *Sarah, plain and tall.* New York: Harper & Row. (M)

Mathis, S. B. (1975). *The hundred penny box.* New York: Viking. (M)

McBratney, S. (1995). *Guess how much I love you.* Cambridge, MA: Candlewick. (P)

Meddaugh, S. (1995). *Hog-eye.* Boston: Houghton Mifflin. (P)

Milne, A. A. (1974). *Winnie-the-Pooh.* New York: Dutton. (P–M)

Naylor, P. R. (1991). *Shiloh.* New York: Atheneum. (M–U)

Sebestyen, O. (1979). *Words by heart.* Boston: Little, Brown. (U)

Whelan, G. (2000). *Homeless bird.* New York: Scholastic. (U)

spacing and variation in the print types and colors. This distinction is especially important for students who are not familiar with script format.

Very few quality scripts are available for elementary students, so students usually prepare their own scripts from books they have read. Some recommended stories are presented in the Classroom Library box above. Laughlin and Latrobe (1989) suggest that students begin by reading the book and thinking about its theme, characters, and plot. Next, students choose an episode to script, and they make copies of the scene and use felt-tip pens to highlight the dialogue. They then adapt the scene by adding narrators' lines to bridge gaps, set the scene, and summarize. Students assume roles and read the script aloud, revising and experimenting with new text until they are satisfied with the script. The final version is typed, duplicated, and stapled into pamphlets. The steps in developing readers theatre performances are shown in the Step by Step feature on page 358.

EFFERENT TALK

Students use efferent talk to inform and to persuade. They use efferent talk in conversations during theme cycles. They also use four other types of efferent talk: show-and-tell, oral reports, interviews, and debates. These activities are more formal presentations, and students prepare and rehearse their talks before giving them in front of an audience.

Readers Theatre

1. **Select a script.** Teachers select a script for students to use, or they work with students to craft a script from a familiar picture-book story or an episode from a chapter book.

2. **Rehearse the performance.** To begin, students choose the parts they will read. One student is needed for each character, plus one for a narrator if the script calls for one. Students read through the script once or twice, then stop to talk about the story. Through this conversation, students gain a clearer understanding of the story and decide how to interpret their characters. After students decide how to use their voices, gestures, and facial expressions to interpret the characters, they read the script one or two more times, striving for accurate pronunciation, strong voice projection, and appropriate inflection. Obviously, less rehearsal is needed for an informal, in-class performance than for a more formal production; nevertheless, interpretations should always be developed as fully as possible.

3. **Stage the performance.** Readers theatre can be performed on a stage or in a corner of the classroom. Students stand or sit in a row and read their lines in the script. They stay in position throughout the performance or enter and leave according to the characters' appearances "on stage." If readers are sitting, they may stand to read their lines; if they are standing, they may step forward to read. The emphasis is not on production quality; rather, it is on the interpretive quality of the readers' voices and expressions. Costumes and props are unnecessary; however, adding a few enhances interest and enjoyment, as long as they do not interfere with the interpretive quality of the reading.

Talking About Content-Area Topics

Students use efferent talk in small-group conversations to accomplish goals, learn information, and work out problems. This talk is an important part of theme cycles. Students talk about concepts they are learning and about issues such as pollution, immigration, nuclear energy, and human rights. The talk can take place when students meet in small groups or get together as a class. In contrast to conversations about literature, in which students use primarily aesthetic talk to create and deepen their interpretations, students use primarily efferent talk to create knowledge and understand relationships among concepts they are learning.

Instructional Conversations. These conversations provide opportunities for students to talk about the main ideas they are learning in theme cycles and enhance students' conceptual learning and their linguistic abilities (Goldenberg, 1992/1993). Like grand conversations, these discussions are interesting and engaging, and students are active participants, building on classmates' ideas with their own comments. Teachers are participants in the conversation, making comments much as the students do, but they also assume the teacher role to clarify misconceptions, ask questions, and provide instruction. Goldenberg has identified these content and linguistic elements of an instructional conversation:

- The conversation focuses on a content-area topic.
- Students activate or build knowledge about the topic during the instructional conversation.
- Teachers provide information and directly teach concepts when necessary.
- Teachers promote students' use of more complex vocabulary and language to express the ideas being discussed.
- Teachers encourage students to provide support of the ideas they present using information found in informational books, content-area textbooks, and other resources in the classroom.
- Students and teachers ask higher-level questions, often questions with more than one answer, during instructional conversations.
- Students participate actively in the instructional conversation and make comments that build on and expand classmates' comments.
- The classroom is a community of learners where both students' and teachers' comments are respected and encouraged.

Researchers have compared the effectiveness of small-group conversations with other instructional approaches and have found that students' learning is enhanced when they relate what they are learning to their own experiences—especially when they do so in their own words (Wittrock & Alesandrini, 1990). Similarly, Pressley (1992) reported that students' learning was promoted when they had opportunities to elaborate ideas through talk. The steps in an instructional conversation are explained in the Step by Step feature on page 360.

After the discussion ends, students often write and draw in learning logs to record the important ideas discussed during the instructional conversation. Students may refer to the brainstormed list or cluster the teacher made during the first part of the discussion.

Instructional conversations are useful for helping students grapple with important ideas they are learning in social studies, science, and other content areas. When students are discussing literature, they usually use grand conversations, which facilitate response to literature. An exception is when students focus on analyzing plot, characters, theme, and other elements of story structure; then they are thinking efferently and they are participating in an instructional conversation, not a grand conversation.

Questioning Strategies. Teachers often use questions to initiate conversations during theme cycles, and the questions teachers ask go beyond literal-level thinking (with single correct answers) to authentic questions that prompt students to analyze and synthesize information and make connections to their own lives.

Here are some examples for a theme cycle on pioneers:

- As part of a conversation introducing a theme cycle on pioneers, teachers ask if there are pioneers today. After students conclude that there are, teachers ask where modern-day pioneers go, what they do, and why they are pioneers.
- After making a list of the reasons why people moved west, teachers ask students which reason seems most important to them.

Step by Step

Instructional Conversations

1. **Choose a focus.** Teachers choose a focus for the instructional conversation, and the focus is often worded in the form of an open-ended question. It should be related to the goals of a theme cycle or to main ideas presented in an informational book or in a content-area textbook.

2. **Activate and build background knowledge.** Teachers present background knowledge in preparation for the discussion; students may read an informational book or selection from a content-area textbook to learn about the topic, or they may view a video about the topic.

3. **Begin the conversation.** Students come together as a class or in smaller groups for the instructional conversation. Teachers begin with the focus they have identified. They make a statement or ask a question, and then students respond, sharing information they have learned, asking questions, and offering opinions. Teachers assist students as they make comments, helping them extend their ideas and use appropriate vocabulary. In addition, teachers write students' comments in a list or on a cluster or other graphic organizer.

4. **Expand the conversation.** After students have discussed the teacher's focus, the conversation continues and moves in other directions. Students may share other interesting information, make personal connections to information they are learning, or ask questions. Teachers may have students do a read-around and share important ideas from their reading.

- After sharing a map of the westward trails that pioneers traveled, teachers ask students to choose a destination and plan their travel along one of the trails.
- As a class, students brainstorm a list of the possessions pioneers carried with them; then students work in small groups to choose the five most important possessions for pioneers traveling to and settling in particular areas.

Wilen (1986) reviewed the research about questioning strategies and offers these suggestions:

- Ask carefully planned questions to organize and direct the lesson.
- Ask clearly phrased questions rather than vaguely worded or multiple questions.
- Sequence questions to move from factual-level questions to higher-level questions that require critical thinking.
- Ask questions to follow up on students' responses.

Teachers need to allow students sufficient time to think about questions and plan their responses. Sometimes the most effective way to do this is to have stu-

K-W-L Charts

1. **Create a large chart.**   Teachers post a large sheet of butcher paper on a wall or bulletin board and divide it into three columns. They label the columns K (or What We Know), W (or What We Wonder/What We Want to Learn), and L (or What We Learned).

2. **Complete the K column.**   At the beginning of the theme cycle, teachers ask students to think about what they know about the topic and brainstorm information for the teacher to record in this column. Sometimes students suggest information that is not correct, and these statements should be turned into questions and added to the W (What We Wonder) column. If it turns out during the unit that some information recorded in the K column is incorrect, it should be corrected immediately on the K-W-L chart so that students don't keep rereading incorrect information.

3. **Complete the W column.**   Teachers write the questions that students ask in the W column. They continue to add questions to the W column throughout the unit.

4. **Complete the L column.**   Toward the end of the theme cycle, teachers ask students to reflect on what they have learned and then record this information in the L column. Teachers do not expect students to answer each of the questions posted in the W column; instead, students focus on the most important and interesting information they have learned.

dents talk about the question in small groups and then report back to the class. It is important to encourage wide participation and interaction among students and to draw in students who do not volunteer contributions. Seating students in a circle is one technique, and having students work in small groups is another. Other ways to promote student involvement are to have students create questions, lead the conversation, and follow up on ideas developed during the conversation. The emphasis in these conversations is on creating knowledge and making connections with information students are learning. Students also use persuasive language as they argue their viewpoints and try to persuade classmates of the importance of the points they make and the issues they discuss.

K-W-L Charts.   K-W-L charts (Ogle, 1986, 1989) are a good way to help students take an active role in recalling and building background knowledge and talking about what they are learning in theme cycles. The letters K, W, and L stand for "What I/We Know," "What I/We Want to Learn" or "What I/We Wonder," and "What I/We Learned." Teachers use these charts at the beginning of theme cycles to help students think about what they will study and to encourage them to ask questions to direct their learning during the theme cycle, and they use them again at the end of the unit to summarize and review students' learning. The procedure is described in the Step by Step feature above.

FIGURE 8-2 *A Second-Grade Class's K-W-L Chart on Penguins*

K What We Know	W What We Wonder	L What We Learned
Penguins are black and white. Penguins are good swimmers and divers. We saw penguins at the zoo. They eat fish. Penguins like to play on ice and snow. Penguins look funny when they walk on little feet.	Are penguins fish or birds? Do penguins live in California? What do penguin babies look like? Do polar bears hunt and kill penguins? Do penguins have enemies? Do penguins ever get cold? How long do penguins live? Can you have a penguin for a pet?	We learned that penguins are birds but they can't fly and they love to swim. Some penguins can swim real fast—25 miles an hour. They have feathers on their bodies. Penguins live at the South Pole. It is called Antarctica. They don't get cold because they have fat and feathers on their bodies to keep warm. Penguins have flippers that look like little wings but they can't fly. Penguins can live for 20 years. The emperor penguin is the largest penguin. It is almost as big as we are. Babies hatch from eggs. They are chicks. The fathers care for eggs until they hatch. The chicks are covered with soft gray feathers called down. The penguin's enemies are leopard seals, killer whales, sharks, and people.

K-W-L charts can be used in several ways. Teachers can make class K-W-L charts with their students, students can work in small groups to make charts, and students can make individual charts in journals or on drawing paper. Class charts work best for younger students or for older students who have not made K-W-L charts before. Middle- and upper-grade students often work with classmates to make group charts on chart paper, or they can make individual K-W-L charts. Figure 8–2 shows a K-W-L chart developed by a second-grade

FIGURE 8-3   *A Middle-Grade Student's K-W-L Chart on Spiders*

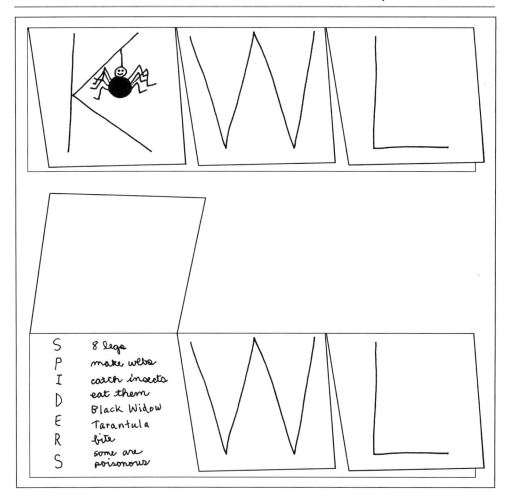

class as they studied penguins, and Figure 8–3 shows an individual K-W-L chart on spiders. The individual chart was made by folding a sheet of paper in half vertically. Next, the student cut three flaps and labeled them "K," "W," and "L," as shown in the top drawing in the figure. Then, the student flipped up the flaps to write on the chart, as shown in the lower picture in the figure.

Show-and-Tell

Daily sharing time is a familiar ritual in many kindergarten and primary-grade classrooms: Children bring favorite objects to school and talk about them. This is a nice bridge between home and school, and show-and-tell is a good introduction to speaking in front of a group.

If sharing time becomes repetitive, children can lose interest, so teachers must play an active role to make sharing a worthwhile activity. Teachers can discuss the roles and responsibilities of both speakers and listeners. A second-grade class developed the list of responsibilities for speakers and listeners

FIGURE 8-4 *A Second-Grade Class List of Responsibilities of Talkers and Listeners*

Our Rules for Show-and-Tell

What a Speaker Does

    Brings something interesting to talk about.

    Brings the same thing only one time.

    Thinks of three things to say about it.

    Speaks loudly so everyone can hear.

    Passes what he or she brought around so everyone can see it.

What Listeners Do

    Be interested.

    Pay attention.

    Listen.

    Ask a question.

    Say something nice.

---

shown in Figure 8–4. This list, with minor variations, has been used with students in upper grades as well.

Some children need prompting even if they have been advised to plan in advance to say two or three things about the object they have brought to school. It is tempting for teachers to speed things up by asking questions and, without realizing it, to answer their own questions, especially for a very quiet child. Show-and-tell could go like this:

Teacher:	Jerry, what did you bring today?
Jerry:	(Holds up a stuffed bear.)
Teacher:	Is that a teddy bear?
Jerry:	Yeah.
Teacher:	Is it new?
Jerry:	(Shakes head yes.)
Teacher:	Can you tell us about your bear?
Jerry:	(Silence.)
Teacher:	Jerry, why don't you walk around and show your bear to everyone?

Jerry needed prompting, but the teacher in this example dominated the conversation and Jerry said only one word—"Yeah." Two strategies may help. First, the teacher talks with children like Jerry and helps them plan something to say. Second, the teacher invites listeners to ask the speakers "5 Ws plus one" questions (who, what, where, when, why, and how).

Classmates are the audience for show-and-tell activities, but often teachers become the focus (Cazden, 1988). To avoid this, teachers join the audience rather than direct the activity. They also limit their comments and allow the student who is sharing to assume responsibility for the activity and the discussion that follows. Students can ask three or four classmates for comments and then choose which student will share next. It is difficult for teachers to share control of their classrooms, but young students are capable of handling the activity themselves.

Show-and-tell can evolve into an informal type of oral report for middle-grade students, especially for students with limited language fluency. When this method is used effectively, older students gain valuable practice talking to classmates in an informal and nonthreatening situation. As with young children's show-and-tell activities, older students bring objects from home to share with classmates. For example, students can talk about a collection of sharks' teeth, a program from an Ice Capades show they attended, a recently found snake skin, or snapshots of a vacation at Yellowstone National Park. Students prepare for their presentations as younger children do, planning what they will say and keeping to two or three main points. They also might want to rehearse their presentations so that they will be confident and fluent presenters.

Oral Reports

Learning how to prepare and present an oral report is an important efferent talk activity for middle- and upper-grade students. But students are often assigned an oral report without any guidance about how to prepare and give one. Too many students simply copy the report verbatim from an encyclopedia and then read it aloud. The result is that students learn to fear speaking in front of a group rather than gain confidence in their oral language abilities.

Students prepare and give reports about topics they are studying in social studies and science. Giving a report orally helps students to learn about topics in specific content areas as well as to develop their speaking abilities. Students need more than just an assignment to prepare a report for presentation on a particular date; they need to learn how to prepare and present an oral report. The four steps in giving reports are listed in the Step by Step feature on page 366.

Students are usually the audience for the oral reports, and members of the audience have responsibilities: They should be attentive, listen to the speaker, ask questions, and applaud the speaker. Sometimes they also provide feedback to speakers about their presentations using a checklist or rubric, but at other times students self-assess the process they used to prepare and give their presentations. The Weaving Assessment Into Practice feature on page 367 presents a self-assessment rubric developed by a fourth-grade class. It lists questions about the students' preparation for the presentation and about the presentation itself.

Interviews

Almost all children see interviews on television news programs and are familiar with the interviewing techniques reporters use. Interviewing is an

Oral Reports

Step by Step

1. **Choose a topic.**   Students begin by brainstorming a list of possible topics related to the theme cycle, and then each student chooses a topic for the report. Next, students inventory, or think over, what they know about their topic and decide what they need to learn about it. Teachers often help students identify several key questions to focus the report.

2. **Gather and organize information.**   Students gather information to answer the key questions using a variety of resources, including informational books, content-area textbooks, the Internet, and encyclopedias. Encyclopedias are a valuable resource, but they are only one possible source, and other reference materials must be available so that students will learn to use them. In addition, students can view videotapes and can interview people in the community who have special expertise on the topic. Students often use clusters or data charts (McKenzie, 1979) to organize the important information for their reports. Figure 8–5 shows a cluster and a data chart for a report on the human body. The three key questions are clear in both graphic organizers.

3. **Develop the report.**   Students review the information they have gathered and decide how best to present it so that the report will be both interesting and well organized. Students can transfer the notes they want to use for their reports from the cluster or data chart onto note cards. Only key words—not sentences or paragraphs—should be written on the cards.

4. **Create visuals.**   Students develop visuals, such as charts, diagrams, maps, pictures, models, and time lines. Visuals provide a crutch for the speaker and add an element of interest for the listeners.

5. **Rehearse the presentation.**   Students choose an interesting fact to begin their presentation, review key points, and read over their note cards. However, they do not read the report verbatim from the note cards. Then students practice giving their report.

6. **Give the presentation.**   Before the presentations begin, teachers teach minilessons on the characteristics of successful presentations. For instance, speakers should talk loudly enough for all to hear, look at the audience, keep to the key points, refer to note cards for important facts, and use the visuals they have prepared.

FIGURE 8-5   *A Cluster and a Data Chart for a Report on the Human Body*

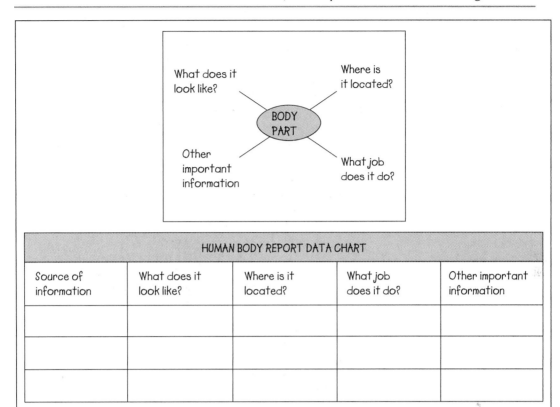

HUMAN BODY REPORT DATA CHART				
Source of information	What does it look like?	Where is it located?	What job does it do?	Other important information

Weaving Assessment Into Practice

A Self-Assessment Rubric for Oral Reports

Name _____   Date _____

Topic _____

	no	1	2	3	4	yes
1. Did you collect enough information on a cluster or data chart?		—	—	—	—	
2. Did you make a useful chart or visual to show during your presentation?		—	—	—	—	
3. Did you rehearse your presentation?		—	—	—	—	
4. Did you speak loudly so everyone could hear?		—	—	—	—	
5. Did you look at the audience?		—	—	—	—	
6. Did you use your visuals?		—	—	—	—	
7. Did you make your main points?		—	—	—	—	
8. How pleased were you with your report?		—	—	—	—	
9. How did the audience respond?		—	—	—	—	

FIGURE 8-6 *A First Grader's Interview Report*

Mr. Kirtley came down.
We asked him questions. He
answered them. He is
blind. His dog's name is
Milo.

exciting language arts activity that helps students refine questioning skills and use oral and written language for authentic purposes (Haley-James & Hobson, 1980).

Interviewing is an important language tool that can be integrated effectively in literature focus units and theme cycles. As part of a theme cycle on school, for example, a class of first graders invited the local high school principal to visit their class to be interviewed. The principal, who had been blinded several years earlier, brought his guide dog with him. The children asked him questions about how visually impaired people manage everyday tasks as well as how he performed his job as a principal. They also asked questions about his guide dog. After the interview, students drew pictures and wrote summaries of the interview. One first grader's report is shown in Figure 8–6.

Or, during a literature focus unit on *Number the Stars* (Lowry, 1989), fifth graders can interview grandparents and great-grandparents about their memories of World War II. After reading excerpts from Studs Terkel's book *Working* (1974), a class of eighth graders interviewed people in the community to learn about their jobs. To begin, students brainstormed a list of 25 questions they might ask people about their jobs. Then they interviewed people they had selected and shared the answers with the class. Afterward, students wrote reports of their interviews, either in the first person, as Terkel did, or in the third person (Bowser, 1993). Students worked in small groups several times during this

Interviews

1. **Choose questions**   Students write a list of questions to ask the person being interviewed. They begin by brainstorming possible questions, and then they narrow the list to the questions that are most likely to elicit useful information. Students should avoid questions that require only yes or no answers. Students often write the questions on note cards, and then they sequence the cards in a reasonable order.

2. **Conduct the interview.**   Students greet the person being interviewed and conduct the interview by asking questions they have prepared. They take notes or tape-record the answers. They ask followup questions about points that are not clear, and if the answer to one question brings up another question that has not been written down, students ask it anyway. Students are polite and are respectful of the answers and opinions of the person being interviewed. At the end of the interview, students thank the person for participating.

3. **Share the results.**   Students share the results of the interview in one of several ways: They may present an oral report, write a report or newspaper article, or make a poster.

project. Before the interviews, they brainstormed questions in small groups, and they met again in small groups to revise and edit their compositions. The papers were both informative and insightful, as this excerpt from one student's report about being a real estate agent shows: "Long and unpredictable hours are what she hates most about her job. You never know how much time you'll be spending with a customer. . . . She does not have close friends at work because the business is so competitive" (Bowser, 1993, p. 40).

One way to introduce interviewing is to watch interviews conducted on a television newscast and discuss what the purpose of the interview is, what a reporter does before and after an interview, and what types of questions are asked. Interviewers use a variety of questions, some to elicit facts and others to probe for feelings and opinions, but all questions are open-ended. Rarely do interviewers ask questions that require only a yes or no answer.

Interviewing involves far more than simply conducting the actual interview. Students prepare for the interview in advance and follow up after the interview by using what they have learned in some way. The steps for interviews are given in the Step by Step feature above.

Teachers assess students' interviews by checking that they followed the three steps of the interview process and by examining the quality of their final products. Similarly, students can assess their own use of the interview process and their reports, much as they assess other types of efferent talk projects.

CLASSROOM LIBRARY

Books That Spark Debates

Armstrong, W. (1969). *Sounder.* New York: Harper & Row. (M–U)

Avi. (1991). *Nothing but the truth.* New York: Orchard. (U)

Babbitt, N. (1975). *Tuck everlasting.* New York: Farrar, Straus & Giroux. (U)

Bauer, M. D. (1986). *On my honor.* Boston: Houghton Mifflin. (M)

Bunting, E. (1991). *Fly away home.* New York: Clarion. (M)

Bunting, E. (1994). *A day's work.* New York: Clarion. (M)

Bunting, E. (1994). *Smoky night.* San Diego, CA: Harcourt Brace. (M)

Byars, B. (1968). *The midnight fox.* New York: Viking. (M)

Clements, A. (1996). *Frindle.* New York: Aladdin. (M–U)

Curtis, C. P. (1995). *The Watsons go to Birmingham–1963.* New York: Delacorte. (M–U)

Fox, P. (1984). *One-eyed cat.* New York: Bradbury. (M–U)

Gantos, J. (2000). *Joey Pigza loses control.* New York: Farrar, Straus & Giroux. (U)

Gardiner, J. R. (1980). *Stone Fox.* New York: Harper & Row. (M)

Haddix, M. P. (1998). *Among the hidden.* New York: Aladdin. (U)

Lowry, L. (1989). *Number the stars.* Boston: Houghton Mifflin. (M–U)

Lowry, L. (1993). *The giver.* Boston: Houghton Mifflin. (U)

Meunier, B. (2003). *Pipiolo and the roof dogs.* New York: Dutton. (M)

Naylor, P. R. (1991). *Shiloh.* New York: Atheneum. (M)

Paterson, K. *The great Gilly Hopkins.* New York: Crowell. (U)

Ryan, P. M. (1998). *Riding Freedom.* New York: Scholastic. (M–U)

Sachar, L. (1998). *Holes.* New York: Farrar, Straus & Giroux. (U)

Speare, E. G. (1983). *The sign of the beaver.* Boston: Houghton Mifflin. (M–U)

Staples, S. F. (1989). *Shabanu: Daughter of the wind.* New York: Knopf. (U)

Steig, W. (1982). *Doctor DeSoto.* New York: Farrar, Straus & Giroux. (M)

Van Allsburg, C. (1979). *The garden of Abdul Gasazi.* Boston: Houghton Mifflin. (M)

Van Allsburg, C. (1985). *The polar express.* Boston: Houghton Mifflin. (M)

Van Allsburg, C. (1992). *The witch's broom.* Boston: Houghton Mifflin. (M)

Debates

Students participate in debates when they are excited about an issue and when most of the students have taken positions on one side of the issue or the other. Students can debate issues related to social studies and science topics, community issues, and current events. Middle- and upper-grade students can also debate topics related to books they are reading. For example, after reading *Tuck Everlasting* (Babbitt, 1975), they might debate whether people should live forever. Books that spark debates are listed in the Classroom Library box above. Upper-grade students have strong feelings about the issues raised in many of these books, and debating provides a forum for thinking about important issues.

As they participate in debates, students learn how to use oral language to persuade their classmates. They must be able to articulate their viewpoints clearly, use information and emotional appeals to support their viewpoints, and think on their feet to respond to the opposing team's questions. The steps in a debate are listed in the Step by Step feature on page 371.

Students who are not participating in the debate often assess their classmates' performance in the debate and determine the winning team. The students can develop an assessment form and award points to each team based on the effectiveness of the team's arguments and manner of presentation.

Debates

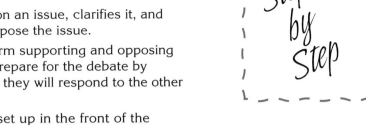

1. **Identify a topic.**　The class decides on an issue, clarifies it, and identifies positions that support or oppose the issue.

2. **Prepare for the debate.**　Students form supporting and opposing teams. Then students in each team prepare for the debate by deciding on their arguments and how they will respond to the other team's arguments.

3. **Conduct the debate.**　A podium is set up in the front of the classroom, and the teacher initiates the debate by asking a student from the supporting side to state that position on the issue. After this opening statement, a student on the opposing side makes a statement. From this point, students take turns going to the podium and speaking in support of or in opposition to the issue. Students who have just made a statement are often asked a question before a student for the other side makes a return statement.

4. **Conclude the debate.**　After students on both sides have presented their viewpoints, one member from each team makes a final statement to sum up that team's position.

DRAMATIC ACTIVITIES

Drama provides a medium for students to use language, both verbal and nonverbal, in a meaningful context. Drama is not only a powerful form of communication, but it is also a valuable way of knowing. When children participate in dramatic activities, they interact with classmates, share experiences, and explore their own understanding. According to Dorothy Heathcote, a highly acclaimed British drama teacher, drama "cracks the code" so that the message can be understood (Wagner, 1976). Drama has this power because it involves both logical, left-brain thinking and creative, right-brain thinking; because it requires active experience (the basic, and first, way of learning); and because it integrates the language arts. Research confirms that drama has a positive effect on both students' oral language development and their literacy learning (Kardash & Wright, 1987; Wagner, 1988). Drama is often neglected, however, because some consider it a nonessential part of the language arts curriculum.

Many dramatic activities that elementary students participate in are informal and spontaneous. Others involve some rehearsal and are presented for an audience. The most formal dramatic activities are theatrical productions, which are polished performances of a play produced on a stage and before a large audience. They require extensive rehearsal and are quite formal. Because the purpose of theatrical productions is a polished presentation, they are audience centered rather than child centered. Instead of encouraging students to be spontaneous and improvisational, they require that students memorize lines. They are not recommended for students in elementary grades unless students write the scripts themselves (Stewig, 1983; Wagner, 1976).

Role-Playing

Students assume the role of another person as they act out stories or reenact historical events. Through role-playing, students step into someone else's shoes and view the world from another perspective. Role-playing activities are usually informal. Students assume roles and then act out the drama as the teacher narrates or guides the dramatization.

Students role-play stories during literature focus units. These activities can be done during the responding, exploring, and applying stages. Teachers often use role-playing as they are reading a story with students to emphasize key points in the story, to clarify misunderstandings, or to deepen students' comprehension. For example, a key point in *Johnny Tremain* (Forbes, 1970) for a role-playing activity occurs when Johnny tragically burns his hand. This moment is important because of the event's ramifications through the rest of the story. Another key point for role-playing occurs when Johnny has given up hope and lies among the graves on Copp's Hill. Because students enjoy the role-playing activity, they often ask to role-play the part about the Boston Tea Party—because it is fun, not because they do not understand.

After reading, students often act out folktales and other stories told in picture books using both dialogue and body movements. Teachers use role-playing to review and sequence the events in the story and to develop students' concept of story. Folktales such as *The Gingerbread Boy* (Galdone, 1975) and *If You Give a Mouse a Cookie* (Numeroff, 1985) are good for younger children to dramatize because they are repetitive. Middle- and upper-grade students act out favorite scenes from longer stories, such as *Shiloh* (Naylor, 1991), *Nightjohn* (Paulsen, 1993), and *The Giver* (Lowry, 1993). Students can read biographies, such as *The Life and Death of Crazy Horse* (Freedman, 1996) and *Mandela: From the Life of the South African Statesman* (Cooper, 1996), and dramatize events from these people's lives.

Students also use role-playing to create dramatic productions of a favorite story as a project. Students follow approximately the same steps they do in storytelling. They choose roles in the story, reread the story, identify key parts to include in the dramatization, collect simple props, and rehearse the story several times. Then they present the story to their classmates.

Role-playing in theme cycles is designed to help students gain insights about how to handle real-life problems and understand historical and current events (Nelson, 1988). Students assume the role of another person—not roles in a story, but rather the roles people play in society—and reenact events they are studying.

Heathcote has developed an innovative approach to role-playing to help students experience and better understand historical events (Wagner, 1976). Through a process she calls "funneling," Heathcote chooses a dramatic focus from a general topic (e.g., ancient Rome, the Civil War, the Pilgrims). She begins by thinking of all the aspects of the general topic and then decides on a dramatic focus—a particular critical moment. For example, using the topic of the Pilgrims, one possible focus is the night of December 20, 1620, 11 weeks after the Pilgrims set sail from England on the *Mayflower* and the night before the ship reached Plymouth.

The improvisation begins when students assume roles; the teacher becomes a character, too. As they begin to role-play the event, questions draw students' attention to certain features and probe their understanding. Questions about the Pilgrims might include:

- Where are you?
- After 11 weeks sailing the Atlantic Ocean, what do you think will happen?
- How are you feeling?
- Why did you leave England?
- What kind of life do you dream of in the new land?
- Can you survive in this cold winter weather?

These questions also provide information by reminding students of the time of year, the problems they are having, and the length of the voyage.

Heathcote recommends that teachers stop sometimes in the middle of role-playing and ask students to write what they are thinking and feeling in a quick-write or simulated-journal entry. As part of the Pilgrim improvisation, students can be asked to write an entry in their simulated journals for December 20, 1620. A simulated-journal entry written by a fourth-grade "Pilgrim" is shown in Figure 8–7. After the writing activity, students continue role-playing.

Heathcote uses drama to begin study on a topic rather than as a culminating activity in which students apply all they have learned because she believes that role-playing experiences stimulate children's curiosity and make them want to read books and learn more about a historical or current event. Whether you use role-playing as an introduction or as a conclusion, it is a valuable activity because students become immersed in the event. By reliving it, they are learning far more than mere facts.

For more information on simulated journals, see Chapter 6, "Personal Writing."

FIGURE 8–7   *A Fourth-Grade Pilgrim's Simulated-Journal Entry*

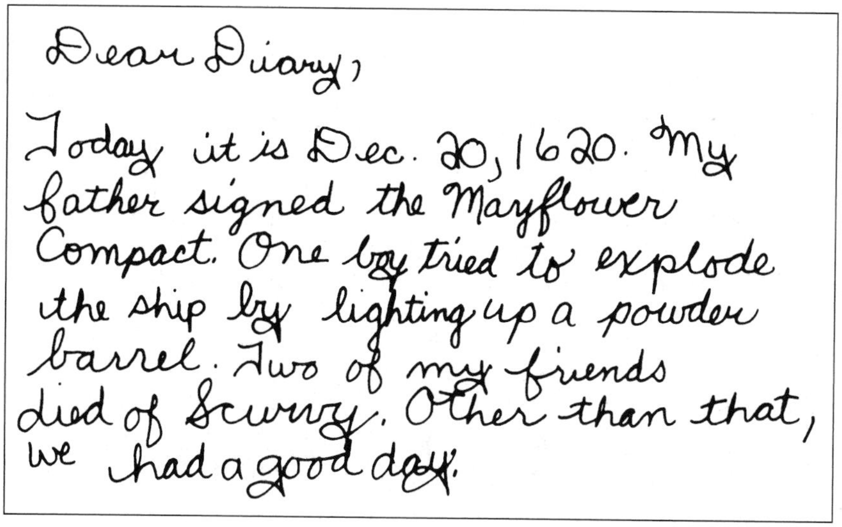

Dear Diary,

Today it is Dec. 20, 1620. My father signed the Mayflower Compact. One boy tried to explode the ship by lighting up a powder barrel. Two of my friends died of Scurvy. Other than that, we had a good day.

Puppets and Other Props

Students create characters with puppets. A second grader pulls a green sock on one hand and a brown sock on the other hand, and with these socks that simply have buttons sewn on for eyes, the characters of Frog and Toad from Arnold Lobel's award-winning books *Frog and Toad Are Friends* (1970) and *Frog and Toad Together* (1972) come to life. The student talks in the voices of the two characters and involves the characters in events from the stories. Whereas adults often feel self-conscious with puppets, children do not.

Children can create puppet shows with commercially manufactured puppets, or they can construct their own. When children create their own puppets, the only limitations are their imaginations, their ability to construct things, and the materials at hand. Puppets can be especially useful with shy students. Puppets can be helpful not only in all types of dramatic activities, but also as a novel way to introduce a language skill, such as use of quotation marks. Teachers can use puppets to improvise a dialogue and then record it using quotation marks.

Simple puppets provide children with the opportunity to develop both creative and dramatic ability. The simpler the puppet, the more is left to the imagination of the audience and the puppeteer. Constructing elaborate puppets is beyond the resources of both teachers and students. The type of puppets the students make, however, depends on how they will be used. Students can construct puppets using all sorts of scrap materials. Following are descriptions for making eight types of hand and finger puppets; the puppets are illustrated in Figure 8–8.

1. Stick puppets.   Stick puppets are versatile and perhaps the easiest to make. Sticks, tongue depressors, dowels, and straws can be used. The rest of the puppet is attached to the stick and is constructed from papier-mâché, Styrofoam balls, pictures students have drawn, or pictures cut from magazines and mounted on cardboard. Students draw or paint the features on the materials they have selected for the head and body. Some puppets may need only a head; others may also need a body. Making stick puppets provides an opportunity to combine art and drama.

2. Paper bag puppets.   These puppets are also simple to make. The paper bags should be the right size to fit students' hands. Paper lunch bags are a convenient size, although smaller bags are better for kindergartners. What characters they portray and what emphasis the students give the size of the character are the determining factors, however. Students place the puppet's mouth at the fold of the paper bag. Then they paint on faces and clothes, add yarn for hair, and attach arms and legs. Students should choose ways to decorate their bag puppets to match the characters they develop.

3. Cylinder puppets.   Cylinder puppets are made from cardboard tubes from bathroom tissue, paper towel, and aluminum foil rolls. The diameter and length of the cylinder determine the size of the puppet. The cylinders can be painted, and various appendages and clothing can be attached. Again, the character's role should determine how the puppet is costumed. Students insert their fingers in the bottom of the cylinder to manipulate the puppet.

4. Sock puppets.   Sock puppets are quite versatile. A sock can be used as is, with button eyes, yarn hair, pipe-cleaner antennae, and other features added. The sock can also be cut at the toe to create a mouth, and whatever else is needed to give the impression of the character can be added.

FIGURE 8-8

Types of Puppets Students Can Make

Stick Puppet

Paper Bag Puppet

Cylinder Puppet

Sock Puppet

Styrofoam Puppet

Paper Plate Puppet

Finger Puppet
(with tabs)

Finger puppet
(from glove finger)

Cloth Puppet

   5. Cup puppets.   Even primary-grade students can make puppets from Styrofoam cups. They glue facial features, hair, wings, and other decorations on the cup. Pipe cleaners, toothpicks, and cotton swabs tipped with glitter can easily be attached to a Styrofoam cup. Then a stick or heavy-duty straw is attached to the inside of the cup as the handle.

   6. Paper plate puppets.   Paper plates can be used for face puppets as well as for masks. Students add junk materials to decorate the puppets, then tape a stick or ruler to the back of the plate as a handle.

   7. Finger puppets.   Students can make several types of finger puppets. For one type, students draw, color, and cut out small figures, then add tabs to either side of the figure and tape the tabs together to fit around the finger. Larger puppets can be taped to fit around the hand. For a second type of finger puppet, students cut the finger section from a glove and add decoration. The pointed part that separates the compartments of an egg carton can also be used for a finger puppet.

8. Cloth puppets. If parents are available to assist with the sewing, students can make cloth puppets. Two pieces of cloth are sewn together on all sides except the bottom; then students personalize the puppets using scraps of fabric, lace, yarn, and other materials.

After students have created their puppets, they can perform the puppet show almost anywhere. They can make a stage from an empty appliance packing crate or an empty television cabinet. They can also drape blankets or cloths in front of classroom tables and desks. They might also turn a table on its side. There may be other classroom objects your students can use as makeshift stages.

Scriptwriting and Theatrical Productions

Scripts are a unique written language form that elementary students need opportunities to explore. Scriptwriting often grows out of role-playing and storytelling. Soon students recognize the need to write notes when they prepare for plays, puppet shows, readers theatre, and other dramatic productions. This need provides the impetus for introducing students to the unique dramatic conventions and for encouraging them to write scripts to present as theatrical productions.

Writing Scripts. Once students want to write scripts, they will recognize the need to add the structures unique to dramatic writing to their repertoire of written language conventions. Students begin by examining scripts. It is especially effective to have students compare narrative and script versions of the same story; for example, Richard George has adapted two of Roald Dahl's fantastic stories, *Charlie and the Chocolate Factory* (1976) and *James and the Giant Peach* (1982), into scripts.

Then students discuss their observations and compile a list of the unique characteristics of scripts. An upper-grade class compiled the list of unique dramatic conventions presented in Figure 8–9.

The next step is to have students apply what they have learned about scripts by writing a class collaboration or group script. The whole class develops a script by adapting a familiar story. As the script is being written, the teacher refers to the chart of dramatic conventions and asks students to check that they are using these conventions. Collaborative writing affords unique teaching opportunities and needed practice for students before they must write individually. After the script is completed, students read it using readers theatre procedures, or produce it as a puppet show or play.

Once students are aware of the dramatic conventions and have participated in writing a class collaboration script, they can write scripts individually or in small groups. Students often adapt familiar stories for their first scripts; later, they will want to create original scripts. An excerpt from "The Lonely Troll," a

FIGURE 8-9   *An Upper-Grade-Class List of Dramatic Conventions*

Everything You Ever Wanted to Know About Scripts

1. Scripts are divided into acts and scenes.
2. Scripts have four parts:
   a. a list of characters (or cast)
   b. the setting at the beginning of each act or scene
   c. stage directions written in parentheses
   d. dialogue
3. The dialogue carries the action.
4. Descriptions and other information are set apart in the setting or in stage directions.
5. Stage directions give actors important information about how to act and how to feel.
6. The dialogue is written like this:
   Character's Name: Dialogue
7. Sometimes a narrator is used to quickly fill in parts of the story.

script written by a team of five upper-grade students, appears in Figure 8–10 as an example of the type of scripts older students can compose. Although most of the scripts they write are narrative, students also create biographical scripts about famous people or informational scripts about science or social studies topics.

Producing Video Scripts.   Students use a similar approach in writing scripts that will be videotaped, but they must now consider the visual component of the film as well as the written script. They often compose their scripts on storyboards, which focus their attention on the camera's view and how the story they are creating will be filmed (Cox, 1985). Storyboards—sheets of paper divided into three sections—are used to sketch in scenes. Students place a series of three or four large squares in a row down the center of the paper, with space for dialogue and narration on the left and shooting directions on the right. Cox compares storyboards to road maps because they provide directions for filming the script. The scene renderings and the shooting directions help students tie the dialogue to the visual images that will appear on the videotape. Figure 8–11 shows a sample storyboard form with an excerpt from a fourth-grade class collaboration script.

The script can be produced several ways—as a live-action play, as a puppet show, or through animation. After writing the script on the storyboards or transferring a previously written script to storyboards, students collect or construct the props they will need to produce the script. Students design a backdrop and collect clothes for costumes. Teachers should encourage students to keep the production details simple. Students should also print the title and credits on large posters to appear at the beginning of the film. After several rehearsals, the students film the script using a video camera.

FIGURE 8-10   *An Excerpt From a Script Written by Upper-Grade Students*

The Lonely Troll

NARRATOR: Once upon a time, in a far, far away land, there was a troll named Pippin who lived all alone in his little corner of the woods. The troll hated all the creatures of the woods and was very lonely because he didn't have anyone to talk to since he scared everyone away. One day, a dwarf named Sam wandered into Pippin's yard and . . .

PIPPIN: Grrr. What are you doing here?

SAM: Ahhhhh! A troll! Please don't eat me!

PIPPIN: Why shouldn't I?

SAM: (Begging) Look, I'm all skin and bones. I won't make a good meal.

PIPPIN: You look fat enough for me. (Turns to audience) Do you think I should eat him? (Sam jumps off stage and hides in the audience.)

PIPPIN: Where did he go? (Pippin jumps off stage and looks for Sam. When he finds Sam, he takes him back on stage, laughing; then he ties Sam up.) Ha, ha, ha. Boy, that sure did tire me out. (Yawn) I'll take a nap. Then I'll eat him later. (Pippin falls asleep. Lights dim. Sam escapes and runs behind a tree. Lights return, and Pippin wakens.)

PIPPIN: (To audience) Where's my breakfast? (Sam peeps out from behind a tree and cautions the audience to be quiet.) Huh? Did someone say he was behind that tree? (Points to tree. Pippin walks around. Sam kicks him in the rear. Pippin falls and is knocked out.)

SAM: I must get out of here, and warn the queen about this short, small, mean, ugly troll. (Sam leaves. Curtains close.)

NARRATOR: So Sam went to tell Queen Muffy about the troll. Meanwhile, in the forest, Pippin awakens, and decides to set a trap for Sam. (Open curtains to forest scene, showing Pippin making a box trap.)

PIPPIN: Ha, ha, ha! That stupid dwarf will come back here looking for me. When he sees this ring, he'll take it. Then, I'll trap him! Ha, ha, ha, ha. (Pippin hides.)

NARRATOR: The dwarf finally reaches Queen Muffy's castle and hurries to tell her his story.

SAM: (Open curtains to Queen Muffy sitting on a throne, eating. Sam rushes in, out of breath.) I have some very important news for you. There's . . .

QUEEN: I don't have time for you.

SAM: But, I . . .

QUEEN: Come, come. Don't bother me with small things.

SAM: There's an ugly old . . .

QUEEN: You're wasting my time.

SAM: I just wanted to warn you, there's a big, ugly, mean . . .

QUEEN: Hurry up.

SAM: . . . man-eating . . .

QUEEN: This had better be important.

SAM: (Angry, he yells) THERE'S A TROLL IN THE FOREST!!!

QUEEN: Who cares if there's a . . . a . . . (Screams) A TROLL!!!

SAM: That's what I've been saying. A troll—in the forest.

QUEEN: Then I must send out my faithful knight . . . Sir Skippy . . . to kill him. I shall offer a reward. (Queen exits.)

FIGURE 8-11 *An Excerpt From a Class Collaboration Storyboard Script*

DIALOGUE	SCENE	SHOOTING DIRECTIONS
Paula: Hurry up, Parker. You'll miss the bus. Parker: Coming! Paula: Here's what we'll do. We'll go to the library and find a book on how to kill witches.	CITY LIBRARY	They ride the bus to the library. Follow them up the stairs into the library.
Parker: I found the book, Paula! Paula: Let's see, here it is! How to kill a witch. Parker: Here's what we'll do. Psst. Psst. Psst. (whispering)	How to Kill Witches	They find the book. Hold book up. Close up Check index to find out how to kill her.

Review

Teachers sustain talk in the elementary classroom because talk has definite benefits for elementary students. Too often, teachers assume that students already know how to talk, so they concentrate on reading and writing. The four types of talk activities—conversations, aesthetic talk, efferent talk, and dramatic activities—are important for developing children's talk, and they also complement students' written language development. The key points in this chapter include:

1. Talk is a necessary ingredient for learning.
2. Students talk in informal conversations as part of all four instructional patterns.
3. In grand conversations, students use aesthetic talk to respond to a book and deepen their understanding.
4. In storytelling and readers theatre activities, students use aesthetic talk to present stories.
5. Students use efferent talk as they participate in instructional conversations.
6. K-W-L charts are a good way to help students talk about what they are learning in a theme cycle.
7. In show-and-tell, oral reports, interviews, and debates, students use efferent talk to inform and persuade listeners.
8. Drama is not only a powerful form of communication, but also a valuable way of knowing.

Visit Chapter 8 on the Companion Website at www.prenhall.com/tompkins to:

• Check your understanding of the concepts presented in the chapter

• Access the Extensions (activities and a list of related readings)

• Link to related websites

9. Students use role-playing and puppets to learn and share their learning in literature focus units and theme cycles.
10. In connection with literature focus units and theme cycles, students can write scripts that they present as a play or on videotape.

Professional References

Bowser, J. (1993). Structuring the middle-school classroom for spoken language. *English Journal, 82,* 38–41.

Busching, B. A. (1981). Readers theatre: An education for language and life. *Language Arts, 58,* 330–338.

Cazden, C. D. (1988). *Classroom discourse: The language of teaching and learning.* Portsmouth, NH: Heinemann.

Cintorino, M. A. (1993). Getting together, getting along, getting to the business of teaching and learning. *English Journal, 82,* 23–32.

Cox, C. (1985). Filmmaking as a composing process. *Language Arts, 62,* 60–69.

Eeds, M., & Wells, D. (1989). Grand conversations: An exploration of meaning construction in literature study groups. *Research in the Teaching of English, 23,* 4–29.

Goldenberg, C. (1992/1993). Instructional conversations: Promoting comprehension through discussion. *The Reading Teacher, 46,* 316–326.

Haley-James, S. M., & Hobson, C. D. (1980). Interviewing: A means of encouraging the drive to communicate. *Language Arts, 57,* 497–502.

Heath, S. B. (1983). Research currents: A lot of talk about nothing. *Language Arts, 60,* 999–1007.

Kardash, C. A. M., & Wright, L. (1987, Winter). Does creative drama benefit elementary school students: A meta-analysis. *Youth Theater Journal,* 11–18.

Kaufman, D. (2000). *Conferences and conversations: Listening to the literate classroom.* Portsmouth, NH: Heinemann.

Kingore, B. W. (1982). Storytelling: A bridge from the university to the elementary school to the home. *Language Arts, 59,* 28–32.

Laughlin, M. K., & Latrobe, K. H. (1989). *Readers theatre for children: Scripts and script development.* Englewood, CO: Libraries Unlimited.

Manna, A. L. (1984). Making language come alive through reading plays. *The Reading Teacher, 37,* 712–717.

McKenzie, G. R. (1979). Data charts: A crutch for helping pupils organize reports. *Language Arts, 56,* 784–788.

Morrow, L. M. (1979). Exciting children about literature through creative storytelling techniques. *Language Arts, 56,* 236–243.

Morrow, L. M. (1985). Reading and retelling stories: Strategies for emergent readers. *The Reading Teacher, 38,* 870–875.

Nelson, P. A. (1988). Drama, doorway to the past. *Language Arts, 65,* 20–25.

Nystrand, M., Gamoran, A., & Heck, M. J. (1993). Using small groups for response to and thinking about literature. *English Journal, 82,* 14–22.

Ogle, D. M. (1986). K-W-L: A teaching model that develops active reading of expository text. *The Reading Teacher, 39,* 564–570.

Ogle, D. M. (1989). The know, want to know, learn strategy. In K. D. Muth (Ed.), *Children's comprehension of text: Research into practice* (pp. 205–223). Newark, DE: International Reading Association.

Peterson, R., & Eeds, M. (1990). *Grand conversations: Literature groups in action.* New York: Scholastic.

Pressley, M. (1992). Encouraging mindful use of prior knowledge: Attempting to construct explanatory answers facilitates learning. *Educational Psychologist, 27,* 91–109.

Shafer, K. (1993). Talk in the middle: Two conversational skills for friendship. *English Journal, 82,* 53–55.

Shuy, R. W. (1987). Research currents: Dialogue as the heart of learning. *Language Arts, 64,* 890–897.

Smith, P. G. (Ed.). (2001). *Talking classrooms: Shaping children's learning through oral language instruction.* Newark, DE: International Reading Association.

Sorenson, M. (1993). Teach each other: Connecting talking and writing. *English Journal, 82,* 42–47.

Stewig, J. W. (1983). *Informal drama in the elementary language arts program.* New York: Teachers College Press.

Wagner, B. J. (1976). *Dorothy Heathcote: Drama as a learning medium.* Washington, DC: National Education Association.

Wagner, B. J. (1988). Research currents: Does classroom drama affect the arts of language? *Language Arts, 65,* 46–55.

Wells, G., & Chang-Wells, G. L. (1992). *Constructing knowledge together: Classrooms as centers of inquiry and literacy.* Portsmouth, NH: Heinemann.

Wilen, W. W. (1986). *Questioning skills for teachers* (2nd ed.). Washington, DC: National Education Association.

Wilkinson, L. C. (1984). Research currents: Peer group talk in elementary school. *Language Arts, 61,* 164–169.

Wittrock, M. C., & Alesandrini, K. (1990). Generation of summaries and analogies and analytic and holistic abilities. *American Research Journal, 27,* 489–502.

Worthy, J., & Prater, K. (2002). "I thought about it all night": Readers theatre for reading fluency and motivation. *The Reading Teacher, 56,* 294–297.

Children's Book References

Babbitt, N. (1975). *Tuck everlasting.* New York: Farrar, Straus & Giroux.

Brett, J. (1989). *The mitten.* New York: Putnam.

Cooper, F. (1996). *Mandela: From the life of the South African statesman.* New York: Philomel.

Danziger, P. (1994). *Amber Brown is not a crayon.* New York: Putnam.

Dahl, R. (1976). *Charlie and the chocolate factory.* New York: Knopf.

Dahl, R. (1982). *James and the giant peach.* New York: Knopf.

dePaola, T. (1978). *Pancakes for breakfast.* New York: Harcourt Brace Jovanovich.

Forbes, E. (1970). *Johnny Tremain: A story of Boston in revolt.* Boston: Houghton Mifflin.

Freedman, R. (1996). *The life and death of Crazy Horse.* New York: Holiday House.

Galdone, P. (1975). *The gingerbread boy.* New York: Seabury.

Lobel, A. (1970). *Frog and Toad are friends.* New York: Harper & Row.

Lobel, A. (1972). *Frog and Toad together.* New York: Harper & Row.

Lowry, L. (1989). *Number the stars.* Boston: Houghton Mifflin.

Lowry, L. (1993). *The giver.* Boston: Houghton Mifflin.

Naylor, P. R. (1991). *Shiloh.* New York: Atheneum.

Numeroff, L. J. (1985). *If you give a mouse a cookie.* New York: Harper & Row.

Paulsen, G. (1993). *Nightjohn.* New York: Delacorte.

Polacco, P. (1988). *Rechenka's eggs.* New York: Philomel.

Soto, G. (1987). *The cat's meow.* New York: Scholastic.

Stanley, D. (1983). *The conversation club.* New York: Macmillan.

Terkel, S. (1974). *Working.* New York: Pantheon.

Van Allsburg, C. (1991). *The wretched stone.* Boston: Houghton Mifflin.

Yorinks, A. (1986). *Hey, Al.* New York: Farrar, Straus & Giroux.

9 Reading and Writing Stories

PATTERNS OF PRACTICE

Mrs. Ochs teaches a literature focus unit on *Number the Stars* (Lowry, 1989), a Newbery award–winning story of two girls, one Christian and one Jewish, set in Denmark during World War II. In her unit, she wants to help her fifth-grade students use their knowledge of genre and story structure to deepen their comprehension of the story. She rereads the story, analyzes the elements of story structure in the book, and considers how she wants to teach the unit. She makes the chart shown on page 384.

Reading and Writing Workshop

Literature Focus Units

Literature Circles

Theme Cycles

To begin the unit, Mrs. Ochs asks students about friendship: "Would you help your friend if he or she needed help?" The students talk about friendship and what it means to them. They agree that they would help their friends in any way they could—helping friends get medical treatment if they were ill, and sharing their lunch if they were hungry, for example. One child volunteers that he is sure that his mom would let his friend's family stay at his house if the friend's house burned down. Then Mrs. Ochs asks, "What if your friend asked you to hold something for him or her, something so dangerous that 60 years ago you could be imprisoned or killed for having it?" Many say they would, but

doubt they would ever be called to do that. Then she shows them a broken star of David necklace, similar to the one on the cover of *Number the Stars,* and one student says, "You're talking about the Nazis and the Jews in World War II." The prereading stage continues for 2 more days as students share what they know about the war, and Mrs. Ochs presents information, reads several picture-book stories about the war, and shows a video.

Mrs. Ochs reads the first chapter of *Number the Stars* aloud to students as they follow along in individual copies of the book. She almost always starts a book this way because she wants to get all students off to a good start and because so many concepts and key vocabulary words are introduced in the beginning of a book. After the first chapter, students continue reading the second chapter. Most of the students read independently, but some read with buddies, and Mrs. Ochs continues reading with a group of the six lowest readers.

Then Mrs. Ochs brings all the students together for a grand conversation. The students make connections between the information they have learned about World War II and the story events. Mrs. Ochs reads aloud *The Yellow Star: The Legend of King Christian X of Denmark* (Deedy, 2000), a picture-book story about the Danish king who defies the Nazis, because the king is the focus of the second chapter. The students predict that the Nazis will take Ellen and her family to a concentration camp even though Annemarie and her family try to hide them. After the grand conversation, the students write in reading logs. For this entry, Mrs. Ochs asks students to write predictions about what will happen in the story based on what they know about World War II and what they read in the first two chapters.

> ### How can teachers facilitate students' comprehension of stories?
>
> As teachers teach literature focus units, they include activities at each stage of the reading process to ensure that all students in their classrooms comprehend what they are reading. This attention to comprehension is essential because when students don't understand what they are reading and can't relate the literature to their own lives and the world around them, the experience has been wasted. As you read this vignette, notice how Mrs. Ochs involves her fifth graders in a variety of language arts activities to deepen their understanding of World War II and facilitate their comprehension of the story, *Number the Stars.*

Mrs. Ochs continues having the students read and respond to the chapters. Some students continue to read independently, but many of the students form reading groups so that they can read and talk about the story as they are reading. Mrs. Ochs continues reading with the lowest readers. The whole class comes together after reading each day to talk about the story in a grand conversation. Afterward, they write in journals.

During the grand conversations, Mrs. Ochs probes their understanding of the story and asks students to think about the role of plot, characters, setting, and other elements of story structure in the story. Mrs. Ochs has taught the students about the elements, so they are able to apply their knowledge to the story they are reading. One day, she asks students about the conflict situation in the story. At first the students say that the conflict is between people—Nazis and Danes—but as they continue talking, they realize that the conflict is not between individual people, but within society.

Element	Story Analysis	Teaching Ideas
Plot	The beginning is before Ellen goes into hiding; the middle is while Ellen is in hiding; and the end is after Ellen and her family leave for the safety of Sweden. The problem is saving Ellen's life. The overarching conflict in the story is conflict with the Nazis, who represent society.	Students need background knowledge about World War II, the Nazis, Jews and the holocaust, and Resistance fighters before reading. There are many details, so it is important to focus on the problem and how it will be solved.
Characters	Annemarie and Ellen are the main characters in this story, and through their actions and beliefs, readers learn that these two girls are much more alike than they are different. These two girls are both courageous, one because she has to be, the other because she chooses to be.	Even though one girl is Christian and one is Jewish, the girls are more alike than they are different. A Venn diagram will emphasize this point. Students might make open-mind portraits from one girl's viewpoint.
Setting	The story is set in Denmark during World War II. The setting is integral to the plot and based on actual events, including fishermen ferrying Jews to safety in Sweden.	Use maps of Europe to locate the setting of the story. Students can draw maps and mark story locations, and they can also mark the spread of the German (and Japanese) forces during the war on a world map.
Point of View	The story is limited omniscient. It is told from the third-person viewpoint, and readers know only what Annemarie is thinking.	Students can retell important events from one of the girls' perspectives or from the parents' or the Nazis' viewpoints.
Theme	This story deals with courage and bravery: the Jews, the fishermen, the Resistance fighters, King Christian X and Danes who wore six-pointed, yellow stars on their clothes, and Annemarie and her family. One theme is that people choose to be courageous when they see others mistreated.	Students focus on the theme as they talk in grand conversations and collect favorite quotes from the story. Students might also read about other people who have been courageous to examine the universal qualities of courage.

Another day, Mrs. Ochs talks about the setting. She asks if this story could have happened in the United States. At first the students say no, because the Nazis never invaded the United States, and they use maps to make their point. But as they continue to talk, students broaden their discussion to the persecution of minorities and conclude that persecution can happen anywhere. They cite two examples—the mistreatment of Native Americans and internment of Japanese Americans during World War II.

During the grand conversation after students finish reading *Number the Stars,* Mrs. Ochs asks about the theme. "Did Lois Lowry have a message in her book? What do you think about the theme?" Several students comment that the theme was that the Nazis were bad people. Others said "innocent people get killed in wars" and "peace is better than war." To move the students forward in their thinking, Mrs. Ochs suggests that one theme is about courage or being brave. She reads two sentences from the book: "That's all that *brave* means— not thinking about the dangers. Just thinking about what you must do" (p. 123). The students agree that both girls and their families were brave. Mrs. Ochs asks students to think back through the story and help her brainstorm a list of all the times they were brave. They brainstormed more than 30 instances of bravery!

Mrs. Ochs and her students continue their discussion about the theme for several more days. Finally, she asks them, "Do you think you're brave? Would you be brave if you were Annemarie or Ellen?" They talk about war and having to be brave in a war. "What about Ellen?" Mrs. Ochs asks. "Did she *have* to be brave?" The students agree that she did. "But what about Annemarie? Couldn't she and her family have stayed safely in Copenhagen?" The students are surprised at first by the question, but through their talk, they realize that Annemarie, her family, and the other Resistance fighters had chosen to be brave.

As the students read *Number the Stars,* Mrs. Ochs also involves them in several exploring-stage activities focusing on the story structure. They mark areas of Nazi and Japanese occupation on world maps and draw maps of Denmark. To compare Annemarie and Ellen, they make Venn diagrams and conclude that the girls are more alike than they are different. One student's Venn diagram is shown here. They also make open-mind portraits of one of the girls,

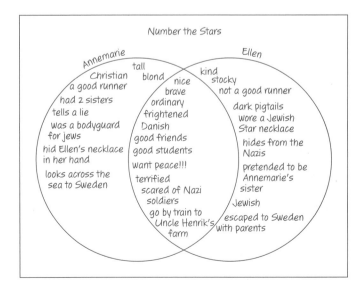

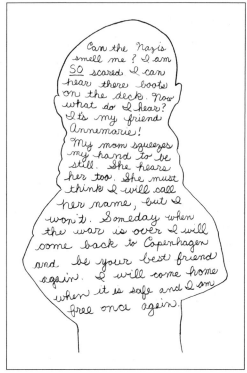

showing what the girl is thinking at several pivotal points in the story. The cover and one page from one student's open-mind portrait of Ellen are shown above.

The students plan an applying-stage activity after the great-grandfather of one of the children comes for a visit. This student brings his great-grandfather to school to talk about his remembrances of World War II, and then the students decide to each interview a grandparent, a great-grandparent, or an elderly neighbor who was alive during the war. The students develop this set of interview questions:

1. What did you do during the war?
2. How old were you?
3. Were you on the home front or the war front?
4. Did you know about the holocaust then?
5. What do you remember most from World War II?

Then each student conducts an interview and writes an essay about the person's wartime experiences using the writing process. They word process their essays so that they have a professional look. Here is one student's essay:

My grandfather Arnold Ott was in college at the time the war started. All of a sudden after Pearl Harbor was attacked, all his classmates started to join the army. He did also and became an engineer that worked on B-24 and B-25 bombers. The military kept sending him to different schools so he would be able to fix all the bombers. He never had to fight because of that. He earned some medals, but he said the real ones were only given

*to those who fought. He said that he was glad that he did not fight be-
cause he had friends that never came back.*

Then Mrs. Ochs duplicates the essays and binds them into books. She also
makes extra copies for the interviewees. The students are so excited about the
people they interviewed and the essays they wrote that they decide to have a
party. They invite the interviewees and introduce them to their classmates, and
they ask the interviewees to autograph the essays they have written about them.

Stories give meaning to the human experience, and they are a powerful way of
knowing and learning. Preschool children listen to family members tell and
read stories aloud, and they have developed an understanding or concept
about stories by the time they come to school. Students use and refine this
knowledge as they read and write stories during the elementary grades. Many
educators, including Jerome Bruner (1986), recommend using stories as a
way into literacy.

 **As you begin
reading this
chapter, you may
want to read the
"Dear Reader"
letter in Chapter 9 on the
Companion Website at
www.prenhall.com/tompkins**

Primary-grade students read and respond to stories such as *Officer Buckle
and Gloria* (Rathmann, 1996), *Where the Wild Things Are* (Sendak, 2003), and
Abuela (Dorros, 1991), and older students read and respond to *Charlotte's Web*
(White, 1980), *The Giver* (Lowry, 1993), and *The Lion, the Witch and the
Wardrobe* (Lewis, 1994). Sometimes teachers call all literature that students
read and write "stories," but stories are a particular type. They have specific
structural elements, including characters and plot.

Students tell and write stories about events in their lives, such as a birthday party, a fishing trip, or a car accident; retell familiar stories, including "The
Gingerbread Man"; and write sequels for stories such as *Jumanji* (Van Allsburg,
1981). The stories that students write reflect the stories they have read. De Ford
(1981) and Eckhoff (1983) found that when primary-grade students read stories in traditional basal reading textbooks, they write stories that reflect the
short, choppy linguistic style of the textbooks, but when students read stories
in trade books, their writing reflects the more sophisticated language structures
and literary style of the trade books. Dressel (1990) also found that the quality
of fifth graders' writing was dependent on the quality of the stories they read or
listened to someone else read aloud, regardless of the students' reading levels.

As you read this chapter, think about these questions:

- How do students develop a concept of story?
- How does students' knowledge of stories affect comprehension?
- How do teachers teach students about story structure?
- How do students read and write stories as part of each of the four
  instructional patterns?

DEVELOPING STUDENTS' CONCEPT OF STORY

Young children have a rudimentary awareness about what makes a story. Knowledge about stories is called a *concept of story*. Children's concept of story includes information about the elements of story structure, such as characters, plot, and setting, as well as information about the conventions authors use. This knowledge is usually intuitive; that is, children are not conscious of what they know. Golden describes children's concept of story as "a mental representation of story structure, essentially an outline of the basic story elements and their organization" (1984, p. 578).

Researchers have documented that children's concept of story begins in the preschool years and that children as young as 2 years old have a rudimentary sense of story (Applebee, 1978; Pitcher & Prelinger, 1963). Children acquire this concept of story gradually, by listening to stories read to them, by reading stories themselves, and by telling and writing stories. Not surprisingly, older children have a better understanding of story structure than do younger children. Similarly, the stories older children tell and write are increasingly more complex; the plot structures are more tightly organized, and the characters are more fully developed. Yet, Applebee found that by the time children who have been read to begin kindergarten, they have already developed a basic concept of what a story is, and these expectations guide them in responding to stories and telling their own stories. He found, for example, that kindergartners could use three story markers: "Once upon a time . . . " to begin a story; the past tense in telling a story; and formal endings such as "The End" or ". . . and they lived happily ever after."

Students' concept of story plays an important role in their comprehension of the stories they read (Mandler & Johnson, 1977; Rumelhart, 1975; Stein & Glenn, 1979), and it is just as important in their writing (Golden, 1984). Students continue to grow in their understanding of stories through reading and writing experiences (Golden, Meiners, & Lewis, 1992). As they respond to and explore stories they are reading and writing, students learn about elements of story structure. Golden and her colleagues conclude that story meaning is dynamic, growing continuously in the reader's mind.

Elements of Story Structure

Stories have unique structural elements that distinguish them from other forms of literature. In fact, the structure of stories is quite complex—plot, characters, setting, and other elements interact with one another to produce a story. Authors manipulate the elements to make their stories complex and interesting. The five most important elements of story structure are plot, characters, setting, point of view, and theme. I explain each element and illustrate how students examine the element using familiar and award-winning trade books.

Plot.   The sequence of events involving characters in conflict situations is the plot. The plot is based on the goals of one or more characters and the processes they go through to attain these goals (Lukens, 2002). The main characters want to achieve a goal, and other characters are introduced to oppose the main characters or prevent them from being successful. The story events are put in motion by characters as they attempt to overcome conflict, reach their goals, and solve their problems.

The most basic aspect of plot is the division of the main events of a story into three parts—beginning, middle, and end. Upper-grade students may sub-

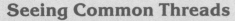

Seeing Common Threads

Why do students need to learn about the elements of story structure?

Tylee Hannigan responds:

There are many reasons why students need to learn the elements of story structure. Understanding the elements of stories helps students comprehend the meaning of stories. If students know the elements of a story when it comes to writing, they are better able to include all of the elements and write a more complete story. Knowing the elements of story structure will also help students perform better on standardized achievement tests. If they are familiar with all of the elements of story structure and they are asked to analyze them and answer questions based on them, they will be more successful. Increased reading comprehension, well-written stories, and improved test scores are all the reasons why I need to focus on story structure in my classroom.

What do you think?

Each chapter presents a question and a response written by one of Dr. Tompkins's students. Consider other comments, or respond to the question yourself, by visiting the Threaded Message Board in Chapter 9 on the Companion Website at www.prenhall.com/tompkins

stitute the terms *introduction, development* or *complication,* and *resolution.* In *The Tale of Peter Rabbit* (Potter, 1902), for instance, one can easily pick out the three story parts: As the story begins, Mrs. Rabbit sends her children out to play after warning them not to go into Mr. McGregor's garden; in the middle, Peter goes to Mr. McGregor's garden and is almost caught; then Peter finds his way out of the garden and gets home safely—the end of the story. Students can cluster the beginning-middle-end of a story using words or pictures, as the cluster for *The Tale of Peter Rabbit* in Figure 9–1 shows.

Specific types of information are included in each of the three story parts. In the beginning, the author introduces the characters, describes the setting, and presents a problem. Together, the characters, setting, and events develop the plot and sustain the theme throughout the story. In the middle, the author adds to events presented in the beginning, with each event preparing readers for what will follow. Conflict heightens as the characters face roadblocks that keep them from solving their problems. Seeing how the characters tackle these problems adds suspense to keep readers interested. In the end, the author reconciles all that has happened in the story, and readers learn whether the characters' struggles are successful.

Conflict is the tension or opposition between forces in the plot, and it is what interests readers enough to continue reading the story. Conflict usually occurs (Lukens, 2002):

- Between a character and nature
- Between a character and society
- Between characters
- Within a character

FIGURE 9-1 *A Beginning-Middle-End Cluster for* The Tale of Peter Rabbit

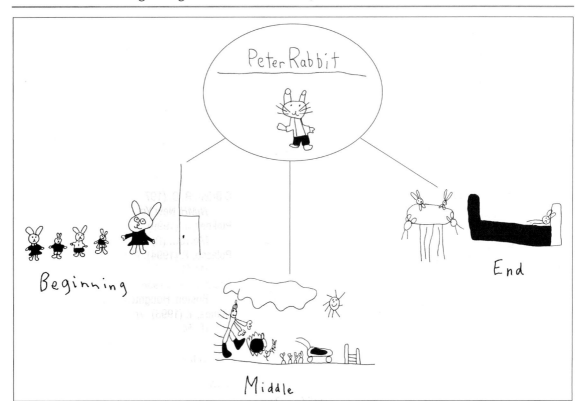

The Classroom Library box on page 391 lists stories representing the four conflict situations.

Conflict between a character and nature occurs in stories in which severe weather plays an important role, such as *Brave Irene* (Steig, 1986), in which Irene endures a snowstorm to deliver a package, and in stories set in isolated geographic locations, such as *Hatchet* (Paulsen, 1987), in which 13-year-old Brian struggles to survive after an airplane crash in the Canadian wilderness. In some stories, a character's activities and beliefs differ from those of other members of the society, and the differences cause conflict between that character and the local society. One example of this type of conflict is in *The Witch of Blackbird Pond* (Speare, 1958), in which Kit Tyler is accused of being a witch because she continues activities that were acceptable in the Caribbean community where she grew up but that are not acceptable in the New England Puritan community that is her new home.

Conflict between characters is a common type of conflict in children's literature. In *Don't Fidget a Feather!* (Silverman, 1994), for example, a duck and a gander challenge each other in a series of contests. In *Catherine, Called Birdy* (Cushman, 1994), set in 1290, high-spirited Birdy outwits her father and finds a husband who pleases her. The fourth type of conflict is conflict within a character, and stories such as *Ira Sleeps Over* (Waber, 1972) and *Chrysanthemum* (Henkes, 1991) provide examples. In *Ira Sleeps Over,* 6-year-old Ira must decide whether to take his teddy bear with him when he goes next door to spend

Stories That Illustrate the Four Types of Conflict

Conflict Between a Character and Nature

George, J. C. (1972). *Julie of the wolves.* New York: Harper & Row. (M–U)

MacLachlan, P. (1994). *Skylark.* New York: HarperCollins. (M)

O'Dell, S. (1960). *Island of the blue dolphins.* Boston: Houghton Mifflin. (M–U)

Paulsen, G. (1987). *Hatchet.* New York: Bradbury Press. (M–U)

Polacco, P. (1990). *Thunder cake.* New York: Philomel. (P–M)

Ruckman, I. (1984). *Night of the twisters.* New York: HarperCollins. (M–U)

Sperry, A. (1968). *Call it courage.* New York: Macmillan. (U)

Steig, W. (1986). *Brave Irene.* New York: Farrar, Straus & Giroux. (P–M)

Conflict Between a Character and Society

Bunting, E. (1995). *Dandelions.* Orlando, FL: Harcourt Brace. (M)

Curtis, C. P. (1995). *The Watsons go to Birmingham—1963.* New York: Delacorte. (M–U)

Lowry, L. (1989). *Number the stars.* New York: Atheneum. (M–U)

Lowry, L. (1993). *The giver.* Boston: Houghton Mifflin. (U)

Meunier, B. (2003). *Pipiolo and the roof dogs.* New York: Dutton. (P)

O'Brien, R. C. (1971). *Mrs. Frisby and the rats of NIMH.* New York: Atheneum. (M)

Pinkney, J. (1999). *The ugly duckling.* New York: Morrow. (P)

Polacco, P. (1994). *Pink and Say.* New York: Philomel. (M–U)

Speare, E. G. (1958). *The witch of Blackbird Pond.* Boston: Houghton Mifflin. (M–U)

Uchida, Y. (1993). *The bracelet.* New York: Philomel. (P–M)

Whelan, G. (2000). *Homeless bird.* New York: Scholastic. (U)

Conflict Between Characters

Blume, J. (1972). *Tales of a fourth grade nothing.* New York: Dutton. (M)

Bunting, E. (1994). *Smoky night.* San Diego, CA: Harcourt Brace. (M)

Cohen, B. (1983). *Molly's pilgrim.* New York: Lothrop, Lee & Shepard. (M)

Creech, S. (2003). *Granny Torrelli makes soup.* New York: HarperCollins. (M)

Cushman, K. (1994). *Catherine, called Birdy.* New York: HarperCollins. (U)

Ehlert, L. (1994). *Mole's hill.* Orlando, FL: Harcourt Brace. (P)

Hesse, K. (2001). *Witness.* New York: Scholastic. (U)

Meddaugh, S. (1995). *Hog-eye.* Boston: Houghton Mifflin. (P)

Naylor, P. R. (1991). *Shiloh.* New York: Atheneum. (M–U)

Rathmann, P. (1995). *Officer Buckle and Gloria.* New York: Putnam. (P)

Silverman, E. (1994). *Don't fidget a feather!* New York: Simon & Schuster. (P)

Zelinsky, P. O. (1986). *Rumpelstiltskin.* New York: Dutton. (P–M)

Conflict Within a Character

Bauer, M. D. (1986). *On my honor.* Boston: Houghton Mifflin. (M–U)

Byars, B. (1970). *The summer of the swans.* New York: Viking. (M)

Henkes, K. (1991). *Chrysanthemum.* New York: Greenwillow. (P)

Jeram, A. (1995). *Contrary Mary.* Cambridge, MA: Candlewick. (P)

Lowry, L. (2003). *The silent boy.* Boston: Houghton Mifflin. (U)

Mead, A. (1995). *Junebug.* New York: Farrar, Straus & Giroux. (U)

Ryan, P. M. (2000). *Esperanza rising.* New York: Scholastic. (M)

Sachar, L. (1998). *Holes.* New York: Farrar, Straus & Giroux. (U)

Waber, B. (1972). *Ira sleeps over.* Boston: Houghton Mifflin. (P)

P = primary grades (K–2); M = middle grades (3–5); U = upper grades (6–8).

the night with a friend. In *Chrysanthemum,* classmates tease a young mouse named Chrysanthemum about her name, and she wishes she had a more common name. Chrysanthemum learns to appreciate her name with the support of an understanding teacher.

The plot is developed through conflict that is introduced in the beginning of a story, expanded in the middle, and finally resolved at the end. Plot development involves four components:

1. *A problem.* A problem that introduces conflict is presented at the beginning of a story.
2. *Roadblocks.* In the middle of the story, characters face roadblocks in attempting to solve the problem.
3. *The high point.* The high point in the action occurs when the problem is about to be solved. This high point separates the middle and end of the story.
4. *Solution.* The problem is solved and the roadblocks are overcome at the end of the story.

The problem is introduced at the beginning of the story, and the main character is faced with trying to solve it. The problem determines the conflict. The problem in Hans Christian Andersen's heartfelt story *The Ugly Duckling* (Pinkney, 1999) is that the big, gray duckling does not fit in with the other ducklings, and conflict develops between the ugly duckling and the other ducks. This is an example of conflict between characters.

After the problem has been introduced, authors use conflict to throw roadblocks in the way of an easy solution. As characters remove one roadblock, the author devises another to further thwart the characters. Postponing the solution by introducing roadblocks is the core of plot development. Stories may contain any number of roadblocks, but many children's stories contain three, four, or five.

In *The Ugly Duckling,* the first conflict comes in the yard when the ducks, the other animals, and even the girl who feeds the ducks make fun of the main character. The conflict is so great that the duckling goes out into the world. Next, conflict comes from the wild ducks and other animals who scorn him, too. Third, the duckling spends a miserable, cold winter in the marsh.

The high point of the action occurs when the solution of the problem hangs in the balance. Tension is high, and readers continue reading to learn whether the main characters solve the problem. With *The Ugly Duckling,* readers are relieved that the duckling has survived the winter, but tension continues because he is still an outcast. Then he flies to a pond and sees some beautiful swans. He flies near to them even though he expects to be scorned.

As the story ends, the problem is solved and the goal is achieved. When he joins the other swans at the garden pond, they welcome him. He sees his reflection in the water and realizes that he is no longer an ugly duckling. Children come to feed the swans and praise the new swan's beauty. The newly arrived swan is happy at last!

Students make a chart called a plot profile to track the tension or excitement in a story (Johnson & Louis, 1987). Figure 9–2 presents a plot profile for *Stone Fox* (Gardiner, 1980), a story about a boy who wins a dogsled race to save his grandfather's farm. A class of fourth graders met in small groups to talk about each chapter, and after these discussions, the whole class came together to decide how to mark the chart. At the end of the story, students analyzed the chart and rationalized the tension dips in chapters 3 and 7: They

FIGURE 9-2 *A Plot Profile for* Stone Fox

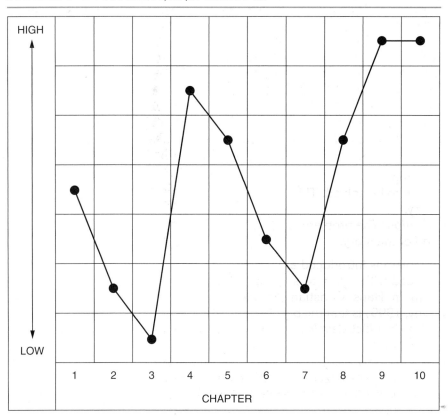

decided that the story would be too stressful without these dips. Also, students were upset about the abrupt ending to the story and wished the story had continued a chapter or two longer so that their tension would have been reduced.

Characters.   Characters, the people or personified animals who are involved in the story, are often the most important element of story structure because many stories are centered on a character or group of characters. In *Catherine, Called Birdy* (Cushman, 1994), for example, the story focuses on Birdy and her determination to outwit her father and not be married off to a revolting, shaggy-bearded suitor.

Usually, one or two well-rounded characters and several supporting characters are involved in a story. Fully developed main characters have many character traits, both good and bad—that is to say, they have all the characteristics of real people. Knowing and inferring a character's traits are important parts of reading. Through character traits, we get to know a character well, and the character seems to come alive. The Classroom Library box on page 394 presents a list of stories with fully developed main characters. Supporting characters may be individualized, but they will be portrayed much less vividly than the main character. The extent to which supporting characters are developed depends on the author's purpose and the needs of the story.

Birdy is the main character in *Catherine, Called Birdy,* and readers get to know her as a real person. Although she is shaped by the culture of medieval

CLASSROOM LIBRARY

Stories With Fully Developed Main Characters

Character	Story
Ramona	Cleary, B. (1981). *Ramona Quimby, age 8.* New York: Morrow. (M)
Bud	Curtis, C. P. (1999). *Bud, not Buddy.* New York: Delacorte. (M–U)
Birdy	Cushman, K. (1994). *Catherine, called Birdy.* New York: HarperCollins. (U)
Lucy	Cushman, K. (1996). *The ballad of Lucy Whipple.* New York: Clarion. (M–U)
Amber	Danziger, P. (1994). *Amber Brown is not a crayon.* New York: Putnam. (M)
Little Willy	Gardiner, J. R. (1980). *Stone Fox.* New York: Harper & Row. (M–U)
Chrysanthemum	Henkes, K. (1991). *Chrysanthemum.* New York: Greenwillow. (P)
Dolores	Howe, J. (1999). *Horace and Morris but mostly Dolores.* New York: Atheneum. (P)
Sarah	MacLachlan, P. (1985). *Sarah, plain and tall.* New York: Harper & Row. (M)
Marty	Naylor, P. R. (1991). *Shiloh.* New York: Atheneum. (M–U)
Karana	O'Dell, S. (1960). *Island of the blue dolphins.* Boston: Houghton Mifflin. (M–U)
Junie	Park, B. (1992). *Junie B. Jones and the stupid smelly bus.* New York: Random House. (P)
Brian	Paulsen, G. (1987). *Hatchet.* New York: Viking. (U)
Babushka	Polacco, P. (1988). *Rechenka's eggs.* New York: Philomel. (P–M)
Officer Buckle	Rathmann, P. (1995). *Officer Buckle and Gloria.* New York: Putnam. (P)
Esperanza	Ryan, P. M. (2000). *Esperanza rising.* New York: Scholastic. (M)
Maria	Soto, G. (1993). *Too many tamales.* New York: Putnam. (P)
Matt	Speare, E. (1983). *The sign of the beaver.* Boston: Houghton Mifflin. (M–U)
Maniac	Spinelli, J. (1990). *Maniac Magee.* New York: Scholastic. (U)
Irene	Steig, W. (1986). *Brave Irene.* New York: Farrar, Straus & Giroux. (P–M)
Cassie	Taylor, M. (1976). *Roll of thunder, hear my cry.* New York: Dial. (U)
Koly	Whelan, G. (2000). *Homeless bird.* New York: Scholastic. (U)
Moon Shadow	Yep, L. (1975). *Dragonwings.* New York: Harper & Row. (U)

England, she challenges the traditional role of "a fine lady" and is determined to marry someone she cares for, not some rich lord of her father's choosing. Through Birdy's journal entries, readers learn about her activities at the manor, how she helps her mother care for sick and injured people, and her beliefs and superstitions. Readers view events in the story through her eyes and sense her wit as she recounts her daily activities. In contrast, the author tells us little about the supporting characters in the story: Birdy's parents, her brothers, the servants, and the peasants who live and work on her father's lands.

Characters are developed in four ways—appearance, action, dialogue, and monologue. Authors present the characters to involve readers in the story's experiences. Similarly, readers notice these four types of information as they read in order to understand the characters.

Authors generally provide some physical description of the characters when they are introduced. Readers learn about characters by the description of their facial features, body shapes, habits of dress, mannerisms, and gestures. Little emphasis is placed on Birdy's appearance, but Birdy writes that she is unattractive. She squints because of poor eyesight and describes herself as tanned and with gray eyes. She often blackens her teeth and crosses her eyes to make herself more unattractive when her father introduces her to potential suitors.

The second way to learn about characters is through their actions, and what a character does is often the best way to know about that character. Birdy writes about picking fleas off her body, making soap and remedies for the sick, doc-

FIGURE 9-3   *An Eighth Grader's Character Traits Chart*

	Will the Real Birdy Please Stand Up?
Trait	Explanation
Defiant	Birdy is defiant because she does not obey her parents. She doesn't want to marry any of the rich men that her father wants her to marry. She does not want to do the needlework that her mother wants her to do. Because she is rebellious, disobedient, and obstinate, she is defiant.
Kindhearted	Birdy is very kindhearted. She is compassionate to the servants and the peasants who are her friends. She treats them like they are as good as her. She is humane because she is like a doctor making medicines and treating sick people. Birdy has a charitable manner; therefore she is kindhearted.
Clever	Birdy is a clever girl. She manages to get rid of her suitors with ingenious plans. She avoids her mother because she is quick-witted. She is smart for someone in the Middle Ages, but not for someone in the year 2000. She can even read and write which is unusual for a girl back then. Because she gets her way most of the time, I think she is clever.

toring with her mother, keeping birds as pets, traveling to a fair and to a friend's castle, and learning how to sew and embroider. She tells how she prefers being outside and how she sneaks away to visit the goat-boy and other friends who work at the manor.

Dialogue is the third way characters are developed. What characters say is important, but so is how they speak. The register of the characters' language is determined by the social situation: A character might speak less formally with friends than with respected elders or characters in positions of authority. The geographic location of the story, the historical period, and the characters' socioeconomic status also determine how characters speak. The language in Birdy's journal entries is often archaic:

> "Mayhap I could be a hermit." (p. 130)
>
> "I am full weary tonight . . . " (p. 131)
>
> "God's thumbs, he looked like my brother Robert!" (p. 132)
>
> "Corpus bones. I utterly loathe my life." (p. 133)

Authors also provide insight into characters by revealing their thoughts through monologue. Birdy shares her innermost thoughts in her journal. Readers know how she attempts to thwart her father's plans to marry her off to a rich lord, her worries about her mother's miscarriages, her love for the goat-boy, and her guilt over meddling in Uncle George's love life.

As students examine the main character of a story in these four ways, they draw conclusions about the character's defining traits. Birdy, for example, is witty, defiant, determined, clever, kindhearted, and superstitious. Teachers work with students to develop a list of character traits, and then students write about one or more of the traits, providing examples from the story to show how the character exemplified the trait. Students can write about character traits in a reading log entry or make a chart. Figure 9–3 shows an eighth grader's chart about Birdy's character traits.

FIGURE 9-4   *An Open-Mind Portrait of Birdy*

Another way students can examine characters and reflect on story events from the character's viewpoint is to draw open-mind portraits. These portraits have two parts: The face of the character is on one page, and the mind of the character is on the second page. The two pages are stapled together, with the mind page under the face page. An eighth grader's open-mind portrait of Birdy is shown in Figure 9–4. This student divided Birdy's mind into two parts—"hate" and "love." In each section, she drew pictures and wrote words about the people, events, and things Birdy hates and loves.

Setting.   In some stories, the setting is barely sketched, and these settings are backdrop settings. The setting in many folktales, for example, is relatively unimportant, and these tales may simply use the convention "Once upon a time . . . " to set the stage. In other stories, the setting is elaborated and integral to the story's effectiveness. These settings are integral settings (Lukens, 2002). A list of stories with integral settings is shown in the Classroom Library box on page 397. The setting in these stories is specific, and authors take care to ensure the authenticity of the historical period or geographic location in which the story is set. Four dimensions of setting are location, weather, time period, and time.

CLASSROOM LIBRARY

Stories With Integral Settings

Babbitt, N. (1975). *Tuck everlasting.* New York: Farrar, Straus & Giroux. (M–U)

Bunting, E. (1994). *Smoky night.* Orlando, FL: Harcourt Brace. (P–M)

Cauley, L. B. (1984). *The city mouse and the country mouse.* New York: Putnam. (P–M)

Choi, S. N. (1991). *Year of impossible goodbyes.* Boston: Houghton Mifflin. (U)

Curtis, C. P. (1995). *The Watsons go to Birmingham—1963.* New York: Delacorte. (M–U)

Curtis, C. P. (1999). *Bud, not Buddy.* New York: Delacorte. (M–U)

George, J. C. (1972). *Julie of the wolves.* New York: Harper & Row. (M–U)

Horvath, P. (2001). *Everything on a waffle.* New York: Farrar, Straus & Giroux. (M–U)

Johnston, T. (1994). *Amber on the mountain.* New York: Dial. (P)

Konigsburg, E. L. (1983). *From the mixed-up files of Mrs. Basil E. Frankweiler.* New York: Atheneum. (M)

Lowry, L. (1989). *Number the stars.* Boston: Houghton Mifflin. (M–U)

MacLachlan, P. (1983). *Sarah, plain and tall.* New York: Harper & Row. (M)

McCloskey, R. (1969). *Make way for ducklings.* New York: Viking. (P)

Meunier, B. (2003). *Pipiolo and the roof dogs.* New York: Dutton. (P)

Myers, W. D. (1988). *Scorpions.* New York: Harper & Row. (U)

Ness, E. (1966). *Sam, Bangs, and moonshine.* New York: Holt, Rinehart and Winston. (P)

Paterson, K. (1977). *Bridge to Terabithia.* New York: Crowell. (M–U)

Paulsen, G. (1987). *Hatchet.* New York: Viking. (U)

Polacco, P. (1988). *The keeping quilt.* New York: Simon & Schuster. (M)

Ringgold, F. (1991). *Tar beach.* New York: Crown. (P–M)

Sachar, L. (1998). *Holes.* New York: Farrar, Straus & Giroux. (U)

Speare, E. G. (1958). *The witch of Blackbird Pond.* Boston: Houghton Mifflin. (M–U)

Speare, E. G. (1983). *The sign of the beaver.* Boston: Houghton Mifflin. (M–U)

Steig, W. (1986). *Brave Irene.* New York: Farrar, Straus & Giroux. (P–M)

Uchida, Y. (1993). *The bracelet.* New York: Philomel. (P–M)

Whelan, G. (2000). *Homeless bird.* New York: Scholastic. (U)

Wilder, L. I. (1971). *The long winter.* New York: Harper & Row. (M)

Location is an important dimension in many stories. For example, the Boston Public Garden in *Make Way for Ducklings* (McCloskey, 1969) and the Alaskan North Slope in *Julie of the Wolves* (George, 1972) are integral to the stories' effectiveness. The settings are artfully described and add something unique to the story. In contrast, many stories take place in predictable settings that do not contribute to their effectiveness.

Weather is a second dimension of setting and, like location, is crucial in some stories. A rainstorm is essential to the plot development in both *Bridge to Terabithia* (Paterson, 1977) and *Sam, Bangs, and Moonshine* (Ness, 1966). At other times, weather is not mentioned because it does not affect the outcome of the story. Many stories take place on warm, sunny days. Think about the impact weather can have on a story; for example, what might have happened if a snowstorm had prevented Little Red Riding Hood from reaching her grandmother's house?

The third dimension of setting is the time period, an important element in stories set in the past or future. If *The Witch of Blackbird Pond* (Speare, 1958) and *Number the Stars* (Lowry, 1989) were set in different eras, for example, they would lose much of their impact. Today, few people would believe that Kit Tyler is a witch or that Jewish people are the focus of government persecution.

In stories that take place in the future, such as *A Wrinkle in Time* (L'Engle, 1962), things are possible that are not possible today.

The fourth dimension, time, includes both time of day and the passage of time. Most stories ignore time of day, except for scary stories that take place after dark. In stories such as *The Ghost-Eye Tree* (Martin & Archambault, 1985), a story of two children who must walk past a scary tree at night to get a pail of milk, time is a more important dimension than in stories that take place during the day, because night makes things scarier.

Many short stories span a brief period of time, often less than a day, and sometimes less than an hour. In *Jumanji* (Van Allsburg, 1981), Peter and Judy's bizarre adventure, during which their house is overtaken by exotic jungle creatures, lasts only the several hours their parents are at the opera. Other stories, such as *Charlotte's Web* (White, 1980) and *The Ugly Duckling* (Pinkney, 1999), span a long enough period for the main character to grow to maturity.

Students can draw maps to show the setting of a story. These maps may show the path a character traveled or the passage of time in a story. Figure 9–5 shows a setting map for *Number the Stars* (Lowry, 1989) that indicates where the families lived in Copenhagen, their trip to a fishing village in northern Denmark, and the ship they hid away on for the trip to Sweden.

Point of View.   Stories are written from a particular viewpoint, and this focus determines to a great extent readers' understanding of the characters and the events of the story. The four points of view are first-person viewpoint, omniscient viewpoint, limited omniscient viewpoint, and objective viewpoint (Lukens, 2002). The Classroom Library box on page 401 presents a list of stories written from each viewpoint.

The first-person viewpoint is used to tell a story through the eyes of one character using the first-person pronoun *I*. In this point of view, the reader experiences the story as the narrator tells it. The narrator, usually the main character, speaks as an eyewitness to and a participant in the events. For example, in *Shiloh* (Naylor, 1991), Marty tells how he works for Judd Travers in order to buy the puppy Travers has mistreated, and in *Abuela* (Dorros, 1991) and the sequel, *Isla* (Dorros, 1995), a girl describes magical flying adventures with her abuela, or grandmother. Many children's books are written from the first-person viewpoint, and the narrator's voice is usually very effective. One limitation is that the narrator must remain an eyewitness.

In the omniscient viewpoint, the author is godlike, seeing and knowing all. The author tells readers about the thought processes of each character without worrying about how the information is obtained. Most stories told from the omniscient viewpoint are chapter books, because revealing the thought processes of each character takes up space. One notable exception is *Doctor De Soto* (Steig, 1982), a picture-book story about a mouse dentist who outwits a fox with a toothache. Steig lets readers know that the fox wants to eat the dentist as soon as his toothache is cured and that the mouse dentist is aware of the fox's thoughts and plans a clever trick. Examples of chapter books written from the omniscient viewpoint are *Tuck Everlasting* (Babbitt, 1975) and *Scorpions* (Myers, 1988).

The limited omniscient viewpoint is used so that readers can know the thoughts of one character. The story is told in the third person, and the author concentrates on the thoughts, feelings, and significant past experiences of the main character or another important character. Many picture-book and chapter-book stories are told from this viewpoint. Lois Lowry uses the limited

FIGURE 9-5   *A Setting Map for* Number the Stars

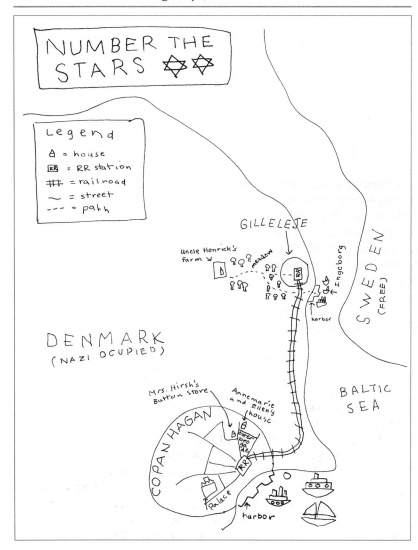

omniscient viewpoint in *The Giver* (1993). Lowry concentrates on the main character, Jonas, using his thoughts to explain Jonas's "perfect" community to readers. Later in the story, Jonas's thoughts reveal his growing dissatisfaction with the community and his decision to escape to Elsewhere with the baby Gabriel.

In the objective viewpoint, readers are eyewitnesses to the story and are confined to the immediate scene. They learn only what is visible and audible, without knowing what any character thinks. Many folktales, such as *Cinderella* (Galdone, 1978) and *The Little Red Hen* (Zemach, 1983), are told from the objective viewpoint. Other picture-book stories, such as *The Tub People* (Conrad, 1989) and *Martha Speaks* (Meddaugh, 1992), are also told from this eyewitness viewpoint. The focus is on recounting events, not on developing the personalities of the characters.

Most teachers postpone introducing the four viewpoints until the upper grades, but younger children can experiment with point of view to understand how the author's viewpoint affects a story. One way to demonstrate point of view is to contrast *The Three Little Pigs* (Galdone, 1970), the traditional version of the story told from an objective viewpoint, with *The True Story of the 3 Little Pigs!* (Scieszka, 1989), a self-serving narrative told by Mr. A. Wolf from a first-person viewpoint. In this unusual and satirical retelling, the wolf tries to explain away his bad image. Even first graders are struck by how different the two versions are and how the narrator filters the information.

Another way to demonstrate the impact of different viewpoints is for students to retell or rewrite a familiar story, such as *Little Red Riding Hood* (Hyman, 1983), from specific points of view—through the eyes of Little Red Riding Hood; her sick, old grandmother; the hungry wolf; or the hunter. As they shift the point of view, students learn that they can change some aspects of a story but not others. To help them appreciate how these changes affect a story, have them choose a story such as *The Lion,* the *Witch and the Wardrobe* (Lewis, 1994), which is told from the omniscient viewpoint, and retell short episodes from the viewpoints of different characters. As students shift to other points of view, they must decide what to leave out according to the new perspective.

A few stories are written from multiple viewpoints. In flip picture books, one version of the story begins at the front of the book, and then the book is flipped over for another story beginning at the back of the book. In Rowland's *Little Red Riding Hood/The Wolf's Tale* (1991), the traditional version begins on one side of the book, the wolf's version on the other. In some chapter books, such as *Bull Run* (Fleischman, 1991), alternating chapters are written from different characters' perspectives. Other stories written from multiple or alternating viewpoints are also listed in the Classroom Library box on page 401.

Theme. The underlying meaning of a story is the theme, and it embodies general truths about human nature (Lehr, 1991). It usually deals with the characters' emotions and values. Themes can be stated either explicitly or implicitly. Explicit themes are stated openly and clearly in the story. Lukens (2002) uses *Charlotte's Web* to point out how one theme of friendship—the giving of oneself for a friend—is expressed as an explicit theme:

Charlotte has encouraged, protected, and mothered Wilbur, bargained and sacrificed for him, and Wilbur, the grateful receiver, realizes that "Friendship is one of the most satisfying things in the world." And Charlotte says later, "By helping you perhaps I was trying to lift up my life a little. Anyone's life can stand a little of that." Because these quoted sentences are exact statements from the text they are called explicit themes. (p. 94)

Implicit themes are suggested rather than explicitly stated in the story. They are developed as the characters attempt to overcome the obstacles that prevent them from reaching their goals. The theme emerges through the thoughts, speech, and actions of the characters as they seek to resolve their conflicts. Lukens also uses *Charlotte's Web* to illustrate implicit themes:

Charlotte's selflessness—working late at night to finish a new word, expending her last energies for her friend—is evidence that friendship is giving oneself. Wilbur's protection of Charlotte's egg sac, his sacrifice of first turn at the slops, and his devotion to Charlotte's babies—giving without any need to stay even or to pay back—leads us to another theme: True friendship is naturally reciprocal. As the two become fond of each other, still another theme emerges: One's best friend can do no wrong. In fact, a best friend is sensational! Both Charlotte and Wilbur believe in these ideas; their experiences verify them. (p. 95)

Stories Illustrating the Four Points of View

First-Person Viewpoint

Creech, S. (2003). *Granny Torrelli makes soup.* New York: HarperCollins. (M)

Curtis, C. P. (1999). *Bud, not Buddy.* New York: Delacorte. (M–U)

Dorros, A. (1991). *Abuela.* New York: Dutton. (P)

Howe, D., & Howe, J. (1979). *Bunnicula: A rabbit-tale of mystery.* New York: Atheneum. (M)

MacLachlan, P. (1985). *Sarah, plain and tall.* New York: Harper & Row. (M)

Meddaugh, S. (1995). *Hog-eye.* Boston: Houghton Mifflin. (P)

Naylor, P. R. (1991). *Shiloh.* New York: Atheneum. (M–U)

Say, A. (1993). *Grandfather's journey.* Boston: Houghton Mifflin. (M)

Scieszka, J. (1989). *The true story of the 3 little pigs!* New York: Puffin. (P–M)

Tunnell, M. O. (1997). *Mailing May.* New York: Greenwillow. (P–M)

Whelan, G. (2000). *Homeless bird.* New York: Scholastic. (U)

Woodruff, E. (1994). *The magnificent mummy maker.* New York: Scholastic. (M–U)

Omniscient Viewpoint

Babbitt, N. (1975). *Tuck everlasting.* New York: Farrar, Straus & Giroux. (M–U)

Grahame, K. (1961). *The wind in the willows.* New York: Scribner. (M)

Lewis, C. S. (1994). *The lion, the witch and the wardrobe.* New York: HarperCollins. (M–U)

Myers, W. D. (1988). *Scorpions.* New York: Harper & Row. (U)

Steig, W. (1982). *Doctor De Soto.* New York: Farrar, Straus & Giroux. (P)

Limited Omniscient Viewpoint

Bunting, E. (1994). *A day's work.* New York: Clarion. (P–M)

Burch, R. (1966). *Queenie Peavy.* New York: Dell. (U)

Cleary, B. (1981). *Ramona Quimby, age 8.* New York: Morrow. (M)

Gardiner, J. R. (1980). *Stone Fox.* New York: Harper & Row. (M)

Lionni, L. (1969). *Alexander and the wind-up mouse.* New York: Pantheon. (P)

Lowry, L. (1993). *The giver.* Boston: Houghton Mifflin. (U)

Paulsen, G. (1987). *Hatchet.* New York: Simon & Schuster. (U)

Ryan, P. M. (2000). *Esperanza rising.* New York: Scholastic. (M)

Sachar, L. (1998). *Holes.* New York: Farrar, Straus & Giroux. (U)

Objective Viewpoint

Brett, J. (1987). *Goldilocks and the three bears.* New York: Putnam. (P)

Cauley, L. B. (1988). *The pancake boy.* New York: Putnam. (P)

Conrad, P. (1989). *The tub people.* New York: Harper & Row. (P–M)

Galdone, P. (1978). *Cinderella.* New York: McGraw-Hill. (P–M)

Pinkney, J. (1999). *The ugly duckling.* New York: Morrow. (P)

Zemach, M. (1983). *The little red hen.* New York: Farrar, Straus & Giroux. (P)

Multiple and Alternating Viewpoints

Avi. (1991). *Nothing but the truth: A documentary novel.* New York: Orchard. (U)

Creech, S. (2000). *The wanderer.* New York: Scholastic. (M–U)

Dorris, M. (1992). *Morning girl.* New York: Hyperion. (U)

Fleischman, P. (1991). *Bull Run.* New York: HarperCollins. (U)

Gray, N. (1988). *A country far away.* New York: Orchard. (P–M)

Hesse, K. (2001). *Witness.* New York: Scholastic. (U)

Rowland, D. (1991). *Little Red Riding Hood/The wolf's tale.* New York: Birch Lane Press. (P–M)

Wolff, V. E. (1998). *Bat 6.* New York: Scholastic. (U)

Step by Step

Sketch-to-Stretch

1. **Read and respond to a story.**   Students read a story or several chapters of a longer book and respond to the story in a grand conversation about literature or in reading logs.

2. **Talk about the themes in the story and ways to symbolize meanings.**   Teachers remind students that there are many ways to represent the meaning of an experience and that they can use lines, colors, shapes, symbols, and words to visually represent what a story means to them. Students and the teacher talk about possible meanings and ways they might visually represent them.

3. **Draw sketches.**   Students work in small groups to draw sketches that reflect what the story means to them. Teachers emphasize that students should focus on the meaning of the story, not on their favorite episode, and that there is no single correct interpretation of the story.

4. **Share sketches with classmates.**   Students meet in small groups to share their sketches and talk about the symbols they used. Teachers encourage classmates to study each student's sketch and tell what they think the student is trying to convey.

5. **Share with the entire class.**   Each group chooses one sketch from the group to share with the class.

6. **Revise sketches and make final copies.**   Some students will want to revise and add to their sketches based on feedback they received and ideas from classmates. Also, students make final copies if the sketches are being used as projects.

Charlotte's Web has several friendship themes, one explicitly stated and others inferred from the text. Stories usually have more than one theme, and their themes usually cannot be articulated with a single word. Friendship is a multi-dimensional theme. Teachers can ask questions during conversations about literature to guide students' thinking as they work to construct a theme (Au, 1992). Students must go beyond one-word labels in describing the theme and construct their own ideas about a theme.

Sketch-to-stretch (Harste, Short, & Burke, 1988; Whitin, 1994, 1996) is a visually representing activity that moves students beyond literal comprehension to think more deeply about the theme of a story. Students work in small groups or individually to draw pictures or diagrams to represent what the story means to them, not pictures of their favorite character or episode. In their sketches, students use lines, shapes, colors, symbols, and words to express their interpretations and feelings. Because students work in a social setting with the support of classmates, they share ideas with each other, extend their understanding, and generate new insights. Students make sketch-to-stretch drawings in reading logs or on posters. The steps in sketch-to-stretch are given in the Step by Step feature above.

Students need many opportunities to experiment with this activity before they move beyond drawing pictures of the story and are able to think symbol-

FIGURE 9–6   *A Fourth Grader's Sketch-to-Stretch Drawing for* The Ballad of Lucy Whipple

ically. It is helpful to introduce this teaching strategy through a minilesson and to draw several sketches together as a class before students do their own sketches. By drawing several sketches, students learn that there is no single correct interpretation, and teachers help students focus on the interpretation rather than on their artistic talents (Ernst, 1993).

As students create symbolic illustrations of books, they probe their understanding of the story and what it means to them (Whitin, 2002). *The Ballad of Lucy Whipple* (Cushman, 1996), for example, is the story of a girl who reluctantly comes with her family to Lucky Diggins, California, during the 1849 Gold Rush. Even though she wants nothing more than to return home to Massachusetts, Lucy makes a new home for herself and finally becomes a "happy citizen" (p. 187) in Lucky Diggins. Figure 9–6 shows a fourth grader's sketch-to-stretch drawing about *The Ballad of Lucy Whipple* that reflects the "home" theme.

In a yearlong study of two seventh-grade language arts classes, Whitin (1996) found that students' use of sketching helped deepen their understanding of theme in the novels they read. Students explored new avenues of expression, such as using color to signify meaning and pie charts to signify feelings. Whitin also had her students write reflections to accompany the sketches. Whitin warns that some upper-grade students view this strategy as an easy form of response and suggests that teachers clarify this misconception early in the school year.

Students also examine the theme as they create quilts. As students design class quilts, the symbols, colors, and quotes they choose reflect their understanding of theme. For example, after reading *Chrysanthemum* (Henkes,

1991), the story of a little girl mouse who is made fun of at school because of her name, and discussing the theme of the story, a second-grade class made a names quilt using construction paper. They decided to emphasize the importance of honoring one another's names in their quilt. The students researched their names, and then each student wrote his or her name and its meaning in a square for the quilt. The teacher also added a square about her first name and because one more square was needed to finish the quilt, one child made a square about Chrysanthemum, the mouse in the story, and her name. They placed the squares next to each other, and around the outside border of the quilt they wrote "Our names are very important to us. We never make fun of anyone's name. Everyone has a beautiful and special name with a story behind it."

Genres

Stories can be categorized in different ways, and one way is according to genres or types of stories (Buss & Karnowski, 2000). Three broad categories are folklore, fantasies, and realism. Traditional stories, including fables, fairy tales, myths, and legends, are folklore. Many of these stories, such as "The Gingerbread Man," "The Tortoise and the Hare," and "Cinderella," were told and retold for centuries before they were written down. Fantasies are make-believe stories. They may be set in imaginary worlds or in future worlds where characters do impossible things. In some fantasies, such as *Bunnicula: A Rabbit-Tale of Mystery* (Howe & Howe, 1979), animals can talk, and in others, the characters travel through time. In *King of Shadows* (Cooper, 1999), for instance, modern-day Nat Field travels to London as part of a drama troupe to perform in the newly built replica of the famous Globe Theatre. After arriving in England, Nat goes to bed ill and awakens after being transported back 400 years to Elizabethan times to perform in the original Globe Theatre with William Shakespeare. Realistic stories, in contrast, are believable. Some stories take place in the past, such as *Crispin: The Cross of Lead* (Avi, 2002), set in medieval England, and *Rodzina* (Cushman, 2003), an orphan train story set in the 1800s. Other stories are set in the contemporary world, such as *Joey Pigza Loses Control* (Gantos, 2000) and *Amber Brown Is Not a Crayon* (Danziger, 1994). Figure 9–7 presents an overview of the story genres. Poetry, biography, and nonfiction are genres, too, and you will learn more about them in upcoming chapters.

Some researchers are currently looking at genres in a much broader way. They have moved beyond the idea of genres as simply categories of children's literature to examine the different patterns or genres of text that young children interact with at home or at school. These genres include magazines, lists, recipes, children's books, workbooks, newspapers, and letters and greeting cards. Through their examination of young children's interaction with genres, Duke and Purcell-Gates (2003) concluded that children develop the understanding that texts have different patterns or genres during the preschool years. Duke and Kays (1998) also found that kindergartners demonstrate their knowledge of genres when they vary how they pretend-read unfamiliar wordless books. These young children pretend-read information books differently than stories. These studies suggest that students come to school with a concept of genre and that through reading and writing experiences and minilessons during the elementary grades, students refine and apply their understanding of genres.

FIGURE 9-7

Story Genres

Category	Genre	Description and Examples
Folklore	Fables	Brief tales told to point out a moral. For example: *Town Mouse, Country Mouse* (Brett, 1994), *Aesop's Fables* (Pinkney, 2000), and *Head, Body, Legs: A Story from Liberia* (Paye & Lippert, 2002).
	Folk and Fairy Tales	Stories in which heroes and heroines demonstrate virtues to triumph over adversity. For example: *The Three Pigs* (Wiesner, 2001), *Beautiful Blackbird* (Bryan, 2003), *The Girl Who Spun Gold* (Hamilton, 2000), and *The Sleeping Beauty* (Hyman, 2000).
	Myths	Stories created by ancient peoples to explain natural phenomena. For example: *King Midas: The Golden Touch* (Demi, 2002), *A Gift from Zeus: Sixteen Favorite Myths* (Steig, 2001), and *The Star-Bearer: A Creation Myth from Ancient Egypt* (Hofmeyr, 2001).
	Legends	Stories, including tall tales, that recount the courageous deeds of people as they struggled against each other or against gods and monsters. For example: *Mystic Horse* (Goble, 2003), *Paul Bunyan: A Tall Tale* (Kellogg, 1984), *The Boy Who Drew Cats* (Hodges, 2002), and *Master Man: A Tall Tale of Nigeria* (Shepard, 2001).
Fantasy	Modern Literary Tales	Stories written by modern authors that exemplify the characteristics of folk tales. For example: *The Runaway Tortilla* (Kimmel, 2000), *Gingerbread Baby* (Brett, 1999), and *Sylvester and the Magic Pebble* (Steig, 1988).
	Fantastic Stories	Imaginative stories that explore alternate realities and contain one or more elements not found in the natural world. For example: *Jeremy Thatcher, Dragon Hatcher* (Coville, 1991) and *Charlotte's Web* (White, 1980).
	Science Fiction	Stories explore scientific possibilities. For example: *Commander Toad in Space* (Yolen, 1980), *The Giver* (Lowry, 1993), and *Stinker From Space* (Service, 1988).
	High Fantasy	These stories focus on the conflict between good and evil and often involve quests. For example: *The Lion, the Witch and the Wardrobe* (Lewis, 1994) and *Harry Potter and the Chamber of Secrets* (Rowling, 1999).
Realism	Contemporary Stories	Stories that portray the real world and contemporary society. For example: *Hatchet* (Paulsen, 1987), *Tales of a Fourth Grade Nothing* (Blume, 1972), and *Locomotion* (Woodson, 2003).
	Historical Fiction	Realistic stories set in the past. For example: *The Watsons Go to Birmingham—1963* (Curtis, 1995), *Sarah, Plain and Tall* (MacLachlan, 1985), and *A Single Shard* (Park, 2001).

Literary Devices

In addition to the five elements of story structure, authors use literary devices to make their writing more vivid and memorable. Without these literary devices, writing can be dull (Lukens, 2002). A list of six literary devices that elementary students learn about is presented in Figure 9–8. Imagery is probably the most commonly used literary device; many authors use imagery as they

FIGURE 9–8

Literary Devices

Comparison	Authors compare one thing to another or view something in terms of something else. When the comparison uses the word *like* or *as*, it is a simile; when the comparison is stated directly, it is a metaphor. For example, "the ocean is like a playground for whales" is a simile; "the ocean is a playground for whales" is a metaphor. Metaphors are stronger comparisons because they are more direct.
Hyperbole	Authors use hyperbole when they overstate or stretch the truth to make obvious and intentional exaggerations for a special effect. "It's raining cats and dogs" and "my feet are killing me" are two examples of hyperbole. American tall tales also have rich examples of hyperbole.
Imagery	Authors use descriptive or sensory words and phrases to create imagery or a picture in the reader's mind. Sensory language stirs the reader's imagination. Instead of saying "the kitchen smelled good as grandmother cooked Thanksgiving dinner," authors create imagery when they write "the aroma of a turkey roasting in the oven filled grandmother's kitchen on Thanksgiving."
Personification	Authors use personification when they attribute human characteristics to animals or objects. For example, "the moss crept across the sidewalk" is personification.
Symbolism	Authors often use a person, place, or thing as a symbol to represent something else. For example, a dove symbolizes peace, the Statue of Liberty symbolizes freedom, and books symbolize knowledge.
Tone	Authors create an overall feeling or effect in the story through their choice of words and use of other literary devices. For example, *Bunnicula: A Rabbit-Tale of Mystery* (Howe & Howe, 1979) and *Catherine, Called Birdy* (Cushman, 1994) are humorous stories, and *Babe the Gallant Pig* (King-Smith, 1995) and *Sarah, Plain and Tall* (MacLachlan, 1985) are uplifting, feel-good stories.

paint rich word pictures that bring their characters and settings to life. Authors use metaphors and similes to compare one thing to another, personification to endow animals and objects with human qualities, and hyperbole to exaggerate or stretch the truth. They also create symbols as they use one thing to represent something else. In Chris Van Allsburg's *The Wretched Stone* (1991), for example, the glowing stone that distracts the crew from reading, from spending time with their friends, and from doing their jobs symbolizes television or, perhaps, computers. For students to understand the theme of the story, they need to recognize symbols. The author's style conveys the tone or overall feeling in a story. Some stories are humorous, some are uplifting celebrations of life, and others are sobering commentaries on society.

Young children focus on events and characters as they read and discuss a story, but during the elementary grades, students become more sophisticated readers. They learn to notice both what the author says and how he or she says it. Teachers facilitate students' growth in reading and evaluating stories by directing their attention to literary devices and the author's style during the responding and exploring stages of the reading process.

Teaching Students About Stories

The most important way that students refine their concept of story is by reading and writing stories, but teachers help students expand their concepts through a variety of activities. As they talk about stories during grand conversations, teachers often draw students' attention to theme and other elements of story structure. And as students develop open-mind portraits, beginning-middle-end clusters, and other diagrams and charts, they are analyzing elements of story structure. In addition, teachers teach minilessons that focus on particular story elements.

Minilessons.   Teachers adapt the teaching strategy set out in Chapter 2 to teach minilessons on the elements of story structure and other procedures, concepts, and strategies and skills related to reading and writing stories. A list of topics for minilessons about stories is presented on pages 408–409, as well as a minilesson that a second-grade teacher taught on theme.

Minilessons about story structure, genres, and literary devices are usually taught during the exploring stage of the reading process, after students have had an opportunity to read and respond to a story and share their reactions. This sequence is important because students need to understand the events of the story before they try to analyze the story at a more abstract level.

Meeting the Needs of Every Student

Stories are a large part of the elementary language arts program, and teachers must find ways to involve all students in successful reading and writing experiences with stories. Some students, however, aren't as knowledgeable about stories as their classmates, and these students often have difficulty comprehending and writing stories. The feature on page 410 suggests that the most important thing teachers can do for struggling students is to read stories aloud to them every day. As they gain more experience with stories and learn about the elements of story structure, these students will be more successful.

Piecing a Lesson Together

Topics on Reading and Writing Stories

Procedures	*Concepts*	*Strategies and Skills*
Make a beginning-middle-end cluster	Concept of story	Visualize
Make a setting map	Beginning-middle-end	Predict and confirm
Make a plot profile	Plot	Empathize with characters
Make an open-mind portrait	Characters	Identify with characters
Do a sketch-to-stretch drawing	Setting	Write dialogue for characters
Design a story quilt	Theme	Notice opposites in the story
Make a class collaboration book	Point of view	Retell the story
Write an innovation on a text	Genres	Monitor understanding
Write a sequel	Literary devices	Connect to one's own life
	Metaphor	Connect to the world
	Simile	Connect to previously read literature
	Hyperbole	Value the story
	Imagery	Evaluate the story
	Personification	
	Symbolism	
	Tone	
	Comprehension	
	Authors	
	Sequels	

Please visit the Companion Website at **www.prenhall.com/tompkins** for a second fully realized minilesson.

THEME

Mrs. Levin's Second Graders Learn About Theme

1. **Introduce the Topic**

   Mrs. Levin's second-grade class has just read *Martha Speaks* (Meddaugh, 1992), the story of a talking dog. Mrs. Levin rereads the last paragraph of the story, which exemplifies the theme, and says, "I think this is what the author, Susan Meddaugh, is trying to tell us—that sometimes we should talk and sometimes we should be quiet. What do you think?" The students agree, and Mrs. Levin explains that the author's message or lesson about life is called the theme.

2. **Share Examples**

   Mrs. Levin shows the students *Little Red Riding Hood* (Galdone, 1974), a story they read earlier in the year, and after briefly reviewing the story, she asks students about the theme of this story. One child quickly responds, "I think the author means that you shouldn't talk to strangers." Another child explains, "Little Red Riding Hood's mom probably tried to teach her to not talk to strangers but Little Red Riding Hood must have forgotten because she talked to the wolf and he was like a stranger." It is a message every child has heard, but they agree that they, too, sometimes forget, just like Little Red Riding Hood.

3. **Provide Information**

   The next day, Mrs. Levin shares three other familiar books and asks students to identify the theme. The first book is *The Three Bears* (Galdone, 1972), and students easily identify the "don't intrude" theme. The second book is *Chrysanthemum* (Henkes, 1991), the story of a young mouse named Chrysanthemum who doesn't like herself after her classmates make fun of her name. The students identify two variations of the theme: "you should be nice to everyone and not hurt their feelings" and "kids who aren't nice get in trouble." The third book is *Miss Nelson Is Missing!* (Allard, 1977), the story of a sweet teacher who transforms herself into a mean teacher after her students refuse to behave. The students identify the theme as "teachers are nice when you behave but they are mean when you are bad."

4. **Supervise Practice**

   Mrs. Levin asks students to choose one of the five stories they have examined and to draw pictures showing the theme. For example, students could draw a picture of Martha using the telephone to report burglars in the house or a picture of themselves ringing the doorbell at a friend's house. Mrs. Levin walks around as students work, helping them add titles to their pictures that focus on the theme of the story.

5. **Reflect on Learning**

   Students share their pictures with the class and explain how the pictures illustrate the theme of the various stories.

Meeting the Needs of Every Student

What Can I Do For the Students In My Class Who Don't Know Much About Stories?

Students who have been read to since they were babies come to school with a great deal of story knowledge, but others who have not been read to—either because they didn't like to sit still long enough to listen to a story or because their parents didn't have books available to read to them or didn't realize how essential early literacy experiences are to school success—are at a disadvantage when it comes to reading and writing stories. The most important thing that teachers can do is to read stories aloud to students every day. During these read alouds, teachers involve students in the reading process. They activate and build students' background knowledge before reading, encourage them to use reading strategies, such as making predictions, during reading, deepen their comprehension through grand conversations, and explore one or more aspects of the story after reading. To build students' story knowledge, teachers take time to explicitly teach about genres, story elements, and literary devices and make connections between stories students are reading and others teachers have read aloud.

Three patterns of practice provide opportunities for students to develop more knowledge about stories. In literature focus units, teachers use direct instruction to teach students about stories, and in literature circles, students work with classmates to apply their knowledge about stories. Students also gain knowledge about stories through reading and writing workshop when they are independently reading self-selected stories and writing stories on self-selected topics.

To investigate other ways to meet the needs of every student, visit the links for this chapter on the Companion Website at www.prenhall.com/tompkins

Companion Website

Assessing Students' Concept of Story

To learn more about reading logs, see Chapter 6, "Personal Writing," and for more information on grand conversations, see Chapter 8, "Sustaining Talk in the Classroom."

Teachers assess students' concept of story in many ways. They observe students as they read and respond to stories. They can note whether students are sensitive to story elements as they talk about stories during grand conversations. Some students talk about the character who is most like them, or they compare two stories they have read. Teachers note whether students use terminology related to story elements: Do they talk about conflict, or the way a story ends? If they are talking about point of view, do they use that term? Teachers also ask questions about story elements during grand conversations and note the responses students make. Students' reading logs also provide evidence of the same sorts of comments and reactions.

Another way students demonstrate their understanding of story elements is by making clusters, charts, and diagrams. These activities are a natural outgrowth of students' responses to a story, not the reason students are reading stories (Urzua, 1992). Teachers also document students' understanding of story elements by examining the stories they have written to see how they have applied their knowledge about stories.

READING STORIES

Students read stories aesthetically, and their concept of story informs and supports their reading. They read popular and award-winning stories together as a class during literature focus units, and they read stories they choose themselves in literature circles and reading workshop. Students use the reading process to read, respond to, explore, and apply their reading, and through these stages of the reading process, they develop and refine their comprehension or understanding of the story. Reading stories with students is more than simply a pleasurable way to spend an hour; it is how classroom communities are created (Cairney, 1992). Reading, writing, and talking about stories are natural extensions of the relationships that students have built together.

To read more about aesthetic reading, see Chapter 3, "The Reading and Writing Processes."

Comprehension

Comprehension is a creative, multifaceted process in which students engage with the text (Tierney, 1990). Teachers often view comprehension as a mysterious process of making meaning. It seems mysterious because it is invisible; some students read and understand what they read, and others seem to read just as well but don't understand what they read. Sometimes comprehension problems relate to students' lack of fluency or limited vocabulary knowledge, but more often than not, students who don't comprehend seem no different from their classmates.

Judith Irwin (1991) defines comprehension as the reader's process of using prior experiences and the author's text to construct meaning that is useful to that reader for a specific purpose. Three factors influence comprehension: the reader, the text, and the purpose. The background knowledge that readers bring to the reading process influences how they understand what they read as well as the strategies they know to use while reading. The text that is being read is the second factor: The author's ideas, the words the author uses to express those ideas, and how the ideas are organized and presented also affect comprehension. The purpose is the third factor: Readers vary the way they read according to their purpose. They read stories and newspapers differently, for example. Readers' comprehension varies because of these three factors.

Louise Rosenblatt (1978) identified two overarching purposes for reading, which she termed the aesthetic and efferent stances. Students use the aesthetic stance when reading stories for pleasure, as opposed to the efferent stance, which they use when reading to remember information. The stance readers take indicates their purpose or the focus of their attention during reading. In her study on the effects of aesthetic and efferent stances on fourth, sixth, and eighth graders' comprehension of stories, Joyce Many (1991) found that students who read aesthetically had higher levels of comprehension.

Aesthetic reading is a personal experience during which readers connect the story they are reading to their own lives and to previous experiences with literature (Rosenblatt, 1978). Readers do not search for the author's "correct" meaning; instead, they create a personal meaning for themselves based on the story events. A story evokes different meanings from different readers, or even from the same reader at different times in his or her life. This view of comprehension is consistent with Judith Irwin's.

Comprehension Processes. Readers do many things as they read in order to comprehend what they are reading. Irwin (1991) has helped to demystify comprehension by identifying five processes of comprehension. To comprehend effectively, readers must use all five processes:

1. *Microprocesses.* Readers chunk ideas into phrases and select what is important from the sentence to keep in short-term memory. Students who chunk ideas into phrases read fluently, not word by word, but students who do not chunk phrases meaningfully have difficulty understanding what they are reading.
2. *Integrative processes.* Readers deal with the semantic and syntactic connections and relationships among sentences, usually sentences within a paragraph. The connections and relationships include pronoun substitutions, synonym substitutions, inferring cause and effect, and recognizing connectives, such as *also, however, because,* and *unless.*
3. *Macroprocesses.* Readers focus on the big picture. They recognize the elements of story structure or other structural patterns and select the most important information to remember.
4. *Elaborative processes.* Readers make personal connections to what they are reading and intertextual connections to other literature they have read. They also personalize their reading when they connect what they are reading to their prior knowledge, make predictions, identify with characters, and visualize what they are reading.
5. *Metacognitive processes.* Readers use strategies to monitor and evaluate their comprehension. Strategies, such as predicting, visualizing, organizing, tapping prior knowledge, and self-questioning, are conscious problem-solving behaviors that students use when reading.

The five comprehension processes along with instructional and assessment activities are described in the LA Essentials box on page 413.

Intertextuality. As students read, they make connections to books they have read previously, and these connections are called intertextuality (de Beaugrande, 1980). Students use intertextuality as they respond to books they are reading by recognizing similarities between characters, plots, and themes. Students also use intertextuality as they incorporate ideas and structures from the stories they have read into the stories they are writing. Five characteristics of intertextuality are (Cairney, 1990, 1992):

1. *Individuality and uniqueness.* Students' literary experiences and the connections they make among them are different.
2. *Dependence on literary experiences.* Intertextuality is dependent on the types of books students have read, their purpose for and interest in reading, and the literary communities to which they belong.
3. *Metacognitive awareness.* Most students are aware of intertextuality and consciously make connections among texts.
4. *Links to concept of story.* Students' connections among stories are linked to their knowledge about literature.
5. *Reading-writing connections.* Students make connections between stories they read and stories they write.

Essentials

The Five Comprehension Processes

Process	Instruction	Assessment
Microprocesses. Readers chunk ideas into phrases within a sentence. Students who read word by word and do not chunk phrases meaningfully have difficulty understanding what they are reading. Similarly, writers chunk ideas into sentences.	Choral reading is a good activity to help children chunk text appropriately because classmates and the teacher model appropriate chunking. Interactive writing and quickwrites are effective ways to develop writing fluency.	Teachers listen to students read aloud and check for appropriate chunking. For writing, they observe students as they write.
Integrative processes. Readers infer connections and relationships between sentences by noticing pronoun substitutions, synonym substitutions, and connectives such as *also, however,* and *unless.* In writing, students also use these substitutions.	Teachers use "close reading" to help students understand these connections by asking questions and directing students' attention to these relationships; for writing, they use sentence-combining activities.	Teachers use "close reading" to check children's ability to use connectives and to understand relationships among words in a paragraph, and they examine the paragraphs students write for these connections.
Macroprocesses. Readers organize and summarize ideas as they read; they look at the big picture of the entire text as well as the smaller units in the text. For writing, they use their knowledge of story, expository text, or poetic structures to organize their compositions.	Students learn about structural patterns of different types of text and draw graphic organizers to visually represent the main ideas. Students also do oral and written retellings and write summaries.	Teachers assess students' knowledge of macrostructures by examining their graphic organizers, their retellings, and their compositions.
Elaborative processes. Readers make connections to their own lives and to other literature. They make predictions, connect their reading to prior knowledge, and identify with characters. In writing, students provide enough details so readers can make connections.	Students learn to make connections as they talk about stories in grand conversations and write in reading logs.	Teachers observe students during grand conversations and read their reading log entries to check for corrections. And teachers monitor students' compositions, checking that they provide detail so readers can make connections.
Metacognitive processes. Readers monitor their comprehension and use problem-solving strategies to read and write effectively.	Teachers model reading strategies by "thinking aloud" as they read aloud and model writing strategies during writing lessons. They provide information about literacy strategies in minilessons.	Teachers observe students and ask them to "think aloud" about the strategies they are using. Teachers also ask students to reflect on their use of strategies during a reading or writing conference.

The sum of students' experiences with literature—including the stories parents have read and told to young children, the books students have read or listened to the teacher read aloud, video versions they have viewed, their concept of story and knowledge about authors and illustrators, and the books students have written—constitute their intertextual histories (Cairney, 1992). Cairney's research indicates that elementary students are aware of their past experiences with literature and use this knowledge as they read and write.

One way teachers encourage students to make intertextual ties is by grouping literature into text sets—collections of three or more books that are related in some way. Possible text sets include:

- Stories written by the same author
- Stories featuring the same character
- Stories illustrating the same theme
- Different versions of a folktale
- Stories and other books related to a theme cycle

As students read and discuss these books, they make connections among them. As students share the connections they are making, classmates gain insights about literature and build on classmates' ideas. Teachers can prompt students and ask them to describe commonalities among the books. Students can also make charts and other diagrams to compare authors, characters, and other aspects of stories.

Literary Opposites. Stories are usually built around opposites or contrasts, and these literary opposites help to create excitement in a story (Temple, 1992). *Where the Wild Things Are* (Sendak, 2003), for example, is built around the contrast between Max's bedroom and the land of the wild things. Whereas his bedroom is safe and secure, where the wild things live is thrilling but a little scary, too. Max's mother sends him to his bedroom for misbehaving, and she is clearly in charge; but when Max becomes king of the wild things, he is in charge. In Phyllis Reynolds Naylor's *Shiloh* (1991), the main characters, Marty Preston and Judd Travers, are opposites: Marty is the "good" character who bravely works for mean-spirited Travers to buy a beagle pup that has been mistreated. Through the experience, Marty learns about human nature and about himself.

Opposites can be between settings, characters, or events in the story; there is more than one opposite in most stories. For example, after reading Steig's *Amos and Boris* (1971), a class of third graders listed these opposites:

big	little
land animal	sea animal
helping	being helped
Amos and Boris	*The Lion and the Mouse*
life	death
forgetting	remembering
hope	hopeless
in the sea	out of the sea
hello	good-bye

FIGURE 9-9 *A Third Grader's Quickwrite About* Amos and Boris

You might think a whale and a mouse are very, very diferent but they are not! They both have hearts full of love for there friends and minds ful of memories. They are mammales too.

Students picked the opposites that seemed most important to them and drew pictures and wrote about them. One student's writing is shown in Figure 9–9. This was a valuable way for students to think deeply about stories and extend their comprehension of the story. Another student made a very interesting intertextual tie between *Amos and Boris* and *The Lion and the Mouse* (Young, 1979), pointing out that the two stories have the same theme—that small, weak creatures can be as powerful as big, strong creatures.

Assessing Students' Comprehension of Stories

Answering comprehension questions or filling in the blanks on worksheets is not adequate for assessing students' comprehension of stories. It is more effective for teachers to monitor and assess students' comprehension through authentic language arts activities, including:

- Listening to students as they talk about stories during grand conversations
- Reading students' entries in reading logs
- Noting students' use of reading strategies while they are reading
- Observing students' participation in exploring activities
- Examining the projects students do (Cairney, 1990)

When students do not successfully comprehend what they are reading, teachers need to more closely investigate students' ability to use each of Irwin's five comprehension processes. Possible assessment activities are suggested in the LA Essentials box on page 413. Once teachers know the processes that students are having difficulty with, they can provide instruction and practice opportunities.

WRITING STORIES

As students read and talk about stories, they learn how writers craft stories. They also draw from stories they have read as they create their own stories, intertwining several story ideas and adapting story elements to meet their own needs (Atwell, 1987; Graves, 1989; Hansen, 1987; Harste, Short, & Burke, 1988; Harwayne, 1992). In his research about intertextuality, Cairney (1990) found that elementary students do think about stories they have read as they write. Blackburn (1985) describes a cycle of intertextuality: Students read and talk about trade books; they weave bits of the stories they have read into the stories they write; they share their compositions; and then bits of these compositions make their way into classmates' compositions. Students make intertextual links in different ways. For example, they:

- Use specific story ideas without copying the plot
- Copy the plot from a story, but add new events, characters, and settings
- Use a specific genre they have studied for a story
- Use a character borrowed from a story read previously
- Write a retelling of the story
- Incorporate content from an informational book into a story
- Combine several stories into a new story

The first two strategies were the ones most commonly used in Cairney's study of sixth graders. The next-to-the-last strategy was used only by less capable readers, and the last one only by more capable readers.

Students incorporate what they have learned about stories when they write stories, and they use the writing process to draft and refine their stories. They write stories as part of literature focus units, during theme cycles, and in writing workshop. Stories are probably the most complex writing form that elementary students use. It is difficult—even for adults—to craft well-formed stories incorporating plot and character development and other elements of story structure.

Writing Retellings of Stories

Elementary students often write retellings of stories they have read and enjoyed. As they retell a story, they internalize the structure of the story and play with the language the author used. Sometimes students work together to write a collaborative retelling, and at other times, they write their own individual retellings.

Students can work together as a group to write or dictate the retelling, or they can divide the story into sections or chapters and have each student or

Conferencing with students.
This teacher asks students to think about the elements of story structure in the stories they are reading during a small-group conference. Students who are each reading a different book during reading workshop come together to talk about how the author of their book crafted the story using plot, characters, setting, point of view, and theme. This conversation is more than a check to make sure students are understanding what they are reading; it is important because students deepen their comprehension and gain new insights as they think and talk about the effect of story elements on the story.

pair of students write a small part. Then the parts are compiled. A class of first graders worked together to dictate their retelling of *Where the Wild Things Are* (Sendak, 2003), which was published as a big book.

Page 1:   Max got in trouble. He scared his dog and got sent to bed.

Page 2:   This room turned into a jungle. It grew and grew.

Page 3:   A boat came for Max. It was his private boat.

Page 4:   He sailed to where the wild things lived.

Page 5:   They made him king of all the wild things.

Page 6:   The wild things had a wild rumpus. They danced and hung on trees.

Page 7:   Max sent them to bed without any supper.

Page 8:   Then Max wanted to come back home. He waved good-bye and sailed home on his boat.

Page 9:   And his dinner was waiting for him. It was still hot from the microwave.

As the first graders dictated the retelling, their teacher wrote it on chart paper. Then they read the story over several times, making revisions. Next, the students divided the text into sections for each page. Then they recopied the text onto each page for the big book, drew pictures to illustrate each page, and added a cover and a title page. Students also wrote their own books, including the major points at the beginning, middle, and end of the story.

Sometimes students change the point of view in their retellings and tell the story from a particular character's viewpoint. A fourth grader wrote this retelling of "Goldilocks and the Three Bears" from Baby Bear's perspective:

One day mom got me up. I had to take a bath. I hate to take baths, but I had to. While I was taking my bath, Mom was making breakfast. When I got out of the tub breakfast was ready. But Dad got mad because his breakfast porridge was too hot to eat. So Mom said, "Let's go for a walk and let it cool." I thought, "Oh boy, we get to go for a walk!" My porridge was just right, but I could eat it later.

When we got back our front door was open. Dad thought it was an animal so he started to growl. I hate it when Dad growls. It really scares me. Anyway, there was no animal anywhere so I rushed to the table. Everybody was sitting down to eat. I said, "Someone ate my porridge." Then Dad noticed someone had tasted his porridge. He got really mad.

Then I went into the living room because I did not want to get yelled at. I noticed my rocking chair was broken. I told Dad and he got even madder.

Then I went into my bedroom. I said, "Someone has been sleeping in my bed and she's still in it." So this little girl with long blond hair raises up and starts to scream. Dad plugged his ears. She jumped up like she was scared of us and ran out of the house. We never saw that little girl again.

Writing Innovations on Texts

Many stories have a repetitive pattern or refrain, and students can use this structure to write their own stories. As part of a literature focus unit on mice, a first-grade class read *If You Give a Mouse a Cookie* (Numeroff, 1985) and talked about the circular structure of the story: The story begins with giving a mouse a cookie and ends with the mouse getting a second cookie. Then first graders wrote stories about what they would do if they were given a cookie. A student named Michelle drew the circle diagram shown in Figure 9–10 to organize her story, and then she wrote this story, which has been transcribed into conventional English spelling:

If you gave Michelle a cookie she would probably want some pop. Then she would want a napkin to clean her face. That would make her tired and she would go to bed to take a nap. Before you know it, she will be awake and she would like to take a swim in a swimming pool. Then she would watch cartoons on T.V. And she would be getting hungry again so she would probably want another cookie.

Judith Viorst's *Alexander and the Terrible, Horrible, No Good, Very Bad Day* (1977) is a more sophisticated pattern story. After reading the book, students often write about their own bad days. A fifth grader named Jacob wrote his version, entitled "Jacob and the Crummy, Stupid, Very Bad Day":

One day I was riding my bike and I fell off and broke my arm and sprained my foot. I had to go to the hospital in an ambulance and get my arm set in a cast and my foot wrapped up real tight in a bandage. I knew it was going to be a crummy, stupid, very bad day. I think I'll swim to China.

Then I had to go to the dentist with my sister Melissa. My sister had no cavities, but guess who had two cavities. I knew it was going to be a crummy, stupid, very bad day. I think I'll swim to China.

My mom felt bad for me because it was such a bad day so she went and bought me a present—two Nintendo games. But my sister started fighting with me and my mom

FIGURE 9-10   *A Circle Diagram for* If You Give a Mouse a Cookie

blamed me for it even though it wasn't my fault. So my mom took the games away. I wonder if there are better sisters in China?

Then I went outside and found out that someone had stolen my bike. It was gone without a trace. It really was a crummy, stupid, very bad day. Now I am going to swim to China for sure.

Writing Sequels

Students often choose to write sequels as projects during literature focus units. For example, after reading *The Sign of the Beaver* (Speare, 1983), students often write sequels in which Matt and Attean meet again. Students write additional adventures about the boa constrictor after reading *The Day Jimmy's Boa Ate the Wash* (Noble, 1980). Many stories lend themselves to sequels, and students enjoy extending a favorite story.

Writing Genre Stories

During some literature focus units, students read books and learn about a particular genre, such as folktales, historical fiction, myths, or fables. After learning about the genre, students try their hand at writing stories that incorporate its characteristics. After reading Gingerbread Man stories, a class of kindergartners dictated this story, which their teacher wrote on chart paper. Interestingly, the students asked their teacher to write the story in two columns. In the left column, the teacher wrote the story, and in the right column, she wrote the refrain:

The Runaway Horse

Once upon a time there was a horse. He jumped over the stable gate and ran away.	Run, run, as fast as you can, you can't catch me!
He meets a farmer. The farmer chases him but the horse runs as fast as the wind.	Run, run, as fast as you can, you can't catch me!
The horse meets a dog. The dog chases him. The horse runs as fast as the wind.	Run, run, as fast as you can, you can't catch me!
The horse meets the wolf. The wolf chases him. The horse runs as fast as the wind.	Run, run, as fast as you can, you can't catch me!
Then the horse meets a fox. And the fox gobbles him up.	Snip, snap, snout, This tale is told out.

A seventh-grade class read and examined myths and compared myths from various cultures. Then they applied what they had learned about myths in this class collaboration myth, "Suntaria and Lunaria: Rulers of the Earth," about the origin of the sun and the moon:

Long ago when gods still ruled the earth, there lived two brothers, Suntaria and Lunaria. Both brothers were wise and powerful men. People from all over the earth sought their wisdom and counsel. Each man, in his own way, was good and just, yet the two were as different as gold and coal. Suntaria was large and strong with blue eyes and brilliantly golden hair. Lunaria's hair and eyes were the blackest black.

One day Zeus, looking down from Mount Olympus, decided that Earth needed a ruler—someone to watch over his people whenever he became too tired or too busy to do his job. His eyes fell upon Suntaria and Lunaria. Both men were wise and honest. Both men would be good rulers. Which man would be the first ruler of the earth?

Zeus decided there was only one fair way to solve his problem. He sent his messenger, Postlet, down to earth with ballots instructing the mortals to vote for a king. There were only two names on the ballot—Suntaria and Lunaria.

Each mortal voted and after the ballots were placed in a secure box, Postlet returned them to Zeus. For seven years Zeus and Postlet counted and recounted the ballots. Each time they came up with the same results: 50% of the votes were for Suntaria and 50% were for Lunaria. There was only one thing Zeus could do. He declared that both men would rule over the earth.

This is how it was, and this is how it is. Suntaria still spreads his warm golden rays to rule over our days. At night he steps down from his throne, and Lunaria's dark, soft night watches and protects us while we dream.

The students incorporated the characteristics of myths in their story. First, their myth explained a phenomenon that has more recently been explained scientifically. Second, the setting is backdrop and barely sketched. Finally, the characters in their myth are heroes with supernatural powers. It is interesting to compare this myth to the sun and moon myths told by aboriginal Australians, Native Americans, Nigerians, and Polynesians collected in *Legends of the Sun and Moon* (Hadley & Hadley, 1983).

Assessing the Stories Students Write

Assessing the stories students write involves far more than simply judging the quality of the finished stories. Assessment also takes into account students' knowledge of story structure as well as the activities they engage in while writing and refining their stories. Teachers consider four components in assessing students' stories: students' knowledge of the elements of story structure, their application of the elements in writing, their use of the writing process, and the quality of the finished stories.

Determining whether students learned about the element and applied what they learned in their stories is crucial in assessing students' stories. Consider the following points:

- Can the student define or identify the characteristics of the element?
- Can the student explain how the element was used in a particular story?
- Did the student apply the element in the story he or she has written?

Teachers assess students' use of the writing process by observing them as they write and by asking these questions:

- Did the student write a rough draft?
- Did the student participate in a writing group?
- Did the student revise the story according to feedback received from the writing group?
- Did the student complete a revision checklist?
- Did the student proofread the story and correct as many mechanical errors as possible?
- Did the student share the story?

The quality of students' stories is difficult to measure. Students who write high-quality and interesting stories use the elements of story structure to their advantage. Their stories are creative and well organized. Ask these questions to assess the quality of children's stories:

- Is the story interesting?
- Is the story well organized?

The assessment and grading of students' stories reflect more than simply the quality of the finished product. They should reflect all four components of students' involvement with stories.

Review

During the elementary grades, students develop their concept of stories as they learn about five elements of story structure: plot, characters, setting, point of view, and theme. Students apply this knowledge as they read and write stories.

They read stories aesthetically and deepen their comprehension as they read and respond to stories. Students use the writing process to write retellings of familiar stories, new versions of stories, sequels, and original stories. Key concepts are:

1. Students acquire a concept of story by reading and writing stories and by learning about the elements of story structure.
2. Stories have unique structural elements that distinguish them from other forms of writing: plot, characters, setting, point of view, and theme.
3. Teachers present minilessons about the elements of story structure, and students apply what they have learned as they read and write stories.
4. Students read stories aesthetically, and their concept of story informs and supports their reading.
5. Comprehension involves three factors: the reader, the text, and the purpose.
6. There are five comprehension processes: microprocesses, integrative processes, macroprocesses, elaborative processes, and metacognitive processes.
7. Teachers involve students in a variety of activities to develop their ability to use all five comprehension processes.
8. When students do not comprehend well, teachers can assess their ability to use each of the five comprehension processes.
9. Students use intertextuality as they incorporate ideas from the stories they have read into the stories they write.
10. Students read and write stories as part of literature focus units, literature circles, reading and writing workshop, and theme cycles.

Visit Chapter 9 on the Companion Website at www.prenhall. com/tompkins to:

- **Check your understanding of the concepts presented in the chapter**
- **Access the Extensions (activities and a list of related readings)**
- **Link to related websites**

Professional References

Applebee, A. N. (1978). *The child's concept of story: Ages 2 to 17.* Chicago: University of Chicago Press.

Atwell, N. (1987). *In the middle: Writing, reading, and learning with adolescents.* Portsmouth, NH: Heinemann.

Au, K. H. (1992). Constructing the theme of a story. *Language Arts, 69,* 106–111.

Blackburn, E. (1985). Stories never end. In J. Hansen, J. Newkirk, & D. Graves (Eds.), *Breaking ground: Teachers relate reading and writing in the elementary school* (pp. 3–13). Portsmouth, NH: Heinemann.

Bruner, J. (1986). *Actual minds, possible worlds.* Cambridge, MA: Harvard University Press.

Buss, K., & Karnowski, L. (2000). *Reading and writing literary genres.* Newark, DE: International Reading Association.

Cairney, T. (1990). Intertextuality: Infectious echoes from the past. *The Reading Teacher, 43,* 478–484.

Cairney, T. (1992). Fostering and building students' intertextual histories. *Language Arts, 69,* 502–507.

de Beaugrande, R. (1980). *Text, discourse and process.* Norwood, NJ: Ablex.

De Ford, D. (1981). Literacy: Reading, writing, and other essentials. *Language Arts, 58,* 652–658.

Dressel, J. H. (1990). The effects of listening to and discussing different qualities of children's literature on the narrative writing of fifth graders. *Research in the Teaching of English, 24,* 397–414.

Duke, N. K., & Kays, J. (1998). "Can I say 'Once upon a time'? ": Kindergarten children's developing knowledge of information book language. *Early Childhood Research Quarterly, 13,* 295–318.

Duke, N. K., & Purcell-Gates, V. (2003). Genres at home and at school: Bridging the known to the new. *The Reading Teacher, 57,* 30–37.

Eckhoff, B. (1983). How reading affects children's writing. *Language Arts, 60,* 607–616.

Ernst, K. (1993). *Picturing learning.* Portsmouth, NH: Heinemann.

Golden, J. M. (1984). Children's concept of story in reading and writing. *The Reading Teacher, 37,* 578–584.

Golden, J. M., Meiners, A., & Lewis, S. (1992). The growth of story meaning. *Language Arts, 69,* 22–27.

Graves, D. H. (1989). *Experiment with fiction.* Portsmouth, NH: Heinemann.

Hansen, J. (1987). *When writers read.* Portsmouth, NH: Heinemann.

Harste, J. C., Short, K. G., & Burke, C. (1988). *Creating classrooms for authors: The reading-writing connection.* Portsmouth, NH: Heinemann.

Harwayne, S. (1992). *Lasting impressions: Weaving literature into writing workshop.* Portsmouth, NH: Heinemann.

Irwin, J. W. (1991). *Teaching reading comprehension processes* (2nd ed.). Boston: Allyn & Bacon.

Johnson, T. D., & Louis, D. R. (1987). *Literacy through literature.* Portsmouth, NH: Heinemann.

Lehr, S. S. (1991). *The child's developing sense of theme: Responses to literature.* New York: Teachers College Press.

Lukens, R. J. (2002). *A critical handbook of children's literature* (7th ed.). New York: HarperCollins.

Mandler, J. M., & Johnson, N. S. (1977). Remembrance of things parsed: Story structure and recall. *Cognitive Psychology, 9,* 111–115.

Many, J. E. (1991). The effects of stance and age level on children's literary responses. *Journal of Reading Behavior, 23,* 61–85.

Pitcher, E. G., & Prelinger, E. (1963). *Children tell stories: An analysis of fantasy.* New York: International Universities Press.

Rosenblatt, L. M. (1978). *The reader, the text, the poem: The transactional theory of the literary work.* Carbondale: Southern Illinois University Press.

Rumelhart, D. (1975). Notes on a schema for stories. In D. G. Bobrow (Ed.), *Representation and understanding: Studies in cognitive science* (pp. 99–135). New York: Academic Press.

Stein, N. L., & Glenn, C. G. (1979). An analysis of story comprehension in elementary school children. In R. O. Freedle (Ed.), *New directions in discourse processing* (pp. 53–120). Norwood, NJ: Ablex.

Temple, C. (1992). Lots of plots: Patterns, meanings, and children's literature. In C. Temple & P. Collins (Eds.), *Stories and readers: New perspectives on literature in the elementary classroom* (pp. 3–13). Norwood, MA: Christopher-Gordon.

Tierney, R. J. (1990). Redefining reading comprehension. *Educational Leadership, 47,* 37–42.

Urzua, C. (1992). Faith in learners through literature studies. *Language Arts, 69,* 492–501.

Whitin, P. E. (1994). Opening potential: Visual response to literature. *Language Arts, 71,* 101–107.

Whitin, P. E. (1996). Exploring visual response to literature. *Research in the Teaching of English, 30,* 114–140.

Whitin, P. E. (2002). Leading into literature circles through the sketch-to-stretch strategy. *The Reading Teacher, 55,* 444–450.

Children's Book References

Allard, H. (1977). *Miss Nelson is missing!* Boston: Houghton Mifflin.

Avi. (2002). *Crispin: The cross of lead.* New York: Hyperion.

Babbitt, N. (1975). *Tuck everlasting.* New York: Farrar, Straus & Giroux.

Blume, J. (1972). *Tales of a fourth grade nothing.* New York: Dutton.

Brett, J. (1999). *Gingerbread baby.* New York: Putnam.

Bryan, A. (2003). *Beautiful blackbird.* New York: Atheneum.

Conrad, P. (1989). *The tub people.* New York: Harper & Row.

Cooper, S. (1999). *King of shadows.* New York: Aladdin.

Curtis, C. P. (1995). *The Watsons go to Birmingham—1963*. New York: Delacorte.

Cushman, K. (1994). *Catherine, called Birdy*. New York: HarperCollins.

Cushman, K. (1996). *The ballad of Lucy Whipple*. New York: Clarion.

Cushman, K. (2003). *Rodzina*. New York: Clarion.

Danziger, P. (1994). *Amber Brown is not a crayon*. New York: Putnam.

Deedy, C. A. (2000). *The yellow star: The legend of King Christian X of Denmark*. Atlanta: Peachtree.

Demi. (2002). *King Midas: The golden touch*. New York: McElderry.

Dorros, A. (1991). *Abuela*. New York: Dutton.

Dorros, A. (1995). *Isla*. New York: Dutton.

Fleischman, P. (1991). *Bull Run*. New York: HarperCollins.

Galdone, P. (1970). *The three little pigs*. New York: Seabury.

Galdone, P. (1972). *The three bears*. New York: Clarion.

Galdone, P. (1974). *Little Red Riding Hood*. New York: McGraw-Hill.

Galdone, P. (1978). *Cinderella*. New York: McGraw-Hill.

Gantos, J. (2000). *Joey Pigza loses control*. New York: Farrar, Straus & Giroux.

Gardiner, J. R. (1980). *Stone Fox*. New York: Harper & Row.

George, J. C. (1972). *Julie of the wolves*. New York: Harper & Row.

Goble, P. (2003). *Mystic horse*. New York: HarperCollins.

Hadley, E., & Hadley, T. (1983). *Legends of the sun and moon*. Cambridge: Cambridge University Press.

Hamilton, V. (2000). *The girl who spun gold*. New York: Scholastic.

Henkes, K. (1991). *Chrysanthemum*. New York: Morrow.

Hodges, M. (2002). *The boy who drew cats*. New York: Holiday.

Hofmeyr, D. (2001). *The star-bearer: A creation myth from ancient Egypt*. New York: Farrar, Straus & Giroux.

Howe, D., & Howe, J. (1979). *Bunnicula: A rabbit-tale of mystery*. New York: Aladdin.

Hyman, T. S. (1983). *Little Red Riding Hood*. New York: Holiday House.

Hyman, T. S. (2000). *The sleeping beauty*. Boston: Little, Brown.

Kellogg, S. (1984). *Paul Bunyan, a tall tale*. New York: Morrow.

Kimmel, E. A. (2000). *The runaway tortilla*. Delray Beach, FL: Winslow Press.

King-Smith, D. (1995). *Babe the gallant pig*. New York: Random House.

L'Engle, M. (1962). *A wrinkle in time*. New York: Farrar, Straus & Giroux.

Lewis, C. S. (1994). *The lion, the witch and the wardrobe*. New York: HarperCollins.

Lowry, L. (1989). *Number the stars*. Boston: Houghton Mifflin.

Lowry, L. (1993). *The giver*. Boston: Houghton Mifflin.

MacLachlan, P. (1985). *Sarah, plain and tall*. New York: Harper & Row.

Martin, B., Jr., & Archambault, J. (1985). *The ghost-eye tree*. New York: Holt, Rinehart and Winston.

McCloskey, R. (1969). *Make way for ducklings*. New York: Viking.

Meddaugh, S. (1992). *Martha speaks*. Boston: Houghton Mifflin.

Myers, W. D. (1988). *Scorpions*. New York: Harper & Row.

Naylor, P. R. (1991). *Shiloh*. New York: Atheneum.

Ness, E. (1966). *Sam, Bangs, and moonshine*. New York: Holt, Rinehart and Winston.

Noble, T. H. (1980). *The day Jimmy's boa ate the wash*. New York: Dial.

Numeroff, L. J. (1985). *If you give a mouse a cookie*. New York: Harper & Row.

Park, L. S. (2001). *A single shard*. New York: Clarion.

Paterson, K. (1977). *Bridge to Terabithia*. New York: Crowell.

Paulsen, G. (1987). *Hatchet*. New York: Viking.

Paye, W., & Lippert, M. H. (2002). *Head, body, legs: A story from Liberia*. New York: Holt.

Pinkney, J. (1999). *The ugly duckling*. New York: Morrow.

Pinkney, J. (2000). *Aesop's fables*. New York: North-South.

Potter, B. (1902). *The tale of Peter Rabbit*. New York: Warne.

Rathmann, P. (1996). *Officer Buckle and Gloria*. New York: Putnam.

Rowland, D. (1991). *Little Red Riding Hood/The wolf's tale*. New York: Birch Lane Press.

Rowling, J. K. (1999). *Harry Potter and the chamber of secrets*. New York: Scholastic.

Scieszka, J. (1989). *The true story of the 3 little pigs!* New York: Viking.

Sendak, M. (2003). *Where the wild things are*. New York: HarperCollins.

Service, P. (1988). *Stinker from space*. New York: Scribner.

Shepard, A. (2001). *Master man: A tall tale of Nigeria*. New York: HarperCollins.

Silverman, E. (1994). *Don't fidget a feather!* New York: Simon & Schuster.

Speare, E. G. (1958). *The witch of Blackbird Pond*. Boston: Houghton Mifflin.

Speare, E. G. (1983). *The sign of the beaver*. Boston: Houghton Mifflin.

Steig, W. (1971). *Amos and Boris*. New York: Farrar, Straus & Giroux.

Steig, W. (1982). *Doctor De Soto*. New York: Farrar, Straus & Giroux.

Steig, W. (1986). *Brave Irene*. New York: Farrar, Straus & Giroux.

Steig, J. (2001). *A gift from Zeus: Sixteen favorite myths*. New York: HarperCollins.

Van Allsburg, C. (1981). *Jumanji*. Boston: Houghton Mifflin.

Van Allsburg, C. (1991). *The wretched stone*. Boston: Houghton Mifflin.

Viorst, J. (1977). *Alexander and the terrible, horrible, no good, very bad day*. New York: Atheneum.

Waber, B. (1972). *Ira sleeps over*. Boston: Houghton Mifflin.

White, E. B. (1980). *Charlotte's web*. New York: HarperCollins.

Wiesner, D. (2001). *The three pigs*. New York: Clarion.

Woodson, J. (2003). *Locomotion*. New York: Putnam.

Yolen, J. (1980). *Commander Toad in space*. New York: Putnam.

Young, E. (1979). *The lion and the mouse*. New York: Putnam.

Zemach, M. (1983). *The little red hen*. New York: Farrar, Straus & Giroux.

10 Reading and Writing Information

PATTERNS OF PRACTICE

Reading and Writing Workshop

Literature Focus Units

Literature Circles

Theme Cycles

Mrs. LaRue's kindergartners have been studying fish for 3 weeks. The theme cycle began when the teacher brought in two goldfish to be class pets. The students were excited and immediately named them; they named the orange one Goldie and the white one Moon. So that the children would know how to care for them, she read aloud *Pet Fish* (Nelson, 2002). After listening to the book, the class wrote about their new pets using interactive writing. The children usually write one sentence on chart paper, but because they had more to write, they wrote the first sentence interactively and then Mrs. LaRue wrote their dictated sentences. Here is their completed chart about "Our New Pets":

We have 2 goldfish named Goldie and Moon. We will take good care of them. We will feed them goldfish food and keep their bowl clean. We will look at them but not touch them.

426

They posted the chart near the fish bowl and reread it each day. With practice, the children learned to pick out some familiar words on the chart, such as *we, good, goldfish, Goldie* and *Moon.*

Mrs. LaRue began a K-W-L chart at the beginning of the theme to record what the children knew about fish and what they wanted to learn. Looking for answers to their questions helped direct the children's attention as they participated in theme-related activities. Today, they are completing the right column of the chart about what they have learned. They have learned so much information to list on the chart that it takes Mrs. LaRue 30 minutes to write their dictated sentences. The completed chart is shown on page 428.

Mrs. LaRue has a text set of books about fish that she has been reading aloud to the kindergartners. The stories, informational books, and poems and rhymes are listed in the box on page 429. The teacher uses the books as springboards to language arts activities. After reading *A Fish Out of Water* (Palmer, 1961), the comical story of a fish that outgrows its bowl because it was fed too much, the children wonder if Goldie and Moon will outgrow their bowl. They talk about the possibility in a grand conversation, and then Mrs. LaRue promises not to let them feed the fish too much food so that they won't get too big. The next day when the children arrive, they are reminded of the story and asked to answer this question on the sign-in chart: *Will Goldie and Moon outgrow their bowl?* The question is written at the top of a two-column chart. The columns are titled *No* and *Yes,* and the children answer the question by writing their first names in the column with their answer.

Can kindergartners read and write information?

Some teachers assume that emergent readers and writers are too young to learn from informational books; they think that stories are more appropriate for young children and that reading and writing information should be postponed until the middle grades. Nothing could be further from the truth! Many young children, especially boys, are very interested in science and social studies topics. In fact, they prefer to read and write about information. As you read this vignette about Mrs. LaRue's kindergarten class, notice how her students listened to information books read aloud and how they wrote informational books.

The Kindergartners' K-W-L Chart About Fish

What We Know About Fish	What We Wonder About Fish	What We Learned About Fish
Fish live in water.	Are sharks fish?	Sharks are fish.
Fish can swim.	How does a fish breathe underwater?	Eels are fish.
Tuna is a fish.	How long does a fish live?	Sea horses are fish, too.
My Grandpa likes to fish.	Why don't fish have arms and legs?	Whales are not fish.
There are different kinds of fish.	Are whales fish?	Crabs are not fish.
Fish are slippery if you hold them.	Where do fish live?	Jelly fish and starfish are not fish either.
You can eat fish.	Do fish sleep?	Fish have backbones.
Fish are pretty.	What do they eat?	Fish breathe through gills.
	Can fish hear me talk?	Fish live any place there is water.
		Some fish like salt water.
		Some fish like fresh water with no salt.
		Fish eat little animals they find in the water.
		Fish eyes don't have eyelids.
		Fish swim by moving their tails.
		When they don't move maybe they are resting or sleeping.
		Fish will die if they are not in the water because they cannot breathe.
		Fish hatch from eggs in the water.
		Fish have all the colors of the rainbow.
		Fishes' skin is covered with scales.
		Fish live in groups called schools.
		Some fish live for 50 years or more.
		Yes, fish can hear.

Mrs. LaRue's Text Set of Books About Fish

Stories

Krudop, W. L. (2000). *The man who caught fish.* New York: Farrar, Straus & Giroux.
Lionni, L. (1973). *Swimmy.* New York: Dragonfly.
Lionni, L. (1974). *Fish is fish.* New York: Dragonfly.
Palmer, H. (1961). *A fish out of water.* New York: Random House.
Pfister, M. (1992). *The rainbow fish.* New York: North-South Books.
Yorinks, A. (1986). *Louis the fish.* New York: Farrar, Straus & Giroux.

Informational Books

Angelfish, C. (1999). *The fish book.* New York: Golden Books.
Arnosky, J. (1993). *Crinkleroot's 25 fish every child should know.* New York: Simon & Schuster.
Cole, J., & Wexler, J. (1984). *A fish hatches.* New York: Morrow.
Ehlert, L. (1992). *Fish eyes: A book you can count on.* San Diego: Harcourt Brace/Voyager.
Evans, M., & Caras, R. A. (2001). *Fish: Pet care guides for kids.* New York: Dorling Kindersley.
Nelson, R. (2002). *Pet fish.* Minneapolis, MN: Lerner.
Pfeffer, W. (1996). *What's it like to be a fish?* New York: HarperCollins.
Sill, C. P. (2002). *About fish: A guide for children.* Atlanta, GA: Peachtree.

Poems and Rhymes

Seuss, Dr. (1960). *One fish two fish red fish blue fish.* New York: Random House.

Several children expect that the goldfish will outgrow their bowl, but most children understand that their pets will stay small.

The children are curious about the parts of a fish, so Mrs. LaRue shows them an illustration of a goldfish in *Fish: Pet Care Guides for Kids* (Evans & Caras, 2001) and identify the fish's body parts—mouth, eyes, scales, gills, fins, tail. Afterward, she draws a picture of goldfish on chart paper and the students use interactive writing to label the parts. Later, many of the children draw or paint their own pictures of fish, and Mrs. LaRue helps them label two or more body parts on their pictures.

Each day, Mrs. LaRue reads a story or informational book about fish. The kindergartners' favorite book was *The Rainbow Fish* (Pfister, 1992), the story of a vain and selfish fish who learns the value of friendship. The children talk about this book in a grand conversation, and later they draw pictures about their favorite part of the story and dictate a sentence for Mrs. LaRue to add to their pictures. The children share their pictures and sentences from the author's chair, and then the teacher compiles them and binds them into a book that is placed in the classroom library for children to "read."

The next day, this question is posted on their sign-in chart: *What did the rainbow fish learn?* The children choose from among these three answers: *To be selfish. To be a friend. To look pretty.* Mrs. LaRue reads the three possible answers to the first few students who arrive in the classroom, and then they read them to the next group and so on until everyone has signed in. The teacher uses the sign-in chart to check her students' comprehension as well as to take attendance and encourage socialization and sharing.

The children learn more about fish at learning centers. Students spend 30 minutes each day working at centers. Mrs. LaRue has set up these eight centers in the classroom:

1. *Science center.* Children use magnifying glasses to closely observe the goldfish, and then they draw pictures of them in their science journals. Models of various fish, charts about fish, and several informational books about fish are also available for children to examine at the center.

2. *Book-making center.* After reading Lois Ehlert's *Fish Eyes: A Book You Can Count On* (1992), the children make their own fish counting books. Some kindergartners make books to count to 5, and others with more interest in writing and knowledge about numbers make books to count to 10. They use a familiar sentence starter, "I see . . . ," and Mrs. LaRue has introduced the words *big* and *little.* Students choose a word card with one of the words to add to their sentence. They write the other words themselves with the assistance of a parent volunteer. One page from a child's book is shown in the box below.

3. *Listening center.* Children listen to cassette tapes of Dr. Seuss's *One Fish Two Fish Red Fish Blue Fish* (1960) and *Fish Is Fish* (Lionni, 1974) and follow along in individual copies of the books.

4. *Storytelling center.* Children use storyboards (pictures from the story backed with cardboard and laminated) from *The Rainbow Fish* (Pfister, 1992) and puppets of the rainbow fish and other fish to retell the story and create new adventures for the rainbow fish.

5. *Sequencing center.* Kindergartners arrange a set of life cycle illustrations cut from a copy of *A Fish Hatches* (Cole & Wexler, 1984) and laminated in order from egg to adult fish.

6. *Sorting center.* Children sort picture cards of fish and other water animals and place the cards with pictures of fish in one pocket chart labeled "Fish," and pictures of animals that aren't fish in the "Not Fish" pocket chart. Pictures of fish include goldfish, swordfish, tuna, trout, shark, clown fish, eel, catfish, and seahorse. Other animal pictures include dolphin,

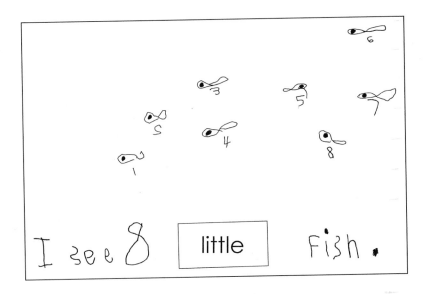

octopus, crab, turtle, clam, whale, jelly fish, lobster, sea otter, sea urchin, and starfish. Mrs. LaRue introduced this center after teaching children that the two characteristics of fish are that they have backbones and breathe with gills. The students practiced identifying and sorting the picture cards with the teacher before working at the center.

7. *Word work center.* Mrs. LaRue teaches phonemic awareness, phonics, and spelling lessons at this center. The children read and recite rhymes about fish, match objects that rhyme, such as *fish* and *dish,* sort pictures and objects that begin with /f/, such as a fish, a fan, and a feather. The children also write letters and words on white boards as Mrs. LaRue teaches handwriting skills at the same time she is teaching phonics and spelling.

8. *Library center.* Children look at fish books from the text set at this center. Each day, a fifth-grade student comes to help out at the center. This student rereads one of the books Mrs. LaRue has already read to interested children while other kindergartners look at books independently.

The highlight of the theme is the day that the children take a field trip to a nearby aquarium to see the different kinds of fish they've been learning about. Mrs. LaRue takes many photos with her digital camera of the children observing the fish and other water animals. After they get back to school, she prints out copies of the photos for the children to examine and talk about. Then each child chooses one photo to use in making a square for their class fish quilt. They glue their photos to the center of 8 by 8-inch squares of light blue construction paper and add a sentence under the photo. Joshua dictates, "Sharks are very dangerous!" Miriam dictates, "I saw lots of shiny sardine fish." Anthony writes, "Jellyfish are beautiful but they're not fish." Some students dictate their sentence for Mrs. LaRue to write, and others write interactively with Mrs. LaRue's assistance. Because these sentences will be read and reread, Mrs. LaRue emphasizes that they should be written with "grown-up" spelling so that everyone can read them. Finally, the kindergartners help the teacher place the

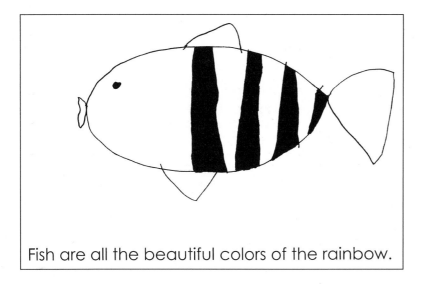

Fish are all the beautiful colors of the rainbow.

photo squares on a bulletin board that she has covered with wrapping paper decorated with fish. They add a title: Our Field Trip to the Aquarium. The finished product is a paper quilt.

Now the theme is coming to an end. After they finish their K-W-L charts, the children work on their culminating project—a collaborative book about fish. Each child dictates one fact about fish, and Mrs. LaRue types their facts on the computer. Students then add a picture to illustrate their fact. Malisa's page is shown in the box on page 431. The teacher compiles the pages, adds a cover, laminates the pages, and binds the book together. Children eagerly listen as Mrs. LaRue shares their published book with the class, clapping with excitement when their page is read. The book is added to their classroom library, and children take turns checking out the book and taking it home to share with their families. Mrs. LaRue has put three blank pages at the back of the book, and families write notes to the class on these pages, congratulating them on making such an interesting and informative book. These kindergartners are proud authors!

As you begin reading this chapter, you may want to read the "Dear Reader" letter in Chapter 10 on the Companion Website at www.prenhall.com/tompkins

It's common to hear teachers say, "I have an exciting story to read to you today about how whales migrate," and, "What a wonderful story you've written, and I learned a lot about baleen whales!" These books about whales may be stories, but it is more likely that they are informational or nonfiction books, because their primary purpose is to provide information. Teachers often use the word *story* as a generic term for all books students read and all books they write, thinking that *story* is an easier term for them to understand. But it is unfair to students to do this. Stories and informational books are different genres, although they overlap. Some informational books, such as *The Magic School Bus Inside a Hurricane* (Cole, 1995), use a storylike format, but the emphasis is on providing information (Freeman & Person, 1992).

Teachers have assumed that constructing stories in the mind is a fundamental way of learning (Wells, 1986). Recent research suggests, however, that children are able to understand and write informational texts as well as they do stories (Pappas, 1991, 1993; Read, 2001; Palmer & Stewart, 2003). Children are interested in learning about their world—about baleen whales, how a road is built, threats to the environment of Antarctica, or Helen Keller's courage—and informational books provide this knowledge.

Students often assume the efferent stance as they read informational books to locate facts, but they do not always do so (Rosenblatt, 1978, 1991). Many times, they pick up an informational book to check a fact, and then they continue reading—aesthetically, now—because they are fascinated by what they are reading. They get carried away in the book, just as they do when reading stories. At other times, students read books about topics they are interested in, and they read aesthetically, engaging in the lived-through experience of reading and connecting what they are reading to their own lives and prior reading experiences.

Russell Freedman, who won the 1988 Newbery Medal for *Lincoln: A Photobiography* (1987), talks about the purpose of informational books and explains that it is not enough for an informational book to provide information: "[An informational book] must animate its subject, infuse it with life. It must create a vivid and believable world that the reader will enter willingly and leave only with reluctance. . . . It should be just as compelling as a good story" (1992, p. 3). High-quality informational books such as Freedman's encourage students to read aesthetically because they engage readers and tap their curiosity. Barbara Moss advocates using informational books for read-alouds and explains that reading nonfiction trade books "has the ever widening effect of a pebble thrown into a pond" (1995, p. 122).

Students also write informational books about concepts and information they are learning during theme cycles. The informational trade books they have read serve as models for their writing, and they organize the information that they present using the same types of patterns or structures used in informational books (Freeman, 1991; Tompkins, Smith, & Hitchcock, 1987).

This chapter focuses on expository text, the type of writing used in informational books. As you continue reading, think about these questions:

◆ How do teachers develop students' knowledge about expository text?

◆ How can teachers facilitate students' reading of informational books?

◆ How can teachers facilitate students' writing of various types of informational writing, including reports and biographies?

DEVELOPING STUDENTS' KNOWLEDGE ABOUT INFORMATIONAL BOOKS

As students read informational books and listen to them read aloud, they learn about the world around them and many other things as well. They learn how to vary their reading depending on their purpose. Sometimes they read informational books from beginning to end as they do stories, or they may use the index to locate a specific topic and then read just that section. They learn how to use an index and a table of contents, and how to read charts, graphs, maps, and diagrams. They also notice the different ways informational books are organized and how authors develop interrelationships among the pieces of information being presented.

Types of Informational Books

There is a new wave of engaging and artistic informational books being published today, and these books show increased respect for children. Peter Roop

(1992) explains that for years, informational books were the "ugly duckling" of children's literature, but now they have grown into a beautiful swan.

Four qualities of informational books are accuracy, organization, design, and style (Vardell, 1991). First and foremost, the facts must be current and complete. These books must be well researched, and, when appropriate, varying points of view should be presented. Stereotypes are to be avoided, and the details in both the text and the illustrations must be authentic. Second, information should be presented clearly and logically, using organizational patterns to increase the book's readability. Third, the design of the book should be eye-catching and should enhance its usability. Illustrations should complement the text, and explanations should accompany each illustration. Last, the book should be written in a lively and stimulating style so as to engage the reader's curiosity and wonder.

Thousands and thousands of informational books are available for elementary students today. Topics range from the earth and astronomy, plants and animals, technology, the arts, geography and history to sports, occupations and careers, social issues, and customs and holidays. Teachers collect and use informational books in the theme cycles they teach, and students often choose to read informational books on topics that interest them during reading workshop.

Many informational books are written in the picture-book format for primary-grade students. Aliki is a respected author of informational books for young children, and her book *Ah, Music* (2003) provides a wealth of visual and textual information about music. Books about animals appeal to children, such as Lois Ehlert's cleverly designed book *Waiting for Wings* (2001), which presents the life cycle of the butterfly, and *Dig, Wait, Listen: A Desert Toad's Tale* (Sayre, 2001), which introduces young children to this desert animal's life cycle and habitat. In addition, *Little Panda: The World Welcomes Hua Mei at the San Diego Zoo* (Ryder, 2001) introduces Hua Mei, the first panda born in captivity in the Western Hemisphere to survive more than 4 days. Other informational books include *So You Want to Be President?* (St. George, 2000), a collection of interesting tidbits of information about the presidents supported with humorous cartoon illustrations, and *Millions to Measure* (Schwartz, 2003), in which Marvelosissimo the Mathematical Magician examines the history of measurement.

Some informational books for older children are also written in the picture-book format, but many others are chapter books with photo illustrations, diagrams, and charts. For example, *Remember the Lusitania!* (Preston, 2003) is a riveting account of the ill-fated 1915 voyage of the British luxury liner, sunk by a German submarine. Russell Freedman's *In the Days of the Vaqueros: America's First True Cowboys* (2001) is a tribute to the early Native American cowmen, and Jim Murphy presents a moving account of the Texas War of Independence showing how accounts differ over time in *Inside the Alamo* (Murphy, 2003). In *The Bald Eagle Returns* (Patent, 2000), the author explains how bald eagles have made a significant comeback in the United States, and in *A Dragon in the Sky: The Story of a Green Darner Dragonfly* (Pringle, 2001), the author tells a richly detailed story of Anax, a green darner dragonfly.

Life stories also are informational books; biographies are one type and autobiographies are another. Life stories being written today are more realistic than those written in the past; they present well-known personalities and common people, warts and all. Jean Fritz's portraits of Revolutionary War figures, such as *Will You Sign Here, John Hancock?* (1976), are among the best known, and middle- and upper-grade teachers often use them in teaching American history. Elementary students read books about both historical personalities and contemporary figures. Historical personalities are profiled in *Saladin: Noble Prince of Islam* (Stanley, 2002), *Abigail Adams* (Wallner, 2001), and *Confucius: The Golden Rule* (Freedman, 2002), and contemporary figures in *Harvesting Hope: the Story of Cesar Chavez* (Krull, 2003), *Light Shining Through the Mist: A Photobiography of Dian Fossey* (Matthews, 1998), and *Martin's Big Words: The Life of Dr. Martin Luther King, Jr.* (Rappaport, 2001). In addition, some collective biographies are available for middle- and upper-grade students, such as *The Signers: The 56 Stories Behind the Declaration of Independence* (Fradin, 2002) and *They Saw the Future: Oracles, Psychics, Scientists, Great Thinkers, and Pretty Good Guessers* (Krull, 1999).

Fewer autobiographies are written for children than for adults, but more are published each year. Autobiographies about authors and illustrators, such as *On the Bus With Joanna Cole* (1996), author of the series of Magic School Bus books, *The True Stories Behind Hatchet and the Brian Books* by Gary Paulsen (2001), Lois Lowry's *Looking Back: A Book of Memories* (1998), and Tomie dePaola's *Things Will NEVER Be the Same* (2003), the fifth book in his autobiographical series, are popular. In addition, many upper-grade students read Francisco Jiménez's moving books about his family's experiences as migrant farm workers, *The Circuit* (1997) and *Breaking Through* (2001).

In addition to these main types of informational books, there are other, more specialized, types. Three types that elementary students read are:

1. Alphabet and counting books.   Although many alphabet and counting books with pictures of familiar objects are designed for young children, others are more sophisticated and provide detailed information on social studies and science topics. In his alphabet book *Illuminations* (1989), Jonathan Hunt describes medieval life, in *Capital! Washington, DC From A to Z* (2003), Laura Melmed takes readers on a tour of our nation's capital, and in *A Swim Through the Sea* (1994), Kristin Joy Pratt describes 26 types of sea creatures, including clown fish and hermit crabs. R. L. Williams demonstrates how to count money in *The Coin Counting Book* (2001), and Ann Herbert Scott cleverly integrates information about cowboys in *One Good Horse: A Cowpuncher's Counting Book* (1990). In some of these books, new terms are introduced and illustrated, and in others, terms are explained in a sentence or a paragraph.

2. Books that present information through a song or poem.   In these powerful books, songs and poems are illustrated with a word, line, or stanza on each page. Together the text and illustrations provide information. In *America the Beautiful* (Bates, 1993), Neil Waldman's expressionistic illustrations highlight 14 natural and man-made wonders, including the Great Smokies and Mesa Verde, and information about each is presented in the back of the book. Jeannette Winter's haunting illustrations underscore the dangers of the Underground Railroad in *Follow the Drinking Gourd* (1988). Henry Wadsworth Longfellow's *The Midnight Ride of Paul Revere* (2000) re-creates the silversmith's historic ride, and historical facts about the event are included in an endnote. Diane Siebert's poem and Wendell Minor's paintings combine to present a powerful portrait in *Sierra* (1991), and Jane Yolen's poem and Laura Regan's illustrations unite to describe the lush rain-forest environment in *Welcome to the Green House* (1993).

    3. Multigenre or combined-text books present information using more than one genre. The Magic School Bus series of science-related books, including *The Magic School Bus in the Rain Forest* (Cole, 1998), and the social studies–related books in the Ms. Frizzle's Adventures series, including *Ms. Frizzle's Adventures: Medieval Castle* (Cole, 2003), are the best-known multigenre books. The main text is presented as a narrative, and the side panels and other special boxes provide additional information. This information is presented as questions and answers, notes, and brief reports written by Ms. Frizzle's students as well as charts, maps, and other diagrams. *The 5,000-Year-Old Puzzle: Solving a Mystery of Ancient Egypt* (Logan, 2002) presents information about the discovery of King Tut's tomb through journal entries, photos, maps, postcards, sidebars, and newspaper articles. By using a combination of genres, the author and illustrator provide multiple viewpoints and enrich their presentation of information in the book. In *Leonardo: Beautiful Dreamer* (Byrd, 2003), boxes with notes, explanations, and excerpts from Leonardo da Vinci's own notes amplify the text. Multigenre books are richly layered texts, often presented in picture-book form. Because of the complexity of the page layout, Chapman and Sopko (2003) compare reading multigenre books to peeling an onion. They recommend that teachers read the books three or four times over a period of several days so that students can fully comprehend and appreciate the book. First, they suggest taking a picture walk to examine the illustrations. Then teachers read the book, focusing on the informational text, and for the second reading, they focus on the narrative text. Finally, they focus on the sketches and borders. Of course, the number of rereadings depends on the students' interests and the complexity of the book.

Expository Text Structures

Just as stories are structured using plot, characters, and the other elements of story structure, informational books are organized or patterned in particular ways called expository text structures. Five of the most common organizational patterns are description, sequence, comparison, cause and effect, and problem and solution (Meyer & Freedle, 1984; Niles, 1974). Figure 10–1 describes these patterns and presents sample passages and cue words that signal use of each pattern. The story-structure patterns interact to create the framework for the story; however, in informational books, expository text structures can be used separately.

Description. Writers describe a topic by listing characteristics, features, and examples in this organizational pattern. Phrases such as *for example* and *characteristics are* cue this structure. Examples of books using description include *Spiders* (Gibbons, 1992), *Where Do Puddles Go?* (Robinson, 1995b), and *Gorillas* (Simon, 2000), and in these books, the authors describe many

FIGURE 10-1

The Five Expository Text Structures

Pattern and Definition	Graphic Organizer	Sample Passage
Description: The author describes a topic by listing characteristics, features, and examples. Cue words are: *for example* *characteristics are*		The Olympic symbol consists of five interlocking rings. The rings represent the five continents—Africa, Asia, Europe, North America, and South America—from which athletes come to compete in the games. The rings are colored black, blue, green, red, and yellow. At least one of these colors is found in the flag of every country sending athletes to compete in the Olympic games.
Sequence: The author lists items or events in numerical or chronological order. Cue words are: *first, second, third* *next* *then* *finally*		The Olympic games began as athletic festivals to honor the Greek gods. The most important festival was held in the valley of Olympia to honor Zeus, the king of the gods. It was this festival that became the Olympic games in 776 B.C. These games were ended in A.D. 394 by the Roman Emperor who ruled Greece. No Olympic games were held for more than 1,500 years. Then the modern Olympics began in 1896. Almost 300 male athletes competed in the first modern Olympics. In the games held in 1900, female athletes were allowed to compete. The games have continued every four years since 1896 except during World War II, and they will most likely continue for many years to come.
Comparison: The author explains how two or more things are alike and/or how they are different. Cue words are: *different* *in contrast* *alike* *same as* *on the other hand*		The modern Olympics is very unlike the ancient Olympic games. Individual events are different. While there were no swimming races in the ancient games, for example, there were chariot races. There were no female contestants, and all athletes competed in the nude. Of course, the ancient and modern Olympics are also alike in many ways. Some events, such as the javelin and discus throws, are the same. Some people say that cheating, professionalism, and nationalism in the modern games are a disgrace to the Olympic tradition. But according to the ancient Greek writers, there were many cases of cheating, nationalism, and professionalism in their Olympics, too.

(continues)

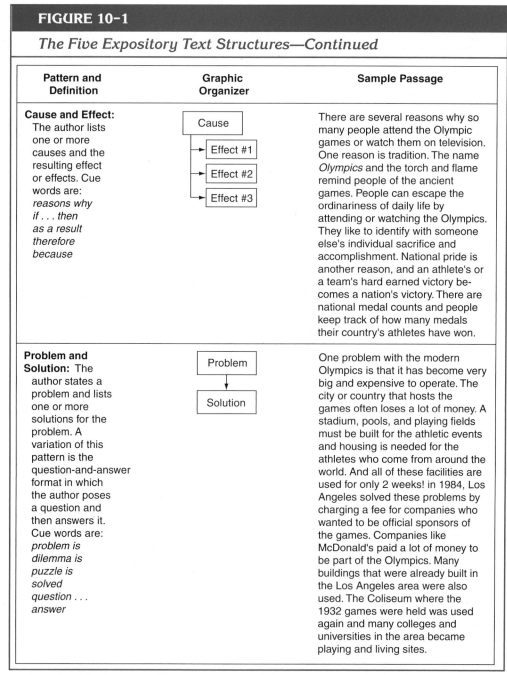

FIGURE 10-1

The Five Expository Text Structures—Continued

Pattern and Definition	Graphic Organizer	Sample Passage
Cause and Effect: The author lists one or more causes and the resulting effect or effects. Cue words are: *reasons why* *if . . . then* *as a result* *therefore* *because*	Cause → Effect #1, Effect #2, Effect #3	There are several reasons why so many people attend the Olympic games or watch them on television. One reason is tradition. The name *Olympics* and the torch and flame remind people of the ancient games. People can escape the ordinariness of daily life by attending or watching the Olympics. They like to identify with someone else's individual sacrifice and accomplishment. National pride is another reason, and an athlete's or a team's hard earned victory be-comes a nation's victory. There are national medal counts and people keep track of how many medals their country's athletes have won.
Problem and Solution: The author states a problem and lists one or more solutions for the problem. A variation of this pattern is the question-and-answer format in which the author poses a question and then answers it. Cue words are: *problem is* *dilemma is* *puzzle is* *solved* *question . . .* *answer*	Problem → Solution	One problem with the modern Olympics is that it has become very big and expensive to operate. The city or country that hosts the games often loses a lot of money. A stadium, pools, and playing fields must be built for the athletic events and housing is needed for the athletes who come from around the world. And all of these facilities are used for only 2 weeks! in 1984, Los Angeles solved these problems by charging a fee for companies who wanted to be official sponsors of the games. Companies like McDonald's paid a lot of money to be part of the Olympics. Many buildings that were already built in the Los Angeles area were also used. The Coliseum where the 1932 games were held was used again and many colleges and universities in the area became playing and living sites.

facets of their topic. When students delineate any topic, such as the Missis-sippi River, eagles, or Alaska, they use description.

Sequence.   Writers list items or events in numerical or chronological order in this pattern. Cue words include *first, second, third, next, then,* and *finally.* Car-oline Arnold describes the steps in creating a museum display in *Dinosaurs All Around: An Artist's View of the Prehistoric World* (1993), and David Macaulay describes how a castle was constructed in *Castle* (1977). Students use

Graphic organizers. *These second graders are working with their teacher to create a cluster to record information they are learning during a theme cycle on animals. They are beginning the cluster after reading a book about different types of animal homes, and as they continue to read books and learn more about animal homes, they will add more information to the cluster. Later they will use the information on the cluster to make posters and write reports. Clusters and other graphic organizers are important note-taking tools for all students, even primary-grade students.*

sequence to write directions for completing a math problem, the stages in an animal's life cycle, or events in a biography.

Comparison.   Writers explain how two or more things are alike or different in this structure. *Different, in contrast, alike, same as,* and *on the other hand* are cue words and phrases that signal this structure. In *Horns, Antlers, Fangs, and Tusks* (Rauzon, 1993), for example, the author compares animals with these distinctive types of headgear, and in *Solid, Liquid, or Gas?* (Robinson, 1995a), the author compares the three states of matter. When students compare and contrast book and video versions of a story, reptiles and amphibians, or life in ancient Greece with life in ancient Egypt, they use this organizational pattern.

Cause and Effect.   Writers describe one or more causes and the resulting effect or effects in this pattern. *Reasons why, if . . . then, as a result, therefore,* and *because* are words and phrases that cue this structure. Explanations of why dinosaurs became extinct, the effects of pollution on the environment, or the causes of the Civil War use the cause-and-effect pattern. Betsy Maestro's *How Do Apples Grow?* (1992) and Paul Showers's *What Happens to a Hamburger?* (1985) are two informational books that exemplify the cause-and-effect structure.

Problem and Solution.   Writers present a problem and offer one or more solutions in this expository structure. In *Man and Mustang* (Ancona, 1992), the author describes the problem of wild mustangs and explains how they are rescued, and in *The Mystery of the Hieroglyphs* (Donoughue, 1999), the author explains how the French archaeologist Jean François Champollion deciphered Egyptian hieroglyphs. A variation is the question-and-answer format, in which the writer poses a question and then answers it; one question-and-answer book is . . . *If You Lived at the Time of Martin Luther King* (Levine, 1990). Cue words and phrases include *the problem is, the puzzle is, solve,* and *question . . . answer.* Students use this structure when they write about why money was invented, saving endangered animals, and building dams to stop flooding. They often use the problem-solution pattern in writing advertisements and in other persuasive writing.

These organizational patterns correspond to the traditional organization of main ideas and details within paragraphs. The main idea is embodied in the organizational pattern, and the details are the elaboration; for example, in the sample passage of the comparison pattern in Figure 10–1, the main idea is that the modern Olympic games are very different from the ancient Olympic games. The details make specific comparisons and contrasts.

Graphic organizers can help students organize and visually represent ideas for the five organizational patterns (Piccolo, 1987; Smith & Tompkins, 1988). Students might use a cluster for description, a Venn diagram or T-chart for comparison, or a series of boxes and arrows for cause and effect (Bromley, 1991; Yopp & Yopp, 2000). Diagrams of a variety of graphic organizers also appear in Figure 10–1. Most of the research on expository text structures has focused on older students' use of these patterns in reading; however, elementary students also use the patterns and cue words in their writing (Langer, 1986; Raphael, Englert, & Kirschner, 1989; Tompkins, 2004).

Even though the expository text structures are used with informational texts, some books that are classified as stories also involve sequence, cause and effect, or one of the other expository text structures. Teachers can point out these structures or use graphic organizers to help students look more closely at the story. The popular *The Very Hungry Caterpillar* (Carle, 1970), for example, involves two sequences: Eric Carle uses sequence to show the development of the caterpillar from egg to butterfly and to list what the caterpillar ate each day. In *The Blue and the Gray* (1996), a story about the construction of a modern interracial community on the site of a Civil War battlefield, Eve Bunting contrasts the misery of the war with the harmony of the neighborhood. The Caldecott Medal book about the riots in Los Angeles, *Smoky Night* (Bunting, 1994), demonstrates cause and effect. Anger causes the riots, and the riots bring hope and understanding. Problem and solution is illustrated in *A New Coat for Anna* (Ziefert, 1986), a story set in war-torn Europe, as Anna's mother makes a series of trades to get a new coat for her daughter.

Teaching Students About Expository Text Structures

Just as teachers teach students about the elements of story structure, teachers point out how authors structure informational books. When students recognize the five expository text structures in books they are reading, they are better able to comprehend what they are reading, and when they structure their in-

Seeing Common Threads

How does understanding expository text structures contribute to students' learning?

Judith Kenney responds:

Expository text structure teaches my students to organize information and write accurate and interesting reports. My fifth-grade students who have a sense of text structure are able to grasp the purpose and main idea of what they are reading rather than just remembering a few unimportant and isolated details. I've noticed that as my students become more comfortable with text structure they begin to use graphic organizers in their content-area learning logs which can then be used to assess their progress and understanding. As my fifth graders incorporate the five expository text structures into their reading and writing they are better able to present a clear, concise, and organized presentation in paragraph form.

What do you think?

Each chapter presents a question and a response written by one of Dr. Tompkins's students. Consider other comments, or respond to the question yourself, by visiting the Threaded Message Board in Chapter 10 on the Companion Website at www.prenhall.com/tompkins

Companion Website

formational writing according to these structures, their writing is easier to understand. Research over the past 20 years has confirmed the importance of teaching students to recognize expository text structures as an aid to reading comprehension and to improve writing effectiveness (Flood, Lapp, & Farnan, 1986; Harvey, 1998; McGee & Richgels, 1985; Robb, 2003).

Examining Expository Text Structures in Informational Books.   Many informational books are clearly organized using one of the expository text structures, and students can identify the pattern because it is signaled by the title, topic sentences, or cue words. The Classroom Library box on page 442 lists books that illustrate each of the five expository text structures. Other books, however, use a combination of two or more structures or may have no apparent structure at all. Sometimes the title of a book incorrectly signals an organizational pattern. When the book doesn't have a clear structure or falsely signals a structure, students are likely to have trouble comprehending and remembering main ideas. Whenever there isn't a clear structure, teachers should provide one through the purpose they set for reading the book.

As teachers share informational books with students, they teach them to identify the expository text structures. Being able to identify the expository structures is not the goal, but when students recognize how a text is structured, they are better able to comprehend what they are reading. Similarly, students learn to diagram each expository text structure using a specific

Informational Books Representing the Expository Text Structures

Description

Arnosky, J. (2002). *All about frogs.* New York: Scholastic. (P–M)

de Bourgoing, P. (1995). *Under the ground.* New York: Scholastic. (P)

Fowler, A. (1996). *Life in a tide pool.* New York: Children's Press. (P)

Gibbons, G. (1995). *Sea turtles.* New York: Holiday House. (P)

Patent, D. H. (1992). *Feathers.* New York: Cobblehill. (M–U)

Pringle, L. (1995). *Coral reefs: Earth's undersea treasures.* New York: Simon & Schuster. (U)

Simon, S. (2000). *Gorillas.* New York: HarperCollins. (M–U)

Wexler, J. (1995). *Sundew stranglers: Plants that eat insects.* New York: Dutton. (U)

Sequence

Aliki. (1992). *Milk from cow to carton.* New York: HarperCollins. (P–M)

Gibbons, G. (1995). *Planet earth/inside out.* New York: Morrow. (M)

Leedy, L. (1993). *Postcards from Pluto: A tour of the solar system.* New York: Holiday House. (P–M)

Provensen, A. (1990). *The buck stops here.* New York: HarperCollins. (M–U)

Steltzer, U. (1995). *Building an igloo.* New York: Holt. (P–M)

Tatham, B. (2002). *Penguin chick.* New York: Harper-Collins. (P)

Wadsworth, G. (1995). *Giant Sequoia trees.* Chicago: Lerner. (P–M)

Comparison

Gibbons, G. (1984). *Fire! Fire!* New York: Harper & Row. (P–M)

Lasker, J. (1976). *Merry ever after: The story of two medieval weddings.* New York: Viking. (M–U)

Markle, S. (1993). *Outside and inside trees.* New York: Bradbury Press. (M)

Rauzon, M. J. (1993). *Horns, antlers, fangs, and tusks.* New York: Lothrop, Lee & Shepard. (P–M)

Robinson, F. (1995). *Solid, liquid, or gas?* Chicago: Children's Press. (P)

Sewall, M. (1995). *Thunder from the clear sky.* New York: Atheneum. (M–U)

Singer, M. (1995). *A wasp is not a bee.* New York: Holt. (P)

Spier, P. (1987). *We the people.* New York: Doubleday. (M–U)

Cause and Effect

Branley, F. M. (1985). *Volcanoes.* New York: Harper & Row. (P–M)

Branley, F. M. (1986). *What makes day and night?* New York: Harper & Row. (P–M)

Casey, D. (1995). *Weather everywhere.* New York: Macmillan. (P)

Heller, R. (1983). *The reason for a flower.* New York: Grosset & Dunlap. (M)

Lauber, P. (1995). *Who eats what? Food chains and food webs.* New York: HarperCollins. (M)

Showers, P. (1985). *What happens to a hamburger?* New York: Harper & Row. (P–M)

Souza, D. M. (1994). *Northern lights.* Minneapolis: Carolrhoda. (U)

Zoehfeld, K. W. (1995). *How mountains are made.* New York: HarperCollins. (M)

Problem and Solution

Arnosky, J. (1995). *I see animals hiding.* New York: Scholastic. (P)

Colman, P. (1995). *Rosie the riveter: Women working on the home front in World War II.* New York: Crown. (U)

Fritz, J. (1987). *Shh! We're writing the Constitution.* New York: Putnam. (M–U)

Geisert, B. (1995). *Haystack.* Boston: Houghton Mifflin. (P)

Heller, R. (1986). *How to hide a whippoorwill and other birds.* New York: Grosset & Dunlap. (P–M)

Lauber, P. (2003). *Who came first? New clues to prehistoric Americans.* Washington, DC: National Geographic Society. (M–U)

Moore, K. (1997). . . . . *If you lived at the time of the American Revolution.* New York: Scholastic. (M–U)

Rounds, G. (1995). *Sod houses on the Great Plains.* New York: Holiday House. (M)

Schanzer, R. (2003). *How Ben Franklin stole the lightning.* New York: HarperCollins. (M)

Continues

CLASSROOM LIBRARY

Informational Books Representing the Expository Text Structures – Continued

Combination

Adkins, J. (2002). *Bridges: From my side to yours.* Brookfield, CT: Millbrook/Roaring Brook Press. (M)

Aliki. (1981). *Digging up dinosaurs.* New York: Harper & Row. (M)

Coombs, K. M. (1995). *Flush! Treating wastewater.* Minneapolis: Carolrhoda. (M–U)

George, J. C. (1995). *Everglades.* New York: HarperCollins. (M)

Guiberson, B. Z. (1991). *Cactus hotel.* New York: Henry Holt. (P–M)

Hoyt-Goldsmith, D. (1992). *Hoang Anh: A Vietnamese-American boy.* New York: Holiday House. (M)

McKissack, P., & McKissack, F. (1995). *Red-tail angels: The story of the Tuskeegee airmen of World War II.* New York: Walker. (U)

Micucci, C. (2003). *The life and times of the ant.* Boston: Houghton Mifflin. (P–M)

Schwartz, D. (2003). *Millions to measure.* New York: HarperCollins. (P–M)

graphic organizer so they will be able to use the structure to help them pick out the main ideas when they are reading. This knowledge pays off as well when students are writing: They apply what they have learned as they organize their writing.

Minilessons.   Teachers present minilessons about the five expository text structures and show students how to use the organizational patterns to improve their reading comprehension as well as to organize their writing. A list of minilesson topics related to expository text structures is presented on pages 444 and 445. Also included with the list of topics is a minilesson a second-grade teacher taught on sequence.

Assessing Students' Use of Expository Text Structures

Teachers can assess how students use expository text structures to comprehend as they read and listen to informational books read aloud. Students should learn to recognize the structural patterns and use graphic organizers to classify information, take notes, and generalize main ideas. Teachers can monitor students as they participate in discussions about informational books and review students' learning log entries during theme cycles to assess their understanding of key concepts and their use of graphic organizers.

Teachers can also assess how well students organize information when they write paragraphs, reports, and other across-the-curriculum pieces. When students write to present information, they:

- Choose the most appropriate structure
- Develop a graphic organizer before writing
- Write a topic sentence that identifies the structure
- Use cue words to signal the structure

These four components can be used to develop a checklist or rubric to assess students' use of expository text structures.

Piecing a Lesson Together

Topics on Expository Text Structures

Procedures	Concepts	Strategies and Skills
Make clusters	Description	Vary reading according to purpose
Make Venn diagrams	Sequence	Locate information using index
Make flowcharts	Comparison	Identify expository text structures
	Cause and effect	Note cue words
	Problem and solution	Use graphic organizers

Please visit the Companion Website at **www.prenhall.com/tompkins** for a second fully realized minilesson.

REPORTS OF INFORMATION

Often, students are not exposed to report writing until they are faced with writing a term paper in high school, at which point they are overwhelmed with learning how to take notes on note cards, organize and write the paper, and compile a bibliography. There is no reason to postpone report writing until students reach high school; students in the elementary grades—even in the primary grades—write both class collaboration and individual reports (Duthie, 1994; Krogness, 1987; Queenan, 1986). Early, successful experiences with informative writing teach students about content-area topics as well as how to interview, collect data, and write reports.

SEQUENCE

Minilesson

Mrs. Miller Introduces Sequencing to Her Second Graders

1. **Introduce the Topic**

   Mrs. Miller explains to her second-grade class that authors organize informational books in special ways. One of those ways is sequence, in which the author puts information in a certain order. She explains that they know many sequences: the numbers 1 to 10, the days of the week, the grades in school, the seasons, and the months of the year.

2. **Share Examples**

   Mrs. Miller explains that she wants her students to be detectives to try to figure out the sequence in *From Plant to Blue Jeans* (L'Hommedieu, 1997). She begins to read the book aloud, and soon the students recognize that it describes the process of making blue jeans, from harvesting the cotton to sewing the fabric pieces into pants.

3. **Provide Information**

   Mrs. Miller explains that authors give some word clues about the sequence. She points out that in *From Plant to Blue Jeans,* the author uses the words *begin, then, last,* and *finally* to structure the book. These special words are called *cue words,* she explains, and other cue words are *first,* *second, third,* and *next.* One student also points out that the title gives you an idea about the sequence. Then Mrs. Miller and the second graders make a poster, listing the steps and adding pictures to illustrate each step of the jeans-making process.

4. **Supervise Practice**

   The next day, Mrs. Miller divides the students into five small groups and passes out one of these books to each group: *Chicken and Egg* (Back & Olesen, 1984), *From Wax to Crayon* (Forman, 1997), *Honeybee* (Watts, 1989), *Postcards from Pluto: A Tour of the Solar System* (Leedy, 1993), and *Let's Find Out About Ice Cream* (Reid, 1996). The students read the book to figure out what is sequenced. Then they make posters, listing the steps in the sequence and drawing pictures to illustrate each step. Afterward, students explain the sequence in their books and share their posters with the class.

5. **Reflect on Learning**

   The students locate other books with the sequence pattern and bring them to show Mrs. Miller. She asks them what they have learned, and they respond that they have learned that some books have a special organization—sequence—but others do not. One student asks, "So just what are the other patterns?"

Visual Reports

Students can report information in charts, maps, flowcharts, and other diagrams as well as through paragraphs. Moline (1995) explains that visual presentations are sophisticated, multilayered reports. Visual reports are used when the information can be presented more effectively through a diagram than through a traditional report. Seven formats for visual reports are clusters, diagrams, flowcharts, data charts, maps, time lines, and cubes; these formats are summarized in the LA Essentials box on page 446. At first thought, these formats might seem easier to produce than written reports, but if they are done properly, they are just as challenging.

Essentials

Seven Ways to Report Information Visually

1. Clusters

Students make weblike diagrams to organize information hierarchies. The topic is listed in a center circle, and main-idea rays are drawn out from it. Then details are added to the main-idea rays. A tree diagram is like a cluster because information is grouped and linked with lines. Tree diagrams look like upside-down trees. The best-known example of a tree diagram is a genealogy chart.

2. Diagrams

Students make diagrams when they add labels to pictures they have drawn. Students can also make more sophisticated diagrams, such as cross-section diagrams and diagrams drawn to scale. In science, for example, students draw cross-section diagrams of a cell or a volcano, and scale diagrams compare the size of the planets.

3. Flowcharts

Students use flowcharts to show the steps in a process. They usually draw a series of boxes and connect the boxes with arrows. One type of flowchart is a circle chart in which the series of boxes are arranged in a circle. Flowcharts are used to show life cycles, food chains, and "how-to" directions.

4. Data Charts

Data charts are tables in which information is sorted into categories and written in cells or sections. The cells are made by dividing the chart into rows and columns. Students write headings for each row and column and record information in each cell. Students use data charts to report detailed information about science and social studies topics. A special kind of data chart is a Venn diagram, in which two topics are compared and contrasted.

5. Maps

Students draw geographic maps as well as other types of maps to show spatial connections. They can draw home, classroom, and community maps as well as maps of the universe or an animal's home.

6. Time Lines

Students draw time lines to record a series of events. They also make special time lines called lifelines to trace the events in a person's life. Students can make multiple time lines for the same time period to compare the influence of one thing on something else.

7. Cubes

Students examine a topic from six perspectives, write paragraphs based on their examinations, and then attach the paragraphs to the six sides of a cube. This three-dimensional visual report helps students look at concepts they are learning in a fresh way. Students create cubes about almost any topic—the Crusades, photosynthesis, the earth, or Plains Indians.

Adapted from Moline, 1995.

The diagrams used for visual reports can be used as learning tools as well as for reports. When students make a flowchart in their learning logs, for example, they are using the flowchart as a graphic organizer to better understand a concept they are learning. Students' diagrams are quickly sketched when they are being used as part of the learning process. In contrast, when students use diagrams for visual reports, they use the writing process to draft, revise, edit, and make a final copy. As reports, visual reports are as formal as other types of reports.

As students develop their visual reports, they consider the layout, how the words and drawings are integrated, and the typography, the type styles they use to communicate meaning (Moline, 1995). As they plan their layout, students consider the arrangement of the diagram on the page, the use of lines, boxes and headings to organize information, and the drawings and colors to highlight key points. Students also consider how they use type styles: They might print some words in all capital letters or highlight key terms, or they might choose a type style for the title that emphasizes the concept. For example, when students make a visual report on ancient Egypt, they use a type style that resembles hieroglyphics for the title. Word processing programs allow students to experiment with a variety of fonts and to use italics and boldface to add emphasis.

Two types of visual reports are clusters and cubes. Clusters are weblike diagrams that students use to gather and organize information (Bromley, 1996; Rico, 1983). The topic is written in a circle centered on a sheet of paper or poster. Main ideas are written on rays drawn out from the circle, and branches with details and examples are added to complete each main idea.

Two clusters are presented in Figure 10–2. The top cluster was developed by a sixth-grade teacher during a theme cycle on birds. The purpose of the cluster was to assist students in categorizing birds such as cardinals, penguins, vultures, chickens, and ducks. As the class talked about the categories, students wrote the names of examples beside each category to complete the cluster. Later in the theme cycle, students each chose one bird to research, and then they presented the results of their research in cluster form. The bottom cluster presents the results of one student's research on bald eagles. The information in the cluster is divided into four categories: life, hunters, symbol, and body; other, more general, information is listed at the top of the figure.

Cubing is a useful procedure for across-the-curriculum theme cycles; middle- and upper-grade students can cube topics such as Antarctica, the United States Constitution, tigers or other endangered animals, the Underground Railroad, and the Nile River. In cubing, students explore a topic they have studied from six dimensions or viewpoints (Neeld, 1986). The name *cubing* comes from the fact that cubes have six sides and students explore the topic from six perspectives in this activity. These six perspectives are:

1. *Description.* Students describe the topic, including its colors, shapes, and sizes.
2. *Comparison.* Students compare the topic to something else. They consider how it is similar to or different from this other thing.
3. *Association.* Students associate the topic to something else and explain why the topic makes them think of this other thing.
4. *Analysis.* Students analyze the topic and tell how it is made or what it is composed of.

FIGURE 10-2 *Two Clusters About Birds*

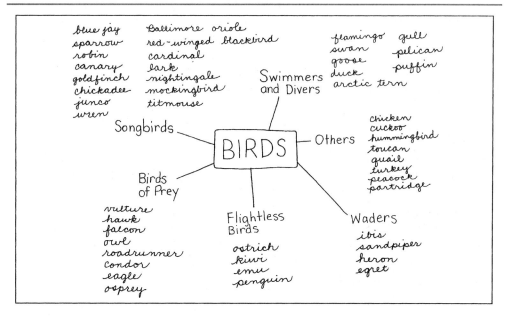

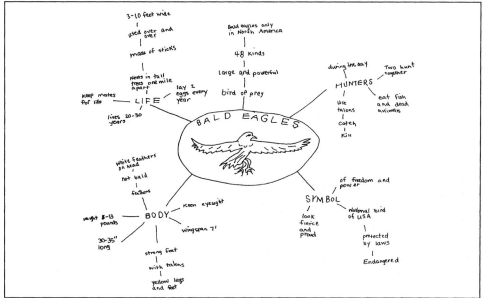

5. *Application.* Students apply the topic and tell how it can be used or what can be done with it.
6. *Argumentation.* Students argue for or against the topic. They take a stand and list reasons to support it.

The steps in cubing are described in the Step by Step feature on page 449.
    What is especially valuable about cubing is that students think about and apply the information they have been learning about a topic in new

Cubing

1. **Choose a topic.**   Students and the teacher choose a topic related to a social studies or science theme. It is important that students are already familiar with the topic.

2. **Examine the topic from each perspective.**   Students divide into six small groups, and each group examines the topic from one of the perspectives.

3. **Draft on each perspective.**   Students brainstorm ideas and use them to develop a paragraph that explores the perspective.

4. **Share drafts with the class.**   Students read their paragraphs to the class, and others react to the ideas and novel connections they have made. Others also may suggest possible revisions.

5. **Revise and edit the paragraphs.**   Students revise, edit, and then make a final copy of their paragraphs to use in the next step.

6. **Construct the cube.**   Students attach the final copies of their paragraphs to a box or construct a cube using cardboard in order to display the cube in the classroom.

ways as they analyze, associate, and consider the other perspectives. Figure 10–3 presents a cubing written by small groups of fifth graders as a review at the end of an across-the-curriculum theme on the American Revolution.

"All About . . . " Books

Contrary to the popular assumption that young children's first writing is narrative, educators have found that kindergartners and first graders write many nonnarrative compositions in which they provide information about familiar topics, including "Signs of Fall," or directions for familiar activities, such as "How to Feed Your Pet" (Bonin, 1988; Sowers, 1985). Many of these writings might be termed "All About . . . " books, and others are informational pieces that children dictate for the teacher to record. These two types introduce young children to informational writing.

In young children's "All About . . . " books, they write an entire booklet on a single topic. Usually one piece of information and an illustration appear on each page. A second grader wrote an "All About . . . " book, "Snowy Thoughts," shown in Figure 10–4. It was written as part of a theme on the four seasons. Even though the student omitted some capital letters and punctuation marks and used invented spelling for a few words in his book, the information can be easily deciphered.

Young children can dictate reports to their teacher, who serves as scribe to record them. After listening to a guest speaker, viewing a film, or reading several books about a particular topic, kindergartners and first graders can dictate

FIGURE 10-3 *A Cubing on the American Revolution*

Describe	The American Revolution was fought from 1775 to 1783 between Britain's Lobster Backs and the young American patriots. From the first major battle of Bunker Hill in 1775 to the battle of Yorktown in 1781, there were many hardships and deaths. The brave Americans continued on in spite of Britain's better supplied army because they wanted freedom, justice, and independence from King George.
Compare	The American Revolution and the Civil War were alike in many ways. They were both fought on American soil. Both wars were fought for people's rights and freedoms. With families fighting against families, these wars were very emotional. The winning side of each war had commanding generals who became presidents of the United States: George Washington and Ulysses S. Grant. The soldiers in the war rallied to the song "Yankee Doodle."
Associate	We celebrate the American Revolution on the 4th of July with fireworks and parades. Fireworks are spectacular things for spectacular days! Rockets shoot into the air like cannonballs! Great big booms and sparkles fall from the sky as people celebrate! Parades remind us of soldiers marching into battle led by flutes, drums, and flags! The 4th of July is a celebration of history.
Analyze	The American Revolution began when King George taxed the colonists too much and did not ask them if they wanted to pay or not. In five years, the Stamp Act, the Townsend Act, the Quartering Act, and the Intolerable Acts were forced on the colonists. This money was to pay for the French and Indian War. This made the colonists angry. One time the colonists dressed up like Indians and threw tea into the Boston Harbor. King George kept on pushing until the colonists revolted and started a war.
Apply	The most important outcome of the American Revolution was the beginning of our 200-year-old country. We enjoy the freedom of speech, religion, and the press. The Constitution grants us a lot of other freedoms, too. This living document has given us the opportunity to be anything we want to be.
Argue for	If we had not fought and won the American Revolution, there would be no United States of America. We would not have the right to speak our minds. We might all have to go to the same church. We would not have freedom or equality. There would be no Liberty Bell or Statue of Liberty. Although war is scary, painful, and violent, if we had the chance to go back, we would go and fight with all our might. We would rather do math problems all day than be ruled by a king.

FIGURE 10-4 *A Second Grader's "All About . . ." Book*

John – David

Snowy
Thoughts

the best thing about
Snow is a Swonman

When it
stats to snow
I think about
having a Snow ball
fight

When its Snowing I
like to play With
my brother.

My favorite swon-day
food is hot sup.

brief reports. A class of kindergartners compiled this book-length report on police officers:

Page 1:   Police officers help people who are in trouble. They are nice to kids. They are only mean to robbers and bad people. Police officers make people obey the laws. They give tickets to people who drive cars too fast.

Page 2:   Men and women can be police officers. They wear blue uniforms like Officer Jerry's. But sometimes police officers wear regular clothes when they work undercover. They wear badges on their uniforms and on their hats. Officer Jerry's badge number is 3407. Police officers have guns, handcuffs, whistles, sticks, and two-way radios. They have to carry all these things.

Page 3:   Police officers drive police cars with flashing lights and loud sirens. The cars have radios so the officers can talk to other police officers at the police station. Sometimes they ride on police motorcycles or on police horses or in police helicopters or in police boats.

Page 4:   Police officers work at police stations. The jail for the bad people that they catch is right next door. One police officer sits at the radio to talk to the police officers who are driving their cars. The police chief works at the police station, too.

Page 5:   Police officers are your friends. They want to help you so you shouldn't be afraid of them. You can ask them if you need some help.

Page 6:   How We Learned About Police Officers for Our Report
　　　　　1.　We read these books:
　　　　　　　Police by Ray Broekel
　　　　　　　What Do They Do? Policemen and Firemen by Carla Greene
　　　　　2.　We interviewed Officer Jerry.
　　　　　3.　We visited the police station.

The teacher read two books aloud to the students, and Officer Jerry visited the classroom and talked to the students about his job. The students also took a field trip to the police station. The teacher took photos of Officer Jerry, his police car, and the police station to illustrate the report. With this background, the students and the teacher together developed a cluster with these five main ideas: what police officers do, what equipment police officers have, how police officers travel, where police officers work, and police officers are your friends. The students added details to each main idea until each one developed into one page of the report. The background of experiences and the clustering activity prepared students to compose their report. After students completed the report, included a bibliography called "How We Learned About Police Officers for Our Report," and inserted the photographs, it was ceremoniously presented to the school library to be enjoyed by all students in the school.

Collaborative and Individual Reports

Toby Fulwiler (1985) recommends that students do "authentic" research in which they explore topics that interest them or hunt for answers to questions that puzzle them. When students become immersed in content-area study, questions arise that they want to explore. Students often begin by writing collaborative or group reports, and then when they know how to write a report, they write individual reports.

A successful first report-writing experience for middle- and upper-grade students is a class collaboration research report: Small groups of students work together to write sections of the report, which are then compiled. Students benefit from writing a group report in two ways: first, because they learn the steps in writing a research report—with the group as a scaffold or support system—before tackling individual reports; and second, because working in groups lets them share the laborious parts of the work.

A group of four fourth graders wrote a collaborative report on hermit crabs. The students sat together at one table and watched hermit crabs in a terrarium. They cared for the crustaceans for 2 weeks and made notes of their observations in learning logs. After this period, the students were bursting with questions about the hermit crabs and were eager for answers. They wanted to know about the crabs' natural habitat, what the best habitat was for them in the classroom, how they breathed air, why they lived in borrowed shells, why one pincer was bigger than the other, and so on. Their teacher provided some answers and directed them to books that would provide additional information. As they collected information, they created a cluster that they taped to the table next to the terrarium. The cluster became inadequate for reporting information, so they decided to share their knowledge by writing a book titled *The Encyclopedia About Hermit Crabs*. Chapters from this book and the cluster used in gathering the information appear in Figure 10–5. The students decided to share the work of writing the book, and they chose four main ideas, one for each to write: what hermit crabs look like, how they act, where they really live, and what they eat. One student wrote each section and returned to the group to share the rough draft. The students gave one another suggestions and made revisions based on the suggestions. Next, they edited their report with the teacher and added an introduction, a conclusion, and a bibliography. Finally, they recopied their report and added illustrations in a cloth-bound book, which they read to each class in the school before putting it in the school library.

Students can organize reports in a variety of formats—formats they see used in informational books. One possibility is a question-and-answer format; another possibility is an alphabet book. A group of fourth-grade students wrote an alphabet book about the California missions, with one page for each letter of the alphabet. The "U" page appears in Figure 10–6.

After students have written reports collaboratively to learn how to gather and organize information and write the information in a report, they are ready to write individual reports. A fourth-grade class began a unit on birds by brainstorming questions they wanted to answer. The teacher encouraged them to search for answers in the books they had checked out of the school and community libraries and during an interview with an ornithologist from the local zoo. Once they learned the answers to their questions, the students were eager to share their new knowledge and decided to write reports and publish them as books.

Each student's book began with a table of contents and contained four or five chapters, a glossary, a bibliography, and an index. An excerpt from one

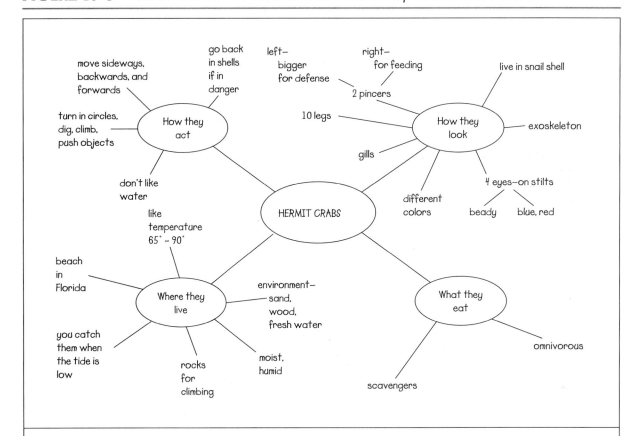

The Encyclopedia About Hermit Crabs

How They Look

Hermit crabs are very much like regular crabs but hermit crabs transfer shells. They have gills. Why? Because they are born in water and when they mature they come to land and kill snails so they can have a shell. They have two beady eyes that look like they are on stilts. Their body is a sight! Their shell looks like a rock. Really it is an exoskeleton which means the skeleton is on the outside. They have two pincers. The left one is bigger so it is used for defense. The right one is for feeding. They also have ten legs.

Where They Live

Hermit crabs live mostly on beaches in Florida where the weather is 65°–90°. They live in fresh water. They like humid weather and places that have sand, wood, and rocks (for climbing on). The best time to catch hermit crabs is at low tide.

What They Eat

Hermit crabs are omnivorous scavengers which means they eat just about anything. They even eat leftovers.

How They Act

Hermit crabs are very unusual. They go back into their shell if they think there is danger. They are funny because they walk sideways, forwards, and backwards. They can go in circles. They can also get up when they get upside down. And that's how they act.

FIGURE 10-6   *The "U" Page From an Alphabet Book on California Missions*

Some of the Indians thought life was UNBEARABLE at the missions. They thought this because they couldn't hunt or do the things they were used to. Once they were at the missions they couldn't leave. They were sometimes beaten if they did.

fourth grader's book on egrets is presented in Figure 10–7. The text was word processed, and then the student added the illustrations.

Multigenre Reports

A report is one genre or kind of writing, and poetry, stories, and journals are other genres. A new approach to report writing is the multigenre report (Romano, 1995, 2000), in which students explore a topic through several genres. Tom Romano (1995) explains, "Each genre offers me ways of seeing and understanding that others do not" (p. 109). Grierson, Anson, and Baird (2002) explain that "research comes alive when students explore a range of alternate genres instead of writing the traditional research report" (p. 51). Students collect a variety of informational materials, including books, textbooks, Internet articles, charts, diagrams, and photos, and then they study the materials. Students write several pieces, including essays, letters, journal entries, stories, and

FIGURE 10-7   *An Excerpt From a Fourth Grader's Report on Egrets*

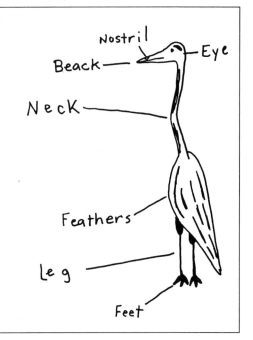

How to Recognize an Egret!

An egret is a bird with white feathers. Some egrets have black and red feathers but the egrets around Marysville are white. They have very long necks and long beaks because they stick their heads under water to catch fish. An egret can be from 20 to 41 inches tall. When they are just standing, they look like in the picture but when they are flying their wing spand can stretch to one-and-a-half feet.

poems; collect photos, charts, and other visual representations; and compile them in a book or display them on a poster. For example, for a multigenre report on the planet Mars, students might include the following pieces:

- An informational essay describing the planet
- A data chart comparing Mars to other planets taken from an informational book students have read
- A photograph of the planet downloaded from the NASA website
- A found poem about Mars with words and phrases taken from a book students have read
- A simulated journal written from the perspective of an astronaut who is exploring the planet

Through these five pieces, students present different kinds of information about the planet, and the report is much more complete than it would have been with just one genre. The LA Essentials box on page 457 lists different genres that can be used for multigenre reports.

Teaching Students to Write Reports

Students learn how to write reports through experience. As they prepare visual reports and write collaborative reports, they learn how to conduct research by posing questions and searching for answers to their questions using multiple resources. They also learn how to organize, draft, and publish a report to share what they have learned. Teachers scaffold students' first report writing experiences to help them develop the knowledge, strategies, and skills to be successful. Perry and Drummond (2002) describe this process as moving from teacher-regulated

Genres for Multigenre Reports

bibliography	Students list the resources they consulted in preparing the paper or poster or list suggested readings related to a topic.
biographical sketch	Students write a biographical sketch of a person related to the topic being studied.
cartoons	Students draw a cartoon or copy a published cartoon from a book or Internet article.
clusters	Students draw clusters or other diagrams to display information concisely.
cubes	Students examine a topic from six perspectives.
data charts	Students create a data chart to list and compare information.
found poems	Students collect words and phrases from a book or article and arrange them to make a poem.
graffiti	Students write words and draw designs to represent the topic visually.
letters	Students write simulated letters or make copies of real letters related to the topic.
lifelines	Students draw lifelines and mark important dates related to a person's life.
maps	Students make copies of actual maps or draw maps related to the topic.
newspaper articles	Students make copies of actual newspaper articles or write simulated articles related to the topic.
open-mind portraits	Students draw open-mind portraits of people related to the topic.
photos	Students download photos from the Internet or make copies of photos in books.
quotes	Students collect quotes about the topic from materials they are reading.
simulated journals	Students write simulated-journal entries from the viewpoint of a person related to the topic.
sketch-to-stretch	Students make sketch-to-stretch drawings to emphasize the theme or key points related to the topic.
stories	Students write stories related to the topic.
time lines	Students draw time lines to sequence events related to the topic.
Venn diagrams	Students draw Venn diagrams to compare the topic with something else.
word wall	Students make an alphabetized word wall of key words related to the topic.

to student self-regulated report writing. They have identified these characteristics of classrooms that promote responsible, independent writers:

1. The classroom is a community of learners where students collaborate and cooperate with classmates.
2. Students are involved in meaningful research activities that require them to think strategically and reflectively.
3. Students increasingly assume responsibility for their learning by making choices, dealing constructively with challenges, and evaluating their work.
4. The evaluation emphasizes both research and the writing process that students use as well as the quality of their finished products.
5. The teacher scaffolds students' learning by providing direct instruction about doing research, modeling the process, having students do research in groups, and gradually releasing responsibility to the students to work independently.

Doing one research project during the school year is not enough. For students to become confident researchers, teachers need to establish a climate of inquiry in their classrooms.

Writing Class Collaboration Reports. Students use the writing process to write class collaboration reports. The steps are listed in the Step by Step feature on page 459.

Report writing has been equated with copying facts out of an encyclopedia, but even elementary students are not too young to understand what plagiarism is and why it is wrong. Even primary-grade students realize they should not "borrow" items belonging to classmates and pretend the items are theirs. Similarly, students should not "borrow" someone else's words, especially without giving credit in the composition. The format of clusters and data charts makes it easier for students to take notes without plagiarizing.

Writing Individual Reports. Writing an individual report is similar to writing a collaborative report. Students continue to design research questions, gather information to answer the questions, and compile what they have learned in a report. However, writing individually demands two significant changes: first, students narrow their topics, and second, they assume the entire responsibility for writing the report. The steps are listed in the Step by Step feature on page 460.

Minilessons. Teachers teach minilessons to prepare students for writing reports. They learn how to make clusters, flowcharts, data charts, and other visual reports, and they learn how to pose research questions and search for answers. A list of minilesson topics related to report writing is presented on pages 462 and 463. Included with the list of minilessons is an outline of Mr. Uchida's minilesson on data charts.

Assessing Students' Reports

Students need to know the requirements for the research project and how they will be assessed and graded. Many teachers distribute a checklist of requirements for the project before students begin working so that the students know

Class Collaboration Reports

1. **Choose a topic.**   Students work in small groups to choose a topic for their sections of the report. If the general topic is the solar system, for example, students can write about Saturn's rings, or they can write to answer this "research" question: Why does Saturn have rings? Students often develop stronger reports when they phrase their topic as a question.

2. **Model how to write a section of the report.**   Students and the teacher choose a topic that none of the groups has chosen to demonstrate the procedure. They work together to gather information, organize it in a data chart, cluster, or other graphic organizer, and write the section of the report on chart paper. Often the teacher takes the students' dictation and does the actual writing in this step to speed up the process. They move through the revising and editing stages of the writing process so that students understand how to develop and refine their section of the report.

3. **Gather and organize information.**   Students working in small groups research their topics using informational books, the Internet, and other resources available in the classroom. The topics provide structure for data collection, because students are looking for specific answers, not randomly writing down information. Students take notes and organize the information using a data chart, cluster, or other graphic organizer. The type of graphic organizer depends on the information being gathered and organized.

4. **Write the sections of the report.**   Students write their sections using the writing process. They write a rough draft and meet with another group to revise their sections. After students have revised their sections, the class comes together and reads the entire report aloud, checking for inconsistencies or redundant passages. Then students edit their sections to correct mechanical errors and meet with the teacher for a final editing.

5. **Compile the report.**   Students compile their sections, and as a class, they design the cover, make the title page and table of contents, write the introduction and conclusion, and compile the bibliography. They also add a list of student authors and place it after the title page or at the back of the report.

6. **Publish the report.**   A final copy, either word processed or handwritten, is produced, and the teacher duplicates and binds copies for each student. In addition, special bound copies can be constructed for the class library or the school library.

Step by Step

Individual Reports

1. **Choose and narrow a topic.** Students choose topics for research reports from a content area, hobbies, or other interests. After choosing a general topic, such as cats or the human body, they narrow the topic so that it is manageable. The broad topic of cats might be narrowed to pet cats or tigers, and the human body to one organ or system.

2. **Design research questions.** Students design research questions by brainstorming a list of questions in a learning log. They review the list, combine some questions, delete others, and finally arrive at four to six questions that they think they can answer and that will be interesting to readers. When they begin their research, they may add new questions and delete others if they reach a dead end.

3. **Gather and organize information.** As in collaborative reports, students use data charts, clusters, or other graphic organizers to gather and organize information. Data charts, with their rectangular spaces for writing information, serve as a transition for upper-grade students between clusters and note cards.

4. **Draft the report.** Students write a rough draft using the information they have gathered. Each research question can become a paragraph or a chapter in the report.

5. **Revise and edit the report.** Students meet in writing groups to share their rough drafts, and then they make revisions based on the feedback they receive from their classmates. After they revise, students use an editing checklist to proofread their reports and correct mechanical errors.

6. **Publish the report.** Students recopy their reports in book format and add illustrations, a title page, a table of contents, and bibliographic information.

what is expected of them and can assume responsibility for completing each step of the assignment. The checklist for an individual report might include these observation behaviors and products:

- Choose a narrow topic.
- Identify four or five research questions.
- Use a cluster to gather information to answer the questions.
- Write a rough draft with a section or a chapter to answer each question.
- Meet in writing groups to share your report.
- Make at least three changes in your rough draft.
- Complete an editing checklist with a partner.
- Add a bibliography.
- Write the final copy of the report.

The checklist can be simpler or more complex depending on students' ages and experiences. Students staple the checklist to the inside cover of the folder in which they keep all the work for the project, and they check off each requirement as they complete it. A checklist enables students to monitor their own work and learn that writing is a process, not just a final product.

After completing the project, students submit their folders to the teacher for assessment. The teacher considers all the requirements on the checklist in determining a student's grade. If the checklist has 10 requirements, each requirement might be worth 10 points, and the grading can be done objectively on a 100-point scale. Thus, if the student's project is complete, the student scores 100, or a grade of A. Points can be subtracted for work that is sloppy or incomplete.

LIFE STORIES

Elementary students learn about the lives of well-known historical personalities, authors and illustrators who write and illustrate books for children, and contemporary personalities as they read biographies and autobiographies. As they read these books and listen to them read aloud, students learn about this genre and examine its structure. These books also serve as models for students' own writing. Biographies and autobiographies are life stories, and they combine expository writing with some elements of narration.

Reading Biographies and Autobiographies

Authors use several approaches in writing biographies and autobiographies (Fleming & McGinnis, 1985). The most common approach is historical: The writer focuses on dates and events and presents them chronologically. Many autobiographies and biographies that span the person's entire life follow this pattern.

A second pattern is the sociological approach, in which the writer describes life during a historical period, providing information about family life, food, clothing, education, economics, transportation, and so on. For instance, *Katie Henio: Navajo Sheepherder* (Thomson, 1995) is a photo documentary that provides a fascinating glimpse into the life of this sheepherder in rural New Mexico.

A third approach is psychological: The writer focuses on conflicts the central figure faces. Conflicts may be with oneself, others, nature, or society. The psychological approach has many elements in common with stories and is most often used in shorter autobiographies and biographies that revolve around particular events or phases in the person's life. One example is *You Want Women to Vote, Lizzie Stanton?* (Fritz, 1995), which is about one of the leaders in the women's rights movement. This book focuses on Lizzie Stanton's role in the suffrage movement; it doesn't recount her entire life.

Biographies are accounts of a person's life written by someone else. Writers try to make the account as accurate and authentic as possible, so they consult a variety of sources of information during their research. The best source, of course, is the biography's subject, and writers can learn many things about the person through an interview. Other primary sources include diaries and letters, photographs, mementos, historical records, and recollections of people who know the person. Examples of secondary sources are books and newspaper articles written by someone other than the biographical subject.

Biographies are categorized as historical or contemporary. Contemporary biographies are written about a living person, especially someone the writer can interview, whereas historical biographies are about people who are no longer alive.

Piecing a Lesson Together

Topics on Reports of Information

Procedures	Concepts	Strategies and Skills
Read charts, diagrams, and maps	Reports versus stories	Design research questions
Make K-W-L charts	Alphabet books	Narrow topics
Draw clusters		Gather information
Draw diagrams		Organize information
Create flowcharts		Take a stand
Write data charts		Summarize
Draw maps		
Draw time lines		
Make cubes		

Please visit the Companion Website at **www.prenhall.com/tompkins** for a second fully realized minilesson.

Although biographies are based on facts, some parts of historical biographies must necessarily be fictionalized. Dialogue and other details about daily life, for example, must often be invented after careful research of the period. In *The Double Life of Pocahontas* (Fritz, 1983), for instance, the author had to take what sketchy facts are known about Pocahontas and make some reasonable guesses to fill in the missing links. To give one example, historians know that

DATA CHARTS

Minilesson

Mr. Uchida Teaches His Fifth Graders How to Write Data Charts

1. **Introduce the Topic**

   Mr. Uchida's fifth graders are preparing to write state reports. They have each chosen a state to research and developed a list of five research questions:

   Who are the people in the state?
   What are the physical features of the state?
   What are the key events in the state's history?
   What is the economy of the state?
   What places should you visit in the state?

   Mr. Uchida explains that students need to collect information to answer each of these five questions, and he has a neat tool to use to collect the data: It's called a data chart.

2. **Share Examples**

   Mr. Uchida shares three sample data charts that his students made to collect information for their state reports last year. He unfolds the large sheets of white construction paper that have been folded into many cells or sections. Each cell is filled with information. The students examine the data charts and read the information in each cell.

3. **Provide Information**

   Mr. Uchida takes a clean sheet of construction paper and folds it into four rows and five columns to create 20 cells. Then he unfolds the paper, shows it to the students, and counts the 20 cells. He explains how he folded the paper and traces over the folded lines so that students can see the cells. Then he writes the five research questions in the cells in the top row. He explains that students will write the information they locate to answer each question in the cells under that question. He demonstrates how to paraphrase information and take notes in the cell.

4. **Supervise Practice**

   Mr. Uchida passes out large sheets of white construction paper and assists students as they divide the sheet into 20 cells and write the research questions in the top row. Then the fifth graders begin to take notes using resources they have collected. Mr. Uchida circulates in the classroom, helping students to locate information and take notes.

5. **Reflect on Learning**

   After several days, Mr. Uchida brings the class together to check on the progress students are making with their data charts. Students show their partially completed charts and talk about their data collection. They ask what to do when they can't find information or when all the information won't fit into one box. Several students comment that they know how they will use their data charts when they begin writing their reports. They will use all the information in one column for one chapter of the report. They are amazed to have made this discovery!

Pocahontas was a young woman when she died in 1617, but they are unsure how old she was when John Smith and the other English settlers arrived in Virginia in 1607. Fritz chose to make her 11 years old when the settlers arrived.

A list of autobiographies and biographies appears in the Classroom Library box on page 464. These life stories feature well-known people such as explorers, kings and queens, scientists, athletes, artists, and movie stars, as well as

CLASSROOM LIBRARY

Life Stories for Elementary Students

Autobiographies

Bunting, E. (1995). *Once upon a time.* Katonah, NY: Richard C. Owen. (M)

Caras, R. (1994). *A world full of animals: The Roger Caras story.* New York: Chronicle Books. (U)

Cleary, B. (1995). *My own two feet: A memoir.* New York: Morrow. (U)

dePaola, T. (2002). *What a year.* New York: Putnam. (P)

Dewy, J. O. (1995). *Cowgirl dreams: A western childhood.* Honesdale, PA: Boyds Mill. (M–U)

Filipovic, Z. (1994). *Zlata's diary: A child's life in Sarajevo.* New York: Viking. (U)

Fritz, J. (1992). *Surprising myself.* Katonah, NY: Richard C. Owen. (M)

Gantos, J. (2002). *Hole in my life.* New York: Farrar, Straus & Giroux. (M–U)

Goble, P. (1994). *Hau kola/Hello friend.* Katonah, NY: Richard C. Owen. (M)

Goodall, J. (1988). *My life with the chimpanzees.* New York: Simon & Schuster. (M)

Howe, J. (1994). *Playing with words.* Katonah, NY: Richard C. Owen. (M–U)

Keller, H. (1980). *The story of my life.* New York: Watermill Press. (M–U)

Nuynh, Q. N. (1982). *The land I lost: Adventures of a boy in Vietnam.* New York: Harper & Row. (M–U)

O'Kelley, M. L. (1983). *From the hills of Georgia: An autobiography in paintings.* Boston: Little, Brown. (P–M–U)

Polacco, P. (1994). *Firetalking.* Katonah, NY: Richard C. Owen. (M)

Zindel, P. (1992). *The pigman and me.* New York: HarperCollins. (M–U)

Biographies

Adler, D. A. (1992). *A picturebook of Anne Frank.* New York: Holiday House. (P)

Adler, D. (1997). *Lou Gehrig: The luckiest man.* San Diego, CA: Harcourt Brace. (M)

Aliki. (1988). *The many lives of Benjamin Franklin.* New York: Simon & Schuster. (M)

Brown, D. (2003). *Mack made movies.* Brookfield, CT: Millbrook/Roaring Brook. (P–M)

Bruchac, J. (1995). *A boy called slow: The true story of Sitting Bull.* New York: Philomel. (P–M)

Cohn, A. L., & Schmidt, S. (2002). *Abraham Lincoln.* New York: Scholastic. (P–M)

Cooper, F. (1994). *Coming home: From the life of Langston Hughes.* New York: Philomel. (M)

Cooper, I. (2003). *Jack: The early years of John F. Kennedy.* New York: Dutton. (M–U)

Freedman, R. (1987). *Lincoln: A photobiography.* New York: Clarion. (M–U)

Freedman, R. (2002). *Confucius: The golden rule.* New York: Scholastic. (M–U)

Fritz, J. (1995). *You want women to vote, Lizzie Stanton?* New York: Putnam. (M)

Giblin, J. C. (1992). *George Washington: A picture-book biography.* New York: Scholastic. (P–M)

Golenbock, P. (1990). *Teammates.* San Diego, CA: Harcourt Brace Jovanovich. (P–M)

McKissack, P. C., & McKissack, F. (1992). *Soujourner Truth: Ain't I a woman?* New York: Scholastic. (M–U)

Meltzer, M. (1992). *Thomas Jefferson: The revolutionary aristocrat.* New York: Franklin Watts. (U)

Mitchell, B. (1986). *Click: A story about George Eastman.* Minneapolis: Carolrhoda. (M)

Orgill, R. (1997). *If I only had a horn: Young Louis Armstrong.* Boston: Houghton Mifflin. (M)

Pinkney, A. D. (2002). *Ella Fitzgerald: The tale of a vocal virtuosa.* New York: Hyperion. (P–M)

Schroeder, A. (1996). *Minty: A story of young Harriet Tubman.* New York: Dial. (M)

Sís, P. (1995). *Starry messenger.* New York: Farrar, Straus & Giroux. (P–M)

Stanley, D. (1994). *Cleopatra.* New York: Mulberry. (M–U)

Stanley, D. (1996). *Leonardo da Vinci.* New York: Morrow. (M)

Stanley, D. (2002). *Saladin: Noble prince of Islam.* New York: HarperCollins. (M–U)

Stanley, D., & Vennema, P. (1992). *Bard of Avon: The story of William Shakespeare.* New York: Morrow. (M)

Stevens, B. (1992). *Frank Thompson: Her Civil War story.* New York: Macmillan. (M–U)

Thomson, P. (1995). *Katie Henio: Navajo sheepherder.* New York: Cobblehill. (M–U)

Winter, J. (2002). *Frida.* New York: Scholastic. (P–M)

"common" people who have endured hardship and shown exceptional courage. Biographers David Adler and Jean Fritz have written many excellent biographies for primary- and middle-grade students, some of which are noted in the list, and numerous authors have written biographies for older students. There are far fewer autobiographies available for children; however, there are a number of autobiographies written by children's authors. The Meet the Author series of autobiographies published by Richard C. Owen is one of the very best.

Teaching Students to Write Autobiographies

When students write autobiographies, they relive and document their lives, usually in chronological order. They describe the memorable events that one would need to know about in order to understand them. Autobiographical writing grows out of children's personal journal entries and "All About Me" books that they write in kindergarten and first grade. Students' own experiences and memories are their primary sources of information for writing.

"Me" Boxes. One way for students to focus on their own lives is to make a "me" box (Fleming, 1985). Students collect objects and pictures representing their families, their hobbies, events in their lives, and special accomplishments. Next, they write explanations or reflections to accompany each object. Then students put all the objects in a shoe box, coffee can, or other container and decorate the outside of the container. Students can use the same approach to make character boxes about a character in a book they are reading or about a historical figure as part of a biography project.

Lifeline Clotheslines. Another strategy students can use to gather and organize information for an autobiography is to collect objects that symbolize their life and hang them on a lifeline clothesline (Fleming, 1985). Next, they write briefly about each object, explaining what the object is and how it relates to their lives, and then they add their explanations to the clothesline, too.

"All About Me" Books. Children in kindergarten and first grade often compile "All About Me" books. These autobiographies usually list information such as the child's birthday, family members, friends, and favorite activities, with drawings as well as text. Figure 10–8 shows two pages from a first grader's "All About Me" book. To write these books, the children and the teacher first decide on a topic for each page; then, after brainstorming possible ideas for the topic, children draw a picture and write about it. Children may also need to ask their parents for information about their birth and events during their preschool years.

Teaching Students to Write Biographies

When students study someone else's life in preparation for writing a biography, they need to become personally involved in the project (Zarnowski, 1988). There are several ways to engage students in biographical study, that is, to help them walk in the subject's footsteps. For contemporary biographies, meeting and interviewing the person is the best way; for other projects, students read books about the person, view videos, dramatize events from the person's life, and write about the person they are studying. An especially valuable activity is

To learn more about teaching students to write biographies, view the CD-ROM that accompanies this text.

FIGURE 10-8   *Two Pages From a First Grader's "All About Me" Book*

This is me wen I'm five. I'm reading a book. MY MOM comes in and puts out my cloths for me to wear but I didn't wat to wear them. I became very picky about my cloths my dad said.

This is my Grammy's house. I have my own room in it. Sometimes I sleep on the love seat. I like to see papa, Sometimes my papa takes me fishing. I love to go fishing. My Grammy makes me feel special.

writing simulated journals, in which students assume the role of the person they are studying and write journal entries just as that person might have.

Students write biographies about living people they know personally as well as about famous personalities. In contrast to the primary sources of information available for gathering information about local people, students may have to depend on secondary sources (e.g., books, magazines, newspapers) for information about well-known and geographically more distant people. Sometimes, however, students can write letters to well-known personalities or perhaps arrange conference telephone calls.

Students learn about authors as real people by reading biographies and autobiographies about them, viewing videotapes and other media presentations of the authors, reading the books the authors have written, and writing letters to them. Christine Duthie (1994) recommends conducting author studies of people such as Gail Gibbons, who writes informational books. Then teachers can connect the author study with learning about expository text structures, research techniques, interviews, and other concepts related to informational books.

Lifelines.   Students sequence the information they gather—about either their life or someone else's—on a lifeline or time line. This activity helps students identify and sequence milestones and other events. They can use the information on the lifeline to identify topics for the life story.

Biography Boxes.   Students can make biography boxes similar to "me" boxes. They begin by identifying items that represent the person, then collect them and put them in a box they have decorated. They also write papers to put with each object, explaining its significance to the person. A fifth grader created a biography box for Paul Revere and decorated the box with aluminum foil, explaining that it looked like silver and Paul Revere was a silversmith. Inside the box, he placed the following items:

- A spoon (to represent his career as a silversmith)
- A toy horse (to represent his famous midnight ride)
- A tea bag (to represent his involvement in the Boston Tea Party)
- A copy of Longfellow's poem "The Midnight Ride of Paul Revere"
- An advertisement for Revere pots and pans (along with an explanation that Paul Revere is credited with inventing the process of layering metals)
- A portrait of the patriot
- Photos of Boston, Lexington, and Concord that were downloaded from the Internet
- A lifeline the student had drawn marking important events in Paul Revere's life

The student wrote a card describing the relationship of each object to Paul Revere and attached it to the item.

Biography Posters.   Students present the information they have learned about the subject of their biography project on a poster. Posters can include a portrait of the person and information about the person's life and accomplishments. Students in an eighth-grade class made a biography quilt with paper squares, and each square was modeled after the illustrations in *My Fellow Americans,* by Alice Provensen (1995). One student's square about Martin Luther King Jr. is presented in Figure 10–9. This student drew a portrait of the civil rights leader set in Washington, D.C., on August 28, 1963, the day he delivered his famous "I Have a Dream" speech. The student also added well-known sayings and other phrases related to Martin Luther King Jr. around the outside.

Multigenre Biography Projects.   Students write and draw a variety of pieces about a person to create a multigenre biography, which is like a multigenre report. Students collect and create some of the following items for a multigenre biography:

lifeline	*collection of objects*
quotations	*simulated journal*
photographs	*found poem or other poem*
open-mind portrait	*story*
report	*poster*

Each item is a complete piece by itself and contributes to the overall impact of the biography. Students compile their biographies on posters or in notebooks.

A seventh-grade class created multigenre biographies. To begin, students read a biography and located additional information about the person from two other sources. Then they created the following pieces for their biography project:

- A lifeline. Students made a lifeline of the person's life, indicating the dates of the person's birth and death and at least 10 key events in the person's life.
- A simulated journal. Students wrote 10 entries spanning the person's entire life.

FIGURE 10-9 *A Biography Poster About Martin Luther King Jr.*

- An open-mind portrait. Students drew a portrait of the person and on separate pages showed what the person was thinking about three key events in his or her life.
- Quotes. Students collected at least three quotes that best illustrated how the person spoke or what the person believed.
- A heart map. Students drew a heart and filled it with pictures and words representing things that really mattered to the person. Figure 10–10 presents excerpts from a seventh grader's multigenre biography project on Maya Angelou.

Meeting the Needs of Every Student

Teachers make adaptations as students read and write informational books so that every student can be successful. It is important to teach students about the genre of informational books and the unique conventions these books have to

FIGURE 10-10   *Excerpts From a Seventh Grader's Multigenre Biography Project on Maya Angelou*

Maya Angelou

In Maya's Heart

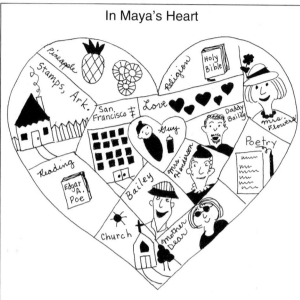

- The pineapple expresses Maya's love for pineapples.
- Ms. Flowers is the woman who gave Maya her first book of poetry.
- Mother Dear is Maya's mother and even though she didn't really raise her, Maya looked up to her.
- Bailey was Maya's brother and they had a strong bond being that they were only one year apart in age.
- Guy is her son and her entire life.

Dear Diary,
One night I was scared and momma let me sleep in the bed with her and Mr. Freeman. Then when momma left early to run an errand, I felt a strange pressure on my left leg. I knew it wasn't a hand because it was much too soft. I was afraid to move and I didn't budge. Mr. Freeman's eyes were wide open with both hands above the covers. He then said, "Stay right here, Rite, I'm not gonna hurt you." I really wasn't afraid, a little curious, but not afraid. Then he left and came back with a glass of water and poured it on the bed. He said, "see how you done peed in the bed." Afterwards, I was confused and didn't understand why Mr. Freeman had held me so gently, then accused me of peeing in the bed.   Marguerite

Dear Diary,
While I was sitting talking to Miss Glory, Mrs. Cullinan called for someone. She said, "Mary P." We didn't know who she was calling, but my name is Marguerite. Now I settled for Margaret, but Mary was a whole nother name. Bailey told me bout Whites and how they felt like they had the power to shorten our names for their convenience. Miss Glory told me her name used to be Hallelujah and Mrs. Cullinan shortened it to Glory. Mrs. Cullinan sent me on an errand, which was a good idea because I was upset and anything was bound to come out of my mouth at the time.
                                                                Marguerite

Dear Diary,
Graduation day was a big event in Stamps. The high school seniors received most of the glory. I'm just a twelve year old 8th grader. I'm pretty high-ranked in my class along with Henry Reed. Henry is also our class valedictorian. The tenth grade teacher helped him with his speech. Momma was even going to close the store. Our graduation dresses are a lemon yellow, but momma added ruffles and cuffs with a crocheted collar. She added daisy embroideries around the trim before she considered herself finished. I just knew all eyes were going to be on me when graduation day came.
                                                                Marguerite

Quotes

"Cleanliness is next to Godliness."

"God blessed everyone with an intelligent mind. Only we can decide how we use it."

help readers—including diagrams, glossaries, and indexes. Students also need to learn about the five expository text patterns because research has shown that less successful readers are not aware of them. Informational books are available on a wide variety of topics and at a range of reading levels, so selecting books that interest students and that are written at their reading levels should not be too difficult.

Teachers can also vary the types of reports that students write so that every student can be successful. Younger students can create "All About . . . " books before they move on to more sophisticated types of reports, and older struggling students can make poster reports and collaborative reports. All students can work together to create alphabet books, multigenre projects, and other class reports. They can also work collaboratively in small groups to write reports. The feature on page 470 provides additional information about working with struggling writers to write collaborative reports.

Meeting the Needs of Every Student

How Can I Help My Struggling Students Who Won't Even Try to Write a Report?

One of the biggest reasons why struggling students aren't successful with report writing is that they don't know how to do it. They don't know how to begin. They don't know how to organize a report or what ideas to include. They don't know about the genre or how to write about information. They don't know how to make maps and diagrams or how to create a table of contents. Writing a report seems like such an enormous undertaking that they feel defeated before they begin. The answer is to write brief collaborative reports. Divide the topic for the report into three sections, and limit the length of each section to a sentence or a paragraph, depending on the students' level. Have the students offer ideas and dictate sentences, but do the writing yourself using the language experience approach. Model how to use the writing process for report writing as you prewrite, draft, revise, and edit the section. Word process the final copy and duplicate copies for students. Give them ideas for adding an illustration or other graphic to the final copy. Repeat the process for the second and third sections, spending a day or two on each section. Then have students compile and number the pages, make a cover, and staple their report booklets together. Your students feel successful, and so do you. Continue to write collaborative reports, and as your students' knowledge and confidence grow, gradually release more responsibility for doing the writing to them.

To investigate other ways to meet the needs of every student, visit the links for this chapter at the Companion Website at www.prenhall com/tompkins

Assessing Students' Life Stories

Students need to know the requirements for their autobiography or biography project, as well as how they will be assessed or graded. A checklist for an autobiography might include the following components:

- Make a lifeline showing at least one important event for each year of your life.
- Draw a cluster showing at least three main-idea topics and at least five details for each topic.
- Write a rough draft with an introduction, three or more chapters, and a conclusion.
- Meet in a writing group to share your autobiography.
- Make at least three changes in your rough draft.
- Complete an editing checklist with a partner.
- Write a final copy with photos or drawings as illustrations.

- Compile your autobiography as a book.
- Decorate the cover.

The checklist for a biography might list the following requirements:

- Learn about the person's life from at least three sources (and no more than one encyclopedia).
- Make a lifeline listing at least 10 important events.
- Write at least 10 simulated-journal entries as the person you are studying.
- Make a cluster with at least three main-idea topics and at least five details for each topic.
- Write a rough draft with at least three chapters and a bibliography.
- Meet in a writing group to share your biography.
- Make at least three changes in your rough draft.
- Complete an editing checklist with a partner.
- Recopy the biography.

Students keep the checklist in their project folders and check off each item as it is completed; at the end of the project, they submit the folders to be assessed or graded. Teachers can award credit for each item on the checklist, as discussed in the section on assessing students' research reports. This approach helps students assume greater responsibility for their own learning and gives them a better understanding of why they receive a particular grade.

Review

Recent research suggests that reading and writing information may be as important for elementary students as reading and writing stories. Students enjoy reading informational books, and they learn about the organization of informational books. This knowledge about text structure supports students' reading and writing. Students write a variety of reports of information, including visual reports, collaborative books, and individual reports. Students also read biographies and autobiographies, and write their own life stories. Important concepts presented in this chapter include:

1. Students read informational books to learn information, and they write informational books to share information with others.
2. Students may use either efferent or aesthetic reading when reading informational books, depending on their purpose for reading.
3. Informational writing is organized into five expository text patterns: description, sequence, comparison, cause and effect, and problem and solution.
4. Students use their knowledge of expository text structures when reading and writing informational books.
5. Students create visual reports using clusters, diagrams, flowcharts, data charts, maps, time lines, and cubes.
6. Students write collaborative reports to learn how to write reports before writing individual reports.
7. Students prepare multigenre papers using a combination of reports, stories, poems, photographs and other illustrations, and other materials.
8. Students make boxes, lifelines, and posters to document events in their own lives and in other people's lives.

Visit Chapter 10 on the Companion Website at www.prenhall. com/tompkins to:

- **Check your understanding of the concepts presented in the chapter**
- **Access the Extensions (activities and a list of related readings)**
- **Link to related websites**

9. Students write autobiographies about events in their own lives and write biographies about both historical and contemporary personalities.
10. Students use the writing process to write reports, autobiographies, and biographies.

Professional References

Bonin, S. (1988). Beyond storyland: Young writers can tell it other ways. In T. Newkirk & N. Atwell (Eds.), *Understanding writing* (2nd ed.) (pp. 47–51). Portsmouth, NH: Heinemann.

Bromley, K. D. (1991). *Webbing with literature: Creating story maps with children's books.* Boston: Allyn & Bacon.

Bromley, K. D. (1996). *Webbing with literature: Creating story maps with children's books* (2nd ed.). Boston: Allyn & Bacon.

Chapman, V. G., & Sopko, D. (2003). Developing strategic use of combined-text trade books. *The Reading Teacher, 57,* 236–239.

Duthie, C. (1994). Nonfiction: A genre study for the primary classroom. *Language Arts, 71,* 588–595.

Fleming, M. (1985). Writing assignments focusing on autobiographical and biographical topics. In M. Fleming & J. McGinnis (Eds.), *Portraits: Biography and autobiography in the secondary school* (pp. 95–97). Urbana, IL: National Council of Teachers of English.

Fleming, M., & McGinnis, J. (Eds.). (1985). *Portraits: Biography and autobiography in the secondary school.* Urbana, IL: National Council of Teachers of English.

Flood, J., Lapp, D., & Farnan, N. (1986). A reading-writing procedure that teaches expository paragraph structure. *The Reading Teacher, 39,* 556–562.

Freedman, R. (1992). Fact or fiction? In E. B. Freeman & D. G. Person (Eds.), *Using nonfiction trade books in the elementary classroom: From ants to zeppelins* (pp. 2–10). Urbana, IL: National Council of Teachers of English.

Freeman, E. B. (1991). Informational books: Models for student report writing. *Language Arts, 68,* 470–473.

Freeman, E. B., & Person, D. G. (Eds.). (1992). *Using nonfiction trade books in the elementary classroom: From ants to zeppelins.* Urbana, IL: National Council of Teachers of English.

Fulwiler, T. (1985). Research writing. In M. Schwartz (Ed.), *Writing for many roles* (pp. 207–230). Upper Montclair, NJ: Boynton/Cook.

Grierson, S. T., Anson, A., & Baird, J. (2002). Exploring the past through multigenre writing. *Language Arts, 80,* 51–59.

Harvey, S. (1998). *Nonfiction matters: Reading, writing, and research in grades 3–8.* York, ME: Stenhouse.

Krogness, M. M. (1987). Folklore: A matter of the heart and the heart of the matter. *Language Arts, 64,* 808–818.

Langer, J. A. (1986). *Children reading and writing: Structures and strategies.* Norwood, NJ: Ablex.

McGee, L. M., & Richgels, D. J. (1985). Teaching expository text structure to elementary students. *The Reading Teacher, 38,* 739–748.

Meyer, B. J., & Freedle, R. O. (1984). Effects of discourse type on recall. *American Educational Research Journal, 21,* 121–143.

Moline, S. (1995). *I see what you mean: Children at work with visual information.* York, ME: Stenhouse.

Moss, B. (1995). Using children's tradebooks as read-alouds. *Language Arts, 72,* 122–126.

Neeld, E. C. (1986). *Writing* (2nd ed.). Glenview, IL: Scott Foresman.

Niles, O. S. (1974). Organization perceived. In H. L. Herber (Ed.), *Perspectives in reading: Developing study skills in secondary schools.* Newark, DE: International Reading Association.

Palmer, R. G., & Stewart, R. A. (2003). Nonfiction trade book use in primary grades. *The Reading Teacher, 57,* 38–48.

Pappas, C. C. (1991). Fostering full access to literacy by including information books. *Language Arts, 68,* 449–462.

Pappas, C. C. (1993). Is narrative "primary"? Some insights from kindergartners' pretend readings of stories and information books. *Journal of Reading Behavior, 25,* 97–129.

Perry, N., & Drummond, L. (2002). Helping young students become self-regulated researchers and writers. *The Reading Teacher, 56,* 298–310.

Piccolo, J. A. (1987). Expository text structures: Teaching and learning strategies. *The Reading Teacher, 40,* 838–847.

Queenan, M. (1986). Finding grain in the marble. *Language Arts, 63,* 666–673.

Raphael, T. E., Englert, C. S., & Kirschner, B. W. (1989). Acquisition of expository writing skills. In J. M. Mason (Ed.), *Reading and writing connections* (pp. 261–290). Boston: Allyn & Bacon.

Read, S. (2001). "Kid mice hunt for their selfs": First and second graders writing research. *Language Arts, 78,* 333–342.

Rico, G. L. (1983). *Writing the natural way.* Los Angeles: Tarcher.

Robb, L. (2003). *Teaching reading in social studies, science, and math.* New York: Scholastic.

Romano, T. (1995). *Writing with passion: Life stories, multiple genres.* Portsmouth, NH: Heinemann/Boynton Cook.

Romano, T. (2000). *Blending genre, alternating style: Writing multigenre papers.* Portsmouth, NH: Heinemann/Boynton Cook.

Roop, P. (1992). Nonfiction books in the primary classroom: Soaring with the swans. In E. B. Freeman & D. G. Person (Eds.), *Using nonfiction trade books in the elementary classroom: From ants to zeppelins*

(pp. 106–112). Urbana, IL: National Council of Teachers of English.

Rosenblatt, L. M. (1978). *The reader, the text, the poem: The transactional theory of the literary work.* Carbondale: Southern Illinois University Press.

Rosenblatt, L. M. (1991). Literature: S.O.S.! *Language Arts, 68,* 444–448.

Smith, P. L., & Tompkins, G. E. (1988). Structured notetaking: A strategy for content area readers. *Journal of Reading, 32,* 46–53.

Sowers, S. (1985). *The story and the "all about" book.* In J. Hansen, T. Newkirk, & D. Graves (Eds.), *Breaking ground: Teachers relate reading and writing in the elementary school* (pp. 73–82). Portsmouth, NH: Heinemann.

Tompkins, G. E. (2004). *Teaching writing: Balancing process and product.* (4th ed.). Upper Saddle River, NJ: Merrill/Prentice Hall.

Tompkins, G. E., Smith, P. L., & Hitchcock, M. E. (1987). *Elementary students' use of expository text structures in report writing.* Paper presented at the National Reading Conference, St. Petersburg Beach, FL.

Vardell, S. M. (1991). A new "picture of the world": The NCTE Orbis Pictus Award for outstanding nonfiction for children. *Language Arts, 68,* 474–479.

Wells, G. (1986). *The meaning makers: Children learning language and using language to learn.* Portsmouth, NH: Heinemann.

Yopp, H. K., & Yopp, R. H. (2000). *Literature-based reading activities* (3rd ed.). Boston: Allyn & Bacon.

Zarnowski, M. (1988, February). The middle school student as biographer. *Middle School Journal, 19,* 25–27.

Children's Book References

Aliki. (2003). *Ah, music.* New York: HarperCollins.

Avi. (1991). *Nothing but the truth.* New York: Avon.

Ancona, G. (1992). *Man and mustang.* New York: Macmillan.

Arnold, C. (1993). *Dinosaurs all around: An artist's view of the prehistoric world.* New York: Clarion.

Back, C., & Olesen, J. (1984). *Chicken and egg.* Englewood Cliffs, NJ: Silver Burdett.

Bates, K. L. (1993). *America the beautiful.* New York: Atheneum.

Bunting, E. (1994). *Smoky night.* San Diego: Harcourt Brace.

Bunting, E. (1996). *The blue and the gray.* New York: Scholastic.

Byrd, R. (2003). *Leonardo: Beautiful dreamer.* New York: Dutton.

Carle, E. (1970). *The very hungry caterpillar.* Cleveland: Collins-World.

Cole, J. (1992). *The magic school bus on the ocean floor.* New York: Scholastic.

Cole, J. (1995). *The magic school bus inside a hurricane.* New York: Scholastic.

Cole, J. (1996). *On the bus with Joanna Cole: A creative autobiography.* Portsmouth, NH: Heinemann.

Cole, J. (1998). *The magic school bus in the rain forest.* New York: Scholastic.

Cole, J. (2003). *Ms. Frizzle's adventures: Medieval castle.* New York: Scholastic.

Cole, J., & Wexler, J. (1984). *A fish hatches.* New York: Morrow.

Colman, P. (1995). *Rosie the riveter: Women working on the home front in World War II.* New York: Crown.

Cowcher, H. (1990). *Antarctica.* New York: Farrar, Straus & Giroux.

dePaola, T. (2003). *Things will NEVER be the same.* New York: Putnam.

Donoughue, C. (1999). *The mystery of the hieroglyphs.* New York: Oxford University Press.

Draper, S. (1994). *Tears of a tiger.* New York: Atheneum.

Ehlert, L. (1992). *Fish eyes: A book you can count on.* San Diego: Harcourt Brace/Voyager.

Ehlert, L. (1996). *Under my nose.* Katonah, NY: Richard C. Owen.

Ehlert, L. (2001). *Waiting for wings.* San Diego: Harcourt Brace.

Evans, M., & Caras, R. A. (2001). *Fish: Pet care guides for kids.* New York: Dorling Kindersley.

Feelings, M. (1971). *Moja means one: Swahili counting book.* New York: Dial.

Forman, M. H. (1997). *From wax to crayon.* New York: Children's Press.

Fradin, D. B. (2002). *The signers: The 56 stories behind the Declaration of Independence.* New York: Walker.

Freedman, R. (1987). *Lincoln: A photobiography.* New York: Clarion.

Freedman, R. (2001). *In the days of the vaqueros: America's first true cowboys.* New York: Clarion.

Freedman, R. (2002). *Confucius: The golden rule.* New York: Scholastic.

Fritz, J. (1976). *Will you sign here, John Hancock?* New York: Coward-McCann.

Fritz, J. (1983). *The double life of Pocahontas.* New York: Putnam.

Fritz, J. (1989). *The great little Madison.* New York: Putnam.

Fritz, J. (1995). *You want women to vote, Lizzie Stanton?* New York: Putnam.

Gibbons, G. (1991). *Surrounded by sea: Life on a New England fishing island.* Boston: Little, Brown.

Gibbons, G. (1992). *Spiders.* New York: Holiday House.

Guiberson, B. Z. (1991). *Cactus hotel.* New York: Henry Holt.

Hunt, J. (1989). *Illuminations.* New York: Bradbury.

Jiménez, F. (1997). *The circuit.* Albuquerque: University of New Mexico Press.

Jiménez, F. (2001). *Breaking through.* Boston: Houghton Mifflin.

Knight, M. B. (1993). *Who belongs here? An American story.* Gardiner, ME: Tulbury House.

Krull, K. (1999). *They saw the future: Oracles, psychics, scientists, great thinkers, and pretty good guessers.* New York: Atheneum.

Krull, K. (2003). *Harvesting hope: The story of Cesar Chavez.* San Diego: Harcourt Brace.

Leedy, L. (1993). *Postcards from Pluto: A tour of the solar system.* New York: Holiday House.

Levine, E. (1990). *. . . If you lived at the time of Martin Luther King.* New York: Scholastic.

L'Hommedieu, A. J. (1997). *From plant to blue jeans.* New York: Children's Press.

Lionni, L. (1974). *Fish is fish.* New York: Dragonfly.

Logan, C. (2002). *The 5,000-year-old puzzle: Solving a mystery of ancient Egypt.* New York: Farrar, Straus & Giroux.

Longfellow, H. W. (2000). *The midnight ride of Paul Revere.* Washington, DC: National Geographic Society.

Lowry, L. (1998). *Looking back: A book of memories.* Boston: Houghton Mifflin.

Macaulay, D. (1977). *Castle.* Boston: Houghton Mifflin.

Maestro, B. (1992). *How do apples grow?* New York: HarperCollins.

Matthews, T. L. (1998). *Light shining through the mist: A photobiography of Dian Fossey.* Washington, DC: National Geographic Society.

Melmed, L. K. (2003). *Capital! Washington, DC from A to Z*. New York: HarperCollins.

Morimoto, J. (1987). *My Hiroshima*. New York: Puffin.

Murphy, J. (2003). *Inside the Alamo*. New York: Delacorte.

Nelson, R. (2002). *Pet fish*. Minneapolis: Lerner.

Palmer, H. (1961). *A fish out of water*. New York: Random House.

Patent, D. H. (2000). *The bald eagle returns*. New York: Clarion.

Paulsen, G. (2001). *Guts: The true stories behind Hatchet and the Brian books*. New York: Delacorte.

Pfister, M. (1992). *The rainbow fish*. New York: North-South Books.

Pratt, K. J. (1994). *A swim through the sea*. Nevada City, CA: DAWN Publications.

Preston, D. (2003). *Remember the Lusitania!* New York: Walker.

Pringle, L. (2001). *A dragon in the sky: The story of a green darner dragonfly*. New York: Scholastic.

Provensen, A. (1995). *My fellow Americans: A family album*. San Diego, CA: Browndeer.

Rappaport, D. (2001). *Martin's big words: The life of Dr. Martin Luther King, Jr*. New York: Hyperion.

Rauzon, M. J. (1993). *Horns, antlers, fangs, and tusks*. New York: Lothrop, Lee & Shepard.

Reid, M. E. (1996). *Let's find out about ice cream*. New York: Scholastic.

Ringgold, F. (1992). *Aunt Harriet's underground railroad in the sky*. New York: Crown.

Robinson, F. (1995a). *Solid, liquid, or gas?* Chicago: Childrens Press.

Robinson, F. (1995b). *Where do puddles go?* Chicago: Childrens Press.

Ryder, J. (2001). *Little panda: The world welcomes Hua Mei at the San Diego Zoo*. New York: Simon & Schuster.

Sayre, A. P. (2001). *Dig, wait, listen: A desert toad's tale*. New York: Greenwillow.

Schwartz, D. M. (2003). *Millions to measure*. New York: HarperCollins.

Scott, A. H. (1990). *One good horse: A cowpuncher's counting book*. New York: Greenwillow.

Seuss, Dr. (1960). *One fish two fish red fish blue fish*. New York: Random House.

Showers, P. (1985). *What happens to a hamburger?* New York: Harper & Row.

Siebert, D. (1991). *Sierra*. New York: HarperCollins.

Simon, S. (1989). *Whales*. New York: Crowell.

Simon, S. (1993). *Mercury*. New York: Morrow.

Simon, S. (2000). *Gorillas*. New York: HarperCollins.

Stanley, D. (2002). *Saladin: Noble prince of Islam*. New York: HarperCollins.

St. George, J. (2000). *So you want to be president?* New York: Philomel.

Thomson, P. (1995). *Katie Henio: Navajo sheepherder*. New York: Cobblehill.

Wallner, A. (2001). *Abigail Adams*. New York: Holiday House.

Watts, B. (1989). *Honeybee*. Englewood Cliffs, NJ: Silver Burdett.

Williams, R. L. (2001). *The coin counting book*. Watertown, MA: Charlesbridge.

Williams, S. A. (1992). *Working cotton*. San Diego: Harcourt Brace Jovanovich.

Winter, J. (1988). *Follow the drinking gourd*. New York: Knopf.

Yolen, J. (1993). *Welcome to the green house*. New York: Putnam.

Ziefert, H. (1986). *A new coat for Anna*. New York: Knopf.

11 Reading and Writing Poetry

PATTERNS OF PRACTICE

Mrs. Harris has a poetry workshop in her sixth-grade classroom several times each year. The poetry workshop lasts one week. Her students read and respond to poems during the reading workshop component, and they write poems during the writing workshop component. Her schedule for a 2-hour poetry workshop is shown in the box on page 478. The first hour is devoted to reading poetry and the second hour to writing poetry. Students have folders for the weeklong poetry unit, and they collect papers to document the week's work in the folders.

During class meetings this week, Mrs. Harris draws students' attention to poetic devices. On Monday, she asks students to think about their favorite poems. What makes a poem a good poem? She reads aloud some favorite poems, and the students mention several poetic devices: rhyme, alliteration, repetition of words and phrases, and onomatopoeia, which they call "sound effects."

On Tuesday, Mrs. Harris focuses on metaphors and similes. She reads aloud these poems from *The Random House Book of Poetry for Children* (Prelutsky,

Reading and Writing Workshop

Literature Focus Units

Literature Circles

Theme Cycles

2000): "The Toaster," "Steam Shovel," "The Dandelion," and "The Eagle." She reads each poem aloud to students and they notice these comparisons: The toaster is compared to a dragon, the steam shovel to a dinosaur, the dandelion to a soldier, and the eagle's dive to a bolt of lightning.

The next day, students come to the class meeting to share poems they have found that have comparisons. Their classmates identify the comparisons. After they discuss the poems, Mrs. Harris explains the terms *metaphor* and *simile* and asks students to classify the comparisons in the poems they have shared.

On Thursday, Mrs. Harris reads aloud "The Night Is a Big Black Cat" (Prelutsky, 2000), a brief, four-line poem comparing night to a black cat, the moon to the cat's eye, and the stars to mice she is hunting in the sky. The students draw pictures illustrating the poem and add the lines or paraphrases of the lines to their pictures. One student's drawing is shown on page 479. On Friday, students finish their pictures and share them with the class.

Mrs. Harris points out the poetry section of the classroom library that has been infused with 75 more books of poetry. Students select books of poetry from the library to read during the independent reading time. Next, she introduces seven recently published books about poetry. *Love That Dog* (Creech, 2001), *Locomotion* (Woodson, 2003), and *A Bird About to Sing* (Montenegro, 2003) are stories written in poetic form about how children use poetry to

> ## How does poetry fit into the four patterns of practice?
>
> Teachers incorporate poetry into all four instructional patterns. They share poems with students on topics related to literature focus units and theme cycles, and in literature circles and reading workshops, students read books of poetry as well as stories and informational books. Students write poems in all four patterns, too. They write poems as projects during literature focus units, literature circles, and theme cycles, and once students learn how to write poetry, they often choose to do so during writing workshop. As you read this vignette, notice how Mrs. Harris adapts reading and writing workshop for her weeklong poetry workshop.

write about their feelings. She also shares Janet Wong's book of poetry with advice about writing poems, *You Have to Write* (2002), and two informational books, *Poetry Matters: Writing a Poem From the Inside Out* (Fletcher, 2002)

Poetry Workshop Schedule	
15 minutes	**Class Meeting** Mrs. Harris leads a whole-class meeting to give a book talk on a new poetry book, talk about a poet, read several favorite poems using choral reading, or talk about a difficult or confusing poem.
30 minutes	**Independent Reading** Students choose books of poetry from the classroom library and read poems independently. As they read, students choose favorite poems and mark them with small sticky notes.
15 minutes	**Sharing** Students form small groups and share favorite poems with classmates. Then several students read their favorite poems aloud to the whole class. They rehearse before reading to the class and try to "read like a poet" with good expression.
15 minutes	**Minilesson** Mrs. Harris teaches minilessons on poetry writing strategies, such as how to use poetic devices, how to arrange the lines of a poem on a page, and how to use "unwriting" to revise poems. She also introduces and reviews poetry formulas during minilessons.
45 minutes	**Writing** Students write lots of rough-draft poems and choose the ones they like best to take through the writing process and publish. Students meet in revising groups and editing conferences with Mrs. Harris and classmates as they polish their poems. On Friday, the students have a poetry reading and they read aloud one of the poems they have written.

and *Troy Thompson's Excellent Peotry (sic) Book* (Crew, 1998), books about how to write poetry that are written for middle school students. She has several copies of each book, and she asks students to choose one to read during the week and to be prepared to participate in a grand discussion about the books on Friday.

During independent reading time, students also read poems and pick their favorites to share with classmates. Students make a list of books they read in their poetry folders. Students also choose their three favorite poems, and Mrs. Harris will make copies of these poems for their poetry folders. For each of their three favorite poems, students write a brief reflection explaining why they like the poem, and they describe poetic devices whenever possible in their explanations.

After reading, students get into small groups to share their favorite poems with classmates, and they rehearse the poem they will read to the whole class. Five or six students read one of their favorite poems aloud each day to the class. During a previous poetry workshop, Mrs. Harris taught the students how to read poetry with expression, or as she says, "like a poet." They know how to vary the speed and loudness of their voices, how to emphasize the rhyme or other important words, and how to pause at the ends of lines or within lines. Mrs. Harris expects students to apply what they have learned when they read

poetry aloud.

During the writing workshop minilessons this week, Mrs. Harris focuses on "unwriting," a strategy students use to revise their poems. On Monday, she shares the rough draft of a color poem she has written. She has written the poem on a transparency and displays it using an overhead projector. She explains that she thinks she has too many unnecessary words in the poem, and she asks the students to help her unwrite it. The students make suggestions, and she crosses out words and substitutes stronger words for long phrases. Together they revise the poem and make it tighter. Mrs. Harris explains that poems are powerful because they say so much using only a few words. She encourages students to use unwriting as they revise their poems.

On Tuesday and Wednesday, Mrs. Harris shares students' rough-draft poems, which she has copied onto transparencies. Then students suggest ways to unwrite their classmates' poems using the same procedure they used on Monday.

Several students ask to learn more about limericks, so on Thursday, Mrs. Harris reviews the limerick form and shares limericks from a book in the classroom library and other limericks that her students wrote in previous years. Then on Friday, students divide into small groups to try their hands at writing limericks. Mrs. Harris moves from group to group, providing assistance as needed. Afterward, they share their limericks with classmates.

Mrs. Harris's students keep writing notebooks in which they record collections of words, quotes from books they read, interesting sentences and descriptions, lists of writing topics, and rough drafts of stories, poems, and other

---

Poetry Workshop Grading Sheet

Name _____   Date _____

Student's Check   **Teacher's Grade**

_____ 1. Read lots of poems. Keep a list of poetry books that you read. (15)   _____

_____ 2. Make copies of three favorite poems and write why you like the poems. (15)   _____

_____ 3. Read one poem aloud to the class. Be sure to read like a poet. (10)   _____

_____ 4. Write rough drafts of at least five poems. (25)   _____

_____ 5. Take one poem through the writing process to publication. (15)   _____

_____ 6. Read one of your poems during the poetry reading on Friday. (10)   _____

_____ 7. Other (10)   _____
        Draw a "night cat" picture.
        Write a limerick in a small group.

---

writings. They also have a paper describing the different types of poems that Mrs. Harris has taught them. During the independent writing time, they often use ideas, words and sentences, or even rough-draft poems in their writing notebooks. Students write lots of rough drafts and then choose the most promising ones to take through the writing process and publish. During the week, they meet in revising groups and editing conferences with Mrs. Harris and a small group of classmates. During the first half of the writing time, Mrs. Harris holds a revising group, and during the second half, she holds an editing group. Students sign up for the groups in advance. Students keep all their drafts of the poems they publish to document their use of the writing process and to trace the development of their poems.

On the last day of the poetry workshop, they type final copies of their poems, which they contribute to the class book of poetry that Mrs. Harris compiles. The students move their desks into a circle and have a poetry reading. They read around, each taking a turn to read aloud one of the poems he or she has written.

Mrs. Harris posts the schedule for poetry workshop in the classroom so that students know what they are to be doing during the 2-hour time block. She also sets out her expectations for students at the beginning of the poetry workshop: They are to read and write lots of poems. She wants them to choose at least three favorite poems from the ones that they read and to take at least one poem that they write through the writing process. She passes out copies of the grading sheet they will use that week, and they place them in their writing folders. This way they know from the first day of the workshop what they are expected to accomplish. A copy of Mrs. Harris's poetry workshop grading sheet is shown on page 480.

As students complete the assignments, they add check marks in the left-hand column. After they finish the unit, they turn in their writing folders with the grading sheet and the papers they completed during the workshop. Mrs. Harris reviews their assignments and awards points to determine the grade using a 100-point grading scale.

- -

Poetry "brings sound and sense together in words and lines," according to Donald Graves, "ordering them on the page in such a way that both the writer and reader get a different view of life" (1992, p. 3). Children are natural poets, and poetry surrounds them as they chant jump-rope rhymes on the playground, clap out the rhythm of favorite poems, and dance in response to songs and their lyrics. Larrick (1991) believes that we enjoy poetry because of the physical involvement the words evoke. Also, people play with words as they invent rhymes and ditties, create new words, and craft powerful comparisons.

As you begin reading this chapter, you may want to read the "Dear Reader" letter in Chapter 11 on the Companion Website at www.prenhall.com/tompkins

No longer is poetry confined to rhyming verse about daffodils, clouds, and love. Both adult and child poets write poems on every imaginable subject—grasshoppers, fire trucks, boa constrictors, spaghetti and meatballs, Jupiter, and grandfathers. These poems tell stories, create images and moods, make us laugh or cry, develop our sense of wonder, and show us the world in a new way (Cullinan, Scala, & Schroder, 1995; Glover, 1999). The definition of poetry, too, has broadened to include songs and raps, word pictures, memories, riddles, observations, questions, odes, and rhymes.

In an article in *Language Arts,* Lisa Siemens (1996) describes how her primary-grade students are immersed in reading and writing poetry. She makes poetry the core of her language arts program, and her students respond enthusiastically. She shares three of her students' descriptions of poetry. One child writes:

> A poem is like a big green dragon waiting to blow fire at the knight who seeks the treasure. (p. 239)

Another child shares:

> Poems are words that you feel and mumble jumble words too, also words that float around in your head. (p. 239)

A third child explains:

> I think poetry is when you wake up and see the sun racing above from the clouds. Poetry is when sunlight and moon shines up together. Poetry is when you go to Claude Monet's garden for the first time and everything is breathtaking. That is what I think poetry is. (p. 239)

Sometimes poems are "a garden of words . . . planted in neat rows, but then again, [they] grow wild and free," according to Nancy Cecil (1994, p. 3). Concrete poems, for example, are drawn like pictures on a page, hink-pinks are brief, rhyming, question-and-answer poems, and found poems are collections of words culled from other texts and arranged on a page. Other poems are written for two readers, and they are arranged in two columns to be read like a musical duet. Possible topics for poems and ways for arranging them on a page are nearly limitless.

The focus of this chapter is on involving students with wordplay and poetry. As you read, think about these questions:

◆ How do teachers encourage students to play with words and express ideas using figurative language?

◆ How do students read and respond to poems?

◆ What kinds of poems do students write?

◆ How can teachers incorporate poetry activities into the four patterns of practice?

PLAYING WITH WORDS

Poet and teacher Georgia Heard calls language "the poet's paint" (1989, p. 65). As students experiment with words, they learn to create images, play with words, and evoke feelings. They laugh with language, experiment with rhyme, and invent new words. These activities provide students with a rich background of experiences for reading and writing poetry, and they gain confidence in choosing the "right" word to express an idea, emphasizing the sounds of words, and expressing familiar ideas with fresh comparisons. A collection of wordplay books that elementary students enjoy is listed in the Classroom Library box on page 483.

Laughing With Language

As children learn that words have the power to amuse, they enjoy reading, telling, and writing riddles and jokes. Linda Gibson Geller (1985) researched children's humorous language and identified two stages of riddle play that elementary students move through: Primary-grade children experiment with the riddle form and its content, and middle- and upper-grade students explore the paradoxical constructions in riddles. Riddles are written in a question-and-answer format, but young children at first may only ask questions, or ask questions and offer unrelated answers. With more experience, students both provide questions and give related answers, and their answers may be either descriptive or nonsensical. An example of a descriptive answer is:

Why did the turtle go out of his shell?
Because he was getting too big for it.

Wordplay Books

Agee, J. (1992). *Go hang a salami! I'm a lasagna hog! and other palindromes.* New York: Farrar, Straus & Giroux. (U)

Agee, J. (2002). *Palindromania!* New York: Farrar, Straus & Giroux. (M–U)

Barrett, J. (1983). *A snake is totally tail.* New York: Atheneum. (P–M)

Bayer, J. (1984). *A my name is Alice.* New York: Dial. (P–M)

Bierhorst, J. (Ed.). (1992). *Lightning inside you: And other Native American riddles.* New York: Morrow. (M–U)

Brown, M. (1983). *What do you call a dumb bunny? And other rabbit riddles, games, jokes, and cartoons.* Boston: Little, Brown. (P–M)

Cole, J., & Calmenson, S. (1995). *Yours till banana splits: 201 autograph rhymes.* New York: Morrow. (M–U)

Cox, J. A. (1980). *Put your foot in your mouth and other silly sayings.* New York: Random House. (P–M)

Degen, B. (1983). *Jamberry.* New York: Harper & Row. (P)

Degen, B. (1996). *Sailaway home.* New York: Scholastic. (P)

Eiting, M., & Folsom, M. (1980). *Q is for duck: An alphabet guessing game.* New York: Clarion. (P–M)

Esbensen, B. J. (1986). *Words with wrinkled knees.* New York: Crowell. (M–U)

Fakih, K. O. (1995). *Off the clock: A lexicon of time words and expressions.* New York: Clarion. (M)

Gwynne, F. (1970). *The king who rained.* New York: Dutton. (M–U)

Gwynne, F. (1976). *A chocolate moose for dinner.* New York: Dutton. (M–U)

Gwynne, F. (1980). *The sixteen hand horse.* New York: Prentice Hall. (M–U)

Gwynne, F. (1988). *A little pigeon toad.* New York: Simon & Schuster. (M–U)

Hall, F., & Friends. (1985). *Sniglets for kids.* Yellow Springs, OH: Antioch. (M–U)

Hall, K., & Eisenberg, L. (1992). *Spacey riddles.* New York: Dial. (P)

Hanson, J. (1972). *Homographic homophones. Fly and fly and other words that look and sound the same but are as different in meaning as bat and bat.* Minneapolis: Lerner. (M)

Hartman, V. (1992). *Westward ho ho ho! Jokes from the wild west.* New York: Viking. (M–U)

Houget, S. R. (1983). *I unpacked my grandmother's trunk: A picture book game.* New York: Dutton. (P–M)

Juster, N. (1982). *Otter nonsense.* New York: Philomel. (P–M)

Kellogg, S. (1987). *Aster Aardvark's alphabet adventures.* New York: Morrow. (P–M)

Lewis, J. P. (1996). *Riddle-icious.* New York: Knopf. (M)

Maestro, G. (1984). *What's a frank Frank? Tasty homograph riddles.* New York: Clarion. (P–M)

McMillan, B. (1990). *One sun: A book of terse verse.* New York: Holiday House. (M)

Merriam, E. (1992). *Fighting words.* New York: Morrow. (P–M)

Most, B. (1992). *Zoodles.* San Diego, CA: Harcourt Brace Jovanovich. (M)

Perl, L. (1988). *Don't sing before breakfast, don't sing in the moonlight.* New York: Random House. (M–U)

Rees, E. (1995). *Fast Freddie frog and other tongue twister rhymes.* Honesdale, PA: Wordsong. (P)

Schwartz, A. (1973). *Tomfoolery: Trickery and foolery with words.* Philadelphia: Lippincott. (M–U)

Schwartz, A. (1982). *The car's elbow and other secret languages.* New York: Farrar, Straus & Giroux. (M–U)

Schwartz, A. (1992). *Busy buzzing bumblebees and other tongue twisters.* New York: HarperCollins. (P–M)

Smith, W. J., & Ra, C. (1992). *Behind the king's kitchen: A roster of rhyming riddles.* Honesdale, PA: Wordsong. (M–U)

Steig, J. (1992). *Alpha beta chowder.* New York: HarperCollins. (P–M)

Terban, M. (1982). *Eight ate: A feast of homonym riddles.* New York: Clarion. (P–M)

Terban, M. (1983). *In a pickle and other funny idioms.* New York: Clarion. (M)

Terban, M. (1985). *Too hot to hoot: Funny palindrome riddles.* New York: Clarion. (M–U)

Terban, M. (1992). *Funny you should ask: How to make up jokes and riddles with wordplay.* New York: Clarion. (M–U)

Terban, M. (1995). *Time to rhyme: A rhyming dictionary.* Honesdale, PA: Wordsong. (M)

Van Allsburg, C. (1987). *The z was zapped.* Boston: Houghton Mifflin. (M)

Wilbur, R. (1995). *Runaway opposites.* San Diego, CA: Harcourt Brace. (P)

Zalben, J. B. (1992). *Lewis Carroll's Jabberwocky.* Honesdale, PA: Boyds Mills Press. (M–U)

P = primary grades (K–2); M = middle grades (3–5); U = upper grades (6–8).

483

A nonsensical answer might involve an invented word. For example:

Why did the cat want to catch a snake?

Because he wanted to turn into a rattlecat (Geller, 1981, p. 672).

Many primary-grade students' riddles seem foolish by adult standards, but wordplay is an important precursor to creating true riddles.

Riddles depend on using metaphors and on manipulating words with multiple meanings or similar sounds. The Opies (1959) identified five riddle strategies that elementary students use:

1. Using multiple referents for a noun: What has an eye but cannot see? A needle.
2. Combining literal and figurative interpretations for a single phrase: Why did the kid throw the clock out the window? Because he wanted to see time fly.
3. Shifting word boundaries to suggest another meaning: Why did the cookie cry? Because its mother was a wafer (away for) so long.
4. Separating a word into syllables to suggest another meaning: When is a door not a door? When it's ajar (a jar).
5. Creating a metaphor: What are polka dots on your face? Pimples.

Children begin riddle play by telling familiar riddles and reading riddles written by others. Several excellent books of riddles to share with elementary students are *Tyrannosaurus Wrecks: A Book of Dinosaur Riddles* (Sterne, 1979), *What Do You Call a Dumb Bunny? And Other Rabbit Riddles, Games, Jokes, and Cartoons* (Brown, 1983), and *Eight Ate: A Feast of Homonym Riddles* (Terban, 1982). Soon children are composing their own by adapting riddles they have read, and others turn jokes into riddles. A third grader wrote this riddle using two meanings for Milky Way:

Why did the astronaut go to the Milky Way?

Because he wanted a Milky Way Bar.

A fifth grader wrote this riddle using the homophones *hair* and *hare:*

What is gray and jumpy and on your head? A gray hare!

The juxtaposition of words is important in many jokes and riddles.

Creating Word Pictures

Children create word pictures by arranging words to make a picture. These word pictures can be single-word pictures or a string of words or a sentence arranged in a picture. Figure 11–1 shows four word pictures. In the upper-left box, a rabbit is drawn using words to describe each of the body parts. The word *whiskers*, for example, is written to form the whiskers. In the upper-right box, the word *nervous* is written concretely. Students can write the names of objects and animals concretely, illustrating features of the named item through the style of the letters. The lower-left box shows the word *bird* written concretely. Also, students can compose a descriptive phrase or sentence and write it in the shape of an object, as the ice-cream cone in the lower-right box in Figure 11–1 illustrates. An asterisk indicates where to start reading the sentence picture.

To make word pictures, students first draw a picture with lines. Next, they place a second sheet of paper over the drawing and replace all or most of

FIGURE 11-1   *Students' Word Pictures*

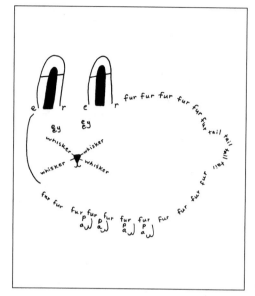

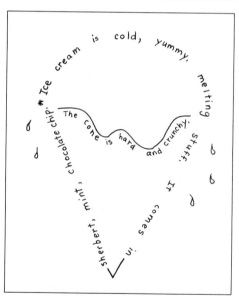

the lines with repeated words. Then students write descriptive words so that the arrangement, size, and intensity of the letters in the word illustrate the meaning.

Experimenting With Rhyme

Because of their experience with Dr. Seuss stories, finger plays, and nursery rhymes, kindergartners and first graders enjoy creating rhymes. When it comes naturally, rhyme adds a delightful quality to children's writing, but when it is equated with poetry, it can get in the way of wordplay and vivid images. The following three-line poem, "Thoughts After a 40-Mile Bike Ride," shows a fifth grader's effective use of rhyme:

My feet
And seat
Are beat.

A small group of first graders created their own version of *Oh, A-Hunting We Will Go* (Langstaff, 1974). After reading the book, they identified the refrain (lines 1, 2, and 5) and added their own rhyming couplets:

Oh, a-hunting we will go,
a-hunting we will go.
We'll catch a little bear
and curl his hair,
and never let him go.

Oh, a-hunting we will go,
a-hunting we will go.
We'll catch a little mole
and put him in a hole,
and never let him go.

Oh, a-hunting we will go,
a-hunting we will go.
We'll catch a little bug
and give him a big hug
and never let him go.

Oh, a-hunting we will go,
a-hunting we will go.
We'll catch a little bunny
and fill her full of honey,
and never let her go.

Oh, we'll put them in a ring
and listen to them sing
and then we'll let them go.

The first graders wrote this collaboration with the teacher taking dictation on a large chart. After the rough draft was written, students reread it, checking the rhymes and changing a word here or there. Then each student chose one stanza to copy and illustrate. The pages were collected and compiled to make a book. Students shared the book with their classmates, with each student reading his or her own page.

Hink-pinks are short rhymes that either take the form of an answer to a riddle or describe something. Hink-pinks are composed with two one-syllable rhyming words; they are called hinky-pinkies when two two-syllable words are used, and hinkity-pinkities with two three-syllable words (Geller, 1981). Two examples of these rhymes are:

Ghost   What do you call an astronaut?
White   A sky guy.
Fright

Other Poetic Devices

Poets choose words carefully. They craft powerful images when they use unexpected comparisons, repeat sounds within a line or stanza, imitate sounds, and repeat words and phrases; these techniques are poetic devices. As students learn about the devices, they appreciate the poet's ability to manipulate a device in poems they read and apply it in their own writing (Cullinan et al., 1995). The terminology is also helpful in response groups when students talk about poems they have read and in writing groups so that students can compliment classmates on the use of a device or suggest that they try a particular device when they revise their writing.

Comparison.   One way to describe something is to compare it to something else. Students can compare images, feelings, and actions to other things using two types of comparisons—similes and metaphors. A simile is an explicit comparison of one thing to another—a statement that one thing is like something else. Similes are signaled by the use of *like* or *as*. In contrast, a metaphor compares two things by implying that one is something else, without using *like* or *as*. Differentiating between the two terms is less important than using comparisons to make writing more vivid; for example, children can compare anger to an occurrence in nature. Using a simile, they might say, "Anger is like a thunderstorm, screaming with thunder-feelings and lightning-words." Or, as a metaphor, they might say, "Anger is a volcano, erupting with poisonous words and hot-lava actions."

To learn more about similes and metaphors, turn back to Chapter 5, "Looking Closely at Words."

Students begin by learning traditional comparisons and idioms, and they learn to avoid stale comparisons, such as "high as a kite," "butterflies in your stomach," and "light as a feather." Then they invent fresh, unexpected comparisons. A sixth grader uses a combination of expected and unexpected comparisons in this poem, "People":

People are like birds
who are constantly getting their feathers ruffled.
People are like alligators
who find pleasure in evil cleverness.
People are like bees
who are always busy.
People are like penguins
who want to have fun.
People are like platypuses—unexplainable!

Alliteration.   Alliteration is the repetition of the initial consonant sound in consecutive words or in words in close proximity. Repeating the initial sound makes poetry fun to read, and children enjoy reading and reciting alliterative verses, such as *A My Name Is Alice* (Bayer, 1984) and *The Z Was Zapped* (Van Allsburg, 1987). After reading one of these books, children can create their own versions. A fourth-grade class created its own version of Van Allsburg's book, which they called *The Z Was Zipped*. Students divided into pairs, and each pair composed two pages for the class book. Students illustrated their letter on the front of the paper and wrote a sentence on the back to describe

FIGURE 11–2   *Two Pages from a Fourth-Grade Class Book of Alliterations*

their illustration, following Van Allsburg's pattern. Two pages from the book are shown in Figure 11–2. Before reading the sentences, examine the illustrations and try to figure out the sentences. These are the students' alliterative sentences:

The D got dunked by the duck.
The T was totally terrified.

Tongue twisters are an exaggerated type of alliteration in which every word (or almost every word) in the twister begins with the same letter. Dr. Seuss compiled an easy-to-read collection of tongue twisters for primary-grade students in *Oh Say Can You Say?* (1979). Anita Lobel's *Alison's Zinnia* (1990) and Steven Kellogg's *Aster Aardvark's Alphabet Adventures* (1987) are two good books of tongue twisters for middle- and upper-grade students. Practice with tongue twisters and alliterative books increases children's awareness of the poetic device in poems they read and write. Few students consciously think about adding alliteration to a poem they are writing, but they get high praise in writing groups when classmates notice an alliteration and compliment the writer on it.

Onomatopoeia.   Onomatopoeia is a device in which poets use sound words to make their writing more sensory and more vivid. Sound words (e.g., *crash, slurp, varoom, meow*) sound like their meanings. Students can compile a list of sound words they find in stories and poems and display the list on a classroom chart or in their language arts notebooks to refer to when they write their own poems.

Peter Spier has compiled two books of sound words; *Gobble Growl Grunt* (1971) is about animal sounds, and *Crash! Bang! Boom!* (1972) is about the sounds people and machines make. Students can use these books to select sound words for their writing. Comic strips are another good source of sound words; children collect frames from comic strips with sound words to add to a classroom chart.

In *Wishes, Lies, and Dreams* (2000), Kenneth Koch recommends having children write noise poems that include a noise or sound word in each line. These first poems often sound contrived (e.g., "A dog barks bow-wow"), but the experience helps children learn to use onomatopoeia, as this poem, "Elephant Noses," dictated by a kindergartner, illustrates:

Elephant noses
Elephant noses
Elephants have big noses
Big noses
Big noses
Elephants have big noses
through which they drink
SCHLURRP

Repetition. Repetition of words and phrases is another device writers use to structure their writing as well as to add interest. Poe's use of the word *nevermore* in "The Raven" is one example, as is the Gingerbread Boy's boastful refrain in "The Gingerbread Boy." In this riddle, a fourth grader uses a refrain effectively:

I am a little man standing all alone
In the deep, dark wood.
I am standing on one foot
In the deep, dark wood.
Tell me quickly, if you can,
What to call this little man
Standing all alone
In the deep, dark wood.
Who am I?
(Answer: a mushroom)

READING POEMS

Children grow rather naturally into poetry. The Opies (1959) have verified what we know from observing children: Children have a natural affinity to verse, songs, riddles, jokes, chants, and puns. Preschoolers are introduced to poetry when their parents repeat Mother Goose rhymes, read *The House at Pooh Corner* (Milne, 1956) and the Dr. Seuss stories, and sing short songs to them. During the elementary grades, youngsters often create jump-rope rhymes and other ditties on the playground.

Types of Poems Children Read

Poems for children assume many different forms. The most common type of poetry is rhymed verse, such as Vachel Lindsay's "The Little Turtle," John Ciardi's "Mummy Slept Late and Daddy Fixed Breakfast," and Robert Louis Stevenson's "Where Go the Boats?" Poems that tell a story are narrative poems; examples are Clement Moore's *The Night Before Christmas*, Robert Browning's *The Pied*

Seeing Common Threads

Given the current emphasis on improving test scores, do you think there is time for poetry in the language arts curriculum?

Laura North writes:

Poetry can be quickly and easily integrated into thematic units to enrich your students' learning. For example, in my second-grade classroom we're learning about the water cycle. My students were having trouble remembering the words *evaporation, condensation,* and *precipitation* so I taught them a poem about the water cycle and they quickly committed those words to memory. In fact, a TV meteorologist came to visit our class and the kids were so excited about what they had learned that they begged to recite the poem for him. Needless to say, he was quite impressed. I believe that reading and writing poetry will prepare my students for the achievement tests because they expand their vocabularies, learn synonyms, and develop higher-level comprehension skills through poetry.

What do you think?

Each chapter presents a question and a response written by one of Dr. Tompkins's students. Consider other comments, or respond to the question yourself, by visiting the Threaded Message Board in Chapter 11 on the Companion Website at www.prenhall.com/tompkins

Piper of Hamelin, and Henry Wadsworth Longfellow's "The Song of Hiawatha." A Japanese form, haiku, is popular in anthologies of poetry for children. Haiku is a three-line poem that contains just 17 syllables. Because of its brevity, it has been considered an appropriate form of poetry for children to read and write. Free verse has lines that don't rhyme, and rhythm is less important than in other types of poetry; images take on greater importance in free-form verse. Langston Hughes's "Subway Rush Hour" and William Carlos Williams's "This Is Just to Say" are two examples of free verse. Other forms of poetry include limericks, a short, five-line, rhymed verse form popularized by Edward Lear (1995), and concrete poems, which are arranged on the page to create a picture or an image. *A Poke in the I* (Janeczko, 2001) is a recent book of concrete poems.

Three types of poetry books are published for children. A number of picture-book versions of single poems (in which each line or stanza is illustrated on a page) are available, such as *Paul Revere's Ride* (Longfellow, 1990). Other books are specialized collections of poems, either written by a single poet or related to a single theme, such as dinosaurs or Halloween. Comprehensive anthologies are the third type of poetry book for children, and they feature 50 to 500 or more poems arranged by category. One of the best anthologies is *The Random House Book of Poetry for Children* (Prelutsky, 2000). A list of poetry books that includes examples of each of the three types is presented in the Classroom Library box on page 491.

CLASSROOM LIBRARY

Poetry Books

Picture Book Versions of Single Poems

Bates, K. L. (2003). *America the beautiful.* New York: Putnam. (M)

Carroll, L. (2003). *Jabberwocky.* Cambridge, MA: Candlewick Press. (M–U)

Frost, R. (1988). (Ill. by E. Young). *Birches.* New York: Henry Holt. (U)

Howitt, M. (2002). *The spider and the fly.* New York: Simon & Schuster. (P)

Lear, E. (1986). (Ill. by L. B. Cauley). *The owl and the pussycat.* New York: Putnam. (P–M)

Longfellow, H. W. (1990). (Ill. by T. Rand). *Paul Revere's ride.* New York: Dutton. (M–U)

Nash, O. (1995). *The tale of Custard the dragon.* Boston: Little, Brown. (P)

Sandburg, C. (1993). *Arithmetic.* New York: Harcourt Brace. (P–M)

Thayer, E. L. (2000). (Ill. by C. Bing). *Casey at the bat: A ballad of the republic sung in the year 1888.* New York: Handprint. (M–U)

Westcott, N. B. (1988). *The lady with the alligator purse.* Boston: Little, Brown. (P)

Specialized Collections

Adoff, A. (1995). *Street music: City poems.* New York: HarperCollins. (P)

Argueta, J. (2001). *A movie in my pillow/Una pelicula en mi almohada: Poems.* San Francisco: Children's Book Press. (P–M)

Carlson, L. M. (Ed.). (1998). *Sol a sol: Bilingual poems.* New York: Henry Holt. (P–M)

Carlson, L. M. (Ed.). (1994). *Cool salsa.* New York: Henry Holt. (M–U)

Fleischman, P. (1988). *Joyful noise: Poems for two voices.* New York: Harper & Row. (M–U)

Florian, D. (2003). *Bow wow meow meow: It's rhyming cats and dogs.* San Diego: Harcourt Brace. (P)

Franco, B. (2003). *Mathematickles!* New York: McElderry. (P–M)

George, K. (2002). *Swimming upstream: Middle school poems.* New York: Clarion. (M–U)

Glaser, I. J. (1995). *Dreams of glory: Poems starring girls.* New York: Atheneum. (M–U)

Herrera, J. F. (1998). *Laughing out loud, I fly.* New York: HarperCollins. (M–U)

Hopkins, L. B. (1995). *Blast off! Poems about space.* New York: HarperCollins. (P)

Hopkins, L. B. (Ed.). (2002). *Hoofbeats, claws and rippled fins: Creature poems.* New York: HarperCollins. (P)

Janeczko, P. B. (Sel.). (1993). *Looking for your name: A collection of contemporary poems.* New York: Orchard Books. (U)

Jones, H. (Ed.). (1993). *The trees stand shining: Poetry of the North American Indians.* New York: Dial. (M–U)

Kennedy, X. J. (2002). *Exploding gray: Poems to make you laugh.* Boston: Little, Brown. (M–U)

Kuskin, K. (2003). *Moon, have you met my mother? The collected poems of Karla Kuskin.* New York: HarperCollins. (M)

Levy, C. (2002). *Poems of our watery world.* New York: Scholastic. (P–M)

Lewis, J. P. (1995). *Black swan/White crow.* New York: Atheneum. (haiku) (M–U)

Livingston, M. C. (Sel.). (1991). *Lots of limericks.* New York: McElderry Books. (M–U)

Mannis, C. D. (2002). *One leaf rides the wind: Counting in a Japanese garden.* New York: Viking. (P–M)

McCord, D. (1974). *One at a time.* Boston: Little, Brown. (M–U)

Myers, W. D. (2003). *blues journey.* New York: Holiday House. (M–U)

Pomerantz, C. (1982). *If I had a paka: Poems in 11 languages.* New York: Greenwillow. (M–U)

Prelutsky, J. (1984). *The new kid on the block.* New York: Greenwillow. (P–M)

Prelutsky, J. (1989). *Poems of A. Nonny Mouse.* New York: Knopf. (P–M)

Prelutsky, J. (2002). *Scranimals.* New York: Greenwillow. (P–M)

Silverstein, S. (1996). *Falling up.* New York: HarperCollins. (P–M)

Swados, E. (2002). *Hey you! C'mere: A poetry slam.* New York: Scholastic. (M–U)

Comprehensive Anthologies

de Regniers, B. S., Moore, E., White, M. M., & Carr, J. (Compilers). (1988). *Sing a song of popcorn: Every child's book of poems.* New York: Scholastic. (P–M–U)

Kennedy, X. J. (Compiler). (1985). *The forgetful wishing well: Poems for young people.* New York: McElderry. (U)

Kennedy, X. J., & Kennedy, D. M. (Compilers). (1999). *Knock at a star: A child's introduction to poetry* (rev. ed.). Boston: Little, Brown. (P–M–U)

Prelutsky, J. (Compiler). (2000). *The Random House book of poetry for children.* New York: Random House. (P–M–U)

FIGURE 11-3	
Adult Poems Recommended for Elementary Students	
Poet	**Poems and/or Books of Poetry**
William Blake	Read "The Lamb," "The Tyger," "The Piper," and other selections from *Songs of Experience* and *Songs of Innocence.* Compare with Nancy Willard's *A Visit to William Blake's Inn: Poems for Innocent and Experienced Travelers* (1981).
e. e. cummings	Enjoy Deborah Kogan Ray's picture-book version of *hist whist* (1989) at Halloween.
Emily Dickinson	Share "I'm Nobody! Who Are You?," "There Is No Frigate Like a Book," and other favorite poems from *I'm Nobody! Who Are You? Poems of Emily Dickinson for Children* (1978) and *A Brighter Garden* (1990).
T. S. Eliot	Try using choral reading to share the poems that inspired the Broadway musical "Cats" in *Old Possum's Book of Practical Cats* (Eliot, 1982).
Robert Frost	Enjoy "The Pasture," "Birches," "Fire and Ice," "Stopping by Woods on a Snowy Evening," and other favorites that are included in *A Swinger of Birches: Poems of Robert Frost for Young People* (1982) and *Poetry for Young People: Robert Frost* (Schmidt, 1994). *Stopping by Woods on a Snowy Evening,* illustrated by Susan Jeffers (2001), and *Birches* illustrated by Ed Young (1988), are delightful picture-book versions of individual poems.
Langston Hughes	Learn about the poet through Alice Walker's biography, *Langston Hughes: American Poet* (2001), and Tony Medina's tribute, *Love to Langston* (2002). Hughes's powerful poems in *The Dream Keeper and Other Poems* (1994) and *The Book of Rhythms* (1995) appeal to middle- and upper-grade students.
Henry Wadsworth Longfellow	Compare the awesome picture-book versions of Longfellow's poem, "The Midnight Ride of Paul Revere," including Ted Rand's (1990), Jeffrey Thompson's (2000), Christopher Bing's (2001), and Charles Santore's (2003) versions, that are currently available. For other poems, check *Poetry for Young People: Henry Wadsworth Longfellow* (Schoonmaker, 1998).
Edgar Allan Poe	Check *The Raven and Other Poems* (Poe, 2002) and *Poetry for Young People: Edgar Allan Poe* (Bagert, 1995) for "Annabel Lee," "The Raven," "The Bells," and spooky poems that upper elementary students love.
Carl Sandburg	Share Ted Rand's stunning picture-book version of "Arithmetic" (1993) as well as poems from these collections: *Poetry for Young People: Carl Sandburg* (Bolin, 1995) and *Rainbows Are Made: Poems of Carl Sandburg* (Hopkins, 1982).
Walt Whitman	Read poems from *Poetry for Young People: Walt Whitman* (Levin, 1997) and *Voyages: Poems of Walt Whitman* (Hopkins, 1988). Also, share Robert Sabuda's striking picture-book version of "I Hear America Singing" (1991).

In addition to poetry written specifically for children, some poetry written for adults can be used effectively with elementary students, especially at upper-grade levels. Apseloff (1979) explains that poems written for adults use more-sophisticated language and imagery and provide children with an early introduction to poems and poets they will undoubtedly study later. For instance, elementary students will enjoy Shakespeare's "The Witches' Song" from *Macbeth* and Carl Sandburg's "Fog." Figure 11–3 lists poems written for adults that may be appropriate with some elementary students.

Children have definite preferences about which poems they like best, just as adults do. Fisher and Natarella (1982) surveyed the poetry preferences of first, second, and third graders; Terry (1974) investigated fourth, fifth, and sixth graders' preferences; and Kutiper (1985) researched seventh, eighth, and ninth graders' preferences. The results of the three studies are important for teachers to consider when they select poems. The most popular forms of poetry were limericks and narrative poems; least popular were haiku and free verse. In addition, children preferred funny poems, poems about animals, and poems about familiar experiences; they disliked poems with visual imagery and figurative language. The most important elements were rhyme, rhythm, and sound. Primary-grade students preferred traditional poetry, middle graders preferred modern poetry, and upper-grade students preferred rhyming verse. The researchers found that children in all three studies liked poetry, enjoyed listening to poetry read aloud, and could give reasons why they liked or disliked particular poems.

Researchers have also used school library circulation figures to examine children's poetry preferences. Kutiper and Wilson (1993) found that the humorous poetry of Shel Silverstein and Jack Prelutsky was the most popular. The three most widely circulated books were *The New Kid on the Block* (Prelutsky, 1984), *Where the Sidewalk Ends* (Silverstein, 1974), and *A Light in the Attic* (Silverstein, 1981). In fact, 14 of the 30 most popular books used in the study were written by these two poets. Both Silverstein and Prelutsky have used rhyme and rhythm effectively in their humorous narrative poems about familiar, everyday occurrences; these are the same qualities that children liked in the earlier poetry preference studies.

Books of poems on almost every possible topic are available for children today: dog poems in *It's About Dogs* (Johnston, 2000), baseball poems in *That Sweet Diamond* (Janeczko, 1998) and *Extra Innings: Baseball Poems* (Hopkins, 1993), penguin poems in *Antarctic Antics* (Sierra, 1998), and food poems in *What's on the Menu?* (Goldstein, 1992) and *Munching: Poems About Eating* (Hopkins, 1985), for example. When teachers know their students well, they can connect them with books of poetry related to their hobbies and interests. Teachers also share poems in connection with theme cycles. During a theme cycle on the desert, for example, they can share poems from *Desert Voices* (Baylor, 1981), *Cactus Poems* (Asch & Levin, 1998), and *Mojave* (Siebert, 1988). Teachers add books of poetry to text sets of books for theme cycles and copy favorite poems on charts or make copies for students to add to their learning logs. Including poems in theme cycles is important because poetry gives students a different perspective on social studies and science concepts.

Children are just as interested in learning about favorite poets as they are about authors who write stories and informational books. When children view poets and other writers as real people, people whom they can relate to and who enjoy the same things they do, they begin to see themselves as poets—a necessary criterion for successful writing. Information about poets is available in *Speaking of Poets: Interviews With Poets Who Write for Children and Young Adults* (Copeland, 1993), *Speaking of Poets 2: More Interviews With Poets Who Write for Children and Young Adults* (Copeland & Copeland, 1994), and *A Jar of Tiny Stars: Poems by NCTE Award-Winning Poets* (Cullinan, 1996). More information is available on the Internet about many contemporary poets. Some poets have their own websites, and information about others is available on children's literature websites, such as The Children's Literature Web Guide at the University of Calgary (www.ucalgary. ca/~dk brown).

Teaching Students to Read and Respond to Poems

In her poem "How to Eat a Poem," Eve Merriam (1966) provides useful advice for students who are reading poems: She says that reading a poem is like eating a piece of fruit, and she advises biting right in and letting the juice run down your chin. The focus is on enjoyment: Children read poems and listen to them read aloud because they are pleasurable activities. With so many poems available for children today, it is easy to find poems that appeal to every child and poems that teachers like, too.

Reading Poetry Aloud. Students should have many, many opportunities to read and listen to poems read aloud. Teachers share poems that they especially like with students, and they read them expressively. Elster and Hanauer (2002) noted these qualities of teachers' expressive reading: slow and melodious reading, stressing and elongating words, adjusting reading speeds, and using musical instruments or props to accompany the reading. Students are not expected to analyze poems; instead, they read poems they like and share their favorite poems with classmates. Poetry sharing does not need to be scheduled for a particular time of day. First thing in the morning or right after lunch is a good time, but because poems can be shared quickly, they can be tied in with almost any activity. Poetry fits into all four patterns of practice: Students can read poems during reading workshop and in connection with literature focus units, literature circles, and theme cycles.

Poetry is intended to be shared orally. It shouldn't be read silently because the words and phrases lose much of their music when they are read with the eyes, not the voice. As teachers and students read poems aloud, they use their voices to enhance the rhyme and rhythm and other poetic elements. According to John Stewig (1981), readers make four types of decisions to increase the effectiveness of their oral presentations:

- Tempo—how fast or slowly to read the lines
- Rhythm—which words to stress or say loudest
- Pitch—when to raise or lower the voice
- Juncture—when and how long to pause

Students experiment with tempo, rhythm, pitch, and juncture as they read poems in different ways during minilessons, and they learn how to vary their reading to make their presentations more interpretive. Students also learn that in some poems, reading speed may be more important and that in other poems, pausing is more important. These considerations reinforce the need to rehearse a poem several times before reading it aloud for classmates. During rehearsal, students experiment with tempo, rhythm, pitch, and juncture to read the poem as effectively as possible.

Teachers read many poems aloud to students, and students read other poems themselves. One way for students to read poems is using choral reading,

Choral Reading

Step by Step

1. **Select a poem to use for choral reading.** Teachers choose a poem or other text and copy it onto a chart or make multiple copies for students to read.

2. **Arrange the text for choral reading.** Teachers work with students to decide how to arrange the poem for reading. They add marks to the chart, or have students mark individual copies so that they can follow the arrangement.

3. **Rehearse the poem.** Teachers read the poem with students several times at a natural speed, pronouncing words carefully. Many teachers stand so that students can see how they move their mouths to form the words as they read.

4. **Have students read the poem aloud.** Teachers emphasize that students pronounce words clearly and read with expression. Teachers can tape-record students' reading so that they can hear themselves, and sometimes students want to rearrange the choral reading after hearing an audiotape of their reading.

in which students take turns reading a poem together. The procedure for choral reading is shown in the Step by Step feature above. Students need multiple copies of the poem for choral reading, or the poem must be displayed on a chart or an overhead projector so that everyone can read it. Then students and the teacher decide how to arrange the poem for choral reading. Students may read the poem aloud together or in small groups, or individual students can read particular lines or stanzas. Four possible arrangements are (Stewig, 1981):

1. *Echo reading.* The leader reads each line, and the group repeats it.
2. *Leader and chorus reading.* The leader reads the main part of the poem, and the group reads the refrain or chorus in unison.
3. *Small-group reading.* The class divides into two or more groups, and each group reads one part of the poem.
4. *Cumulative reading.* One student or one group reads the first line or stanza, and another student or group joins in as each line or stanza is read so that a cumulative effect is created.

Choral reading makes students active participants in the poetry experience, and it helps them learn to appreciate the sounds, feelings, and magic of poetry. Two books of award-winning poems written specifically for choral reading are *I Am Phoenix: Poems for Two Voices* (Fleischman, 1985), a collection of poems about birds, and *Joyful Noise: Poems for Two Voices* (Fleischman, 1988), a collection of poems about insects. Many other poems can be used for choral reading; try, for example, Shel Silverstein's "Boa Constrictor," Karla

Kuskin's "Full of the Moon," Laura E. Richards's "Eletelephony," and Eve Merriam's "Catch a Little Rhyme."

English learners who speak Spanish will enjoy reading poems that incorporate some Spanish words, such as Gary Soto's *Neighborhood Odes* (1992) and *Canto Familiar* (1995) and Juan Felipe Herrera's *Laughing Out Loud, I Fly* (1998). The Spanish words are translated in a glossary, so even non-Spanish speakers can understand the poems. Other books of poetry are bilingual; the poems are printed side-by-side in Spanish and English, such as *Sol a Sol: Bilingual Poems* (Carson, 1998), *From the Bellybutton of the Moon and Other Summer Poems/Del Ombligo de la Luna y Otros Poemas de Verano* (Alarcon, 1998), and *The Tree Is Older Than You Are* (Nye, 1995). Students can read these poems in either language, or alternate reading one line in English and the next in Spanish.

Teachers begin by reading favorite poems aloud to students and hanging charts with the poems written on them in the classroom. After doing this for several days, teachers point out a collection of poetry books in the classroom library and invite students to prepare a poem to share with the class the next day. Before long, students will be eagerly volunteering to read poems to the class. A list of guidelines for reading poems with children is presented in the LA Essentials box on page 497.

Responding to Poems. After reading, students respond to the poem they have read or listened to someone else read aloud. Sometimes the response is brief, with students talking informally about the poem, sharing connections to their own lives or expressing whether they liked it. At other times, students may explore the poem, choose favorite lines, or illustrate it.

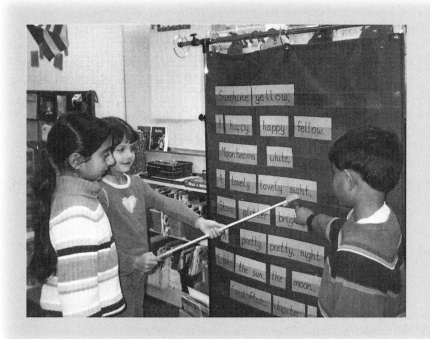

Reading poems. These children are rereading a poem their teacher recently introduced to the class. Through this reading practice, these first graders learn high-frequency words and develop reading fluency as well as an awareness of poetic devices. After reading the poem, the children take the sentence strips out of the pocket chart, shuffle them, and then resequence them on the pocket chart. Sometimes they decide that they prefer their arrangement to the poet's. In another week of practice, their teacher will cut apart the words on each strip, and children can practice resequencing the words in each line.

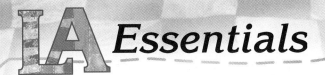

Essentials

Guidelines for Reading Poems

1. Reading Aloud

Read poetry aloud, not silently, in order to appreciate the cadence of the words. Even if students are reading independently, they should speak each word, albeit softly or in an undertone.

2. Expression

Teach students how to read a poem with expression, how to emphasize the rhythm and feel of the words, and where to pause.

3. Song Tunes

Have children sing poems to familiar tunes, such as "Twinkle, Twinkle Little Star" or "I've Been Working on the Railroad." Let the students experiment to find a tune that fits the line structure of the poem and then sing the poem to the tune.

4. Rehearsal

Have readers rehearse poems several times before reading aloud so that they can read fluently and with expression. In other words, encourage students to read "poetically."

5. Poetry Books

Include a collection of poetry books in the classroom library for children to read during reading workshop and other independent reading times.

6. Memorization

Rarely assign students a particular poem to memorize; rather, encourage children who are interested in learning a favorite poem to do so and to share it with class members. Soon memorizing poetry will become a popular classroom activity.

7. No Analysis

Don't expect children to analyze the meaning of a poem or its rhyme scheme; instead, talk with them about poems they like and why they like them.

8. Author Units

Teach author units to focus on a poet, such as Dr. Seuss, Jack Prelutsky, or Gary Soto. Have students read the poet's poems and learn about his or her life through biographies and Internet resources.

9. Display Poems

Copy and display poems on chart paper or on sentence strips in pocket charts for students to read and enjoy.

One way students explore familiar poems is to sequence the lines of a poem. Teachers can copy the lines of the poem on sentence strips (long strips of chart paper), and students sequence the lines in a pocket chart or by lining up around the classroom. Or, teachers can enlarge the text of the poem on a copy machine and then cut the lines apart. Then students arrange the lines in order on a tray or cookie sheet and read the familiar poem. As students sequence the poem, they check a copy of the poem posted in the classroom, if necessary. For a more challenging activity, teachers can cut apart the words on each line so that students build the poem word by word. Through these sequencing activities, students have opportunities to practice word-identification skills and experiment with the syntactic structure of poems.

During poetry units, students often create projects. They use drama, art, and music activities to extend their interpretations of favorite poems. For instance, students can role-play Kuskin's "I Woke Up This Morning" or construct monster puppets for the Lurpp creature in Prelutsky's "The Lurpp Is on the Loose." Students may also compile picture-book versions of narrative poems with one line or stanza on each page. Students add an illustration for each page to complete the book. A page from a third-grade class book illustrating Shel Silverstein's "Hug O' War" (1974) is shown in Figure 11–4.

Some students enjoy compiling anthologies of their favorite poems. This activity often begins quite naturally when students read poems. They copy favorite poems to keep, and soon they are stapling their collections together to make books. Copying poems can also be a worthwhile handwriting activity because students are copying something meaningful to them, not just words and sentences in a workbook. In *Pass the Poetry, Please!* poet and anthologist Lee Bennett Hopkins (1987) suggests setting up a dead tree branch or an artificial Christmas tree in the classroom as a "poetree" on which students can hang copies of their favorite poems for classmates to read and enjoy. A list of additional ways students respond to poems is presented in the LA Essentials box on page 499.

FIGURE 11–4   *An Excerpt From a Third-Grade Class Book Illustrating Shel Silverstein's Poem "Hug O' War"*

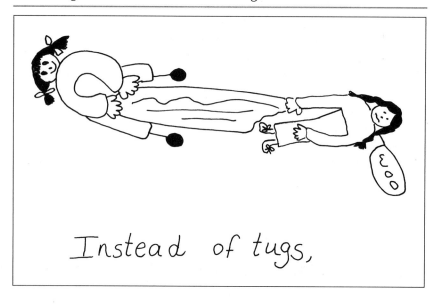

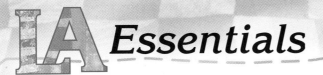

Essentials

Ways to Respond to a Poem

1. Students read the poem aloud to classmates. They read "poetically," with expression.

2. Students perform the poem using puppets or pantomime as a tape recording is played aloud.

3. Students write a reading log entry, discussing what the poem brings to mind or why they like it.

4. Students arrange the poem for choral reading and with classmates present it to the class. They may also choose appropriate background music for the presentation.

5. Students identify a favorite line in a poem and explain why they like it, either by talking to a classmate or in a double-entry journal.

6. Students draw or paint a picture of an image the poem brings to mind and write a favorite line or two from the poem on the picture. Or, students can write the favorite line on a sentence strip (long strip of chart paper). Then the line is read aloud during sharing time and added to a bulletin board of favorite lines.

7. Students make a picture book with lines or a stanza of the poem written on each page and illustrated.

8. Students choose a favorite line and use it in a poem they are writing.

9. Students make a mobile with stanzas cut apart and hung together with pictures.

10. Students "can," "box," or "bag" a poem by decorating a container and inserting a copy of the poem and two items related to it.

11. Students or the teacher writes the poem on word cards, and then students "build" the poem, sequencing the cards in a pocket chart.

12. Students enlarge a copy of the poem on a copy machine and then cut apart the words and sequence them on their desks. Sometimes students decide to arrange the words differently than the way the poet wrote them because they like their arrangement better!

13. Students read other poems written by the same poet.

14. Students research the poet using biographies and Internet resources.

15. Students write a letter to the poet and mail it.

16. Students make a cluster on a topic related to the poem.

17. Students write a poem on the same topic or following the format of the poem they have read.

18. Students dramatize the poem with a group of classmates.

19. Students make a poster to illustrate the poem and attach a copy of the poem to it.

20. Students add the poem to a personal notebook of favorite poems.

Piecing a Lesson Together

Topics on Reading Poetry

Procedures	Concepts	Strategies and Skills
Read a poem interpretively	Poetry	Vary tempo
Do choral reading	Rhymed verse	Emphasize rhythm
Share poems	Narrative poems	Vary pitch
Respond to poems in quickwrites	Free verse	Stress juncture
Discuss poems	Concrete poems	
Do a project	Information about poets	
Compile an anthology	Arrangements for choral reading	

Please visit the Companion Website at **www.prenhall.com/tompkins** for a second fully realized minilesson.

Teaching Minilessons. Teachers present minilessons to teach students about how to read and respond to poems. Minilessons cover procedures, concepts, and strategies and skills related to reading poetry. They also teach students to identify and appreciate comparisons, alliteration, and other types of wordplay in poems. A list of topics for minilessons is presented on these pages. Also included is a minilesson about how to read a poem interpretively.

READING POEMS

Minilesson

Mr. Johnston Teaches His Third Graders How to Read Poems Interpretively

1. **Introduce the Topic**

   Mr. Johnston places a transparency of "A Pizza the Size of the Sun" by Jack Prelutsky (1996) on the overhead projector and reads it aloud in a monotone voice. He asks his third graders if he did a good job reading the poem, and they tell him that his reading was boring.

2. **Share Examples**

   Mr. Johnston asks what he could do to make his reading better, and they suggest that he read with more expression. He asks the students to tell him which words he should read more expressively and marks their changes on the transparency. He reads the poem again and students agree that it is better. Then students suggest he vary his reading speed and he marks their changes on the transparency. He reads the poem a third time, incorporating more changes. They agree that his third reading is the best!

3. **Provide Information**

   Mr. Johnston praises his students for their suggestions; they did help him make this reading better. Then he asks what he can do to make his reading more interesting, and they suggest:

   - Read some parts loud and some parts soft
   - Read some parts fast and some parts slow
   - Change your voice for some words

4. **Supervise Practice**

   Mr. Johnston divides students into small groups and passes out transparencies of other poems. Students in each group decide how to read the poem and mark parts they will read in special ways. Mr. Johnston circulates around the classroom as students work, providing assistance as needed. Then students display their poems on the overhead projector and read them aloud with expression.

5. **Reflect on Learning**

   Mr. Johnston asks students to talk about what they have learned. One student explains that there are two ways of reading: One is boring and the other is fun. They have learned how to read the fun way so that they can share their enjoyment of poems with others.

Assessing Students' Experiences With Poems

Teachers assess students' experiences with poetry in several ways. They observe students as they are involved in poetry-reading activities, and keep anecdotal notes of students as they read and respond to poems and share poems they like with classmates. They read students' reading logs and monitor the projects they create. Teachers can also conference with students and ask them about favorite poems to assess their interest in poetry. They also notice students' attention to how poets use wordplay and poetic devices. Students can also write reflections about their learning and work habits during the poetry activities, and these reflections provide valuable assessment information.

WRITING POEMS

Children can write poetry! They write funny verses, vivid word pictures, powerful comparisons, and expressions of deep sentiment. The key to successful poetry is poetic formulas. These formulas serve as scaffolds, or temporary writing frameworks, so that students focus on ideas rather than on the mechanics of writing poems (Cecil, 1994). In some formula poems, students begin each line with particular words, as with color poems; in some, they count syllables, as in haiku; and in others, they follow rhyming patterns, as in limericks.

Many types of poetry do not use rhyme, and rhyme is the sticking point for many would-be poets. In searching for a rhyming word, children often create inane verse, for example:

I see a funny little goat
Wearing a blue sailor's coat
Sitting in an old motorboat.

Of course, children should be allowed to write rhyming poetry, but rhyme should never be imposed as a criterion for acceptable poetry. Children should use rhyme when it fits naturally into their writing. When children write poetry, they are searching for their own voices, and they need freedom to do that.

Five types of poetic forms are formula poems, free-form poems, syllable- and word-count poems, rhymed poems, and model poems. Elementary students' poems illustrate each poetic form. Kindergartners' and first graders' poems may seem little more than lists of sentences compared to the more sophisticated poems of older students, but the range of poems effectively shows how students in kindergarten through eighth grade grow in their ability to write poetry through these writing activities.

Formula Poems

The poetic forms may seem like recipes, but they are not intended to be followed rigidly. Rather, they provide a scaffold, organization, or skeleton for students' poems. After collecting words, images, and comparisons through brainstorming or another prewriting strategy, students craft their poems, choosing words and arranging them to create a message. Meaning is always most important, and form follows the search for meaning. Perhaps a better description is that children "dig for poems" (Valentine, 1986) through words, ideas, poetic forms, rhyme, rhythm, and conventions.

Poet Kenneth Koch (2000), working with students in the elementary grades, developed some simple formulas that make it easy for nearly every child to become a successful poet. These formulas call for students to begin every line the same way or to insert a particular kind of word in every line. The formulas use repetition, a stylistic device that is more effective for young poets than rhyme. Some forms may seem more like sentences than poems, but the dividing line between poetry and prose is a blurry one, and these poetry experiences help children move toward poetic expression.

"I Wish . . . " Poems. Children begin each line of their poems with the words "I wish" and complete the line with a wish (Koch, 2000). In a second-grade class collaboration, children simply listed their wishes:

I wish I had all the money in the world.
I wish I was a star fallen down from Mars.
I wish I were a butterfly.
I wish I were a teddy bear.
I wish I had a cat.
I wish I were a pink rose.
I wish it wouldn't rain today.
I wish I didn't have to wash a dish.
I wish I had a flying carpet.
I wish I could go to Disney World.
I wish school was out.
I wish I could go outside and play.

After this experience, students choose one of their wishes and expand on the idea in another poem. Brandi expanded her wish this way:

I wish I were a teddy bear
Who sat on a beautiful bed
Who got a hug every night
By a little girl or boy
Maybe tonight I'll get my wish
And wake up on a little girl's bed
And then I'll be as happy as can be.

Color Poems. Students begin each line of their poems with a color. They can use the same color in each line or choose a different color (Koch, 2000). For example, a class of seventh graders wrote about yellow:

Yellow is shiny galoshes
splashing through mud puddles.
Yellow is a street lamp
beaming through a dark, black night.
Yellow is the egg yolk
bubbling in a frying pan.
Yellow is the lemon cake
that makes you pucker your lips.
Yellow is the sunset
and the warm summer breeze.
Yellow is the tingling in your mouth
after a lemon drop melts.

Students can also write more complex poems by expanding each idea into a stanza, as this poem about black illustrates:

Black is a deep hole
sitting in the ground
waiting for animals
that live inside.
Black is a beautiful horse
standing on a high hill
with the wind
swirling its mane.
Black is a winter night sky
without stars
to keep it
company.
Black is a panther
creeping around a jungle
searching for
its prey.

Hailstones and Halibut Bones (O'Neill, 1989) is another source of color poems; however, O'Neill uses rhyme as a poetic device, and it is important to emphasize that students' poems need not rhyme.

Writing color poems can be coordinated with teaching young children to read and write color words. Instead of having kindergartners and first graders read worksheets and color pictures in the designated colors, students can create color poems in booklets of paper stapled together. They write and illustrate one line of the poem on each page.

Five-Senses Poems.   Students write about a topic using each of the five senses. Sense poems are usually five lines long, with one line for each sense, as this poem, "Being Heartbroken," written by a sixth grader demonstrates:

Sounds like thunder and lightning
Looks like a carrot going through a blender
Tastes like sour milk
Feels like a splinter in your finger
Smells like a dead fish
It must be horrible!

It is often helpful to have students develop a five-senses cluster and collect ideas for each sense. Students select from the cluster the strongest or most vivid idea for each sense to use in a line of the poem.

"If I Were . . . " Poems.   Children write about how they would feel and what they would do if they were something else—a tyrannosaurus rex, a hamburger, or sunshine (Koch, 2000). They begin each poem with "If I were" and tell what it would be like to be that thing. For example, 7-year-old Robbie wrote about what he would do if he were a dinosaur:

If I were a tyrannosaurus rex
I would terrorize other dinosaurs
And eat them up for supper.

In composing "If I were . . . " poems, students use personification, explore ideas and feelings, and consider the world from a different vantage point. Students can also write poems from the viewpoint of a book character. Fifth graders, for example, wrote this short poem after reading *Number the Stars* (Lowry, 1989):

If I were Annemarie,
I'd be brave.
I'd hide my friends,
and trick those Nazi soldiers.
I would lie if I had to.
If I were Annemarie,
I'd be brave.

Definition Poems.   Students experiment with comparisons as they write definition poems. The teacher or students begin by identifying a topic, such as anger or liberty; then students brainstorm descriptions and examples, which often employ metaphors or similes. Students pick their most powerful definitions and create the poem, beginning each line with the topic and the word *is*. A group of second graders wrote the following poem as a part of their weather unit. Before discussing what causes thunder, they brainstormed a list of possible explanations for this phenomenon:

Thunder is someone bowling.
Thunder is a hot cloud bumping against a cold cloud.
Thunder is someone playing basketball.
Thunder is dynamite blasting.
Thunder is a brontosaurus sneezing.
Thunder is people moving their furniture.
Thunder is a giant laughing.
Thunder is elephants playing.
Thunder is an army tank.
Thunder is Bugs Bunny chewing his carrots.

Students often write powerful poems using this formula once they move beyond the cute "Happiness is . . . " and "Love is . . . " patterns.

Preposition Poems.   Students begin each line of preposition poems with a preposition. This pattern often produces a delightful poetic effect. A seventh grader wrote this preposition poem about Superman:

Within the city
In a phone booth
Into his clothes
Like a bird
In the sky
Through the walls
Until the crime
Among us
is defeated!

It is helpful for children to brainstorm a list of prepositions to refer to when they write preposition poems. Students may find that they need to ignore the formula for a line or two to give the content of their poems top priority, or they may mistakenly begin a line with an infinitive (e.g., *to say*) rather than a preposition. These forms provide a structure or skeleton for students' writing that should be adapted as necessary.

Acrostic Poems. Students write acrostic poems using key words. They choose a key word and write it vertically on a sheet of paper. Then they create lines of poetry, each one beginning with a letter of the word or words they have written vertically. Students can use their names during a unit on autobiography or names of characters during a literature focus unit. For example, after reading *Officer Buckle and Gloria* (Rathmann, 1995), the story of a police officer and his dog who give safety speeches at schools, a small group of first graders wrote this acrostic using the dog's name, Gloria, for the key word written vertically.

Gloria
Loves to do tricks.
Officer Buckle tells safety
Rules at schools.
I wish I had
A dog like Gloria.

Another small group composed this acrostic using the same word written vertically:

Good dog Gloria
Likes to help
Officer Buckle teach safety
Rules to boys and girls.
I promise to remember
All the lessons.

Free-Form Poems

Students choose words to describe something and put the words together to express a thought or tell a story, without concern for rhyme or other arrangements. The number of words per line and the use of punctuation vary. In the following poem, an eighth grader poignantly describes loneliness concisely, using only 15 well-chosen words:

A lifetime
Of broken dreams
And promises
Lost love
Hurt
My heart
Cries
In silence

Students can use several methods for writing free-form poems. They can select words and phrases from brainstormed lists and clusters, or they can write a paragraph and then "unwrite" it to create the poem by deleting unnecessary words. They arrange the remaining words to look like a poem.

Concrete Poems. Students create concrete poems through art and the careful arrangement of words on a page. Words, phrases, and sentences can be written in the shape of an object, or word pictures can be inserted within poems written left to right and top to bottom. Concrete poems are extensions of the word pictures discussed earlier. Two concrete poems are shown in Figure 11–5. In "Ants," the words *ants, cake,* and *frosting* create the image of a familiar picnic scene, and in "Cemetery," repetition and form create a reflection of peace.

FIGURE 11-5 *Students' Concrete Poems*

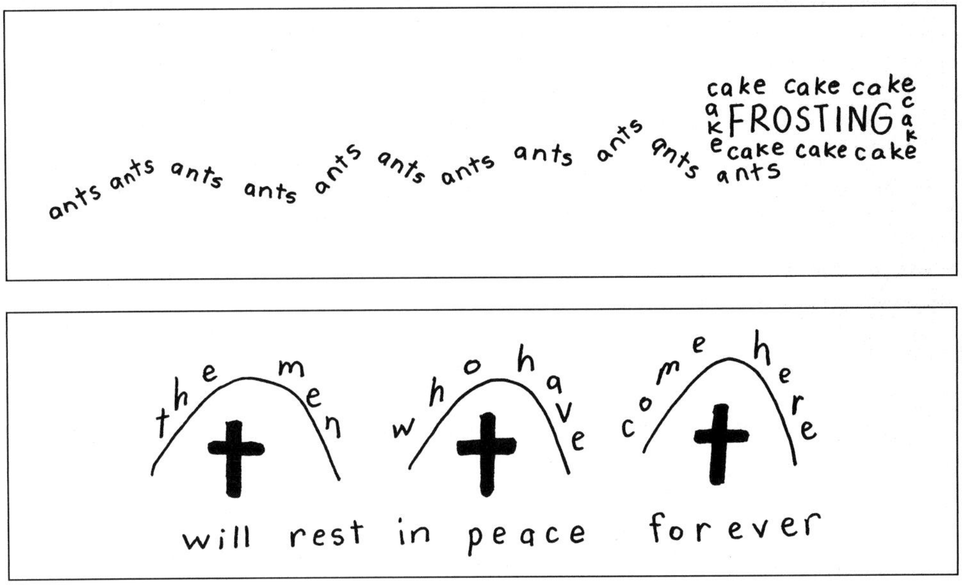

Three books of concrete poems are *Splish Splash: Poems* (Graham, 1994), *Seeing Things* (Froman, 1974), and *A Poke in the I* (Janeczko, 2001).

Found Poems. Students create poems by culling words from other sources, such as stories, songs, and informational books. They collect words and phrases as they read and then arrange them to make a poem. A sixth grader wrote this poem after reading *Hatchet* (Paulsen, 1987), the story of a boy who survives for months in the wilderness after his plane crashes:

He was 13.
Always started with a single word:
Divorce.
An ugly word,
A breaking word, an ugly breaking word.
A tearing ugly word that meant fights and yelling.
Secrets.
Visitation rights.
A hatchet on his belt.
His plane.
The pilot had been sighted.
He rubbed his shoulder.
Aches and pains.
A heart attack.
The engine droned.
A survival pack which had emergency supplies.
Brian Robeson
Alone.
Help, p-l-e-a-s-e.

When they compose found poems, students have the opportunity to experiment with vocabulary and language structures that are more sophisticated than they might write themselves. These poems also document students' understanding of the stories and other texts they have read.

Poems for Two Voices.   A unique type of free verse is poems for two voices. These poems are written in two columns, side by side, and the columns are read together by two readers. One reader (or group) reads the left column, and the other reader (or group) reads the right column. Sometimes readers alternate when they read, but when readers both have words—either the same words or different words—written on the same line, they read them simultaneously so that the poem sounds like a musical duet.

Two books of poems for two readers are Paul Fleischman's *I Am Phoenix: Poems for Two Voices* (1985), which is about birds, and the Newbery Medal–winning *Joyful Noise: Poems for Two Voices* (1988), which is about insects. And, if two voices aren't enough, Fleischman has also written *Big Talk: Poems for Four Voices* (2000) for upper-grade students.

Students, too, can write poems for two voices. A third-grade class wrote this poem for two voices about whales as part of their across-the-curriculum theme on the ocean:

Whales	Whales
dive deep	dive deep
into the ocean	
	then surface for air
breathing	
	through blowholes
always	always
swimming	looking for food
looking for food	swimming
whales	whales
mammals	
	look like fish
but they aren't	but they aren't
two groups	two groups
baleen whales	
	toothed whales
the humpback whale	
	a baleen whale
fast swimmer	fast swimmer
little beluga whale	
	a toothed whale
all white	
	very unusual
the blue whale	
	a baleen whale
the biggest	
	of all
big blue	big blue
killer whale	
	a toothed whale
black and white	white and black
dangerous attacker	dangerous attacker
whales	whales

Lorraine Wilson (1994) suggests that topics with contrasting viewpoints are the most effective. Students can also write poems from two characters' viewpoints. For example, after reading *Officer Buckle and Gloria* (Rathmann, 1995), a second-grade class wrote this poem for two voices. The voice on the left is Officer Buckle's and the voice on the right is Gloria the dog's:

I am Officer Buckle.	
	I am Gloria,
	a police dog in the K-9.
I teach safety tips	I teach safety tips
to boys and girls.	to boys and girls.
I say,	
"Keep your shoelaces tied."	
	I do a trick.
I say,	
"Do not go swimming	
during electrical storms."	
	I do a trick.
I say,	
"Stay away from guns."	
	I do a trick.
Bravo!	Bravo!
Everyone claps.	Everyone claps.
Do the kids love me?	
	Yes, they do.
No, the kids love you more.	
	The kids love both of us.
We're buddies!	We're buddies!
Always stick with your buddy.	Always stick with your buddy.

Syllable- and Word-Count Poems

Haiku and other syllable- and word-count poems provide a structure that helps students succeed in writing; however, the need to adhere to these poems' formulas may restrict freedom of expression. In other words, the poetic structure may both help and hinder. The exact syllable counts force students to search for just the right words to express their ideas and feelings and provide a valuable opportunity for students to use thesauri and dictionaries.

Haiku. The most familiar syllable-counting poem is haiku (high-KOO), a Japanese poetic form consisting of 17 syllables arranged in three lines of 5, 7, and 5 syllables. Haiku poems deal with nature and present a single, clear image. Haiku is a concise form, much like a telegram. A fourth grader wrote this haiku poem about a spider web she saw one morning:

Spider web shining
Tangled on the grass with dew
Waiting quietly.

Books of haiku to share with students include *Black Swan/White Crow* (Lewis, 1995), *Cool Melons—Turn to Frogs!* (Gollub, 1998), *Spring: A Haiku Story* (Shannon, 1996), and *Shadow Play: Night Haiku* (Harter, 1994). The photographs and artwork in these trade books may give students ideas for illustrating their haiku poems.

Tanka. Tanka (TANK-ah) is a Japanese verse form containing 31 syllables arranged in five lines, 5-7-5-7-7. This form is similar to haiku, but with two additional lines of 7 syllables each. An eighth grader wrote this tanka poem about stars, which was published in her middle school anthology:

The summer dancers
Dancing in the midnight sky,
Waltzing and dreaming.
Stars glistening in the night sky.
Wish upon a shooting star.

Cinquain.   A cinquain (SIN-cane) is a five-line poem containing 22 syllables in a 2-4-6-8-2 syllable pattern. Cinquain poems often describe something, but they may also tell a story. Have students ask themselves what their subject looks like, smells like, sounds like, and tastes like, and record their ideas using a five-senses cluster. The formula is as follows:

Line 1: a one-word subject with two syllables

Line 2: four syllables describing the subject

Line 3: six syllables showing action

Line 4: eight syllables expressing a feeling or an observation about the subject

Line 5: two syllables describing or renaming the subject

Here is a cinquain poem written by an upper-grade student:

Wrestling
skinny, fat
coaching, arguing, pinning
trying hard to win
tournament

If you compare this poem to the cinquain formula, you'll notice that some lines are short a syllable or two. The student bent some of the guidelines in choosing words to create a powerful image of wrestling; however, the message of the poem is always more important than adhering to the formula.

An alternate cinquain form contains five lines, but instead of following a syllable count, each line has a specified number of words. The first line contains a one-word title; the second line has two words that describe the title; the third line has three words that express action; the fourth line has four words that express feelings; and the fifth line contains a two-word synonym for the title.

To learn more about the parts of speech, turn to Chapter 13, "Learning About Grammar and Usage."

Diamante.   Iris Tiedt (2002) invented the diamante (dee-ah-MAHN-tay), a seven-line contrast poem written in the shape of a diamond. This poetic form helps students apply their knowledge of opposites and parts of speech. The formula is as follows:

Line 1: one noun as the subject

Line 2: two adjectives describing the subject

Line 3: three participles (ending in -ing) telling about the subject

Line 4: four nouns (the first two related to the subject and the second two related to the opposite)

Line 5: three participles telling about the opposite

Line 6: two adjectives describing the opposite

Line 7: one noun that is the opposite of the subject

A third-grade class wrote this diamante poem about the stages of life:

Baby

wrinkled tiny

crying wetting sleeping

rattles diapers money house

caring working loving

smart helpful

Adult

Notice that the students created a contrast between *baby,* the subject represented by the noun in the first line, and *adult,* the opposite in the last line. This contrast gives students the opportunity to play with words and apply their understanding of opposites. The third word in the fourth line, *money,* begins the transition from *baby* to its opposite, *adult.*

Rhymed Verse Forms

Several rhymed verse forms, such as limericks and clerihews, can be used effectively with middle- and upper-grade students. It is important that teachers try to prevent the forms and rhyme schemes from restricting students' creative and imaginative expression.

Limericks.   The limerick is a form of light verse that uses both rhyme and rhythm. The poem consists of five lines; the first, second, and fifth lines rhyme, and the third and fourth lines rhyme with each other and are shorter than the other three. The rhyme scheme is a-a-b-b-a, and a limerick is arranged this way:

Line	Rhyme
1_____	a
2_____	a
3_____	b
4_____	b
5_____	a

The last line often contains a funny or surprise ending, as in this limerick written by an eighth grader:

There once was a frog named Pete
Who did nothing but sit and eat.
He examined each fly
With so careful an eye
And then said, "You're dead meat."

Writing limericks can be a challenging assignment for many upper-grade students, but middle-grade students can also be successful with this poetic form, especially if they write a class collaboration.

Limericks are believed to have originated in the city of Limerick, Ireland, and were first popularized over a century ago by Edward Lear (1812–1888).

Poet X. J. Kennedy (1999) describes limericks as the most popular type of poem in the English language today. Introduce students to limericks by reading aloud some of Lear's verses so that students can appreciate the rhythm of the verse. Two collections of Lear's limericks are *Daffy Down Dillies: Silly Limericks by Edward Lear* (Lear, 1995) and *Lots of Limericks* (Livingston, 1991). Children also enjoy the playfulness of John Ciardi's verses in *The Hopeful Trout and Other Limericks* (1989). Arnold Lobel has also written a book of unique pig limericks, *Pigericks* (1983). After reading Lobel's pigericks, students often write "birdericks" or "fishericks."

Clerihews.   Clerihews (KLER-i-hyoos), four-line rhymed verses that describe a person, are named for Edmund Clerihew Bentley (1875–1956), a British detective writer who invented the form. The formula is as follows:

> *Line 1: the person's name*
>
> *Line 2: the last word rhymes with the last word in the first line*
>
> *Lines 3 and 4: the last words in these lines rhyme with each other*

Clerihews can be written about anyone—historical figures, characters in stories, and even the students themselves. A sixth grader named Heather wrote this clerihew about Albert Einstein:

Albert Einstein
His genius did shine.
Of relativity and energy did he dream
And scientists today hold him in high esteem.

Model Poems

Students model their poems on poems composed by adult poets, as Kenneth Koch suggested in *Rose, Where Did You Get That Red?* (1990). In this approach, students read a poem and write their own, using some of the words and the theme expressed in the model poem. For other examples of model poems, see Paul Janeczko's *Poetry from A to Z: A Guide for Young Writers* (1994) and Nancy Cecil's *For the Love of Language* (1994).

Apologies.   Using William Carlos Williams's "This Is Just to Say" as the model, children write a poem in which they apologize for something they are secretly glad they did (Koch, 1990). Middle- and upper-grade students are familiar with offering apologies and enjoy writing humorous apologies. A seventh grader, for example, wrote this apology poem, "The Truck," to his dad:

Dad,
I'm sorry
that I took
the truck
out for
a spin.
I knew it
was wrong.
But . . .
the exhilarating
motion was
AWESOME!

FIGURE 11-6   *A Comparison Chart Created After Reading Anastasia Krupnik*

Rules About Writing Poetry

Mrs. Westvessel's Rules	Our Rules
1. Poems must rhyme.	1. Poems do not have to rhyme.
2. The first letter in each line must be capitalized.	2. The first letter in each line does not have to be capitalized.
3. Each line must start at the left margin.	3. Poems can take different shapes and be any-where on a page.
4. Poems must have a certain rhythm.	4. You hear the writer's voice in a poem—with or without rhythm.
5. Poems should be written about serious things.	5. Poems can be about anything—serious or silly things.
6. Poems should be punctuated like other types of writing.	6. Poems can be punctuated in different ways or not be punctuated at all.
7. Poems are failures if they don't follow these rules.	7. There are no real rules for poems, and no poem is a failure.

dents to write poems. Students write poems during writing workshop and as part of literature focus units, literature circles, and theme cycles. A list of guidelines for writing poetry is shown in the LA Essentials box on page 516.

Minilessons.   Teachers use minilessons to introduce students to poetic forms and write collaborative poems for practice before they write poems independently. Class collaborations are crucial because they are a practice run for children who are not sure what to do. The 5 minutes it takes to write a class collaboration poem can be the difference between success and failure for students. Teachers also teach other topics related to writing poetry. They teach minilessons on the poetic devices and how to incorporate them into the poems that students write, how to arrange lines of poetry for the greatest impact, and how to punctuate and capitalize poems, for example. A list of topics for minilessons related to writing poetry and a sample minilesson are presented on pages 518–519.

Teaching minilessons about writing poetry is important; it is not enough simply to provide opportunities for students to experiment with poetry. Georgia Heard (1989) emphasizes the importance of teaching students about line breaks and white space on the page. Young children often write poems with the same page arrangement as stories, but as they gain more experience reading poems and experimenting with line breaks, they shape their poems to emphasize rhythm and rhyme, images, and poetic devices. Students learn that there are not right or wrong ways to arrange a poem on a page, but that the way the lines are broken affects both how the poem looks and how it sounds when read aloud.

Publishing Students' Poems.   Students use the writing process to draft and refine their poems; the final stage of the writing process is publishing. It's an

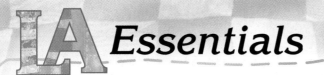

LA Essentials

Guidelines for Writing Poems

1. **Concept of Poetry**

   Explain what poetry is and what makes a good poem. Too often, students assume that all poems must rhyme, are written on topics such as love and flowers, must be punctuated in a particular way, or have other restrictions.

2. **Poetry Books**

   Set out books of poetry in a special section of the classroom library. Students learn about poetry through reading, and some poems can serve as models for the poems students write.

3. **Model Poems**

   Encourage students to write poems that model or incorporate a line from a poem they've read.

4. **Formulas**

   Teach students 5 to 10 formulas to use when they write poems so that they have a range of formulas from which to choose. At the same time, it is important that students know that they can break the formulas in order to express themselves more effectively.

5. **Minilessons**

   Present minilessons on comparison, alliteration, onomatopoeia, and repetition, and encourage students to use poetic devices other than rhyme.

6. **Wordplay**

   Encourage students to play with words, invent new words, and create word pictures as they write poems.

7. **Projects**

   Have students write poetry as part of literature focus units, literature circles, and theme cycles. Students can write found poems using excerpts from books, write poems about characters in stories, and write poems about topics related to themes.

8. **Celebrations**

   Have students share their poems in the author's chair, and post these "published" poems on a "poet-tree," a dead branch, displayed in the classroom.

9. **Anthologies**

   Create a class anthology of students' poems, and make copies of the anthology for each student.

important step because it brings closure to the writing process, students are motivated by sharing and by receiving their classmates' approval, and they gather ideas they can use in their own writing as they listen to and read their classmates' poems. Students share their poetry in two ways—by reading it aloud to classmates and by sharing written copies of their poems for classmates to read.

The most common way that students share their poems is by reading them aloud from the author's chair. Classmates listen to the poems read aloud and then offer compliments about what they liked about the poem—the student's choice of words, topic, use of poetic devices and poetry forms. Another way that students share their poems with classmates is through a read-around, as Mrs. Harris's students did in the vignette at the beginning of the chapter.

Students compile their poems into books that they place in the classroom library for classmates to read. Teachers also display copies of students' poems, often accompanied by an illustration, on a wall of the classroom and then have a gallery walk for students to read and respond to the poems. If there isn't enough space in the classroom to display the students' work for the gallery walk, teachers can post poems in the hallway or place them on students' desks. Students move from poem to poem and read and respond to it using small sticky notes that they attach to the edge of the student's paper or on the wall next to the paper. The steps in conducting a gallery walk are shown in the Step by Step feature on page 520. This activity can be completed much more quickly than if each student were to share his or her poem in front of the class, and because classmates will view their work, students are often more motivated than when the teacher will be the only audience.

Meeting the Needs of Every Student

Teachers can introduce poetry using song lyrics, use choral reading, and make other adaptations so that all students can read poems successfully. They can use interactive writing and collaborative writing activities so that all students can write poems successfully, although many teachers question why they should take time for poetry when their struggling students read and write below grade-level standards. In addition, state and federally mandated achievement tests increase the pressure that teachers feel to teach the basics. The Meeting the Needs of Every Student feature on page 521 explains why poetry is important for all students, especially struggling readers and writers.

Assessing the Poems Students Write

As teachers read, respond to, and assess the poems that students write, they need to recognize the nuggets of promise in the poems and support and build on them, instead of noticing children's lack of adult conventions (Tway, 1980). Donald Graves (1992) recommends that teachers focus on the passion and wonder in students' writing and on students' unique ability to make the common seem uncommon. Teachers can also notice the specific details,

Piecing a Lesson Together

Topics on Writing Poetry

Procedures	Concepts	Strategies and Skills
Write formula poems	Poetic forms	Use poetic forms
Write "I wish . . ." poems		Create sensory images
Write color poems		Paint word pictures
Write five-senses poems		Unwrite
		Use model poems
Write "If I were . . ." poems		Write rhymes
Write preposition poems		Punctuate poems
Craft found poems		Capitalize poems
Write free-form poems		Arrange poems on the
Design concrete poems		page
Write haiku poems		
Write cinquain poems		
Write diamante poems		
Write limericks		
Write clerihews		
Write model poems		

Please visit the Companion Website at **www.prenhall.com/tompkins** for a second fully realized minilesson.

strong images, wordplay, comparisons, onomatopoeia, alliteration, and repetitions of words and lines that students incorporate in their poems.

The poetic formulas discussed in this chapter provide options for students as they experiment with ways to express their thoughts. Although children experiment with a variety of forms during the elementary grades, it is not necessary to test their knowledge of particular forms. Knowing that haiku is a

FIVE-SENSES POEM

Ms. Yang Teaches Her First Graders to Write Five-Senses Poems

1. Introduce the Topic

Ms. Yang explains that her first graders are going to write a five-senses poem. She asks them to name the five senses and writes the words on the chalkboard and adds a small picture to illustrate each one.

2. Share Examples

Next, Ms. Yang reads aloud several five-senses poems that her students wrote last year; one is about a baby, another is about a tiger, and a third is about a pumpkin. After she reads each poem, she asks students to guess what is described in each poem. They guess the answers easily.

3. Provide Information

Ms. Yang opens a bag with five apples and explains that they will write five-senses poems about apples. The first step, she explains, is to draw a data chart. She draws a chart with five columns, one for each sense, on a large sheet of butcher paper. She writes the five senses, one at the top of each column. Then she asks the students to brainstorm words to describe apples. First they consider the "see" column. Students say that apples are round and shiny, red on the outside, and white on the inside; have a star in the middle; and have

stems. Ms. Yang records the students' ideas on the chart. Then they collect words for the other four columns. When they get to the "taste" column, Ms. Yang cuts several apples into sections for students to taste. After they finish the data chart, the first graders choose words from each column to craft this poem about apples, which Ms. Yang writes on chart paper:

Red on the outside,
White on the inside,
And a star in the middle.
It's round like a ball,
Smooth to touch.
Yummy to munch.
When you bite in—
Crunch! Crunch!

Ms. Yang planned to write one line about each of the five senses, but as students suggested lines, the poem changed form.

4. Supervise Practice

The first graders write their own apple poems using words from the data chart. Some students write individual poems, and others write with a classmate, munching on apple slices as they write.

5. Reflect on Learning

After students read their poems aloud to classmates, Ms. Yang collects them to make a class book.

Japanese poetic form composed of 17 syllables arranged in three lines will not make a child a poet. Descriptions of the forms should instead be posted in the classroom or added to language arts notebooks for students to refer to as they write.

Assessing the quality of students' poems is especially difficult, because poems are creative combinations of wordplay, poetic forms, and poetic devices.

Gallery Walks

Step by Step

1. **Display the work.** Students and the teacher post the work on classroom walls or place it on desks in preparation for the gallery walk.

2. **Provide comment sheets.** Teachers give students small sticky notes on which to write comments about each student's work. Students attach notes with their comments to the edges of classmates' work.

3. **Give directions for the gallery walk.** Teachers explain the purpose of the gallery walk, how to view and/or read the work, and what comments to make to classmates. Teachers also set time limits and direct students to visit three, five, eight, or more students' work, if there is not time to read everyone's work.

4. **Model how to view, read, and respond.** The teacher models how to behave during the gallery walk using one or two students' work as examples.

5. **Direct the flow of traffic.** Teachers direct students as they move around the classroom, making sure that all students' work is viewed, read, and responded to and that comments are supportive and useful.

6. **Bring closure to the gallery walk.** Teachers ask students to move to their own art or writing projects and look at the comments, questions, or other responses they have received. Often one or two students will share their responses or comment on the gallery walk experience.

Instead of trying to give a grade for quality, teachers can assess students on other criteria:

- Has the student experimented with the poetic form presented in a minilesson?
- Has the student used the process approach in writing, revising, and editing the poem?
- Has the student used wordplay or another poetic device in the poem?

Teachers also ask students to assess their own progress in writing poems. Students choose their best efforts and poems that show promise. They can explain which writing strategies they used in particular poems and which poetic forms they used.

Students keep copies of their poems in their writing folders or poetry booklets so that they can review and assess their own work. They may also place copies of some poems in their language arts portfolios. If a grade for quality is absolutely necessary, students should choose several of the poems in their writing folders for the teacher to evaluate.

Meeting the Needs of Every Student

Shouldn't My Struggling Students Be Doing Something More Important Than Reading and Writing Poetry?

You might argue that there is so much language arts instruction that your struggling students need that they don't have time for poetry, but that's a fallacy. The most important reason why poetry is important for struggling students is that poetry offers them a unique opportunity to be successful. Struggling students aren't successful very often in school, but when they are successful, they become more interested and motivated to learn. There are specific benefits for reading, too. Students develop reading fluency as they practice reading a favorite poem in preparation for reading it aloud to the class, and they learn about figurative language and inferential comprehension as they think about the meaning of a poem. Students use other language arts as they read and respond to poetry: They might memorize a favorite poem and recite it expressively, adding background music or digital photographs to accompany it. Or, they might share a poem written in their native language and then translate it for the class. There are benefits for writing as well. Many struggling students avoid long writing assignments. Because poems are shorter than many other compositions, students often find them easier to write. Struggling students' poems are usually better organized than other compositions because they use familiar poetic forms to structure their writing. The quality of their poems is often remarkable. They draw images with words, combine words in fresh, unexpected ways, and create a strong voice through their writing; in fact, students often surprise themselves with the poems they write.

To investigate other ways to meet the needs of every student, visit the links for this chapter on the Companion Website at www.prenhall.com/tompkins

Companion
Website

Review

Poetry is an important part of the language arts curriculum. Elementary students participate in wordplay activities and read and write poetry as part of literature focus units, reading and writing workshop, and theme cycles. The important concepts presented in this chapter include:

1. Wordplay activities with riddles, comparisons, rhyme, and other poetic devices provide the background of experiences students need for reading and writing poetry.
2. Three types of poetry books published for children are picture-book versions of single poems, specialized collections of poems, and comprehensive anthologies of poems.
3. Elementary students have definite opinions about the types of poems they like best.

Visit Chapter 11 on the Companion Website at www.prenhall. com/tompkins to:

• **Check your understanding of the concepts presented in the chapter**

• **Access the Extensions (activities and a list of related readings)**

• **Link to related websites**

4. The focus in teaching students to read and respond to poems is enjoyment.
5. Tempo, rhythm, pitch, and juncture are four considerations when reading poetry aloud.
6. Choral reading is an effective way for students to read poetry aloud.
7. Students read poems during reading workshop and in connection with literature focus units, literature circles, and theme cycles.
8. Students can write poems successfully using poetic formulas in which they begin each line with particular words, count syllables, or create word pictures.
9. Because rhyme is a sticking point for many, students should be encouraged to experiment with other poetic devices in their writing.
10. Students write poetry during writing workshop and as part of literature focus units, literature circles, and theme cycles.

Professional References

Apseloff, M. (1979). Old wine in new bottles: Adult poetry for children. *Children's Literature in Education, 10,* 194–202.

Cecil, N. L. (1994). *For the love of language: Poetry for every learner.* Winnipeg, Canada: Peguis.

Copeland, J. S. (1993). *Speaking of poets: Interviews with poets who write for children and young adults.* Urbana, IL: National Council of Teachers of English.

Copeland, J. S., & Copeland, V. L. (1994). *Speaking of poets 2: More interviews with poets who write for children and young adults.* Urbana, IL: National Council of Teachers of English.

Cullinan, B. E., Scala, M. C., & Schroder, V. C. (1995). *Three voices: An invitation to poetry across the curriculum.* York, ME: Stenhouse.

Elster, C. A., & Hanauer, D. I. (2002). Voicing texts, voices around texts: Reading poems in elementary school classrooms. *Research in the Teaching of English, 37,* 89–134.

Fisher, C. J., & Natarella, M. A. (1982). Young children's preferences in poetry: A national survey of first, second, and third graders. *Research in the Teaching of English, 16,* 339–354.

Geller, L. G. (1981). Riddling: A playful way to explore language. *Language Arts, 58,* 669–674.

Geller, L. G. (1985). *Word play and language learning for children.* Urbana, IL: National Council of Teachers of English.

Glover, M. K. (1999). *A garden of poets: Poetry writing in the elementary classroom.* Urbana, IL: National Council of Teachers of English.

Graves, D. H. (1992). *Explore poetry.* Portsmouth, NH: Heinemann.

Heard, G. (1989). *For the good of the earth and sun: Teaching poetry.* Portsmouth, NH: Heinemann.

Hopkins, L. B. (1987). *Pass the poetry, please!* New York: Harper & Row.

Koch, K. (2000). *Wishes, lies, and dreams.* New York: Harper Perennial.

Koch, K. (1990). *Rose, where did you get that red?* New York: Vintage.

Kutiper, K. (1985). *A survey of the poetry preferences of seventh, eighth, and ninth graders.* Unpublished doctoral dissertation, University of Houston.

Kutiper, K., & Wilson, P. (1993). Updating poetry preferences: A look at the poetry children really like. *The Reading Teacher, 47,* 28–35.

Larrick, N. (1991). *Let's do a poem! Introducing poetry to children.* New York: Delacorte.

Opie, I., & Opie, P. (1959). *The lore and language of school children.* Oxford: Oxford University Press.

Siemens, L. (1996). "Walking through the time of kids": Going places with poetry. *Language Arts, 73,* 234–240.

Stewig, J. W. (1981). Choral speaking: Who has the time? Why take the time? *Childhood Education, 57,* 25–29.

Terry, A. (1974). *Children's poetry preferences: A national survey of upper elementary grades* (NCTE Research Report No. 16). Urbana, IL: National Council of Teachers of English.

Tiedt, I. (2002). *Tiger lilies, toadstools, and thunderbolts: Engaging K–8 students with poetry.* Newark, DE: International Reading Association.

Tway, E. (1980). How to find and encourage the nuggets in children's writing. *Language Arts, 57,* 299–304.

Valentine, S. L. (1986). Beginning poets dig for poems. *Language Arts, 63,* 246–252.

Wilson, L. (1994). *Write me a poem: Reading, writing, and performing poetry.* Portsmouth, NH: Heinemann.

Children's Book References

Alarcon, F. X. (1998). *From the bellybutton of the moon and other summer poems/Del ombligo de la luna y otros poemas de verano.* San Francisco: Children's Book Press.

Asch, F., & Levin, T. (1998). *Cactus poems.* San Diego: Harcourt Brace.

Bagert, B. (Ed.). (1995). *Poetry for young people: Edgar Allan Poe.* Pittsburgh, PA: Sterling House.

Bayer, J. (1984). *A my name is Alice.* New York: Dial.

Baylor, B. (1981). *Desert voices.* New York: Scribner.

Bolin, F. S. (Ed.). (1995). *Poetry for young people: Carl Sandburg.* Pittsburgh, PA: Sterling House.

Brown, M. (1983). *What do you call a dumb bunny? And other rabbit riddles, games, jokes, and cartoons.* Boston: Little, Brown.

Carlson, L. M. (Ed.). (1998). *Sol a sol: Bilingual poems.* New York: Henry Holt.

Ciardi, J. (1989). *The hopeful trout and other limericks.* Boston: Houghton Mifflin.

Creech, S. (2001). *Love that dog.* New York: HarperCollins.

Crew, G. (1998). *Troy Thompson's excellent peotry (sic) book.* Victoria, Australia: Lothian.

Cullinan, B. E. (Ed.). (1996). *A jar of tiny stars: Poems by NCTE award-winning poets.* Honesdale, PA: Boyds Mill Press.

Eliot, T. S. (1982). *Old possum's book of practical cats.* San Diego: Harcourt Brace.

Fleischman, P. (1985). *I am phoenix: Poems for two voices.* New York: Harper & Row.

Fleischman, P. (1988). *Joyful noise: Poems for two voices.* New York: Harper & Row.

Fleischman, P. (2000). *Big talk: Poems for four voices.* Cambridge, MA: Candlewick Press.

Fletcher, R. (2002). *Poetry matters: Writing a poem from the inside out.* New York: HarperCollins.

Froman, R. (1974). *Seeing things: A book of poems.* New York: Crowell.

Frost, R. (1988). *Birches* (E. Young, Illus.). New York: Holt.

Frost, R. (2001). *Stopping by woods on a snowy evening* (S. Jeffers, Illus.). New York: Dutton.

Goldstein, B. S. (Sel.). (1992). *What's on the menu?* New York: Viking.

Gollub, M. (1998). *Cool melons—turn to frogs!* New York: Lee and Low.

Graham, J. B. (1994). *Splish splash: Poems.* New York: Ticknor.

Harter, P. (1994). *Shadow play: Night haiku.* New York: Simon & Schuster.

Herrera, J. F. (1998). *Laughing out loud, I fly.* New York: HarperCollins.

Hopkins, L. B. (Sel.). (1982). *Rainbows are made: Poems of Carl Sandburg.* New York: Harcourt Brace.

Hopkins, L. B. (Sel.). (1985). *Munching: Poems about eating.* Boston: Little, Brown.

Hopkins, L. B. (Sel.). (1988). *Voyages: Poems of Walt Whitman.* San Diego: Harcourt Brace.

Hopkins, L. B. (1992). *Questions: Poems.* New York: HarperCollins.

Hopkins, L. B. (Sel.). (1993). *Extra innings: Baseball poems.* San Diego: Harcourt Brace.

Hopkins, L. B. (1994). *Weather.* New York: HarperCollins.

Hopkins, L. B. (1995). *Blast off! Poems about space.* New York: HarperCollins.

Hughes, L. (1994). *The dream keeper and other poems*. New York: Knopf.

Hughes, L. (1995). *The book of rhythms*. New York: Oxford University Press.

Janeczko, P. B. (1994). *Poetry from A to Z: A guide for young writers*. New York: Bradbury.

Janeczko, P. B. (1998). *That sweet diamond*. New York: Atheneum.

Janeczko, P. B. (2001). *A poke in the I*. Cambridge, MA: Candlewick Press.

Johnston, T. (2000). *It's about dogs*. San Diego: Harcourt Brace.

Kellogg, S. (1987). *Aster Aardvark's alphabet adventures*. New York: Morrow.

Kennedy, X. J., & Kennedy, D. M. (1999). *Knock at a star: A child's introduction to poetry* (rev. ed.). Boston: Little, Brown.

Langstaff, J. (1974). *Oh, a-hunting we will go*. New York: Atheneum.

Lear, E. (1995). *Daffy down dillies: Silly limericks by Edward Lear*. Honesdale, PA: Wordsong.

Levin, J. (Ed.). (1997). *Poetry for young people: Walt Whitman*. Pittsburgh, PA: Sterling House.

Lewis, J. P. (1995). *Black swan/white crow*. New York: Atheneum.

Livingston, M. C. (Sel.). (1991). *Lots of limericks*. New York: McElderry.

Lobel, A. (1983). *Pigericks: A book of pig limericks*. New York: Harper & Row.

Lobel, A. (1990). *Alison's zinnia*. New York: Greenwillow.

Longfellow, H. W. (1990). *Paul Revere's ride*. New York: Dutton.

Longfellow, H. W. (2001). *The midnight ride of Paul Revere* (C. Bing, Illus.). New York: Handprint.

Longfellow, H. W. (2003). *Paul Revere's ride: The landlord's tale* (C. Santore, Illus.). New York: HarperCollins.

Lowry, L. (1979). *Anastasia Krupnik*. Boston: Houghton Mifflin.

Lowry, L. (1989). *Number the stars*. Boston: Houghton Mifflin.

Medina, T. (2002). *Love to Langston*. New York: Lee & Low.

Merriam, E. (1966). *It doesn't always have to rhyme*. New York: Atheneum.

Milne, A. A. (1956). *The house at Pooh Corner*. New York: Dutton.

Montenegro, L. N. (2003). *A bird about to sing*. Boston: Houghton Mifflin.

Nye, S. S. (1995). *The tree is older than you are*. New York: Simon & Schuster.

O'Neill, M. (1989). *Hailstones and halibut bones: Adventures in color*. Garden City, NJ: Doubleday.

Paulsen, G. (1987). *Hatchet*. New York: Viking.

Poe, E. A. (2002). *The raven and other poems*. New York: Scholastic.

Prelutsky, J. (Sel.). (2000). *The Random House book of poetry for children*. New York: Random House.

Prelutsky, J. (1984). *The new kid on the block*. New York: Greenwillow.

Prelutsky, J. (1996). *A pizza the size of the sun*. New York: Greenwillow.

Rathmann, P. (1995). *Officer Buckle and Gloria*. New York: Putnam.

Schmidt, G. D. (Ed.). (1994). *Poetry for young people: Robert Frost*. Pittsburgh, PA: Sterling House.

Schoonmaker, F. (Ed.). (1998). *Poetry for young people: Henry Wadsworth Longfellow*. Pittsburgh, PA: Sterling House.

Seuss, Dr. (1979). *Oh say can you say?* New York: Beginner Books.

Shannon, C. (1996). *Spring: A haiku story*. New York: Greenwillow.

Siebert, D. (1988). *Mojave*. New York: HarperCollins.

Sierra, J. (1998). *Antarctic antics: A book of penguin poems*. San Diego: Harcourt Brace.

Silverstein, S. (1974). *Where the sidewalk ends*. New York: Harper & Row.

Silverstein, S. (1981). *A light in the attic*. New York: Harper & Row.

Soto, G. (1992). *Neighborhood odes*. San Diego: Harcourt Brace.

Soto, G. (1995). *Canto familiar*. San Diego: Harcourt Brace.

Spier, P. (1971). *Gobble growl grunt*. New York: Doubleday.

Spier, P. (1972). *Crash! Bang! Boom!* New York: Doubleday.

Sterne, N. (1979). *Tyrannosaurus wrecks: A book of dinosaur riddles*. New York: Crowell.

Terban, M. (1982). *Eight ate: A feast of homonym riddles*. New York: Clarion.

Thompson, J. (2000). *The midnight ride of Paul Revere*. Washington, DC: National Geographic Society.

Van Allsburg, C. (1987). *The Z was zapped*. Boston: Houghton Mifflin.

Viorst, J. (1981). *If I were in charge of the world and other worries*. New York: Atheneum.

Walker, A. (2001). *Langston Hughes: American poet*. New York: HarperCollins/Amistad.

Whitman, W. (1991). *I hear America singing* (R. Sabuda, Illus.). New York: Philomel.

Willard, N. (1981). *A visit to William Blake's inn: Poems for innocent and experienced travelers*. New York: Harcourt Brace.

Wong, J. S. (2002). *You have to write*. New York: McElderry.

Woodson, J. (2003). *Locomotion*. New York: Putnam.

12 Learning to Spell Conventionally

Reading and Writing Workshop

Literature Focus Units

Literature Circles

Theme Cycles

The 28 students in Mr. Martinez's fourth-grade classroom participate in a 30-minute spelling lesson sandwiched between reading and writing workshop. During this time, the teacher assigns spelling words, and students practice them for the Friday test. Mr. Martinez uses the words from a textbook spelling program, and each week's list of words focuses on a topic—*r*-controlled vowels or compound words, for example. Mr. Martinez introduces the topic through a series of lessons a week in advance so that his students will understand the topic and be familiar with the words before they study them for the spelling test.

During the first semester, students studied vowel patterns (e.g., *strike, each*), *r*-controlled vowels (e.g., *first*), diphthongs (e.g., *soil*), more sophisticated consonant spellings (e.g., *edge, catch*), words with silent letters (e.g., *climb*), and homophones (e.g., *one–won*). Now in the second semester, they are learning two-syllable words. They have studied compound words (e.g., *headache*) and words with inflectional suffixes (e.g., *get–getting*), and now the

topic is irregular verbs. Irregular verbs is a difficult topic because students need to know the verb forms as well as how to spell the words.

Because the students' spelling levels range from second to sixth grade, Mr. Martinez has divided them into three groups. Each month, the groups choose new food-related names for themselves. This month, the names are types of pizza. Earlier in the year, they chose fruit names, Mexican food names, vegetable names, cookie names, and snack names. Of course, at the end of the month, they sample the foods. Mr. Martinez calls these food names his "secret classroom management tool" because students behave and work hard in order to participate in the tasting.

Students in the Pepperoni Pizza group spell at the second-grade level, and they are studying *r*-controlled vowels. They have already studied two-letter spelling patterns, and now they are learning three-letter patterns. This week the focus is on *ear* and *eer* patterns. Students in the Sausage Pizza group are at and almost at grade level. They are reviewing ways to spell/ou/. Students in the Hawaiian Pizza group are above-grade-level spellers. They are studying Latin root words and examining noun and verb forms of these words. This week's focus is spelling/shun/. Mr. Martinez meets with each group twice a week, and each group has a folder of activities to work on between meetings. Some of these group meetings are held during the spelling period (usually on Thursdays), and others are squeezed into reading and writing workshop. The teacher also encourages students to look for words they are studying in the books they're reading and to use them in their writing. They bring their examples to share at these meetings.

> **H***ow can teachers incorporate textbooks into their spelling programs?*
>
> Teaching spelling is more than having students memorize a list of words and take a test on Friday. Students need to learn spelling concepts—not just practice words—in order to develop into competent spellers. In addition, a single list of words is usually not appropriate for all students in a class because students' level of spelling development varies. As you read this vignette about Mr. Martinez's spelling program, notice how he teaches spelling concepts, incorporates the textbook's weekly lists of spelling words, and takes into account students' levels of spelling development.

This Week's Spelling List			
All Pizzas	Pepperoni Pizzas	Sausage Pizzas	Hawaiian Pizzas
*forget	*year	*smooth	educate
*forgot	fear	*group	*education
*forgotten	deer	soup	observe
*know	beard	*moving	*observation
*knew	*cheer	wood	admit
*known	*hear	would	*admission
*throw			
*threw			
*thrown			
*break			
*broke			
*broken			

* = words on the spelling test

This week's spelling list is shown in the box above. The irregular verbs in the "All Pizzas" column are taken from the spelling textbook. All students study the words in the "All Pizzas" column, and students in each group also study their own list of words. Students study between 15 and 20 words each week, and they spell 15 words on the Friday test. When they are studying more than 15 words, as they are this week, students don't know which words will be on the test, but the asterisks in the box indicate which words Mr. Martinez plans to use.

Mr. Martinez and his students are involved in three types of activities during the 30-minute spelling period: He teaches lessons on the weekly topic, students study words for the weekly spelling test, and students meet in small groups to study other spelling topics. The schedule is:

Monday	15 min.	Introduce the topic for the week
	15 min.	Have students take the pretest and self-check it
Tuesday	20 min.	Teach a lesson on the week's topic
	10 min.	Have students practice spelling words
Wednesday	15 min.	Teach a lesson on the week's topic
	15 min.	Have students take the practice test and self-check it
Thursday	20 min.	Work with small groups on other spelling topics
	10 min.	Have students practice spelling words
Friday	10 min.	Give spelling test
	20 min.	Review topic for the week and/or meet with small groups

This is the fourth week that Mr. Martinez is teaching verbs. During the first week, students brainstormed verbs and Mr. Martinez listed them on one of four charts: verbs that do not change form (e.g., *set, hurt*), regular verbs (e.g., *walk–walked*), irregular verbs with three forms (e.g., *do–did–done*), and irregular verbs with two forms (e.g., *sell–sold*). The students reviewed verbs that do not change form and regular verbs that form the past and past participle forms by adding-*ed*. That week, students were tested on words with inflectional suffixes, the topic taught the previous week. Regular verbs were tested the week after they were taught. For the next 2 weeks, students studied irregular verbs with three forms. Because it was a difficult concept for many of the students, Mr. Martinez took 2 weeks to teach it. Students sorted the words into present, past, and past participle columns as shown in the box on page 530, practiced spelling the words on white boards, and created posters using the words in sentences. One student chose *eat–ate–eaten* and wrote this paragraph:

> *I like to EAT m & ms. They are my favorite candy. I ATE a whole bag of m & ms yesterday. Now I have a stomachache because I have EATEN too much candy.*

The students created their posters during writing workshop. They used the writing process to draft and refine their sentences, word processed them, enlarged them to fit their posters, and printed them out. After sharing them during a spelling lesson, the students posted them on a wall in the classroom.

This week, the focus changes to irregular verbs with two forms, such as *sleep–slept, leave–left,* and *buy–bought.* On Monday, they review the list of verbs they created several weeks ago that is shown on page 531. Mr. Martinez observes that students are already familiar with these irregular verbs; the only difficult one is *wind–wound.* The students are familiar with the nouns *wind* and *wound,* but they don't know the verbs *wind* and *wound.* Mr. Martinez explains each word:

Wind *(noun; pronounced with a short* i*): air in motion*

Wind *(verb; pronounced with a long* i*): to coil or wrap something or to take a bending course*

Wound *(verb—past tense of* wind; *the* ou *is pronounced as in* cow*): having coiled or wrapped something or to have taken a bending course*

Wound *(noun; the* ou *is pronounced as in* moon*): an injury*

He sets out these objects to clarify the words: a small alarm clock to wind, a map showing a road that winds around a mountain, wind chimes to show the wind's motion, a skein of yarn to wind, and an elastic bandage to wind around a wound. The students examine each item and talk about how it relates to one or more of the words. Clayton explains the bandage and manages to include all four words:

> *OK. Let's say it is a windy day. The* wind *could blow you over and you could sprain your ankle. I know because it happened to me. A sprain is an injury like a* wound *but there's no blood. Well, then you get a bandage and you put it around your ankle like this [he demonstrates as he talks]: You* wind *it around and around to give your ankle some support. Now [he says triumphantly], I have* wound *the bandage over the* wound.

On Tuesday, the students play the "I'm thinking of . . . " game to practice the words on the Irregular Verbs With Two Forms chart. They are familiar with the game and eager to play it. Mr. Martinez begins, "I'm thinking of a word where you delete one vowel to change the spelling from present to past tense." The students identify *bleed–bled* and *meet–met.* Next, he says, "I'm thinking of a word where you add one letter to the present-tense verb to spell the past tense form," and the students identify *mean–meant.*

Word Sort of Irregular Verbs With Three Forms

Present	Past	Past Participle
forget	forgot	forgotten
eat	ate	eaten
sing	sang	sung
write	wrote	written
break	broke	broken
throw	threw	thrown
forgive	forgave	forgiven
grow	grew	grown
fly	flew	flown
take	took	taken
steal	stole	stolen
freeze	froze	frozen
go	went	gone
bite	bit	bitten
fall	fell	fallen
get	got	gotten
see	saw	seen
ride	rode	ridden

Irregular Verbs With Two Forms

*sleep–slept	meet–met	*leave–left	*bring–brought
shine–shone	fight–fought	*wind–wound	*buy–bought
*catch–caught	pay–paid	mean–meant	hang–hung
bleed–bled	*teach–taught	creep–crept	*build–built
dig–dug	tell–told	*think–thought	sell–sold
make–made	keep–kept	*sweep–swept	say–said

* = word (past-tense form) on next week's spelling list

Then the students take turns being the leader. Simone begins, "I'm thinking of a word where you change one vowel for the past tense." The students identify *dig–dug, hang–hung,* and *shine–shone.* Next, Erika says, "I'm thinking of a word where you change one consonant to make past tense," and the students answer *build–built* and *make–made.* Joey offers, "I'm thinking of a verb where you change the *i* to *ou* to get the past tense." The students identify four pairs: *wind–wound, think–thought, bring–brought,* and *fight–fought.* Then, Camille says, "I'm thinking of a verb where you take away an *e* and add a *t* to make the past tense," and the students reply *keep–kept, sweep–swept, sleep–slept,* and *creep–crept.* The students continue the game until they have practiced all the verbs.

Today Mr. Martinez distributes white boards to the class. He says the past-tense form of an irregular verb and students write both the present- and past-tense forms, without looking at the chart, unless they need help: *slept, taught, paid, bought, built,* and *left.* Many of the words he chooses are the ones that will be on next week's spelling list, but he also includes other words from the list. After they write each pair of words, the students hold up their white boards so that Mr. Martinez can check their work. He reviews how to form a letter or points out an illegible letter when necessary.

After 15 minutes of practice, the students return to their desks to take the practice test on this week's words. Mr. Martinez reads the list aloud while the students write using blue pens, and then he places a transparency with the words on the overhead projector so students can check their own tests. The students put away their blue pens and get out red pens to check their papers, so cheating is rarely a problem. Mr. Martinez walks around the classroom to monitor students' progress.

---

arctic	consciousness	embarrass	grammar	ingenious
liquefy	marshmallow	occasion	professor	souvenir

Which of these words are spelled correctly? If you are like most people, you may be confused about the spelling of one or more of them. All of them are spelled correctly, but it's easy to question the spelling of some words, especially if you expect pronunciation to determine spelling. English is not a purely phonetic language, and many words, such as *souvenir,* reflect their origins in other languages.

 As you begin reading this chapter, you may want to read the "Dear Reader" letter in Chapter 12 on the Companion Website at www.prenhall.com/tompkins

Spelling is a tool for writers that allows them to communicate convention-ally with readers. As Graves explains: "Spelling is for writing. Children may achieve high scores on phonic inventories or weekly spelling tests, but the ul-timate test is what the child does under 'game conditions,' within the process of moving toward meaning" (1983, pp. 193–194). Rather than equating spelling instruction with weekly spelling tests, students need to learn to spell words conventionally so that they can communicate effectively through writ-ing. English spelling is complex, and attempts to teach spelling through weekly lists have not been very successful. Many students spell the words correctly on the weekly test, but they continue to misspell them in their writing.

As you continue reading this chapter, consider these questions:

◆ How do children learn to spell?

◆ How can teachers determine students' level of spelling development?

◆ How should spelling be taught?

◆ How can teachers make weekly spelling tests more effective?

CHILDREN'S SPELLING DEVELOPMENT

Turn to Chapter 5, "Looking Closely at Words," for more information on the etymology of words.

The alphabetic principle suggests a one-to-one correspondence between phonemes and graphemes, but English spelling is phonetic only about half the time. Other spellings reflect the language from which a word was borrowed. For example, *alcohol,* like most words beginning with *al-,* is an Arabic word, and *homonym,* like most words with *y* where *i* would work, is a Greek word. Other words are spelled to reflect semantic relationships, not phonological ones. The spelling of *national* and *nation* and of *grade* and *gradual* indicates related meanings even though there are vowel or consonant changes in the pronunci-ations of the word pairs. If English were a purely phonetic language, it would be easier to spell, but at the same time, it would lose much of its sophistication.

See Chapter 4, "Emerging Into Literacy," for more information about young children's writing.

Elementary students learn to spell the phonetic elements of English as they learn about phoneme-grapheme correspondences, and they continue to refine their spelling knowledge through reading and writing. Children's spelling that reflects their growing awareness of English orthography is known as invented spelling, and during the elementary grades, children move from using scribbles and single letters to represent words through a series of stages until they adopt conventional spellings.

What Is Invented Spelling?

Children create unique spellings, called invented spellings, based on their knowledge of English orthography. Charles Read (1975, 1986), one of the first researchers to study preschoolers' efforts to spell words, discovered that they used their knowledge of phonology to invent spellings. These children used let-ter names to spell words, such as U (you) and R (are), and they used consonant sounds rather consistently: GRL (girl), TIGR (tiger), and NIT (night). The preschoolers used several unusual but phonetically based spelling patterns to represent affricates. They spelled *tr* with *chr* (e.g., CHRIBLES for *troubles*) and *dr* with *jr* (e.g., JRAGIN for *dragon*), and they substituted *d* for *t* (e.g., PREDE for *pretty*). Words with long vowels were spelled using letter names: MI (my), LADE (lady), and FEL (feel). The children used several ingenious strategies to spell words with short vowels. The 3-, 4-, and 5-year-olds rather consistently selected letters to represent short vowels on the basis of place of articulation in the mouth. Short *i* was represented with *e* as in FES (fish), short *e* with *a* as in LAFFT (left), and short *o* with *i* as in CLIK (clock). These spellings may seem odd to adults, but they are based on phonetic relationships. The children often omitted nasals within words (e.g., ED for *end*) and substituted *-eg* or *-ig* for *-ing* (e.g., CUMIG for *coming* and GOWEG for *going*). Also, they often ignored the vowel in unaccented syllables, as in AFTR (after) and MUTHR (mother).

These children developed strategies for their spellings based on their knowledge of the phonological system and of letter names, their judgments of phonetic similarities and differences, and their ability to abstract phonetic information from letter names. Read suggested that from among the many phonetic properties in the phonological system, children abstract certain phonetic details and preserve others in their invented spellings.

Stages of Spelling Development

Based on Read's seminal work, other researchers began to systematically study the development of children's spelling abilities. Henderson and other researchers (Beers & Henderson, 1977; Gentry, 1981; Templeton, 1979; Zutell, 1979) have studied the manner in which children proceed developmentally from invented spelling to conventional spelling.

Based on observations of children's spellings, researchers have identified five stages that children move through on their way to becoming conventional spellers, and at each stage, they use different types of strategies. The stages are: emergent spelling, letter name spelling, within-word spelling, syllables and affixes spelling, and derivational relations spelling (Bear, Invernizzi, Templeton, & Johnston, 2004). The characteristics of each of the five stages of spelling development are summarized in the LA Essentials box on page 534.

Emergent Spelling.   Children string scribbles, letters, and letterlike forms together, but they do not associate the marks they make with any specific phonemes. Emergent spelling represents a natural, early expression of the alphabet and other concepts about writing. Children may write from left to right, right to left, top to bottom, or randomly across the page. Some emergent spellers have a large repertoire of letter forms to use in writing, whereas others repeat a small number of letters over and over. Children use both upper- and lowercase letters, but they show a distinct preference for uppercase letters. Toward the end of this stage, children are beginning to discover how spelling works and that letters represent sounds in words. This stage is typical of preschoolers, ages 3 to 5. During the emergent stage, children learn:

- The distinction between drawing and writing
- The formation of upper- and lowercase letters
- The direction of writing on a page
- Some letter-sound matches

Letter Name Spelling.   Children learn to represent phonemes in words with letters, indicating that they have a rudimentary understanding of the alphabetic

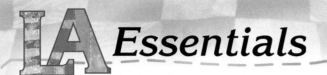

LA Essentials

Characteristics of the Stages of Spelling Development

Stage 1: Emergent Spelling

Children string scribbles, letters, and letterlike forms together, but they do not associate the marks they make with any specific phonemes. This stage is typical of 3- to 5-year-olds. Children learn:

- the difference between drawing and writing
- the formation of letters
- the direction of writing on a page
- some letter-sound matches

Stage 2: Letter Name Spelling

Children represent phonemes in words with letters. At first, their spellings are quite abbreviated, but they learn to use consonant blends and digraphs and short-vowel patterns to spell words. Spellers are 5- to 7-year-olds. Children learn:

- the alphabetic principle
- consonant sounds
- short-vowel sounds
- consonant blends and digraphs

Stage 3: Within-Word Spelling

Students learn long-vowel patterns and *r*-controlled vowels, but they may confuse spelling patterns and spell *meet* as *mete,* and they reverse the order of letters, such as *form* for *from* and *gril* for *girl.* Spellers are 7- to 9-year-olds, and they learn these concepts:

- long-vowel spelling patterns
- *r*-controlled vowels
- complex consonant patterns
- diphthongs

Stage 4: Syllables and Affixes Spelling

Students learn to spell multisyllabic words. They also add inflectional endings (e.g., *-es, -ed, -ing*), use apostrophes in contractions, and differentiate between homophones, such as *your–you're.* Spellers are often 9- to 11-year-olds, and they learn these concepts:

- inflectional endings
- syllabication
- contractions
- homophones
- possessives

Stage 5: Derivational Relations Spelling

Students explore the relationship between spelling and meaning and learn that words with related meanings are often related in spelling despite changes in sound (e.g., *wise–wisdom, sign–signal, nation–national*). They also learn about Latin and Greek root words and derivational affixes (e.g., *amphi-, pre-, -able, -tion*). Spellers are 11- to 14-year-olds. Students learn these concepts:

- consonant and vowel alternations
- Latin affixes and root words
- Greek affixes and root words
- etymologies

Adapted from Bear, Invernizzi, Templeton, and Johnston, 2004.

principle—that a link exists between letters and sounds. Spellings are quite abbreviated and represent only the most prominent features in words. Examples of stage 2 spelling are DA (day), KLZ (closed), BAD (bed), and CLEN (clean). Many children continue to write mainly with capital letters. These spellers use a letter-name strategy: They slowly pronounce words they want to write, listening for familiar letter names and sounds. Spellers at this stage are 5- to 7-year-olds. During the letter name stage, students learn:

- The alphabetic principle
- Consonant sounds
- Short-vowel sounds
- Consonant blends and digraphs

Within-Word Spelling.   Children's understanding of the alphabetic principle is further refined in this stage as they learn how to spell long-vowel patterns, diphthongs and the less common vowel patterns, and r-controlled vowels (Henderson, 1990). Examples of within-word spelling include LIEV (live), SOPE (soap), HUOSE (house), and BERN (burn). Students experiment with long-vowel patterns and learn that words such as *come* and *bread* are exceptions that do not fit the vowel patterns. Children may confuse spelling patterns and spell *meet* as METE, and they reverse the order of letters, such as FORM for *from* and GRIL for *girl*. Students also learn about complex consonant sounds, including *-tch* (*match*) and *-dge* (*judge*), and they learn about diphthongs (*oi/oy*) and other less common vowel patterns, including *au* (*caught*), *aw* (*saw*), *ew* (*sew, few*), *ou* (*house*), and *ow* (*cow*). Students also become aware of homophones and compare long- and short-vowel combinations (*hop–hope*) as they experiment with vowel patterns. Spellers at this stage are typically 7- to 9-year-olds, and they learn these spelling concepts:

- Long-vowel spelling patterns
- *R*-controlled vowels
- More complex consonant patterns
- Diphthongs and other less common vowel patterns

Syllables and Affixes Spelling.   The focus in this stage is on syllables and the spellings used where two syllables join together. Students apply what they have learned about one-syllable words to multisyllabic words, and they learn to break words into syllables. They learn about inflectional endings (*-s, -es, -ed,* and *-ing*) and rules about consonant doubling, changing the final *y* to *i,* or dropping the final *e* before adding an inflectional suffix. They also learn about homophones, compound words, possessives, and contractions. They learn some of the more common derivational prefixes and suffixes. Examples of syllables and affixes spelling include EAGUL (eagle), MONY (money), GETING (getting), BABYIES (babies), THEIR (there), CA'NT (can't), and BE CAUSE (because). Spellers in this stage are generally 9- to 11-year-olds. Students learn about these concepts during the syllables and affixes stage of spelling development:

- Inflectional endings (*-s, -es, -ed, -ing*)
- Syllabication
- Contractions
- Homophones
- Possessives

Derivational Relations Spelling. Students explore the relationship between spelling and meaning during the derivational relations stage, and they learn that words with related meanings are often related in spelling despite changes in vowel and consonant sounds (e.g., *wise–wisdom, sign–signal, nation–national*) (Templeton, 1983). Examples of spelling errors include: CRITISIZE (criticize), APPEARENCE (appearance), and COMMITTE or COMMITEE (committee). The focus in this stage is on morphemes, and students learn about Greek and Latin root words and affixes. They also begin to examine etymologies and the role of history in shaping how words are spelled. They learn about eponyms (words from people's names), such as *maverick* and *sandwich*. Spellers at this stage are 11- to 14-year-olds. Students learn these concepts at this stage of spelling development:

- Consonant alternations (e.g., *soft–soften, magic–magician*)
- Vowel alternations (e.g., *please–pleasant, define–definition, explain–explanation*)
- Greek and Latin affixes and root words
- Etymologies

Teachers do many things to scaffold children's spelling development as they move through the stages of spelling development, and the kind of support they provide depends on students' stage of development. As young children scribble, for example, teachers encourage them to use pencils, not crayons, for writing, to differentiate between drawing and writing. Letter name spellers notice words in their environment, and teachers help children use these familiar words to choose letters to represent the sounds in the words they are writing. As students enter the syllables and affixes stage, teachers teach syllabication rules, and in the derivational relations stage, they teach students about root words and the variety of words created from a single Latin or Greek root word. For example, from the Latin root word *-ann* or *-enn*, meaning "year," students learn these words: *annual, centennial, biannual, millennium, anniversary, perennial,* and *sesquicentennial.* Figure 12–1 presents a list of guidelines for supporting children's spelling development at each stage.

Analyzing Children's Spelling Development

Teachers analyze the spelling errors in children's compositions by classifying them according to the five stages of spelling development. This analysis will provide information about the child's current level of spelling development and the kinds of errors the child makes. Knowing the stage of a student's spelling development helps teachers choose the appropriate type of instruction.

A personal journal entry written by Marc, a first grader, is presented in the Weaving Assessment Into Practice feature on page 539. He reverses *d* and *s,* and these two reversals make his writing more difficult to decipher. Here is a translation of Marc's composition:

Today a person at home called us and said that a bomb was in our school and made us go outside and made us wait a half of an hour and it made us waste our time on learning. The end.

Marc was writing about a traumatic event, and it was appropriate for him to use invented spelling in his journal entry. Primary-grade students should write using

Ways to Support Children's Spelling at Each Stage of Development

Stage 1: Emergent Spelling
Allow the child to experiment with making and placing marks on the paper.
Suggest that the child write with a pencil and draw with a crayon.
Model how adults write.
Point out the direction of print in books.
Encourage the child to notice letters in names and environmental print.
Ask the child to talk about what he or she has written.

Stage 2: Letter Name Spelling
Sing the alphabet song and name letters of the alphabet with children.
Show the child how to form letters in names and other common words.
Demonstrate how to say a word slowly, stretch it out, and isolate beginning, middle, and ending sounds in the word.
Use Elkonin boxes to segment words into beginning, middle, and ending sounds.
Post high-frequency words on a word wall.
Teach lessons on consonants, consonant digraphs, and short vowels.
Write sentences using interactive writing.

Stage 3: Within-Word Spelling
Teach lessons on long-vowel spelling rules, vowel digraphs, and *r*-controlled vowels.
Encourage students to develop visualization skills in order to recognize whether a word "looks" right.
Teach students to spell irregular high-frequency words.
Focus on silent letters in one-syllable words (e.g., *k*now, li*gh*t).
Have students sort words according to spelling patterns.
Have students make words using magnetic letters and letter cards.
Introduce proofreading so students can identify and correct misspelled words in compositions.
Write sentences using interactive writing.

Stage 4: Syllables and Affixes Spelling
Teach students to divide words into syllables and the rules for adding inflectional endings.
Teach schwa sound and spelling patterns (e.g., *handle*).
Teach homophones, contractions, compound words, and possessives.
Sort two-syllable words and homophones.
Have students make words using letter cards.
Teach proofreading skills and encourage students to proofread all writings.

Stage 5: Derivational Relations
Teach root words and derivational affixes.
Make clusters with a root word in the center and related words on rays.
Teach students to identify words with English, Latin, and Greek spellings.
Sort words according to roots or language of origin.
Have students check the etymologies of words in a dictionary.

invented spelling, and correct spelling is appropriate when the composition will "go public." Prematurely differentiating between "kid" and "adult" spelling interferes with children's natural spelling development and makes them dependent on adults to supply the adult spelling.

Spelling can be categorized using a chart, also shown in the feature on page 539, to gauge students' spelling development and to anticipate upcoming changes in their spelling strategies. Teachers write the stages of spelling development across the top of the chart and list each misspelled word in the student's composition under one of the categories, ignoring proper nouns. When teachers are scoring young children's spellings, they often ignore capitalization errors and poorly formed or reversed letters, but when scoring older students' spellings these errors are considered.

Perhaps the most interesting thing about Marc's writing is that he spelled half the words correctly even though at first reading it might seem that he spelled very few words correctly. Marc wrote this paper in January of his first-grade year, and his spellings are typical of first graders. Of his misspellings, eight were categorized as letter name spelling, and another eight were within-word spellings. This score suggests that he is moving into the within-word stage.

Marc is clearly using a sounding-out strategy, which is best typified by his spelling of the word *learning*. His errors suggest that he is ready to learn CVCe and other long-vowel spelling patterns and *r*-controlled vowels. Marc spells some high-frequency words phonetically, so he would benefit from more exposure to high-frequency words, such as *was* and *of*. Marc also spelled *today* and *outside* as separate words, so he is ready to learn about compound words.

Marc pronounced the word MAKBE as "maked" and the DE is a reversal of letters, a common characteristic of within-word spelling. Based on this categorization of Marc's spelling errors, he would benefit from instruction on high-frequency words, the CVCe long-vowel spelling pattern, *r*-controlled vowels, and compound words. His teacher should also monitor his *b/d* and *s/z* reversal problem to see if it disappears with more writing practice. It is important, of course, to base instructional recommendations on more than one writing sample. Teachers should look at three or more samples to be sure the recommendations are valid.

Older students' spelling can also be analyzed the same way. Fifth-grade Eugenio wrote the "Why My Mom Is Special" essay shown in the Weaving Assessment Into Practice feature on page 540. Eugenio is Hispanic; his native language is Spanish, but he is now fully proficient in English. His writing is more sophisticated than Marc's, and the spelling errors he makes reflect both his use of longer, more complex words and his pronunciation of English sounds.

All but one of Eugenio's spelling errors are classified at either the within-word stage or the syllables and affixes stage. His other error, classified at the letter name stage, is probably an accident because when he was asked, he could spell the word correctly.

Eugenio's within-word stage errors involve more complex consonant and vowel spelling patterns. Eugenio has moved beyond spelling *because* as BECUZ, but he still must learn to replace the *u* with *au* and the *z* with *s*. His spelling of *shoes* as SHOSE is interesting because he has reversed the last two letters. He doesn't recognize that, however, when he is questioned. Instead, his focus is on representing the /sh/ and the /oo/ sounds correctly. His spelling of both *school* and *career* seem to be influenced by his pronunciation. The /sh/ sound

An Analysis of a First Grader's Spelling

Tobay a perezun at home kob
uz anb seb that a bome wuz in
on skuwl anb mab uz go at zib
anb makbe uz wat a haf uf
a awr anb it mab uz wazt on
time on loren ee ing.

THE eNb

Emergent	Letter Name	Within-Words	Syllables and Affixes	Derivational Relations
	KOB/called	BOME/bomb	TO BAY/today	
	SEB/said	OR/our	PEREZUN/person	
	WUZ/was	SKUWL/school	MAKBE/maked	
	MAB/made	AT SIB/outside		
	WAT/wait	UF/of		
	HAF/half	AWR/hour		
	MAB/made	OR/our		
	WAZT/waste	LORENEEING/learning		

Data Analysis		Conclusions
Emergent	0	Marc's spelling is at the Letter Name and Within-Word stages. From his misspellings, he is ready for the following instruction:
Letter Name	8	
Within Word	8	• high-frequency words
Syllables and Affixes	3	• CVCe spellings
Derivational Relations	0	• r-controlled vowels
Correctly spelled words	22	• compound words
Total words in sample	41	He also reverses *b/d* and *s/z*.

An Analysis of a Fifth Grader's Spelling

My mom is specil to me. she gave me everething when I was small. When she gets some mony she byes me pizza. My mom is specil to me becuze she taks me anywhere I want to get some nike shose. She byes me some.

My mom changed my life. She is so nice and loveble. She cares what I am doing in shool. She cares about my grades. I will do anything for mom. I would get a ceriar. Maybe I could be a polisman. That is why I think she is so nice.

Emergent	Letter Name	Within-Words	Syllables and Affixes	Derivational Relations
	TAKS/takes	BECUZE/because SHOSE/shoes SHOOL/school CERIAR/career POLISMAN/policeman	SPECIL/special EVERETHING/everything MONY/money BYES/buys SPECIL/special BYES/buys LOVEBLE/lovable	

Data Analysis

Emergent	0
Letter Name	1
Within Word	5
Syllables and Affixes	7
Derivational Relations	0
Correctly spelled words	82
Total words in sample	95

Conclusions

Eugenio's spelling is at the syllables and affixes stage. Based on this sample, this instruction is suggested:

- dividing words into syllables
- compound words
- using *y* at the end of 1- and 2-syllable words
- homophones
- suffixes

is difficult for him, as it is for many children whose first language is Spanish, and he doesn't recognize that *school* begins with /sk/, not /sh/. Eugenio pronounces the first syllable of *career* as he spelled it, and he explains that it was a hard word but it looks right to him. These comments suggest that Eugenio understands that spelling has both phonetic and visual properties. In the word *policeman,* Eugenio used *s* rather than *ce* to represent the /s/. Even though it is a compound word, this word is classified at this level because the error has to do with spelling a complex consonant sound.

The largest number of Eugenio's spelling errors fall in the syllables and affixes stage. Most of his errors at this stage deal with spelling multisyllabic words. In SPECIL, Eugenio has misspelled the schwa sound, the vowel sound in unaccented syllables of multisyllabic words. In *everything,* Eugenio wrote *e* instead of *y* at the end of *every.* What he did not understand is that the long *e* sound at the end of a two-syllable word is usually represented by *y.* Eugenio spelled *money* as MONY. It's interesting that he used *y* to represent the long *e* sound here, but in this case, *ey* is needed. BYES for *buys* is a homophone error, and all homophone errors are classified as this stage even though they are one-syllable words. Eugenio's other spelling error at this stage is LOVEBLE. Here he added the suffix -*able* but misspelled it. He wasn't aware that he added a suffix. When he was asked about it, he explained that he sounded it out and wrote the sounds that he heard. It is likely that he also knows about the -*ble* end-of-word spelling pattern because if he had spelled the suffix phonetically, he probably would have written LOVEBUL.

Even though Eugenio has a number of errors at both the within word and syllables and affixes stages, Eugenio's spelling can be classified at the syllables and affixes stage because most of his errors are at that stage. Based on this one writing sample, it appears that he would benefit from instruction on dividing words into syllables, compound words, using *y* at the end of one- and two-syllable words, homophones, and suffixes. These instructional recommendations should not be based on only one writing sample; they should be validated by examining several other writing samples.

TEACHING SPELLING IN THE ELEMENTARY GRADES

The goal of spelling instruction is to help students develop what Hillerich (1977) calls a "spelling conscience"—a positive attitude toward spelling and a concern for using standard spelling. Two dimensions of a spelling conscience are understanding that standard spelling is a courtesy to readers and developing the ability to proofread to spot and correct misspellings.

Students need to learn that it is unrealistic to expect readers to try to decipher numerous misspelled words. This dimension of a spelling conscience develops as students write frequently and for varied audiences. As students move from writing for themselves to writing to communicate with others, they internalize this concept. Teachers help students recognize the purpose of conventional spelling by providing meaningful writing activities directed to a variety of genuine audiences.

Components of the Spelling Program

A comprehensive spelling program has 10 components, including reading and writing opportunities, making-words activities, proofreading, and using the dictionary. These components are summarized in the LA Essentials box on page 543.

Daily Writing Opportunities.   Providing opportunities for students to write every day is prerequisite to any spelling program. Spelling is a writer's tool, and it is best learned through the experience of writing. Students who write daily and invent spellings for unfamiliar words move naturally toward conventional spelling. When they write, children guess at spellings using their developing knowledge of sound-symbol correspondences and spelling patterns. Most of the informal writing students do each day doesn't need to be graded, and spelling errors should not be marked. Learning to spell is a lot like learning to play the piano. These daily writing opportunities are the practice sessions, not the lesson with the teacher.

When students use the writing process to develop and polish their writings, emphasis on conventional spelling belongs in the editing stage. Through the process approach, children learn to recognize spelling for what it is—a courtesy to readers. As they write, revise, edit, and share their writing with genuine audiences, students understand that they need to spell conventionally so that their audience can read their compositions.

Daily Reading Opportunities.   Reading plays an enormous role in students' learning to spell. As they read, students store the visual shapes of words. The ability to recall how words look helps students decide when a spelling they are writing is correct. When students decide that a word doesn't look right, they can rewrite the word several ways until it does look right, ask the teacher or a classmate who knows the spelling, or check the spelling in a dictionary.

To read more about word walls, turn back to Chapter 5, "Looking Closely at Words."

Word Walls.   One way to direct students' attention to words in books they are reading or in social studies and science theme cycles is through the use of word walls. Students and the teacher choose words to write on word walls, large sheets of paper hanging in the classroom. Then students refer to these word walls for word-study activities and when they are writing. Seeing the words posted on word walls, clusters, and other charts in the classroom and using them in their writing help students learn to spell the words.

Teachers also hang word walls with high-frequency words (Cunningham, 1995; Marinelli, 1996). Researchers have identified the most commonly used words and recommend that elementary students learn to spell 100 to 500 of these words because of their usefulness. The 100 most frequently used words represent more than 50% of all the words children and adults write (Horn, 1926)! Figure 12–2 lists the 100 most frequently used words, and Figure 12–3 presents a second list of 100 useful words for students in the middle and upper grades. Some teachers type the alphabetized word list on small cards—personal word walls—that students keep at their desks to refer to when they write (Lacey, 1994).

Making Words.   Students arrange and rearrange a group of letter cards to spell words (Cunningham & Cunningham, 1992). Primary-grade students can use the letters s, p, i, d, e, and r to spell *is, red, dip, rip, sip, side, ride,* and *ripe.*

Essentials

Components of a Comprehensive Spelling Program

1. **Writing**

   Students write informally in journals and use the writing process to draft, revise, and edit writing every day.

2. **Reading**

   Students develop visual images of words as they read a variety of books each day.

3. **Word Walls**

   Students and the teacher post high-frequency words, words related to books they are reading, and words related to theme cycles in alphabetical order on word walls in the classroom.

4. **Making Words**

   Students participate in making-words activities in which they arrange letter cards to spell increasingly longer and more complex words.

5. **Word Sorts**

   Students sort word cards into two or more categories to focus on particular spelling patterns.

6. **Proofreading**

   Students learn to proofread their own compositions to locate and then correct spelling errors.

7. **Dictionaries**

   Students learn to use dictionaries to locate the spellings of unknown words.

8. **Spelling Options**

   Students explore the variety of ways phonemes are spelled in English in order to know options they have for spelling sounds in words.

9. **Root Words and Affixes**

   Students learn about root words and affixes and use that knowledge to spell multisyllabic words.

10. **Spelling Strategies**

    Students learn strategies, including "think it out," to spell unknown words.

FIGURE 12-2   *The 100 Most Frequently Used Words*

A	B	C	D	E
a and about are after around all as am at an	back be because but by	came can could	day did didn't do don't down	

F	G	H	I	J
for from	get got	had his have home he house her how him	I into if is in it	just

K	L	M	N	O
know	like little	man me mother my	no not now	of our on out one over or

P	QR	S	T	U
people put		said saw school see she so some	that think the this them time then to there too they two things	up us

V	W	X	Y	Z
very	was when we who well will went with were would what		you your	

With the letters *t, e, m, p, e, r, a, t, u, r,* and *e,* a class of fifth graders spelled these words:

> *1-letter words:* a
>
> *2-letter words:* at, up
>
> *3-letter words:* pet, are, rat, eat, ate, tap, pat
>
> *4-letter words:* ramp, rate, pare, pear, meat, meet, team, tree
>
> *5-letter words:* treat
>
> *6-letter words:* temper, tamper, mature, repeat, turret
>
> *7-letter words:* trumpet, rapture
>
> *8-letter words:* repeater
>
> *9-letter words:* temperate, trumpeter

FIGURE 12-3   *100 High-Frequency Words for Older Students*

A	B	C	D	E
a lot	beautiful	caught	decided	either
again	because	certain	desert-dessert	embarrassed
all right	belief	close-clothes	different	enough
although	believe	committee	discussed	especially
another	beneath	complete	doesn't	etc.
anything	between			everything
around	board-bored			everywhere
	breathe			excellent
	brought			experience
F	**G**	**H**	**I**	**J**
familiar		hear-here	immediately	
favorite		heard-herd	interesting	
field		height	it's-its	
finally		herself		
foreign		himself		
friends		humorous		
frighten		hungry		
K	**L**	**M**	**N**	**O**
knew-new	language	maybe	necessary	once
know-no	lying		neighbor	ourselves
knowledge				
P	**QR**	**S**	**T**	**U**
particular	quiet-quite	safety	their-there-they're	until
people	really	school	themselves	usually
piece-peace	receive	separate	though	
please	recommend	serious	thought	
possible	remember	since	threw-through	
probably	restaurant	special	throughout	
	right-write	something	to-two-too	
		success	together	
V	**W**	**X**	**Y**	**Z**
	weight		your-you're	
	were			
	we're			
	where			
	whether			
	whole-hole			

The procedure for making words is explained in the Step by Step feature on page 546.

Teachers often introduce making words as a whole-class lesson and then set the cards and the word list in a center for students to use again independently or in small groups. Teachers can use almost any words for making-words activities, but words related to literature focus units and theme cycles work best. The words *spider* and *temperature* were selected from science theme cycles.

Step by Step

Making Words

1. **Make letter cards.**   Teachers prepare a set of small letter cards (1- to 2-inch square cards) for students to use in word-making activities. For high-frequency letters (vowels, *s, t,* and *r*), they make three or four times as many letter cards as there are students in the class. For less frequently used letters, teachers make one or two times as many letter cards as there are students in the class. They print the lowercase letter form on one side of the letter cards and the uppercase form on the other side. They package cards with each letter separately in small boxes, plastic trays, or plastic bags. Teachers may also want to make a set of larger letter cards (3- to 6-inch square cards) to display in a pocket chart or on a chalk tray during the activity.

2. **Choose a word for the activity.**   Teachers choose a word or spelling pattern to use in the word-making activity and have a student distribute the needed letter cards to individual students or to small groups of students.

3. **Name the letter cards.**   Teachers ask students to name the letter cards and arrange them on one side of their desks.

4. **Make words using the cards.**   Students use the letter cards to spell a particular word or words containing two, three, four, five, six, or more letters or using a particular spelling pattern. For example, students might use letter cards (*a, d, g, i, n, n, o, s, t, t, u*) to spell these three-letter words: *sit, tan, out, not, and, dog.* Then students use the same letter cards to spell four-letter words (e.g., *sing, nuts, said*), five-letter words (e.g., *stand, doing, giant*), and longer words until they use all of the letters to spell *outstanding.* Or, with a different set of cards, students might spell *at* and then add a beginning letter to spell *cat, hat,* or another rhyming word. With other letter cards, students might spell *rid* and *fed* and then change the words to *ride* and *feed* to practice ways to spell long-vowel sounds. The teacher monitors students' spellings and encourages them to fix any misspelled words. As students spell the words, a student or the teacher can arrange the large letter cards to spell the same words or record the spellings on chart paper or on the chalkboard.

5. **Share word cards.**   Teachers show word cards with some of the words that students have made. They ask students to read the words and place them in a pocket chart or on the chalk tray. After reading all of the words, teachers point out particular spelling patterns and group the word cards according to the patterns.

FIGURE 12-4 *A Word Sort on* R-Controlled Vowels

ar	are	air	ar + e	others
shark	hare	chair	large	are
yard	square	stairs	carve	heart
jar	bare	flair		their
sharp		hair		there
hard		pair		bear

Word Sorts.   Students use word sorts to compare and contrast spelling patterns as they sort a pack of word cards. Teachers prepare word cards for students to sort into two or more categories according to vowel patterns, affixes, root words, or another spelling concept (Bear et al., 2004). Sometimes teachers tell students what categories to use, making the sort a closed sort; at other times, students determine the categories themselves, making the sort an open sort. Students can sort word cards and then return them to an envelope for future use, or they can glue the cards onto a sheet of paper. Figure 12–4 shows a word sort for *r*-controlled vowels. In this sort, students work in small groups to pronounce the words and sort them according to how the *r*-controlled vowel is spelled.

Proofreading.   Proofreading is a special kind of reading that students use to locate misspelled words and other mechanical errors in their rough drafts. As

Making words. *These second graders are using small plastic letters to spell words. Children often benefit more by manipulating plastic letters than by writing lists of words—in part because making words is a fun, playlike activity and partly because students actually do spell more words this way than through more traditional spelling activities. Through making words, children examine spelling patterns and practice spelling high-frequency words. When teachers participate in the activity by asking children to switch letters or substitute one letter for another, they take advantage of teachable moments.*

See Chapter 3, "The Reading and Writing Processes," to read more about proofreading and editing.

students learn about the writing process, they are introduced to proofreading. In the editing stage, they receive more in-depth instruction about how to use proofreading to locate spelling errors and then correct these misspelled words (Wilde, 1996). Through a series of minilessons, students can proofread sample student papers and mark misspelled words. Then, working in pairs, students can correct the misspelled words.

Proofreading should be introduced in the primary grades. Young children and their teachers proofread class collaboration and dictated stories together, and students can be encouraged to read over their own compositions and make necessary corrections soon after they begin writing. In this way, students accept proofreading as a natural part of both spelling and writing. Proofreading activities are more valuable for teaching spelling than dictation activities, in which teachers dictate sentences for students to write and correctly capitalize and punctuate. Few people use dictation in their daily lives, but students use proofreading skills every time they polish a piece of writing.

To learn more about children's dictionaries, turn back to Chapter 5, "Looking Closely at Words."

Dictionaries. Students need to learn how to locate the spelling of unknown words in the dictionary. Of the approximately 750,000 entry words in an unabridged dictionary, students typically learn to spell 3,000 through weekly spelling tests by the end of eighth grade—leaving 747,000 words unaccounted for! Obviously, students must learn how to locate the spellings of some additional words. Although it is relatively easy to find a "known" word in the dictionary, it is hard to locate an unfamiliar word, and students need to learn what to do when they don't know how to spell a word. One approach is to predict possible spellings for unknown words, then check the most probable spellings in a dictionary. This procedure involves six steps:

1. Identify root words and affixes.
2. Consider related words (e.g., *medicine–medical*).
3. Determine the sounds in the word.
4. Generate a list of possible spellings.
5. Select the most probable alternatives.
6. Consult a dictionary to check the correct spelling.

The fourth step, during which students develop a list of possible spellings using their knowledge of both phonology and morphology, is undoubtedly the most difficult. Phoneme-grapheme relationships may rate primary consideration in generating spelling options for some words; root words and affixes or related words may be more important in determining how other words are spelled.

Spelling Options. In English, there are alternative spellings for many sounds because so many words borrowed from other languages retain their native spellings. There are many more options for vowel sounds than for consonants. Even so, there are four spelling options for /f/(*f, ff, ph, gh*). Spelling options sometimes vary according to position in a syllable or word. For example, *ff* and *gh* are used to represent /f/ only at the end of a syllable or word, as in *cuff* and *laughter.* Common spelling options for phonemes are listed in Figure 12–5.

Teachers point out spelling options as they write words on word walls and when students ask about the spelling of a word. They can also use a series of minilessons to teach upper-grade students about these options. During each minilesson, students focus on one phoneme, such as /f/ or /ar/, and as a class or small group develop a list of the various ways the sound is spelled in English, giving examples of each spelling. A sixth-grade chart on long *i* is presented in Figure 12–6 with lists of one-syllable and multisyllable words. The location of the long *i* sound in the word is also marked on the chart.

Root Words and Affixes.   Students learn about roots and affixes as they read and spell longer, multisyllabic words. Teaching root words helps students unlock meaning when they read and spell the words correctly when they write. Consider the Latin root word *terra,* meaning "earth." Middle- and upper-grade students learn to read and spell these *terra* words and phrases: *terrarium, all-terrain vehicles, subterranean, territory, terrace,* and *terrier dogs.* Lessons about root words merge instruction about vocabulary and spelling.

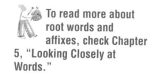 To read more about root words and affixes, check Chapter 5, "Looking Closely at Words."

Children learn to spell inflectional suffixes, such as the plural -*s* marker and the past tense -*ed* marker, in the primary grades, and in the middle and upper grades, they learn about derivational prefixes and suffixes and how they affect meaning. They learn to recognize the related forms of a root word, for example: *educate, uneducated, educator, education, educational.*

Students also learn rules for spelling suffixes. For example, the -*able* suffix is added to *read* to spell *readable,* but the -*ible* suffix is added to *leg-* (a Latin root word that is not a word in English) to spell *legible.* The rule is that -*able* is added to complete words and -*ible* is added to word parts. In other words, such

FIGURE 12–5

Common Spelling Options for Phonemes

Sound	Spellings	Examples	Sound	Spellings	Examples
long a	a-e	date	short oo	oo	book
	a	angel		u	put
	ai	aid		ou	could
	ay	day		o	woman
ch	ch	church	ou	ou	out
	t(u)	picture		ow	cow
	tch	watch	s	s	sick
	ti	question		ce	office
long e	ea	each		c	city
	ee	feel		ss	class
	e	evil		se	else
	e-e	these		x(ks)	box
	ea-e	breathe	sh	ti	attention
short e	e	end		sh	she
	ea	head		ci	ancient
f	f	feel		ssi	admission
	ff	sheriff	t	t	teacher
	gh	cough		te	definite
	ph	photograph		ed	furnished
j	ge	strange		tt	attend
	g	general	long u	u	union
	j	job		u-e	use
	dge	bridge		ue	value
k	c	call		ew	few
	k	keep	short u	u	ugly
	x	expect, luxury		o	company
	ck	black		ou	country
	qu	quite, bouquet		u	union
l	l	last		u-e	use
	ll	allow	y	y	yes
	le	automobile		i	onion
m	m	man		ue	value
	me	come		ew	few
	mm	comment	z	z	zoo
n	n	no		s	present
	ne	done		se	applause
long o	o	go		ze	gauze
	o-e	note	syllabic l	le	able
	ow	own		al	animal
	oa	load		el	cancel
short o	o	office		il	civil
	a	all	syllabic n	en	written
	au	author		on	lesson
	aw	saw		an	important
oi	oi	oil		in	cousin
	oy	boy		contractions	didn't
long oo	u	cruel		ain	certain
	oo	noon	r-controlled	er	her
	u-e	rule		ur	church
	o-e	lose		ir	first
	ue	blue		or	world
	o	to		ear	heard
	ou	group		our	courage

FIGURE 12-6 *Sixth Graders' Chart of Spelling Options for Long* i

Spelling	Examples	Location		
		Initial	Medial	Final
i	child, climb, blind, wild, hire		x	
	idea, Friday, microwave, lion, gigantic, rhinoceros, variety, triangle, siren, liar, rabbi	x	x	x
i-e	smile, bride, drive, write		x	
	criticize, impolite, beehive, paradise, valentine, capsize, ninety, sniper, united, decide		x	x
ie	pies, lie, die		x	x
	untie			x
ei	none			
	feisty, seismograph		x	
igh	high, sight, knight, bright		x	x
	knighthood, sunlight		x	
eigh	height		x	
	none			
y	why, my, by, try, fly			x
	July, nylon, crying, xylophone, unicycle, notify, dynamite, skyscraper, hydrogen		x	x
y-e	byte, types, hype, rhyme		x	x
	paralyze, stylist		x	x
ye	dye, rye			x
	goodbye			x
eye	eye			x
	eyeball, eyelash	x		
ui	none			
	guidance		x	
ui-e	guide			x
	none			
uy	guy, buy			x
	buyer		x	

as *lovable,* the final *e* in *love* is dropped before adding *-able* because *a* serves the same function in the word, and in *huggable,* the *g* is doubled before adding *-able* because the *u* in *hug* is short. Through a combination of wide reading and minilessons, students learn about root words and affixes, and they use this knowledge to expand their vocabularies.

Turn back to Chapter 1, "Learning and the Language Arts," to learn more about strategies.

Spelling Strategies.   Students need to develop a repertoire of strategies in order to spell unfamiliar words (Laminack & Wood, 1996; Wilde, 1993). Some of these spelling strategies are:

- Inventing spellings for words, based on phonological, semantic, and historical knowledge of words.
- Proofreading to locate and correct spelling errors.
- Locating words on word walls and other charts.
- Predicting the spelling of a word by generating possible spellings and choosing the best alternative.
- Breaking words into syllables and spelling each syllable.
- Applying affixes to root words.
- Spelling unknown words by analogy to known words.
- Locating the spelling of unfamiliar words in a dictionary or other resource book.
- Writing a string of letters as a placeholder to stand for an unfamiliar word in a rough draft.
- Asking the teacher or a classmate how to spell a word.

Instead of giving the traditional "sound it out" advice when students ask how to spell an unfamiliar word, teachers should help them use a strategic approach: Teachers should encourage students to "think it out." This advice reminds students that spelling involves more than phonological information and suggests a more strategic approach.

Minilessons

Teachers teach students about spelling procedures, concepts, and strategies and skills during minilessons. A list of topics for spelling minilessons is presented on pages 554 and 555, along with a second grade teacher's minilesson on the "think it out" strategy.

Weekly Spelling Tests

Many teachers question the use of spelling tests to teach spelling, because research on children's spelling development suggests that spelling is best learned through reading and writing (Gentry & Gillet, 1993; Wilde, 1993). In addition, teachers complain that lists of spelling words are unrelated to the words students are reading and writing, and the 30 minutes of valuable instructional time spent each day in completing spelling textbook activities is excessive. Weekly spelling tests, when they are used, should be individualized so that children learn to spell the words they need for their writing.

In an individualized approach to spelling instruction, students choose the words they will study, and many of the words they choose are words they use in their writing projects. Students study five to eight specific words during the

Seeing Common Threads

Why aren't spelling tests a complete spelling program?

Deby Wyrick responds:

Every teacher can tell you stories about students who get 100% on every spelling test and spell the same words wrong in their daily writing. This waves a big red flag that something is not working and that something is standardized spelling tests. Effective teachers use more than just spelling tests to teach spelling and they use more than scores on spelling tests to assess students' learning. Effective teachers are assessing where their students are and are scaffolding them to the next step developmentally with appropriate instructional strategies. Students spell words according to their stage of spelling development and teachers can assess students' development using samples of their writing to see what progress has been made. From these assessments teachers can develop a comprehensive spelling program for each student.

What do you think?

Each chapter presents a question and a response written by one of Dr. Tompkins's students. Consider other comments, or respond to the question yourself, by visiting the Threaded Message Board in Chapter 12 on the Companion Website at www.prenhall.com/tompkins

Companion Website

week using a specific study strategy. This approach places more responsibility on students for their own learning, and when students have responsibility, they tend to perform better. The guidelines for using individualized spelling tests are provided in the LA Essentials box on page 556.

Teachers develop a weekly word list of 25 to 50 words of varying levels of difficulty from which students select words to study. Words for the master list are drawn from words students needed for their writing projects during the previous week, high-frequency words, and words related to literature focus units and theme cycles ongoing in the classroom. Words from spelling textbooks can also be added to the list, but they should never make up the entire list. The master word list can be used for minilessons during the week. Students can look for phoneme-grapheme correspondences, add words to charts of spelling options, and note root words and affixes.

On Monday, the teacher administers the pretest using the master list of words, and students spell as many of the words as they can. Students correct their own pretests, and from the words they misspell, each student chooses 5 to 10 words to study. They make two copies of their study list. Students number their spelling words using the numbers on the master list to make it easier to take the final test on Friday. Students keep one copy of the list to study, and the teacher keeps the second copy.

Researchers have found that the pretest is a critical component in learning to spell. The pretest eliminates words that students already know how to spell

Piecing a Lesson Together

Topics on Spelling

Procedures	Concepts	Strategies and Skills
Locate words on a word wall	Alphabetic principle	Invent spellings
Locate words in a dictionary	"Kid" or invented	Use placeholders
Use a thesaurus	spelling	Sound it out
Study a spelling word	Homophones	
Analyze spelling errors	Root words and affixes	*Think it out*
	Spelling options	Visualize words
	High-frequency words	Spell by analogy
	Dictionary	Apply affixes
	Thesaurus	Proofread
	Contractions	Apply capitalization rules
	Compound words	
	Possessives	

Please visit the Companion Website at **www.prenhall.com/tompkins** for a second fully realized minilesson.

so that they can direct their study toward words that they don't know yet. More than half a century ago, Ernest Horn recommended that the best way to improve students' spelling was for them to get immediate feedback by correcting their own pretests. His advice is still sound today.

Students spend approximately 5 to 10 minutes studying the words on their study lists each day during the week. Research shows that instead of busywork activities, such as using their spelling words in sentences or gluing yarn in the

"THINK IT OUT"

Minilesson

Mrs. Hamilton Teaches the "Think It Out" Strategy to Her Second Graders

1. **Introduce the Topic**

   Mrs. Hamilton asks her second graders how to spell the word *because,* and they suggest these options: *beecuz, becauz, becuse,* and *becuzz.* She asks the students to explain their spellings. Aaron explains that he sounded the word out and heard *bee* and *cuz.* Molly explains that she knows there is no *z* in *because* so she spelled it *becuse.* Other students explain that they say the word slowly, listening for all the sounds, and then write the sounds they hear. Mrs. Hamilton explains that this is a good first-grade strategy, but now she is going to teach them an even more important second-grade strategy called "think it out."

2. **Share Examples**

   Mrs. Hamilton asks students to observe as she spells the word *make.* She says the word slowly and writes *mak* on the chalkboard. Then she explains, "I sounded the word out and wrote the sounds I heard, but I don't think the word is spelled right because it looks funny." The children agree and eagerly raise their hands to supply the right answer. "No," she says, "I want to 'think it out.' Let's see. Hmmm. Well, there are vowel rules. The *a* is long so I could add an *e* at the end of the word." The students clap, happy that she has figured out the spelling of the word. She models

the process two more times, spelling *great* and *running.*

3. **Provide Information**

   Mrs. Hamilton shares a chart she has made with the steps in the "think it out" strategy:

   1. Sound the word out and spell it the best you can.
   2. Think about spelling rules to add.
   3. Look at the word to see if it looks right.
   4. If it doesn't look right, try to change some letters, ask for help, or check the dictionary.

   The students talk about how Mrs. Hamilton used the strategy to spell *make, great,* and *running.*

4. **Supervise Practice**

   Mrs. Hamilton passes out white boards and dry-erase pens for the students to use as they practice the strategy. The students write *time, what, walked, taking, bread,* and *people* using the "think it out" strategy. As they move through each step, they hold up their white boards to show Mrs. Hamilton their work.

5. **Reflect on Learning**

   Mrs. Hamilton ends the minilesson by asking students what they learned, and they explain that they learned the grown-up way to spell words. They explain the steps this way: First they sound it out, then they look it out, and then they think it out.

shape of the words, it is more effective for students to use this strategy for practicing spelling words:

1. Look at the word and say it to yourself.
2. Say each letter in the word to yourself.
3. Close your eyes and spell the word to yourself.
4. Write the word, and check that you spelled it correctly.
5. Write the word again, and check that you spelled it correctly.

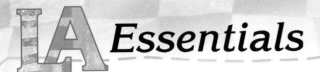 *Essentials*

Guidelines for Individualized Spelling Tests

1. **Master List**

   Teachers prepare a master list of 20–50 words, depending on students' grade level and the range of spelling levels in the classroom. Words on the list are drawn from spelling textbooks, words students misspell in their writing, and spelling skills being taught and reviewed.

2. **Pretest**

   On Monday, students take a pretest of the 20–50 words on the master list, and they self-correct their pretests immediately after they take them using red pens.

3. **Words to Study**

   Students choose 5 to 10 words to study from the words they misspelled on the pretest.

4. **Study Lists**

   Students make two study lists, one to take home and one to use at school.

5. **Study Strategy**

   Students use this strategy to study the words each day during the week:

   Look at the word and say it to yourself.
   Say each letter in the word to yourself.
   Close your eyes and spell the word to yourself.
   Write the word, and check that you spelled it correctly.
   Write the word again, and check that you spelled it correctly.

   They study their spelling words this way rather than by writing sentences or stories using the words.

6. **Practice Test**

   Students work with a partner to give each other a practice test during the week to check their progress in learning to spell the words.

7. **Posttest**

   On Friday, students take a posttest of the words they have practiced. Teachers collect the tests and grade them themselves.

8. **Next Week's Words**

   Teachers make a list of words that students misspell to include on their master list for the following week.

This strategy focuses on the whole word rather than breaking it apart into sounds or syllables. During a minilesson at the beginning of the school year, teachers explain how to use the strategy, and then they post a copy of the strategy in the classroom. In addition to this word-study strategy, sometimes students trade word lists with a partner on Wednesday or Thursday and give each other a practice test.

A final test is administered on Friday. The teacher reads the master list, and students write only those words they have practiced during the week. To make it easier to administer the test, students first list the numbers of the words they have practiced from their study lists on their test papers. Any words that students misspell should be included on their lists the following week.

This individualized approach is recommended instead of a textbook approach. Typically, textbooks are arranged in weeklong units, with lists of 10 to 20 words and practice activities that often require at least 30 minutes per day to complete. Research indicates that only 60 to 75 minutes per week should be spent on spelling instruction, however; greater periods of time do not result in improved spelling ability (Johnson, Langford, & Quorn, 1981). Moreover, many textbook activities focus on language arts skills that are not directly related to learning to spell.

The words in each unit are often grouped according to spelling patterns or phonetic generalizations, even though researchers question this approach unless teachers teach students about the pattern and provide practice activities as Mr. Martinez did in the vignette at the beginning of the chapter. Otherwise, students memorize the rule or spelling pattern and score perfectly on the spelling test but later are unable to choose among spelling options in their writing. For example, after learning the *i-e* vowel rule and the *-igh* spelling pattern in isolation, students are often stumped about how to spell a word such as *light*. They have learned two spelling options for /i/, *i-e* and *-igh,* and *lite* is an option, one they often see in their environment. Instead of organizing words according to phonetic generalizations and spelling rules, teachers should teach minilessons and point out the rules as they occur when writing words on word walls.

Meeting the Needs of Every Student

Spelling can be adapted to meet the needs of all students, but the single most important adaptation teachers can make is to match spelling instruction to students' stage of spelling development. Teachers need to analyze their struggling students' spelling according to the five stages of spelling development, identify the spelling patterns and rules of the words that students misspell, and then plan instruction to teach those patterns and rules. Even with systematic instruction, some students will struggle with *r*-controlled vowels, the schwa sound, adding suffixes, and multisyllabic words. The Meeting the Needs of Every Student feature on page 558 addresses another common problem: students who misspell many words because they continue to depend on the "sound it out" strategy. Instruction is only part of the answer: students also need daily reading and writing experiences to become conventional spellers.

Assessing Students' Progress in Spelling

Grades on weekly spelling tests are the traditional measure of progress in spelling, and the individualized approach to spelling instruction provides this

Meeting the Needs of Every Student

How Can I Help My Struggling Students Who Still Use Invented Spelling?

Don't blame invented spelling! Students invent spellings whenever they attempt to spell unfamiliar words. They apply their knowledge of English orthography and spell the words the best they can. What you're concerned about is that your students' invented spellings aren't getting more sophisticated. Students' invented spellings shouldn't remain constant. In first grade, for example, a child might spell *would* as *wud,* and in second grade, as *wood.* By third grade, that child might spell it correctly, or at least the incorrect spelling is closer to correct, such as *woud* or *wuold.* Sometimes students get stuck and continue to sound out the spellings of familiar words that they should have learned. That's why it's important that you take action. Here's what you can do:

1. Analyze your students' stage of spelling development, and let the errors guide your instruction.

2. Teach the "think it out" strategy. First, students sound the word out, next they apply their knowledge of spelling patterns and rules to deduce the probable spelling, and finally, they check it to be sure it looks right. "Sound it out" is only the first step in the strategy.

3. Regularly teach minilessons on spelling patterns and other spelling skills to your struggling students.

4. Post on word walls in the classroom the high-frequency words that your students can't spell, have students practice spelling them, and insist that they spell these words, many of which can't be sounded out, correctly when they write.

Through these steps, your students' spelling should improve.

To investigate other ways to meet the needs of every student, visit the links for this chapter on the Companion Website at www.prenhall.com/tompkins

Companion Website

convenient way to assess students. This method of assessing student progress is somewhat deceptive, however, because the goal of spelling instruction is not simply to spell words correctly on weekly tests but to use the words, spelled conventionally, in writing. Samples of student writing should be collected periodically to determine whether words that were spelled correctly on tests are being spelled correctly in writing projects. If students are not applying in their writing what they have learned through the weekly spelling instruction, they may not have learned to spell the words after all.

When students perform poorly on spelling tests, consider whether faulty pronunciation or poor handwriting is to blame. Ask students to pronounce words they habitually misspell to see if their pronunciation or dialect differences may be contributing to spelling problems. Students need to recognize that pronunciation does not always predict spelling. For example, in some parts of the United States, people pronounce the words *pin* and *pen* as though they were spelled with the same vowel, and sometimes we pronounce *better* as though it were spelled *bedder* and *going* as though it were spelled *goin'*. Also, ask students to spell orally the words they spell incorrectly in their writing to see whether handwriting difficulties are contributing to spelling problems. Sometimes a minilesson on how to connect two cursive letters (e.g., *br*) or a reminder about the importance of legible handwriting will solve the problem.

It is essential that teachers keep anecdotal information and samples of children's writing to monitor their overall progress in spelling. Teachers can examine error patterns and spelling strategies in these samples. Checking to see if students have spelled their spelling words correctly in writing samples provides one type of information, and examining writing samples for error patterns and spelling strategies provides additional information. Fewer misspellings do not necessarily indicate progress, because to learn to spell, students must experiment with spellings of unfamiliar words, which will result in errors from time to time. Students often misspell a word by misapplying a newly learned spelling pattern. The word *extension* is a good example: Middle-grade students spell the word EXTENSHUN, then change their spelling to EXTENTION after they learn the suffix -*tion*. Although they are still misspelling the word, they have moved from using sound-symbol correspondences to using a spelling pattern—from a less sophisticated spelling strategy to a more sophisticated one.

Students' behavior as they proofread and edit their compositions also provides evidence of spelling development. They should become increasingly able to spot misspelled words in their compositions and to locate the spelling of unknown words in a dictionary. It is easy for teachers to calculate the number of spelling errors students have identified in proofreading their compositions and to chart students' progress in learning to spot errors. Locating errors is the first step in proofreading; correcting the errors is the second step. It is fairly simple for students to correct the spelling of known words, but to correct unknown words, they must consider spelling options and predict possible spellings before they can locate the words in a dictionary. Teachers can document students' growth in locating unfamiliar words in a dictionary by observing their behavior when they edit their compositions.

Teachers can use the writing samples they collect to document children's spelling development. They can note primary-grade students' progression through the stages of invented spelling by analyzing writing samples using a chart such as the ones in the Weaving Assessment Into Practice Features on pages 539 and 540 to determine a general stage of development. Students in the middle and upper grades can use this chart to analyze their own spelling errors.

Review

Spelling is a language tool, and through instruction in spelling, students learn to communicate more effectively. During the elementary grades, students learn to spell conventionally. The key concepts discussed in this chapter are:

Visit Chapter 12 on the Companion Website at www.prenhall. com/tompkins to:

- **Check your understanding of the concepts presented in the chapter**
- **Access the Extensions (activities and a list of related readings)**
- **Link to related websites**

1. Students move through a series of five stages of spelling development.
2. In the first stage, emergent spelling, students string scribbles, letters, and letterlike forms together with little or no understanding of the alphabetic principle.
3. In the second stage, letter name spelling, students learn to represent phonemes in the beginning, middle, and end of words with letters.
4. In the third stage, within-word spelling, students learn to spell long-vowel patterns, *r*-controlled vowels, and complex consonant combinations.
5. In the fourth stage, syllables and affixes, students learn to spell two-syllable words and add inflectional endings.
6. In the fifth stage, derivational relations, students learn that multisyllabic words with related meanings are often related in spelling despite changes in vowel and consonant sounds.
7. Teachers can analyze students' misspellings to determine their stage of spelling development and plan appropriate instruction.
8. Spelling instruction includes daily opportunities to read and write, word walls, word-making and word-sort activities, proofreading, dictionary use, and instruction in spelling options, root words and affixes, and other spelling concepts.
9. Teachers teach minilessons about strategies for spelling unfamiliar words as well as other spelling procedures, concepts, and strategies and skills.
10. Weekly spelling tests, when they are used, should be individualized so that students learn to spell words they do not already know how to spell.

Professional References

Bear, D. R., Invernizzi, M., Templeton, S., & Johnston, F. (2004). *Words their way: Word study for phonics, vocabulary, and spelling instruction* (3rd ed.). Upper Saddle River, NJ: Merrill/Prentice Hall.

Beers, J. W., & Henderson, E. H. (1977). A study of developing orthographic concepts among first graders. *Research in the Teaching of English, 11,* 133–148.

Cunningham, P. M. (1995). *Phonics they use: Words for reading and writing* (2nd ed.). New York: HarperCollins.

Cunningham, P. M., & Cunningham, J. W. (1992). Making words: Enhancing the invented spelling-decoding connection. *The Reading Teacher, 46,* 106–115.

Gentry, J. R. (1981). Learning to spell developmentally. *The Reading Teacher, 34,* 378–381.

Gentry, J. R., & Gillet, J. W. (1993). *Teaching kids to spell.* Portsmouth, NH: Heinemann.

Graves, D. H. (1983). *Writing: Teachers and children at work.* Portsmouth, NH: Heinemann.

Henderson, E. H. (1990). *Teaching spelling* (2nd ed.). Boston: Houghton Mifflin.

Hillerich, R. L. (1977). Let's teach spelling—not phonetic misspelling. *Language Arts, 54,* 301–307.

Horn, E. (1926). *A basic writing vocabulary.* Iowa City: University of Iowa Press.

Johnson, T. D., Langford, K. G., & Quorn, K. C. (1981). Characteristics of an effective spelling program. *Language Arts, 58,* 581–588.

Lacey, C. (1994). *Moving on in spelling: Strategies and activities for the whole language classroom.* New York: Scholastic.

Laminack, L. L., & Wood, K. (1996). *Spelling in use: Looking closely at spelling in whole language classrooms.* Urbana, IL: National Council of Teachers of English.

Marinelli, S. (1996). Integrated spelling in the classroom. *Primary Voices K–6, 4,* 11–15.

Read, C. (1975). *Children's categorization of speech sounds in English* (NCTE Research Report No. 17). Urbana, IL: National Council of Teachers of English.

Read, C. (1986). *Children's creative spelling.* London: Routledge & Kegan Paul.

Templeton, S. (1979). Spelling first, sound later: The relationship between orthography and higher order phonological knowledge in older students. *Research in the Teaching of English, 13,* 255–265.

Templeton, S. (1983). Using the spelling/ meaning connection to develop word knowledge in older students. *Journal of Reading, 27,* 8–14.

Wilde, S. (1993). *You kan red this! Spelling and punctuation for whole language classrooms, K–6.* Portsmouth, NH: Heinemann.

Wilde, S. (1996). A speller's bill of rights. *Primary Voices K–6, 4,* 7–10.

Zutell, J. (1979). Spelling strategies of primary school children and their relationship to Piaget's concept of decentration. *Research in the Teaching of English, 13,* 69–79.

13 Learning About Grammar and Usage

Reading and
Writing
Workshop

Literature
Focus
Units

Literature
Circles

Theme
Cycles

M r. Keogh's fifth graders are reading *Poppy* (Avi, 1995), the story of a little deer mouse named Poppy who outwits Mr. Ocax, a great horned owl. Mr. Keogh introduced the novel to the class, and they read the first chapter together. Then the students continued reading and talking about the book in small groups that operate like literature circles. The teacher brings the students back together for activities and minilessons on vocabulary and grammar and for other exploring-stage activities.

The students list important words from the story on the word wall posted in the classroom after reading each chapter or two, and as the words are listed, the teacher asks students to identify their parts of speech. Even though the book is rich with adverbs, few are chosen for the word wall, so Mr. Keogh begins adding some, such as *profoundly, sufficiently,* and *ravenously.*

For the first grammar activity, Mr. Keogh has students work in small groups to make a list of 10 nouns, 10 adjectives, 10 verbs, and 10 adverbs from the word wall. The teacher walks around the classroom, monitoring students' progress, answering questions, and referring students to the novel to see how a word was used or to the dictionary to check the part of speech. The students

find that some of the words are tricky because they are written in isolation on the word wall. An example is *fake*. It can be used in two ways: as an adjective in *the fake owl* and as a noun in *it was a fake*. Mr. Keogh allows the students to list it either way, but they have to be able to defend their choice. This activity serves as a good review for students.

Next, Mr. Keogh creates a word sort activity using words from the groups' lists. Students cut the word cards apart and sort them into noun, adjective, verb, and adverb categories. Students practice several times with pairs before they glue the cards down into the categories. One student's completed word sort is shown at the top of page 564.

The next day, the students create sentences using one or more words from each category on their word sort. They can also add words to complete the sentences. The first sentences they create, *Mr. Ocax shrieked furiously from the abandoned tree* and *Mr. Ocax shrieked harshly under the crescent moon,* are predictable. Mr. Keogh encouraged the fifth graders to experiment with more creative ways to use the words, the way Avi did in *Poppy*. The students work with partners to create these sentences:

> **H**ow can teachers teach grammar as part of literature focus units?
>
> Traditionally, teachers taught grammar by having their students complete exercises in a textbook. The problem was that students didn't apply what they were practicing orally or in writing. A newer approach is to teach grammar more authentically through books students are reading and through their writing. The focus on grammar fits into the exploring stage of the reading process and the editing stage of the writing process. In this vignette, you'll see how Mr. Keogh incorporates grammar instruction into a literature focus unit. The students experiment with arranging words and phrases into more sophisticated sentences than they normally say or write.

Delicate little Poppy swiveled nervously on one foot, searching the sky for Mr. Ocax.

The man snatched the motionless whirligig from the corn field while his girl friend watched nervously.

Harshly Mr. Ocax snatched the appetizing little mouse named Poppy from the slippery moss-covered rock.

The porcupine named Ereth skittered desperately past the abandoned log and into the protection of Dimwood Forest.

Nouns	Adjectives	Verbs	Adverbs
Mr. Ocax	crescent	shrieked	enormously
whirligig	charred	hunched	cautiously
dignity	appetizing	roosting	furiously
Poppy	motionless	luxuriating	harshly
porcupine	perplexed	saunter	desperately
notion	porcupine-quill	surveyed	deftly
Ereth	wary	skittered	stately
privacy	abandoned	swiveling	profoundly
effrontery	delicate	plunged	nervously
camouflage	fake	snatch	entirely

They write their sentences on sentence strips and post them in the classroom to reread. The next day, Mr. Keogh has them reread the sentences and use green crayons to mark the subject and blue crayons to mark the verb.

Next, Mr. Keogh teaches a series of lessons on prepositional phrases. The students create a list of prepositions that is posted in the classroom, and then they collect prepositional phrases from the novel. Each group culls prepositional phrases from a different chapter. Some of the students confuse prepositional phrases with infinitive verbs (e.g., *he tried to run*), so Mr. Keogh moves around the classroom, explaining infinitives and deleting them from their lists. Then he asks each group to choose five prepositional phrases and use them to complete a chart. The chart made by the group collecting prepositional phrases from Chapter 9 is shown here. In the first column of the chart, students write the preposition; in the second column, they write the entire prepositional phrase; and in the third column, they create a sentence using the prepositional phrase. They share their charts and post them in the classroom.

Preposition	Prepositional Phrase	Used in a Sentence
on	on a succulent dandelion stem	Poppy climbed on a succulent dandelion stem.
over	over Farmer Lamout's fields	The great horned owl flew over Farmer Lamout's fields.
in	in the Gray House attic	She found them in the Gray House attic.
above	above water	Poppy tried to keep her head above water.
below	below the surface	Poppy sank below the surface.

spread his wings	on a branch	triumphantly	with his piercing gaze
soundlessly	a long, low cry of triumph	surveyed	called
from right to left	and	of an old charred oak	he
back into the air	perched	Mr. Ocax	into the night air
swiveled his head	when	smiled	Dimwood Forest
ruled	the great horned owl	as	soared

The next day, they reread the sentence strips they created earlier and use a different color of crayon to underline the prepositional phrases they find. They also add more prepositional phrases to the sentences and color-code them, too.

After this review of the parts of speech, Mr. Keogh changes his focus to sentences. He has created a pack of word and phrase cards to use in reviewing simple sentences, sentence fragments, and compound sentences. He also includes *as* and *when* cards in the pack so his students can build complex sentences, even though they are not expected to learn this concept in fifth grade. Students cut apart a sheet of cards to use in making sentences about Mr. Ocax. A copy of the sheet of cards is shown above.

First, the fifth graders use the cards to create these simple sentences:

The great horned owl ruled Dimwood Forest.

He swiveled his head from right to left.

The great horned owl smiled into the night air.

Soundlessly, the great horned owl soared into the night air.

With his piercing gaze, Mr. Ocax ruled Dimwood Forest triumphantly.

After they create each sentence, Mr. Keogh asks them to identify the subject and the verb. To simplify the process, students color their subject cards green and their verb cards blue. They continue to sort the cards and identify the adverbs and prepositional phrases and the one conjunction card in the pack. Next he asks them to create sentence fragments. They create these examples and identify whether the subject or verb is missing:

When Mr. Ocax soared into the night air.

Soundlessly, swiveled his head from right to left with his piercing gaze.

The students save their packs of cards in small, self-sealing plastic bags, and the next day, they continue this activity. Mr. Keogh asks them to use the *and* card in their sentences, and they create these sentences with compound predicates:

> *Mr. Ocax swiveled his head from right to left and surveyed Dimwood Forest.*

> *The great horned owl called a long, low cry of triumph, spread his wings, and soared back into the air.*

> *He spread his wings soundlessly and soared back into the air.*

The students identify the subject and verbs in the sentences to figure out that these sentences have compound predicates. They try to make a sentence with a compound subject but find that they can't with the word cards they have.

Next Mr. Keogh asks them to craft compound sentences using two subjects and two verbs, and they arrange these sentences:

> *The great horned owl perched on a branch of an old charred oak, and he surveyed Dimwood Forest.*

> *The great horned owl called a long, low cry of triumph, and he soared soundlessly into the night air.*

> *Mr. Ocax surveyed Dimwood Forest triumphantly, and he smiled.*

After they share each sentence, Mr. Keogh asks the students to identify the subjects and verbs. Several students make additional word cards so that they can create the compound sentences they want:

> *The great horned owl spread his wings, and he flew up high into the night sky.*

> *Mr. Ocax blinked his large round eyes, and he watched a little mouse named Poppy.*

"Let's make some even more interesting sentences," Mr. Keogh suggests as he asks them to use the *as* or *when* cards in their sentences. They create these complex sentences:

> *With his piecing gaze, Mr. Ocax surveyed Dimwood Forest as he perched on a branch.*

> *When he called a long, low cry of triumph, Mr. Ocax surveyed Dimwood Forest and soared into the night air.*

> *Mr. Ocax smiled triumphantly as he ruled Dimwood Forest.*

> *As the great horned owl called a long, low cry of triumph, he perched on a branch of an old charred oak.*

> *Mr. Ocax smiled as he soundlessly spread his wings and soared back into the air.*

The students identify the subjects and verbs in the sentences, and at first they assume the sentences are compound sentences. Mr. Keogh explains that these sentences are called *complex sentences*: They have one independent clause and one dependent clause. He explains that the clauses beginning with *as* or *when* are called dependent clauses because they cannot stand alone as sentences. The students color these two cards red so that they will stand out in a sentence.

Several days later, Mr. Keogh repeats the process with a pack of cards with words and phrases about Poppy. The students practice arranging the cards to make simple, compound, and complex sentences, and they keep a list of the sentences they make in their reading logs.

For one of the projects at the end of the book, the students write a character sketch about Mr. Ocax or Poppy. Mr. Keogh explains that in a character sketch, students do three things:

1. Describe what the character looks like.
2. Describe what the character did.
3. Identify one character trait the character exemplified, such as being smart, brave, or determined.

This writing project grows out of the vocabulary and grammar activities. The students are encouraged to use words they've been arranging as well as other words from the word wall in their character sketches. The students work through the writing process as they brainstorm ideas and words, write a draft, meet with revising and editing partners, and conference with Mr. Keogh. The teacher's focus is on making sure that the students include all three components in their character sketches and that they incorporate words and phrases from the novel in their writing. The students are not plagiarizing because they are not copying directly from the novel; instead, they are using newly learned words and phrases from charts in the classroom in their writing. Then they make their final copies.

Here is Darla's character sketch about Poppy:

Poppy was a *dainty* little girl mouse. She looked like a mouse. Her fur was *orange-brown,* and she had a *plump belly* that was white. She had a *tiny nose, pink toes,* and a very long *tail.* On her nose was a scar made by a *great horned owl* named Mr. Ocax. Her *ears were long,* and *her eyes were dark, almost round.*

Mr. Ocax *ruled* over the entire *territory* where Poppy lived. He controlled them *with pure power and fury.* They had to get his *permission* to do anything or else they were his *dinner.* He said he protected them from the *vicious* porcupine who lived in Dimwood Forest, but he was lying. One day Poppy met Ereth, the porcupine. He told her that he eats bark, not mice. Mr. Ocax had to stop Poppy or she would tell everyone that he was *a liar and a bully.* He would not be *king* anymore. Many times the owl tried to catch Poppy, but she always escaped. Then he tricked her and caught her. *Bravely* she stuck her *porcupine-quill* sword into his *left claw.* That's how she escaped. Mr. Ocax was not so lucky. His flying was *totally out of control* because of the pain in his claw, and he *slammed into the salt* lick. It was the violent death he deserved.

Poppy was a brave little mouse. I think she was a hero. That might surprise you because she *was trembling with fear* every time she confronted the owl who *looked like death* to her. What she did was she pretended to be brave. To be a coward was bad. She said it is *hard to be brave, but harder to be a coward.* She risked her life, but now her whole family was safe.

Because of the vocabulary and grammar activities, Darla's writing is stronger with more sophisticated language and more specific words. The italicized words and phrases in her writing came from the novel and were collected on charts or sentence strips posted in the classroom.

As you begin reading this chapter, you may want to read the "Dear Reader" letter in Chapter 13 on the Companion Website at www.prenhall.com/tompkins

Grammar is probably the most controversial area of language arts. Teachers, parents, and the community disagree about the content of grammar instruction, how to teach it, and when to begin teaching it. Some people believe that formal instruction in grammar is unnecessary—if not harmful—during the elementary grades; others believe that grammar instruction should be a key component of language arts instruction. Before getting into the controversy, let's clarify the terms *grammar* and *usage*. *Grammar* is the description of the syntax or structure of a language and prescriptions for its use (Weaver, 1996). It involves principles of word and sentence formation. In contrast, *usage* is correctness, or using the appropriate word or phrase in a sentence. It is the socially preferred way of using language within a dialect. *My friend, she; the man brung;* and *hisself* are examples of Standard English usage errors that elementary students sometimes make. Fraser and Hodson explain the distinction between grammar and usage this way: "Grammar is the rationale of a language; usage is its etiquette" (1978, p. 52).

Children learn the structure of the English language—its grammar—intuitively as they learn to talk; the process is an unconscious one. They have almost completed it by the time they enter kindergarten. The purpose of grammar instruction, then, is to make this intuitive knowledge about the English language explicit and to provide labels for words within sentences, parts of sentences, and types of sentences. Children speak the dialect that their parents and community members speak. Dialect, whether Standard English or nonstandard English, is informal and differs to some degree from the written Standard English, or book language, that students will read and write in elementary school (Edelsky, 1989; Pooley, 1974).

Children demonstrate their knowledge of grammar when they make reading miscues (Goodman, 1965). A miscue is a departure from the words in the text, and as students read aloud, they sometimes read a different word from the word printed in the text. For example, second graders sometimes substitute *dad* for *father* and *mom* for *mother* when reading "When bath time was over, the Tub People always lined up along the edge of the bathtub—the father, the mother, the grandmother, the doctor, the policeman, the child, and the dog" in Pam Conrad's *The Tub People* (1989, n.p.). Or upper-grade students read " 'Please,' he begged, 'take some of the pain' " for " 'Please,' he gasped, 'take some of the pain' " when reading Lois Lowry's *The Giver* (1993, p. 118). These miscues indicate that students have an intuitive sense of grammar that they draw upon as they read. In the second-grade example, students substituted nouns for nouns, and in the upper-grade example, they substituted a verb for a verb.

During the elementary grades, students refine their knowledge of grammar as they learn to read and write, but teachers disagree about whether to teach grammar, and if grammar is to be taught, how it should be taught. As you read this chapter, think about the role of grammar in the language arts program. Use these three questions to guide your reading:

◆ What are the components of grammar?

◆ Why should grammar be taught in the elementary grades?

◆ How should teachers teach grammatical concepts?

GRAMMATICAL CONCEPTS

The five most common types of information about grammar taught during the elementary grades are parts of speech, parts of sentences, types of sentences, capitalization and punctuation, and usage. These components are summarized in the LA Essentials box on page 570.

Parts of Speech

Grammarians have sorted English words into eight groups, called parts of speech: nouns, pronouns, verbs, adjectives, adverbs, prepositions, conjunctions, and interjections. Words in each group are used in essentially the same way in all sentences. Nouns and verbs are the basic building blocks of sentences. Nouns are words that name a person, a place, or a thing. Concepts, such as love, are nouns, too. Pronouns substitute for nouns. Verbs are words that show action or link a subject to another word in the sentence. Adjectives, adverbs, and prepositions build on and modify the nouns and verbs. Adjectives are words that describe a noun or a pronoun, and adverbs describe a verb, an adjective, or another adverb. Prepositions are words that show position or direction, or how words are related to each other. They introduce prepositional phrases.

The last two parts of speech are conjunctions and interjections. Conjunctions connect individual words, groups of words, and sentences, and interjections express strong emotion or surprise. They are set off with exclamation points or commas.

Consider this sentence: *Hey, did you know that it rains more than 200 days a year in a tropical rain forest and that as much as 240 inches of rain fall each year?* All eight parts of speech are represented in this sentence. *Rain forest, days, year, inches,* and *rain* are nouns, and *you* and *it* are pronouns. *Tropical* is an adjective describing *rain forest,* and *each* is an adjective describing *year.* The verbs are *did know, rains,* and *fall. More than* is an adverb modifying *200 days* and *as much as* is an adverb modifying *240 inches.* They both answer the question "how much." *Of* and *in* are prepositions, and they introduce prepositional phrases. The conjunction *and* joins the two dependent clauses. The first word in the sentence, *hey,* is an interjection, and it is set off with a comma. The LA Essentials box on page 571 reviews the eight parts of speech.

Parts of Sentences

A sentence is made up of one or more words to express a complete thought and, to express the thought, must have a subject and a predicate. The subject

Essentials

Components of Grammar Instruction

1. Parts of Speech

The eight parts of speech are nouns, pronouns, adjectives, verbs, adverbs, prepositions, conjunctions, and interjections. Children learn to identify the parts of speech in order to understand the role of each part of speech in a sentence.

2. Parts of Sentences

Simple sentences can be divided into the subject and the predicate. The subject is the noun or pronoun and words or phrases that modify it, and the predicate is the verb and the words or phrases that modify it. Children learn to identify subjects and predicates in order to check for subject-verb agreement and to determine sentence types.

3. Types of Sentences

Sentences can be classified according to structure and purpose. The structure of a sentence may be simple, compound, complex, or compound-complex, according to the number and type of clauses. The purpose of a sentence can be to make a statement (declarative sentence), ask a question (interrogative sentence), make a command (imperative sentence), or express strong emotion or surprise (exclamatory sentence).

4. Capitalization and Punctuation

Capitalization and punctuation marks are often used to mark the beginning and the end of a sentence. The first word in a sentence is capitalized, and periods, question marks, and exclamation points are used to mark the end of a sentence. In the elementary grades, students learn to use capital letters and punctuation marks to indicate the structure of the sentences they write.

5. Usage

Standard English is the English used by educated people in speaking and writing; however, many people speak dialects, or nonstandard varieties of English. Children come to school speaking the language used by their families, and those children who speak nonstandard varieties learn Standard English through reading and writing activities. Children learn, for example, to use past-tense and plural markers, subject-verb agreement, pronoun-antecedent agreement, and objective/subjective pronouns.

Essentials

The Eight Parts of Speech

Words are used in different ways in English. The eight parts of speech are used to label these roles.

Noun	A word used to name something—a person, a place, or a thing. A proper noun names a particular person, place, or thing and is capitalized. Examples: *Abraham Lincoln, United States, Kleenex.* In contrast, a common noun does not name a particular person, place, or thing and is not capitalized. Examples: *pilot, city, sandwich, courage.*
Pronoun	A word used in place of a noun. Examples: *I, you, it, me, who.*
Adjective	A word used to describe a noun or a pronoun. Adjectives can be common or proper, and proper adjectives are capitalized. Examples: *the, American, fastest, slippery-fingered, better.* Some words can be either adjectives or pronouns; they are adjectives if they come before a noun and modify it, and they are pronouns if they stand alone. Examples: *This girl is my friend. This is my friend. Is that his wallet? Is that his?*
Verb	A word used to show action or state of being. Examples: *eat, saw, think, is.* A verb's form varies depending on its number (singular or plural) and tense (present, past, future). Examples: *eat, eats, ate, have eaten.* Some verbs are auxiliary, or helping, verbs; they are used to help form some tenses or voice. Examples: *is, are, was, were, will, can, have, would.* Voice is either active or passive. The subject of the verb is doing something when the voice is active. Example: *The comic told a joke.* The subject of the verb is being acted upon when the voice is passive. Example: *A joke was told by the comic.* To form a passive verb, a form of the *be* verb is added to the past participle.
Adverb	A word used to modify a verb, an adjective, or another adverb. An adverb tells how, when, where, why, how often, and how much. Examples: *quickly, now, outside, well, loudly.*
Preposition	A word or group of words used to show position, direction, or how two words or ideas are related to each other. For example: *at, with, to, from, between.*
Conjunction	A word used to connect words and groups of words. Examples: *and, but, or, either-or, because, when.* The three types of conjunctions are: coordinating conjunctions, which connect equivalent words, phrases, or clauses; correlative conjunctions, which are used in pairs; and subordinating conjunctions, which connect two clauses that are not equally important.
Interjection	A word or phrase used to express strong emotion and set off by commas or an exclamation point. Examples: *Wow! Hey, how are you? Cool, dude!*

names who or what the sentence is about, and the predicate includes the verb and anything that completes or modifies it. In a simple sentence with one subject and one predicate, everything that is not part of the subject is part of the predicate. Consider this sentence about the rain forest: *Most rain forests are found in warm, wet climates near the equator.* The subject is *most rain forests* and the rest of the sentence is the predicate.

Types of Sentences

Sentences are classified in two ways. First, they are classified according to structure, or how they are put together. The structure of a sentence may be simple, compound, complex, or compound-complex, according to the number and type of clauses. A clause consists of a subject and a predicate, and there are two types of clauses. If the clause presents a complete thought and can stand alone as a sentence, it is an independent clause. If the clause is not a complete thought and cannot stand alone as a sentence, it is a dependent clause—it depends on the meaning expressed in the independent clause. An example of an independent clause is *Tropical rain forests are the most complex ecosystems on earth,* and an example of a dependent clause is *Because tropical rain forests are the most complex ecosystems on earth.* This dependent clause cannot stand alone as a sentence; it must be attached to an independent clause. For example: *Because tropical rain forests are the most complex ecosystems on earth, scientists are interested in studying them.* The independent clause, which could stand alone as a sentence, is *scientists are interested in studying them.*

A simple sentence contains only one independent clause, and a compound sentence is made up of two or more independent clauses. A complex sentence contains one independent clause and one or more dependent clauses. A compound-complex sentence contains two or more independent clauses and one or more dependent clauses. Can you identify which of these sentences are simple, compound, complex, and compound-complex?

1. Although a tropical rainforest is a single ecosystem, it is composed of four layers.
2. The tallest trees in the rain forest grow to be about 300 feet tall, and they form the top, emergent layer.
3. The next level is the canopy, and it is alive with activity as hummingbirds, woodpeckers, tree frogs, and monkeys go from flower to flower and branch to branch.
4. Vines, ferns, and palms grow in the understory.
5. Few flowers bloom in the understory because sunlight does not shine through the leaves of the canopy.
6. The bottom layer is the forest floor; mosses, fungi, and other parasitic plants grow here.

The fourth sentence is simple, the second and sixth sentences are compound, the first and fifth sentences are complex, and the third sentence is compound-complex.

Second, sentences are classified according to their purpose or the type of message they contain. Sentences that make statements are declarative, those that ask questions are interrogative, those that make commands are imperative, and those that communicate strong emotion or surprise are exclamatory. The purpose of a sentence is often signaled by the punctuation mark placed at the end of the sentence. Declarative sentences and some imperative sentences are marked with periods, interrogative sentences are marked with question marks, and exclamatory sentences and some imperative sentences are marked with exclamation points.

Capitalization and Punctuation

During the elementary grades, students learn that capital letters divide sentences and signal important words within sentences (Fearn & Farnan, 1998). Consider how the use of capital letters affects the meaning of these three sentences:

> *They were going to the white house for dinner.*
> *They were going to the White house for dinner.*
> *They were going to the White House for dinner. (Wilde, 1992, p. 18)*

Capital letters also express loudness of speech or intensity of emotion because they stand out visually.

Children often begin writing during the preschool years using only capital letters; during kindergarten and first grade, they learn the lowercase forms of letters. They learn to capitalize *I,* the first word in a sentence, and names and other proper nouns and adjectives. By the upper elementary grades, the most common problem is overcapitalization, or capitalizing too many words in a sentence, as in this example: *If the Tropical Rain Forest is destroyed, the Earth's climate could get warmer, and this is known as the Greenhouse Effect.* This problem tends to persist into adolescence and even into adulthood because students have trouble differentiating between common and proper nouns (Shaughnessy, 1977). Too often, students assume that important words in the sentence should be capitalized.

It's a common assumption that punctuation marks signal pauses in speech, but punctuation plays a greater role than that, according to Sandra Wilde (1992). Punctuation marks both signal grammatical boundaries and express meaning. Some punctuation marks indicate sentence boundaries. Periods, question marks, and exclamation points mark sentence boundaries and indicate whether a sentence makes a statement, asks a question, or expresses an exclamation. In contrast, commas, semicolons, and colons mark grammatical units within sentences.

Quotation marks and apostrophes express meaning within sentences. Quotation marks are used most often to indicate what someone is saying in dialogue, but a more sophisticated use is to express irony, as in *My son "loves" to wash the dishes.* Apostrophes are used in contractions to join two words and in possessive nouns to show relationships. Consider the different meanings of these phrases:

> *The monkey's howling (and it's running around the cage).*
> *The monkey's howling (annoyed us; we wanted to kill it).*
> *The monkeys' howling (annoyed us; we wanted to kill them).*
> *(We listened all night to) the monkeys howling. (Wilde, 1992, p. 18)*

Learning centers. *These first graders experiment with end-of-sentence punctuation marks at a learning center. The sentences they're working with were written during a minilesson several days ago. As they work collaboratively to identify the punctuation marks, reread the sentences, and choose the appropriate punctuation marks, they are learning more than they would by working individually to complete a worksheet. Teachers can make the center activities self-checking, too, so that students will know immediately if they are correct, and can get help from classmates or the teacher if they are not correct.*

Researchers have documented that learning to use punctuation is a developmental process. Beginning in the preschool years, children notice punctuation marks and learn to discriminate them from letters (Clay, 1991; Ferreiro & Teberosky, 1982). In kindergarten and first grade, children are formally introduced to the end-of-sentence punctuation marks and learn to use them conventionally about half the time (Cordeiro, Giacobbe, & Cazden, 1983). Many beginning writers use punctuation marks in more idiosyncratic ways, such as between words and at the end of each line of writing, but over time, children's usage becomes more conventional. Edelsky (1983) looked at first-through third-grade bilingual writers and found similar developmental patterns for second-language learners.

Usage

To read more about dialects, check Chapter 1, "Learning and the Language Arts."

Students come to school speaking dialects or varieties of English that their parents speak, and sometimes these dialects differ from Standard English; they are nonstandard. Students may use double negatives rather than single negatives so that they say *I ain't got no money* instead of *I don't have any money.* Or they may use objective pronouns instead of subjective pronouns so that they say *Me and him have dirt bikes* instead of *He and I have dirt bikes.*

FIGURE 13-1

Ten Usage Errors That Middle- and Upper-Grade Students Can Correct

1. Irregular Verb Forms	Students form the past tense of irregular verbs as they would a regular verb; for example, some students might use *catch + ed* to make *catched* instead of *caught*, or *swim + ed* to make *swimmed* instead of *swam*.
2. Past-Tense Forms	Students use present-tense or past-participle forms in place of past-tense forms, such as *I ask* for *I asked, she run* for *she ran,* or *he seen* for *he saw*.
3. Nonstandard Verb Forms	Students use *brung* for *brought* or *had went* for *had gone*.
4. Double Subjects	Students use both a noun and a pronoun in the subject, such as *My mom she*.
5. Nonstandard Pronoun Forms	Students use nonstandard pronoun forms, such as *hisself* for *himself, them books* for *those books,* and *hisn* for *his*.
6. Objective Pronouns for the Subject	Students use objective pronouns instead of subjective pronouns in the subject, such as *Me and my friend went to the store* or *Her and me want to play outside*.
7. Lack of Subject-Verb Agreement	Students use *we was* for *we were* and *he don't* for *he doesn't*.
8. Double Negatives	Students use two negatives when only one is needed; for example, *I don't got none* and *Joe don't have none*.
9. Confusing Pairs of Words	Some students confuse word pairs, such as *learn–teach, lay–lie,* and *leave–let*. They might say *I'll learn you to read,* instead of *I'll teach you to read, go lay down* instead of *go lie down,* and *leave me do it* instead of *let me do it*. Other confusing pairs include *bring–take, among–between, fewer–less, good–well, passed–past, real–really, set–sit, than–then, who–which–that, who–whom, it's–its,* and *your–you're*.
10. *I* as an Objective Pronoun	Students incorrectly use *I* instead of *me* as an objective pronoun. Students say or write *It's for Bill and I* instead of *It's for Bill and me*.

Adapted from Pooley, 1974, and Weaver, 1996.

Students who speak nonstandard dialects learn Standard English forms as alternatives to the forms they already know. Rather than trying to substitute their standard forms for students' nonstandard forms, teachers can explain that Standard English is the language of school. It is the language used in books, and students can easily locate Standard English examples in books they are reading. Calling Standard English "book language" also helps to explain the importance of proofreading to identify and correct usage errors in the books that students are writing. Moreover, many Standard English usage errors are status marking, and upper-grade students need to understand that Standard English is the language of privilege and prestige and that they can add Standard English to their repertoire of language registers. Figure 13–1 lists 10 types of usage errors that middle- and upper-grade students can learn to correct.

TEACHING GRAMMAR IN THE ELEMENTARY GRADES

For many years, grammar was taught using language arts textbooks. Students read rules and definitions, copied words and sentences, and marked them to apply the concepts presented in the text. This type of activity often seemed meaningless to students. A more effective approach is to connect grammar with reading and writing activities and to teach minilessons about the function of words in sentences and ways to arrange words into sentences (Cullinan, Jaggar, & Strickland, 1974; Tompkins & McGee, 1983).

Lucy McCormick Calkins has argued for more than 20 years that "basic skills belong in context" (1980, p. 567). The ability to use Standard English grammatical constructions effectively is best fostered by teaching them in the context of their use. Reggie Routman (1996) recommends that teachers do the following to teach skills:

- Model effective use of grammar skills.
- Raise expectations and hold students accountable for work done accurately and neatly.
- Teach minilessons using children's writing and excerpts from books students are reading.
- Teach students to proofread their writing to locate and correct errors.
- Encourage students to self-assess their work.
- Share research with parents about the importance of teaching the grammar and usage skills in context.
- Value students' effective use of grammar and usage.

In the vignette at the beginning of the chapter, Mr. Keogh followed many of these recommendations as he taught grammar as part of a literature focus unit.

Skills that are taught in isolation are not used as consistently or effectively as skills taught when students are using oral and written language in meaningful, functional, and genuine ways (Routman, 1996). The position taken in this book is that grammar be taught as part of reading and writing activities. Guidelines for teaching grammar are listed in the LA Essentials box on page 577.

Why Teach Grammar?

Teachers, parents, and the community at large cite many reasons for teaching grammar. First, using Standard English is the mark of an educated person, and students should know how to use Standard English. Many teachers feel that teaching grammar will help students understand sentence structure and form sentences to express their thoughts. Another reason is that parents expect that grammar will be taught, and teachers must meet these expectations. Other teachers explain that they teach grammar to prepare students for the next grade or for instruction in a foreign language. Others pragmatically rationalize grammar instruction because it is a part of norm-referenced achievement tests mandated by state departments of education.

Language arts textbooks have traditionally emphasized grammar; often, more than half the pages have been devoted to drills on parts of speech, parts

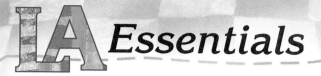

Essentials

Guidelines for Teaching Grammar

Teachers follow these guidelines as they teach grammar to their students.

1. Minilessons

Teachers teach minilessons on grammar and usage concepts and have students locate examples of grammar and usage concepts they are learning in books they are reading and books they are writing.

2. Concept Books

Teachers share concept books when students are studying parts of speech, and students also create their own concept books.

3. Sentence Collection

Students collect favorite sentences from books they are reading and use the sentences for grammar and usage activities.

4. Sentence Manipulation

Students use sentences from books they are reading for sentence unscrambling, sentence imitating, sentence combining, and sentence expanding activities.

5. New Versions of Books

Young children write innovations, or new versions of books, using patterns in books they have read.

6. Posters

Students make grammar posters to visually represent parts of speech, sentence types, or usage rules they are learning.

7. Proofreading

Students need to learn how to proofread so that they can locate and correct grammar and usage errors in their own writing.

8. Standard English Alternative

Teachers explain that Standard English is the language of school and is one way of speaking and writing. It is important that students understand that the purpose of grammar instruction is to expand their repertoire of language options, not to replace their home language.

Seeing Common Threads

Should grammar be taught?

Kristi Garcia responds:

I think grammar should be taught but it should be taught in context. Today children watch TV more than ever. Their role models are cartoon characters and sports heroes. They are not always the best models for Standard English. People with poor grammar are perceived as uneducated or unintelligent. Therefore, it becomes the responsibility of the classroom teacher to ensure that students are taught Standard English. Textbooks and dittos are not effective because they are not meaningful to students. When teaching grammar to students through the use of books and other texts, the task becomes meaningful and aids students in understanding new concepts.

What do you think?

Each chapter presents a question and a response written by one of Dr. Tompkins's students. Consider other comments, or respond to the question yourself, by visiting the Threaded Message Board in Chapter 13 on the Companion Website at www.prenhall.com/tompkins

Companion Website

of sentences, and sentence types. Many teachers and parents assume that the content of a language arts textbook indicates what the curriculum should be, but it is important to separate the two so that the textbook is only one of many resources for implementing the curriculum.

Conventional wisdom is that knowledge about grammar and usage should improve students' oral language and writing, but research since the early 20th century has not confirmed this assumption. In 1936, for example, the National Council of Teachers of English (NCTE) passed a resolution against the formal teaching of grammar, and based on their review of research conducted before 1963, Braddock, Lloyd-Jones, and Schoer concluded that "the teaching of formal grammar has a negligible or, because it usually displaces some instruction and practice in actual composition, even a harmful effect on the improvement of writing" (1963, pp. 37–38). Since then, other studies have reached the same conclusion, and the NCTE resolution has been reaffirmed again and again (Hillocks, 1987; Hillocks & Smith, 2003; Weaver, 1996).

Despite the controversy about teaching grammar and its value for elementary students, grammar is a part of the elementary language arts curriculum and will undoubtedly remain so for some time. Given this fact, it is only reasonable that grammar should be taught in the most beneficial manner possible. Researchers suggest that integrating grammar study with reading and writing produces the best results (Beers, 2001; Noguchi, 1991; Noyce & Christie, 1983; Weaver, McNally, & Moerman, 2001). They view grammar as a tool for writers and recommend integrating grammar instruction with the revising and editing stages of the writing process.

Teaching Grammar Through Reading

Students learn many things about the structure of the English language through reading. They learn more sophisticated academic language, a more formal register than they speak, and sophisticated ways of phrasing ideas and arranging words into sentences. In *Aunt Flossie's Hats (and Crab Cakes Later)* (Howard, 1991), for example, Susan tells about a visit to her great-aunt and how she and her sister play with her great-aunt's hats: "One Sunday afternoon, I picked out a wooly winter hat, sort of green, maybe" (p. 11). This sentence is particularly rich in modifiers: The hat is wooly, it is a winter hat, and may be green—sort of.

Charlotte Zolotow uses a sophisticated sentence form in *This Quiet Lady* (1992). On each page, the core sentence, "This girl is my mother," is expanded to chronicle the stages and events in a mother's life. The second page describes the mother when she was a girl: "This curly-haired little girl with the doll drooping from her hand is my mother" (n.p.).

Students often read sentences that are longer than the ones they speak and learn new ways to string words into sentences. In *Chrysanthemum* (Henkes, 1991), the story of a mouse named Chrysanthemum who loves her name until she starts school and is teased by her classmates, the author uses a combination of long and short sentences very effectively: "Chrysanthemum could scarcely believe her ears. She blushed. She beamed. She bloomed" (n.p.).

Students read sentences exemplifying all four sentence types in many books. One example is the Caldecott Medal–winning *Officer Buckle and Gloria* (Rathmann, 1995), the story of a police officer and his dog, Gloria. "Officer Buckle loved having a buddy" and "That night Officer Buckle watched himself on the 10 o'clock news" (n.p.) are statements, or declarative sentences. "How about Gloria?" and "Could she come?" (n.p.) are questions, or interrogative sentences. Officer Buckle's safety tips, such as "Keep your shoelaces tied" and "Do not go swimming during electrical storms!" (n.p.), are imperative sentences. The children loved Gloria and her tricks, and they cheered, "Bravo!" (n.p.)—an example of an exclamation, or exclamatory sentence.

Students read simple, compound, complex, and compound-complex sentences in books. William Steig includes all of these types of sentences in his Caldecott Medal book, *Sylvester and the Magic Pebble* (1969):

Simple Sentence: *"Suddenly Mr. Duncan saw the red pebble" (n.p.).*

Compound Sentence: *"He felt he would be a rock forever and he tried to get used to it" (n.p.).*

Complex Sentence: *"When he was awake, he was only hopeless and unhappy" (n.p.).*

Compound-Complex Sentence: *"If he hadn't been so frightened, he could have made the lion disappear, or he could have wished himself safe at home with his father and mother" (n.p.).*

It might seem surprising, but many books for young children include complex and compound sentences. In Lois Ehlert's *Mole's Hill* (1994), for example, Fox snarls, "Where there's a mole, there's a mess" (n.p.). In Numeroff's *If You Give a Mouse a Cookie* (1985), the book begins, "If you give a mouse a cookie, he's going to ask for a glass of milk" (n.p.). It is less common to find compound sentences in books for young children, but here is one example: in Eric Carle's *The Very Quiet Cricket* (1990), children repeat the refrain "The little cricket wanted to answer, so he rubbed his wings together. But nothing happened. Not a sound" on every page. For the sake of sentence length, many authors break would-be compound sentences into two simple sentences.

Chapter books often include examples of all sentence types. On the first page of *The Giver* (Lowry, 1993), for instance, there are examples of simple, compound, and complex sentences:

> Simple Sentence: *"But the aircraft a year ago had been different."*
>
> Compound Sentence: *"It was almost December, and Jonas was beginning to be frightened."*
>
> Complex Sentence: *"Frightened was the way he had felt a year ago when an unidentified aircraft had overflown the community twice."*

And on the second page, there is an example of a compound-complex sentence: "His parents were both at work, and his little sister, Lily, was at the Childcare Center where she spent her after-school hours."

Students can pick out the subjects and predicates in these sentences. The subject in "Officer Buckle loved having a buddy" (n.p.) is "Officer Buckle," and the remainder of the simple sentence is the predicate. In "He felt he would be a rock forever and he tried to get used to it" (n.p.), a compound sentence, there are two independent clauses, and "he" is the subject of each clause. The first clause of "If you give a mouse a cookie, he's going to ask for a glass of milk" (n.p.) is a dependent clause, and the subject is "you." The second clause is an independent clause, and the subject is "he" (the mouse).

Some authors write dialogue and other text in nonstandard English that is appropriate to the characters and the setting they are creating. In *Shiloh* (Naylor, 1991), for example, the story of a boy named Marty who will do anything to save a beagle puppy, Marty says, "Thinking don't cost nothing" (p. 31), and this language is appropriate for the rural setting of the book. The same is true in *Mississippi Bridge* (Taylor, 1990), which is set in the rural South during the 1930s. This story is about African Americans having to give up their seats on the bus to white people. The bus driver says, "Ain't I done tole you to get off this bus?" (p. 46), and, "I gots to go on this bus" (p. 47), when he forces Josias to get off the bus so that more white passengers can get on. When the bus goes over a bridge during a storm, it's one of the people who was denied a seat who jumps into the raging river to try to save the people on the bus. Jeremy, the character telling the story, runs to get help after the accident and tells his father, "The bus, it done gone off the bridge!" (p. 55). Understanding that authors (and all language users) make choices about Standard and nonstandard English according to the situation in which it is used is important in helping students who speak nonstandard English become aware of Standard English options.

One way to help students focus on sentences in stories is sentence collecting (Speaker & Speaker, 1991). Students collect favorite sentences and share them with classmates. They copy their sentences on chart paper or on long strips of tagboard and post them in the classroom. Students and the teacher talk about the merits of each sentence, focus on word choice, and analyze the sentence types. Through this discussion, students gradually learn to comprehend more syntactically complex sentences. Students can cut the words in the sentences apart and rebuild them, either in the author's original order or in an order that appeals to them. These sentences can also be used in teaching minilessons.

Teaching Grammar Through Writing

Not only do students notice the way the sentences are phrased in the books they read or listen to read aloud, but they also use the structures in books they are writing. Kathy Egawa (1990) reports that a first grader used the structure and rhythm of Jane Yolen's *Owl Moon* (1987) in writing a book called *Salamander Sun. Owl Moon* begins this way: "It was late one winter night, long past my bedtime when Pa and I went owling" (n.p.). The child's book, written in invented spelling, begins this way: "It was lat one spring afternoon a long time after lunch when ma tact me sawlumendering" (Egawa, 1990, p. 586). This first grader was not plagiarizing Yolen's book, but adapting and incorporating the structure and voice into his own writing.

Teachers use a problem-solving approach to deal with usage errors during the editing stage of the writing process. Students hunt for errors, trying to make their papers "optimally readable" (Smith, 1982). They recognize that it is a courtesy to readers to make their papers as correct as possible. During editing, classmates note errors and correct each other's papers, and teachers point out other errors. Sometimes teachers explain the correction (e.g., the past tense of *bring* is *brought,* not *brung*), and at other times, they simply mark the correction, saying, "We usually write it this way."

> **Check Chapter 3, "The Reading and Writing Processes,"** for more information on the editing stage of the writing process, as well as on proofreading.

Teaching the Parts of Speech

Students can learn about parts of speech through minilessons and reading and writing activities. They can locate examples of the parts of speech in books they are reading so that they will understand that authors use parts of speech to express their ideas. They can read grammar concept books, including the popular books by author-illustrator Ruth Heller, and make their own books, too. Students can write sentences and experiment with words to see how parts of speech are combined to form sentences. These activities are described in the following sections.

Collecting Parts of Speech. Students work in small groups to identify words representing one part of speech or all eight parts of speech from a book they are reading. A group of fifth graders identified the following words representing each part of speech from Van Allsburg's *The Polar Express* (1985):

- Nouns: *train, children, Santa Claus, elves, pajamas, roller coaster, conductor, sleigh, hug, clock, Sarah*
- Pronouns: *we, they, he, it, us, you, his, I, me*
- Verbs: *filled, ate, flickered, raced, were, cheered, marched, asked, pranced, stood, shouted*
- Adjectives: *melted, white-tailed, quiet, no, first, magical, cold, dark, polar, Santa's*

FIGURE 13-2 *An Excerpt From a Second-Grade Class Book on Adjectives*

- Adverbs: *soon, faster, wildly, apart, closer, alone*
- Prepositions: *in, through, over, with, of, in front of, behind, at, for, across, into*
- Conjunctions: *and, but*
- Interjections: *oh, well, now*

After identifying the parts of speech, teachers can make word cards and students can sort the words according to the part of speech. Because some words, such as *melted* and *hug,* can represent more than one part of speech, depending on how the word is used in the sentence, teachers must choose words for this activity carefully or use the words in a sentence on the word card so that students can classify them correctly.

After collecting words representing one part of speech from books they are reading or from books they have written, students can create a book using some of these words. Figure 13–2 shows the cover and a page from an alphabet book focusing on adjectives that second graders developed.

Reading and Writing Grammar Concept Books. Students examine concept books that focus on one part of speech or another grammatical concept. For example, Brian Cleary describes adjectives and lists many examples in *Hairy, Scary, Ordinary: What Is an Adjective?* (2000). After students read the book and identify the adjectives, they can make posters or write their own books about the parts of speech. Useful books for teaching parts of speech are listed in the Classroom Library box on page 583.

Grammar Concept Books

Nouns

Cleary, B. P. (1999). *A mink, a fink, a skating rink: What is a noun?* Minneapolis: Carolrhoda. (M)

Heller, R. (1987). *A cache of jewels and other collective nouns.* New York: Grosset & Dunlap. (M–U)

Heller, R. (1990). *Merry-go-round: A book about nouns.* New York: Grosset & Dunlap. (M–U)

Hoban, T. (1981). *More than one.* New York: Greenwillow. (P)

MacCarthy, P. (1991). *Herds of words.* New York: Dial. (M)

Terban, M. (1986). *Your foot's on my feet! and other tricky nouns.* New York: Clarion. (M)

Verbs

Beller, J. (1984). *A-B-Cing: An action alphabet.* New York: Crown. (P–M)

Burningham, J. (1986). *Cluck baa, jangle twang, slam bang, skip trip, sniff shout, wobble pop.* New York: Viking. (P–M)

Cleary, B. P. (2001). *To root, to toot, to parachute: What is a verb?* Minneapolis: Carolrhoda. (M)

Heller, R. (1988). *Kites sail high: A book about verbs.* New York: Grosset & Dunlap. (M–U)

Maestro, B., & Maestro, G. (1985). *Camping out.* New York: Crown. (P–M)

Neumeier, M., & Glasser, B. (1985). *Action alphabet.* New York: Greenwillow. (M)

Rotner, S. (1996). *Action alphabet.* New York: Atheneum. (P–M)

Schneider, R. M. (1995). *Add it, dip it, fix it: A book of verbs.* Boston: Houghton Mifflin. (M)

Shiefman, V. (1981). *M is for move.* New York: Dutton. (P–M)

Terban, M. (1984). *I think I thought and other tricky verbs.* New York: Clarion. (M)

Adjectives

Boynton, S. (1983). *A is for angry: An animal and adjective alphabet.* New York: Workman. (M–U)

Cleary, B. P. (2000). *Hairy, scary, ordinary: What is an adjective?* Minneapolis: Carolrhoda. (M)

Heller, R. (1989). *Many luscious lollipops: A book about adjectives.* New York: Grosset & Dunlap. (M–U)

Hubbard, W. (1990). *C is for curious: An ABC book of feelings.* San Francisco: Chronicle. (M)

Maestro, B., & Maestro, G. (1979). *On the go: A book of adjectives.* New York: Crown. (P–M)

Conjunctions

Heller, R. (1998). *Fantastic! Wow! And unreal! A book about interjections and conjunctions.* New York: Penguin. (M–U)

Pronouns

Cleary, B. P. (2004). *I and you and don't forget who: What is a pronoun?* Minneapolis: Carolrhoda. (M)

Heller, R. (1997). *Mine, all mine: A book about pronouns.* New York: Grosset & Dunlap. (M–U)

Prepositions

Berenstain, S., & Berenstain, J. (1968). *Inside, outside, upside, down.* New York: Random House. (M)

Cleary, B. P. (2002). *Under, over, by the clover: What is a preposition?* Minneapolis: Carolrhoda. (M)

Heller, R. (1995). *Behind the mask: A book of prepositions.* New York: Grosset & Dunlap. (M–U)

Hoban, T. (1991). *All about where.* New York: Greenwillow. (P)

Lillie, P. (1993). *Everything has a place.* New York: Greenwillow. (P)

Adverbs

Cleary, B. P. (2003). *Dearly, nearly, insincerely: What is an adverb?* Minneapolis: Carolrhoda. (M)

Heller, R. (1991). *Up, up and away: A book about adverbs.* New York: Grosset & Dunlap. (M–U)

Interjections

Heller, R. (1998). *Fantastic! Wow! And unreal! A book about interjections and conjunctions.* New York: Penguin. (M–U)

P = primary grades (K–2); M = middle grades (3–5); U = upper grades (6–8).

FIGURE 13-3   *An Eighth-Grade Poster on Adverbs*

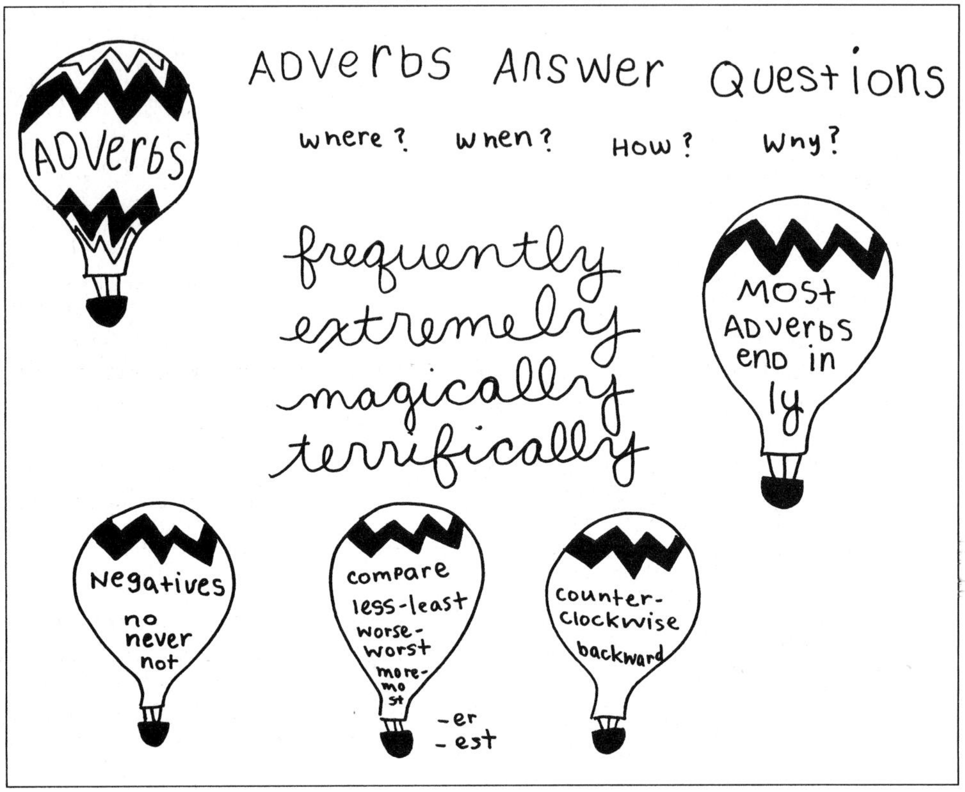

Students in an eighth-grade class divided into small groups to read Ruth Heller's books about parts of speech, including *Up, Up and Away: A Book About Adverbs* (1991), *Mine, All Mine: A Book About Pronouns* (1997), *Behind the Mask: A Book of Prepositions* (1995), and *Merry-Go-Round: A Book About Nouns* (1990). After reading one of her books, students made a poster with information about the parts of speech, which they presented to the class. The students' poster for adverbs is shown in Figure 13–3. Later, students divided into small groups to do a word sort. In this activity, students cut apart a list of words and sorted them into groups according to the part of speech. All the words had been taken from posters that students created, and students could refer to the posters if needed.

Experimenting With Sentence Slotting.   Students experiment with words and phrases to see how they function in sentences by filling in sentences that have slots, or blanks. Sentence slotting teaches students about several different grammatical concepts. They can experiment with parts of speech using a sentence like this:

The snake slithered _____ the rock.

> *over*
>
> *around*
>
> *under*
>
> *to*

Students brainstorm a number of words to fill in the slot, all of which will be prepositions; adjectives, nouns, verbs, and adverbs will not make sense. This activity can be repeated to introduce or review any part of speech.

Sentence slotting also demonstrates to students that some parts of speech can substitute for each other. In the following sentence, common and proper nouns as well as pronouns can be used in the slot:

_____ *knew more safety tips than anyone else in Napville.*

The man

Officer Buckle

He

The police officer

A similar sentence-slotting example demonstrates how phrases can function as an adverb:

The dog growled _____.

> *ferociously*
>
> *with his teeth bared*
>
> *daring us to reach for his bone*

In this example, the adverb *ferociously* can be used in the slot, as well as prepositional and participial phrases.

Sentences with an adjective slot can be used to show that phrases function as adjectives. The goal of this activity is to demonstrate the function of words in sentences. Many sentence-slotting activities, such as the last example, also illustrate that sentences become more specific with the addition of a word or phrase. The purpose of these activities is to experiment with language; they should be done with small groups of students or the whole class, not as worksheets.

Teaching Students to Manipulate Sentences

Students experiment with or manipulate sentences when they rearrange words and phrases in a sentence, combine several sentences to make a single, stronger sentence, or write sentences based on a particular sentence pattern. Through these activities, students learn about the structure of sentences and experiment with more sophisticated sentences than they might otherwise write.

Students in the primary grades often create new books or "innovations" using the structure in repetitive books. Young children create new verses for *Mary Wore Her Red Dress* (Peek, 1985) when they are studying colors, and they write their own versions of *Brown Bear, Brown Bear, What Do You See?* (Martin, 1983) and the sequel *Polar Bear, Polar Bear, What Do You Hear?* (Martin, 1992). Similarly, middle-grade students write new verses following the rhyming pattern in Laura Numeroff's *Dogs Don't Wear Sneakers* (1993) and the sequel, *Chimps Don't Wear Glasses* (1995).

A third-grade class used Numeroff's frame to write verses, and one small group composed this verse, rhyming *TV* and *bumblebee:*

Ducks don't have tea parties,
Lions don't watch TV,
And you won't see a salamander
being friends with a bumblebee.

FIGURE 13-4

Killgallon's Four Types of Sentence Manipulation

Teachers choose sentences from a book students are reading for these sentence-manipulation activities. It is important that the book used for these activities is well written and that teachers choose powerful sentences for students to manipulate.

1. Sentence Unscrambling
Teachers choose a long sentence from a book students are reading and break the sentence into phrases. Then students reassemble the sentence to examine how the author structures sentences. Sometimes students duplicate the author's sentence, but at other times, they create an original sentence that they like better.

2. Sentence Imitating
Teachers choose a sentence with an interesting structure from a book students are reading to imitate. Then students create a new sentence on a new topic that imitates the structure and style of the original sentence.

3. Sentence Combining
Teachers choose a conceptually dense sentence from a book students are reading and break the sentence into three or more simple sentences. Then students combine and embed the simple sentences to re-create the author's original sentence. They compare their sentence with the original sentence.

4. Sentence Expanding
Teachers choose a sentence from a book students are reading and shorten the sentence to make an abridged version. Then students expand the abridged sentence, trying to re-create the author's original sentence, or write a new sentence, trying to match the author's style.

Adapted from Killgallon, 1997, 1998.

Another group wrote this verse, rhyming *cars* and *bars:*

Sea otters don't go to church,
Hummingbirds never drive cars,
And you won't see a hermit crab
munching on candy bars.

Middle- and upper-grade students can choose a favorite sentence and imitate its structure by plugging in new words. Stephen Dunning calls this procedure "copy changes" (Dunning & Stafford, 1992). For example, eighth graders chose sentences from *The Giver* (Lowry, 1993) for copy changes. The original sentence was "Dimly, from a nearly forgotten perception as blurred as the substance itself, Jonas recalled what the whiteness was" (p. 175). A student created this sentence using the sentence frame: "Softly, from a corner of the barn as cozy and warm as the kitchen, the baby kitten mewed to its mother."

Don Killgallon (1997, 1998) recommends that teachers help students examine how authors write sentences through four types of activities: sentence unscrambling, sentence imitating, sentence combining, and sentence expanding. Sentence imitating is like the innovations and copy changes discussed earlier. Through sentence manipulation, students learn new syntactic structures and practice ways to vary the sentences they write. These four types of sentence manipulation are summarized in Figure 13–4.

Sentence Unscrambling. Teachers choose a sentence from a book students are reading and divide it into phrases. Then they present the phrases in a random order to students, and the students unscramble the sentence and re-arrange it in the author's original order. Although older students can do this activity with a list of phrases written on the chalkboard or on a sheet of paper, younger students need to have the phrases written on sentence strips so that they can actually arrange and rearrange the phrases until they are satisfied with the order. After unscrambling the phrases, students compare their rearrangement with the author's. They may duplicate the author's sentence or create an original sentence that they like better.

Here is a sentence from E. B. White's *Charlotte's Web* (1980), broken into phrases and scrambled:

in the middle of the kitchen
teaching it to suck from the bottle
a minute later
with an infant between her knees
Fern was seated on the floor

Can you unscramble the sentence? E. B. White's original is: "A minute later Fern was seated on the floor in the middle of the kitchen with an infant between her knees, teaching it to suck from the bottle" (pp. 6–7).

Sentence Imitating. Students choose a sentence from a book they are reading and then write their own sentence imitating the structure of the one they have chosen. Here is an original sentence from *Charlotte's Web:* "Avery noticed the spider web, and coming closer, he saw Charlotte" (p. 71). Can you create a sentence on a new topic that imitates E. B. White's sentence structure, especially the "and coming closer" part? A class of sixth graders created this imitation: *The fox smelled the poultry, and coming closer, he saw five juicy chickens scratching in the dirt.* Here is another sentence from *Charlotte's Web:* "His medal still hung from his neck; by looking out of the corner of his eye he could still see it" (p. 163). Sixth graders also created this imitation: *The message was still stuck in the keyhole; using a magnifying glass the little mouse could still read those awful words.*

Teachers begin sentence imitating by having students collect favorite sentences as they read, and then write them on sentence strips to post in the classroom and in their reading logs. After students gain experience collecting sentences, the teacher introduces sentence imitation as an oral activity. The teacher chooses a sentence from those posted on the classroom wall, reads it, and then orally creates a new sentence using the same structure. The teacher says this new sentence aloud and points out that this sentence follows the structure of the sentence posted on the wall. Then the teacher invites students to pick a sentence and create a new one using the same structure. Some students will quickly pick up on the idea and create sentences to share with the class. With practice, more and more students will join in on the activity.

Sentence Combining. Students combine and rearrange words in sentences to make the sentences longer and more conceptually dense (Strong, 1996). The goal of sentence combining is for students to experiment with different ways to join and embed words. Teachers choose a sentence from a book students are reading and break it apart into short, simple sentences. Then students combine the sentences, trying to recapture the author's original sentence. For example, try your hand at combining these short sentences that were taken from a more complex sentence written by E. B. White:

> *No one ever had such a friend.*
>
> *The friend was so affectionate.*
>
> *The friend was so loyal.*
>
> *The friend was so skillful.*

The original sentence from *Charlotte's Web* is: "No one ever had such a friend—so affectionate, so loyal, and so skillful" (p. 173). You might wonder whether the *and* before *so skillful* is necessary. Students often discuss why the author added it.

Try this more complex sentence-combining activity, again using a sentence from *Charlotte's Web*:

> *They explored their home.*
>
> *They crawled here and there.*
>
> *They waved at Wilbur.*
>
> *They crawled up and down.*
>
> *They trailed tiny draglines behind them.*
>
> *They crawled around and about.*
>
> *They crawled for several days and several nights.*

The original sentence is: "For several days and several nights they crawled here and there, up and down, around and about, waving at Wilbur, trailing tiny draglines behind them, and exploring their home" (p. 178).

Sentence Expanding.   Teachers choose a rich sentence from a book students are reading and present an abridged version to students. Then students expand the sentence so that the words and phrases they add blend in with the author's sentence. An abridged sentence from *Charlotte's Web* is:

> *There is no place like home. . . .*

Here is the original: "There is no place like home, Wilbur thought, as he placed Charlotte's 514 unborn children carefully in a safe corner" (p. 172). A sixth grader wrote this expansion: *There is no place like home, like his home in the barn, cozy and warm straw to sleep on, the delicious smell of manure in the air, Charlotte's egg sac to guard, and his friends Templeton, the goose, and the sheep nearby.* Even though it is not the same as E. B. White's original sentence, the student's sentence retains the character of E. B. White's writing style.

These sentence-manipulation activities fit easily into exploring activities during the reading process. Whether students are involved in a literature focus unit, literature circles, or reading workshop, they often collect favorite sentences in their reading logs. Then students can use some of the sentences they have collected for these activities.

Minilessons

Teachers identify topics for grammar minilessons in two ways. The preferred way is to identify concepts by assessing students' writing and noting what types of grammar and usage errors they are making. Another way is to choose topics from lists of skills they are expected to teach at their grade level. The topics can be taught to the whole class or to small groups of students. Atwell (1987) suggests using minilessons because of their immediate connections to reading and writing.

Worksheets are not recommended for minilessons; instead, excerpts from books students are reading or from students' own writing are used. Students can write words on cards and manipulate them to form sentences, or they can write sentences on overhead transparencies to share with classmates. Teachers introduce a concept and its related terminology; then they provide opportunities for students to experiment with sentence construction. A list of topics for minilessons is suggested on pages 590 and 591, and a sample minilesson on combining sentences is also included in the feature.

Meeting the Needs of Every Student

The goal of grammar instruction is to increase students' ability to structure and manipulate sentences and to expand their repertoire of sentence patterns. Teaching grammar is a controversial issue, and it is especially so for students whose native language is not English or for students who speak a nonstandard form of English. The best way to promote students' language development is to encourage all students to talk freely in the classroom; and in classrooms where teachers have created a community of learners, students do feel comfortable talking, whether or not they speak standard English. In the past, researchers have recommended that teachers not correct students' talk so as to not embarrass them; however, teachers are finding that many English learners want to be corrected so that they can learn to speak standard English correctly and do well in school (Scarcella, 2003). Teachers can correct grammatical errors in students' talk and writing and explain rules affecting the grammatical constructions, but they also need to provide direct instruction through minilessons for English learners and other students who do not speak and write standard English. The Meeting the Needs of Every Student feature on page 592 provides suggestions for working with English learners. The rationale for providing direct instruction is that many English learners have not been successful in acquiring standard English through naturalistic approaches alone.

Assessing Students' Knowledge About Grammar

The best gauge of students' knowledge of grammar is how they arrange words into sentences as part of genuine communication projects. Teachers can develop checklists of grammar and usage skills to teach at a particular grade level, or they can list errors they observe in students' writing. Then teachers observe students as they write and examine their compositions to note errors, plan and teach minilessons based on students' needs, note further errors, plan

Piecing a Lesson Together

Topics on Grammar and Usage

Procedures	Concepts	Strategies and Skills
Sort parts of speech	Parts of speech	Write complete sentences
Unscramble sentences	Contractions	Rearrange sentences
Imitate sentences	Possessives	Vary sentence length
Combine sentences	Comparisons and superlatives	Proofread to locate usage errors
Expand sentences	Subject and predicate	
	Simple sentences	
	Compound sentences	
	Complex sentences	
	Compound-complex sentences	
	Declarative sentences	
	Interrogative sentences	
	Imperative sentences	
	Exclamatory sentences	
	Punctuation	
	Capitalization	

 Please visit the Companion Website at **www.prenhall.com/tompkins** for a second fully realized minilesson.

and teach other minilessons, and so on. As teachers identify grammar and usage problems, they should plan minilessons to call students' attention to the problems that make a bigger difference in writing (Pooley, 1974). For example, in the sentences "Mom leave me go outside" and "I fell off of my bike," the use of *leave* for *let* is a more important problem than the redundant use of *of*.

Review

Grammar is the description of the structure of a language and the principles of word and sentence formation. Even though grammar is a controversial topic,

COMBINING SENTENCES   Minilesson

Mrs. Reeves's Third Graders Learn to Combine Sentences

1. Introduce the Topic

Mrs. Reeves makes a transparency of this paragraph and shares it with her third-grade class:

Recess is good. It is the best time of the day. I like to run. I like to kick the ball. It is fun. I like to play ball games like soccer. I like to play hard. I like to win. I dream of being on the winning team. I wish recess was longer. I wish it was two hours long.

She explains that this paragraph is like many of the paragraphs that her students write. She asks them to tell her what is good about the paragraph and what they think should be changed. That the paragraph sticks to one topic is a plus, and the students agree that the "I like" sentences are repetitive and boring.

2. Share Examples

Mrs. Reeves explains that they can revise the paragraph and put some of the sentences together to make the paragraph more interesting. Here is their revision:

Recess is the best time of the day. I like to play ball games like soccer. Running and kicking are fun. I like to play hard and win. I dream of being on the winning team. I wish recess was two hours long.

3. Provide Information

Mrs. Reeves explains to students that what they did is called sentence combining. They can combine sentences to make them more interesting and reword them to vary the words in the sentence.

4. Supervise Practice

Mrs. Reeves divides the class into small groups and gives each group of students another paragraph to revise. She circulates as students work and provides assistance as needed. After they revise their sentences, students in each group share their revised paragraphs.

5. Reflect on Learning

Mrs. Reeves asks the students to reflect on this lesson by rereading the paragraphs she gave them and their revised paragraphs. She asks, "Which one is better?" The students respond that their revised paragraphs are better because the sentences are not as repetitive and boring.

---

the position in this text is that grammar should be taught within the context of authentic reading and writing activities rather than using workbooks. The key concepts discussed in this chapter are:

1. Grammar is the structure of language, whereas usage is the socially accepted way of using words in sentences.
2. Parts of speech, parts of sentences, sentence types, capitalization and punctuation, and usage are the five components of grammar instruction.
3. The eight parts of speech are nouns, pronouns, verbs, adjectives, adverbs, prepositions, conjunctions, and interjections.
4. The two parts of a sentence are the subject and the predicate.

Meeting the Needs of Every Student

How Should I Teach Grammar to My English Learners?

In addition to involving students in a wide variety of talk, reading, and writing activities, teachers should regularly teach minilessons on grammar topics to English learners. The best way to choose topics for the minilessons is to identify the kinds of errors students are making and then teach lessons on those topics. In addition, teachers usually choose topics from state and district-level curriculum guides. Ten of the most common topics are:

Plurals	Prepositions
Verb tenses	Subject-verb agreement
Irregular verbs	Negatives
Contractions	Comparatives
Possessives	Articles

Teachers use the same approach for grammar minilessons that they use for other types of lessons. They introduce the topic using grammatical terms, provide examples from books students are reading and from students' own oral language and writing, explain the rules or provide guidelines for choosing the correct forms, involve students in practice exercises, and monitor students as they apply what they are learning in talk and writing activities. Learning to speak, read, and write standard English takes time, and it's unrealistic to assume that students will learn a grammar topic through a single minilesson. What's important is that teachers regularly teach standard English to their English learners and expect them to assume responsibility for learning it.

To investigate other ways to meet the needs of every student, visit the links for this chapter on the Companion Website at www.prenhall.com/tompkins

Companion Website

Visit Chapter 13 on the Companion Website at www.prenhall. com/tompkins to:

- **Check your understanding of the concepts presented in the chapter**
- **Access the Extensions (activities and a list of related readings)**
- **Link to related websites**

5. Sentences can be classified according to structure: simple, compound, complex, or compound-complex.
6. Sentences can be classified according to purpose: declarative, interrogative, imperative, or exclamatory.
7. Teaching grammar is a controversial topic, but teachers are expected to teach grammar even though research has not documented its usefulness.
8. Grammar should be taught in the context of reading and writing activities.
9. Teachers use sentences from books students are reading and sentences from students' own writing for grammar instruction.
10. Teachers deal with students' usage errors more effectively as part of the editing stage of the writing process than by correcting students' oral language.

Professional References

Atwell, N. (1987). *In the middle: Writing, reading, and learning with adolescents.* Portsmouth, NH: Heinemann.

Beers, K. (2001). Contextualizing grammar. *Voices from the middle, 8*(3), 4.

Braddock, R., Lloyd-Jones, R., & Schoer, L. (1963). *Research in written composition.* Champaign, IL: National Council of Teachers of English.

Calkins, L. M. (1980). When children want to punctuate: Basic skills belong in context. *Language Arts, 57,* 567–573.

Clay, M. M. (1991). *Becoming literate: The construction of inner control.* Portsmouth, NH: Heinemann.

Cordeiro, P., Giacobbe, M. E., & Cazden, C. (1983). Apostrophes, quotation marks, and periods: Learning punctuation in the first grade. *Language Arts, 60,* 323–332.

Cullinan, B. E., Jaggar, A., & Strickland, D. (1974). Oral language expansion in the primary grades. In B. Cullinan (Ed.), *Black dialects and reading.* Urbana, IL: National Council of Teachers of English.

Dunning, S., & Stafford, W. (1992). *Getting the knack: 20 poetry writing exercises.* Urbana, IL: National Council of Teachers of English.

Edelsky, C. (1983). Segmentation and punctuation: Developmental data from young writers in a bilingual program. *Research in the Teaching of English, 17,* 135–136.

Edelsky, C. (1989). Putting language variation to work for you. In P. Rigg & V. G. Allen (Eds.), *When they don't all speak English: Integrating the ESL student into the regular classroom* (pp. 96–107). Urbana, IL: National Council of Teachers of English.

Egawa, K. (1990). Harnessing the power of language: First graders' literature engagement with *Owl moon. Language Arts, 67,* 582–588.

Fearn, L., & Farnan, N. (1998). *Writing effectively: Helping children master the conventions of writing.* Boston: Allyn & Bacon.

Ferreiro, E., & Teberosky, A. (1982). *Literacy before schooling.* Portsmouth, NH: Heinemann.

Fraser, I. S., & Hodson, L. M. (1978). Twenty-one kicks at the grammar horse. *English Journal, 67,* 49–53.

Goodman, K. S. (1965). A linguistic study of cues and miscues in reading. *Elementary English, 42,* 639–643.

Hillocks, G., Jr. (1987). *Research on written composition: New directions for teaching.* Urbana, IL: National Conference on Research in English and the ERIC Clearinghouse on Reading and Communication Skills.

Hillocks, G., Jr., & Smith, M. W. (2003). Grammars and literacy learning. In J. Flood, D. Lapp, J. R. Squire, & J. M. Jensen (Eds.), *Handbook of research on teaching the English language arts* (2nd ed.) (pp. 721–737). Mahwah, NJ: Erlbaum.

Jaggar, A. (1980). Allowing for language differences. In G. S. Pinnell (Ed.), *Discovering language with children* (pp. 25–28). Urbana, IL: National Council of Teachers of English.

Killgallon, D. (1997). *Sentence composing for middle school.* Portsmouth, NH: Heinemann.

Killgallon, D. (1998). Sentence composing: Notes on a new rhetoric. In C. Weaver (Ed.), *Lessons to share: On teaching grammar in context* (pp. 169–183). Portsmouth, NH: Heinemann.

Noguchi, R. R. (1991). *Grammar and the teaching of writing: Limits and possibilities.* Urbana, IL: National Council of Teachers of English.

Noyce, R. M., & Christie, J. F. (1983). Effects of an integrated approach to grammar instruction on third graders' reading and writing. *Elementary School Journal, 84,* 63–69.

Pooley, R. C. (1974). *The teaching of English usage.* Urbana, IL: National Council of Teachers of English.

Routman, R. (1996). *Literacy at the crossroads: Crucial talk about reading, writing, and other teaching dilemmas.* Portsmouth, NH: Heinemann.

Scarcella, R. C. (2003). *Accelerating academic English: A focus on the English learner.* Oakland: Regents of the University of California.

Shaughnessy, M. P. (1977). *Errors and expectations: A guide for teachers of basic writing.* New York: Oxford University Press.

Smith, F. (1982). *Writing and the writer.* New York: Holt, Rinehart and Winston.

Speaker, R. B., Jr., & Speaker, P. R. (1991). Sentence collecting: Authentic literacy events in the classroom. *Journal of Reading, 35,* 92–95.

Strong, W. (1996). *Writer's toolbox: A sentence-combining workshop.* New York: McGraw-Hill.

Tompkins, G. E., & McGee, L. M. (1983). Launching nonstandard speakers into standard English. *Language Arts, 60,* 463–469.

Weaver, C. (1996). *Teaching grammar in context.* Portsmouth, NH: Heinemann.

Weaver, C., McNally, C., & Moerman, S. (2001). To grammar or not to grammar: That is *not* the question! *Voices from the middle, 8*(3), 17–33.

Wilde, S. (1992). *You kan red this! Spelling and punctuation for whole language classrooms, K–6.* Portsmouth, NH: Heinemann.

Children's Book References

Avi. (1995). *Poppy.* New York: Orchard.

Carle, E. (1990). *The very quiet cricket.* New York: Philomel.

Cleary, B. P. (2000). *Hairy, scary, ordinary: What is an adjective?* Minneapolis: Carolrhoda.

Conrad, P. (1989). *The tub people.* New York: Harper & Row.

Ehlert, L. (1994). *Mole's hill.* Orlando: Harcourt Brace.

Heller, R. (1990). *Merry-go-round: A book about nouns.* New York: Grosset & Dunlap.

Heller, R. (1991). *Up, up and away: A book about adverbs.* New York: Grosset & Dunlap.

Heller, R. (1995). *Behind the mask: A book of prepositions.* New York: Grosset & Dunlap.

Heller, R. (1997). *Mine, all mine: A book about pronouns.* New York: Grosset & Dunlap.

Henkes, K. (1991). *Chrysanthemum.* New York: Greenwillow.

Howard, E. F. (1991). *Aunt Flossie's hats (and crab cakes later).* New York: Clarion.

Lowry, L. (1993). *The giver.* Boston: Houghton Mifflin.

Martin, B., Jr. (1983). *Brown bear, brown bear, what do you see?* New York: Holt, Rinehart and Winston.

Martin, B., Jr. (1992). *Polar bear, polar bear, what do you hear?* New York: Holt, Rinehart and Winston.

Naylor, P. R. (1991). *Shiloh.* New York: Atheneum.

Numeroff, L. J. (1985). *If you give a mouse a cookie.* New York: Harper & Row.

Numeroff, L. J. (1993). *Dogs don't wear sneakers.* New York: Simon & Schuster.

Numeroff, L. J. (1995). *Chimps don't wear glasses.* New York: Simon & Schuster.

Peek, M. (1985). *Mary wore her red dress.* New York: Clarion.

Rathmann, P. (1995). *Officer Buckle and Gloria.* New York: Putnam.

Steig, W. (1969). *Sylvester and the magic pebble.* New York: Simon & Schuster.

Taylor, M. D. (1990). *Mississippi bridge.* New York: Dial.

Van Allsburg, C. (1985). *The polar express.* Boston: Houghton Mifflin.

White, E. B. (1980). *Charlotte's web.* New York: HarperCollins.

Yolen, J. (1987). *Owl moon.* New York: Philomel.

Zolotow, C. (1992). *This quiet lady.* New York: Greenwillow.

14 Developing Legible Handwriting

PATTERNS OF PRACTICE

Reading and Writing Workshop

Literature Focus Units

Literature Circles

Theme Cycles

Ms. Boland's seventh graders—a class of Mexican American English learners—are reading *The Circuit* (1997), a collection of autobiographical stories by Francisco Jiménez about his life as a child of migrant farm workers in California. These students understand the poverty Francisco describes in the book, and they can relate to his family's frequent moves: Many of these students change schools more than once a year. Many of their parents or other relatives have picked cotton, grapes, and strawberries. In fact, a few of the seventh graders work in the fields themselves during the summer. One day after school, Sergio stops by to ask if he can keep his book because "it's the truest book I read, and I never have a book of my own." The copies the students are reading are school property, but Ms. Boland digs through her classroom library to find a copy of her own to give him.

Ms. Boland uses shared reading to read the stories with her students in class, and then they reread them independently for homework. After reading each story, they talk about it in a grand conversation. She's teaching them to

be active readers by making predictions and connections while they're reading and talking about the story. She has introduced the three kinds of connections, and there is a chart in the classroom with three sections, labeled personal, world, and literary connections. Whenever a student makes a connection, Ms. Boland writes the student's connection on the chart. The students have made many connections to their own lives, but they have also made other kinds of connections. In the world connections category, students thought of California's controversial law allowing illegal aliens to get driver's licenses and President Bush's guest workers plan. In the literary connections category, several students remembered their sixth-grade teacher reading aloud *Esperanza Rising* (Ryan, 2000), another story about migrant workers in California.

Although Ms. Boland is pleased with the students' involvement in reading and talking about *The Circuit,* their reading log entries are another story: She's frustrated because she can't read their illegible handwriting. Almost every student's handwriting is hard to read because the writing is very small and the letters aren't formed correctly; it's difficult to tell the difference between the letters *e* and *i* and *l* and *b*. Some students mix upper- and lowercase letters and move back and forth between cursive and manuscript forms in the same sentence. She brings the students together for a frank discussion about their handwriting, and she shares examples from their reading logs that she's made into overhead transparencies. An excerpt from one student's reading log is shown in the box on page 598. It reads:

How important is handwriting instruction?

Over the past decade, many teachers have paid less attention to teaching handwriting. There are many reasons for this: Teachers are more involved in sharing literature with students through literature focus units and literature circles, they are involving students in reading and writing workshop, and they are paying more attention to preparing students for state-mandated tests. What are the effects of this decreased attention to handwriting? As you read this vignette about Ms. Boland's seventh graders who have poor handwriting skills, think about the effects of deemphasizing handwriting instruction and what elementary teachers can do about it.

I predict that Francisco is going to be something great when he grows up. I liked it when his mom gave them gifts for Christmas. I wasn't sure that the dad had found work.

598 CHAPTER 14 Developing Legible Handwriting

The ideas are good, but the handwriting seems rushed and careless, with poorly formed letters. The most interesting thing is that this student's uppercase *I* looks like a lowercase *b*.

Ms. Boland explains the importance of legible handwriting, and tells the students they won't get credit for their work if she can't read it. The students agree that their handwriting is hard to read, and they explain why. Isabel says, "I do it so you don't know my words are wrong." Other students agree that their illegible handwriting covers their spelling errors. Moises and Jesus add that nobody ever taught them how to do cursive handwriting. That's the opening Ms. Boland was waiting for: She asks them if they would like to learn how to make their handwriting more legible. The students say yes; they are eager to learn better handwriting skills.

Ms. Boland visits with the wife of a colleague who teaches third grade for advice about teaching handwriting and a quick review of how to form manuscript and cursive letters. Here are the third-grade teacher's suggestions:

1. Demonstrate good handwriting when you write on the chalkboard and call students' attention to the fact that the handwriting is legible.
2. Teach minilessons on handwriting skills.
3. Demonstrate how to form manuscript and cursive letters, and for cursive, show students how to connect the letters.
4. Let students choose to use manuscript or cursive handwriting for writing assignments, but insist that their handwriting be legible.
5. Conference with individual students about specific handwriting problems.
6. Make legible handwriting part of the grade for each assignment.

Ms. Boland borrows a set of small dry-erase boards, pens, and erasers for the students to use to practice writing letters during minilessons, and she also goes to the local school-supply store to purchase large manuscript and cursive handwriting charts to post in the classroom and small cards with handwriting forms for the students to keep in their notebooks to refer to whenever they are writing.

First, Ms. Boland reviews manuscript handwriting forms in a minilesson. She talks about the basic strokes—straight lines, curves, and circles—and demonstrates how to form several uppercase and lowercase letters using the basic strokes. Next, she asks students to practice forming each letter on their dry-erase boards. The students are hesitant to try to form letters she hasn't modeled, so Ms. Boland spends 20 minutes each day for a week demonstrating a few letters and having the students practice them.

After reviewing all of the manuscript upper- and lowercase letters, she asks the students to each choose a favorite sentence from *The Circuit* to copy in their best manuscript handwriting in their reading logs. The students take the assignment seriously and work for nearly a half hour carefully copying their chosen sentence. Ms. Boland circulates around the classroom, providing assistance to students who are unsure how to form particular letters. She uses a dry-erase board to demonstrate how to form the letters and points out when students use uppercase letters unnecessarily within sentences. They continue copying sentences for several days, and then students submit their best handwriting sample for Ms. Boland to grade. She marks each incorrectly or poorly formed letter with a red pen and grades the papers this way: 0–1 error = A, 2–3 errors = B, 4–5 errors = C, and so on. No students had more than four errors. One student's manuscript handwriting paper is shown in the box below. His only error was to capitalize the *F* in *fence,* but he does need to keep the same slant through the entire sentence.

> We walked along the wire wall until Papá spotted a small hole underneath the Fence.

Along with the handwriting minilessons, Ms. Boland and her students continue reading and discussing the stories in *The Circuit*. She asks them to write their journal entries legibly using the manuscript handwriting form. Students are required to recopy any illegible entries. Bobby, Roxana, and Jaime continue to struggle with manuscript handwriting so they come in during lunch for extra assistance. The students create sentences and then they write them on dry-erase boards, following Ms. Boland's model.

Ms. Boland introduces cursive handwriting by demonstrating how she writes her name in cursive. She writes several students' names in cursive on the chalkboard, and then while the students write reading log entries, she moves around the classroom demonstrating for each student how to write his or her name in cursive handwriting. Next, she teaches a series of minilessons on forming the cursive lowercase and uppercase letters, as she did for manuscript handwriting. Then the students copy favorite sentences they have chosen from *The Circuit* in cursive handwriting, and Ms. Boland again collects their best sample to grade. Several students' handwriting receives an A, but most students receive a C. They will continue to practice cursive handwriting. One student's sentence is shown in the box below; this is one of the better samples. This student's only problem was forming the lowercase *k*.

> At the end of the day I was tired and disappointed I had not piched as much cotton as I had wanted to.

At the end of reading *The Circuit,* Ms. Boland teaches the students how to write found poems by collecting words and phrases from the book and arranging them to create a free-form poem. Here is one student's found poem:

La Frontera
Spotted a small hole underneath the fence.
Take care of Trampita
Someday I will pick cotton with you.
First year of school
The more she spoke, the more anxious I became.
Torita, the little bull
Prayed for him in front of a faded picture
Of the Virgen de Guadalupe.
Watched our neighbor's goldfish
Called it "el Angel de Oro."
Received a bag of candy.
"Feliz Navidad, Vieja."
Love El Perico
Buried El Perico in a cigar box.
Sacks for picking cotton
Picked without a sack.
From Jalisco.
Yes, I like corridos.

Students use the writing process to draft and refine their poems, and they have a final editing conference with Ms. Boland in which she helps them correct spelling and grammar errors. She also urges them to use their best handwriting for their final copies. The quality of their handwriting is one item on the rubric that she uses to grade their poems.

Every student's final copy is legible, and the poems demonstrate their understanding of *The Circuit.* The students are very proud of their poems, and the language is more sophisticated than what students ordinarily use. A few spelling and grammar errors remain in their final copies, but their handwriting is much easier to read.

Now the students know Ms. Boland is serious about legible handwriting, and their handwriting is improving. Even the students' parents have noticed the improvement and are thanking her.

As you begin reading this chapter, you may want to read the "Dear Reader" letter in Chapter 14 on the Companion Website at www.prenhall.com/tompkins

Handwriting is a tool for writers. Donald Graves explains: "Children win prizes for fine script, parents and teachers nod approval for a crisp, well-crafted page, a good impression is made on a job application blank . . . all important elements, but they pale next to the substance they carry" (1983, p. 171). Even though the message is more important than the formation of letters, handwriting is still an essential communication tool, and handwriting instruction should not be ignored. Graves (1994) urges teachers to keep handwriting in perspective.

It is important to distinguish between writing and handwriting: Writing is the substance of a composition, and handwriting is the formation of alphabetic symbols on paper. Students need to develop a legible style of handwriting so that they will be able to participate fully in all written-language activities.

The goal in handwriting instruction is to help students develop legible forms to communicate effectively through writing. The two most important criteria in determining quality in handwriting are legibility (the writing can be easily and quickly read) and fluency (the writing can be easily and quickly written). Even though a few students take great pleasure in developing flawless handwriting skills, most of them feel that handwriting instruction is boring and unnecessary. It is imperative, therefore, to recognize the functional purpose of handwriting and convey to students the importance of developing legible handwriting. Writing for genuine audiences is the best way to convey the importance of legibility. A letter sent to a favorite author that is returned by the post office because the address is not decipherable or a child's published hardcover book that sits unread on the library shelf because the handwriting is illegible makes clear the importance of legibility. Illegible writing means a failure to communicate—a harsh lesson for a writer!

As you continue reading, think about these questions:

◆ What handwriting forms do elementary students learn?

◆ How does children's handwriting develop in the elementary grades?

◆ How do teachers teach and assess handwriting?

HANDWRITING FORMS

Two forms of handwriting are currently used in elementary schools: manuscript, or printing, and cursive, or connected writing. These are illustrated in Figure 14–1. Typically, students in the primary grades learn and use the manuscript form; they switch to cursive handwriting in second or third grade. In the middle and upper grades, students use both handwriting forms.

Manuscript Handwriting

Until the 1920s, students learned only cursive handwriting. Marjorie Wise is credited with introducing the manuscript form for primary-grade students in 1921 (Hildreth, 1960). Manuscript handwriting is considered better for young children because they seem to lack the necessary fine motor control and eye–hand coordination for cursive handwriting. In addition, manuscript handwriting is similar to the type style in primary-level reading textbooks. Only two lowercase letters, *a* and *g,* are usually different in typed and handwritten forms. The similarity may actually facilitate young children's introduction to reading because it enhances letter recognition (Adams, 1990).

FIGURE 14-1

Manuscript and Cursive Handwriting Forms

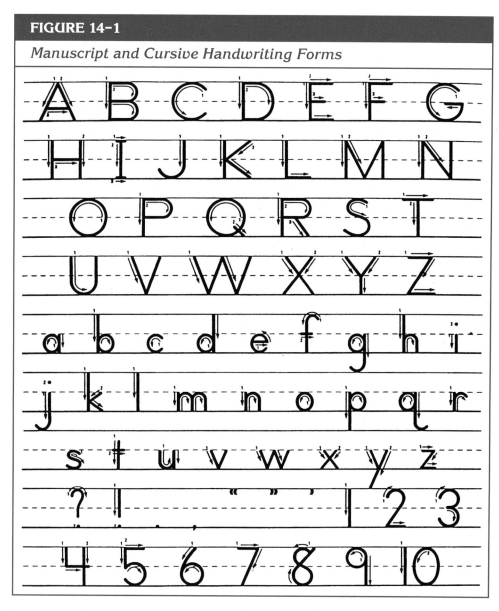

Used with permission of the publisher, Zaner-Bloser, Inc., Columbus, OH, copyright 2003. From *Handwriting: A Way to Self-Expression,* by Clinton Hackney.

Barbe and Milone (1980) suggest several additional reasons that students in the primary grades should learn manuscript before cursive handwriting. First, manuscript handwriting is easier to learn. Studies show that young children can copy letters and words written in the manuscript form more easily than those written in the cursive form. Also, young children can form the vertical and horizontal lines and circles of manuscript handwriting more easily than the cursive strokes. Furthermore, manuscript handwriting is more legible than cursive handwriting. Because it is easier to read, signs and advertisements are printed in letter forms closely approximating manuscript handwriting. Finally, people are often requested to print when completing applications and other forms. For these reasons, manuscript handwriting has become the preferred

FIGURE 14–1 *Continued*

handwriting form for young children as well as a necessary handwriting skill for older children and adults.

Students' use of the manuscript form often disappears in the middle grades after they have learned cursive handwriting. It is essential that middle- and upper-grade teachers learn and use the manuscript form with their students so that it remains an option. Second and third graders learn cursive handwriting, a new form, just when they are becoming proficient in the manuscript form, so it is not surprising that some students want to switch back and forth between the two. The need to develop greater writing speed is often given as the reason for the quick transfer to cursive handwriting, but research does not show that one form is necessarily written more quickly than the other.

There have also been criticisms of the manuscript form. A major complaint is the reversal problem caused by some similar lowercase letters; *b* and *d* are particularly confusing. Detractors also argue that using both the manuscript and cursive forms in the elementary grades requires teaching students two totally different kinds of handwriting within the span of several years.

They also complain that the "circle and sticks" style of manuscript handwriting requires frequent stops and starts, thus inhibiting a smooth and rhythmic flow of writing.

Cursive Handwriting

When most people think of handwriting, the cursive or connected form comes to mind. The letters in cursive handwriting are joined together to form a word with one continuous movement. Children often view cursive handwriting as the grown-up type. Primary-grade students often attempt to imitate this form by connecting the manuscript letters in their names and other words before they are taught how to form and join the letters. Awareness of cursive handwriting and interest in imitating it are indicators that students are ready for instruction.

D'Nealian Handwriting

D'Nealian handwriting is an innovative manuscript and cursive handwriting program developed by Donald Neal Thurber, a teacher in Michigan. The D'Nealian handwriting forms are shown in Figure 14–2. In the manuscript form, letters are slanted and formed with a continuous stroke; in the cursive form, the letters are simplified, without the flourishes of traditional cursive. Both forms were designed to increase legibility and fluency and to ease the transition from manuscript to cursive handwriting.

The purpose of the D'Nealian program was to mitigate some of the problems associated with the traditional manuscript form (Thurber, 1987). D'Nealian manuscript uses the same basic letter forms that students will need for cursive handwriting, as well as the slant and rhythm required for cursive. Another advantage of the D'Nealian style is that the transition from manuscript to cursive involves adding only connective strokes to most manuscript letters. Only five letters—*f, r, s, v,* and *z*—are shaped differently in the cursive form. Research has not yet documented that D'Nealian is better than the traditional manuscript form even though many elementary teachers prefer it (Graham, 1992).

CHILDREN'S HANDWRITING DEVELOPMENT

During the elementary grades, children grow from using scribbles and letterlike forms in kindergarten to learning the manuscript handwriting form in the primary grades and the cursive form beginning in the middle grades. Students in the middle and upper grades use both forms interchangeably for a variety of handwriting tasks. Examples of children's handwriting from kindergarten through eighth grade are shown in Figure 14–3. The excerpts were selected from letters.

Handwriting Before First Grade

Children's handwriting grows out of their drawing activities. Young children observe words all around them in their environment: McDonald's, Coke,

FIGURE 14-2

D'Nealian Manuscript and Cursive Handwriting Forms

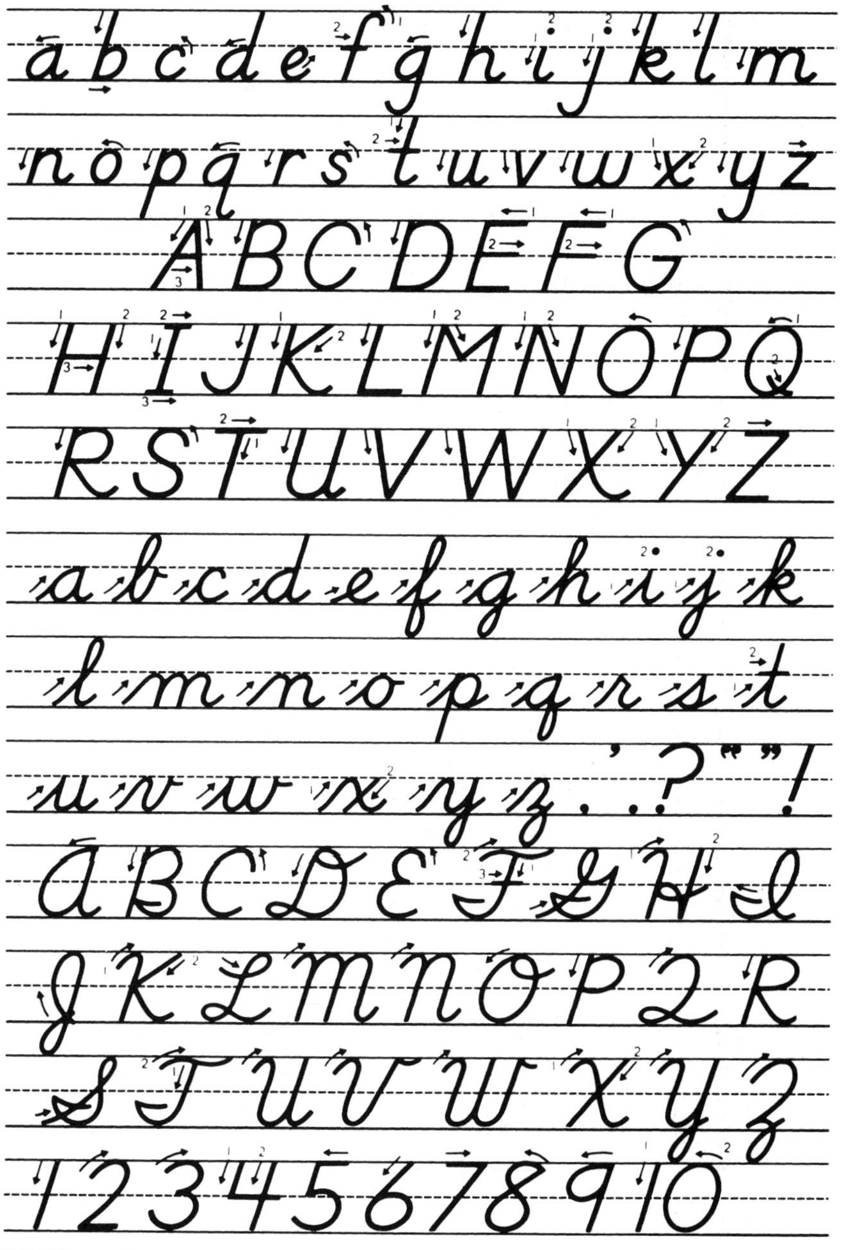

Source: D'Nealian is a registered trademark of Donald Neal Thurber, Copyright © 1999 by Scott, Foresman and Company.

FIGURE 14-3 *Examples of Children's Handwriting*

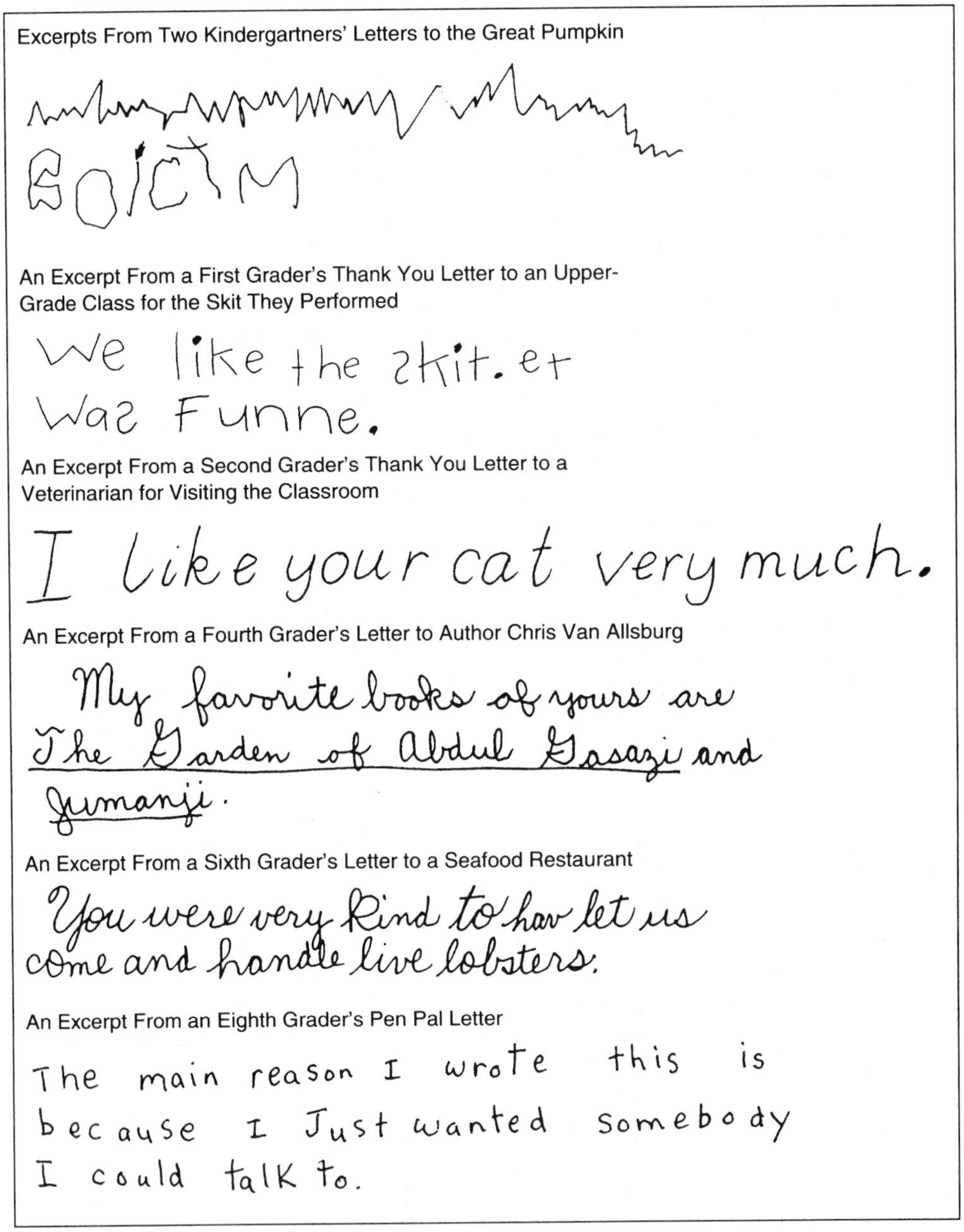

Excerpts From Two Kindergartners' Letters to the Great Pumpkin

[handwritten scribbles]

ΒΟΙĊΤΜ

An Excerpt From a First Grader's Thank You Letter to an Upper-Grade Class for the Skit They Performed

We like the zkit. et Waz Funne.

An Excerpt From a Second Grader's Thank You Letter to a Veterinarian for Visiting the Classroom

I like your cat very much.

An Excerpt From a Fourth Grader's Letter to Author Chris Van Allsburg

My favorite books of yours are The Garden of Abdul Gasazi and Jumanji.

An Excerpt From a Sixth Grader's Letter to a Seafood Restaurant

You were very kind to hav let us come and handle live lobsters.

An Excerpt From an Eighth Grader's Pen Pal Letter

The main reason I wrote this is because I just wanted somebody I could talk to.

STOP. They also observe parents and teachers writing messages. From this early interest in written words and communicating through writing, preschoolers begin to write letterlike forms and scribbles. In kindergarten, children watch the teacher transcribe language experience stories, and they begin to copy their names and familiar words. Once they are familiar with some of the letters, they use invented spelling to express themselves in writing. Through this drawing-reading-writing-handwriting connection, youngsters discover that they can experiment with letters and words and communicate through written language. Handwriting becomes the tool for this written communication.

Young children enter kindergarten with different backgrounds of handwriting experience. Some 5-year-olds have never held a pencil, and many others have written cursivelike scribbles or manuscript-letter-like forms. Some preschoolers have learned to print their names and some other letters. Handwriting in kindergarten typically includes three types of activities: stimulating children's interest in writing, developing their ability to hold writing instruments, and refining their fine motor control. Adults are influential role models in stimulating children's interest in writing. They record children's talk and write labels on signs. They can also provide paper, pencils, and pens so that children can experiment with writing. Students develop the ability to hold a pencil or other writing instrument by adults' modeling and through numerous opportunities to experiment with pencils, pens, paintbrushes, crayons, and other writing instruments.

Handwriting instruction in kindergarten usually focuses on teaching children to form upper- and lowercase letters and to print their names. Handwriting is linked with writing at all grade levels, even in kindergarten. Young children write labels, draw and write stories, keep journals, and write other messages (Klein & Schickedanz, 1980). The more they write, the greater their need becomes for instruction in handwriting. Writers need to know how to grip a pencil, form letters, and leave space between letters and words. Instruction is necessary so that students do not learn bad habits that later must be broken. Students often devise rather bizarre ways to form letters, and these bad habits can cause problems when they need to develop greater writing speed.

Handwriting in the Primary Grades

Formal handwriting instruction begins in first grade. Students learn how to form manuscript letters and space between them, and they develop skills related to the six elements of legibility. A common handwriting activity requires students to copy short writing samples from the chalkboard, but this type of activity is not recommended. For one thing, young children have great difficulty with far-to-near copying (Lamme, 1979); a piece of writing should be placed close to the child for copying. Children can recopy their own compositions, language experience stories, and self-selected writing samples; other types of copying should be avoided. It is far better for children to create their own writing than to copy words and sentences they may not even be able to read!

Special pencils and handwriting paper are often provided for handwriting instruction. Kindergartners and first graders have commonly been given "fat" beginner pencils because it has been assumed that these pencils are easier for young children to hold; however, most children prefer to use regular-sized pencils that older students and adults use. Moreover, regular pencils have erasers! Research now indicates that beginner pencils are not better than regular-sized pencils for young children (Graham, 1992). Likewise, there is no evidence that specially shaped pencils and small writing aids that slip onto pencils to improve children's grips are effective.

Many types of paper, both lined and unlined, are used in elementary classrooms. Paper companies manufacture paper lined in a range of sizes. Typically, paper is lined at 2-inch intervals for kindergartners and at $7/8$- to $3/8$-inch intervals for older students. Lined paper for first and second graders has an added midline, often dotted, to guide students in forming lowercase letters. Sometimes

Seeing Common Threads

Is cursive handwriting still necessary in this age of technology?

Nancy Hill responds:

Even with all the contemporary ways of creating text, we still need cursive handwriting to allow for basic communication between people. It is important that people be able to write neatly and quickly in order to get their meaning across to the reader. People who cannot write legibly do not get their message across to others. Fair or not, a person's handwriting is used to make judgments about him or her. Neat and precise handwriting is often considered the sign of well-educated, organized people who care about their work. Cursive handwriting is important because it allows people to communicate more quickly with others or to take notes about something that should not be missed.

What do you think?

Each chapter presents a question and a response written by one of Dr. Tompkins's students. Consider other comments, or respond to the question yourself, by visiting the Threaded Message Board in Chapter 14 on the Companion Website at www.prenhall.com/tompkins

a line appears below the baseline to guide placement of letters such as lower-case *g, p, q,* and *y* that have "tails" that drop below the baseline. The few research studies that have examined the value of lined paper in general and paper lined at specific intervals offer conflicting results. One study suggests that younger children's handwriting is more legible when they use unlined paper and that older children's is better when they use lined paper (Lindsay & McLennan, 1983). Most teachers seem to prefer that students use lined paper for handwriting activities, but students easily adjust to whichever type of writing paper is available. Children often use rulers to line their paper when they are given unlined paper, and, likewise, they ignore the lines on lined paper if the lines interfere with their drawing or writing.

Transition to Cursive Handwriting

Students' introduction to cursive handwriting typically occurs in the second semester of second grade or the first semester of third grade. Parents and students often attach great importance to the transition from manuscript to cursive, thus adding unnecessary pressure for the students. Beverly Cleary's *Muggie Maggie* (1990) describes the pressure one child feels. The time of transition is usually dictated by tradition rather than by sound educational theory. All students in a school or school district are usually introduced to cursive handwriting at the same time, regardless of their interest in making the change.

Some students indicate an early interest in cursive handwriting by trying to connect manuscript letters or by asking their parents to demonstrate how to write their names. Because of individual differences in motor skills and levels of interest in cursive writing, it is better to introduce some students to cursive handwriting in first or second grade while providing other students with additional time to refine their manuscript skills. These students then learn cursive handwriting in third or fourth grade.

Cursive handwriting does not replace manuscript handwriting. While they are learning cursive handwriting, children continue to use manuscript handwriting part of the time. Because manuscript handwriting is easier for students to form and to read, they often use the manuscript form when they write during theme cycles. Also, because manuscript handwriting looks more like the type used in books, students reinforce their knowledge of content-area vocabulary as they use manuscript writing.

The practice of changing to cursive handwriting only a year or two after children learn the manuscript form is receiving increasing criticism. The argument has been that students need to learn cursive handwriting as early as possible because of their increasing need for handwriting speed. Because of its continuous flow, cursive handwriting was thought to be faster to write than manuscript; however, research suggests that manuscript handwriting can be written as quickly as cursive handwriting (Jackson, 1971). The controversy over the benefits of the two forms and the best time to introduce cursive handwriting is likely to continue.

Handwriting in the Middle and Upper Grades

Students are introduced to the cursive handwriting form in second and third grades. Usually, the basic strokes that make up the letters (e.g., slant stroke, undercurve, downcurve) are taught first. Next, the lowercase letters are taught in isolation, and then the connecting strokes are introduced. Uppercase letters are taught later because they are used far less often and are more difficult to form. Which cursive letters are most difficult? The lowercase *r* is the most troublesome letter. The other lowercase letters students frequently form incorrectly are *k, p,* and *z.*

After students have learned both manuscript and cursive handwriting, they need to review both forms periodically. By this time, too, they have firmly established handwriting habits, both good and bad. At the middle- and upper-grade levels, emphasis is on helping students diagnose and correct their handwriting trouble spots so that they can develop a legible and fluent handwriting style. Older students both simplify their letter forms and also add unique flourishes to their handwriting to develop their own trademark styles.

Teachers often insist that students demonstrate their best handwriting every time they pick up a pencil or pen. This requirement is unrealistic; certainly there are times when handwriting is important, but at other times speed or other considerations outweigh neatness. Children need to learn to recognize two types of writing occasions—private and public. Legibility counts in public writing, but when students make notes for themselves or write a rough draft of a composition, they are doing private writing and should decide for themselves whether neatness is important.

A review of the sequence of children's handwriting development is presented in the LA Essentials box on page 610.

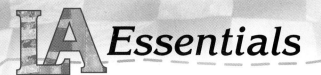
Essentials

Sequence of Children's Handwriting Development

1. Handwriting Before First Grade

Teachers teach basic handwriting skills during kindergarten.

- Children learn how to hold a pencil.
- Children learn to recognize and form upper- and lowercase letters.
- Children learn to write their names and other common words.

2. Handwriting in the Primary Grades

Primary-grade students develop legible manuscript handwriting.

- Children learn to form upper- and lowercase manuscript letters and space between letters.
- Children often use "fat" beginner pencils even though research does not support this practice.
- Children use wide, lined paper with a dotted midline to guide them in forming lowercase letters.

3. Transition to Cursive Handwriting

Teachers teach students to both read and write cursive handwriting because it is a new writing system.

- Students are introduced to cursive handwriting in second or third grade.
- Students learn to read cursive writing.
- Students learn to form upper- and lowercase letters and to join letters.
- Students continue to use manuscript writing during the transition, especially for writing related to theme cycles.

4. Handwriting in the Middle and Upper Grades

Teachers expect students to use both manuscript and cursive handwriting in daily writing activities.

- Students have learned both manuscript and cursive handwriting forms.
- Students develop their own trademark styles.
- Students vary the legibility and neatness of their handwriting for private and public writing.

TEACHING HANDWRITING IN THE ELEMENTARY GRADES

Handwriting is best taught in separate periods of direct instruction and teacher-supervised practice. As soon as skills are taught, they should be applied in real-life writing activities. Busywork assignments, such as copying sentences from the chalkboard, lack educational significance. Moreover, students may develop poor handwriting habits or learn to form letters incorrectly if they practice without direct supervision. It is much more difficult to correct bad habits and errors in letter formation than to teach correct handwriting in the first place.

Elements of Legibility

For students to develop legible handwriting, they need to know what qualities or elements determine legibility and then to analyze their own handwriting according to these elements (Hackney, 1993). The six elements of legible handwriting are:

1. *Letter formation.* Letters are formed with specific strokes. Letters in manuscript handwriting are composed of vertical, horizontal, and slanted lines plus circles or parts of circles. The letter *b,* for example, is composed of a vertical line and a circle, and *M* is composed of vertical and slanted lines. Cursive letters are composed of slanted lines, loops, and curved lines. The lowercase cursive letters *m* and *n,* for instance, are composed of a slant stroke, a loop, and an undercurve stroke. An additional component in cursive handwriting is the connecting stroke used to join letters.
2. *Size and proportion.* During the elementary grades, students' handwriting becomes smaller, and the proportional size of uppercase to lowercase letters increases. First graders' uppercase manuscript letters are twice the size of their lowercase letters. When second- and third-grade students begin cursive handwriting, the proportional size of letters remains 2:1; later, the proportion increases to 3:1 for middle- and upper-grade students.
3. *Spacing.* Students should leave adequate space between letters in words and between words in sentences. Spacing between words in manuscript handwriting should equal one lowercase letter *o,* and spacing between sentences should equal two lowercase *o*s. The most important aspect of spacing within words in cursive handwriting is consistency. To correctly space between words, the writer should make the beginning stroke of the new word directly below the end stroke of the preceding word. Spacing between sentences should equal one uppercase letter *O,* and the indent for a new paragraph should equal two uppercase letter *O*s.
4. *Slant.* Letters should be consistently parallel. Letters in manuscript handwriting are vertical, and in the cursive form, letters slant slightly to the right. To ensure the correct slant, right-handed students tilt their papers to the left, and left-handed students tilt their papers to the right.
5. *Alignment.* For proper alignment in both manuscript and cursive handwriting, all letters should be uniform in size and consistently touch the baseline.
6. *Line quality.* Students should write at a consistent speed and hold their writing instruments correctly and in a relaxed manner to make steady, unwavering lines of even thickness.

Piecing a Lesson Together

Topics on Handwriting

Procedures	Concepts	Strategies and Skills
Grip a pencil	Legibility	Determine purpose of
Form letters	Manuscript handwriting	handwriting
Space between letters	Cursive handwriting	Choose manuscript or
Size of letters	Public and private	cursive
Make letters parallel	handwriting	Apply elements of legibility
Write manuscript letters		Personalize handwriting
Write cursive letters		
Make letters touch the		
baseline		
Keep letters same size		
Make lines steady and of		
even thickness		
Self-assess handwriting		
problems		

Please visit the Companion Website at
www.prenhall.com/tompkins for a second fully
realized minilesson.

Correct letter formation and spacing receive the major focus in handwriting instruction during the elementary grades. Although the other four elements usually receive less attention, they, too, are important in developing legible handwriting.

Minilessons

Handwriting, like other components of language arts, is taught in minilessons. Brief lessons and practice sessions taught several times a week are more effective than a single, lengthy period weekly or monthly. Regular handwriting in-

LETTER FORMATION

Minilesson

Ms. Thomas Teaches Her First Graders Manuscript-Letter Formation

1. **Introduce the Topic**

   Ms. Thomas brings her first graders together on the rug for handwriting practice and passes out a small white board, pen, and eraser to each child. They begin by rereading the class news chart that they wrote the day before using interactive writing. Ms. Thomas explains that she wants to practice three lowercase letters—*m, n,* and *u*—that the children had difficulty writing the previous day.

2. **Share Examples**

   Ms. Thomas rereads the chart and asks students to point out the three letters when they notice them in the class news chart. She asks one student to underline each word the students point out. Children point out these words: *and, made, not, when, never, some, then, you, your,* and *wanted.* After reading the entire chart, the students agree that these letters are important because they are used so often in their writing.

3. **Provide Information**

   Ms. Thomas demonstrates how to form each of the letters for students by writing the letter

on a white board and verbalizing the strokes she is making. Then the children practice writing the letters on their white boards as Ms. Thomas observes them. She assists several students in holding their pencils correctly, and she demonstrates again for several students who are continuing to have trouble writing the letters.

4. **Supervise Practice**

   Once she is satisfied that each student can form the three letters and differentiate among them, Ms. Thomas asks students to write several of the underlined words on their white boards as she observes. She provides immediate feedback to students who are not forming the letters correctly or who make the letters too large.

5. **Reflect on Learning**

   After this brief review, Ms. Thomas asks students to remember what they learned about forming these letters when they are writing. The children name all the occasions they have during the day to remember how to form the letters when they are writing—when they write books at the writing center, when they write in journals, and when they do interactive writing.

struction is necessary when teaching the manuscript form in kindergarten and first grade and the cursive form in second or third grade. In the middle and upper grades, instruction focuses on specific handwriting problems that students demonstrate and periodic reviews of both handwriting forms.

A list of minilesson topics is presented in the box on these pages, and a sample lesson on teaching manuscript-letter formation in first grade is also shown. The teacher introduces the handwriting skill and then supervises as students practice it.

Research has shown the importance of the teacher's active involvement in handwriting instruction and practice. Teachers often print or write handwriting samples in advance on practice sheets. Then they distribute the sheets and ask students to practice a handwriting skill by copying the model they have written. Observing "moving" models—that is, having students watch the teacher write the handwriting sample—is of far greater value than copying models that have already been written (Wright & Wright, 1980). Moving models are possible when the teacher circulates around the classroom, stopping to demonstrate a procedure, strategy, or skill for one student and moving to assist another; circling incorrectly formed letters and marking other errors with a red pen on completed handwriting sheets is of little value. As in the writing process, the teacher's assistance is far more worthwhile while the students are writing, not after they have completed writing.

As Graves said, "Handwriting is for writing" (1983, p. 171), and for the most meaningful transfer of skills, students should be involved in writing for various purposes and for genuine audiences. Students apply their handwriting procedures, strategies, and skills whenever they write, and the best way to practice handwriting is through writing.

Working With Left-Handed Writers

Approximately 10% of the U.S. population is left-handed, and there may be two or three left-handed students in most classrooms. Until 1950 or so, teachers insisted that left-handed students use their right hands for handwriting because left-handed writers were thought to have inferior handwriting skills. Parents and teachers are more realistic now and accept children's natural tendencies for left- or right-handedness. In fact, research has shown that there is no significant difference in the quality or speed of left- and right-handed students' writing (Groff, 1963).

Most young children develop handedness—the preference for using either the right or the left hand for fine motor activities—before entering kindergarten or first grade. Teachers must help those few students who have not already developed handedness to choose and consistently use one hand for handwriting and other fine motor activities. The teacher's role consists of observing the student's behavior and hand preference in play, art, writing, and playground activities. Over a period of days or weeks, the teacher observes and notes which hand the child uses in activities such as building with blocks, throwing and catching balls, cutting with scissors, holding a paintbrush, manipulating clay, and pouring water or sand.

During the observation period, teachers may find that a child who has not established hand preference uses both hands interchangeably; for example, a child may first reach for several blocks with one hand and then reach for the next block with the alternate hand. During drawing activities, the child will sometimes switch hands every few minutes. In this situation, the teacher consults the child's parents and asks them to observe and monitor the child's behavior at home, noting hand preferences when the child eats, brushes teeth, turns on the television, opens doors, and so on. The teacher, the child, and the child's parents should then confer and—based on the results of joint observations, the handedness of family members, and the child's wishes— make a tentative decision about hand preference. At school, teacher and child will work closely together so that the child will use only the chosen hand. As long as the child continues to use both hands interchangeably, neither hand will develop the prerequisite fine motor control for handwriting, so teachers should postpone handwriting instruction until the child develops a dominant hand.

Teaching handwriting to left-handed students is not simply the reverse of teaching handwriting to right-handed students (Howell, 1978). Left-handed students have unique handwriting problems, and special adaptations of the procedures for teaching right-handed students are necessary. Many of the problems that left-handed students have can actually be made worse by using the procedures designed for right-handed writers (Harrison, 1981). Special adjustments are necessary to allow left-handed students to write legibly, fluently, and with less fatigue.

The basic difference between right- and left-handed writing is physical orientation: Right-handed students pull their arms toward their bodies as they write, whereas left-handed writers push away. As left-handed students write, they move their left hand across what they have just written, often covering it. Many children adopt a "hook" position to avoid covering and smudging what they have written. Because of their different physical orientation, left-handed writers need to make three major types of adjustments:

1. *Holding pencils.* Left-handed writers should hold pencils or pens an inch or more farther back from the tip than right-handed writers do. This change helps them see what they have just written and avoid smearing their writing. Left-handed writers need to work to avoid hooking their wrists. They keep their wrists straight and elbows close to their bodies to avoid the awkward hooked position. Practicing handwriting on the chalkboard is one way to help them develop a more natural style.

2. *Tilting paper.* Left-handed students should tilt their writing papers slightly to the right, in contrast to right-handed students, who tilt their papers to the left. Sometimes it is helpful to place a piece of masking tape on the student's desk to indicate the proper amount of tilt.

3. *Slanting letters.* Whereas right-handed students are encouraged to slant their cursive letters to the right, left-handed writers often write vertically or even slant their letters slightly backward. Some handwriting programs recommend that left-handed writers slant their cursive letters slightly to the right as right-handed students do, but others advise teachers to permit any slant between vertical and 45 degrees to the left of vertical (Howell, 1978).

Diagnosing and Correcting Handwriting Problems

Students use the six elements of legibility to diagnose their handwriting problems. Primary-grade students, for example, can check to see if they have formed a particular letter correctly, if the round parts of letters are joined neatly, and if slanted letters are joined in sharp points. Older students can examine a piece of handwriting to see if their letters are consistently parallel and if the letters touch the baseline consistently. A checklist for evaluating manuscript handwriting is shown in the Weaving Assessment Into Practice feature on page 616. Checklists can also be developed for cursive handwriting. It is important to involve students

Weaving Assessment Into Practice

A Checklist for Assessing Manuscript Handwriting

Name _____

Writing Project_____

Date _____

_____ 1.   Did I form my letters correctly?
Did I start my line letters at the top?
Did I start my circle letters at 1:00?
Did I join the round parts of the letters neatly?
Did I join the slanted strokes in sharp points?

_____ 2.   Did my lines touch the midline or top line neatly?

_____ 3.   Did I space evenly between letters?

_____ 4.   Did I leave enough space between words?

_____ 5.   Did I make my letters straight up and down?

_____ 6.   Did I make all my letters sit on the baseline?

in developing the checklists so that they appreciate the need to make their hand-writing more legible.

Another reason students need to diagnose and correct their handwriting problems is that handwriting quality influences teacher evaluation and grading. Researchers have found that teachers consistently grade papers with better handwriting higher than papers with poor handwriting, regardless of the content (Graham, 1992). Students in the elementary grades are not too young to learn that poor or illegible handwriting may lead to lower grades.

Keyboarding: An Alternative to Handwriting

To become efficient computer users, elementary students need to develop keyboarding skills. Students with good keyboarding skills can use the computer more easily for word processing, to write e-mail messages, and to create HyperStudio projects. Keyboarding is also faster than writing by hand. In the upper elementary grades, students can learn to type 20 to 25 words per minute, but they handwrite only 10 to 15 words in the same amount of time (National Business Education Association, 1997).

Informal keyboarding instruction begins in the primary grades. Students become familiar with the keyboard and learn basic hand positioning. They learn to keep their right hands on the right of the keyboard and their left hands on the left side. They learn simple keyboarding skills. They learn to keep their

Keyboarding. These two fifth graders are learning to position their fingers on the home-row keys and the location of the letters on the keyboard. It's important that middle-grade students learn keyboarding skills so that they can word process their compositions quickly and accurately. Through a combination of instruction from the teacher and practice using a computer keyboarding program, they learn touch-typing skills and to look at the screen rather than their fingers while typing. In addition, they develop proper posture while working at the computer so that they won't become fatigued.

fingers on the home-row keys (asdfghjkl;) and to type with more than one finger. Students also learn proper posture: They sit directly in front of the computer and keep their feet on the floor.

In third or fourth grade, students receive formal keyboarding lessons. Through a series of lessons, students learn touch typing and to look mainly at the screen rather than at their fingers while typing. It is crucial that students develop good touch-typing skills and avoid bad habits that inhibit efficient use of the keyboard. Students often practice keyboarding using AlphaSmart or another portable keyboard because a full computer is not needed. Guidelines for teaching keyboarding skills are presented in the LA Essentials box on page 618.

Students can learn keyboarding through teacher-directed lessons or using software packages. The Kid Keys software package is recommended for primary students. This package includes lessons on becoming familiar with the letter positions on the keyboard and games using keyboarding skills to make music. The Mavis Beacon Teaches Typing software package is recommended for students in third grade and above. The lessons teach fundamental keyboarding skills at several levels of difficulty and offer games to reinforce the skills.

Even though voice-recognition systems may someday replace the need for computer keyboards, keyboarding skills are still essential.

Meeting the Needs of Every Student

The goal of handwriting instruction is for every student to develop legible and fluent handwriting. Students' handwriting does not need to match textbook samples, but it does need to be easy to read and quickly produced. When students are writing for genuine audiences, their handwriting is likely to be better

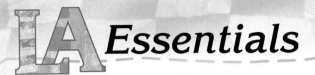

Essentials

Guidelines for Successful Keyboarding

Students need to sit correctly at the computer and learn touch-typing skills in order to be successful and avoid problems related to computer work.

1. **Body Position**

   Students sit up straight and directly in front of the keyboard, aligning the center of their bodies with the *j* key.

2. **Foot Position**

   Students keep their feet flat on the floor, about a hand span's distance apart.

3. **Back Position**

   Students keep their backs straight and lean slightly forward.

4. **Arm Position**

   Students keep their arms and shoulders relaxed and their elbows close to the body.

5. **Wrist Position**

   Students keep their wrists straight.

6. **Home-Row Keys**

   Students anchor their fingers on the home-row keys (*asdfghjkl;*). They use their thumbs to press the space bar and their little fingers to press the shift and return keys.

7. **Finger Position**

   Students keep their fingers in a well-curved position and use a snap stroke to press the keys.

8. **Touch Typing**

   Students learn touch typing and other special computer-related keyboard features.

9. **Eye Position**

   Students keep their eyes on the screen or the text they are typing onto the computer.

10. **Speed and Accuracy**

    Students develop typing speed and accuracy through practice and using the computer for authentic writing activities.

National Business Education Association, 1997.

Meeting the Needs of Every Student

If Students Type Their Compositions on the Computer, How Will They Develop Legible Handwriting Skills?

It's a good idea to have students word process their compositions because students like word processing, and it makes their compositions look professional. Having the opportunity to use the computer often increases students' interest in writing. This is especially important for struggling students who typically have fewer opportunities to use the computer because they are often slower getting their writing done. It's not a question of helping students develop either legible handwriting or keyboarding skills: Your students need both.

Students rarely develop legible handwriting by simply being told to write neatly. They need to understand why legibility is important and to take pride in their work. During the elementary grades, students should learn how to do both manuscript and cursive handwriting. Some students, however, don't apply what they are learning, and their handwriting is hard to read. They need additional instruction, regular feedback about handwriting, and daily practice opportunities. Writing the final copy of a composition is probably not a good practice activity because compositions are usually quite long and students are often under pressure to get the final copy finished. Shorter pieces of writing are better for handwriting practice; for example, writing journal entries, copying favorite sentences from books, making charts and posters, and practicing spelling words are appropriate activities.

Like handwriting, keyboarding also needs to be taught. It's important that students learn how to type using all 10 fingers and have many, many opportunities to practice the skills they are learning so that they become fluent typists.

To investigate other ways to meet the needs of every student, visit the links for this chapter on the Companion Website at www.prenhall.com/ tompkins

Companion Website

than when they are writing for themselves. It is important that students understand and differentiate between public and private occasions for writing. For students who have difficulty with handwriting, the D'Nealian handwriting program may be more effective because the letter forms are simplified. Students with severe handwriting problems can use computers with word-processing programs to produce most of their written work. Suggestions for teaching both handwriting and keyboarding skills are presented above. Teachers also need to adapt handwriting instruction for left-handed students.

Review

Handwriting is a tool for writers, and during the elementary grades, students learn both manuscript and cursive handwriting. The emphasis in handwriting instruction is on legibility rather than on imitating handwriting models perfectly; students need to learn how to write so that their writing can be easily read. The key concepts discussed in this chapter are:

1. Students learn two handwriting forms—manuscript and cursive—during the elementary grades.
2. Students learn manuscript handwriting or printing in kindergarten and first grade.
3. Research has shown that pencil size and the use of lined paper do not affect handwriting quality.
4. Students learn cursive or connected handwriting in second or third grade.
5. During the upper elementary grades, students practice both handwriting forms and learn to use them for different purposes.
6. A transitional handwriting form is D'Nealian, which simplifies students' transition from manuscript to cursive handwriting.
7. The six elements of handwriting are letter formation, size and proportion, spacing, slant, alignment, and line quality.
8. The most important component of handwriting instruction is that the teacher demonstrate handwriting and provide feedback during the lesson.
9. Handwriting instruction must be linked with writing at all grade levels.
10. Students should learn to self-assess their handwriting and identify ways to improve its legibility.

Visit Chapter 14 on the Companion Website at www.prenhall. com/tompkins to:

- **Check your understanding of the concepts presented in the chapter**
- **Access the Extensions (activities and a list of related readings)**
- **Link to related websites**

Professional References

Adams, M. J. (1990). *Beginning to read: Thinking and learning about print.* Cambridge, MA: MIT Press.

Barbe, W. B., & Milone, M. N., Jr. (1980). *Why manuscript writing should come before cursive writing* (Zaner-Bloser Professional Pamphlet No. 11). Columbus, OH: Zaner-Bloser.

Graham, S. (1992). Issues in handwriting instruction. *Focus on Exceptional Children, 25,* 1–14.

Graves, D. H. (1983). *Writing: Teachers and children at work.* Portsmouth, NH: Heinemann.

Graves, D. H. (1994). *A fresh look at writing.* Portsmouth, NH: Heinemann.

Groff, P. J. (1963). Who writes faster? *Education, 83,* 367–369.

Hackney, C. (1993). *Handwriting: A way to self-expression.* Columbus, OH: Zaner-Bloser.

Harrison, S. (1981). Open letter from a left-handed teacher: Some sinistral ideas on the teaching of handwriting. *Teaching Exceptional Children, 13,* 116–120.

Hildreth, G. (1960). Manuscript writing after sixty years. *Elementary English, 37,* 3–13.

Howell, H. (1978). Write on, you sinistrals! *Language Arts, 55,* 852–856.

Jackson, A. D. (1971). *A comparison of speed of legibility of manuscript and cursive handwriting of intermediate grade pupils.* Unpublished doctoral dissertation, University of Arizona. Dissertation Abstracts, 31, 4384A.

Klein, A., & Schickedanz, J. (1980). Preschoolers write messages and receive their favorite books. *Language Arts, 57,* 742–749.

Lamme, L. L. (1979). Handwriting in an early childhood curriculum. *Young Children, 35,* 20–27.

Lindsay, G. A., & McLennan, D. (1983). Lined paper: Its effects on the legibility and creativity of young children's writing. *British Journal of Educational Psychology, 53,* 364–368.

National Business Education Association. (1997). *Elementary/middle school keyboarding strategies guide* (2nd ed.). Reston, VA: Author.

Thurber, D. N. (1987). *D'Nealian handwriting (Grades K–8).* Glenview, IL: Scott, Foresman.

Wright, C. D., & Wright, J. P. (1980). Handwriting: The effectiveness of copying from moving versus still models. *Journal of Educational Research, 74,* 95–98.

Children's Book References

Cleary, B. (1990). *Muggie Maggie.* New York: Morrow.

Jiménez, F. (1997). *The circuit: Stories from the life of a migrant child.* Albuquerque: University of New Mexico Press.

Ryan, P. M. (2000). *Esperanza rising.* New York: Scholastic.

15 Putting It All Together

PATTERNS OF PRACTICE

Reading and Writing Workshop

Literature Focus Units

Literature Circles

Theme Cycles

Mrs. McNeal's first graders are studying the solar system. At the beginning of the theme cycle, the children listed what they knew about the planets on a K-W-L chart and brainstormed a list of questions, and at the end of the theme, they will finish the chart by adding what they've learned. A word wall also went up at the beginning of the theme, and students added the names of the planets, *astronaut, moon, ring, asteroid, alien, comet,* and other new words to the word wall. They also added small illustrations to make identifying the words easier.

Each morning, the first graders sign in when they arrive in the classroom. Mrs. McNeal makes daily sign-in sheets on a large sheet of drawing paper by writing a theme-related question at the top of the paper and two or three possible answers at the bottom. The students read the question and possible answers and sign in by writing their names in a column above the answer they think is correct. Today's question is: *What makes the moon shine?* The three possible answers are: *The sun makes it shine, It has its own light,* and *The earth makes it shine.* Most of the students guess that it has its own light, but they

aren't sure. The purpose of the question was to pique the students' interest, and Mrs. McNeal reads aloud Gail Gibbons's *The Moon Book* (1997) so the students can find out if they are right. They learn, of course, that the moon reflects the sun's light. Earlier in the theme cycle after she introduced the nine planets, Mrs. McNeal asked, *How many planets are there?* on the daily sign-in chart to check the students' understanding. The possible answers were *5, 9,* and *10.* On another day she asked, *Which one of these is a star?* The possible answers were *sun, asteroid,* and *Mercury.*

Mrs. McNeal has been reading aloud stories, informational books, and poems from a text set of books about the solar system, and she and the class have been talking about the stories and poems in grand conversations and about the informational books in instructional conversations. A list of the books in Mrs. McNeal's text set is shown in the box on page 625. After they read a book, the students have been writing paragraphs to define and explain concepts they are

How do students use the six language arts during theme cycles?

Students use the six language arts—listening, talking, reading, writing, viewing, and visually representing—as tools for learning and to document their learning during social studies and science theme cycles. For example, they talk and listen as they participate in instructional conversations, read text sets of books related to the theme, write in learning logs, reports, and multigenre projects, view photos, diagrams, and maps, and make posters and artifacts. As you read this vignette, notice how Mrs. McNeal provides opportunities for her students to use the six language arts as they learn about the solar system.

learning. The students choose the three most important pieces of information, arrange them into sentences, and combine the sentences to make a paragraph. Here are four of their paragraphs:

Rocket

A rocket is a machine that goes into space. It carries astronauts. They study outer space.

Moon

The moon is a ball of rock. It goes around the earth. It has no air or atmosphere.

Asteroids
Asteroids are chunks of rock and metal. They orbit around the sun.
Many asteroids are in the asteroid belt between Mars and Jupiter.

The Inner Planets
The inner planets are Mercury, Venus, Earth, and Mars. They are
closest to the sun. All four are made of rock.

The students write the paragraphs on chart paper using interactive writing, and Mrs. McNeal supervises their work, making corrections and teaching spelling, capitalization, and punctuation skills as needed. It's important that the paragraphs are written conventionally because they are posted in the classroom for students to read and reread.

Mrs. McNeal hangs a framed print of Vincent Van Gogh's painting "Starry Night" in the classroom and reads excerpts from *The First Starry Night* (Isom, 1997) to introduce the painting. The students like the sparkling effect in the painting, and as they continue to talk about it, Mrs. McNeal collects their words and helps them arrange the words to make a poem to Vincent Van Gogh:

To Vincent Van Gogh
Twinkle, twinkle little stars.
Sparklers in the night.
Bright! Brighter!! Brightest!!!
We see your stars and love them, too.
Twinkle, twinkle, little stars.

The students fold sheets of drawing paper in half. On the outside, they use crayons to re-create Van Gogh's painting, and on the inside, they copy the poem or create their own poems. Then Mrs. McNeal arranges the students' art around Van Gogh's painting.

The first graders participate in other theme-related activities at eight centers that Mrs. McNeal has set up in her classroom. Students participate in all of the centers, with certain ones assigned each day. They go to some centers only once a week and others, such as the research center, more often. The centers are:

1. *Art center.* Students use paint to create a map of the solar system with a parent-volunteer's assistance at this center. They dip 10 round sponges of varying sizes (one for the sun and nine for the planets) into paint and stamp them on a wide sheet of construction paper; students dip the largest sponge into yellow paint and stamp it at the left side of the paper, and then they stamp the nine planets in order away from the sun. After the paint dries, the students label the planets, add moons, rings, and the asteroid belt using marking pens.
2. *Listening center.* Each week, the students listen to a different book from the text set of books about the solar system and draw pictures and write words to complete a chart about the book. This week, they're listening to Frank Asch's *The Sun Is My Favorite Star* (2000).

Text Set of Books About the Solar System

Leveled Books
Berger, M. (1995). *Out in space.* New York: Newbridge Educational Publishing.
Biddulph, F., & Biddulph, J. (1992). *Earth and moon.* Bothell, WA: The Wright Group.
Cutting, B., & Cutting, J. (1992a). *Exploring space.* Bothell, WA: The Wright Group.
Cutting, B., & Cutting, J. (1992b). *What is in space?* Bothell, WA: The Wright Group.
Cutting, J. (1988). *Space journey.* Bothell, WA: The Wright Group.

Stories
Asch, F. (1978). *Moon bear.* New York: Atheneum.
Asch, F. (1982). *Happy birthday, moon.* Englewood Cliffs, NJ: Prentice Hall.
Asch, F. (2000). *The sun is my favorite star.* New York: Scholastic.
Carle, E. (1986). *Papa, please get the moon for me.* Natick, MA: Picture Book Studio.
Coffelt, N. (1993). *Dogs in space.* San Diego: Harcourt Brace.
Harper, C. M. (2002). *There was a bold lady who wanted a star.* Boston: Little, Brown.
Hopkinson, D. (1999). *Maria's comet.* New York: Atheneum.
Polacco, P. (1987). *Meteor!* New York: Putnam.

Informational Books
Barton, B. (1988). *I want to be an astronaut.* New York: HarperCollins.
Brandley, F. M. (1981a). *The planets in our solar system.* New York: HarperCollins.
Brandley, F. M. (1981b). *The sky is full of stars.* New York: HarperCollins.
Brandley, F. M. (1984). *Is there life in outer space?* New York: HarperCollins.
Brown, P. (1993). *Moon jump: A cowntdown.* New York: Puffin.
Cole, J. (1990). *The magic school bus lost in the solar system.* New York: Scholastic.
Fowler, A. (1991). *The sun is always shining somewhere.* Chicago: Childrens Press.
Fowler, A. (1992). *The sun's family of planets.* Chicago: Childrens Press.
Gibbons, G. (1992). *Stargazers.* New York: Scholastic.
Gibbons, G. (1993). *The planets.* New York: Holiday House.
Gibbons, G. (1997). *The moon book.* New York: Holiday House.
Jeunesse, G., & Verdet, J. (1995). *The universe.* New York: Scholastic.
Krulik, N. E. (1991). *My picturebook of the planets.* New York: Scholastic.
Leedy, L. (1993). *Postcards from Pluto: A tour of the solar system.* New York: Scholastic.
Rockwell, A. (1999). *Our stars.* New York: Scholastic.
Young, R. (1990). *A trip to Mars.* New York: Orchard.

Poems
Barner, B. (2002). *Stars! Stars! Stars!* San Francisco: Chronicle Books.
Livingston, M. C. (1988). *Space songs.* New York: Holiday House.

---

3. *Writing center.* The students make a pattern book based on Pat Hutchins's *Rosie's Walk* (1968), a story the first graders know well. Mrs. McNeal writes one line on each page of the book, omitting the last word or phrase. She compiles the pages and binds the book together so that all students have to do is supply the underlined word

or phrase and add an illustration to complete the page. Here is Jacky's completed book:

My star and I traveled through <u>space</u>
Across the <u>clouds</u>
Around the <u>moon</u>
Over the <u>stars</u>
Past the <u>space shuttle</u>
Under the <u>meteors</u>
Through the <u>milky way</u>
And I got back in time for my <u>birthday.</u>

The underlined words are the words that Jacky chose for her book. After she finished her book, she put it in her personal box of books to read and reread at home and during the first 10 minutes of the school day. Students make a new book every week to add to their collections, so that by the end of the school year, they have 30 books or more that they can read independently.

4. *Word wall center.* Students use a pointer to reread the words on the solar system word wall. Then they participate in other activities, including writing the words on white boards, spelling them with magnetic letters, and matching word cards to pictures.

5. *Research center.* Students write and illustrate books about the solar system at the research center. Every other day, Mrs. McNeal focuses on one of the planets and records information about the planet on a large data chart hanging on the wall next to the center. The completed data chart is shown on page 627. Then students each write a paragraph-long report about the planet that contains three facts. Students refer to the chart as they write their reports, and through this activity, they are practicing what they've been learning about writing paragraphs with three facts. Alex's report about Jupiter is shown in the box on page 628. He has incorporated three facts from the data chart, and most of the words are spelled correctly because he could check the spellings on the data chart. Mrs. McNeal has introduced the idea of indenting the first line in a paragraph, but Alex didn't think to do that. After the students have written reports about all nine planets, their reports are compiled and published as a book.

6. *Computer center.* Students use the Internet to check the NASA website for photos of the planets taken by Voyager and other spacecraft, and the National Geographic site for a virtual tour of the solar system. Mrs. McNeal has bookmarked these two sites, and students navigate the World Wide Web with the assistance of a Technology Liaison from the local high school.

7. *Library center.* Students read books from the solar system text set at this center. They are especially interested in reading and rereading the leveled books and in poring over the photos in the informational books.

8. *Poetry center.* In small groups, students reread poems about the sun, moon, and planets written on chart paper that they have practiced reading as a class. They also take the poems written on sentence strips out of pocket charts, rearrange the lines to create new versions of each poem, and read them. This is a favorite center because one student gets to pretend to be Mrs. McNeal and use a pointer to direct the other children in the group as they read the poems.

Data Chart on the Planets							
Planet	Where is it?	How big is it?	Does it have moons or rings?	Is it hot or cold?	What does it look like?	Is there life?	Other facts
Mercury	first, closest to the sun	second smallest	no	roasting hot or freezing cold	dry, airless, rocky, lots of craters	no	about the size of our moon
Venus	second	about the size of earth	no	hotter than an oven	thick, yellow clouds and tall mountains	no	air is poisonous, easiest planet to see in the sky
Earth	third	a middle-sized planet	1 moon	just right for life	made of rock and mostly covered with oceans	yes	we live here
Mars	fourth	half the size of earth	2 tiny moons	colder than earth	red dirt desert and pink sky	no	nickname is the Red Planet because of rusty iron in the soil
Jupiter	fifth, outside the asteroid belt	biggest planet, the "king"	16 moons 2 rings	cold	giant ball of gas, has a great red spot, covered with clouds	no	all the other planets could fit inside it
Saturn	sixth	second biggest planet	17 moons thousands of rings	very cold	giant ball of gas, covered with clouds	no	most beautiful planet
Uranus	seventh	third biggest planet	15 moons 10 rings	freezing cold	giant ball of gas, bluish-green color	no	lies on its side, spins differently
Neptune	eighth	fourth biggest planet	8 moons 4 rings	freezing cold	giant ball of gas, also bluish-green color, has a great dark spot	no	takes a rocket 8 years to go from Neptune to the sun
Pluto	ninth, farthest from the sun	smallest planet	1 moon	coldest planet	hard, frozen snowball	no	takes 248 years to go around the sun

Mrs. McNeal has a magnetized white board that she uses to direct students to centers, and students check off the centers they complete on a chart hanging near the white board so that Mrs. McNeal can keep track of their work. At the end of each week, students are expected to have completed six of the eight centers, including the art, writing, and research centers.

As they approach the end of the theme cycle, Mrs. McNeal brings the class together to talk about their final project to extend their learning and demonstrate all they have learned. They talk about several possibilities, but they decide to invite their parents to come to the classroom on Friday afternoon to listen to oral presentations about the planets and to see their work. They divide into groups of two or three, and each group chooses one planet to report on. They make posters with drawings of the planet and three facts about it. They check the information on the data chart and practice what they will say. They also ask Mrs. McNeal to take the parents on a tour of the classroom, showing them their books, charts, centers, and other activities. Many parents, grandparents, and

Jupiter is a giant ball of gas. It is outside the asroid belt. Did you no all the other planets could fit inside it?

friends come to the after-school presentation, and the students share their posters and give their presentations. The parents are impressed with all that their children have learned, especially the new information about the planets' rings and moons that the NASA spacecraft have discovered.

Teachers often search for the one best way to develop units or design language arts instruction, but there is no one best way. Instead, teachers pick and choose from thousands of books, activities, and assignments as they plan literature focus units, literature circles, reading and writing workshop, and theme cycles. In this text, you've read about these components of language arts instruction:

As you begin reading this chapter, you may want to read the "Dear Reader" letter in Chapter 15 on the Companion Website at www.prenhall.com/tompkins

- Creating a community of learners
- The reading and writing processes
- Language arts procedures, concepts, skills, and strategies
- Word walls and vocabulary activities
- Journals and other ways to use writing as a learning tool
- Three purposes for listening

- Grand conversations and other talk and drama activities
- Language arts centers
- Reading and writing stories and learning about the structure of stories
- Reading and writing information and learning about expository text structures
- Reading and writing poetry and learning about poetic forms and stylistic devices
- Spelling, handwriting, and grammar

Teachers pick and choose among these components as they plan for instruction. Choosing to have students write in reading logs or create a story quilt is not necessarily better than having students write sequels or collect sentences from a book to examine sentence structure. Teachers begin with frameworks for the three instructional approaches and then select literature, activities, and assignments based on their instructional goals and beliefs about how children learn.

As teachers gain experience developing units, they often go beyond the "What shall I do with this book?" or "What shall I teach in this unit?" questions to think about the choices they make as they plan instruction and teach (McGee & Tompkins, 1995). Teachers need to think about why students should choose many of the books they read and why skill and strategy instruction should be taught in context. Through this reflection, teachers realize how theories about how children learn, along with their instructional goals, provide the foundation for language arts instruction (Zarrillo, 1989).

As you continue reading, think about how you will organize for language arts instruction and how you will design literature focus units, literature circles, reading and writing workshop, and theme cycles. Consider these key points:

◆ How do teachers design, teach, and assess literature focus units?

◆ How do teachers organize, monitor, and assess literature circles?

◆ How do teachers set up, manage, and assess reading and writing workshop?

◆ How do teachers develop, teach, and assess theme cycles?

LITERATURE FOCUS UNITS

Teachers plan literature focus units featuring popular and award-winning stories for children and adolescents. Some literature focus units feature a single book, either a picture book or a chapter book, whereas others feature a text set of books for a genre unit or an author study unit. Figure 15–1 presents a list of trade books, genres, and authors recommended for literature focus units for kindergarten through eighth grade. During these units, students move through the five stages of the reading process as they read and respond to stories, learn reading and writing skills and strategies, and engage in language arts activities.

FIGURE 15–1

Recommended Books, Genres, and Authors for Literature Focus Units

Books	Genres	Authors and Illustrators

Primary Grades (K–2)

Books	Genres	Authors and Illustrators
Brett, J. (1989). *The mitten.* New York: Putnam.	Number books	Jan Brett
Carle, E. (1970). *The very hungry caterpillar.* Cleveland: Collins-World.	Folk tales	Eric Carle
Dorros, A. (1991). *Abuela.* New York: Dutton.	Pattern stories	Donald Crews
Galdone, P. (1972). *The three bears.* New York: Clarion.	Alphabet books	Tomie dePaola
Henkes, K. (1991). *Chrysanthemum.* New York: Greenwillow.	Fairy tales	Dr. Seuss
Hutchins, P. (1968). *Rosie's walk.* New York: Macmillan.	Biographies	Lois Ehlert
Lester, H. (1988). *Tacky the penguin.* Boston: Houghton Mifflin.		Mem Fox
Lionni, L. (1969). *Alexander and the wind-up mouse.* New York: Knopf.		Tana Hoban
Most, B. (1978). *If the dinosaurs came back.* San Diego, CA: Harcourt Brace.		Steven Kellogg
Noble, T. H. (1980). *The day Jimmy's boa ate the wash.* New York: Dial.		James Marshall
Numeroff, L. (1985). *If you give a mouse a cookie.* New York: Harper & Row.		Bill Martin and John Archambault
Rylant, C. (1985). *The relatives came.* New York: Bradbury Press.		Patricia and Frederick McKissack
Stevens, J., & Crummel, S. S. (1999). *Cook-a-doodle-doo.* San Diego, CA: Harcourt Brace.		Bernard Most
		Bernard Waber
		Audrey and Don Wood

Middle Grades (3–5)

Books	Genres	Authors and Illustrators
Barrett, J. (1978). *Cloudy with a chance of meatballs.* New York: Macmillan.	Biographies	Byrd Baylor
Blume, J. (1972). *Tales of a fourth grade nothing.* New York: Dutton.	Fables	Beverly Cleary
Cleary, B. (1981). *Ramona Quimby, age 8.* New York: Morrow.	Native American myths	Paula Danziger
Coerr, E. (1977). *Sadako and the thousand paper cranes.* New York: Putnam.	Poetry	Jean Fritz
Cohen, B. (1983). *Molly's pilgrim.* New York: Morrow.	Tall tales	Paul Goble
Creech, S. (2003). *Granny Torrelli makes soup.* New York: HarperCollins.	Wordplay books	Eloise Greenfield
Gardiner, J. R. (1980). *Stone Fox.* New York: Harper & Row.		Patricia MacLachlan
Lowry, L. (1989). *Number the stars.* Boston: Houghton Mifflin.		Patricia Polacco
MacLachlan, P. (1985). *Sarah, plain and tall.* New York: Harper & Row.		Jack Prelutsky
Naylor, P. R. (1991). *Shiloh.* New York: Macmillan.		Cynthia Rylant
Speare, E. G. (1983). *The sign of the beaver.* Boston: Houghton Mifflin.		Jon Scieszka
White, E. B. (1952). *Charlotte's web.* New York: Harper & Row.		William Steig
		R. L. Stine
		Marvin Terban
		Chris Van Allsburg
		Jane Yolen

FIGURE 15–1

Recommended Books, Genres, and Authors for Literature Focus Units—Continued

Books	Genres	Authors and Illustrators
Upper Grades (6–8)		
Avi. (1991). *Nothing but the truth.* New York: Orchard.	Science fiction	Lloyd Alexander
Babbitt, N. (1975). *Tuck everlasting.* New York: Farrar, Straus & Giroux.	Myths Poetry	Avi Christopher Paul Curtis
Curtis, C. P. (1999). *Bud, not Buddy.* New York: Delacorte.		Russell Freedman Karen Hesse
Fox, L. (1984). *One-eyed cat.* New York: Bradbury Press.		David Macaulay Walter Dean Myers
George, J. C. (1972). *Julie of the wolves.* New York: Harper & Row.		Scott O'Dell Katherine Paterson
Hesse, K. (2001). *Witness.* New York: Scholastic.		Gary Paulsen Richard Peck
Hinton, S. E. (1967). *The outsiders.* New York: Viking.		Jerry Spinelli Yoshiko Uchida
L'Engle, M. (1962). *A wrinkle in time.* New York: Farrar, Straus & Giroux.		Laurence Yep Paul Zindel
Lewis, C. S. (1994). *The lion, the witch and the wardrobe.* New York: HarperCollins.		
Lowry, L. (1993). *The giver.* Boston: Houghton Mifflin.		
Paulsen, G. (1987). *Hatchet.* New York: Viking.		
Sachar, L. (1998). *Holes.* New York: Farrar, Straus & Giroux.		
Taylor, M. (1976). *Roll of thunder, hear my cry.* New York: Dial.		
Whelan, G. (2000). *Homeless bird.* New York: Scholastic.		

How to Develop a Literature Focus Unit

Teachers develop a literature focus unit through an eight-step series of activities, beginning with choosing the literature for the unit, continuing to identify and schedule activities, and ending with deciding how to assess students' learning. Whether teachers are using trade books or textbook selections, they develop a unit using these steps to meet the needs of their students. Effective teachers do not simply follow directions in basal reader teachers' manuals and literature focus unit planning guides that are available for purchase in school-supply stores. Teachers need to make the plans themselves because they are the ones who best know their students, the reading materials they have available, the time available for the unit, the skills and strategies they want to teach, and the language arts activities they want to use.

Usually literature focus units featuring a picture book are completed in 1 week, and units featuring a chapter book are completed in 2, 3, or 4 weeks. Genre and author units may last 2, 3, or 4 weeks. Rarely, if ever, do literature

To read more about literature focus units, turn back to Chapter 2, "Teaching and Assessing Language Arts," and the full-color insert on literature focus units.

focus units continue for more than a month. When teachers drag a unit out for 6 weeks, 2 months, or longer, they risk killing students' interest in the particular book or, worse yet, their love of literature.

The steps in developing a literature focus unit are outlined in the LA Essentials box on page 633 and described more fully in the following sections.

Step 1: Select the Featured Book.   Teachers begin by selecting the featured book for the literature focus unit. The literature may be a story in a picture book format, a chapter book, or a story selected from a basal reading textbook. The reading materials should be high-quality literature and should often include multicultural selections. Sometimes teachers select several related stories—books representing the same genre, books written by the same author for an author study, or books illustrated by the same artist for an illustrator study. Teachers collect multiple copies of the book or books for the literature focus unit. When teachers use trade books, they have to collect class sets of the books for the unit. In some school districts, class sets of selected books are available for teachers. However, in other school districts, teachers have to request that administrators purchase multiple copies of books or buy them themselves through book clubs. When teachers use picture books, students can share books so only half as many books as students are needed.

Once the book (or books) is selected, teachers collect related books for the text set. Books for the text set include:

- Other versions of the same story
- Books written by the same author
- Books illustrated by the same artist
- Books with the same theme
- Books with similar settings
- Books in the same genre
- Informational books on a related topic
- Books of poetry on a related topic

Teachers collect one or two copies of 10, 20, 30, or more books for the text set, which they add to the classroom library during the focus unit. Books for the text set are placed on a special shelf or in a crate in the library center. At the beginning of the unit, teachers do a book talk to introduce the books in the text set, and then students read them during independent reading time.

Step 2: Develop a Unit Plan.   Teachers read or reread the selected book or books and then think about the focus they will use for the unit. Sometimes teachers focus on an element of story structure, the historical setting, wordplay, the author or genre, or a concept or topic related to the book, such as weather or life in the desert.

After determining the focus, teachers think about which activities they will use at each of the five stages of the reading process. Questions that teachers can ask themselves at each stage are listed in Figure 15–2. Teachers often jot notes on a chart divided into sections for each stage. Then they use the ideas they have brainstormed as they plan the unit. Usually teachers do not use all the brainstormed activities in the literature focus unit, but they select the most important ones according to their focus and the available time. Teachers do not omit any of the stages, however, in an attempt to make more time available for activities during any one stage.

Virtual Field Experience
How to Use the Accompanying CD-ROM

Familiarity with the practice of teaching is essential to effective teacher development. Simply reading and researching is not enough. Witnessing meaningful teaching first-hand, observing master teachers, and reflecting on the actions, decisions, and artistry behind good teaching can bring you further along on your journey toward becoming a better teacher yourself.

While practice in living classrooms is an integral part of teacher preparation, you need another way to uncover the deep meaning in the layers of content, pedagogy, culture, and environment in real classrooms. There should be a way to stop the action, review it, hold it up for scrutiny, and look at the action from various points of view. And there is such a way—through virtual classroom experiences.

With this CD you have immediate access to living classroom examples of teaching and learning in literacy instruction. The examples provide context and anchor thinking in the realities of authentic classrooms.

The CD allows you to see wholes and parts, hear and read a variety of stakeholder perspectives, manipulate and create your own grouping of virtual classroom experiences, and assess the depth of your comprehension of the rich instructional layers inherent in these dynamic lessons.

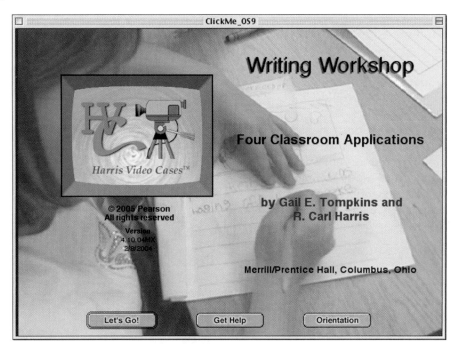

To make the most of your virtual classroom experience, you'll need to understand all the options available to you on this CD. You can begin by simply examining the four different classrooms and watching each lesson. But to truly uncover the layers of teacher decision making, theoretical connections, and pedagogy, you'll want not only to look closely at specific pieces of footage, analyzing each clip as well as the stakeholder perspectives, but also to manipulate and rework the clips for the layered information each holds.

Creating your own study

As you review each classroom lesson, generate questions and answers to illustrate the layers of instruction you observe in each lesson. The following are some questions to consider.

- What elements of planning does each teacher use?
- What specific language arts concepts does each lesson cover?
- What makes each lesson effective for learning?
- How does the developmental level of each group of children dictate the way each teacher executes her lesson?

Study Builder

To create your own study, begin by clicking on the Study Builder button on the navigation bar.

Begin with your own question, then look for answers in the numerous video clips provided. Compare and contrast teaching and learning principles as they are applied with students at different levels of intellectual, emotional, and physical development. Focus on these or any other question by isolating clips in which the teaching supplies answers.

A total of eight clips can be used in each of your studies. Isolate and sequence clips from the 24 archived clips provided. Drag and drop your selected clips onto an open slot in the grid, then save and name your study. Now you're ready to finish by customizing your study under the Custom Studies button.

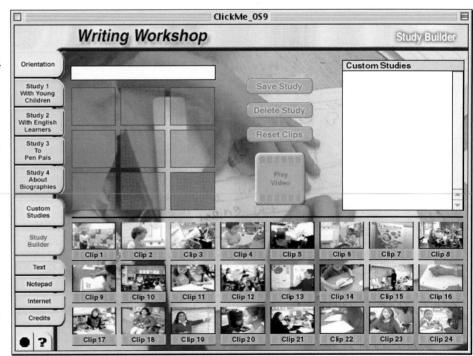

Step by Step

1. Decide on a question
2. Select clips that focus on that query
3. Drag and drop the clips into the eight open slots
4. Name the study
5. Save the study
6. Move on to the Custom Studies step

For a more complete walk-through of this module, click on the help (?) button, then on Study Builder under Help Topics.

Using the Features of the CD

CUSTOM STUDIES
The Custom Studies section allows you to customize your personal studies with your own comments, lesson plans, and quotes from the text of the CD. We will cover this in detail as well.

STUDY BUTTONS
The CD illustrates a teacher and students engaged in various aspects of literacy learning. Each teaching topic has its own button on the navigation bar on the left of the screen. By clicking on the topic of your choice, you move into the specific video clips and discussions of that topic.

VIDEO CLIPS
Each topic includes nine video clips. Individual clips are labeled according to the topics illustrated. Simply click on the thumbnail of one clip to watch the video segment. Across the bottom of the video screen you'll find buttons that allow you to pause, fast forward, and rewind the clip.

STUDY BUILDER
The Study Builder feature helps you to create your own study lesson using the video clips provided on the CD. We will discuss this in detail in a moment.

TEXT BUTTON
The text of the commentators for the CD is provided in this area, available for copying and pasting to your own study.

NOTEPAD BUTTON
This feature allows you to take notes, copy and paste material from other sources, and save your ideas and insights. Each time you create something in the Notepad, you can save it individually to your hard drive or a disk, and then start a new file to jot down other ideas.

INTERNET BUTTON
Clicking on the Internet button launches an Internet browser, allowing you to visit the links provided or insert an Internet address and go to discussion groups, e-mail, or other relevant sites that pertain to literacy.

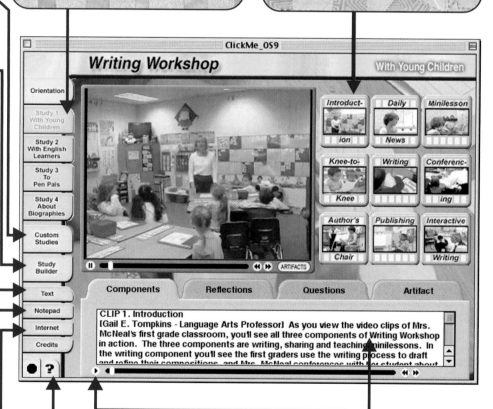

HELP TOPICS
The ? button provides a wealth of clear, step-by-step information. Clicking on the ? button will open up the help file, where you will find explanations and directions for every button and a guided tour through using the CD and building your own study.

REFLECTION COMMENTS
As soon as a specific video clip is highlighted, comments from various stakeholders become available. Click the arrow at the bottom to begin the audio.

Custom Study

To customize your study, click on Custom Studies. Click on the name of your saved study in the Custom Studies field. Move to the Custom Study Commentary section and add your own comments concerning each clip and the way it fits into your study. You can also use the Internet or Text buttons to copy and paste materials from those sources that relate to your study.

Each custom study you create can be used to fulfill an assignment or become part of your electronic teaching portfolio. Create as many custom studies as you like and examine your own understanding of any number of teaching strategies, techniques, and concerns.

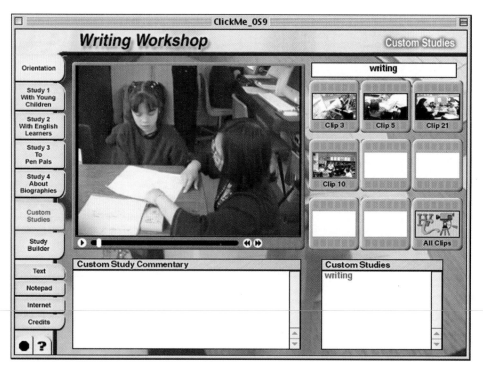

Step by Step

1. Open saved study
2. Click on chosen clip
3. Add comments of your own or pull comments from the Internet or Text buttons
4. When you've added all your elements, save your study to your own hard drive or disk

The Custom Studies tutorial found on the Help screen provides a helpful reminder should you need a bit of assistance creating your study.

Steps in Developing a Literature Focus Unit

Teachers follow these eight steps as they develop literature focus units featuring a picture book, a chapter book, an author, or a genre.

1. **Literature Selection**

   Select the piece of literature to be featured in the literature focus unit and obtain a class set of books.

2. **Unit Plan**

   Develop the teaching plan for the literature focus unit.

3. **Strategies and Skills**

   Identify the language arts strategies and skills to teach during the unit.

4. **Technology Resources**

   Locate technology resources related to the featured book.

5. **Six Language Arts**

   Incorporate activities representing all six language arts into the teaching plan.

6. **Grouping**

   Coordinate whole-class, small-group, and individual grouping patterns with the activities.

7. **Schedule**

   Create a time schedule and lesson plans.

8. **Assessment**

   Plan how students' work will be assessed, and make an assignment checklist or other grading sheet.

FIGURE 15-2

Questions to Use in Developing Literature Focus Units

1. Prereading
   - What background knowledge do students need before reading?
   - What key concepts and vocabulary should I teach before reading?
   - How will I introduce the story and stimulate students' interest for reading?
   - How will I assess students' learning?

2. Reading
   - How will students read this story?
   - What reading strategies and skills will I model or ask students to use?
   - How can I make the story more accessible for less capable readers and English learners?

3. Responding
   - Will students write in reading logs? How often?
   - Will students participate in grand conversations? How often?
   - What scenes from the book will students want or need to dramatize?

4. Exploring
   - What words might be added to the word wall?
   - What vocabulary activities might be used?
   - Will students reread the story?
   - What skill and strategy minilessons might be taught?
   - How can I focus students' attention on words and sentences in the book?
   - How will books from the text set be used?
   - What can I share about the author, illustrator, or genre?

5. Applying
   - What projects might students choose to pursue?
   - How will books from the text set be used?
   - How will students share projects?

Check Chapter 1, "Learning and the Language Arts," for more information about strategies and skills.

Step 3: Identify Language Arts Strategies and Skills to Teach. Teachers decide which strategies and skills to teach using the book. Their choice is dependent on the students' observed needs, opportunities afforded by the book, and school district requirements. Sometimes teachers plan minilessons to teach skills and strategies directly. At other times, they plan to model how to use the skills and strategies as they read aloud or to ask students to share how they use the skills and strategies during grand conversations.

Step 4: Locate Technology Resources. Teachers locate technology resources to use in the unit, including CD-ROM and video versions of stories for students to view and compare to the book version, audiotapes of stories to use at listening centers, and author information and interviews on videotapes and on the Internet. Teachers also plan how they will use computers for writing and researching activities and cameras for photographic essays related to the unit.

To review the six language arts, check Chapter 1, "Learning and the Language Arts."

Step 5: Incorporate Activities Representing All Six Language Arts. Teachers review the plans they are developing to make sure that students have opportunities to engage in listening, talking, reading, writing, viewing, and visually representing activities during the literature focus unit. Of course, not all six language arts fit into every unit, but for most units they do.

Step 6: Coordinate Grouping Patterns With Activities.

Teachers think about how to incorporate whole-class, small-group, buddy, and individual activities into their unit plans. It is important that students have opportunities to read and write independently as well as to work with small groups and to come together as a class. If the piece of literature that students are reading will be read together as a class, then students need opportunities to reread it with a buddy or independently or to read related books independently. These grouping patterns should be alternated during various activities in the unit. Teachers often go back to their planning sheet and highlight activities with colored markers according to grouping patterns.

Step 7: Create a Time Schedule.

Teachers create a time schedule that allows students sufficient time to move through the five stages of the reading process and to complete the activities planned for the focus unit. Literature-based reading programs require large blocks of time, at least 2 hours, in which students read, listen, talk, and write about the literature they are reading.

Using this block of time, teachers complete weekly lesson plans, and the activities they include represent each of the five stages of the reading process. The stages are not clearly separated and they overlap, but preparing, reading, responding, exploring, and extending activities are included in the lesson plan.

Step 8: Plan for Assessment.

Teachers often distribute unit folders for students to use. They keep all work, reading logs, reading materials, and related materials in the folder. Then at the end of the unit, students turn in their completed folders for teachers to evaluate. Keeping all the materials together makes the unit easier for both students and teachers to manage.

Teachers plan ways to document students' work at centers or on projects during a literature focus unit. The Weaving Assessment Into Practice feature on page 636 shows a literacy centers assessment checklist prepared in booklet form for a first-grade literature focus unit on *The Mitten* (Brett, 1989). Students color in the mitten on each page as they complete work at the center.

Teachers also plan ways to document students' learning and to assign grades. One form of record keeping is an assignment checklist. This sheet is developed with students and distributed at the beginning of the literature focus unit. Students keep track of their work during the unit and sometimes negotiate to change the sheet as the unit evolves. Students keep the lists in unit folders, and they mark off each item as it is completed. At the end of the unit, students turn in their completed assignment checklist and other completed work.

An assignment checklist for an upper-grade literature focus unit on *The Giver* (Lowry, 1993), a story about a "perfect" community that isn't, is presented in the Weaving Assessment Into Practice feature on page 637. Although this list does not include every activity students are involved in, it does list the activities and other assignments that the teacher holds students accountable for. Students complete the checklist on the left side of the sheet and add titles of books and other requested information. The teacher awards points (up to the number listed in parentheses) on the lines on the right side of the sheet, and totals the number of points on the bottom of the page. Then the total score can be translated into a letter grade or other type of grade.

A Centers Assessment Booklet for a Unit on **The Mitten**

"The Mitten"

Centers Booklet

Retelling Center

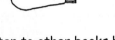

Use puppets and pictures to tell "The Mitten" story.

Word Work Center

Make words using magnetic letters.

Listening Center

Listen to other books by Jan Brett.

Writing Center

Write books about "The Mitten" or books about the animals in the story.

Reading Center

Compare the three "The Mitten" stories and pick your favorite one.

Knitting Center

Learn to knit with Tasha's mom.

Sorting Center

Sort the phonics objects and word cards into buckets.

Weaving Assessment Into Practice

An Upper-Grade Assignment Checklist *for* The Giver

Name _____

Student's
Check   Points

_____   1. Read *The Giver.*   _____

_____   2. Write at least ten entries in your reading log. Use a double-entry format
            with quotes and your connections. (20)   _____

_____   3. Participate in small-group grand conversations   _____

_____   4. Create a storyboard. Chapter # _____ (10)   _____

_____   5. Make an open-mind portrait of Jonas with four mind pages. (10) _____

_____   6. Write an essay about the theme of the book. (10)   _____

_____   7. Choose and analyze ten words from the word wall according to
            prefix, root word, and suffix. (10)   _____

_____   8. Read one book from the text set. Write a brief summary in your reading log
            and compare what you learned about societies with *The Giver.* (10)   _____

            Title _____

            Author _____

_____   9. Make a square for the class story quilt. (5)   _____

_____ 10. Create a project and share it with the class. (25)   _____

            Project _____   _____

            Date shared _____

                                                                Total _____

A Primary-Grade Literature Focus Unit on The Mitten

Jan Brett's *The Mitten* (1989), a cumulative picture-book story about a series of animals who climb into a mitten that a little boy has dropped in the snow on a cold winter day, is the featured selection in literature focus units taught in many primary-grade classrooms. A planning cluster for a literature focus unit on *The Mitten* is shown in Figure 15–3. Teachers use the big book version of *The Mitten* to introduce the unit and to examine Brett's innovative use of borders. Students use the teacher's collection of stuffed animals and puppets representing the animals in the story—a mole, a rabbit, a hedgehog, an owl, a badger, a fox, a bear, and a mouse—as they retell the story. Students read the story several times—in small groups with the teacher, with partners, and independently. The teacher also reads aloud several other versions of the story, including *The Woodcutter's Mitten* (Koopmans, 1990) and *The Mitten* (Tresselt, 1964), and students make a chart to compare the versions. The teacher presents mini-lessons on phonemic awareness and phonics skills, creates a word wall, and

FIGURE 15–3   *A Planning Cluster for a Primary-Grade Unit on* The Mitten

Word Wall

A	acorn	M	meadow mouse
B	Baba		mitten
	badger		mole
	bear		muzzle
	bear's nose	N	Nicki
	big kickers	O	owl
	borders	PQ	prickles
C	commotion	RS	sheep
	cozy		snowshoe rabbit
D	diggers		stretched
	drowsy		swelled
E	enormous sneeze		swooped down
F	fox	T	trotted
G	glinty talons		tunneling along
	glove	UV	Ukraine
	grandmother	WX	whiskers
HIJ	hedgehog		wool
K	knitted		wriggled
L	lumbered by	YZ	yarn

Other Books by Jan Brett

Armadillo rodeo. (1995). New York: Putnam.
Berlioz the bear. (1991). New York: Putnam.
Gingerbread baby. (1999). New York: Putman.
Goldilocks and the three bears. (1987). New York: Putnam.
The hat. (1997). New York: Putnam.
The owl and the pussycat. (1991). New York: Putnam.
Town mouse, country mouse. (1994). New York: Putnam.
Trouble with trolls. (1992). New York: Putnam.

Big Book

Introduce the story using the big book version of the book (published by Scholastic) and shared reading.

Author Study

• Read other books by Jan Brett.
• Visit her website at www.JanBrett.com.
• Examine Brett's use of borders in her books and have students create borders in the books they write.
• Write letters to the author.

Compare Versions of the Story

Read these versions and make a chart to compare them with Brett's version:

Koopmans, L. (1990). *The woodcutter's mitten.* New York: Crocodile Books.
Tresselt, A. (1964). *The mitten.* New York: Lothrop, Lee & Shepard.

The Mitten

Vocabulary Activities

• Post an alphabetized word wall.
• Make colorful word posters in the shape of a mitten.
• Sort words according to "mitten" and "animal" categories or using phonics categories.

Research

• Research the animals in the story.
• Create a semantic feature analysis to compare the animals.
• Write a class book about one of the animals.
• Research sheep, wool, and yarn using these books:

Fowler, A. (1993). *Wooly sheep and hungry goats.* Chicago: Children's Press.
Mitgutsch, A. (1975). *From sheep to scarf.* Minneapolis: Carolrhoda.

Sequencing Activities

• Sequence events using storyboards cut from two copies of the book, backed with cardboard and laminated.
• Dramatize the story with puppets or stuffed animals.
• Create a circle diagram of the story. Have students draw pictures of each event and post them in a circle, beginning and ending with the grandmother.

Writing Activities

• Write a class collaboration retelling of the story.
• Create a found poem using words and phrases from the book.
• Write letters to the author.
• Create a story quilt with a mitten design on each square and a sentence about the book.

involves students in word-study activities. Students participate in sequencing and writing activities and learn about knitting from a parent volunteer. The teacher also sets out a text set of other books by Jan Brett and reads some of the books aloud to students. As their application project, students divide into small groups to research one of the animals mentioned in the story. Fifth graders work with the primary-grade students as they research the animals and share what they learn on large posters.

An Upper-Grade Literature Focus Unit on The Giver

Upper-grade students spend 3 or 4 weeks reading, responding to, exploring, and extending their understanding of Lois Lowry's Newbery Medal book, *The Giver* (1993). Lowry creates a "perfect" community in which the people are secure but regulated. Jonas, the main character, is chosen to be a leader in the community, but he rebels against the society and escapes. To introduce this book, teachers might connect the book to the United States Constitution and the Bill of Rights, or discuss the problems in U.S. society today and ask students to create a perfect society. Or, students might think about how their lives would be different in a world without colors, like Jonas's.

Students can read the story together as a class, in small groups with the teacher or in literature study groups, with buddies, or independently. Students come together to discuss the story in grand conversations and deal with the complex issues presented in the book in both small groups and whole-class discussions. They also write in reading logs. Teachers identify skills and strategies to model during reading and to teach in minilessons. Students write important words from the story on the word wall and engage in a variety of vocabulary activities. Students also learn about the author and examine the story structure in the book. After reading, they can do a choral reading, create a story quilt, compare U.S. society with the society described in the book, and create other projects. Figure 15–4 shows a planning cluster for *The Giver.*

LITERATURE CIRCLES

Students divide into small groups, and they read and respond to a self-selected book together during a literature circle (Evans, 2001; Frank, Dixon, & Brandts, 2001). Students read independently, and then they come together to participate in grand conversations to discuss the book. They also write in reading logs and sometimes create projects related to the book. For students to be successful in literature circles, a community of learners is essential. Students need to develop responsibility, learn how to work in a small group with classmates, and participate in group activities.

How to Organize for Literature Circles

Teachers move through a series of steps as they prepare for literature circles. Even though students assume leadership roles and make a number of decisions as they participate in literature circles, the success depends on the teacher's planning and the classroom community that has been created. The LA Essentials box on page 641 outlines the steps in organizing literature circles.

For more information on literature circles, turn back to Chapter 2, "Teaching and Assessing Language Arts," and the full-color insert on literature circles.

FIGURE 15-4   A Planning Cluster for an Upper-Grade Unit on The Giver

Introducing the Book

- Read the book when studying ancient civilizations and focus on the traits of a civilization.
- Discuss the problems in U.S. society, and ask students to create a perfect society.
- Create a world with no colors.
- Share objects from a book box, including an apple, a bicycle, a sled, the number 19, a stuffed bear or other "comfort object," and a kaleidoscope of colors.

Story Structure Activities

- Create a set of storyboards, one for each chapter, with a good title for the chapter, a picture, and a summarizing paragraph.
- Create a plot diagram to graph the highs and lows of the book.
- Make an open-mind portrait with several mind pages to track Jonas's thinking through the book.
- Compare Jonas's character to Kira's in Lowry's *Gathering Blue* (2000) or that of another familiar character.
- Draw a setting map of the story.
- Analyze the theme of the book and create a story quilt to represent it.

Vocabulary Activities

- Post an alphabetized word wall in the classroom, and have students make individual word walls.
- Draw word clusters.
- Sort words according to "Jonas," "Giver," and "Community" categories.
- Teach minilessons on dividing long words into syllables or identifying root words and affixes (e.g., obediently, distrustful, apprehensive).
- Teach minilessons on etymology (e.g., English, Latin, and Greek words).
- Collect powerful sentences and write them on sentence strips.

Comparing Societies

Students read a book about U.S. democratic society and compare it to the perfect society in *The Giver*.

Cowman, P. (1995). *Strike! The bitter struggle of American workers from colonial times to the present.* New York: Millbrook.

Fleming, R. (1995). *Rescuing a neighborhood: The Bedford-Stuyvesant Volunteer Ambulance Corps.* New York: Walker.

Haskins, J. (1993). *The march on Washington.* New York: HarperCollins.

Hoose, P. (1993). *It's our world, too! Stories of young people who are making a difference.* New York: Joy Street.

Meltzer, M. (1990). *Crime in America.* New York: Morrow.

The Giver

Author Information

- Collect information about Lois Lowry, including "Newbery Acceptance" by Lois Lowry, published in the July/August 1994 issue of *Horn Book* (pp. 414–422).
- Read other books by the author, including *Number the Stars* (1989) and *Gathering Blue* (2000).
- Write letters to the author.

Grand Conversations

- Have students share their ideas about the chapters they have read.
- Have students choose an appropriate title for the chapter.
- Have students share favorite sentences from the chapter.
- Have students make predictions about the next chapter.

Reading Log

- Keep a simulated journal, written from Jonas's viewpoint, after reading each chapter.
- Write a double-entry journal with quotes from the story in one column and personal connections or predictions in the other column.

Writing Projects

- Write found poems, "I Am" poems, or other poems.
- Write an essay comparing Jonas's society with ours.
- Write a reaction to this quote: "The greatest freedom is the freedom of choice."
- Write a simulated letter from one character to another in the story.
- Write a prequel or a sequel to the story.

Word Wall

A	anguished assignment	PQ	permission precision punishment
B	bicycle		
CD	ceremony community	R	Receiver regret released ritual
EF	Elders elsewhere		
GH	Gabe guilt	S	sameness stirrings successor
I	ironic		
JK	Jonas	T	transgression transmit tunic
L	luminate		
M	memories		
N	Nurturer	UV	
O	obediently obsolete	WX	
		YZ	yearning

 *Essentials*

Steps in Organizing Literature Circles

Teachers follow these steps as they choose books and plan literature circles.

1. **Books**

   Choose six or seven titles and collect five or six copies of each book for students to read.

2. **Groups**

   Organize the circles by giving book talks and having students sign up for the book they want to read.

3. **Roles**

   Decide on roles for group members and clearly explain the responsibilities of each role.

4. **Schedule**

   Set the schedule for literature circles and have students in each small group decide how they will schedule reading, discussion, and other work times.

5. **Grand Conversations**

   Conduct grand conversations to monitor students' reading and support students as they respond to and deepen their understanding of the book.

6. **Reading Logs**

   Set guidelines for how often students will write in reading logs and the types of entries they will make.

7. **Projects**

   Decide whether students will develop projects after reading the book, and if so, the types of projects they will pursue.

8. **Assessment**

   Plan ways to monitor students as they read and respond to the book in small groups.

Step 1: Choose Books.   Teachers choose five, six, or seven titles and collect six copies of each book. Then they give a book talk about each book, and students sign up for the book they want to read. One way to do this is to set each book on the chalk tray and have students sign their names on the chalkboard above the book they want to read. Or, teachers can set the books on a table and place a sign-up sheet beside each book. Students take time to preview the books, and then they select the book they want to read. Once in a while, students don't get to read their first-choice book, but they can always read it later during another literature circle or during reading workshop.

Sometimes teachers choose unrelated books, but at other times, they choose related books for literature circles. For example, first graders might choose and read various Dr. Seuss stories, third graders might read different versions of a fairy tale, such as "The Three Little Pigs," and sixth graders might read survival stories. A list of suggested text sets for literature circles is presented in the Classroom Library box on page 643.

Step 2: Organize the Circles or Groups.   The books in the text set often vary in length and difficulty, but students are not placed in groups according to their reading levels. Students choose the books they want to read, and as they preview the books they consider how good a fit the book is, but that is not their only consideration. They often choose to read the book they find most interesting or the book their best friend has chosen. Students can usually manage whatever book they choose because of support and assistance from their group or through plain and simple determination. Once in a while, teachers counsel students to choose another book or provide an additional copy of the book to practice at home or to read with a tutor at school.

Step 3: Decide on Roles for Group Members.   Teachers must decide how to structure the literature circles and what roles students will assume. Sometimes students form a group, and students choose their own group leader, or a natural leader emerges when they first get together; however, at other times, teachers identify the group leader. In addition to the leadership role, each student in the group may assume a role, and students also select these during the first meeting of the group. When teachers have students assume roles, they must clearly outline the responsibilities of each group member. Teachers often spend a great deal of time at the beginning of the school year teaching students how to fulfill the responsibilities of each role.

Students assume various roles in the group to facilitate their understanding of the book they are reading. Students complete their responsibilities after reading and share their work with their classmates when they meet. These roles include:

- Passage master, who chooses several passages to read aloud to the group during the grand conversation
- Word wizard, who explains the meaning of key words in the text
- Connector, who finds connections between the book and the children's lives
- Summarizer, who prepares a brief summary of the text to share with the group
- Artist, who draws a picture about the text
- Investigator, who locates and shares background information about the text

Text Sets for Literature Circles

PRIMARY GRADES

Dr. Seuss Stories
Green eggs and ham. (1960). New York: Random House.
One fish, two fish, red fish, blue fish. (1960). New York: Random House.
Hop on pop. (1963). New York: Random House.
The cat in the hat. (1967). New York: Random House.
The foot book. (1968). New York: Random House.

Frog and Toad Books
Clarke, B. (1990). *Amazing frogs and toads.* New York: Knopf.
Lobel, A. (1970). *Frog and Toad are friends.* New York: Harper & Row.
Mayer, M., & Mayer, M. (1975). *One frog too many.* New York: Dial.

Pallotta, J. (1990). *The frog alphabet book.* Watertown, MA: Charlesbridge.
Yolen, J. (1980). *Commander Toad in space.* New York: Coward-McCann.

Versions of "The Three Little Pigs"
Bishop, G. (1989). *The three little pigs.* New York: Scholastic Hardcover.
Lowell, S. (1992). *The three little javelinas.* Flagstaff, AZ: Northland.
Marshall, J. (1989). *The three little pigs.* New York: Dial.
Scieszka, J. (1989). *The true story of the 3 little pigs!* New York: Viking.
Trivizas, E. (1993). *The three little wolves and the big bad pig.* New York: McElderry Books.

MIDDLE GRADES

Magic School Bus Books
Cole, J. (1987). *The magic school bus inside the earth.* New York: Scholastic.
Cole, J. (1989). *The magic school bus inside the human body.* New York: Scholastic.
Cole, J. (1990). *The magic school bus lost in the solar system.* New York: Scholastic.
Cole, J. (1992). *The magic school bus on the ocean floor.* New York: Scholastic.
Cole, J. (1994). *The magic school bus in the time of the dinosaurs.* New York: Scholastic.
Cole, J. (1999). *The magic school bus and the electric field trip.* New York: Scholastic.

Cole, J. (2001). *The magic school bus explores the senses.* New York: Scholastic.

Tall Tales
Isaacs, A. (1994). *Swamp angel.* New York: Dutton.
Kellogg, S. (1984). *Paul Bunyan.* New York: Morrow.
Kellogg, S. (1986). *Pecos Bill.* New York: Morrow.
Kellogg, S. (1992). *Mike Fink.* New York: Morrow.
Lester, J. (1994). *John Henry.* New York: Dial.

Beverly Cleary Books
Henry and Ribsy. (1954). New York: Morrow.
The mouse and the motorcycle. (1965). New York: Morrow.
Ramona and her father. (1975). New York: Morrow.
Ramona Quimby, age 8. (1981). New York: Morrow.
Dear Mr. Henshaw. (1983). New York: Morrow.

UPPER GRADES

Arthurian Legends
Andronik, C. M. (1989). *Quest for a king: Searching for the real King Arthur.* New York: Atheneum.
Pyle, H. (1984). *The story of King Arthur and his knights.* New York: Scribner.
Riordan, J. (1982). *Tales of King Arthur.* New York: Macmillan.
Sutcliff, R. (1980). *The light beyond the forest: The quest for the Holy Grail.* New York: Dutton.
Tennyson, A. L. (1986). *The lady of Shalott.* Oxford, England: Oxford University Press.
Yolen, J. (2003). *Sword of the rightful king: A novel of King Arthur.* San Diego, CA: Harcourt Brace.

Survival Stories
George, J. C. (1972). *Julie of the wolves.* New York: Harper & Row.
Hamilton, V. (1971). *The planet of Junior Brown.* New York: Macmillan.

Lowry, L. (1993). *The giver.* Boston: Houghton Mifflin.
Paulsen, G. (1987). *Hatchet.* New York: Viking.
Sperry, A. (1940). *Call it courage.* New York: Macmillan.

Ancient Egypt
Bradshaw, G. (1991). *The dragon and the thief.* New York: Greenwillow.
Carter, D. S. (1987). *His majesty, Queen Hatshepsut.* New York: HarperCollins.
Dexter, C. (1992). *The gilded cat.* New York: Morrow.
Logan, C. (2002). *The 5,000-year-old puzzle: Solving a mystery of Ancient Egypt.* New York: Farrar, Straus & Giroux.
McMullan, K. (1992). *Under the mummy's spell.* New York: Farrar, Straus & Giroux.
Snyder, Z. K. (1967). *The Egypt game.* New York: Atheneum.

Some teachers use the same roles for each literature circle during the school year, but other teachers vary the roles based on the demands of the book.

Step 4: Set the Schedule. Teachers set a time schedule for the literature circle and then each small group of students decides how to use the time to read the book and participate in grand conversations. During group meetings, teachers often participate in grand conversations and add their ideas to the discussion. They also monitor that students are completing their reading assignments and fulfilling the responsibilities of their roles. While the teacher meets with one group, the other groups read independently or participate in other activities.

Chapter 8, "Sustaining Talk in the Classroom," presents more information on grand conversations.

Step 5: Conduct Grand Conversations. Students alternate reading and discussing the book in grand conversations. At the beginning of the literature circle, students decide how often to meet for grand conversations and how much of the book to read before each discussion. Sometimes teachers participate in the conversations and sometimes they don't. When the teachers are participants, they participate as fellow readers who share joys and difficulties, insights and speculations. They also help students develop literary insights by providing information, asking insightful questions, and guiding students to make comments. Eeds and Peterson (1991) advise that teachers need to listen carefully to what students say as they talk about a book, and label what students are talking about when appropriate.

Check Chapter 6, "Personal Writing," to read more about reading logs.

Step 6: Write in Reading Logs. Teachers make decisions about the types of entries they want students to make as they read a book during a literature circle. Students often write in reading logs as part of literature circles. Sometimes students write entries in their logs after each chapter, and at other times, they write once a week. Students may write their reactions to the chapters they have read or write about issues that arose during the grand conversation. Students may also write predictions, collect vocabulary words, and record powerful sentences from the book in their journals. Depending on the complexity of the book and the issues the teacher wants students to think about, the teacher may ask students to reflect on and write about specific topics after reading particular chapters.

For a list of project ideas, turn back to Chapter 3, "The Reading and Writing Processes."

Step 7: Decide on Projects. Reading and responding are the heart of literature circles, but sometimes students also prepare projects to celebrate the reading experience. Students can make puppets, write a poem, dramatize an event from the story, make a story quilt, read another book by the same author, or complete another project. Teachers consider the types of experiences that might be most beneficial for students, or they may decide to have students choose their own projects.

Step 8: Plan for Assessment. Teachers also plan how they will monitor and assess students' learning during the literature circle. Most teachers monitor students as they move around the classroom and participate in grand conversations. They can also check students' reading logs and the work they complete in the various roles. Many teachers also use a calendar or assignment sheet to assess students' work. A fifth-grade grading sheet is shown in the Weaving Assessment Into Practice feature on page 645.

A Fifth-Grade Grading Sheet for Literature Circles

ASSESSMENT CHECK

Name _____   **Book** _____

Circle Members

1. _____   3. _____   5. _____

2. _____   4. _____   6. _____

Write a schedule of your activities. What was your role?

M	T	W	T	F

M	T	W	T	F

M	T	W	T	F

Reflect on your work in this literature circle. Score yourself, and then write about your work on the back of this sheet.

1. Read the book.   A   B   C   D

2. Complete your group role.   A   B   C   D

3. Participate in grand conversations.   A   B   C   D

4. Write in your reading log.   A   B   C   D

5. Make a group project.   A   B   C   D

6. Share your project.   A   B   C   D

READING AND WRITING WORKSHOP

Nancie Atwell (1987) introduced reading workshop as an alternative to traditional reading instruction. In reading workshop, students read books that they choose themselves and respond to books through writing in reading logs and conferencing with teachers and classmates. This approach represents a change in what we believe about how children learn and how literature is used in the classroom. Atwell developed reading workshop with her middle-school students, but it has been adapted and used successfully at every grade level, first through eighth (Hornsby, Sukarna, & Parry, 1986; McWhirter, 1990). There are several versions of reading workshop, but they usually contain these components: reading, sharing, minilessons, and reading aloud to students.

Writing workshop is similar to reading workshop, except that the focus is on writing. Students write on topics that they choose themselves, and they assume ownership of their writing and learning (Atwell, 1987; Calkins, 1994; Graves, 1994; Hornsby et al., 1986). At the same time, the teacher's role changes from that of being a provider of knowledge to that of serving as a facilitator and guide. The classroom becomes a community of writers who write and share their writing. There is a spirit of pride and acceptance in the classroom.

Writing workshop is a 60- to 90-minute period scheduled each day. During this time, students are involved in three components: writing, sharing, and minilessons. Sometimes a fourth activity, reading aloud to students, is added to writing workshop when it is not used in conjunction with reading workshop.

Establishing a Workshop Environment

Teachers begin to establish the workshop environment in their classroom from the first day of the school year by providing students with choices, time to read and write, and opportunities for response. Through their interactions with students, the respect they show to students, and the way they model reading and writing, teachers establish the classroom as a community of learners.

Teachers develop a schedule for reading and writing workshop with time allocated for each component, or they alternate between the two types of workshops. In their schedules, teachers allot as much time as possible for students to read and write. After developing the schedule, teachers post it in the classroom, talk with students about the activities, and discuss their expectations with students. Teachers teach the workshop procedures and continue to model them as students become comfortable with the routines (Kaufman, 2001). As students share what they are reading and writing at the end of workshop sessions, their enthusiasm grows and the workshop approaches are successful.

Students keep two folders—one for reading workshop and one for writing workshop. In the reading workshop folder, students keep a list of books they have read, notes from minilessons, reading logs, and other materials. In the writing workshop folder, they keep all rough drafts and other compositions. They also keep a list of all compositions, topics for future pieces, and notes from minilessons. They also keep language arts notebooks in which they jot down images, impressions, dialogue, and experiences that they can build on for writing projects (Calkins, 1991).

How to Set Up a Reading Workshop

Teachers move through a series of steps as they set up their classroom, prepare students to work independently in the classroom, and provide instruction. The steps are summarized in the LA Essentials box on page 648.

To read more about reading workshop, see Chapter 2, "Teaching and Assessing Language Arts," and the full-color insert on reading and writing workshop.

Step 1. Collect Books for Reading Workshop. Students read all sorts of books during reading workshop, including stories, informational books, biographies, and books of poetry. They also read magazines. Most of their reading materials are selected from the classroom library, but students also bring books from home and borrow books from the public library, the school library, and classmates. Students read many award-winning books during reading workshop, but they also read series of popular books and technical books related to their hobbies and special interests. These books are not necessarily the same ones that teachers use for literature focus units, but students often choose to reread books they read earlier in the school year or during the previous year in literature studies.

Teachers need to have literally hundreds of books in their class libraries, including books written at a range of reading levels, in order to have enough books so that every student can read during reading workshop. Primary teachers often worry about finding books that their emerging readers can handle independently. Wordless picture books in which the story is told entirely through pictures, alphabet and number books, pattern and predictable books, and books the teacher has read aloud several times are often the most accessible for kindergartners and first graders. Primary-grade children often read and reread easy-to-read books such as books in the Scholastic Bookshelf series and the Wright Group's Story Box kits.

Teachers introduce students—especially reluctant readers—to the books in the classroom library so that they can more effectively choose books to read during reading workshop. The best way to preview books is using a very brief book talk to interest students in the book. In book talks, teachers tell students a little about the book, show the cover, and perhaps read the first paragraph or two (Prill, 1994/1995). Teachers also give book talks to introduce text sets of books, and students give book talks as they share books they have read with the class during the sharing part of reading workshop.

Step 2: Teach Reading Workshop Procedures. Students need to learn how to choose books, write responses to books they are reading, share books they have finished reading, and conference with the teacher, as well as other procedures related to reading workshop. Some of these procedures need to be taught before students begin reading workshop, and others can be introduced and reviewed as minilessons during reading workshop.

Step 3: Identify Topics for Minilessons. Minilessons are an important part of reading workshop because the workshop approach is more than reading practice. Instruction is important, and minilessons are the teaching step. Teachers present minilessons on reading workshop procedures and on reading concepts, strategies, and skills. Teachers identify topics for minilessons based on what they observe students doing during reading workshop, the questions students ask, and the skills and strategies teachers are expected to introduce,

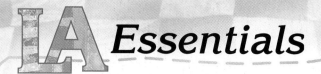

Essentials

Steps in Setting Up a Reading Workshop

Teachers follow these steps to set up a writing workshop.

1. **Books**

   Collect a wide variety of books at varying reading levels for students to read, including stories, informational books, poems, and other resources, and place them on a special shelf in the classroom library.

2. **Workshop Procedures**

   Teach reading workshop procedures so that students know how to choose and respond to books, participate in conferences, and share books they have read. Reading workshop operates much more smoothly when students are familiar with the procedures.

3. **Minilesson Topics**

   Identify topics for minilessons to teach during reading workshop while anticipating that other topics will arise from skills and strategies that students are using but are confusing.

4. **Read-Aloud Books**

   Choose read-aloud books to introduce students to new genres, authors, literary elements, or series stories that they might want to continue reading on their own.

5. **Schedule**

   Design a reading workshop schedule that incorporates reading, sharing, minilessons, and reading aloud to students.

6. **Conferences**

   Plan a schedule for conferences so that you can talk with students individually or in small groups about the books they are reading and monitor their comprehension.

7. **Assessment**

   Plan ways to monitor students' work and assess their reading with state-of-the-class charts, observations, and conferences.

practice, or review at their grade levels. Teachers use examples from books students are reading, and students are often asked to reflect on their own reading processes. These minilessons can be taught to the whole class, small groups, or individual students, depending on which students need the instruction.

Step 4: Choose Books to Read Aloud to Students. When teachers include the reading aloud component with reading workshop, they carefully choose the books they will read. These books may be more difficult than those students can read independently, or they may be chosen to introduce students to a genre, an author, or a literary element. Sometimes teachers read aloud the first book in a series and then invite students to continue reading the sequels themselves. Teachers choose books to read aloud for a variety of specific instructional purposes.

Step 5: Design a Schedule for Reading Workshop. Teachers examine their daily schedule, consider the other language arts activities in which their students are involved, decide how much time is available for reading workshop, and allocate time to each of the reading workshop components. Some teachers make reading and writing workshop their entire language arts program. They begin by reading aloud a book, chapter by chapter, to the class and talking about the book in a grand conversation for the first 30 minutes of reading workshop. During this time, teachers focus on modeling reading strategies and talking about elements of story structure during the grand conversations. For the next 45 to 50 minutes, students read self-selected books independently. The teacher conferences with small groups of students as they read and presents minilessons to small groups of students as needed. Then students spend the next 15 to 20 minutes writing in reading logs about their reading. Often teachers have students keep double-entry journals in which they record quotes from the story in one column and react to the quotes in the other column. Sharing is held during the last 15 minutes, and students do book talks about books they have finished reading.

Other teachers coordinate reading workshop with literature focus units. For example, they decide to allocate one hour to reading workshop at the beginning of their language arts block. Students begin with 30 minutes of independent reading and then use the next 10 minutes to share books they have finished reading with the class. The last 20 minutes are used for a minilesson. Then students move into a literature focus unit for the next 90 minutes. In some classrooms, teachers alternate reading and writing workshop, either by month or by grading period.

Step 6: Plan for Conferencing. During reading workshop, students are reading independently, and teachers must find ways to monitor their progress. Many teachers begin each reading period by moving around the classroom to check that students have chosen books and are reading purposefully and then use the rest of the reading period for individual and small-group conferences. Teachers create conference schedules and meet with students on a regular basis, usually once a week, to talk about their reading and reading skills and strategies, listen to them read excerpts aloud, and make plans for the next book. Teachers take notes during these conferences in folders they keep for each student.

Step 7: Plan for Assessment. Teachers use a classroom chart to monitor students' work on a daily basis. At the beginning of reading workshop, students or the teacher record on a class chart what book students are reading and the activity in which they are currently involved. Atwell (1987) calls this chart "the state of the class." Teachers can review students' progress and note which students need to meet with the teacher or receive additional attention. When students fill in the chart themselves, they develop responsibility for their actions and a stronger desire to accomplish tasks they set for themselves.

To monitor primary-grade students, teachers often use a pocket chart and have students place a card in their pocket, indicating whether they are reading or responding during reading workshop or at which stage of the writing process they are working during writing workshop.

Teachers take time during reading workshop to observe students as they interact and work together in small groups. Researchers who have observed in reading and writing workshop classrooms report that some students, even as young as first graders, are excluded from group activities because of sex, ethnicity, or socioeconomic status (Henkin, 1995; Lensmire, 1992). The socialization patterns in elementary classrooms seem to reflect society's patterns. Henkin recommends that teachers be alert to the possibility that boys might share books only with other boys or that some students won't find anyone willing to be their editing partner. If teachers see instances of discrimination in their classrooms, they should confront it directly and work to foster a classroom environment where students treat each other equitably.

How to Set Up a Writing Workshop

To learn more about writing workshop, turn back to Chapter 2, "Teaching and Assessing Language Arts," and the full-color insert on reading and writing workshop.

As teachers set up a writing workshop classroom, they collect writing supplies and materials for making books for the writing center. Teachers set out different kinds of paper—some lined and some unlined—and various writing instruments, including pencils and red and blue pens. Bookmaking supplies include cardboard, contact paper, cloth, and wallpaper for book covers, stencils, stamps, art supplies, and a saddleback stapler and other equipment for binding books. Teachers also set up a bank of computers with word-processing programs and printers or arrange for students to have access to the school's computer lab. Teachers encourage students to use the classroom library, and many times, students' writing grows out of favorite books they have read.

Teachers also think about the classroom arrangement. Students sit at desks or tables arranged in small groups as they write. The teacher circulates around the classroom, conferencing briefly with students, and the classroom atmosphere is free enough that students converse quietly with classmates and move around the classroom to collect materials at the writing center, assist classmates, or share ideas. There is space for students to meet for writing groups, and often a sign-up sheet for writing groups is posted in the classroom. A table is available for the teacher to meet with individual students or small groups for conferences, writing groups, proofreading, and minilessons.

To learn more about setting up a writing workshop, view the CD-ROM that accompanies this text.

In addition to collecting supplies and arranging the classroom, teachers need to prepare students for writing workshop and make plans for the instruction. The steps in setting up a writing workshop are summarized in the LA Essentials box on page 651.

Essentials

Steps in Setting Up a Writing Workshop

Teachers follow these steps to set up a writing workshop.

1. **Writing Process**

   Teach the stages of the writing process so that students understand how to develop and refine a composition.

2. **Workshop Procedures**

   Teach writing workshop procedures so that students know how to meet in revising groups, sign up for conferences, and publish their writing, for example. For students to be successful, it is essential that they know the procedures they will be expected to use.

3. **Minilesson Topics**

   Identify topics for minilessons to teach during writing workshop while anticipating that other topics will arise from skills and strategies that students are using but are confusing.

4. **Schedule**

   Design a writing workshop schedule that includes writing, sharing, and teaching minilessons. Consistency is important so that students know what is expected of them and can develop a routine.

5. **Conferences**

   Plan how you will conference in small groups and individually with students so that you can monitor their work, provide feedback about their writing, and assess their progress.

6. **Sharing**

   Include opportunities for students to share their published writing with classmates.

7. **Assessment**

   Plan to monitor and assess students' work using state-of-the-class reports, conferences, writing-process checklists, and rubrics.

FIGURE 15–5 *A Seventh-Grade Class's Guidelines for Writing Workshop*

Ten Writing Workshop Rules

1. Keep everything in your writing folder.
2. Write rough drafts in pencil.
3. Double-space all rough drafts so you will have space to revise, and only write on one side of a page.
4. Revise in blue ink.
5. Edit in red ink.
6. Show your thinking and never erase except on the final copy.
7. Don't throw anything away—keep everything.
8. Date every piece of writing.
9. Keep a record of the compositions you write in your writing folder.
10. Work hard!

Chapter 3, "The Reading and Writing Processes," presents the five stages of the writing process.

Step 1: Teach the Stages of the Writing Process. Teachers often begin writing workshop by teaching or reviewing the five stages of the writing process, setting guidelines for writing workshop, and taking students through one writing activity together.

Step 2: Teach Writing Workshop Procedures. Teachers need to explain how students will meet in groups to revise their writing, how to sign up for a conference with the teacher, how to proofread, how to use the publishing center, and other procedures used in writing workshop. A set of guidelines for writing workshop that one seventh-grade class developed is presented in Figure 15–5.

Step 3: Identify Topics for Minilessons. As with reading workshop, teachers teach minilessons during writing workshop. Teachers present minilessons on procedures related to writing workshop and writing concepts, skills, and strategies that students can apply in their own writing. Some topics for minilessons come from teachers' observations of students as they write, questions students ask, and topics identified in grade-level curriculum guides.

Teachers also share information about authors and how they write during minilessons. For students to think of themselves as writers, they need to know what writers do. Each year, there are more autobiographies written by authors. Tomie dePaola has written a popular series of autobiographical picture-book stories for young children, including *Things Will NEVER Be the Same* (2003), and Lois Lowry has written *Looking Back: A Book of Memories* (1998). Each chapter focuses on a memory prompted by a photo; this is a format students can imitate when they write autobiographies. A number of well-known authors and illustrators are profiled in the Meet the Author series published by Richard C. Owen, including *Can You Imagine* by Patricia McKissack (1997), *If You Give an Author a Pencil* by Laura Numeroff (2003), *One Man Show* by Frank Asch (1997), *From Paper Airplanes to Outer Space* by Seymour Simon (2000), and *Firetalking* (1994) by Patricia Polacco (1994). Students like these picture-book autobiographies because they provide interesting information, and the authors come to life through the color photographs on each page. They can be read aloud to primary students, and older students can read them independently. Video productions about authors and illustrators are also available. For example, in the 27-minute video *Eric Carle: Picture Writer* (1993), Eric Carle demonstrates how he uses paint and collage to create the illustrations for his popular picture books.

Step 4: Design a Writing Workshop Schedule.   An important instructional decision that teachers make is how to organize their daily schedule and what portion of the language arts block to allocate to reading and writing workshop. Some teachers make reading and writing workshop the focus of their language arts program. During the writing workshop portion, students move through the writing process as they write on self-selected topics for 45 or 50 minutes. The teacher meets with small groups of students or with individual students as they draft, revise, and edit their compositions during this writing time. Next, teachers use a 15- to 30-minute block of time for minilessons, and they present minilessons on writing workshop procedures and writing concepts, skills, and strategies to the whole class, small groups of students, or individual students as needed. Sharing is held during the last 15 minutes, and students read their finished compositions aloud to classmates, often sitting in the author's chair.

Other teachers coordinate writing workshop with literature focus units. For example, they may allocate the last hour of their language arts block for reading and writing workshop, and alternate reading workshop and writing workshop by month or by grading period. Another way some teachers allocate time for writing workshop is during the last week of a literature focus unit, when students are developing a writing project. For example, in the literature focus unit on *The Mitten* discussed earlier in this chapter, primary-grade students use a writing workshop approach as they research one of the animals mentioned in the story and create posters to share what they learn.

Step 5: Plan for Conferencing.   Teachers conference with students as they write. Many teachers prefer moving around the classroom to meet with students rather than having the students come to a table to meet with them. Too often, a line forms as students wait to meet with the teacher, and students lose precious writing time. Some teachers move around the classroom in a regular pattern, meeting with one-fifth of the students each day. In this way, they can conference with every student during the week.

Other teachers spend the first 15 to 20 minutes of writing workshop stopping briefly to check on 10 or more students each day. Many use a zigzag pattern to get to all parts of the classroom each day. These teachers often kneel down beside each student, sit on the edge of the student's seat, or carry their own stool to each student's desk. During the 1- or 2-minute conferences, teachers ask students what they are writing, listen to students read a paragraph or two, and then ask what they plan to do next. Then these teachers use the remaining time during writing workshop to more formally conference with students who are revising and editing their compositions. Students often sign up for these conferences. Teachers make comments to find strengths, ask questions, and discover possibilities during these revising conferences. Some teachers like to read the pieces themselves, whereas others like to listen to students read their papers aloud. As they interact with students, teachers model the kinds of responses that students are learning to give to each other.

As students meet to share their writing during revising and editing, they continue to develop their sense of community. They share their rough drafts with classmates in writing groups composed of four or five students. In some classrooms, teachers join in the writing groups whenever they can, but students normally run the groups themselves. They take turns reading their rough drafts to one another and listen as their classmates offer compliments and suggestions for revision. In other classrooms, students work with one partner to edit their writing, and they often use red pens.

After proofreading their drafts with a classmate and then meeting with the teacher for a final editing, students make the final copy of their writing. Students often want to put their writing on the computer so that their final copy will appear professional. Many times, students compile their final copy to make a book during writing workshop, but sometimes they attach their writing to artwork, make a poster, write a letter that is mailed, or perform a script as a skit or puppet show. Not every piece is published, however. Sometimes students decide not to continue with a piece of writing. They file the piece in their writing folders and start something new.

Check Chapter 3, "The Reading and Writing Processes," to learn more about how to use the author's chair.

Step 6: Include Sharing.   For the last 10 to 15 minutes of writing workshop, students gather together as a class to share their new publications and make other, related announcements. Younger students often sit in a circle or gather together on a rug for sharing time. If an author's chair is available, each student sits in the special chair to read his or her composition. After reading, classmates clap and offer compliments. They may also make other comments and suggestions, but the focus is on celebrating completed writing projects, not on revising the composition to make it better. Classmates help celebrate after the child shares by clapping, and perhaps the best praise is having a classmate ask to read the newly published book.

Step 7: Plan for Assessment.   Teachers monitor students' work in several ways. They monitor students' progress from day to day with a state-of-the-class report; an excerpt from a fifth-grade writing workshop chart is shown in the Weaving Assessment Into Practice feature on page 655. Teachers can also use the chart to award weekly effort grades, to have students indicate their need to conference with the teacher, or to have students announce that they are ready

An Excerpt From a Fifth-Grade State-of-the-Class Chart

Names	Dates 10/18	10/19	10/20	10/21	10/22	10/25	10/26	10/27
Antonio	4 5	5	5	6	7	8	8	89
Bella	2	2	2 3	2	2	4	5	6
Charles	8 9 1	3 1	1	2	2 3	4	5	67
Dina	6	6	6	7 8	8	91	1	23
Dustin	78	8	8	8	8	8	91	1
Eddie	23	2	24	56	8	91	12	23
Elizabeth	7	6	7	8	8	8	9	12
Elsa	2	3	45	56	67	8	8	91

Code:

1 = Prewrite

2 = Draft

3 = Conference

4 = Writing Group

5 = Revise

6 = Edit

7 = Conference

8 = Make Final Copy

9 = Publish

to share their writing. Teachers can also develop writing-process checklists that students can use to keep track of their work, and they regularly conference with students about their writing. In addition, teachers can use rubrics to assess the quality of students' published compositions.

THEME CYCLES

Theme cycles are interdisciplinary units that integrate reading and writing with social studies, science, math, and other curricular areas (Altwerger & Flores, 1994; Kucer, Silva, & Delgado-Larocco, 1995). Sometimes they focus on one curricular area, such as a theme cycle on insects or the Revolutionary War, and at other times, they extend across most or all of the school day and students are involved in planning the direction for the theme. Topics for these extended theme cycles are broad and encompass many possible directions for exploration, such as houses and homes and people who have changed the world.

Students take part in planning the theme cycles and identifying some of the questions they want to explore and activities that interest them (Cordeiro, 1995; Lindquist & Selwyn, 2000). Students are involved in authentic and

Seeing Common Threads

How does integrating the language arts in theme cycles increase students' learning?

Laura Presno responds:

Students' learning in any subject is enhanced with oral language, reading, and writing experiences. In other words, students learn better when they talk about what they are learning and when they read and write. They learn the subject better and their language arts skills are reinforced. For example, if fourth graders are learning about the California Gold Rush of 1849, why not go beyond reading the textbook and have your students read a story and keep a "character" diary of events? Even though they are fictional, they are related to actual occurrences. This allows students to go beyond the textbook and to delve into the period to witness historical events. Even though it takes more time to plan themes, it is worth it because students learn so much more.

What do you think?

Each chapter presents a question and a response written by one of Dr. Tompkins's students. Consider other comments, or respond to the question yourself, by visiting the Threaded Message Board in Chapter 15 on the Companion Website at www.prenhall.com/tompkins

meaningful learning activities, not reading chapters in content-area textbooks in order to answer the questions at the end of the chapter. Textbooks might be used as a resource, but only as one of many available resources. Students explore topics that interest them and research answers to questions they have posed and are genuinely interested in answering. Students share their learning at the end of the theme cycle and are assessed on what they have learned as well as on the processes they used in learning and working in the classroom.

How to Develop a Theme Cycle

Turn back to Chapter 2, "Teaching and Assessing Language Arts," for more information about theme cycles. Also see the full-color insert on the theme cycle.

To begin planning a theme cycle, teachers choose the general topic and then identify three or four key concepts that they want to develop through the theme. The goal of a theme cycle is not to teach a collection of facts, but to help students grapple with several big understandings (Tunnell & Ammon, 1993). Next, teachers identify the resources that they have available for the theme and develop their teaching plan. Ten steps in developing a theme cycle are summarized in the LA Essentials box on page 657.

Step 1: Collect a Text Set.   Teachers collect stories, poems, informational books, magazines, newspaper articles, and reference books for the text set related to the theme. The text set is placed in the special area for materials related to the theme in the classroom library. Teachers plan to read some books aloud to students, some will be read independently, and others students will read together as shared or guided reading. These materials can also be used

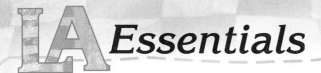

LA Essentials

Steps in Developing a Theme Cycle

1. **Text Set**

   Collect a text set of stories, information books, poems, and Internet resources to use in the theme cycle. Set out the print materials on a special shelf in the classroom library, and bookmark the Internet resources on the computers in the classroom.

2. **Listening Center**

   Set up a listening center and collect recordings of various books in the text set.

3. **Textbooks**

   Coordinate content-area textbook reading with other activities in the theme cycle.

4. **Technology Resources**

   Locate Internet and other technology resources and plan ways to integrate them into the theme cycle.

5. **Word Walls**

   Identify potential words for the word wall and activities to teach those words.

6. **Learning Logs**

   Plan how students will use learning logs as a tool for learning.

7. **Strategies and Skills**

   Identify language arts strategies and skills to teach.

8. **Talk and Visually Representing Activities**

   Too often, teachers forget to include these two language arts in theme cycles. Plan ways to involve students in talk activities, such as instructional conversations, dramatization, and oral presentations, and in visually representing activities, such as graphic organizers, posters, and quilts.

9. **Projects**

   Brainstorm possible projects students can create to apply their learning, but usually allow students some choice in which projects they develop.

10. **Assessment**

    Plan how you will monitor and assess students' learning using assignment checklists, rubrics, and other assessment tools.

for minilessons, to teach students, for example, about reading strategies and expository text structures. Other books can be used as models or patterns for writing projects. Teachers also write the poems on charts to share with students or arrange a bulletin-board display of the poems.

Step 2: Set Up a Listening Center.   Teachers select recordings to accompany stories or informational books or create their own tapes so that absent students can catch up on a book being read aloud day by day. Also, the recordings can be used to provide additional reading experiences for students who listen to a recording when they read or reread a story or informational book.

Step 3: Coordinate Content-Area Textbook Readings.   Teachers can teach theme cycles without textbooks; however, when information is available in a literature or content-area textbook, it can be used. Upper-grade students, in particular, read and discuss concepts presented in textbooks or use them as a reference for further study.

Step 4: Locate Technology Resources.   Teachers plan the videotapes, CD-ROM, charts, time lines, maps, models, posters, and other displays to be used in connection with the theme cycle. Children view videos and explore Internet sites to provide background knowledge about the theme, and other materials are used in teaching the key concepts. Materials can be viewed or displayed in the classroom, and students can make other materials during the theme cycle.

Chapter 5, "Looking Closely at Words," presents information about word walls and related vocabulary activities.

Step 5: Identify Potential Words for the Word Wall.   Teachers preview books in the text set and identify potential words for the word wall. This list of potential words is useful in planning vocabulary activities, but teachers do not use their word lists simply for the classroom word wall. Students and the teacher develop the classroom word wall together as they read and discuss the key concepts and other information related to the theme.

For more information on learning logs, see Chapter 6, "Personal Writing."

Step 6: Plan How Students Will Use Learning Logs.   Teachers plan for students to keep learning logs in which students take notes, write questions, make observations, clarify their thinking, and write reactions to what they are learning during theme cycles (Tompkins, 2004). They also write quickwrites and make clusters to explore what they are learning.

Step 7: Identify Language Arts Strategies and Skills to Teach.   Teachers plan minilessons to teach literacy skills and strategies, such as expository text structures, how to use an index, skimming and scanning, how to write an alphabet book, and interviewing techniques. Minilessons are taught using a whole-part-whole approach so that students can apply what they are learning in reading and writing activities.

Step 8: Plan Talk and Visually Representing Activities.   Students use talk and visually representing to learn during the theme cycle and to demonstrate their learning (Erickson, 1988; Nelson, 1988; San Jose, 1988). These are possible activities:

- Give oral reports.
- Interview someone with special expertise on the theme.

- Participate in a debate related to the theme.
- Create charts and diagrams to display information.
- Role-play a historical event.
- Assume the role of a historical figure.
- Participate in a readers theatre presentation of a story or poem.
- Tell or retell a story, biography, or event.
- Use a puppet show to tell a story, biography, or event.
- Make a quilt with information or vocabulary related to the theme.
- Write and perform a skit or play.

Step 9: Brainstorm Possible Projects Students May Create. Teachers think about possible projects students may choose to develop to apply and personalize their learning during theme cycles. This advance planning makes it possible for teachers to collect needed supplies and to have suggestions ready to offer to students who need assistance in choosing a project. Students work on projects independently or in small groups and then share the projects with the class at the end of the theme cycle. Projects involve one or more of the six language arts. Some suggestions are:

Check Chapter 3, "The Reading and Writing Processes," for a list of project ideas.

- Read a biography related to the theme cycle.
- Create a poster to illustrate a key concept.
- Write and mail a letter to get information related to the theme.
- Write a story related to the theme.
- Perform a readers theatre production, puppet show, or other dramatization.
- Write a poem, song, or rap related to the theme.
- Write an "All About . . . " book or a report about one of the key concepts.
- Create a commercial or advertisement related to the theme.
- Create a tabletop display or diorama about the theme.

Step 10: Plan for Assessment. Teachers consider how they will monitor and assess students' learning as they make plans for activities and assignments. In this way, teachers can explain to students at the beginning of the theme cycle how they will be assessed and can check that their assessment will emphasize students' learning of the key concepts and important ideas. An assignment checklist for a theme cycle about flight for middle-grade students is shown in the Weaving Assessment Into Practice feature on page 660.

Using Content-Area Textbooks

Content-area textbooks are often difficult for students to read—more difficult, in fact, than many informational books. One reason textbooks are difficult is that they briefly mention many topics without developing any of them. A second reason is that content-area textbooks are read differently than stories. Teachers need to show students how to approach content-area textbooks and teach them how to use specific expository-text reading strategies and procedures to make comprehension easier. Figure 15–6 presents guidelines for using content-area textbooks.

Teachers can make content-area textbooks more readable and show students ways to remember what they have read. Some activities are used before reading and others after reading. The before-reading activities are used to help

An Assignment Checklist for a Middle-Grade Theme Cycle on Flight

Name _____ Date _____

	Excellent	Good	Fair	Poor
1. Make a K-W-L chart on flight.	____	____	____	____
2. Read five books on flight and write a note card on each one.	____	____	____	____
3. Write ten pages in your learning log.	____	____	____	____
4. Make a word wall on flight with 50 words.	____	____	____	____
5. Make a cluster about birds.	____	____	____	____
6. Make a time line about flight.	____	____	____	____
7. Write a compare-contrast essay on birds and airplanes.	____	____	____	____

_____ Prewriting
_____ Drafting
_____ Revising
_____ Editing
_____ Publishing

8. Make a report poster on flight. Choose four ways to share information.	____	____	____	____

_____ report   _____ diagram   _____ photo
_____ poem   _____ picture   _____ quote
_____ story   _____ Internet   _____ other

students activate prior knowledge, set purposes for reading, or build background knowledge. The after-reading activities help students identify and remember main ideas and details. Other activities are used when students want to locate specific information. Seven activities to make content-area textbooks more readable are:

1. *Preview.* Teachers introduce the reading assignment by asking students to note main headings in the chapter and then skim or rapidly read the chapter to get a general idea about the topics covered in the reading assignment.
2. *Prereading plan (PReP).* Teachers introduce a key concept discussed in the reading assignment and ask students to brainstorm words and ideas related to the concept before reading (Langer, 1981).
3. *Anticipation guides.* Teachers present a set of statements on the topic to be read. Students agree or disagree with each statement and then read the assignment to see if they were right (Head & Readence, 1986).
4. *Exclusion brainstorming.* Teachers distribute a list of words, most of which are related to the key concepts to be presented in the reading assignment. Teachers ask students to circle the words that are related to

FIGURE 15-6

Guidelines for Using Content-Area Textbooks

1. Comprehension Aids
Teach students how to use the comprehension aids in content-area textbooks, including chapter overviews; headings that outline the chapter; helpful graphics, such as maps, charts, tables, graphs, diagrams, photos, and drawings; technical words defined in the text; end-of-chapter summaries; and review questions.

2. Questions
Divide the reading of a chapter into sections. Before reading each section, have students turn the section heading into a question and read to find the answer to the question. As they read, have students take notes about the section, and then after reading, answer the question they created using the section heading.

3. Expository Text Structures
Teach students about expository text structures and assist them in identifying the patterns used in the reading assignment, especially cause and effect or problem and solution, before reading.

4. Vocabulary
Introduce only the key terms as part of a presentation or discussion before students read the textbook assignment. Present other vocabulary during reading, if needed, and after reading, develop a word wall with all important words.

5. Key Concepts
Have students focus on key concepts or the big ideas instead of trying to remember all the facts or other information.

6. Content-Area Reading Techniques
Use content-area reading techniques, such as PReP, exclusion brainstorming, and anticipation guides, to help students identify and remember main ideas and details after reading.

7. Headings
Encourage students to use headings and subheadings to select and organize relevant information. The headings can be used to create a semantic map, and students can add details as they read.

8. Listen-Read-Discuss Format
Use a listen-read-discuss format. First, the teacher presents the key concepts orally, and then the students read and discuss the chapter. Or, have students read the chapter as a review activity rather than as the introductory activity.

a key concept and then read the assignment to see if they circled the right words (Johns, Van Leirsburg, & Davis, 1994).

5. *Clusters.* Teachers distribute a cluster, map, or other graphic organizer with main ideas marked. Students complete the graphic organizer by adding details after reading each section.

6. *Note taking.* Students develop an outline by writing the headings and then take notes after reading each section.

7. *Scanning.* Students reread quickly to locate specific information.

Students in the upper grades also need to learn how to use the SQ3R study strategy, a five-step technique in which students survey, question, read, recite, and review as they read a content-area reading assignment. This study strategy was devised in the 1930s and has been researched and thoroughly documented as a very effective technique when used properly (Anderson & Armbruster, 1984; Caverly & Orlando, 1991). Teachers introduce the SQ3R study strategy and provide opportunities for students to practice each step. At first, students can work together as a class as they use the technique with a text the teacher is reading to students. Then students can work with partners and in small groups before using it independently. Teachers need to emphasize that if students simply begin reading the first page of the assignment without doing the first two steps, they won't be able to remember as much of what they read. Also, when students are in a hurry and skip some of the steps, the technique will not be as successful.

Sometimes content-area textbooks are used as the entire instructional program in social studies or science, but that's not a good idea. Textbooks typically only survey topics; other instructional materials are needed to provide depth and understanding. Students need to read, write, and discuss topics. It is most effective to use the reading process and then extend students' learning with projects. Developing theme cycles and using content-area textbooks as one resource are a much better idea. Tierney and Pearson (1992) recommend that teachers shift from teaching *from* textbooks to teaching *with* textbooks and incorporate other types of reading materials and activities into theme cycles.

A Middle-Grade Theme Cycle on Flight

Middle-grade students connect science and language arts in a theme cycle on flight. To begin the theme, students and the teacher create a K-W-L chart and students write facts about how birds and airplanes fly, space flight, and famous aviators. They also identify questions they will investigate during the theme. The teacher sets out a text set of stories, poems, and informational books about flight that students will read during the theme. Some of the books are on tape or CD, and students can listen to them at the listening center. Students list important words about flight on a word wall and participate in a variety of vocabulary activities. Students research flight-related questions using books and Internet resources and through interviews with a pilot, flight attendant, astronaut or other knowledgeable person. Students present oral reports or prepare multigenre papers to share what they learn. A planning cluster for a theme cycle on flight is presented in Figure 15–7.

Review

Designing language arts instruction that reflects the theory and research about language and how children learn is an important responsibility. Teachers follow a series of steps to develop literature focus units, literature circles, reading and writing workshop, and theme cycles. Ten key concepts presented in this chapter are:

1. Teachers develop literature focus units featuring award-winning and other high-quality books that students could not read independently.
2. Teachers develop activities using all five stages of the reading process for literature focus units.
3. Teachers organize for literature circles so that students can read and respond to self-selected books in small groups.
4. Teachers help students create a community of learners in order for them to work successfully in small groups.

Books

Bellville, C.W. (1993). *Flying in a hot air balloon.* Minneapolis: Carolrhoda.

Bernhard, E. (1994). *Eagles: Lions of the sky.* New York: Holiday House.

Borden, L. (1998). *Good-bye, Charles Lindbergh: Based on a true story.* New York: McElderry.

Busby, P. (2003). *First to fly: How Wilbur and Orville Wright invented the airplane.* New York: Crown.

Johnston, S.A. (1995). *Raptor rescue: An eagle flies free.* New York: Dutton.

Kalman, B. (1998). *How birds fly.* New York: Crabtree.

Lopez, D. (1995). *Flight.* New York: Time-Life.

Maynard, C. (1995). *Airplane.* London: Dorling Kindersley.

Peters, L.W. (1994). *This way home.* New York: Holt.

Ryan, P.M. (1999). *Amelia and Eleanor go for a ride: Based on a true story.* New York: Scholastic.

Weiss, H. (1995). *Strange and wonderful aircraft.* Boston: Houghton Mifflin.

Yolen, J. (2003). *My brothers' flying machine: Wilbur, Orville, and me.* Boston: Little Brown.

Word Wall

AB	airflow	H	helicopters
	airfoil	I	instruments
	airplane	JK	jet
	airport		jet stream
	altitude	L	landing
	Amelia Earhart		lift
	astronauts	MNO	migration
	aviation	PQ	passengers
	aviator		pilot
C	Charles Lindbergh		pitch
	Chuck Yeager		propeller
	controls	RS	roll
D	drag		rudder
E	engine	TUV	takeoff
F	FAA		thrust
	flapping wings		tilt
	flight attendant	WX	weight
	flightless		wing
	flyways		Wright brothers
	fuselage	YZ	yaw
G	glide		

Charts and Diagrams

- Make a time line of the history of flight.
- Draw diagrams of birds' wings or airplanes.
- Make a Venn diagram comparing birds and airplanes.
- Make a data chart of information about animals that fly, including birds, bats, insects, and fish.

Multigenre Papers

- Prepare a multigenre report about flight.
- Prepare a multigenre biography of an aviator, such as the Wright brothers, Chuck Yeager, Charles Lindbergh, or Amelia Earhart.

Vocabulary Activities

- Post words on an alphabetized word wall hanging in the classroom.
- Use words on the word wall for a minilesson on dividing words into syllables.
- Make word clusters and hang them on airplane and bird mobiles.

Flight

K-W-L Charts

- Post a K-W-L chart on the wall and complete the sections together as a class.
- Have students make individual flip-book K-W-L charts.

Interviews

- Interview a pilot, flight attendant, astronaut, zookeeper, ornithologist, or someone else knowledgeable about flight.
- Participate in an on-line interview of a pilot or astronaut.

Learning Logs

- Have students keep learning logs with notes, drawings, maps, diagrams, vocabulary words, and other information.

Internet

- Have students use yahooligans.com or another search engine designed for children to learn about flight on the Internet.
- Have students participate in an on-line interview of a pilot, astronaut, or other person involved with flight.

Oral Presentations

- Have students present oral reports about an airplane, bird, or aviator.
- Have students do an oral presentation of a poem from Fleischman, P. (1985). *I Am Phoenix: Poems for Two Voices.* New York: Harper Collins.

Visit Chapter 15 on the Companion Website at www.prenhall. com/tompkins to:

- Check your understanding of the concepts presented in the chapter

- Access the Extensions (activities and a list of related readings)

- Link to related websites

5. Teachers organize reading and writing workshop with plenty of time for reading and writing, and present minilessons on procedures, skills, and strategies.

6. Teachers provide opportunities for students to read and write independently during reading and writing workshop.

7. Teachers can adapt and combine literature focus units, literature circles, reading and writing workshop, and theme cycles to fit the needs of their students and their curriculum.

8. Teachers focus on several key concepts as they develop theme cycles.

9. Content-area textbooks can be used as one resource in theme cycles, but they should never be the only resource.

10. Teachers design assignment checklists for all four instructional approaches that students complete to document their learning.

Professional References

Altwerger, B., & Flores, B. (1994). Theme cycles: Creating communities of learners. *Primary Voices K–6, 2,* 2–6.

Anderson, T. H., & Armbruster, B. B. (1984). Studying. In P. D. Pearson, R. Barr, M. L. Kamil, & P. Mosenthal (Eds.), *Handbook of reading research* (pp. 657–679). New York: Longman.

Atwell, N. (1987). *In the middle: Writing, reading, and learning with adolescents.* Portsmouth, NH: Heinemann.

Calkins, L. M. (1991). *Living between the lines.* Portsmouth, NH: Heinemann.

Calkins, L. M. (1994). *The art of teaching writing* (2nd ed.). Portsmouth, NH: Heinemann.

Caverly, D. C., & Orlando, V. P. (1991). Textbook study strategies. In D. C. Caverly & V. P. Orlando (Eds.), *Teaching reading and study strategies at the college level* (pp. 86–165). Newark, DE: International Reading Association.

Cordeiro, P. (Ed.). (1995). *Endless possibilities: Generating curriculum in social studies and literacy.* Portsmouth, NH: Heinemann.

Eeds, M., & Peterson, R. (1991). Teacher as curator: Learning to talk about literature. *The Reading Teacher, 45,* 118–126.

Erickson, K. L. (1988). Building castles in the classroom. *Language Arts, 65,* 14–19.

Evans, K. S. (2001). *Literature discussion groups in the intermediate grades: Dilemmas and possibilities.* Newark, DE: International Reading Association.

Frank, C. R., Dixon, C. N., & Brandts, L. R. (2001). Bears, trolls, and pagemasters: Learning about learners in book clubs. *The Reading Teacher, 54,* 448–462.

Graves, D. H. (1994). *A fresh look at writing.* Portsmouth, NH: Heinemann.

Head, M. H., & Readence, J. E. (1986). Anticipation guides: Meaning through prediction. In E. K. Dishner, T. W. Bean, J. E. Readence, & D. W. Moore (Eds.), *Reading in the content areas* (2nd ed.) (pp. 229–234). Dubuque, IA: Kendall/Hunt.

Henkin, R. (1995). Insiders and outsiders in first-grade writing workshops: Gender and equity issues. *Language Arts, 72,* 429–434.

Hornsby, D., Sukarna, D., & Parry, J. (1986). *Read on: A conference approach to reading.* Portsmouth, NH: Heinemann.

Johns, J. L., Van Leirsburg, P., & Davis, S. J. (1994). *Improving reading: A handbook of strategies.* Dubuque, IA: Kendall/Hunt.

Kaufman, D. (2001). Organizing and managing the language arts workshop: A matter of motion. *Language Arts, 79,* 114–123.

Kucer, S. B., Silva, C., & Delgado-Larocco, E. L. (1995). *Curricular conversations: Themes in multilingual and monolingual classrooms.* York, ME: Stenhouse.

Langer, J. A. (1981). From theory to practice: A prereading plan. *Journal of Reading, 25,* 152–157.

Lensmire, T. (1992). *When children write.* New York: Teachers College Press.

Lindquist, T., & Selwyn, D. (2000). *Social studies at the center: Integrating kids, content, and literacy.* Portsmouth, NH: Heinemann.

McGee, L. M., & Tompkins, G. E. (1995). Literature-based reading instruction: What's guiding the instruction? *Language Arts, 72,* 405–414.

McWhirter, A. M. (1990). Whole language in the middle school. *The Reading Teacher, 43,* 562–565.

Nelson, P. A. (1988). Drama, doorway to the past. *Language Arts, 65,* 20–25.

Prill, P. (1994/1995). Helping children use the classroom library. *The Reading Teacher, 48,* 363–364.

San Jose, C. (1988). Story drama in the content areas. *Language Arts, 65,* 26–33.

Tierney, R. J., & Pearson, P. D. (1992). Learning to learn from text: A framework for improving classroom practice. In E. K. Dishner, T. W. Bean, J. E. Readence, & D. W. Moore (Eds.), *Reading in the content areas: Improving classroom instruction* (pp. 85–99). Dubuque, IA: Kendall-Hunt.

Tompkins, G. E. (2004). *Teaching writing: Balancing process and product* (4th ed.). Upper Saddle River, NJ: Merrill/Prentice Hall.

Tunnell, M. O., & Ammon, R. (Eds.). (1993). *The story of ourselves: Teaching history through children's literature.* Portsmouth, NH: Heinemann.

Zarrillo, J. (1989). Teachers' interpretations of literature-based reading. *The Reading Teacher, 43,* 22–28.

Children's Book References

Asch, F. (1997). *One man show.* Katonah, NY: Richard C. Owen.

Asch, F. (2000). *The sun is my favorite star.* New York: Scholastic.

Brett, J. (1989). *The mitten.* New York: Putnam.

Bunting, E. (1994). *Smoky night.* San Diego: Harcourt Brace.

Bunting, E. (1995). *Once upon a time.* Katonah, NY: Richard C. Owen.

dePaola, T. (2003). *Things will NEVER be the same.* New York: Putnam.

Fritz, J. (1992). *Surprising myself.* Katonah, NY: Richard C. Owen.

Gibbons, G. (1997). *The moon book.* New York: Holiday House.

Goble, P. (1994). *Hau kola/Hello friend.* Katonah, NY: Richard C. Owen.

Hutchins, P. (1968). *Rosie's walk.* New York: Macmillan.

Isom, J. S. (1997). *The first starry night.* Watertown, MA: Charlesbridge.

Koopmans, L. (1990). *The woodcutter's mitten.* New York: Crocodile Books.

Lowry, L. (1993). *The giver.* Boston: Houghton Mifflin.

Lowry, L. (1998). *Looking back: A book of memories.* Boston: Houghton Mifflin.

McKissack, P. (1997). *Can you imagine.* Katonah, NY: Richard C. Owen.

Numeroff, L. (2003). *If you give an author a pencil.* Katonah, NY: Richard C. Owen.

Polacco, P. (1994). *Firetalking.* Katonah, NY: Richard C. Owen.

Simon, S. (2000). *From paper airplanes to outer space.* Katonah, NY: Richard C. Owen.

Tresselt, A. (1964). *The mitten.* New York: Lothrop, Lee & Shepard.

INDEX